Public Management

Public Management: A Three-Dimensional Approach

CAROLYN J. HILL
Georgetown University

LAURENCE E. LYNN JR.
University of Chicago
University of Texas at Austin

A Division of SAGE
Washington, D.C.

CQ Press
2300 N Street, NW, Suite 800
Washington, DC 20037

Phone: 202-729-1900; toll-free, 1-866-4CQ-PRESS (1-866-427-7737)

Web: www.cqpress.com

Permissions for copyrighted material are continued on page 465, which is to be considered an extension of the copyright page.

Cover design: Archeographics, Washington, DC
Composition: Auburn Associates, Inc., Baltimore, Maryland

♾ The paper used in this publication exceeds the requirements of the American National Standard for Information Sciences—Permanence of Paper for Printed Library Materials, ANSI Z39.48-1992.

Printed and bound in the United States of America

12 11 10 09 08 1 2 3 4 5

Library of Congress Cataloging-in-Publication Data

Hill, Carolyn J.

Public management : a three-dimensional approach / Carolyn J. Hill, Laurence E. Lynn.

p. cm.

Includes bibliographical references and index.

ISBN 978-0-87289-348-1 (alk. paper)

1. Public administration—United States. 2. United States—Politics and government. I. Lynn, Laurence E., 1937– II. Title.

JK421. H55 2008

351.73—dc22 2008048762

For Max and Ada

Contents

Tables, Figures, and Boxes

TABLES

FIGURES

BOXES

Concepts in Action

How the World Works

Rule of Law

Preface

Public Management: A Three-Dimensional Approach was born of the conviction that effective public management and competent public managers are essential not only to achieving the duly authorized goals of public policy but also to maintaining the legitimacy of administration within America's scheme of constitutional governance. Imparting a sense of urgency to this project were the stories of mismanagement and incompetence at every level of government over the past decade. Policies, organizations, and public officials have failed, all with consequences ranging from unfortunate on a local level to egregious on a global level. Because such failures diminish Americans' trust in government, we want to help our readers acquire the motivation, skills, and values that will enable them to contribute to more effective governance at a time when such contributions are badly needed.

But failures are far from the whole story, and we can point to many examples of successful policies, organizations, and individuals. As a matter of fact, the daily business of government at all levels is performed with commendable competence by officials committed to public service. The bottom line is that the American administrative state works, if not always brilliantly. That this is true attracts little media, interest group, or citizen attention, however. "Another good day at the office" is not a compelling story; but excuses that cavalierly explain mismanagement as "stuff happens" hardly mollify citizens who, hard-pressed to meet the demands of daily living, correctly resent misuses of their tax dollars.

What we have come to know, all too well, is that public management in our democracy can be daunting. Indeed, to manage effectively in a regime of separated powers and checks and balances entails intellectual and practical challenges that are exceptional among modern industrial democracies. Educating individuals to meet these challenges is the goal of public affairs education, and it is our purpose in writing this book.

We define "management" as ensuring that the allocation and use of resources available to the government are directed toward the achievement of lawful public policy goals. To manage in the public sector requires an understanding of how three distinct dimensions—administrative structures and processes, organizations and their cultures, and individual public managers and their skills and values—interact to produce results that approximate what citizens and their representatives expect from their governments.

We attempt to prepare students for the challenges of public management by pursuing two overarching objectives: (1) to show students that effective public management in the real world requires critical analytical thinking and the ability to incorporate such thinking into persuasive arguments on behalf of managerial solutions, strategies, and decisions; and (2) to bring the need for such skills to vivid life through the liberal use of cases, examples, and insightful anecdotes of public management in practice.

OUR APPROACH TO TEACHING PUBLIC MANAGEMENT

The approach we take draws on Laurence Lynn's thirty-five years of experience teaching both public management and policy analysis to students in professional master's degree programs (experience that, in turn, was grounded on his own years as a senior federal policy and budget official). Over that time, he has tried several approaches to teaching public management; we have based this book on one developed and used by Lynn in the last half-dozen years and recently used by Carolyn Hill. It has worked well for us, and we believe it can work for instructors teaching public management in graduate programs in public administration, public policy, and public affairs. This approach characterizes public management as a multidimensional endeavor requiring critical analytical skill, brought to life through examples of actual public management practice.

A further aspect of our approach is its emphasis on the rule of law. Far too many texts, whatever methods they use to prepare professionals for practice, view laws, rules, courts, and legality as specialized topics, thus giving short shrift to how the rule of law influences professional work. These books may deal with particular laws, lawsuits, and court decisions in the context of considering specific managerial problems, but they do not discuss the relationship of managerial practice to lawfulness and to upholding the Constitution, which the public manager's oath of office requires. In this book, adhering to the rule of law is regarded as the foundation of public management, and we consider in detail what that proposition means.

Public management is not only thoughtful deliberation and the lawful action that proceeds from it, however. It is also rhetoric, the ability to use language effectively in political and organizational contexts to bring others to agreement and action. The "method" of this book is argument, an idea fully developed in the text. We believe that the ability to make evidence-based arguments is fundamental to the practice of public management (indeed, it is fundamental to all forms of public service) in a democracy. Cognitive skills—the ability to reason and explain—are not always given appropriate emphasis in domains such as public management, where behavioral skills—supervision, teamwork, motivation, conflict management, and leadership—are regarded as essential. These behavioral skills *are* essential, and our hope is that students are given opportunities to develop such skills in their professional training. But reasoned persuasion is a too-little-recognized prerequisite for managerial effectiveness. It is, moreover, a skill that can be practiced and effectively developed in the classroom.

OUR ARGUMENT FOR THIS BOOK

One of the key points in this book is that developing clear, well-reasoned, and persuasive arguments is a cornerstone of responsible public management. The book therefore begins with a straightforward claim: Public managers who are able to use all three dimensions of public management to address the issues and problems they confront, whether routine or extraordinary, will perform more effectively than those who cannot distinguish these dimensions or who use them inappropriately. In a nutshell, three-dimensional public management is better public management.

The reason for making this claim is also straightforward. Because the administrative system is embedded within complex political and legal processes having constitutional origins, public officials in managerial roles have neither the broad discretion nor the clear bottom line that provide a focus for business management. Public managers cannot simply resort to "technical rationality" or rely on "leadership." Instead, their decisions are constrained by laws, policies, organizational cultures, and legal precedents, and their actions and the consequences they produce are subject to critical scrutiny from legislators, interest groups, courts, the media, and their own employees.

The reader will find the evidence for this claim and the reasoning supporting it in the scores of examples, case studies, stories, and references that are included or cited throughout the book. From the analyses of the structural, cultural, and craft elements of real-world managerial activity emerges a strong sense of their specific importance, used singly or in combination. Public managers who, *in extremis,* have the ability to consider all three dimensions of public management are, the evidence suggests, more likely to cope with a crisis, reform an agency, or reach a politically and legally satisfactory resolution to a vexing problem.

The warrant or theory justifying the link between the book's claim and its evidence is in the logic of governance discussed in chapter 4 and the theoretical reasoning on which it is based. That body of theory postulates that citizens are linked to the activities and performance of their governments through layers of institutions established according to general principles of delegation and control or accountability. No approach to public management that fails to incorporate the resulting logic of governance into its analysis and prescriptions will adequately recognize the kinds of pressures that constitute the reality of day-to-day public management.

ORGANIZATION OF THE BOOK

To develop the approach just described, we have organized the book as follows. The first four chapters cover what we regard as the basics. Chapter 1 describes what we mean by the term "public management." Chapter 2 provides rationales and definitions for three dimensions of public management: structure, culture, and craft. Chapter 3 elaborates the method of reasoned argument as an essential managerial skill. Chapter 4 explains the pervasive importance of the rule of law and its implications for public management.

The next three chapters provide extended consideration of each public management dimension. Chapter 5 discusses the structural dimension; chapter 6 explains the meaning of culture as both an individual and organizational phenomenon; and chapter 7 is about managerial craft: the contribution of managers as individuals in their own right. Each chapter includes specific theories, frameworks, concepts, ideas, and heuristics, as well as numerous examples to illustrate the many specific aspects of each dimension.

The final three chapters provide metaperspectives on public management. Chapter 8 elaborates on the notion of accountability in the public sector; chapter 9 discusses public management reform and its role in American politics; and chapter 10 pulls the various strands of the book together in discussing what it means to be a three-dimensional public manager.

HOW THIS BOOK DIFFERS FROM OTHER TEXTBOOKS

This book differs in significant ways from other textbooks used in introductory courses on public administration and management in professional master's degree programs. One reason for differences across texts is that authors have different disciplinary orientations. Instructors whose backgrounds differ from ours—we consider ourselves to be political economists—might not agree with our emphasis, for example, on the hierarchical nature of governance or on the analytic value of the principal-agent model. Anticipating this reality, we have tried to let the practical challenges of public management, rather than the preoccupations of our own academic field, govern our selection of concepts, heuristics, and examples. Although the assumption of rationality can be insightful in certain applications, we also discuss equally insightful kinds of psychosocial considerations that affect decision making. We think that applications of principal-agent logic, suitably qualified, can enlighten practice, but we include other models of human interaction as well. We cannot expect instructors to change their academic stripes, but we do hope they will consider the pedagogical value of concepts that they may not use as scholars.

We also acknowledge the differences in how instructors conceive of the nature of professional education; that is, on the answer to the question: How can students at the master's level best be prepared for the professional practice of public management? Our approach is based on our answer: by helping students acquire critical analytical and rhetorical skills appropriate to addressing public management's distinctive challenges, through the use of the method of argument, and through familiarity and facility with the process of applying frameworks and heuristics to particular problems.

Some instructors consider the goal of master's education in public management to be familiarizing students with research literature relating to the subject of public management and to suggest applications of the theories and empirical findings of that literature to public management. Their students are encouraged, in effect, to think like applied social scientists. As practicing social scientists, we have the utmost respect for rigorous research, and the book introduces and draws heavily on it. We believe, however, that master's-level graduates of a professional program who are not familiar with *all* that is known in an academic field or subfield still are able to think critically and analytically about public management problems. Knowing and applying research literature is a means to an end for practice, not an end in itself. Mastery of an insightful heuristic, together with intellectual curiosity about where helpful answers to managerial challenges may lie, is more likely to assist real-time thinking than mere mastery of the full realm of academic knowledge.

Yet another view of the purpose of master's education in public management is that it should familiarize students with the administrative state's architecture and functions, which provide the context for professional practice and the profession of public administration. As with rigorous social science, we do not stint in our respect for the importance of a working knowledge of the institutions of American governance and the critical importance of public service values. But we believe that being able to describe institutions is of less immediate import to professional practice than knowing how the details of institutions can be a source both of management problems and of solutions to them.

A third view of the purpose of master's-level education in public management is that it should show how individual personality, skill, aspiration, and character—enlightened by knowledge of the "best practices" of successful managers—can contribute to effective governmental performance. Many books, therefore, have a "nuts-and-bolts" orientation, emphasizing popular topics such as handling the press, working with politicians, dealing with unpleasant people, managing one's boss, fostering teamwork, negotiating, and the like. These skills are important and may enable a particular public manager to handle a situation successfully. But teaching these skills typically involves constructing principles of effective practice from the analysis of cases, examples, and personal experience. Such case-based and experience-based analyses often take institutional and organizational constraints as given. Our analyses of cases and personal experience assume that management is three-dimensional and must not overemphasize individual managers, however charismatic they may be. We are also skeptical of the value of universal principles of effective practice; good managers will violate them as the situation requires.

Our approach emphasizes the acquisition of critical analytical skills that are appropriate for addressing public management's distinctive challenges in our constitutional scheme of governance. Our choice of emphasis, analytic framework, and text organization inevitably means that familiar subjects—budgeting, human resources administration, information management, outsourcing, change management, and analysis and decision making—are woven into discussions of the three dimensions. Frequent cross-references to various topics appear throughout the book, emphasizing the multidimensional nature of particular issues. This treatment reflects our view that the appropriate use of these kinds of specialized functions is intrinsic to managing in three dimensions rather than an end in itself.

TEACHING AND LEARNING WITH THIS BOOK

This book is designed for a semester-long course (or a two-quarter course sequence) on public management at the master's degree level. Supplemented by other readings, it also might be suitable for a doctoral seminar on the subject and, possibly, for advanced undergraduates studying American politics and government. The book is appropriate for pre-career students and those with some or considerable experience in the public sector (many of whom return to school to develop conceptual foundations for their careers), as most contemporary public management classes include both types of students. Although the emphasis is on management in the public sector, students whose interests lie primarily in the nonprofit sector also will find material of value to them.

In developing the text, we confronted two additional issues. First, where do particular topics that many instructors regard as important to public management, such as budgeting, change, leadership, and ethics, belong? We decided on the primary locations of various topics based on our judgment as to how they would best fit into the conceptual and narrative flow of the book. Because a great many of these topics are themselves multidimensional, however, we have included numerous cross-references throughout the book.

Second, how should we choose from among the wide array of concepts and heuristics that might be included? We attempted to balance a number of criteria: significance, analytical value, and what works well in the classroom. We added citations in endnotes of additional resources that an instructor might find useful. Other topics and readings that appeal to individual instructors can be incorporated in a syllabus at appropriate points in the course. Some instructors may choose a different balance and spend an entire class period discussing contracting, while others may devote less time to this structural feature and instead emphasize networks and network management strategies.

To facilitate an interactive, experiential process of teaching and learning, each chapter offers some "hooks" and motivations for class discussion. These are of several types. First are examples and stories of varying lengths to illustrate concepts, ideas, and arguments. These examples are based on, or actually taken from, media accounts, official reports, and, in some cases, academic research publications. Such illustrative materials provide a basis for class discussion of the ideas and arguments to which they relate. Instructors might consider developing pre-class assignment questions based on the examples or encouraging students to find others.

An issue that always arises in selecting examples is the balance to be struck between successes and failures. This is a subject of lively controversy, with some arguing that failures are more enlightening and others that successes are more inspiring. We like the anecdote about the Dutch national soccer team's persistent failure to win important matches because of its inability to make penalty kicks. After a coaching strategy of having players study film of successful kicks did not improve matters, team officials decided—with better results—to study film of failed kicks and point out why they failed. While we include both successes and failures throughout the book, we did not hesitate to choose failures—often referred to in the literature as "fiascos"—as a basis for drawing lessons from complex situations.

The conceptual boxes found in each chapter not only illustrate concepts discussed in the text but also provide points of departure for classroom discussion. The introduction to the material in each box establishes connections between the box and the chapter narrative. We view these boxes as essential to engaging with the conceptual discussion. Students will have an incentive to read and think about them if instructors routinely use them as a basis for class discussion.

These boxes are of three types:

- CONCEPTS IN ACTION: These boxes contain applications of concepts discussed in the text that stand out in news stories, opinion pieces, government reports, and other public sources. Their purpose is to show how academic concepts that students often regard as remote from the real world actually come into play in sense making, deliberation, and decision making concerning public management.

- HOW THE WORLD WORKS: These boxes are stories, observations, or examples from published sources that illustrate "the world as it really is," that is, how human nature creates conundrums, irony, and surprise in the practice of public management. A central premise of the book is that theories and concepts can powerfully illuminate the underlying logic of public action. These "how the world works" boxes, however, are reminders that theory cannot fully explain the variety, complexity, and idiosyncrasy of human and organizational behavior.
- RULE OF LAW: These boxes contain excerpts from statutes, regulations, court decisions, and other legal documents that illuminate the immediacy of how the rule of law affects public management and public managers.

Both the conceptual boxes and the examples in the text tend to be weighted more toward national or federal government issues than toward state or local issues. Although a somewhat more even balance is in principle desirable, the actual balance reflects the fact that public management issues at the federal level and situations occurring in cities such as New York, Los Angeles, and Washington, D.C., tend to be more widely publicized, better documented, and more accessible and even familiar to students in many different settings. We hope that instructors will supplement our examples with stories from state and local settings that reflect local interests and concerns.

Third, following the main text of each chapter is a section titled "Analysis and Argument: Test Your Understanding." These end-of-chapter exercises either present a case or example or refer instructors and students to the URL of a case that is available online or that may be purchased from the Kennedy School of Government Case Program. Each case is accompanied by a series of questions that may be assigned as preparation for class discussion or as the basis of a written assignment. In general, readers are asked to analyze the case using the concepts presented in the chapter and to practice the method of argument in their responses. We have used these cases in our courses and have found them to work well.

For class discussions and assignments, students can be encouraged to exercise the "method" of the course—that is, use the tools described in chapter 3 to analyze the arguments made by public managers, elected officials, researchers, and others—or to develop their own arguments as they analyze examples and cases. Specific ideas for how to incorporate this method throughout the course are described in chapter 3.

We have found it helpful to maintain an explicit relationship between the flow of course material and the real world of public management. Students tend to react well to regular discussions of "public management in the news," based on news items that illustrate course themes and ideas. Students might be asked to submit news items for inclusion in this segment of class discussion. Involvement and interaction among students outside of class may be enhanced by using Blackboard or social bookmarking sites to post and discuss such items.

We intend for this book to be used as a platform for different types of applications and different types of pedagogical strategies. The three dimensions of public management and the method of argument provide the fundamental framing devices around which a course can be structured.

Our premise is that there is more rational, or at least systematic, thinking in public affairs than may be apparent from media accounts. The institutional framework of American governments tends toward reasoned explanations and justifications for policies and budgets. Making persuasive arguments does matter in practice; and, to the extent it does, that is healthy for democratic governance.

But emotions, deeply held convictions, and prior experience and beliefs matter, too. We need to understand that emotions, obligations, and values; intuition, self-interest, and psychological biases; and commitments to excellence, efficiency, and the public good affect choice and action in all branches and at all levels of government. And we need to incorporate this reality into managerial analysis and argument. This does not mean that managers should appeal to emotions instead of to common sense and considerations of efficiency and effectiveness. It means that managers should understand how particular arguments are likely to be filtered through the values and emotions of citizens, legislators, and public officials. As the account in chapter 10 shows, Paul Vallas, an emotional man, was effective because his arguments reflected a causal understanding of school improvement that was persuasive.

When all is said and done, public management is about making good on those values and commitments that have been given expression in public policies and laws, about satisfying citizens' expectations that their governments will perform honestly and effectively. Doing so is a matter of personal character and democratic values, about caring and serving, but it is more than that. Public managers are at the vortex of America's uniquely complex constitutional scheme, with the intense cross-pressures created by its separation of powers and checks and balances. To be effective requires intellectual, behavioral, and emotional strengths of a high—in many cases an extraordinary—order. But that is the kind of challenge the Founders of the Republic created. And there are few deeper satisfactions than meeting such challenges successfully.

ACKNOWLEDGMENTS

We gratefully acknowledge all that we have learned from our students—Laurence Lynn at the Bush School of Government and Public Service at Texas A & M University and Carolyn Hill at the Georgetown Public Policy Institute (GPPI)—who, at times unwittingly, assisted us in developing the three-dimensional approach. We received invaluable research assistance from master's students at the Bush School and GPPI: Robbie Waters Robichau, Nancy Chan, Troy Scott, and Jake Ward. We were able to improve the manuscript and sharpen our arguments based on the comments of the following reviewers: Amy Donahue, University of Connecticut; Mark Imperial, University of North Carolina, Wilmington; Ed Jennings, University of Kentucky; Mary Kirlin, California State University, Sacramento; Julia Mahler, George

Mason University; Don Moynihan, University of Wisconsin, Madison; and Larry O'Toole, University of Georgia. We also benefited from close readings of the manuscript by William T. Gormley Jr., Alisa K. Hicklin, and Megan Aghazadian. We are grateful to Anthony M. Bertelli and Ted Gayer for offering useful feedback on specific sections.

From CQ Press, we thank Charisse Kiino for her faith in this project and for guidance and good advice from start to finish, Kristine Enderle and Allison McKay for their help and patience in preparing this book for publication, Managing Editor Steve Pazdan and Marketing Manager Christopher O'Brien for all they do to make it all happen, and Erin Snow for her efforts and advice concerning marketing. Thanks also to Carolyn Goldinger for her meticulous and indefatigable copyediting, Mary Mortenson for her superb craft in preparing the indexes, and Kerry Kern for her good humor and attention to detail while seeing the book through production.

Finally, the forbearance and sustained support of our spouses, Patricia R. Lynn and Andreas W. Lehnert, were the *sine qua nons* of completing this project. We love them.

1 What Is Public Management?

At 6:30 p.m. on Thursday, August 25, 2005, Hurricane Katrina made its first landfall on the coast of Florida with wind speeds of approximately 80 mph, making it a category 1 hurricane. On Monday, August 29, at 6:10 a.m., Katrina made its second landfall in southeastern Louisiana, and shortly thereafter, its third landfall on the Louisiana-Mississippi border. Although it had reached category 5 intensity on Sunday, Katrina was a category 3 hurricane, packing 125 mph winds, when it struck the Louisiana coast. A combination of hurricane-force winds, a deluge of rain, and the storm surge of the waters of the Gulf of Mexico overwhelmed New Orleans's system of protective levees, theoretically designed to withstand category 3 storms, and exposed large areas of the city to catastrophic flooding and devastated the coasts of Louisiana and Mississippi. The aftermath of Hurricane Katrina and the response to it by officials at federal, state, and local levels of government, as well as by the private sector, continues to affect the lives of those in its path.

PUBLIC MANAGEMENT'S PERFECT STORM

The story of Hurricane Katrina is partly about politics—especially the politics of public works spending by the U.S. Army Corps of Engineers and of intergovernmental relations—and partly about policy—especially policies concerning governmental responsibilities for emergency management. It is foremost, however, a story about public management and public managers, about what was done prior to, during, and after the storm—and why—by officials with managerial responsibilities. In many ways, Hurricane Katrina was public management's perfect storm: a confluence of events, politics, policies, and personalities that pushed America's system of governance, like

New Orleans's levee system, beyond its breaking point and in the process exposed its fundamental weaknesses.

Katrina revealed, first, that command and communications structures were inadequate to cope with a hurricane of Katrina's magnitude and, in all likelihood, with disasters and terrorist incidents of similar magnitude. Second, it revealed that in some cases the organizational cultures of the entities charged with responding to such incidents impeded their ability to rise to the enormous challenges because the kinds of coordination and collaboration that could have saved lives were subordinated to narrow agency interests and standard operating procedures. Yet in other cases, organizational cultures enabled and encouraged entrepreneurial and life-saving responses by their professional staffs. Finally, the storm revealed what many would call failures of leadership, but which, perhaps even more ominously, actually constituted an inability to apply existing skills and expertise on the part of numerous officials whom the public has a right to expect will do just that—because it is their job.

Structure

A factor that this book calls "structure"—the formal and lawful delegations of specific responsibilities to designated officials and organizations—figures prominently in the Katrina story, especially those related to command and communications. The emergency management community had long anticipated the possibility that just such a severe hurricane would strike New Orleans with devastating consequences. In fact, only the year before, federal, state, and local officials had conducted an exercise, "Hurricane Pam," that simulated a category 3 hurricane and its effects on New Orleans and predicted evacuation failures and other problems that occurred in Katrina's aftermath. But follow-up on the Hurricane Pam exercise was weak, and when Katrina struck, the emergency procedures, plans, and prior agreements in place were ill-equipped to cope with an incident of this magnitude.

In the aftermath of Katrina, the U.S. Senate and the U.S. House of Representatives conducted detailed investigations and issued reports on the events leading up to and following the disaster.[1] Most of the 186 numbered findings in the Senate report address issues related to structure, and the overwhelming majority identified failures in those structures or in their interpretation. These include the following:

> 14. Confusion, ambiguity, and uncertainty characterized the perceptions of the Army Corps of Engineers, the local levee boards, and other agencies with jurisdiction over the levee system of their respective responsibilities, leading to failures to carry out comprehensive inspections, rigorously monitor system integrity, or undertake needed repairs [p. 590]. . . .
>
> 35. Although the Hurricane Pam exercise, among other things, put FEMA [Federal Emergency Management Agency] on notice that a storm of Katrina's magnitude could have catastrophic impact on New Orleans, Michael Brown and FEMA failed to do the necessary planning and preparations:
> a. to train or equip agency personnel for the likely needed operations;
> b. to adequately prearrange contracts to transport necessary commodities;

c. to pre-position appropriate communications assets; or
d. to consult with DOD [Department of Defense] regarding back-up capability in the event a catastrophe materialized, among other deficiencies [p. 592]. . . .

69. The National Communications System failed to develop plans to support first-responder communications, assess the damage to the communications systems, and maintain awareness of the federal government's available communications assets. Local governments either had inadequate plans or were unable to rapidly repair damage to their first responder communications systems [p. 595]. . . .
83. The NRP [National Response Plan] does not adequately address the organizational structure and the assets needed for search and rescue in a large-scale, multi-environment catastrophe. Under the NRP, Emergency Support Function 9 (ESF-9, Urban Search and Rescue) is focused on missions to rescue people in collapsed structures. ESF-9 gives the U.S. Coast Guard a support role for water rescue. However, the NRP does not provide a comprehensive structure for water and air rescues, which constituted a significant portion of the necessary search-and-rescue missions in the Katrina response [p. 596]. . . .
121. Early in the response, Mississippi recognized how severely Katrina had disrupted the state's infrastructure, and the resulting inability of many residents of south Mississippi to travel to the Points of Distribution to acquire life-saving supplies. The resulting "push" of supplies by the National Guard to residents was crucial to preventing additional hardship in south Mississippi [p. 599]. . . .
145. While some active-duty and National Guard units are designed and structured to deploy rapidly as part of their military missions, the Department of Defense is not organized, funded, or structured to act as a first responder for all domestic catastrophic disasters [p. 601]. . . .
174. Due to lack of planning and preparation, much of FEMA's initial spending was reactive and rushed, resulting in costly purchase decisions and utilization of no-bid, sole-source contracts that put the government at increased risk of not getting the best price for goods and services [p. 604]. . . .
176. The NRP lacked clarity on a number of points, including the role and authorities of the Principal Federal Official and the allocation of responsibilities among multiple agencies under the Emergency Support Functions, which led to confusion in the response to Katrina. Plan ambiguities were not resolved or clarified in the months after the NRP was issued, either through additional operational planning or through training and exercises [p. 604]. . . .

The examples in this section emphasize how structure—including the rule of law—shaped and constrained the activities of public officials in planning for and responding to Hurricane Katrina. As the next sections will show, two other aspects of public management were also factors in the response to Katrina. "Culture" and "craft," along with structure, form the framework for this book.

Culture

Culture encompasses the norms, values, and standards of conduct that provide meaning, purpose, and a source of motivation to individuals working within an organizational unit.

Culture is fundamental to an organization's capacity to carry out its lawful responsibilities. At least some of the failed coordination among local, state, and federal agencies that might have contributed to a joint rescue effort can be traced to ingrained organizational cultures and institutional histories that emphasized turf protection and short-term organizational interests at the expense of addressing the immediate needs of citizens and communities in the storm-ravaged areas. The lack of coordination or communication regarding responsibility for the levees, mentioned in finding 14 in the Senate report, can likely be traced to turf protection and short-term interests.

Although organizational cultures contributed to or compounded structural (and craft) failures before and after Katrina, positive responses by employees in public, nonprofit, and for-profit organizations, stemming partly from their strong organizational cultures, helped alleviate the highly visible suffering and prevented further loss of life. Intergovernmental cooperation resulted in a relatively smooth and successful evacuation by vehicle according to the "Contraflow" plan for more than 1 million people.[2] The U.S. Coast Guard, an "independent" agency within the U.S. Department of Homeland Security (DHS), quickly deployed resources as they were needed during and after the storm, rescuing more than thirty thousand people. As one Web site reported:

> During Katrina, the only thing senior Coast Guard Commanders wanted to know from their field commanders was what they needed to do their job. In normal operations, the Coast Guard does not rescue people from rooftops and deposit them on highways, but the trained and skilled officers and enlisted men and women on the ground were in the best position to figure out what needed to be done in New Orleans, and were empowered to do it. Admiral Thad Allan's first act when he visited New Orleans—immediately after relieving Michael Brown as the Primary Federal Official—was to hold a closed door meeting of the parish presidents to find out what he needed to do to help them respond to the devastation in their Parishes. It was a telling comparison of organizational cultures. While Brown was on the cell phone to the White House or the governor's office, Allan saw his immediate role required him to be in a hot room listening to the people who owned the problem.[3]

The Senate report described other examples of how organizational culture influenced response to the storm and its aftermath:

> 87. The individuals working on behalf of federal, state, and local agencies to rescue victims worked in chaotic situations often at great risk to themselves. Yet search-and-rescue resources, including boats and helicopters, were insufficient despite the accelerated deployment through the first week of the landfall [p. 596]. . . .
>
> 122. The federal government's medical response suffered from a lack of planning, coordination, and cooperation, particularly between the U.S. Department of Health and Human Services (HHS) and the Department of Homeland Security [p. 599]. . . .
>
> 134. The NOPD [New Orleans Police Department] was overwhelmed by Katrina. Under extraordinarily difficult circumstances, most of its officers performed their duties [p. 600]. . . .

148. On the whole, the performance of the individual Coast Guard personnel, sailors, soldiers, airmen, and Marines—active, Guard, and Reserve—was in keeping with the high professional standards of the United States military, and these men and women are proud of their service to help the victims of this natural disaster [p. 601]. . . .

Many of these examples show how organizational culture interacted with structure in shaping the preparation for and response to Katrina. In some cases, culture impeded the effective use of structures, while in others, organizational cultures were instrumental in overcoming structural constraints, enabling more effective responses and reflecting initiative by individuals exercising responsible professional judgment.

Craft

Craft refers to public managers' attempts to influence government performance through the force of their personal efforts in goal setting, exemplary actions, leadership, and the like. Even with structural and cultural failures working against them, managers are expected to exercise their organizational and personal skills in times of crisis to learn about the issues, overcome obstacles, make decisions, and solve problems. Again, the Senate report details a number of examples of managerial craft at all levels; as with structure, most findings (though not all) focused on managerial failures to exercise craft responsibly and effectively:

25. Governor [Kathleen] Blanco and Mayor [Ray] Nagin failed to meet expectations set forth in the National Response Plan to coordinate state and local resources "to address the full spectrum of actions" needed to prepare for and respond to Hurricane Katrina. Funding shortages and inadequacies in long-term planning doomed Louisiana's preparations for Katrina [p. 591]. . . .
34. Secretary [Michael] Chertoff appointed a field commander, [FEMA director] Michael Brown, who was hostile to the federal government's agreed-upon response plan and therefore was unlikely to perform effectively in accordance with its principles. Some of Secretary Chertoff's top advisors were aware of these issues but Secretary Chertoff has indicated that he was not. Secretary Chertoff should have known of these problems and, as a result, should have appointed someone other than Brown as Principal Federal Official [p. 592]. . . .
53. Michael Brown, FEMA's director, was insubordinate, unqualified, and counterproductive, in that he:
    a. sent a single employee, without operational expertise or equipment and from the New England region to New Orleans before landfall;
    b. circumvented his chain of command and failed to communicate critical information to the Secretary;
    c. failed to deliver on commitments made to Louisiana's leaders for buses;
    d. traveled to Baton Rouge with FEMA public-affairs and congressional-relations employees and a personal aide, and no operational experts;
    e. failed to organize FEMA's or other federal efforts in any meaningful way; and

f. failed to adequately carry out responsibilities as FEMA's lead official in the Gulf before landfall and when he was appointed as the Principal Federal Official after landfall [p. 593]. . . .

155. During this initial period after landfall, a number of military commanders within the services were proactive, identifying, alerting, and positioning assets for potential response, prior to receiving requests from FEMA or specific orders. Many of these preparations proved essential to the overall response; however, they reflected the individual initiative of various commanders rather than a pre-planned, coordinated response as is necessary for a disaster of this magnitude [p. 602]. . . .

177. Although DHS was charged with administering the plan and leading the response under it, DHS officials made decisions that appeared to be at odds with the NRP, failed to fulfill certain responsibilities under the NRP on a timely basis, and failed to make effective use of certain authorities under the NRP [p. 604]. . . .

186. Where and when personnel with experience and training on NIMS ICS [National Incident Management System Incident Command System] were in control with an adequate number of trained support personnel, coupled with the discipline to adhere to the doctrine of NIMS ICS, it made a positive difference in the quality and success of implementing an incident command structure, establishing a unified command, and the response [p. 605]. . . .

The House report on Katrina, *A Failure of Initiative,* offered this definition of initiative: "The power or ability to begin or follow through energetically with a plan or task; enterprise and determination." Its text used the terms *management, manager,* or *managers* more than five hundred times, concluding that "fundamental changes in disaster management are needed."

How should policymakers and public managers think about, let alone accomplish, changes in public management as fundamental as those called for by the House report? The issues raised for managing the response to emergencies such as Katrina might appear to be so specialized as to hold few lessons for public management in less dire circumstances. Yet Katrina reveals in sharp relief the capacity or incapacity of governments to manage in ways that citizens and their representatives have a right to expect.

The following questions apply to Katrina, but go further: How do policymakers and public managers address legal, command, and organizational structures that fail? How do they address organizational cultures labeled as "risk-averse," with employees who are unwilling to act if doing so would expose them to criticism later? How do they encourage and ensure responsible initiative? How do they address managerial issues such as adequate staffing, staff meetings, conference calls, reports, and timely communications? How can policymakers ensure that these interdependent aspects of public management create a system of public management practice throughout the federal system—because similar questions arise at state and local levels of government—that not only performs the daily work of government but also responds effectively to extraordinary events?

This book addresses these and many other issues of public management. It puts forward a way of thinking about public management and public management reform that is conducive to identifying effective solutions to government performance problems. It identifies concepts and tools of public management and illustrates their application to the kinds of issues and problems that constitute the life of the typical public manager. Using conceptual tools of public management analysis, this book argues for a perspective on public management that fully comprehends the three dimensions of public management: structure, culture, and craft.

First, this introductory chapter presents a brief overview of the history of administration and management of public programs, especially in the U.S. context. Next, different definitions of public management and administration are discussed, and a specific definition is presented that will be used throughout the book. To help make concrete the types of settings and individuals that are the book's focus, the chapter then describes the types of organizations where public managers work, the jobs they perform, and how politics, policy, and leadership affect public managerial practice. Next, the chapter describes the distinctive challenges public managers often face, followed by a discussion of the types of people who become public managers. Differences and similarities between public and private management (in theory and in practice) are reviewed. The chapter concludes with an overview of the book. The end-of-chapter exercise is to apply the ideas and concepts introduced in this chapter to analyze the public management aspects of the case of four young girls whose bodies were found in January 2008 in Washington, D.C.

THE AMERICAN PROBLEM: LEGITIMIZING THE STATE

It is instructive to remember that competent administration was a revolutionary ideal at the country's founding. The American revolutionaries' indictment of British colonial rule primarily concerned the abuse of administrative powers.[4] "[King George] has erected a multitude of new offices," complained the authors of the Declaration of Independence in 1776, "and sent hither swarms of officers to harass our people and eat out their substance." The revolutionary spirit of popular grievance in the face of oppressive or incompetent administration has never faded into the complacent attitudes toward bureaucracy found in Great Britain, continental Europe, Japan, and elsewhere. Working toward governance that is under the firm control of the people and their representatives and that performs to their expectations is the enduring project of American democracy.

Although the revolutionaries' indictment of British colonial rule primarily concerned the abuse of administrative powers, the founders were clearer about what they did not want in their institutional arrangements than about what they did want. What they did not want was a European-style centralized government with unreviewable prerogatives. "[T]he revolt against the old administrative order planted the seeds of a new administrative order without very much conscious attempt to pattern after foreign systems." [5]

Following a scheme of Montesquieu, the founders created a separation of powers: three distinct branches of government whose responsibilities are, respectively, legislative, executive, and judicial. At the same time, to ensure that no one branch assumed superordinate power, the constitutional scheme includes numerous checks and balances and permits many others. According to Article 2, Section 2, all offices must be created by law, that is, by

Congress, a power formerly vested in the Crown. The Constitution thereby gives Congress a basis, in the view of public administration and constitutional scholar John A. Rohr, "for the aggressive role it has always taken in investigating and, in some cases, in managing the activities of executive departments." Further, according to Rohr, by establishing an independent judiciary, the founders created an arrangement whereby the courts "tend to shape administrative agencies in their own image and likeness." [6] Thus, the powers of the three branches are both separated and shared.

The Constitution therefore has the effect of institutionalizing competition among the three branches of government over the extent of their respective powers. Each branch, as Rohr puts it, is to be strong, but not too strong. Public administration and management in America must continuously establish their legitimacy with the political branches of government, before the courts, and in the minds of citizens, all of which have historically been skeptical of authority delegated to unelected officials. Of necessity, American public management is intensely political and almost invariably on the defensive with respect to the kinds of criticism of government that a pluralist, decentralized democracy tends to generate.[7]

From the outset, Europeans saw American government as unique. German philosopher Georg Wilhelm Friedrich Hegel and French political historian Alexis de Tocqueville both depicted America as "essentially a stateless society, devoid of an occupationally distinct administrative class or even a noticeable institutional separation between government and society." [8] So, too, did American students of government. According to political scientists Joel Aberbach and Bert Rockman, America's uniqueness lies in the fact that "its institutional pathways are so convoluted [that is, lines of authority are unclear and confusing] and . . . its parts tend to dominate the whole." Combining federal, state, and local levels, America boasts more units of government, by far, than any other nation.[9]

The early study of public administration in the United States during the Progressive era and after World War I was concerned primarily with identifying organizational structures and principles to ensure efficient delivery of the expanding array of public services that growing urban populations and business elites demanded. Later, as the administrative state at all levels was maturing, attention began to be directed toward the practice of public management, toward what public managers do and how they do it, and toward the identification of best practices, the management strategies and techniques that had proven successful in particular situations. More recently, attention has focused on the formation and significance of organizational cultures—the beliefs and values that infuse public organizations and their employees—that can either inhibit or further the accomplishment of public purposes.

WHAT IS PUBLIC MANAGEMENT?

Definitions of public management abound. Public administration scholars George Frederickson and Kevin Smith define public management as "the formal and informal processes of guiding human interaction toward public organizational objectives." [10] Political scientist James Q. Wilson has described public management as "a world of settled institutions designed to allow imperfect people to use flawed procedures to cope with insoluble problems."[11] Seminal public management researcher Richard Elmore asserts that the term can be used in three different senses: "It describes a distinctive point of view toward graduate education for the public service. It describes what people actually do when they engage in that activity. And it describes a body of knowledge and skills, some of which can be imparted by education."[12] Summarizing the views of organizers of a conference on research in the subject, Barry Bozeman put forth this definition: "Public management research entails a focus on strategy (rather than on managerial processes), on interorganizational relations (rather than intraorganizational relations), and on the intersection of public policy and management."[13]

As the above examples make clear, definitions differ on what is the essence of the subject. A perspective that offers some additional insight is that public managers may be characterized either as **creatures** of their environments—primarily influenced and constrained by laws and rules—or as **creators** of roles for themselves and of organizational priority and capacity. The approaches that emphasize the creature aspects of public management call attention to structural arrangements such as hierarchical chains of command. In these accounts, attention may focus on components such as bureaus, offices, and job descriptions. In a related vein, explanations that focus on the functions that all managers perform also emphasize public managers as creatures of formal authority.

A well-known paper written for President Franklin D. Roosevelt's "Committee on Administrative Management" illustrates the creature perspective. Luther Gulick depicted public managers as obediently carrying out specific functions necessary to the operation of public departments and bureaus: planning, organizing, staffing, directing, coordinating, reporting, and budgeting, summarizing them as POSDCORB.[14] What is the job of the public manager? asked Gulick. His answer: POSDCORB. Another example of this approach is Henry Mintzberg's listing of ten roles common to the work of all managers, public and private, divided into three groups: interpersonal (figurehead, liaison, leader), informational (monitor, disseminator, spokesman), and decisional (improver/changer, disturbance handler, resource allocator, negotiator).[15] As creatures of their environments—subservient to political, legal, and organizational influences—managers do create strategies and choose techniques to accomplish the purposes of public policy, but the balance of compliance and creativity is determined largely by the political and legal environment.

In contrast, approaches to public management that view public managers as creators tend to assume that environmental constraints provide wide latitude for managerial judgment, especially for managers in senior positions. In accounts that emphasize network relationships, for example, the focus may be on how managers use their discretion to create formal or informal patterns of coordination among and within organizations, as well as "micro-networking" of individuals working within and across organizational boundaries.[16] In these approaches, public managers create opportunities, policy, direction, administrative structures, and organizational relationships for those whom they manage and with whom they interact.

To illustrate the "creator" perspective, Elmore notes that "in the actual work of public managers, the technical core [the service-delivery process] becomes less important with increasing responsibility while the institutional, substantive, and influence domains become more critical, both to the performance of individuals and to the functioning of government."[17] Herbert Simon's approach is to emphasize motives and emotion in managerial decision making: "Perhaps the most useful way to think about emotion in relation to administration and to decision-making in organizations is to think of it as a force that helps direct actions toward particular goals by holding attention on them and the means of their realization."[18] These means may include overcoming institutional constraints, perhaps through networking, rather than passively accepting them.

Throughout this book, the public manager is viewed as neither solely creature (primarily influenced and constrained by structural arrangements and roles) nor solely creator (of opportunities and context) but as both creature and creator. And **public management** is defined as: *the process of ensuring that the allocation and use of resources available to the government are directed toward the achievement of lawful public policy goals.* This definition sees the public manager as both creature—of politics, law, structures, and roles—and creator—of strategies, capacity, and results.

Ensuring encompasses oversight and accountability, as well as the specification and provision of structures that enable, constrain, and support the tasks of fulfilling the goals of public policy. This process is the shared, formal responsibility of legislators, elected executives and their appointed and career subordinates, agencies and offices specifically charged with oversight, advisory bodies, and the courts. It is also the informal responsibility of private "watchdog" organizations, interest groups, and others with a stake in policy achievement. The political nature of public management distinguishes it from private management, as will be argued more fully later in this chapter.

Directing encompasses the formal, informal, guiding, discretionary, and motivational responsibilities of public executives and their appointed and career subordinates in the public organizations that exist to achieve public policy goals. This process applies as well to their agents—contractors and grantees—in the private sector.

Ensuring and directing do not occur in a vacuum. They occur in a specific organizational and political context that is characterized both by internal capacity and culture and by external influences and realities. In particular, public management necessarily occurs within the American constitutional scheme, which features the separation of powers among three branches of government; checks and balances, which prevent the branches from encroaching on each other; and federalism, which assigns powers to the federal government and reserves all other power for the states and for the people.

The story of Hurricane Katrina reveals serious failures of ensuring and directing: ensuring failures because the necessary authority and organization for an effective response had not been provided, and directing failures because the authority and organization that were provided, as flawed as they were shown to be, were used ineffectively by public managers. The preparation for and response to Katrina occurred within—and revealed the determinative significance of—the legal and political context in which public management is practiced in the United States. Katrina's public management "perfect storm" occurred because public managers were constrained to performing roles as creatures and, in many cases, failed to respond adequately in their roles as creators. In chapter 2, where this book's three-dimensional approach to public management is developed more fully, the ideas of public managers as creatures and creators—as actors who enable and direct in particular organizational, political, and legal contexts—is revisited.

WHERE DO PUBLIC MANAGERS WORK?

Public managers work in the departments, agencies, bureaus, and offices of federal, state, and local governments. The responsibilities of these organizations vary widely: from providing basic public services, such as education, fire-fighting, and law enforcement, to regulating environmental pollution and the safety of coal mines, gathering and analyzing intelligence, and fighting wars. Their characteristics—size in terms of budgets and personnel, diversity of mission, complexity of tasks, degree of centralization or decentralization, extent and sources of political support—vary widely as well, but the secretary of defense and the official in charge of a local animal control office are both public managers.

Public management scholars have attempted to create analytic rather than simply descriptive perspectives on the organizations where public managers work and, by implication, on the nature of public management jobs. The best known of these analytic perspectives is James Q. Wilson's popular monograph *Bureaucracy: What Government Agencies Do and Why They Do It.* Wilson identifies four types of public organizations, defined as different combinations of two factors: outputs—the nature of the day-to-day work, or the operational activities of the organization—and outcomes—the nature of the impact of this work on individuals and society.[19]

In Wilson's **production organizations,** outputs and outcomes are easily observed and relatively easily measured. Public managers can, within the constraints of their political contexts, more readily pursue the goal of efficient operations. Wilson cites the Internal Revenue Service (IRS) and the Social Security Administration (SSA) as production organizations. For **procedural organizations,** outputs are observable by managers but outcomes may be far less observable or measurable. Here, Wilson cites human service organizations such as mental health agencies, where treatments can be observed but impacts on patients or clients may be difficult to identify. In procedural organizations, public managers tend to focus on measuring work activity rather than outcome achievement.

Wilson's **craft organizations** are the opposite of procedural organizations in that their operational activities are difficult to observe but the outcomes are more readily observable. Wilson points to investigative agencies whose operations may be less standardized and are conducted in the field, such as those that regulate mines, slaughterhouses, and assembly lines. Public managers in these organizations may allow considerable discretion to employees in the field and seek to earn their trust. Finally, **coping organizations** are those for which neither operational activities nor their impacts are observable. Wilson sees police departments and public schools, especially in urban areas, as coping organizations. Here the public managers may face chronic conflict with operational personnel and external stakeholders, and their jobs are often regarded as impossible, a phenomenon discussed further in chapter 10.

CONCEPTS IN ACTION

Outputs, Outcomes, and Managerial Action

Using James Q. Wilson's framework to classify an organization as either production, procedural, craft, or coping is only a first step in analyzing the kinds of issues that a manager in such an organization might face. Even if measures of input, output, and impact are available, as the following excerpt implies, the manager faces the question of how to interpret this information and pursue appropriate action.

Many universities would originally only measure "inputs"—that is, the grades and tests scores of incoming students. "No one was actually focused on how many students stayed or how they learned," [Gene Tempel, director of Indiana University's Center on Philanthropy] says. Eventually, schools began measuring "outcomes" to calculate the number of graduates going on to obtain high-paying jobs or higher degrees. "But the final question is," Tempel says, "What impact is this student having on society—how many of our alumni are doing what? For instance, how many of them patented inventions to treat diseases?" This kind of data can be incredibly important to a school. At the same time, it is also the most difficult to interpret. Can a university actually take credit for a graduate's achievements later in life? If so, how much? And if a school solves the credit equation, how does it reproduce that success with its current students?

Source: Jon Gertner, "For Good, Measure," *New York Times,* March 9, 2008.

Another approach to analyzing the differences in public organizations is that of British political scientist Patrick Dunleavy. He distinguishes several types of agencies depending on how their resources are allocated to three different types of budget: the **core budget,** which are the direct operating costs, such as the salaries of employees and ordinary operating expenses; the agency or **bureau budget,** which includes agency overhead expenses, such as management information systems and space rental, and the noncore costs of serving clients, such as medications; and the **program budget,** or the funds appropriated to the agency but passed through to other government agencies.[20]

Dunleavy's argument is that managerial incentives and tasks differ depending on the structure of the agency's budget. Pressures to maximize budgets tend to be greater in agencies with relatively large core budgets than in agencies with relatively large program budgets, where increases are passed through to other organizations and individuals. Therefore, public management behavior is likely to vary by the type of agency in which managers work. Dunleavy identifies five different types of agencies: delivery, regulatory, transfer, contract, and control.

Delivery agencies are characterized by absolutely and relatively large core budgets and are analogous to Wilson's production agencies. These are classic bureaucracies, where agency employees serve the public: the Federal Bureau of Prisons and state-run institutions such as prisons and mental hospitals. **Regulatory agencies** have absolutely small but relatively large core budgets. Examples include the U.S. Mine Safety and Health Administration and state insurance commissions, small organizations whose missions are carried out largely by agency employees. **Transfer agencies,** such as the SSA and state agencies administering welfare programs for the poor, have relatively small core budgets but absolutely large bureau/agency budgets, and most agency outlays consist of payments to individuals.

Contract agencies have relatively large program budgets but, because of the need to write contracts and supervise contractors, significant core budgets. Examples are the National Aeronautics and Space Administration (NASA), which has a sizable staff to oversee contractors who manufacture space vehicles, and the National Institutes of Health, which has a sizable intramural research program and a larger research program based in the scientific community. Finally, **control agencies** have relatively and absolutely large program budgets. Examples are the Federal Highway Administration, which channels funds to state transportation agencies for highway and road construction and maintenance, and state agencies administering public education programs and channeling funds to local school districts. Additional types or subtypes of control agencies include revenue-collection agencies such as the IRS, trading agencies such as the Power Marketing Administration, and servicing or housekeeping agencies such as the General Services Administration.

Classification schemes like those of Wilson, Dunleavy, or others, can provide an analytic perspective on where public managers work and can be used to identify the types of constraints and opportunities they may encounter, the types of work they are likely to do, and the challenges they are likely to face. These classifications can be used to analyze the kinds of structural, cultural, and craft issues that confront public managers.

WHAT DO PUBLIC MANAGERS DO?

Within the different types of organizations such as those described above are the actual jobs of public managers. Gordon Chase and Elizabeth Reveal provide a snapshot of the scope of positions filled by public managers:

> Typically, agency heads, commissioners, cabinet members, and people of similar rank are considered "public managers." . . . But public managers are of more humble rank as well; in fact, a public manager is anyone who has responsibility for spending public

> monies and directing public employees toward ends authorized by chief executives and legislatures or mandated by courts. Public managers can be police chiefs or insurance commissioners, school principals or hospital administrators, welfare supervisors or prison wardens; or any of the thousands of other public servants responsible for everything from water to roads, mental health to education.[21]

Within a department or program, managerial jobs may consist of a single position or a hierarchy of senior- and mid-level managers with responsibility for overseeing or implementing a particular program or function. An example of a single position would be the manager for environmental services in a small city or town, who is primarily concerned with refuse collection and recycling waste. In a hierarchical system, consider the managerial structure for implementing Head Start, a federally funded program that offers education, nutrition, and social services to low-income preschoolers. The program is under the auspices of HHS, and its services are delivered by public, nonprofit, and for-profit sector providers at the local level. Head Start programs are funded by federal-to-local grants administered by the appropriate HHS regional office.

The secretary of HHS is ultimately responsible for Head Start, among many other programs. As depicted in Figure 1.1, the chain of managerial delegation at the federal, state, and local levels for Head Start flows from the secretary to the assistant secretary for the Administration for Children and Families to the director of the Office of Head Start.[22] This office in Washington, D.C., is responsible for the development of regulation and policy, program oversight and monitoring, and budget, as well as direction of twelve regional offices. Within each regional office, a regional program manager reports to the Office of Head Start.

The regional program managers administer the local grants. Each local grantee has a management structure commensurate with its size of enrollment and complexity. In New York City the Administration for Children's Services (ACS) is responsible for overseeing Head Start programs. In addition to Head Start, the ACS director is responsible for overseeing family court legal services, child protection, and foster care programs, and other programs and services. Next in the chain of delegation is the deputy commissioner for child care and Head Start, and next is an assistant commissioner for Head Start. At the front lines of service delivery and responsible for its implementation is a public manager, the director of a particular Head Start program in a particular location.

The chain of delegation—from the secretary of HHS to the director of the Office of Head Start to the regional program manager to the assistant commissioner for Head Start in New York City down to the local managers who oversee program implementation—illustrates the scope of managerial positions involved in implementing a single program. Not every public program includes such an extensive managerial structure, but others may require even more complex structures.

Whether public managers work under a simple or complex managerial structure, their choices and actions are constrained by factors that are beyond their control. A manager must conform to mandates, laws, and guidelines established by political processes or by higher-

FIGURE 1.1 Managerial Hierarchy: National, Regional, and Local Managerial Positions in the Head Start Program

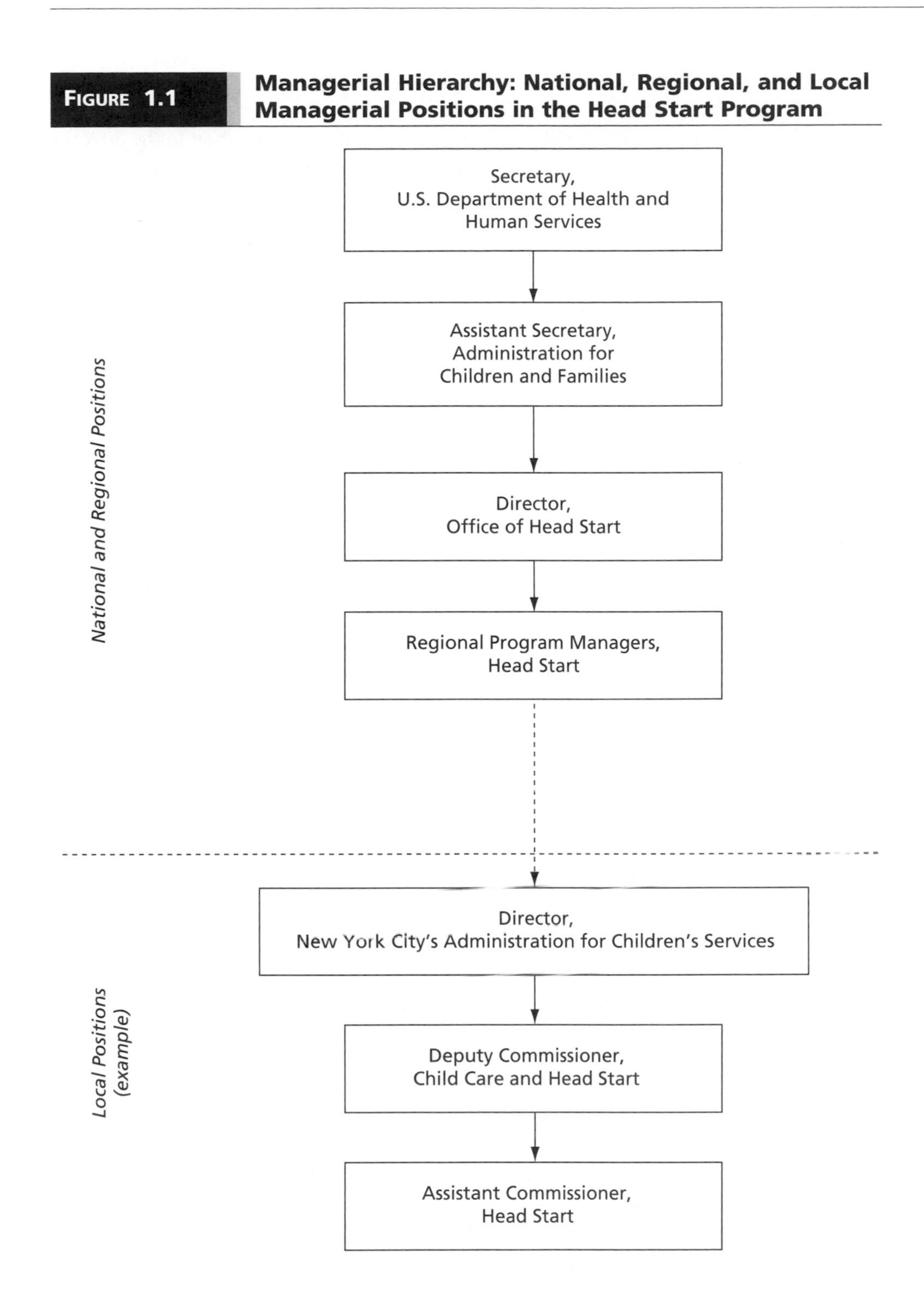

level policymakers.[23] The American system of checks and balances, with its multiple points of involvement by politically motivated actors, introduces additional constraints and accountability channels to which public managers must adhere. In addition to the directive activities uniquely associated with management, the job of a public manager may at times also enter the realms of politics, policymaking, and institutional leadership. Each of these roles makes a distinctive contribution to the public manager's job.

The domain of **politics** is concerned principally with the distribution and use of power over the resources of the nation, summed up nicely in the title of political scientist Harold Lasswell's seminal text, *Politics: Who Gets What, When, How.*[24] According to the U.S. Constitution, citizens have sovereign power, and their wishes are given expression through elected representatives in the political branches of government. The focus of politics is therefore on broad purposes and on governmental processes—that which gives voice to citizen preferences, traditionally referred to as "the public will," and which allocates resources among political jurisdictions, interests, policies, and programs.

The domain of **policymaking** is concerned with making these political purposes specific, choosing from among alternative courses of action those that reflect the values, interests, and facts of given situations and of the actors involved. Therefore, policymaking involves the subject matter or substance of governmental activity, with making specific choices concerning substance that are manifested in statutes, appropriations, organizations, regulations, budgets, strategies, and precedent-setting decisions. Policymaking is certainly influenced by political values and processes, but the reverse is also true: As E. E. Schattschneider observed, "New policies create a new politics." [25]

In the context of a particular setting, situation, program, policy, or discussion, leaders clarify purposes and incite others to take action toward a focused goal. James MacGregor Burns wrote that leadership occurs "when persons with certain motives and purposes mobilize, in competition or conflict with others, institutional, political, psychological, and other resources so as to arouse, engage, and satisfy the motives of followers . . . in order to realize goals mutually held by both leaders and followers." [26] Leadership is essential when purposes are unclear, when a sense of direction is absent, when the situation is characterized by confusion and conflict, or when motivation is lacking.

Public managers, then, have the responsibility for the accomplishment of public purposes. Yet managing is not simply a matter of carrying out the instructions of politicians and policymakers. An early view in U.S. public administration, known as the "politics-administration dichotomy" (discussed further in chapter 8) was that politics and administration could (and should) be separated.[27] This sentiment reflected in part a desire to eliminate corruption from the administration of public programs and in part the era's emphasis on the science of administration.

Today, more than a century later, the possibility and advisability of maintaining such a dichotomy have, for the most part, been dismissed. Politics and policymaking produce mandates that are almost always ambiguous, subject to conflicting interpretations, politically controversial, and inadequately supported with resources and structures of communication and cooperation. Under these circumstances, management consists of making concrete decisions within the limits of delegated discretion and motivating subordinates and others to act. Management therefore must be both substantive and instrumental. As depicted in Figure 1.2, through the authority delegated to public managers, the domain of public management can, depending on the situation, include politics, policymaking, and leadership. In other words, public management can be not only about conducting the public's business, but also about helping to define what the public's business actually entails.

Political scientist Terry Moe's theory of public bureaucracy illustrates the interplay of public management with politics and public policymaking.[28] Moe's starting point is that organizations created in the public sphere are characterized by four elements not found in market relationships: public authority, a political rather than technical/economic basis for organizational design, political uncertainty, and political compromise. Together, these four characteristics result in the creation of organizations, programs, and managerial roles that would not be favored if the decisions of political and interest group actors were solely driven by economic or **technical rationality.** The resulting structures, Moe argues, instead reflect **political rationality.**

FIGURE 1.2 **The Domain of Public Management**

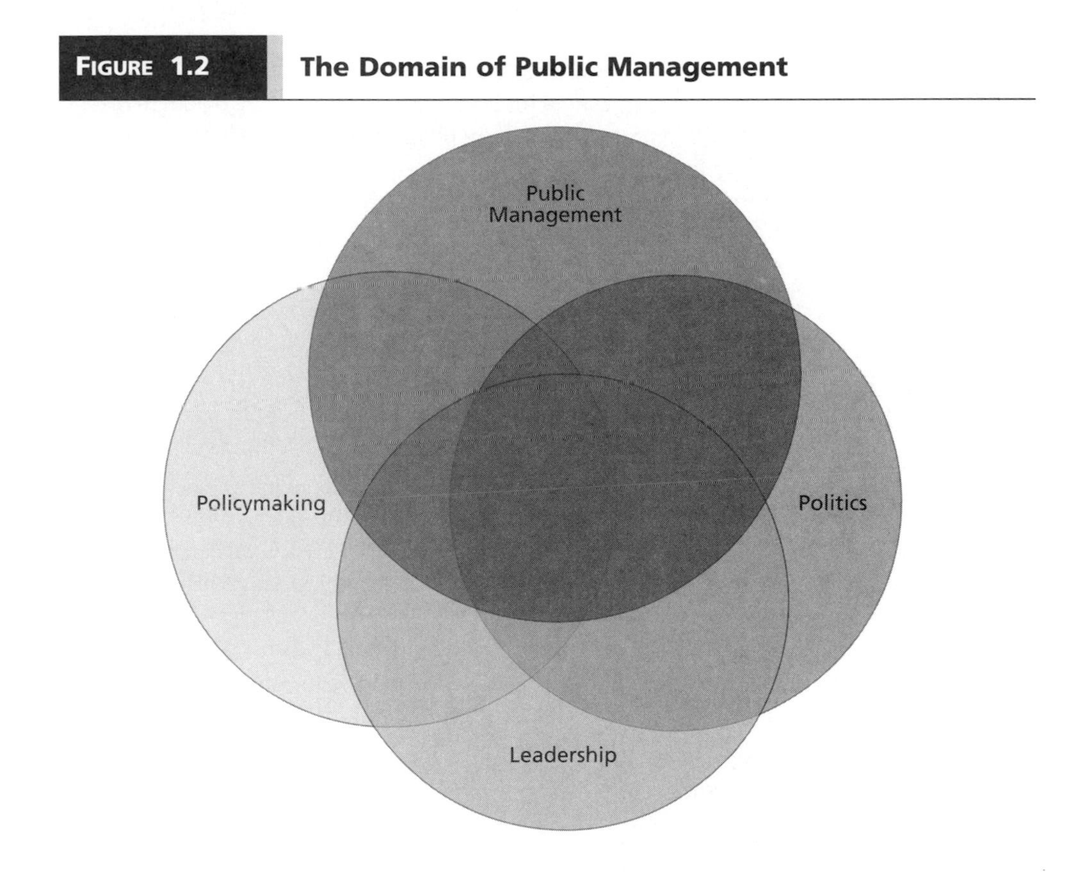

CONCEPTS IN ACTION

Technical Rationality and Political Rationality

The excerpt below is from a Government Accountability Office report on the experiences of Defense Department managers in weapons systems programs. The report describes the constraints, cross-pressures, and continual competition for funding the managers face. Such characteristics would be unlikely had the programs been designed with technical rationality in mind; instead, these pressures almost certainly are products of a system driven by political rationality.

Program managers themselves believe that rather than making strategic investment decisions, [the Department of Defense] starts more programs than it can afford and rarely prioritizes them for funding purposes. The result is a competition for funds that creates pressures to produce optimistic cost and schedule estimates and to overpromise capability. . . . Moreover, once programs begin, the program manager is not empowered to execute the program. In particular, program managers cannot veto new requirements, control funding, or control staff. . . . Program managers also believe that they are not sufficiently supported once programs begin. In fact, they must continually advocate for their programs in order to sustain support. . . . [P]rograms are incentivized to suppress bad news and to continually produce optimistic estimates—largely due to continual funding competition.

Source: U.S. Government Accountability Office, *Best Practices: Better Support of Weapon System Program Managers Needed to Improve Outcomes,* GAO-06-110, 2005.

> Bureaucratic structure emerges as a jerry-built fusion of congressional and presidential forms, their relative roles and particular features determined by the powers, priorities, and strategies of the various designers. The result is that each agency, whatever the technical requirements of effective organization might seem to be, cannot help but begin life as a unique structural reflection of its own politics.[29]

Public managers therefore are constrained by the structures bequeathed to them by the political and policymaking process. "As a result of regime restraints and the politics they authorize, the public manager may have to deal with inadequate resources, unreasonable or unrealistic workload or reporting requirements, inconsistent guidance, or missions defined so as to be virtually unachievable." [30]

Yet using the authority delegated to them and opportunities inherent in managerial roles, public managers can become politically influential:

> Once an agency is created, the political world becomes a different place. Agency bureaucrats are now political actors in their own right: they have career and institutional interests that may not be entirely congruent with their formal missions, and they have powerful resources—expertise and delegated authority—that might be employed toward these "selfish" ends. They are new players whose interests and resources alter the political game.[31]

In describing what public managers do, this section has discussed the kinds of positions they hold as illustrated by the Head Start program. It also discussed the broad directive activities in their role as managers and their other roles—politician, policymaker, and leader. Working in environments that are products of *political rationality,* not solely *technical rationality,* public managers face particular challenges in navigating this terrain.

WHAT KINDS OF CHALLENGES DO PUBLIC MANAGERS CONFRONT?

In every organization, whether public or private, managers routinely encounter problems—of resources, personnel, priorities, technology, and task organization—that arise within their areas of authority and that are more or less within their power to solve. For this kind of problem, the extent of organizational interdependence is often low, meaning that the organization does not need the support of other organizations to take effective action, and therefore managerial focus and accountability are primarily internal to the organization.

Yet decisions for "routine" managerial tasks can have consequences, especially in government. When managers at U.S. Citizenship and Immigration Services diverted staff from processing applications to the heavier burden of completing security checks on the applicants, the processing time increased dramatically despite promises to cut waiting times in half.[32]

During the relatively routine activity of moving a spacecraft at Lockheed-Martin (a NASA contractor) in 2003, the staff ignored several of the procedures and checks in place for this task. Only six people were present instead of the required eleven; the NASA quality assurance team member arrived late and signed off on already completed steps he had not observed; the cart to be used to move the spacecraft was not inspected at the time of the move; and the visual observation by one staff person that "something looked different" about the cart was ignored. The cart collapsed when the spacecraft was loaded onto it, causing $200 million in damage.[33]

The consequences of mismanaging "routine" tasks may range from the merely regrettable—lost time to complete an assignment—to dire, involving significant waste of public resources or even the loss of life, if failure to follow agency standard operating procedures leads to child abuse or a missed opportunity to arrest a dangerous criminal. The point is that managers can take steps to prevent future occurrences of similar problems. They can reallocate internal resources, arrange for additional training, or punish lax performance. In fact, managerial actions almost certainly ensure that such adverse events do not happen more often.

The potential consequences of managerial action are compounded, however, when public managers operate in situations that are extraordinary in scope and complexity and beyond their ability to resolve on their own. Consider the circumstances the FEMA director faced during Hurricane Katrina and its aftermath. The extent of organizational interdependence was high, meaning that coordination and collaboration was essential, and the director was accountable to a broad array of constituencies beyond the boundaries of his agency. Katrina taught Americans that the actions of public managers have social, economic, and public policy implications that may include the well-being of individuals and communities, the security of the nation, prospects for life and death of employees and citizens, and the reputation of government for competence in accomplishing public purposes. Within this broad characterization, a number of **distinctive challenges of public management** can be identified.

First, public managers may confront situations whose causes and solutions lie in significant part outside the boundaries of their formal authority and even beyond the reach of their influence. In such situations managers require extensive voluntary cooperation from other officials who are likely to have different interests and priorities. The managers may need to share information in an attempt to "connect the dots" and develop a full understanding and assessment of a situation. The identification, apprehension, and prosecution of the so-called Beltway snipers in the Washington, D.C., metropolitan area in 2002, who killed ten people and critically injured three others, required the cooperation of police departments from three different jurisdictions, the Justice Department, state attorneys general, state and local crime laboratories, officers of the courts, human service workers, and members of the public without any formal structures of interjurisdictional coordination and little or no history of informal cooperation.

Second, public managers may be under pressure to satisfy the expectations of powerful actors within and outside of their jurisdictions—legislators and legislative committees, interest groups, judges, and elected executives—that are often in conflict. The Environmental Protection Agency (EPA) has conducted years of study and public comment solicitation regarding cleanup of polychlorinated biphenyls (PCBs) that pollute the Hudson River. General Electric Company, source of the PCBs, has opposed the plan for dredging the river, challenging the scientific evidence on the harmfulness of PCBs and arguing that natural processes would be sufficient to flush them out. The debate has involved local, state, and federal elected officials, as well as lawsuits and administrative law hearings.

Third, public managers may be responsible for ensuring the accountability of subordinate agents inside and outside of government over whom their authority, formal and informal, may be ill-defined or nonexistent. When reconstruction of damaged property began in Afghanistan and Iraq, the United States relied on often hastily arranged, opportunistic relationships with dispersed networks of contractors that lacked formal accountability structures and that blurred the distinction between public and private liability. These circumstances resulted in numerous investigations carried out by the Office of the Special Inspector General for Iraq Reconstruction, the Defense Contract Audit Agency, the Government Accountability Office, and the inspectors general of agencies involved in reconstruction. Their findings of malfeasance and mismanagement have led to arrests and convictions.

A fourth challenge is that public managers often learn about serious problems within their jurisdictions from media reports or legislative inquiries that are based on information leaked by their own subordinates, uncovered by investigative reporters using Freedom of Information Act authority, or legally provided by whistleblowers inside their organizations. Managers are put on the defensive and expected to respond before they can acquire an adequate understanding of situations that may be spinning out of their control. The death of Buumba, a zebra at the National Zoo in Washington, D.C., set in motion a series of allegations, investigations (including one by the National Academy of Sciences), and damaging revelations of internal management policies and actions. The zoo director resigned amid considerable acrimony and controversy.

Fifth, public managers may receive warnings of immediate but poorly defined threats, vulnerabilities, or breakdowns in operations. They must then decide whether to take action and, if so, what kinds of action to take, in situations where the costs of acting, the uncertainties associated with any action, and the consequences of being wrong are all extraordinarily high. Telecommunications workers inspecting a cable running through an abandoned concrete tunnel under the Chicago River discovered a leak described as "a tree-like piling piercing through the tunnel roof with a mound of mud slowly growing at its base."[34] The damage may have been caused by construction work at a nearby bridge. They forwarded a videotape to the supervisor of Chicago's Department of General Services, who placed it in his desk drawer. Although officials claimed that the situation was not serious and that they did not want to spend $10,000 maintaining a tunnel that was never used, they nevertheless began a bid process to repair the tunnels. While these managers were planning to contract for repairs in accordance with established operating procedures, within months the leak widened and finally ruptured on April 13, 1992, at 5:57 a.m., flooding the central business district (the famous Loop). The damage required expensive repairs and cleanups and provoked reprisals by the mayor against those (notably the acting transportation commissioner, a thirty-year city employee) held responsible for failure to take timely action.

Sixth, public managers must contend with their permanent employees' ingrained values and beliefs, which have become dysfunctional and yet are stubbornly resistant to change. Investigations of the *Columbia* space shuttle accident and of intelligence collection and analysis activities prior to the U.S. invasion of Iraq focused on how the institutionalized values of agency personnel—the organizational cultures of NASA, the FBI, the CIA, and other agencies—influenced their judgments and conclusions. They tended to screen out dissonant information that did not fit prevailing patterns of belief, but their decisions had unfortunate, possibly preventable, consequences.

A final distinctive challenge of public management mentioned here (there are undoubtedly others) is that public managers may find themselves in a situation characterized by sudden or sharp shifts in priorities or tasks. As agencies such as FEMA were incorporated into the newly formed Department of Homeland Security, their focus was abruptly reoriented away from their usual priorities and toward homeland security and combating terrorism. The consequences, as seen in the Katrina response, can be severe if adjustments are not made rapidly and successfully so that confusion over mission, goals, and means is minimized.

These kinds of complex, sometimes intractable, public management challenges underlie many of the high-profile public affairs stories of recent years: prisoner abuse at Abu Ghraib, Guantánamo Bay, and other U.S. detention facilities; a second fatal accident in NASA's space shuttle program; ongoing and seemingly irresolvable management problems at the IRS and the FBI; intelligence failures preceding the 9/11 terrorist attacks and the American-led invasion of Iraq; the management of war and reconstruction in Afghanistan and Iraq; and continuing controversies associated with implementation of the No Child Left Behind Act and the Medicare prescription drug program. Efforts by policymakers to effectively address these and the less dire challenges that arise throughout American government require sophisticated analysis and public managers who can formulate and execute complex strategies of amelioration.

Such efforts are vindicated by the numerous public management success stories: the largely effective management of the anthrax crisis by officials of the U.S. Postal Service from October through December 2001; the success of Mayor Rudolph Giuliani's administration, particularly, Chief of Police William Bratton, in developing an exemplary management system, known as CompStat, that was associated with reducing crime in New York City; Oklahoma's use of an innovative performance contracting scheme, which brought about a dramatic transformation in the philosophies of nonprofit agencies serving profoundly disabled people, significantly improving their quality of life; and the success of James Lee Witt, director of the then–cabinet-level FEMA from 1993 to 2001, in transforming the agency from a political dumping ground into a widely respected emergency services organization. These stories illustrate how—even in the face of distinctive challenges of public management—combinations of effective enabling structures, deliberate attention to the transformation of organizational cultures, and skilled managers can, in normal circumstances and under pressure, bring about transformative changes in public management.

Addressing public management challenges is not simply a concern of technocrats, consultants, or scholars who study government. Indeed, public management competence has become a matter of high political importance and has led to reforms emanating from both the legislative and executive branches. Congress passed the Government Performance and Results Act (GPRA) in 1993, and more recently has attempted to restructure and redirect the national intelligence community and the agencies concerned with homeland security. President George W. Bush's management agenda featured accelerated privatization, the linking of program performance to budget making, and performance-based personnel system reforms. These and other legislative and executive initiatives, discussed in chapter 9, are visible manifestations of deep and broad efforts to improve governmental performance through better management.

WHAT KIND OF PEOPLE BECOME PUBLIC MANAGERS?

What do we know about the kind of men and women who serve as public managers? Ideally we would like to know about their backgrounds and qualifications, about what motivates them to work in the public sector, and about their craftsmanship, noting in particular what sets them apart from managers in the private sector. Unfortunately, the kind of systematic information needed to answer such questions is unavailable or incomplete, but some insights into how public managers feel about their work and their characteristic behaviors can be gleaned from a large survey of federal employees conducted by the U.S. Office of Personnel Management and from research.

Evidence from the Federal Human Capital Survey

The 2006 Federal Human Capital Survey surveyed more than 220,000 federal employees working in different departments and small/independent agencies across the nation. Although these results may not be generalizable to public employees at other levels of government, a number of findings from the survey are notable:

- Approximately 90 percent of all respondents believe their work is important; 83 percent like the kind of work they do; and close to 73 percent report getting a sense of personal accomplishment from their work.
- Nearly half of those surveyed reported having high levels of respect for their organization's senior leaders, but less than 40 percent reported that their leaders generated high levels of motivation and commitment to the workforce.
- When asked about the level of good work being done by their immediate supervisor/team leader, 66 percent of respondents were positive. But only 47 percent of respondents were satisfied with the communication they received from management about what was going on in the organization, and only 41 percent were satisfied with the policies and practices of their senior leaders.
- Eighty-three percent reported that the people they worked with cooperated to get the job done, but only 39 percent believed that creativity and innovation were rewarded; 32 percent believed that personnel decisions were based on merit; 30 percent felt that differences in performance were recognized in a meaningful way; and just 29 percent believed that proper action was taken to deal with poor performers.[35]

Insights from Research

One explanation and description of the kinds of people who become public managers can be found in the public service motivation literature, which holds that individual interests, norm-based motives, and affective motives are related to the choice of careers in the public sector.[36] The public service motivation framework as well as others that explore links between values, motives, professional training, and other aspects of public service are discussed further in chapter 6.

At this point, some insights into the matter can be gained from individual research studies, but with the caution that their findings may not be generalizable to all types of public managers. Joel Aberbach, Robert Putnam, and Bert Rockman found that American bureaucratic elites—that is, senior officials—at the federal level are, like their European counterparts, from the *crème de la crème* of society, although not as *un*representative of society as a whole as European bureaucrats. American bureaucracies are much less centrist and "much more reflective of the vivid hues of the full national ideological spectrum than are the rather pastel European bureaucracies, and the general image of the U.S. career civil service is slightly pinker [more politically liberal] than its European counterparts." Furthermore, "American career officials are as actively involved with members of Congress as are the political executives" and intensely involved with interest groups. "[T]he independence of Congress from the executive induces American bureaucrats to build support for their own interests from clientele groups who can wield influence on Capitol Hill. . . . Institutional incentives generate entrepreneurial instincts in American bureaucrats." [37]

In *Unsung Heroes,* Norma M. Riccucci presents the results of her study of six members of the federal Senior Executive Service, a group she calls "execucrats" because they are both public executives and career bureaucrats, responsive to their political environments and to their life-long professional commitments. Unlike political appointees, who tend to be outsiders and transients, execucrats are part of the permanent government. They play direct and indirect roles in policymaking and implementation, and their contributions are often significant. She finds that their effectiveness depends on some familiar factors: political skills, management and leadership skills, opportunities for achieving goals, experience, technical expertise, strategies, and personality. Riccucci calls the managers she studied "unsung heroes" for their achievements.[38]

In her study, *How Do Public Managers Manage?* Carolyn Ban concentrated on how federal public managers (117 managers in four agencies) cope with the constraints imposed by the personnel system and, in a related vein, by the budgetary and procurement systems. In general, public managers complain about the constraints imposed by functional systems, but they react to them in different ways. A significant number of managers attempt to cope creatively with such constraints, incurring the costs of doing so, although they will be reluctant to act unless they have the backing of their superiors. Others do not make the effort to overcome constraints and therefore are tied down by them. How public managers cope with difficult employees, for example, may depend on whether the organization's culture is supportive of their being proactive in personnel matters.[39]

Jane Hannaway studied managerial behavior in a public school system. She described the administrative system as having "neither clear guidelines nor unambiguous feedback to direct their behavior. Because of the numerous daily demands on their time, public managers in this setting tended to react selectively and sequentially to issues as they arose." Upper-level managers, Hannaway found, "keep pretty much to themselves, interacting mainly with each other. They do not seem to put much effort into reaching down into the organization, probably because they do not place a high value on what those in lower levels have to say. And lower-level managers are hesitant to interact with their superiors, especially about matters about which they are uncertain." [40]

In general, according to Laurence Lynn, case studies reveal that public managers have many different kinds of goals, including ensuring service quality and access, enforcing due process in administration, taking entrepreneurial initiatives, and building political support for their programs. Lynn quotes Douglas Yates: "Bureaucracies tend gradually to enlarge their roles over a wide spectrum of policymaking functions—spending money, designing new programs and bureaucratic units, developing new regulations, expanding their evaluation of lower-level governments, and increasing their control of the flow of information." [41]

Though the picture is incomplete, available evidence suggests that public managers are anything but passive role players. They care about their work and seek to make positive contributions to their organizations.

PUBLIC AND PRIVATE MANAGEMENT: DIFFERENCES AND SIMILARITIES

An enduring question in public management research and practice is whether management in the public sector is fundamentally different from **management in the private sector.** Are the environments and functions of managers more alike across the sectors than they are different? Or do basic differences characterize the two sectors, justifying different preparation for, and execution of, public managerial responsibilities?

Arguing that the interests of public and private organizations are fundamentally different, political scientist Frank Goodnow noted in 1893: "In transacting its business, [the government's] object is not usually the acquisition of gain but the furtherance of the welfare of the community. This is the great distinction between public and private business." [42] In a later expression of the same idea, Graham Allison argued that although some similarities exist between public and private management, the differences are far more important.[43] But, on the basis of exhaustive review of research on similarities and differences between the sectors, public management scholars Hal Rainey and Young Han Chun argue that although differences exist, they should not be overemphasized lest the generic aspects of "management" be obscured.[44]

Fundamental Differences in Public and Private Sector Activity

Two fundamental factors suggest why the interests of public and private sectors are different: the political and legal forces that create public organizations and the existence of market failures.

The first of these factors, which will be discussed at length in chapter 4, is constitutional. By design, executive authority in government is shared among the executive, legislative, and judicial branches and levels of government; public management is relatively constrained and necessarily governed by incentives that are basically political. Donald Kettl and James Fesler put it this way: "Public organizations exist to administer the law, and every element of their being—their structure, staffing, budget, and purpose—is the product of legal authority."[45] This produces the phenomenon of political rationality.

The second factor is the public and private sector organizations' response to **market failures,** which result when a free market produces inefficient resource allocations. Private, profit-seeking firms operate under maxims of technical rationality and harness individual self-interest and the flexibility inherent in market choice-making to direct resources to uses that, at least in theory, maximize efficiency. Yet private firms do not produce socially optimal levels of output for some types of goods, which creates the justification for their provision (and possibly their production) by the public sector. Public goods, externalities, and information problems are central concepts to an understanding of market failures.[46]

Public goods are "nonrival in consumption"; that is, their consumption by one person does not affect the amount that others can consume. Often, the goods are "nonexcludable" as well, meaning that it is difficult or impossible to restrict the availability of the good to everyone once it is made available to anyone. Familiar examples of such goods are the national security afforded by maintenance of military forces and the illumination afforded by streetlights. If private providers were left to produce goods with these characteristics, those who benefit from them might decline to pay for them; that is, they might "free ride" on the outlays of those who do pay. The providers would undersupply the good; they prefer to have neighbors invest in streetlights instead of installing them in front of their own homes. The public sector, therefore, would need to step in to ensure an adequate supply. Many goods exhibit varying degrees of nonrivalry or nonexcludability—television broadcasts, to which access might be either unrestricted or only on a pay-per-view basis—and thus the potential role for the public sector in supplying them may be less clear. Reflecting the "grayness" of this issue is that the Public Broadcasting Service has both ardent supporters and dedicated opponents.

Externalities are additional benefits or costs that may occur as the result of production or consumption of a good that are not fully reflected in its cost. Goods with positive externalities, including vaccinations against contagious diseases such as the flu, result in benefits that are not fully reaped by the producer or consumer, and thus private producers tend to underproduce such goods; not enough people receive the flu vaccine because they only consider the health benefits to themselves. Goods with negative externalities, such as the emission of greenhouse gasses and the use of PCBs by production processes, result in costs or harms that are not fully borne by the producer or consumer, and these types of goods tend to be overproduced.

Information problems—in particular, **information asymmetries** and **imperfect information**—are present when the parties involved in a transaction have different information about the good or service, and it may be impossible or costly for producers to know everything about their consumers. A classic example arises in the provision of insurance against job loss or poor health where the public sector provides unemployment insurance, welfare, and Medicaid. Information problems also arise in cases where it may be impossible or costly for consumers to become well-informed about the choices they face or whether they have received what they have paid for. Private sector producers might exploit information asymmetries or imperfect information in ways that are dangerous or harmful, leading to a role for the public sector in regulating or providing such goods. The Consumer Product Safety Commission and the Food and Drug Administration (FDA) play such a role. In recent years, the FDA has been under pressure to ensure that pharmaceutical manufacturers supply consumers of already-approved prescription drugs with up-to-date information concerning harmful side effects, information manufacturers are reluctant to provide voluntarily.

Distributional inequity may occur even when markets are performing efficiently. In other words, the public's preferences regarding the fair distribution of income and wealth, or access to particular goods and services such as primary health care, are not guaranteed even if classic market failures are absent. Private producers have little or no incentive to address issues of poverty or wealth inequality or, more specifically, to create an adequate supply of affordable housing or health insurance. Therefore, a potential role is created for the public sector either in subsidizing the production of such goods or, as is the case with Medicare health insurance, in actually providing them.

To address the provision of public goods, the amelioration of information asymmetries, and the assurance of distributional equity, public organizations are often created to accomplish what markets cannot or will not. Public organizations rebalance and redirect resource use in ways that are thought by their proponents to secure higher levels of social welfare than what unregulated private markets, driven by material self-interest, would produce. The choice between private and public organizations, however, need not be so stark. Nonprofit organizations, which are private but forbidden from distributing profits to officers or members, also respond to market failures. (Nonprofits are discussed further in chapter 5.) In addition, policymakers and private resource owners may rely on forms of organization or policy tools, such as vouchers or performance contracts, that attempt to combine the advantages of government and markets: the power of public authority to marshal resources and set terms for their use and the power of interest-driven voluntary choice to direct resources to their best uses subject to those terms.

Although market failures are widely recognized and studied and provide justification for what has been called "positive government," Charles Wolf has emphasized the potential importance of **nonmarket failures** when public organizations regulate or produce goods or services.[47] He points to four primary sources of nonmarket failures: disconnects between the raising and spending of revenues; "internalities" and organizational goals such as budget growth and information control; derived externalities, which are the unintended consequences of public sector provision and production, such as the urban sprawl associated with public highway construction; and distributional inequities, intentional and unintentional, that may result from the need to ration publicly financed goods and services. These problems arise, Wolf argues,

> because the supply and demand characteristics associated with their output are different. Because measures of output are often so hard to define, because feedback and signaling from "consumers" are lacking or unreliable, internal standards for nonmarket organizations cannot be derived from these sources. Furthermore, because there are usually no competing producers, the incentive created by competition to develop internal standards that will control costs is weakened. Under these circumstances, nonmarket agencies often develop internalities that do not bear a very clear or reliable connection with the ostensible public purpose that the agencies were intended to serve.[48]

In addition to the supply and demand conditions for goods and services financed or produced by the public sector, Wolf argues that these nonmarket failures are also a function of the political processes that create public organizations; the separation of payment for and receipt of benefits provided by the public sector; the difficulties of measuring output; the production of such goods by a monopolistic public agency, such as the Veterans Health Administration; uncertainties regarding production technologies for many goods provided by the public sector; and the absence of assured processes for terminating ineffective programs with politically influential constituencies.

This section described the fundamental differences that characterize public and private sector activity: The legal bases of public programs and market failures provide justification for how the environments and activities of public and private management are likely to be different. Empirical evidence also can be brought to bear on the question, discussed in the next section.

Managing in the Public and Private Sectors: Claims and Empirical Evidence

In a seminal study of the sectoral differences in managing, Graham Allison discussed why public and private management are "fundamentally alike in all unimportant respects." He described three primary areas along which management in the sectors might be compared: strategy (establishing organizational objectives and operational plans); internal components (organizing and staffing, personnel management systems, and measuring performance); and external constituencies (communicating and coordinating with other organizations as well as with other units within the organization, and communicating with the press and the public). By informally comparing the jobs of a public and private manager—the EPA director and the chief executive officer of American Motors—Allison concluded that "public and private management are at least as different as they are similar, and that the differences are more important than the similarities."[49] He argued that public management could be best improved by specific research on the subject, lesson-drawing from actual practice of public managers, and the select application of private sector management practices and principles.

More recently, the push to improve government performance (discussed in chapters 8 and 9) has prompted arguments that public organizations can be, and should be, run more like businesses. In other words, the argument is that public and private management may in fact be different, but they should not be as different as they are. In this view, running gov-

CONCEPTS IN ACTION

Comparing Public and Private Management

Robert E. Rubin served during the Clinton administration as director of the National Economic Council from January 1993 to January 1995 and as secretary of the Treasury from January 1995 to July 1999. Prior to his arrival in Washington, Rubin had worked at Goldman Sachs on Wall Street since 1966, most recently as co-chairman. The following excerpt from an article by Al Hunt at the end of Rubin's tenure conveys the secretary's views on the similarities and differences of managing in the public and private sectors.

As one of the few to rise to the very top in both Wall Street . . . and Washington, he [Rubin] sees some similarities between these two disparate worlds: There is a premium on good decision-making (he devoted an entire commencement speech at the University of Pennsylvania last month to decision-making), and on human relations.

But, he acknowledges, the differences are more profound. "A much broader range of views and life experiences are relevant to decisions you make here," notes the 60-year-old outgoing Treasury chief. "The range of issues you confront on Wall Street is really very narrow."

As much as he thrived at Goldman Sachs, his Washington years have been more interesting and rewarding, if not more enriching: "It's a remarkably stimulating experience. I was told whatever intellectual capital you have wears down; you don't have the time to build it up. I think just the opposite. You constantly evolve trying to do things and get things done. It's a dynamic process."

Further, he believes the caliber of people in government is just as high as on Wall Street or anywhere else. "If you take the senior people in this administration and put them together and called them a firm, they would be the equal in terms of ability, commitment and effectiveness to any firm I've ever encountered."

A big difference is the press. "Here, the role of the media is integral," he says, while on Wall Street it usually is peripheral. Although few officials have received better coverage, Mr. Rubin worries about the superficiality of much of the public dialogue.

Source: Albert R. Hunt, "Reflections of a Heavyweight," *Wall Street Journal,* July 1, 1999.

ernment more like a business involves practices such as "steering instead of rowing," decentralizing authority, maintaining a focus on the customer, measuring performance and concentrating on outcomes rather than outputs, and using market mechanisms instead of being guided by rules and regulations or other bureaucratic mechanisms.[50] The Clinton administration's Reinventing Government initiative and the passage of the GPRA reflected many of the ideas associated with this perspective, as did the New Public Management reforms of governments around the world (all discussed at greater length in chapter 9).[51]

Since the 1980s empirical research has examined the basis for claims of similarities or differences between the sectors. Barry Bozeman mapped "degrees of publicness" across public and private sector organizations.[52] The argument is that sectoral distinctions—public, nonprofit, for-profit—based on law are not as significant as the source of organizational authority, in particular, whether that authority tends to be primarily consumers or politicians or, in the case of nonprofits, donors.

Another important source of evidence regarding the differences between public and private management comes from the review of empirical research comparing public and private management conducted by Hal Rainey and Young Han Chun.[53] The authors first describe the differences between the sectors that researchers and practitioners often report. One difference is the environments in which public and private managers operate: Public organizations seldom sell a product or service, and they have few incentives for efficient production. Another difference lies in the types and character of the transactions between organizations and their external environments, which means greater scrutiny of public organizations. In addition are the differences in organizational roles, structures, and processes, such as expectations for accountability and fairness, diverse and unclear goals, constraints on authority imposed by political actors, red tape and procedural delays, incentive structures, and values and attitudes. Many of these differences were touched on in the previous section's discussion of political and legal bases of public organizations as well as market and nonmarket failures.

Some differences between the sectors are obvious and need not be subjected to empirical tests to be proven, while others can be settled only by empirical examination. Rainey and Chun's review of the research finds conflicting conclusions across studies: Some claims about differences between the sectors are supported by empirical evidence, such as more red tape and personnel administration problems in the public sector, but others are not. For example, Rainey and Chun find mixed evidence as to whether public sector managers have higher or equal levels of work satisfaction than managers in the private sector. Public manager work satisfaction is as high as their counterparts in the private sector, but public managers tend to express specific dissatisfactions with work.[54] For both public and private managers, being able "to make a difference" in the work of their organization shows a strong relationship to job satisfaction.[55]

A study by Santa Falcone found that public managers tended to be older and more educated than private sector managers.[56] Further, younger public managers reported having slightly higher job satisfaction than their private sector counterparts, but older public sector managers were less satisfied with their jobs than business executives. Another study found that employees in government ranked interesting work first, followed by good pay and job security as most important to them.[57] This same study found that supervisors in the public sector ranked flexibility as more important than supervisors in the private sector. Worldwide, large portions of public sector employees "fall into advanced phases of burnout," with burnout in the U.S. public sector not being "appreciably worse than in business." [58]

In a comparison of government-wide and private sector responses to the Federal Human Capital Survey, private sector employees reported higher satisfaction in the job performance of their immediate supervisor/team leader, information received from management about what was going on, and overall satisfaction with their organization, but a lower percentage reported liking the kind of work they do.[59]

Summing Up

It is certainly true that senior executives in virtually all types of complex organizations have common preoccupations with goals, people, organizational resources, task accomplishment, and constituencies. They must spend much of their time meeting with people with whom they must compromise to achieve their goals; they must choose a leadership style that motivates rather than inhibits subordinates; and they must deal with substantive and organizational complexities. Yet Rainey and Chun conclude:

> Numerous studies have found that public managers' general roles involve many of the same functions and role categories as those of managers in other settings but with some distinctive features: a more political expository role, involving more meetings with and interventions by external interest groups and political authorities; more crisis management and "fire drills"; greater challenge to balance external political relations with internal management functions.[60]

Where does this mass of evidence, claims, and counterclaims leave those who are trying to understand the differences and similarities between the sectors? The answer is that there is no simple answer; comparisons must necessarily be qualified. Lynn sums up the matter as follows:

> The two sectors are constituted to serve different kinds of societal interests, and distinctive kinds of skills and values are appropriate to serving these different interests. The distinctions may be blurred or absent, however, when analyzing particular managerial responsibilities, functions and tasks in particular organizations. The implication of this argument is that lesson drawing and knowledge transfer across sectors is likely to be useful and should never be rejected on ideological grounds.[61]

PUBLIC MANAGEMENT AND PUBLIC ADMINISTRATION: A DISTINCTION WITHOUT A DIFFERENCE?

This book is about public management. Could it also (or instead) be a text about **public administration?** [62] Is the history of public administration the same as the history of public management? Reference sources such as the *Oxford English Dictionary* and Black's *Law Dictionary* often use the term *administration* to define *management* and vice versa.[63]

Scholars differ as to whether the two concepts are distinguishable. Writers in the first half of the twentieth century, such as Leonard White, Henri Fayol, Roscoe Martin, Paul Van Riper, and Dwight Waldo, tended to view public management and public administration as synonymous, or alternatively held that management was the more overarching construct. More recently, scholars such as Hal Rainey, James Perry, Kenneth Kraemer, Mark Moore, and others tend to view public administration as the overarching construct, with public management being "novel and subordinate or specialized." [64] Lynn characterizes the different concepts of public management:

> For some, public management is irredeemably associated with "managerialism," an ideologically motivated effort to substitute corporate sector values and instrumental notions of efficiency for an ethical commitment by the state and its officers to service and collective justices, in the process transforming active citizens into passive consumers. For others, public management invites an undue focus on actors in managerial roles to the exclusion of the organization and institutions and systems that constrain and enable managerial behavior. For still others, for whom government is about politics and policy, public management is nothing more than traditional public administration with a fashionable new label, a domain for technocrats and mavens of government operations: the public sector equivalent of industrial engineering.[65]

In the absence of agreement on the primacy of either public administration or public management, terms such as *administrative management* or the plural *public management and administration* may bridge the divide. In this book, such terms will be used, and the terms *public administration* and *public management* often will be used interchangeably.

ORGANIZATION OF THE BOOK

This book's basic analytic framework is described in chapter 2, which argues that addressing managerial problems typically requires consideration of what chapter 1 has termed structure, culture, and craft. These are, respectively, organizational structures and processes that distribute authority, responsibility, resources, and access to information in ways that further policy and organizational goals; organizational cultures that reflect employees infused with beliefs and values that contribute to the organization's reputation for reliability and competent performance; and responsible judgment on the part of individual public managers concerning priorities, strategies, and methods to advance the achievement of those goals.[66]

Viewed from the perspective of individual public managers, effectiveness requires skills in analytical reasoning to construct persuasive arguments—what might be termed *persuasive rhetoric*—about how managerial problems and dilemmas might be defined, addressed, and prevented. Following this idea, chapter 3 is a "tools" chapter that provides a guide for engaging in critical analytical thinking with respect to public management issues. Its foundation is a definition for "argument" that originated with philosopher Stephen Toulmin and applies not only to managerial arguments but also to arguments found in academic articles, official reports, legislative testimony, and other sources of public deliberation.

Chapter 4 addresses the basic assumption that public management in the United States is conditioned by the constitutional scheme of governance: the rule of law. The authority and legitimacy of public management are derived from and are ultimately accountable to constitutionally recognized institutions: elected legislatures, elected executives, and judicial institutions, all of which are both prescribed by the Constitution and operate under its aegis. The chapter shows how the Madisonian interplay of faction and power establishes the political context of public management; the separation of powers among legislative, executive, and judicial branches creates tensions and dilemmas for public managers; and a hierarchical backbone that structures public management is created by the lawmaking and fiscal powers assigned to legislatures and the power of judicial review undertaken by the courts in accordance with the Constitution.

The next three chapters address each of the three dimensions of public management in detail. Chapter 5 discusses theories and functional aspects of formal authority, or structure. It addresses the enabling and constraining structures and processes that are formally mandated in legislation, guidelines, regulations, and court orders and the resultant realities and incentives faced by public managers and their subordinates. It discusses core concepts such as transaction costs, principal-agent relationships, and contracts; how structures may affect bureaucratic behavior; and third-party governance, including contracting out and nonprofit organizations. It revisits the issue of political rationality in the context of understanding the structural dimension of public management.

Chapter 6 addresses the institutionalized values and organizational cultures that emerge within organizations, such as ingrained views and habitual behaviors of field-level workers, middle managers, and career officials. These values and cultures may stem from professional training—for example, for attorneys, economists, or budgeters—or they may come from on-the-job experiences and routines. Discussed here are the shared norms, values, and understandings that provide meaning, purpose, and motivation to individuals in their roles as employees of an organizational unit, as well as values, ethics, and motives unique to individuals in their own right. Culture may work two ways—as a source of stability, motivation, and reliability or as an obstacle to change.

A third dimension—the craft of public management—is addressed in chapter 7. This chapter takes an actor-focused view of public management drawing on heuristics from the literature on public management as individual decision, choice, and behavior. It discusses the attributes, skills, and craftsmanship of individual men and women in managerial roles in government, such as cabinet officers, heads of field offices, city managers, and program managers, who operate within systems of formal authority.

Cutting across all three dimensions of public management is managerial accountability, one of the oldest, and at the same time, most elusive, issues in the field. How might public managers be held accountable to the constitutional authority that authorizes their work?

What is the meaning of managerial responsibility in public service? Chapter 8 considers the influences on and solutions to accountability suggested by each of the three dimensions of public management.

While some aspects of public management such as accountability are enduring, the shape and emphases of public management are constantly changing. Chapter 9 traces the most recent developments and intentional efforts to reform and reshape public management. Beginning in the 1970s political parties and policymakers around the world, confronting the growing expenditure demands of the modern welfare state against the background of fiscal shortages, became increasingly committed to public management reforms that would reduce the size and cost of government and create structural incentives for public managers to emphasize efficiency and performance. By the 1990s this movement had been labeled "New Public Management," and its influence, under the more general heading of managerialism, has been present in American and European governments ever since. This chapter discusses the principal reform concepts and techniques and evidence concerning their effects on the size and cost of government.

In the final chapter, the essential and interactive aspects of the three dimensions of public management are brought together. Do citizens prefer to have public managers who are entrepreneurial and visionary, who take risks on behalf of creating public value? Or, do they prefer public managers to take care that the laws are faithfully executed, minimizing instability and emphasizing reliability and transparency? Popular rhetoric may favor the former, but individuals in their roles as citizens and taxpayers are likely to favor the latter. What are the tensions inherent in such preferences, and how do they play out in specific situations? How can current and future public managers balance these tensions? Chapter 10 builds on the various ideas and themes in the previous chapters to illustrate these tensions and discusses three-dimensional management, or "managing in the black."

Because the vast majority of public managers are employed by organizations, the text adopts the organization as the primary unit of analysis. "Organization" in this sense does not solely connote formally separate entities. It may also refer to entities such as departments, agencies, bureaus, offices, contractors, or nonprofit organizations. Ideas such as coordinated or networked management are explored, but interorganizational issues are viewed from the perspective of organizational participants and their motivations and incentives to participate (or not) in such arrangements.

Throughout the text, the ideas and themes are illustrated with or applied to examples from real public management situations, case materials, academic research, and official reports and documents drawn from national, state, and local levels of government. Some of the problems and their illustrations are "high level"—reforming the FBI, ensuring safe space shuttle operations, ensuring service quality and effectiveness by child welfare agencies—to illustrate the multidimensional character and importance of the sociopolitical context in which public managers operate. Other problems and illustrations have more instrumental or operational orientations—instituting performance measurement, contracting, interagency coordination—to illustrate the managerial dilemmas that arise within a hierarchical yet decentralized, pluralistic political system. The examples describe both "successes" and "failures." Successes can inspire, motivate, and exemplify. But, as it is often easier to learn from failure than from success, the examples are weighted toward the former.

This text characterizes public management as a multifaceted endeavor, emphasizing the fundamental dimensions that define, constrain, and enable its practice: structure, culture, and craft. It traces the authority of public management to the rule of law, emphasizes management analysis that utilizes the method of argument, and describes frameworks and concepts upon which practitioners can draw. In the final analysis, the primary goal of this book is to improve the practice of public management by assisting readers to become better prepared for its intellectual and rhetorical challenges.

Key Concepts

creatures
creators
public management
ensuring
directing
production organizations
procedural organizations
craft organizations
coping organizations
core budget
bureau budget
program budget
delivery agencies
regulatory agencies
transfer agencies
contract agencies
control agencies
politics
policymaking
technical rationality
political rationality
distinctive challenges of public management
management in the private section
market failures
public goods
externalities
information asymmetries
imperfect information
distributional inequity
nonmarket failures
public administration

Analysis and Argument: Test Your Understanding

On January 9, 2008, the bodies of four young girls (ages five, six, eleven, and sixteen) were found in a Washington, D.C., house by U.S. marshals. The officers were performing a routine search as they served an eviction notice to its occupant, Banita Jacks. Jacks—the mother of the four girls—was charged with their murder. Authorities estimated she had been living in the house with the girls' corpses since at least September 2007, and perhaps as long as eight months, since May 2007.

Two days after the bodies were found, D.C. mayor Adrian Fenty released a timeline beginning in December 2005 and ending in January 2008 that described contacts between the family and five D.C. government agencies: the Child and Family Services Agency, D.C. public schools, the police department, the Department of Human Services, and the Department of Health. On January 13, demonstrating his pledge to "create a more responsive, accountable government," Fenty fired six child welfare workers because they " 'just didn't do their job.' "[67]

After reviewing the sources listed below, answer the following questions. Use concepts introduced in this chapter as well as specific evidence from the news and other sources regarding the case to support your answers.

1. What aspects of formal structure, organizational culture, and managerial competence and judgment do you identify in this case? As part of answering this question, identify the public managers and the frontline workers, where they work, and the roles they play.
2. Using the aspects you identified in the previous question, consider the following questions:
    a. Was it within any D.C. government agency's power to have prevented the deaths of the four girls? Why or why not?
    b. Which of the distinctive challenges of public management, discussed in this chapter, are illustrated by this case?
    c. Would the outcome have been the same had the private sector (for-profit or nonprofit organizations) run the agencies with which the family interacted? Why or why not?
    d. Who should be held accountable for the girls' deaths? Why?
3. Drawing on your analysis above, what changes should be implemented to reduce the likelihood of tragedies like this happening again? Can the possibility of such tragedies be completely eliminated?

Detailed information about the case can be found in various news accounts and from postings on the Web sites of the mayor and the Child and Family Services Agency.

News Reports and Opinions

Allison Klein and Joshua Zumbrun, "Bodies of 4 Girls Found in SE Home: Deaths Treated as Homicides," *Washington Post,* January 10, 2008, A01, http://www.washingtonpost.com/wp-dyn/content/article/2008/01/09/AR2008010901413.html.

Allison Klein, Keith L. Alexander, and Sue Anne Presley Montes, "SE Woman Says Four Daughters Were 'Possessed': Girls Might Have Died in May," *Washington Post,* January 11, 2008, A01, http://www.washingtonpost.com/wp-dyn/content/article/2008/01/10/AR2008011001174.html.

Sue Anne Pressley Montes, "Fenty Describes Missteps Before Girls Died: After Efforts to Help, Agency Erred in Closing Cases, Mayor Says," *Washington Post,* January 12, 2008, A01, http://www.washingtonpost.com/wp-dyn/content/article/2008/01/11/AR2008011101761.html.

Petula Dvorak and David Nakamura, "Fenty Fires 6 in Girls' Deaths: Four Children Had Not Been Seen for Months," *Washington Post,* January 15, 2008, A01, http://www.washingtonpost.com/wp-dyn/content/article/2008/01/14/AR2008011401001.html.

Richard Wexler, "Fenty's Unthinking Ax," *Washington Post,* January 16, 2008, A15, http://www.washingtonpost.com/wp-dyn/content/article/2008/01/15/AR2008011502862.html.

Keith L. Alexander and Petula Dvorak, "D.C. Court Also at Fault in Girls' Deaths, Judge Says," *Washington Post,* January 16, 2008, B01, http://www.washingtonpost.com/wp-dyn/content/article/2008/01/15/AR2008011503769.html.

David Nakamura, "Fenty Seeks to Inspire, but Instead Infuriates," *Washington Post,* January 20, 2008, C01, http://www.washingtonpost.com/wp-dyn/content/article/2008/01/19/AR2008011902286.html.

Keith L. Alexander and Petula Dvorak, "D.C. Could Have Done More to Help 4 Sisters, Families Say," *Washington Post,* February 28, 2008, http://www.washingtonpost.com/wp-dyn/content/article/2008/02/27/AR2008022703313.html.

Petula Dvorak, "Surge in Caseload Has Put Agency in 'Crisis,' Court Told," *Washington Post,* April 2, 2008, B04, http://www.washingtonpost.com/wp-dyn/content/article/2008/04/01/AR2008040102053.html.

Sue Anne Pressley Montes, "Paper Trail for Contracts Falls Short, Auditor Says," *Washington Post,* April 13, 2008, C05, http://www.washingtonpost.com/wp-dyn/content/article/2008/04/12/AR2008041201916.html.

Petula Dvorak, "Agency Reopens Six Abuse Cases," *Washington Post,* May 3, 2008, B04, http://www.washingtonpost.com/wp-dyn/content/article/2008/05/02/AR2008050203683.html.

Sample Sources from Mayor Adrian Fenty's Office and from the D.C. Child and Family Services Agency

"Fenty Presents Timeline of District Government Contact with Jacks Family," News Release from Office of Mayor Adrian Fenty, January 11, 2008. http://www.dc.gov/mayor/news/release.asp?id=1204&mon=200801.

"Fenty Puts Forth Actions to Address Shortfalls in City's Child Welfare Agency," News Release from Office of Mayor Adrian Fenty, January 14, 2008. http://www.dc.gov/mayor/news/release.asp?id=1205&mon=200801.

Child and Family Services Agency, http://cfsa.dc.gov/cfsa/site/default.asp.

2 Public Management's Three Dimensions

On February 1, 2003, the National Aeronautics and Space Administration (NASA) space shuttle *Columbia* disintegrated while returning to earth after a sixteen-day scientific mission, known within NASA as STS-107, killing its seven crew members. On the day of the accident, NASA administrator Sean O'Keefe appointed a board to investigate it. On August 28, the twelve-member Columbia Accident Investigation Board (CAIB), chaired by retired admiral Harold Gehman, an experienced investigator and military commander, issued a report containing a detailed analysis of the accident's causes and twenty-nine recommendations as to what NASA should do to ensure the space shuttle program's safe return to flight.

The *Columbia* accident and its aftermath constitute a quintessential public management story. Unlike Hurricane Katrina, however, this public management episode played out within the context of a single federal agency.

Immediately after the accident, NASA came under intense scrutiny from Congress, the print and broadcast media, a variety of interest groups, and a shocked public. Many remembered an earlier similar accident: the explosion of the space shuttle *Challenger* shortly after launch in 1986, which also killed its seven-member crew. That accident, too, had been the subject of a detailed investigation resulting in a report. The Report of the Presidential Commission on the Space Shuttle *Challenger* Accident, known as the Rogers Report after its chair, former secretary of state William P. Rogers, recommended numerous changes to improve the safety of manned space flight.[1] The Rogers Report was followed a year later by an evaluation of how well its recommendations had been implemented.[2] How was it possible, many asked about the *Columbia* accident, for history to repeat itself so soon with such tragic consequences?

In the view of Laurence Mulloy, former *Challenger* project leader, "If—and this is a big if, with big capital letters in red—if the cause of the

Columbia accident is the acceptance of debris falling off the tank in ascent, and impacting on the orbiter, and causing damage to the tiles—if that turns out to be the cause of the accident, then the lesson we learned in Challenger is forgotten, if it was ever learned." [3] The *Challenger* accident had resulted from mission managers overruling engineers' warnings concerning air temperatures at launch that were lower than design tolerances for launch equipment. Officials responsible for the *Columbia* launch were anxious to forestall similar allegations of ignoring expert advice. But Mulloy's suspicions turned out to be correct.

Much of the scrutiny of the *Columbia* accident focused on the technical cause of the orbiter's disintegration. Eighty-two seconds after launch a piece of insulating foam had detached from one of the solid rocket boosters and struck the leading edge of one of the orbiter's wings, creating a hole that would allow superheated air generated during reentry to penetrate the vehicle's protective shield and cause fatal structural damage. But significant attention was also devoted to what were termed "management issues."

Newspapers soon reported that less than a year before the accident, in April 2002, Richard Blomberg, the former chairman of the NASA-appointed Aerospace Safety Advisory Panel, had reported to NASA officials and to a congressional committee "the strongest safety concern the Panel has voiced in the 15 years I was involved with it." The problem, said Blomberg, "is that the boundary between safe and unsafe operations can seldom be quantitatively defined or accurately predicted. Even the most well meaning managers may not know when they cross it." [4] An article titled "Shuttle Shakeup Eyed for Cost, Safety Goals" in the September 23, 2002, issue of *Aviation Week & Space Technology* reported on a recently completed Rand Corporation study that found that contract management and safety reform were essential across all U.S. manned space projects.[5]

At issue in these revelations was NASA management during the period between the two space shuttle accidents when, in Blomberg's view, the agency had possibly crossed the line into unsafe operations because, as the CAIB report would later put it, the agency was trying to accomplish too many missions with too few budgetary and human resources. Thus, it was implied, structural constraints, ingrained behaviors within NASA, and management strategies and actions (or inactions) were all implicated in what appeared to be a repetition of the *Challenger* disaster.

When it was created, the CAIB was criticized by interest groups such as the nonprofit Freedom of Information Center and the Project on Government Secrecy at the Federation of American Scientists for its lack of independence: Its members were appointed and paid by NASA—that is, they were federal employees—and, for this reason, public law allowed the board to operate in relative secrecy. In fact, Admiral Gehman had to fight with NASA officials to ensure his board's autonomy and adequate resources to support its work. Its report, however, largely dispelled any concerns about its independence. An editorial in the respected British scientific journal *Nature* said:

> [T]he investigative board charged with finding the causes of February's explosion of the space shuttle *Columbia* turned in about as good a report last week as anyone could

> have asked. In clear, direct language, the panel . . . spelled out what has gone wrong—technically, politically, even sociologically—with the space-shuttle programme since its inception almost 30 years ago. . . . Gehman's report accurately describes the dysfunctional relationship that has developed between the space agency and those in the White House and Congress who fund it. . . . The agency got into the dangerous habit of promising what it could not deliver. Meanwhile, NASA's overseers in the White House and Congress, who surely suspected that the agency was stretched too thin, suppressed their own doubts.[6]

In addition to its analysis of technical issues, such as the prevention of foam shedding from the rocket boosters, the CAIB report addressed issues not only of management but also what it called, in scores of references, NASA's "culture." (Chapter 7 of the report is titled "The Organizational Causes.") The report pointed out that shuttle program managers were responsible for schedule, cost, *and* safety of flight. Combining these responsibilities had the practical effect of shifting the burden of proof on flight safety matters from those responsible for operations to those responsible for the safety of a flight. Had safety-of-flight decisions been independent of the management of flight operations, then operations managers would have been required to prove to the independent authority that a mission was safe.

The report also pointed out that bureaucratic distance and rank—that is, the organization of the formal hierarchy—impeded communications among engineers and managers who needed to discuss issues informally with each other; instead, dissonant information was brushed aside, and dissenters were inhibited from "jumping" the chain of command by going over the heads of superiors who had shown no inclination to listen to them. The report also noted that administrative decisions requiring subjective judgments—applying criteria for determining acceptable risk, safety-of-flight status, conditions for mandatory review, and the existence of an anomaly or a deviation from a norm or rule—were manipulated by managers in the interest of maintaining flight schedules. Managers also were found to have failed to properly evaluate past experience or to examine the assumptions underlying recommendations or unanimous opinions.

Of immediate interest to the CAIB investigators were the reactions of NASA officials during *Columbia*'s mission, particularly those officials constituting the Mission Management Team, to the intensely felt concerns of agency and contractor engineers that the orbiter might have been fatally damaged by the foam strike, which would jeopardize the vehicle's reentry unless corrective measures were taken. Evidently, these internecine conflicts and their potentially dire implications never reached O'Keefe or other top officials during the sixteen days of the mission. Even if they had, NASA had no contingency plans to rescue a mortally damaged orbiter in flight, possibly explaining mission management's inclinations to downplay the seriousness of the foam strike, because nothing could be done about it. Contributing to this disinclination to take corrective action was that foam strikes had become so common during previous shuttle operations as to be considered normal and, therefore, not safety-of-flight issues.

HOW THE WORLD WORKS

Return to Flight Task Force Report

No doubt anticipating that the conclusions of the Columbia Accident Investigation Board (CAIB) concerning the causes of the *Columbia* accident might be sharply critical, NASA administrator Sean O'Keefe appointed the Return to Flight Task Group (RTFTG) in June 2003, under the authority of the Federal Advisory Committee Act, to monitor compliance with the report's recommendations. Following three interim reports, the RTFTG's final report, issued on August 17, 2005, was predictably more sympathetic to NASA because it was more under O'Keefe's control than was the CAIB. Unlike the CAIB report, the RTFTG report concluded that NASA was substantially complying with the spirit and intent of recommendations in Adm. Harold Gehman's report.

The Task Group feels that NASA has met the intent of the CAIB management recommendations, although all of them remain works in progress. The establishment of an Independent Technical Authority within the Chief Engineer's office moves technical requirements out of the direct control of the Space Shuttle Program management chain. This provides a check-and-balance when it becomes necessary to approve waivers or deviations to a technical requirement, since the Independent Technical Authority is not constrained by budget or schedule pressures that may be present within the program. Although initiated prior to the release of the CAIB report, the establishment of the NASA Engineering and Safety Center (NESC) has created an independent body that provides technical assessments across the Agency. A restructured Safety and Mission Assurance (SMA) organization increases the independence of SMA personnel. Reorganizing the systems engineering and systems integration activities within the Space Shuttle Program clears up several ambiguities that led to confused communications between elements.

The Mission Management Team (MMT), much maligned by the CAIB, has been reconstituted and has undergone extensive training, with multiple simulations of alternative scenarios, including consideration of the use of the International Space Station as a safe haven for the crew of a damaged Orbiter, and the launch of a rescue mission. Refurbished facilities for the MMT provide a more conducive environment for their deliberations during each flight. It appears to the Task Group that the changes to the MMT have revitalized this group, but we stress that NASA must not allow this capability to atrophy as it had prior to the Columbia accident.

Publicly, NASA has said that the first two return-to-flight missions are "test flights" to assess the performance of the modified External Tank and to evaluate repair materials and techniques on orbit. In reality, however, the flights are planned as much for servicing the International Space Station as for testing. NASA intends to carefully monitor the performance and condition of the Space Shuttle during these two flights. For example, the launch rules require specific daylight conditions at the Kennedy Space Center and during External Tank separation to facilitate detailed imagery of the Orbiter and External Tank.

Risk acceptance and management are fundamental to leadership in hazardous technical activities and are the ultimate responsibility of any leader. Very few human endeavors, particularly related to high-energy activities involving advanced technologies, are completely free of risk. Space flight in general, and human space flight in particular, is such that it is impossible to drive the risk to zero. While the return-to-flight efforts have eliminated or minimized many known risks, Space Shuttle missions will always be "accepted risk" operations. This requires that the people involved understand, document, and ultimately accept the risk associated with that activity. NASA must be vigilant to prevent the development of a false sense of security by accepting faulty assumptions, or otherwise inappropriate analyses, to justify return to flight and continued Space Shuttle operations.

Source: *Final Report of the Return to Flight Task Group* (Washington, D.C., 2005), 13–14.

To analyze the *Columbia* space shuttle accident, an investigator might view NASA as an organization with a formal structure that defined functions and assigned responsibilities and rules for performing them. Analysis might focus on the location of the space shuttle program within the NASA chain of command and the relation of the safety-of-flight function to operations management. Or analysis might focus on what the CAIB report called NASA's culture—the beliefs and values of NASA's various employees that, because they came into conflict, jeopardized the mission of the space shuttle program. Or analysis might be concerned with the actions and decisions of NASA's administrator, Sean O'Keefe, or of Linda Ham, head of the Mission Management Team, or of flight director Leroy Cain, or of other officials whose priorities and decisions influenced the outcome.

But no one of these perspectives in and of itself provides an adequate basis for the kind of analysis needed to understand the complex challenges of public management involved in the *Columbia* accident or to provide useful guidance to public management practice. In fact, the danger in a one-dimensional approach to public management analysis and practice, whether by managers, elected officials, or judges, is the possibility of seriously misdiagnosing the underlying problem and therefore of taking inappropriate corrective measures. An agency might decide to concentrate on hiring better managers instead of tackling problems with norms of conduct that have become dysfunctional. Or it could impose new rules where additional managerial discretion is needed. For this reason, as the CAIB recognized, multiple dimensions of public management must be considered to understand the *Columbia* accident.

As is the case with the response to Hurricane Katrina, however, NASA's handling of the *Columbia* shuttle flight and its aftermath is not unique. NASA management confronted the challenge of balancing safety-of-flight concerns with the maintenance of the flight schedules necessary to achieve program goals; in other words, it needed to decide how much risk to take. Consider the following examples of substantive challenges that managers in the public sector must confront:

- ensuring that urban police departments under pressure to control crime also respect the civil rights of the citizens they are sworn to protect;
- changing the missions of federal and state agencies responsible for homeland security from prosecuting criminals to preventing acts of terrorism in the first place;
- introducing new information technologies to improve the effectiveness of organizations whose employees might perceive the change as threatening to their security and importance to the organization;
- achieving an appropriate balance between protecting children from harm and strengthening and unifying troubled families in the administration of child welfare policies and programs that call for removing children from homes if circumstances justify it; and
- managing regulatory agencies to achieve a reasonable balance between promoting and negotiating voluntary compliance with regulations and impartially detecting and punishing violators in areas such as airline, mine, and consumer product safety.

The list recalls the distinctive managerial challenges discussed in chapter 1. The solutions are likely to require some combination of interorganizational cooperation, satisfaction of diverse expectations, accountability to various stakeholders, coping with unexpected and unwelcome developments, evaluating advice of uncertain quality and reliability, and mobilizing skeptical employees to cooperate with managerial goals.

Workable solutions that have a reasonable likelihood of success are usually far from obvious, however. Do the policies governing agency operations enable or stand in the way of needed change? Are assignments of responsibilities to and within the agency and resources available to the agency—financial, human, and technical—adequate to meeting organizational objectives? Will agency personnel accept new directions or must internal resistance be overcome? Do public managers have the motivation, knowledge, and skills to discover and accomplish what needs to be done to reach the objectives? Successfully meeting the distinctive challenges of public management requires appropriate levels of delegation and oversight by policymakers, organizations whose employees can adapt to new circumstances while maintaining or improving reliability and quality of service, and high levels of political and administrative skill, commitment, and creativity on the part of public managers.

The kinds of questions that should be answered when confronting difficult public management problems require policymakers and managers, as well as the advisers and staffs that support them, to have the inclinations and skills needed to address them effectively. Public managers must be able to identify the political interests—who wants what, when, and how from government—that may be at stake. Political savvy is always necessary in the public sector. But politics is not enough. Responsible public officials must also be able to think systematically and analytically about the origins or causes of management problems and to formulate and weigh alternative solutions in terms of their likely consequences for fulfilling the public's interests at stake. This kind of public management analysis requires, in turn, a multidimensional frame of reference that directs attention to the most important factors present in complex management situations.

This chapter is organized as follows. First, it discusses several popular approaches to multidimensional management analysis. Next is a definition of the particular three-dimensional approach that is the framework of this text—that is, viewing public management through the dimensions of structure, culture, and craft. These dimensions will be illustrated with facts from the *Columbia* case and with additional examples. The chapter concludes by discussing what it means in practice to "think in three dimensions" and the potential importance of doing so. The end-of-chapter exercise applies three-dimensional analysis to the United Nations' Oil-for-Food Program, which was created to facilitate the flow of humanitarian goods and services to the Iraqi people under Saddam Hussein's regime but which yielded mixed results.

WHAT IS MULTIDIMENSIONAL PUBLIC MANAGEMENT?

Multidimensional thinking has long been popular in the literature of organizations and management. Among the earliest and still most popular of these analyses is that of Graham T. Allison in *The Essence of Decision: Explaining the Cuban Missile Crisis.*[7] The book attempts to explain or interpret that historic episode in crisis management, when the Soviet Union and the United States were on the brink of nuclear war, by using three different models, each incorporating its own logic: a rational choice model, which assumes calculated rationality on the part of participants; a bureaucratic politics model, which assumes that behavior reflects the interplay of faction and power within the government; and an organizational process model, which assumes that behavior reflects the institutionalized administrative routines of the various agencies involved.

Another example of a multidimensional framework is Gareth Morgan's *Images of Organization,* which offers a rich array of metaphors for viewing organizations from different perspectives.[8] Organizations can be viewed as mechanisms, organisms, brains, cultures, political systems, psychic prisons, flux and transformation, and instruments of domination. Such metaphors, Morgan argues, create ways of seeing and shaping organizational life and of thinking and acting in creative ways.

A third example is Henry Mintzberg's "Managing Government, Governing Management." Among the most influential of management scholars, Mintzberg puts forward five models of government, each marked "by its own way of organizing governments and controlling authority, or *superstructure,* and the activities of its agencies, or *microstructure.* (The budget authority would be part of the former, for example; an environmental protection agency an example of the latter.)"[9] His five models are: government-as-machine; government-as-network; performance-control; virtual-government; and normative-control.

A final example of multidimensional thinking is found in *Reframing Organizations: Artistry, Choice, and Leadership,* in which Lee G. Bolman and Terrence E. Deal articulate four frames within which organizations may be analyzed: structural, human resource, political, and symbolic.[10] By reframing, Bolman and Deal mean managers' ability to shift perspectives from one frame to another in order to broaden and to deepen their insights into the issues and problems they face. In these authors' view, managers do not use enough frames, and often use only one. Being able to reframe problems and issues overcomes rigidities of thought and perception. Managers train themselves to see the layers or dimensions of a problem instead of leaping to a conclusion based on preconceptions and an unduly limited frame of reference. (Reframing is discussed further in chapters 7 and 10.)

All of these multidimensional approaches are insightful and might be used to advantage in evaluating complex public management situations. In comparison to these approaches, however, the three-dimensional approach of this book has unique appeal for general public management analysis because it resonates with familiar attitudes and beliefs that underlie debates over public management problems, a point that will be developed further in the next section.

THE THREE-DIMENSIONAL APPROACH

One popular approach to public management analysis is to focus on a public agency's legal authority and the formal allocation of responsibilities and resources to departments, bureaus, and offices. The early twentieth-century study of public management was originally concerned with creating organizational structures and functions that would ensure efficient performance by America's newly emerging administrative state. Such an analysis might evaluate the way responsibilities are assigned and how well channels of communication, deliberation, and decision making work. The **unit of analysis** for this approach, that is, the entity for which data are collected and analyzed, is the organization as a whole and the structures, functions, and processes by which the work of the organization gets done.

As the study of organizations became more sophisticated beginning in the 1930s, attention began to focus on the beliefs, values, and norms that govern and motivate employee behavior—to what was first termed the "informal organization" and is now often referred to as "organizational culture"—and that can either inhibit or advance the fulfillment of the public's interests. In this approach, the units of analysis are the organization's employees, who are seen as individuals with needs and values of their own.

With the administrative state at all levels of government—federal, state, and local—growing and maturing during the middle decades of the twentieth century, attention began to be directed toward the practice of public management, toward "what public managers do and how they do it," and toward how executives and subordinate officials might manage more effectively and efficiently within their political and organizational environments. In this approach, individual managers are the primary units of analysis. In comparing the actions and decision making of actual managers with "best practices" in the field, the emphasis, to use the distinction drawn in chapter 1, is on managers as creators rather than as passive creatures of administrative systems.

These three approaches to public management are not discrete—unique and unconnected—rather, they are separable but interdependent dimensions of public management. Shorthand terms for these three interdependent dimensions are, as indicated in chapter 1, *structure, culture,* and *craft.* These three dimensions are depicted in Figure 2.1. While each dimension is shown to have significant independent influence on public management, the three dimensions also overlap. A public management problem can, in principle, involve any two dimensions, as will be discussed further in chapters 5 through 7 and in chapter 10. The most demanding challenges, depicted in black at the center of the diagram, involve all three dimensions. In chapter 10, public policymakers and managers who must integrate factors from all three dimensions will be said to be "managing in the black."

The various types of overlaps have a logic that links them. Structural delegations of authority and assignments of responsibility within an organization provide the framework for the formation of organizational cultures and subcultures and for the directive activities—

FIGURE 2.1 **Public Management's Three Dimensions**

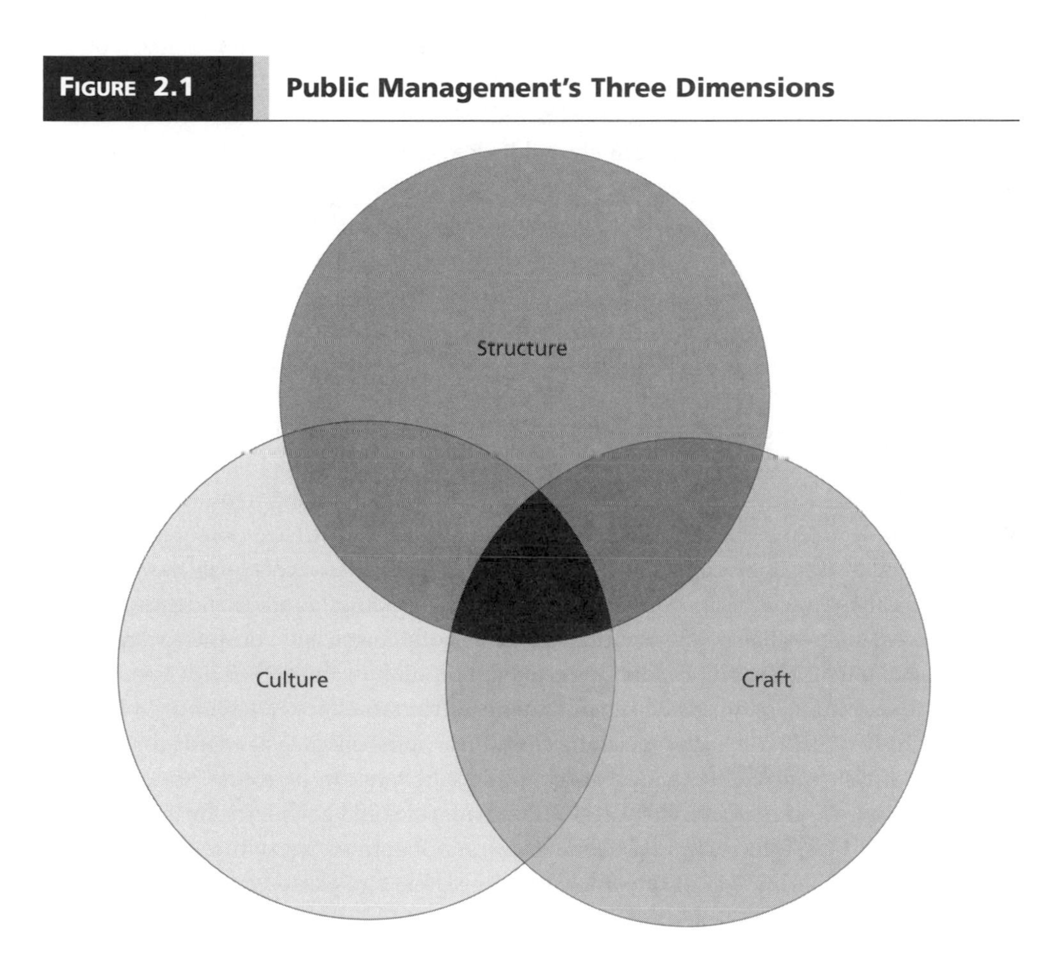

that is, the craft—of public managers. Whether they are entering government as outsiders or are being promoted to new levels of responsibility from within an agency, public managers typically confront a status quo of formally structured, culturally influenced organizational capacities, a status quo that provides the point of departure for their directive activities. Viewed as such, managers may be characterized as creatures of the structural and cultural environments in which they find themselves. Managerial craft may, however, seek to alter that status quo in order to enhance organizational capacity. Through this dimension the specific focus is on the role of managers as creators, who may be able to influence structure and culture, as well as relationships and opportunities. Following this logic, the order of discussion of public management's three dimensions will be structure, culture, and, finally, craft.

Structure

As a dimension of public management, **structure** is defined as lawfully authorized delegations to administrative officials of the authority and responsibility to take action on behalf of policy and program objectives. (Further elaboration and discussion of this definition is in chapter 5.) Structure therefore encompasses how a level of government is organized by law into departments, commissions, and other independent offices with specific authority to act. It further encompasses the agencies, bureaus, and regional and local offices within departments or commissions that have been created by law, executive order, and duly authorized managerial decisions.

Considerations of structure enter into the analysis of the *Columbia* accident in the delegation of two responsibilities to shuttle program managers—meeting flight schedules and the safety of flights—instead of giving these functions separate status. As a consequence of this structural arrangement, these managers could on their own authority choose to take chances with the safety of a flight in order to maintain flight schedules and stay within budget. Moreover, there were no authorized communication channels within NASA for dissident views on issues concerning safety. NASA's structure gave senior officials no opportunity to make a different decision about the flight.

In practice, structures are defined in the provisions of authorizing statutes; in approved legislative budgets; in executive orders, regulations, and rules that have the force of law; in decisions and directives by executives and managers within their spheres of authority; and in injunctions and consent decrees—agreements reached by plaintiffs and defendants pursuant to settling lawsuits—approved by courts. Structures both enable and constrain what public agencies and public managers can do. Delegated responsibilities and authorities may include, among other things, creating additional administrative structures; establishing planning, decision making, and communication processes; prescribing specific standards for the performance of functions and tasks; and allocating specific levels of personnel and budgetary resources to agency offices and activities together with rules and guidelines for their use.

Creating formal structures and processes by means of authorizing statutes and operating budgets is the most direct form of control that legislators and elected executives have over public policy implementation, which accounts for the popularity of legislative and executive reorganizations of public agencies, the drafting of detailed legislation defining managerial responsibilities, and the use of budgetary "earmarks" to direct resources to specified projects and activities. The creation of the Department of Homeland Security in November 2002 out of twenty-two agencies formerly scattered across the federal government and the reorganization of the national intelligence community's fifteen separate agencies—most within the Department of Defense—under a new director of national intelligence in April 2005 are vivid examples of how Congress favored far-reaching (and, in both cases, centralizing) structural change in order, legislators believed, to streamline accountability to Congress. Despite the distinct limits to the effectiveness of structures as mechanisms for controlling the exercise of managerial discretion, there is no doubt that structures generally have a significant influence on what governments do and how they do it.

Consider the following three illustrations of how structures affect government operations and outcomes. First, decisions on which drugs can be reimbursed by the Medicare program are partly governed by national standards and partly by two dozen or so government-contracted private insurers who handle physician and hospital claims for groups of states and are empowered to establish local rules concerning which medications are covered and which are not. This particular arrangement reflects a political bargain struck between the federal government and the American Medical Association, which opposed the British-style nationalization of health care and the standardization of medical practice. The consequence is that drug coverage is governed by more than nine thousand local medical review policies that make up the largely secret world of local health care cost controls. Practitioners and patients' advocates do not know what the rules are and are not allowed to comment on them before they are promulgated.[11] One result is regulatory confusion and uncertainty that in turn affect medical practice and patient health in hard-to-determine ways.

The second is the Texas legislature's creation of new structures and processes for the delivery of health and human services. In 2003 the legislature mandated the consolidation of the ten state health and human service agencies into four agencies under the umbrella Health and Human Services Commission. The stated goals of the reorganization were to improve client services, reduce administrative costs, strengthen accountability, and ensure that tax dollars were spent more effectively. One change was that the Department of Health, part of the Department of Mental Health and Mental Retardation, and the Commission on Alcohol and Drug Abuse would become the Department of State Health Services. Of the Texas human services reorganization, observers noted that "the bureaucracy is subject to the overlapping control (through the constitution, and state and federal laws) of a broad range of institutions, interest groups and individuals. . . . [T]hough several of the changes made were dramatic, they did not undo the multiple layers of control over these agencies. Nor did reorganization involve reworking the rest of the state bureaucracy."[12] Controversies also arose over whether the state saved any money.

CONCEPTS IN ACTION

Can Structure Become an Impediment?

In her testimony before the 9/11 Commission on April 7, 2004, National Security Advisor Condoleezza Rice used the term *structure* forty times, *system* five times, *culture* five times, and *institution* two times. The concept of structure and its popularity among policymakers seeking leverage over governmental performance is illustrated by the following response by Rice to a question posed by commission vice chair Lee H. Hamilton:

Mr. Hamilton: [Y]ou suggest in your statement—and I want you to elaborate on this, if you want to—that in hindsight . . . better information about the threats would have been the single-most important thing for us to have done . . . prior to 9/11—would have been better intelligence, better information about the threats. Is that right? Are there other things that you think stand out?

Ms. Rice: I believe that the absence of light, so to speak, on what was going on inside the country, the inability to connect the dots, was really structural. We couldn't be dependent on chance that something might come together. And the legal impediments and the bureaucratic impediments—but I want to emphasize the legal impediments—to keep the FBI and the CIA from functioning really as one, so that there was no seam between domestic and foreign intelligence, was probably the greatest one. The director of Central Intelligence and, I think, [FBI] Director Freeh had an excellent relationship. They were trying hard to bridge that seam. I know that Louis Freeh had developed legal attaches abroad to try to help bridge that. But when it came right down to it, this country, for reasons of history, and culture, and therefore, law, had an allergy to the notion of domestic intelligence, and we were organized on that basis. And it just made it very hard to have all of the pieces come together.

Source: Hearing of the National Commission on Terrorist Attacks upon the United States, Witness: Dr. Condoleezza Rice, Assistant to the President for National Security Affairs; Chair: Thomas H. Kean; Vice Chair: Lee H. Hamilton, April 8, 2004, Washington, D.C., http://govinfo.library.unt.edu/911/archive/hearing9/9-11Commission_Hearing_2004-04-08.pdf.

The third example of how structure affects government operations and outcomes—this one positively so—concerns Walter Reed Army Medical Center in Washington, D.C. Beginning in February 2007, a series of investigative reports in the *Washington Post* revealed serious neglect, mistreatment, and substandard care provided to soldiers at Walter Reed who were recovering from wounds suffered in Afghanistan and Iraq, especially those soldiers being treated as outpatients. Under intense criticism and pressure to improve care for "wounded warriors," the army created a new organizational unit, the Warrior Transition Brigade, to which all outpatients would be assigned. The brigade's "squad leaders" and "case managers" would be responsible for monitoring each patient's circumstances and needs. In addition, brigade physicians and staff were to work with hospital specialists in preparing patient care plans. The new structure was designed to ensure that an adequate number of qualified personnel would have as their sole responsibility the well-being of outpatient soldiers being treated at Walter Reed. Within several months, a total of thirty-five similar transition care units had been created at other U.S. Army medical centers. Within a year of its creation, the Walter Reed unit was regarded as a success, having proven its value in preventing wounded soldiers from getting lost in the system. Surveys revealed significant improvements in patient satisfaction with the care they were receiving.[13]

In these three examples, elected and appointed officials reallocated responsibilities for policy implementation among subordinate departments and offices and private, mainly nonprofit, contractors with the professed purpose of achieving more effective and efficient programmatic performance. Decentralizing prescription drug reimbursement policies would prevent arbitrary rigidity in medical practice. A unit with sole responsibility for outpatient care would enhance patients' well-being. Offices and agencies grouped together would be more likely to coordinate their activities and cut costs. Whether the expected benefits from such reorganizations actually materialize is another matter, however. In most cases of structural change, including these, no mechanisms are created to measure, monitor, or evaluate the results, and reported successes are often the self-serving claims of those who initiated or who stand to benefit from the changes. Choices of organizational arrangements ordinarily reflect political rationality, discussed in chapter 1, more than they reflect commitments to technical rationality and demonstrated results.

Culture

As a dimension of public management, **culture** may be defined as "institutionalized values." This definition requires clarification, however.

An **institution** may be defined as an organization infused with durable values. **Institutionalization** is the process by which the members of an organization "acquire values that go beyond the technical requirements of organizational tasks." [14] In another expression of this concept, institutionalization is "the emergence of orderly, stable, socially integrating patterns out of unstable, loosely organized, or narrowly technical activities." [15] The importance of institutionalized values therefore is that they constitute a unifying source of meaning and purpose that formal structures of authority and assignments of responsibility cannot provide by themselves.

In the context of organizations, it has become common (indeed fashionable) to talk about institutionalized values as organizational cultures. The term *organizational culture* is often used to describe values that are admirable or widely held to be legitimate. The dedication and seeming selflessness of public school teachers, emergency room doctors and nurses, and those who place themselves in danger in service to others are widely admired. Organizations may be spoken of as having high morale, a strong sense of commitment, or *esprit de corps.* As the story of the *Columbia* accident reveals, however, institutionalized values may at times be inimical to accomplishing important goals or to a manager's need to respect and balance differing values. Organizational cultures may or may not reflect or even acknowledge values prevailing in the community or in the wider society, which can create tensions between public agencies and those who depend on them, tensions that managers may seek to reduce. In other words, a strong organization culture may be a good thing or a bad thing.

Defining culture as institutionalized values, then, refers to those norms, beliefs, and standards of conduct that provide meaning, purpose, and a source of motivation to individuals working within an organizational unit and, therefore, may contribute in both positive and negative ways to an organization's capacity to carry out its lawful responsibilities. (Further discussion of this definition is in chapter 6.)

Considerations of culture enter into the analysis of the *Columbia* accident in several ways: as the institutionalized values among shuttle program managers that subordinated safety to maintenance of flight schedules and budgets, in the reluctance of NASA employees to speak up forcefully in opposition to these values, and in the acceptance of risks to flight safety from debris strikes as normal and acceptable. Moreover, these aspects of NASA's culture had structural origins. The CAIB report on the accident emphasized problems with NASA's culture:

> [P]eople who work at NASA have the legendary can-do attitude, which contributes to the agency's successes. But it can also cause problems. When workers are asked to find days of margin [unprogrammed days prior to a launch deadline, which provide a cushion against uncertainty], they work furiously to do so and are praised for each extra day they find. But those same people (and this same culture) have difficulty admitting that something "can't" or "shouldn't" be done, that the margin has been cut too much, or that resources are being stretched too thin. No one at NASA wants to be the one to stand up and say, "We can't make that date." [16]

A further example of the culture foundations of the *Columbia* accident is the

> unofficial hierarchy among NASA programs and directorates that hindered the flow of communications. The effects of this unofficial hierarchy are seen in the attitude that members of the Debris Assessment Team held. Part of the reason they chose the institutional [that is, staying within their own organization] route for their [request for additional photographs of damage to the shuttle] was that without direction from the Mission Evaluation Room and Mission Management Team, they felt more comfortable with their own chain of command, which was outside the Shuttle Program. Further, when asked by investigators why they were not more vocal about their concerns, Debris Assessment Team members opined that by raising contrary points of view about Shuttle mission safety, they would be singled out for possible ridicule by their peers and managers.[17]

A large, complex department or agency may contain many organizational subcultures that have formed around the missions, tasks, and contexts of subordinate organizational units. The Department of Homeland Security is such an organization, including as it does the many distinctive subcultures of the administrative units incorporated within it, such as customs, immigration, and border patrol officials; Coast Guard officers; airport security personnel; intelligence analysts; and emergency management officials. The challenge facing senior executives in such diverse departments or agencies, which also include, among others, state and local law enforcement, environmental protection, and health and human services agencies, is to overcome the fragmentation and "stove pipe" parochialism of subordinate, specialized subcultures on behalf of broad, overarching organizational values and purposes.

As an extensive research literature shows, organizational cultures are not beyond political and managerial influence. By creating and reassigning responsibilities and authorizing new avenues of communication, structural changes can initiate cultural change. So, too, can the actions of public managers in defining and exemplifying particular standards or norms of conduct. Cultural changes can be furthered through personnel selection and training. Influencing established, durable cultures is likely to be a complicated process, however. As Anne Khademian notes, "Institutionalized values cannot be changed merely by dictate from a leader to employees. Employees must embrace and practice the changes sought by a leader. . . . A program commitment changes when all participants involved in a public program embrace the change as an alternative means to do the work." [18]

Organizational cultures can affect government performance in both negative and positive ways. An example of the negative occurred on the night of April 23, 1998, when three black teenagers and one Hispanic teenager in a rented van were stopped on the New Jersey Turnpike by state troopers. Claiming that the van backed toward them, the troopers opened fire, wounding basketball players heading south for a series of games. In defense of the troopers' actions, the state police superintendent characterized minority groups, incorrectly, as being largely responsible for drug trafficking, revealing that a culture of racial bias existed within his organization, whereupon he was fired. Attorney General Peter Verniero admitted that citizens were stopped and/or searched on the New Jersey Turnpike based on the color of their skin. Sued by the federal government, the state of New Jersey entered into a consent decree with the Justice Department in December 1999, one element of which was an independent monitor to review and analyze implementation of its numerous remedial provisions. To gather data, video cameras were installed in the front of the patrol cars to tape troopers as they engaged drivers. In accepting a plea bargain in another lawsuit concerning the shooting of minority motorists in 2001, two troopers acknowledged that the state police taught racial profiling, that supervisors encouraged it, and that they and others tried to cover up racial profiling by providing false stop data. Two months later, the New Jersey Supreme Court, noting "widespread abuse of our existing laws," outlawed "consent searches" where no reasonable suspicion exists. The consequence of a culture that tolerated racial profiling was detailed interventions by higher levels of government and by the courts, restricting the discretion of law enforcement officers.

HOW THE WORLD WORKS

The Freedom to Ignore Good Advice

The power of an independent entity to influence public agency administration may be limited because its members are outsiders with no direct role in the agency. The Columbia Accident Investigation Board (CAIB) might have believed that applying the concept of culture was necessary to NASA reform, but NASA's Return to Flight Task Group—a more agency-oriented group—was not, and did not have to be, convinced of that point and could resist it, steering clear of the issue of NASA's culture, as the following excerpt suggests.

The CAIB used the term "culture" throughout its report, although there are neither specific recommendations to change culture nor any suggestions on how this might be accomplished. Therefore, organizational culture, although important, was not considered a return-to-flight issue and was not evaluated by the Task Group.

Source: *Final Report of the Return to Flight Task Group* (Washington, D.C., 2005), 18.

Culture can also affect performance in positive ways. The Department of the Army's Armament Research, Development and Engineering Center (ARDEC) was the first government agency to receive the globally recognized Malcolm Baldrige National Quality Award in 2007.[19] Established by Congress in 1987, the award promotes the competitiveness of U.S. technology by honoring organizations that have achieved high standards of performance management and product quality. ARDEC director Joseph Lannon said the agency had been working for many years to establish the performance measurements that won it the award. "We've been at this for over 15 years," he said. "It's not something you can plan for overnight. It takes time, and it takes a culture change to accept the processes you put into place and get buy-in from the workforce. . . . We reached the tipping point a very short time ago." Donelle Denery, who manages ARDEC's performance excellence programs, said the agency was able to promote new management programs by getting almost total participation from managers. "When you have the room full of the 30 senior leaders and you ask who has taken Lean Six Sigma training [an approach to achieving a rapid improvement in quality] and who has their certification, 98 percent of the hands in the room go up," she said. "We walk the talk." Lannon said the arrival of a new generation of scientists and engineers also helped speed the transformation to a performance culture. "They don't have the set practices that a seasoned workforce has," Lannon said. "They're ripe for change. That actually affects the dynamics of your whole organization. They bring challenges to the existing workforce that didn't exist before, and they bring tremendous amounts of energy. We looked at it as an opportunity."

Each of these examples, as well as the *Columbia* accident, illustrates how informally constituted "orderly, stable, socially integrating patterns" of belief and behavior—patterns that constitute organizational cultures—can influence an organization's actions in ways that have significant negative or positive implications for its effectiveness. In some organizations, cultures legitimize behaviors that avoid actions that risk loss of influence and turf. The culture primarily protects the organization's sphere of authority. In other organizations, institutionalized values may justify behaviors that are unduly risky in order to achieve important organizational purposes. Altering the beliefs and values that come to constitute culture—altering beliefs that lead to overt or tacit discrimination or hostile work environments—may be achievable through employing the conventional instruments of management such as personnel recruitment, training, promotion, and discipline; monitoring, evaluation, and reporting; and allocations of responsibility, resources, and support. These instruments bring about change in no straightforward fashion, however, with the consequence that organizational cultures have the power to undermine both structural strategies and managerial ambition and entrepreneurship.

Craft

Even if delegations of authority to subordinate officials are specific and prescriptive, the need for managerial judgment is inevitable for several reasons:

1. Officials are often expressly delegated the authority to make judgments, especially when legislators lack the expertise or inclination to be specific, or legislative language may not preclude them from making such judgments.
2. Statutory delegations may be ambiguous, incomplete, or inconsistent, leaving public managers little choice but to exercise judgment concerning how policy and program implementation are to proceed.
3. Even when the rules and standards governing managerial behavior are clear, whether and how to apply them to specific cases or contexts may require managerial or supervisory judgment.

Depending on their skills, intuitions, inclinations, and values, individual managers almost always have the latitude to exert an independent influence on policy implementation and government performance through the decisions they make and the actions they take. As a dimension of public management, **craft** is defined as the ways public managers attempt to influence government performance through their own personal efforts in the form of directive activity. (Further discussion of this definition is in chapter 7.)

Craft enters into the analysis of the *Columbia* accident in the judgments made by individual NASA officials, including the head of the Mission Control Team, to ignore what amounted to dire warnings by the agency's own advisers of threats to the safety of the shuttle program in general and to the *Columbia* flight in particular. Considerations of craft enter into the aftermath of the accident in the efforts of individual NASA officials to restrict the independence of the CAIB and to create an implementation evaluation team that would be sympathetic to NASA.

The appointment of the individuals who will exercise managerial judgment is therefore an important responsibility of political and managerial leadership. To a considerable extent, patronage enters into the selection of the most senior executives and managers. Elected executives have the authority to appoint such officials, subject, in many cases, to the advice and consent of a legislative body, and their choices may be, but need not be, based on candidates' competence or on the specific skills required. Filling managerial positions in the career civil service is largely a function of public personnel systems, where criteria relating to relevant experience, seniority, credentials, and demonstrated competence have varying weights. In general, managerial competence matters to government performance, but the effort to see that competent people fill the positions can be a hit-or-miss proposition.

The following shows how managerial craft had a negative effect. The former director of operations for the Staten Island Ferry Division of the New York City Department of Transportation pleaded guilty to negligent manslaughter in a 2003 ferry crash that killed eleven passengers. Prosecutors contended that "[h]is executive or managerial negligence was a cause of the crash." The accident occurred when the single pilot of the vessel lost consciousness as it cruised at full speed toward the dock. Having only one pilot on board violated the two-pilot rule, which requires two employees capable of navigating the ferry to be in the wheelhouse when it is in operation. The guilty official "drafted a series of standard operating procedures in 2002 that confirmed the existence of the two-pilot rule. He acknowledged, however, that he never distributed the procedures, trained his staff in their use or made sure the two-pilot rule was followed." [20] Managerial slovenliness contributed to the deaths of eleven people.

Another example concerns a Texas state official responsible for overseeing the safety of railroad crossings. He admitted during court proceedings that he had signed sworn statements concerning the installation of warning signs at railroad crossings. The affidavits he signed were drafted largely by officials in the rail industry and contained information and representations that the state official had not verified or could not verify. The affidavits had become an issue in lawsuits against railroads for deaths at rail crossings that were allegedly unsafe. The railroads had sought the state affidavits to prove that federal funds available for the purpose had actually been spent on installing railroad warning signs, a fact that limits the railroads' liability in lawsuits. The state manager's justification for failing to verify the facts in the affidavits was that he believed he was protecting the state from lawsuits arising from grade crossing collisions, but the effect of his actions was also to protect the railroads, leaving accident victims without redress.

HOW THE WORLD WORKS

What You See May Not Be What You Get

What the public sees in a public manager may be quite different from what insiders see in the course of prolonged first-hand experience. Managerial reputations may or may not reflect actual competence. Despite extensive media attention to his management of the Pentagon from 2001 through 2006, Secretary of Defense Donald Rumsfeld's managerial type and style remained elusive. The *Washington Post* reporters conducted extensive interviews for their story, but name no names.

[N]early two dozen current and former top officers and civilian officials said in interviews that there is a huge discrepancy between the outside perception of Rumsfeld—the crisp, no-nonsense defense secretary who became a media star through his briefings on the Afghan war—and the way he is seen inside the Pentagon. Many senior officers on the Joint Staff and in all branches of the military describe Rumsfeld as frequently abusive and indecisive, trusting only a tiny circle of close advisers, seemingly eager to slap down officers with decades of distinguished service. The unhappiness is so pervasive that all three service secretaries are said to be deeply frustrated by a lack of autonomy and contemplating leaving by the end of the year.

Source: Vernon Loeb and Thomas E. Ricks, "Rumsfeld's Style, Goals Strain Ties In Pentagon: 'Transformation' Effort Spawns Issues of Control," *Washington Post,* October 16, 2002, Sec. A.

Managerial craft can influence performance for the better, as well. Appointed to the position of secretary of the Department of Energy at the beginning of President George W. Bush's second term, Samuel W. Bodman began earning plaudits for his style of public management. With experience as an academic, in the financial services sector, and as a senior official in Bush's first term, Bodman regularly met with more than twenty top department officials to learn what was going on in the department and to encourage communication among managers. Said the Democratic staff director for the Senate Energy and Natural Resources Committee, "While they certainly support very strongly the president's initiatives relating to energy, they are not big ideologues. They are very interested and willing to work with both sides of the aisle on the Hill." [21] Similar plaudits were earned by Mark McClellan, a physician and health economist who served as head of the Centers for Medicare and

Medicaid Services from 2004 to 2006. Upon resigning, he was praised in a *New York Times* editorial for "step[ping] in to solve problems" and for "focusing on important policy issues and responding to valid complaints." [22]

In each of these examples, individual public managers' personal judgments and skills—or the lack thereof—had demonstrable consequences for their agencies. Their qualities of mind, temperament, and character, and their capacity for analysis and sound judgment, can have life and death implications, affect the distribution of rewards and punishments among citizens, and influence communications and the flow of information that are at the heart of policymaking and the successful promotion of organizational change. Within frameworks of formal authority, individuals can matter, for good or for ill, by the choices they make concerning what will be done and how it will be done.

THINKING IN THREE DIMENSIONS

As the examples in the preceding section suggest, each of public management's three dimensions can matter, perhaps decisively, to organizational effectiveness and to the achievement of public purposes. But, public management hardly ever *is* one-dimensional. To address real questions about achieving effective public management—How can policymakers act to improve the performance of agencies providing health and human services? How can individual public managers within NASA be persuaded to achieve an appropriate balance between mission safety and schedule maintenance? Will restrictions on the discretion and increased surveillance of police officers be sufficient to end racial profiling in law enforcement?—it is necessary for public managers to comprehend how all three dimensions interact.

Adequately addressing managerial problems typically requires awareness and often the use of all three of these dimensions: organizational structures and processes that distribute information, responsibility, and resources in ways that further policy and organizational goals; employees infused with beliefs, values, and motivation that enhance the organization's reputation for reliability and for skilled and conscientious performance; and responsible judgment by individual public managers concerning priorities, strategies, and methods to advance the achievement of those goals and to build organizational capacity. This kind of three-dimensional thinking about complex management challenges, intended to provide the intellectual foundations for managerial practice, is the goal of **public management analysis.**

The CAIB report reflected the concept of three-dimensional awareness of the safety-of-flight issues confronting NASA management:

> Policy constraints affected the Shuttle Program's organization culture, its structure, and the structure of the safety system. The three combined to keep NASA on its slippery slope toward Challenger and Columbia. NASA culture allowed flying with flaws when problems were defined as normal and routine; the structure of NASA's Shuttle Program blocked the flow of critical information up the hierarchy, so definitions of risk continued unaltered. Finally, a perennially weakened safety system, unable to critically analyze and intervene, had no choice but to ratify the existing risk assessments on these two problems.[23]

In other words, structures and cultures were such that managers perceived that they "had no choice" but to do what they did. Their craft, in other words, was stultified by structure and culture.

This three-dimensional approach is particularly useful for public management analysis because it relates well to public debates about management issues. The structural dimension is similar to the well-known rational/legal perspective first set forth by Max Weber and the basis for policymakers' preference for organizational solutions to management problems.[24] The cultural dimension reflects the growing popularity of the idea that steering government involves far more than demanding compliance with directives by public employees who inevitably have minds, motives, interests, and values of their own. The craft dimension reflects the tendency in American public life to assign responsibility for success and failure to specific individuals and to create heroes and scapegoats. The insights and lessons from three-dimensional analysis are sufficiently intuitive and "nonacademic" to be attractive to those who have actual responsibilities for addressing management problems in the public sector.

Another advantage of the three-dimensional approach is that it enhances appreciation of the different kinds and sources of public management knowledge. (See chapter 7 for further discussion of this point.) Such knowledge can be experiential, that is, derived from the actual experience of public managers and from the observation of real world activity. It can be academic/empirical, that is, derived from theory-based analysis of statistical data and observational information. Or it can be normative or ideological, that is, derived from principled belief systems or from established norms and standards. Its academic sources can be research that is based in social and behavioral science disciplines and fields, such as economics, political science, sociology, organizational theory, cultural anthropology, and social and cognitive psychology, among others. To put it another way, in addition to being multidimensional, public management is inherently multimethod and interdisciplinary; no one type of knowledge or understanding will suffice to comprehend and resolve complex problems.

Good public management analysis will typically employ a portfolio of theoretical concepts in evaluating a complex problem. Consider *Columbia* once again. The CAIB report adduced several theoretical concepts to help interpret the factual evidence the board had assembled. For example, NASA management's acceptance of the debris strike (which is not supposed to occur) as a normal occurrence was regarded as what sociologist Diane Vaughan has called the "normalization of deviance," an aspect of NASA's culture that had also been present prior to the 1986 *Challenger* accident.[25]

The report also invoked "high reliability theory" (discussed further in chapter 6) which argues that "organizations operating high-risk technologies, if properly designed and managed, can compensate for inevitable human shortcomings, and therefore avoid mistakes that under other circumstances would lead to catastrophic failures." [26] "Additionally," according to the CAIB report, "organizational theory, which encompasses organizational culture, structure, history, and hierarchy, is used to explain the *Columbia* accident, and, ultimately . . . to produce an expanded explanation of the accident's causes." [27] Commentary on this incident also invoked the concept of "groupthink" (discussed further in chapter 7), that is, collective decision making such as that by the STS-107 Mission Management Team, characterized by uncritical acceptance of or conformity to particular points of view.

The CAIB explicitly chose theoretical concepts that were thought to illuminate the underlying causes of that particular incident. "To develop a thorough understanding of accident causes and risk, and to better interpret the chain of events that led to the Columbia accident, the Board turned to the contemporary social science literature on accidents and risk and sought insight from experts in High Reliability, Normal Accident, and Organizational Theory." [28] The key to an incisive public management analysis is selecting concepts and ideas that are especially appropriate for illuminating the problem at hand. Accordingly, in subsequent chapters of this book, concepts that can be applied to a wide variety of management issues, drawn from many fields and disciplines, will be introduced, explained, and illustrated with examples of their application. Together these concepts constitute a basic portfolio for public management analysis. The portfolio includes:

- Structure—delegation and control, the logic of governance and derived checks and balances (chapter 4) and constraining and enabling structures, transaction costs, the principal-agent model, street-level bureaucracy, nonprofit organizations, and the hollow state (chapter 5).
- Culture—trust and reputation, commitments, values, ethics, motives, high-reliability organizations, gift exchanges, and public service bargains (chapter 6).
- Craft—departures from rationality (including bounded rationality and groupthink), managerial type, decision making, framing and reframing, backward mapping, and contextual leadership (chapter 7).

Public management analysis, then, involves not only the habitual resort to three-dimensional thinking but also the insightful use of a portfolio of theoretical concepts and heuristics that can lead to a more thorough, in-depth understanding of the role of structure, culture, and craft in causing—and addressing—specific management challenges.

In chapter 10, a model deliberative process is presented; it outlines a step-by-step approach to conducting a three-dimensional public management analysis that can be the foundation of sound arguments on behalf of management strategies that address public management's distinctive challenges. To build toward that analytical capacity, chapters 5, 6, and 7 focus on each dimension of structure, culture, and craft, individually. Chapter 10 brings together analysis across all three dimensions, along with other major issues raised in the preceding chapters, including the rule of law, accountability, and reform. The method of argument is used throughout the book.

Key Concepts

multidimensional thinking
unit of analysis
structure
culture
institution
institutionalization
craft
public management analysis

Analysis and Argument: Test Your Understanding

The now-defunct "oil-for-food program" administered by the United Nations for the benefit of the Iraqi people under Saddam Hussein's regime is widely regarded as a public management failure. UN Secretary General Kofi Annan appointed a committee to investigate what went wrong. Read the case below and answer the following questions, using as the frame for your answers public management's three dimensions. If possible, read chapter 1 (pages 7–65) in Volume I, "The Report of the Committee," of the Independent Inquiry Committee's report, http://www.iic-offp.org/documents/Sept05/Mgmt_V1.pdf.

1. Given the way the program was structured, could better management—better craft—on the part of managers within the UN Secretariat have ensured a basically honest program, undistorted by member country interests? Why or why not? What if anything, specifically, might have been done differently?
2. Consider the diversity of interests among its members and the organizational cultures of the United Nations and its Security Council. Do you think it is possible for the UN to create and administer an effectively managed program? Why or why not?
3. The recommendations in the committee's report focus almost entirely on structural issues. Why do you think the committee focused on these issues? What if any recommendations might address culture or craft issues that you identified?
4. Do you need additional information to do a good public management analysis of this program? What would it be, and where might you find such information?
5. After all is said and done, did the benefits to the Iraqi people from the oil-for-food program outweigh the costs in terms of propping up Saddam Hussein's regime and of corruption in the award of contracts? In other words, on balance was the program a success, not a failure? Which dimension or dimensions of public management seemed most influential in your assessment?

The United Nations Oil-for-Food Program

Iraq under Saddam Hussein was placed under United Nations sanctions following the 1991 Gulf War. UN member states were prohibited from trading with Iraq, except for essential foods and medicines, until the regime had effectively disarmed. To alleviate the hardships that sanctions imposed on the Iraqi people—the Iraqi regime diverted relief goods—in 1995 the UN Security Council passed Resolution 986, authorizing the oil-for-food program, whereby Iraqi oil could be sold to foreign buyers so long as the proceeds were used primarily to import food, medicines, and other relief goods at fair market prices. The program began operations in October 1997, and the first shipments of food arrived in March 1998. When the program was in full operation, approximately 60 percent of Iraq's 26 million people, according to one estimate, were solely dependent on rations from it.

UN Secretary General Kofi Annan suspended the program in 2003, shortly before coalition forces attacked Iraq for failure to comply with UN resolutions. After Saddam's regime fell as a result of U.S. military operations, the oil-for-food program came under intense scrutiny because of allegations, long voiced by American conservatives, that, with the complicity of UN officials, Saddam had been able to skim billions of dollars from the program by collecting bribes and kickbacks from purchasers of oil and vendors of relief supplies. A UN independent inquiry committee led by Paul Volcker, former chairman of the Federal Reserve System, investigated these allegations and produced a detailed report in October 2005 (http://www.iic-offp.org/story27oct05.htm). Other investigations were conducted by the Government Accountability Office (www.gao.gov/cgi-bin/getrpt?GAO-06-711T) and by the interim Iraq Governing Council.

The oil-for-food program was organized by the UN Secretariat and administered by the Office of the Iraq Program (OIP), which came to be headed by Annan's appointee, Benon Sevan. The OIP director had as his primary goal ensuring a flow of relief supplies into Iraq. Sevan reported directly to Annan, who would, in turn recommend the program's continuation to the Security Council every six months, in effect approving Saddam's "distribution plans" for relief supplies. Revenues from authorized exports of oil, eventually totaling $65 billion, were paid into a UN escrow account and dispersed primarily for relief supplies. These funds also paid for Gulf War reparations to Kuwait, the weapons inspection program, and the program's administrative expenses, which gave these claimants a stake in the program. Shipments of raw foodstuffs were immediate, but most relief items were subject to a review process that could take six months. Items deemed to have any potential application in chemical, biological, or nuclear weapons systems development were not available to the regime, regardless of their stated purpose.

In the negotiations that led to the creation of the program, Saddam was persuaded to cooperate by being given the authority to select the contractors who purchased oil and who imported regulated relief supplies as well as a say in the selection of the bank that would finance the transactions. His regime made these selections with due regard for their political implications. The bank, Banque Nationale de Paris, moreover, had conflicting loyalties: to the UN for maintaining transparency in all transactions and to its customers for maintaining the confidentiality of their business arrangements.

The OIP was ostensibly responsible for examining these contracts for price and quality. Beginning in 1999 the OIP had the power to approve contracts for a range of items without approval from the UN Security Council. According to the GAO, however, "the Office of the Iraq Program lacked clear authority for rejecting commodity contracts based on pricing concerns." [29] The GAO also noted the lack of authority over price and quality by the customs contractor at the border and the lack of independence and resources of the UN's internal auditor, which "identified hundreds of weaknesses and irregularities in its reports" to no apparent effect on program administration. General oversight of the OIP was the responsibility of the UN Security Council acting as a "sanctions committee." This committee was charged with monitoring oil smuggling, screening contracts for items that could have military uses, and approving oil and commodity contracts. Any committee member could put a "hold" on contracts for various reasons, and members could block a proposed action by the sanctions committee by offering objections. For the most part, however, the committee watched out especially for so-called dual-use items: goods that might be used to make weapons. Scrutiny of all other trade was much less observant and, after May 2002, was formally made the responsibility of the UN Secretariat.

The members of the sanctions committee were evidently mindful of their own countries' national interests and ensured access to the program by their contractors. Records of the Iraqi oil ministry contained evidence that hundreds of contractors and officials in France, Germany, China, the United States, and other countries benefited from the oil-for-food program and, therefore, from Saddam's kickback schemes. Payments for an oil allocation significantly exceeded the actual cost of the oil, with the difference used for "surcharges" to Saddam and a handsome profit to the purchaser. The Volcker committee estimated that nearly $230 million in illicit payments were made to Saddam's regime. Relief supplies could be overpriced, with the difference, again, being divided between the regime and the vendor, and the Volcker committee estimated that Saddam's regime received $1.5 billion in kickbacks from relief goods suppliers.

According to an account in the *Washington Times,* other beneficiaries, in the form of oil allocations, included "former French Interior Minister Charles Pasqua (12 million barrels); Patrick Maugein, CEO of the oil company Soco International and financial backer of French President Jacques Chirac (25 million); former French Ambassador to the United Nations Jean-Bernard Merimee (11 million); Indonesian President Megawati Sukarnoputri (10 million); and Syrian businessman Farras Mustafa Tlass, the son of longtime Syrian Defense Minister Mustafa Tlass (6 million). Leith Shbeilat, chairman of the anti-corruption committee of the Jordanian Parliament, received 15.5 million." [30] When other contractors complained to their governments that they were being shaken down, their governments were reluctant to act, often saying, "We don't want to know this." Self-interest guided sanctions committee responses to complaints: the United States, for example, wanted to sanction Syria but not Jordan or Turkey, but such a selective action was blocked by Russia and France, who said that Syria should not be singled out.

Some critics emphasized poor leadership by Annan and Sevan as a principal source of the program's troubles. One allegation was that UN officials, unsympathetic in principle to the sanctions and disinclined to impose rigorous oversight, were, in effect, collaborating with Saddam. The size and nature of authorized trade expanded steadily from 1998 on, to the regime's considerable benefit. As one account put it, "the UN gave to Saddam the entire import-export franchise for Iraq, taking upon itself the responsibility for ensuring that he would use this arrangement to help Iraq's 26 million people. The success of the program depended wholly on the UN's integrity, competence, and willingness to prevent Saddam from subverting the setup to his own benefit." [31] The UN Secretariat maintained a substantial staff in Iraq and had knowledge of the oil-for-food program's detail and regime practices.

Sevan, who had introduced greater secrecy into the program—information on the identities of individual contractors or the price, quality, or quantity of goods involved in any given deal was not disclosed—was said to have benefited personally from an oil-export voucher issued by Saddam, but this allegation was never proved. By 2000 he was said to be reacting to complaints about the kickback schemes by instructing complainants "to submit formal documents to the

Security Council through their countries' UN missions (something they had no incentive to do since Saddam would most likely have responded by scrapping the deals altogether)." [32]

In September 2005 Volcker's committee issued its report, "The Management of the United Nations Oil-For-Food Programme." Its broad conclusion was that:

> [i]n the final analysis, Mr. Sevan ran a $100 billion Programme with very little oversight from the supervisory authority that created his position and OIP. Through a combination of an unclear reporting structure, a lack of supervision by [the secretary general's office], and a general unwillingness to recognize and address significant issues on the part of the Secretary-General and Deputy Secretary-General, Mr. Sevan had substantial autonomy to shape the Programme's direction. He failed to resist and challenge the Iraqi regime's rampant sanctions violations through which the regime diverted millions of dollars away from the humanitarian effort. He failed to properly investigate and monitor sanctions violations. And he failed to disclose pertinent information to the [sanctions committee] about the actions by the Iraqi regime.[33]

3 Analysis and Argument in Public Management

To a significant extent, discussion of public programs and policies and their implementation takes the form of argument: discourse intended to persuade policymakers, employees, and stakeholders of a particular point of view and to build political and organizational support for it. Reasoned persuasion is, and should be, a central part of the job for public managers. Effective public management requires not only intellectual skill, that is, the ability to think analytically, but the incorporation of such thinking into convincing arguments regarding the strategies and options about which decisions must be reached and actions taken.[1] In other words, among the requisite skills of effective public management is what may be termed rhetorical skill: the ability to communicate persuasively.

More than a half-century ago, political scientist Arthur Macmahon pointed to the central role of argument in the public sphere: "The essence of rational structure for any purpose frequently lies in recognizing how far administration is an argumentative as well as a deliberative process that goes on within the frame of legislation."[2] Put differently, arguments made by policymakers and public managers to justify or persuade are fundamental to conducting the public's business in a republican democracy.

How can public managers improve their rhetorical skill? Two complementary tools for doing so form the foundation of this book: the three-dimensional analytic framework—structure, culture, and craft—described in chapter 2, and the method of argument. The three dimensions framework provides a context within which sound arguments can be constructed, and the method of argument described in this chapter draws on and implements the analytical thinking that takes place using those dimensions. Together, the tools of the three-dimensional framework and the method of argument equip public managers to address distinctive challenges with both intellectual and rhetorical skill.

To make the concept of persuasive argument concrete, consider the following three examples. The first is a speech by David Walker, who was the comptroller general of the United States from November 1998 to May 2008. He made the case that the U.S. government is on a "burning platform," facing fiscal imbalances that threaten the country's future economic strength and ability to continue to fund government programs, affecting the well-being of Americans. He argued that factors such as rising health care costs, demographic shifts (especially the aging of the baby boom generation out of the workforce), and expenditures on homeland security, along with the structure of the current tax system, will increase strains on the ability of U.S. government to meet its obligations. Depending on productivity growth is not a viable strategy, Walker said.

> The official U.S. gross debt now stands at about $7 trillion, which works out to about $24,000 for every man, woman, and child in this country. But if you factor in items such as unfunded promises for future Social Security and Medicare benefits, the burden for every American rises to more than $140,000. Our government has already committed itself to more than $40 trillion in IOUs in current dollars—an amount equal to 18 times the current federal budget or 3½ times the current GDP. According to the most recent Medicare trustees' report, the cost of the new Medicare prescription drug benefit alone may exceed $8 trillion in current dollars over 75 years.
>
> Although an improving economy will help, we will not be able to grow our way out of the problem. Closing our fiscal gap would require double-digit economic growth every year for the next 75 years. By any measure, that is unrealistic. Even during the boom years of the 1990s, the economy on average grew only 3.2 percent annually.
>
> Long-term simulations from GAO paint a chilling picture. By 2040, if we continue on our present course, we will have to cut federal spending by more than half or raise taxes to more than two and a half times today's level to balance the budget. At that point, the federal government would be reduced to doing little more than paying off the interest on the national debt.[3]

To move off this "burning platform," Walker maintained that government financial reporting and disclosure need to be more transparent, government program and spending priorities need to be reviewed, the tax system needs to be overhauled, and entitlement programs need to be reformed—especially Social Security and Medicare. Undertaking such reforms sooner rather than later, he believed, will reduce the need for more drastic measures years from now. Before his fifteen-year term as comptroller general expired, Walker left to become president and CEO of the Peterson Foundation, which will "focus on drawing attention to and solving the most critical social, economic and environmental problems that threaten the nation's economy and imperil the American way of life for future generations." [4] In explaining his early exit from the Government Accountability Office, Walker cited the opportunities in his new position to better advocate and advance his positions—that is, to advance his arguments.[5]

The second example of argument is the defense of wiretaps by former attorney general Alberto Gonzales. A December 2005 *New York Times* story revealed that the National

Security Agency (NSA) had been wiretapping certain telephone calls between persons in the United States and persons in other countries. These wiretaps had been conducted without the authorization of the Foreign Intelligence Surveillance Court, whose approval was typically required for such surveillance. Administration officials—including President Bush, Vice President Cheney, Attorney General Gonzales, and Gen. Michael Hayden, the principal deputy director for national intelligence—defended the wiretaps over the next two months in a series of interviews and speeches. Among them, Gonzales offered the following remarks:

> [T]he Justice Department thoroughly examined this program against al Qaeda, and concluded that the President is acting within his power in authorizing it. These activities are lawful. . . . The terrorist surveillance program is firmly grounded in the President's constitutional authorities. No other public official—no mayor, no governor, no member of Congress—is charged by the Constitution with the primary responsibility for protecting the safety of all Americans—and the Constitution gives the President all authority necessary to fulfill this solemn duty. . . .
>
> The President's authority to take military action—including the use of communications intelligence targeted at the enemy—does not come merely from his inherent constitutional powers. It comes directly from Congress as well.
>
> Just a few days after the events of September 11th, Congress enacted a joint resolution to support and authorize military response to the attacks on American soil. In this resolution, the Authorization for Use of Military Force, Congress . . . authoriz[ed] the President to, quote, "use all necessary and appropriate force against those nations, organizations, or persons he determines planned, authorized, committed, or aided the terrorist attacks" in order to prevent further attacks on the United States. . . .
>
> In [*Hamdi v. Rumsfeld*, 2004], the Supreme Court confirmed that the expansive language of the Resolution—"all necessary and appropriate force"—ensures that the congressional authorization extends to traditional incidents of waging war. And, just like the detention of enemy combatants approved in Hamdi, the use of communications intelligence to prevent enemy attacks is a fundamental and well-accepted incident of military force.
>
> This fact is borne out by history. This Nation has a long tradition of wartime enemy surveillance—a tradition that can be traced to George Washington, who made frequent and effective use of secret intelligence, including the interception of mail between the British and Americans.
>
> And as long as electronic communications have existed, the United States has conducted surveillance of those communications during wartime—all without judicial warrant. In the Civil War, for example, telegraph wiretapping was common, and provided important intelligence for both sides. In World War I, President Wilson ordered the interception of all cable communications between the United States and Europe; he inferred the authority to do so from the Constitution and from a general congressional authorization to use military force that did not mention anything about such surveillance. So too in World War II; the day after the attack on Pearl Harbor, President Roosevelt authorized the interception of all communications traffic into and out of the United States.[6]

The use of wiretaps continued to be controversial despite Gonzales's attempts to explain them. Following further controversies during his tenure as attorney general, most notably the dismissal of at least seven U.S. attorneys for political reasons, Gonzales resigned in September 2007.

The third example of argument is Chicago mayor Richard M. Daley's explanation for an initiative to assist ex-offenders after their release from prison. The mayor convened the Mayoral Policy Caucus on Prisoner Reentry in May 2004, and in January 2006 the caucus issued a report with recommendations regarding employment, health, family, and community safety initiatives related to prisoner reentry.[7] The following "Message from the Mayor" appears on the city's Web site describing the initiative:

> The issue of prisoner reentry has taken on new urgency in recent years, as tens of thousands of formerly incarcerated individuals have returned to our city seeking a fresh start. For too long, the challenges facing these individuals were largely ignored.
>
> The dimensions of the problem are clear. This year alone, more than 21,000 people will return to Chicago after their release from prison. Many will return to their same neighborhoods, often jobless, without a place to live and lacking the basic skills they need. Few receive any help in turning their lives around. We need to promote and develop concrete, pragmatic measures that will address the challenges they face every day.
>
> When we talk about lending a hand to these individuals, we do so always with the understanding that some have committed serious crimes. Their problems often are not high on most lists of priorities. And there are certainly citizens who believe that these former criminals do not deserve our attention or concern.
>
> But the approach we have been taking has not worked. If we expect the 14-year drop in our city's crime rate to continue, if we expect to keep our city strong and growing, we must make a renewed commitment to successfully reintegrate the formerly incarcerated into our communities.
>
> These individuals have paid their debt to society and are looking forward to contributing to their families and neighborhoods as law-abiding, hard-working, tax-paying citizens. They are entitled to be treated fairly in issues of employment, education, health care, housing and all other areas of daily life, and we should not hesitate to make sure that they have the necessary tools to succeed.
>
> The fact is that when people with criminal records succeed, we all succeed. Our families, our neighborhoods and our city's economy all benefit when formerly incarcerated individuals achieve their independence and lead healthy, responsible, crime-free lives. With more and more men and women coming to our city after their release from the criminal justice system, we must all do a better job at recognizing their special challenges. These programs are a critical first step in that process.[8]

To date, the main parts of the recommendations that have been implemented are a new set of city of Chicago hiring guidelines for reviewing applicants with criminal convictions, as well as a number of employment initiatives through the city departments of Environment, Fleet Management, Revenue, and Streets and Sanitation, as well as the mayor's Office of Workforce Development.[9]

These examples of public discourse show how policymaking is conducted through the use of argument. Making a sound argument does not guarantee that a manager's desired course of action will come to pass or that that action will produce an effective or efficient outcome. Yet the absence of sound analysis and argument can substantially decrease a public manager's effectiveness. In this sense, developing skills in analysis and argument is a necessary condition for effective public management. It follows that building skills in making sound arguments and in recognizing them when made by others should be among the foundations of public management training and practice.

The chapter is organized as follows. First, the method of argument based on the work of philosopher Stephen Toulmin is described, and the elements are traced back to the three examples above. The chapter next considers the roles of argument and analysis in public management and discusses causal reasoning, the importance of warrants (an element of argument), and the processes of constructing, conveying, and critiquing arguments. The method of argument in practice is discussed next, and finally the use of argument is emphasized as a tool for sound public management analysis. The end-of-chapter exercise asks readers to identify the elements of argument in Washington, D.C., schools chancellor Michelle Rhee's testimony before the city council on her proposed employment policy changes for the nonunion workforce in the school district's central office.

A METHOD OF ARGUMENT

In each of the examples, a public official or policy entrepreneur is making an argument. In most cases, a clear point is stated; it is backed up with reasons that support the main point; facts or data are provided that relate to those reasons and points; a general principle is stated or implied that links the evidence with the main point; and potential criticisms are addressed. Together, these five components constitute the **method of argument.** Based on the work of Stephen Toulmin, these components are referred to, respectively, as claim, reason, evidence, warrant, and acknowledgment and response.[10] Appropriate qualifications on each element should be scrupulously noted. The elements are illustrated in Figure 3.1.

A **claim** is the main point or idea being advanced. Ideally, a claim is clear and succinct, not meandering or convoluted. A claim can be thought of as the "topic sentence" of the argument—the "big picture." A claim might be thought of as a building's exterior that provides the main frame or structure for the argument. Claims are supported by **reasons** that are intended to convince the reader or listener that the claim can be believed. Reasons are analogous to the interior walls and floors of a building, providing support for the claim. Specific facts, data, and other information that further support the claim constitute **evidence.** Evidence pertains directly to the reasons and the claim being made. Evidence is analogous to the foundation of a building; it supports the reasons and claims, just as the foundation supports the interior and exterior structures of a building. It may be difficult to distinguish between reasons and evidence. Wayne Booth, Gregory Colomb, and Joseph M. Williams offer the following guidance:

FIGURE 3.1 Elements of an Argument

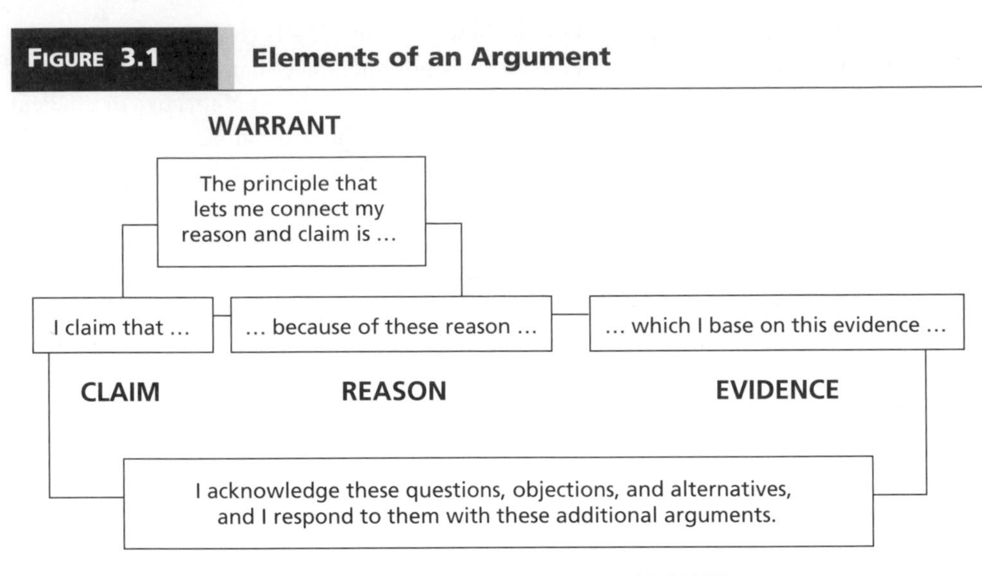

Source: Joseph M. Williams, Gregory G. Colomb, Jonathan D'Errico, and Karen Tracey, *The Craft of Argument, with Readings* (New York: Longman, 2003), 35.

> In some contexts, the words [*reasons* and *evidence*] seem interchangeable:
>
> You have to base your claim on good reasons.
>
> You have to base your claim on good evidence.
>
> But they are not synonyms. Compare these two sentences:
>
> I want to see the evidence that you base your reason on.
>
> I want to see the reason that you base your evidence on.
>
> That second sentence seems a bit odd because we don't base evidence on reasons; we base reasons on evidence.
>
> - Reasons state why readers should accept a claim. Researchers can think up reasons; they don't think up evidence (or at least they do so at their own risk).
> - Evidence is what readers accept as fact, at least for the moment. They think of evidence as "hard" reality, evident to anyone able to observe it.
>
> So when you assemble the elements of your argument, you must start with one or more reasons, but you must base each reason on its own foundation of fact.[11]

The next primary element of argument is the **warrant,** which is a statement of a general principle that justifies the linkages between a particular claim and its reasons and evidence. Just as a building without a roof will not hold up under extreme conditions, an argument without a warrant is incomplete, perhaps flawed. Because they are the most problematic element of a persuasive argument, warrants are discussed in greater detail later in this chapter.

Finally, **acknowledgment and response** is a stage of argument in which responses of various audiences for the argument are anticipated and answered. This stage is likely to involve further reasons, evidence, and warrants. The use of acknowledgments and responses in an argument is important to fair, dispassionate analysis. Such back-and-forth—with other participants in the discourse, supporters, critics, even the merely curious—is part of the process of argumentation, reasoning, and decision making. It lends rationality to the process, involving "argument and counterargument, with the just and fair weighing of conflicts of evidence, and of conflicts of desires." [12] Even though such exchanges bring out the conflicts and disagreements among actors, they need not be contentious. As Joseph M. Williams and Gregory G. Colomb point out, "the language we use about *having* an argument pictures it as combat. But when we describing *making* one, we sound less like combatants than builders." [13]

To think more clearly about the five elements of argument just described, consider the three examples from the beginning of the chapter. In the first, the comptroller general argues that the United States is on a burning platform (claim), because fiscal imbalances are increasing due to deficit spending, demographic shifts, and unsustainable tax structure (reasons). Specific historical and projected spending and revenue figures are used to back up these reasons (evidence). Implied but not specifically stated in Walker's argument are two ideas or principles: (1) marked shifts in revenue sources and spending patterns indicate a crisis; and (2) whenever deficits exist or grow, it is not possible or advisable to continue to operate in the same way (warrants). The projections and conclusions are based on current spending and revenue patterns, coupled with demographic projections. If actions are taken that change spending or revenue in the shorter term, then the picture currently painted for the longer term may not be as bleak (acknowledgment and response).

In the second example, Attorney General Gonzales argues that the NSA wiretaps of phone calls between the United States and other countries were in fact legal (claim), because the Constitution grants the president the responsibility for protecting U.S. citizens, and because a joint resolution of Congress authorized the president to "use all necessary and appropriate force" to prevent terrorist attacks (evidence). Gonzales further argues that the congressional resolution with regard to a military response in fact covered communications intelligence (reason), citing previous instances of the presidential use of such powers during the Revolutionary War, Civil War, World War I, and World War II (evidence). Underlying Gonzales's argument is a general principle that whenever the Constitution grants power to an actor or institution, the actions of that actor or institution that are consistent with that power are legal (warrant). His speech also provides examples of acknowledgment and response:

> Some have suggested that the Force Resolution did not authorize intelligence collection inside the United States. That contention cannot be squared with the reality of the 9/11 attacks, which gave rise to the Resolution, and with the language of the authorization itself, which calls on the President to protect Americans both "at home and abroad" and to take action to prevent further terrorist attacks "against the United States." It's also contrary to the history of wartime surveillance, which has often involved the interception of enemy communications into and out of the United States.[14]

In the third example, Mayor Daley argues that Chicago must develop specific, pragmatic initiatives to assist a growing population of ex-offenders who return to the city after spending time in prison (claim), because they often "return to their same neighborhoods, often jobless, without a place to live and lacking the basic skills they need" (reason). He argues that "when people with criminal records succeed, we all succeed" (warrant). To give a sense of the magnitude of the issue, Daley states that in the current year, more than twenty-one thousand ex-offenders will be released from prison and return to Chicago (evidence). The issue of assisting ex-prisoners is controversial, because of their criminal past and the preferred use of resources in other areas (acknowledgment). But past treatment (that is, ignoring the problem) has not been successful and new initiatives are needed (response).

These three examples provide only part of the argument made by the actors in each case. For the Chicago initiatives, much of the detailed argument that supports the program is contained in the Final Report of the Mayoral Policy Caucus on Prisoner Reentry, not in the brief "Message from the Mayor" posted on the city's Web site. In fact, arguments are almost always more complex than a single claim, reason, piece of evidence, warrant, and acknowledgment and response. Multiple instances of each element may occur, and subarguments may be present; indeed, reasons may themselves become claims for a subargument. As arguments grow more complex, the ability to clearly convey one's own reasoning and to identify the reasoning of others becomes all the more important.

Merely presenting an argument that contains a claim, reason, evidence, warrant, and acknowledgment and response does not guarantee either the argument's validity or its success in winning over intended audiences. The Social Security system has not been reformed either in response to Walker's arguments or to the arguments of others; the legality of the NSA wiretaps remained highly controversial despite the administration's arguments; and Chicago has not adopted all of Mayor Daley's initiatives. But the argument that is complete, containing all the formal elements, has a better chance of being clearly understood and can contribute more usefully to debate on the matter at hand.

A final note: Application and usefulness of the method of argument is not at all unique to public management. The method is applicable to all kinds of settings and situations. This text on public management devotes special attention to the method of argument because, as noted at the beginning of the chapter, discussion of public programs and policies and their implementation often takes the form of argument, and honing this rhetorical skill increases a public manager's chances of being effective.

THE PROCESSES OF ANALYSIS AND ARGUMENT

Effective public managers think analytically about topics ranging from whether and how to contract out the production of public services, how to recruit and motivate employees, how to organize successful collaborations, how to allocate scarce budgetary resources, and how to manage a specific program. Their analyses support informed decisions regarding courses of action on these and many other matters.

As already noted, thinking analytically and arguing persuasively are complementary skills. The skill needed to think analytically, Giandomenico Majone points out in his book *Evidence, Argument, and Persuasion in the Policy Process,* "are not algorithmical [reducible to rote procedure] but argumentative: the ability to probe assumptions critically, to produce and evaluate evidence, to keep many threads in hand, to draw for an argument from many disparate sources, to communicate effectively." [15] The processes of argument and analysis are inextricably related: Analysis supports arguments, and arguments are the outcomes of analysis.

Typically, the goal of analysis is to identify correlational or causal relationships that can inform decision or action—that is, to identify principles or causes that account for the evidence, then to draw appropriate conclusions. Specifying the mechanisms, and in many cases the warrants, that link claims and reasons is a fundamental part of this process.

Causal Reasoning

The nature of "causal" relationships has been the subject of discussion and argument for centuries, and no single definition of a cause exists. The conception of causality in recent years has tended to be characterized by four emphases: clearly distinguishing correlation and causality; focusing on short, not long, causal chains; distinguishing necessary and sufficient conditions for causality; and viewing causality in terms of probabilities rather than certainties.[16]

In the hard sciences, a **causal relationship** is defined as occurring when a cause is both necessary and sufficient for producing the effect, where a necessary condition "must be present for an event to occur" and a sufficient condition "guarantees that the event will occur whenever it is present[, but] the event may occur in its absence." [17] In the social sciences, it is extremely difficult (if ever possible) to identify both necessary and sufficient conditions linking a purported cause and its effect(s). An alternative, commonly used, and relatively straightforward conception of causality, articulated by Paul Lazarsfeld, points to three elements that must be present to establish a causal effect.

1. The cause must happen before the effect.
2. An empirical association must exist between the cause and the effect.
3. Other explanations of the cause-effect relationship must be eliminated (that is, spurious or confounding factors must be ruled out).[18]

If one can think of an additional characteristic or factor that is not accounted for in the analysis, and if it is related both to the characteristic being considered as well as to the outcome, then a causal relationship between the hypothesized cause and the observed effect cannot be established.

To see how these ideas might apply in managerial practice, consider the following. An elementary school principal—public school principals are public managers—wants to improve the performance of students in her school. By looking through the school's administrative records from the past two years, the principal notices that students whose teachers went to the state's flagship public university tend to score higher on standardized tests than do students whose teachers attended other universities. The principal concludes that she should hire only graduates from the state university so that performance of students in her school will improve. To analyze whether the relationship between the purported cause (teacher attends state's flagship university) and effect (student performance improves) is causal or not, Lazarsfeld's criteria can be applied.

The first criterion holds because teachers attend the state university before they teach at the school and therefore before student performance is assessed. The second criterion also holds because the principal's analysis detects an empirical association between the source of the teachers' degree and student performance. The third criterion likely does not hold. It may be the case that better-performing students are placed in the elementary classrooms of the state university teachers to begin with. Or perhaps particular types of individuals whose characteristics lead them to be more effective teachers choose to go to the state university. So it is not the state university per se, but the characteristics of individuals who choose to go there, that is linked to student performance. Or perhaps the state university has a particularly effective approach to elementary education; other universities that use that approach produce equally effective teachers, but no teachers from those universities happen to be in the elementary school at the current time. All of these situations describe spurious factors that prevent concluding that a cause-effect relationship exists between a teacher graduating from a particular university and improved student performance in that teacher's classroom.

Another useful way to think about causal relationships is the **counterfactual** or what the outcome would have been in the absence of the hypothesized cause. Now the question becomes: What would student performance have been had the students and their teachers been the same in all other respects *except* that the teachers did not go to the state university? This counterfactual condition is impossible to create because those same exact teachers could not have attended both the state university and another university at the very same time. The field of program evaluation is focused on constructing appropriate approximations of counterfactuals so that the causal effects of programs, policies, and other interventions can be identified. From that literature, it is well-established that the ideal counterfactual is approximated through randomly assigning some subjects to receive an intervention, such as attending the state university, and others to not receive it by going to another university.

Even though most situations encountered by public managers will not have the benefit of random assignment to establish counterfactuals, public managers and analysts of public management can still use the *concept* of the counterfactual to think critically about the relationship between specific evidence or causes and presumed effects. In justifying the need for the NSA wiretaps, Attorney General Gonzales and other administration officials point to the successful acts of terrorism that might have occurred had such surveillance mechanisms not been deployed.

Argument based on the notion of cause-and-effect reasoning based on evidence from research is not without its critics. Some scholars believe that the analytic concepts and methods of the social sciences are an inappropriate source of evidence for claims about how management strategies cause outcomes. The reason is that such methods require the use of concepts or constructs that are "socially constructed," that is, they reflect the values and biases of researchers rather than so-called objective reality.[19] Such critics might point out that Chicago's policy of ensuring "fair treatment" of "the formerly incarcerated" by helping them lead "responsible lives" is loaded with value judgments and incorporates causal reasoning that may very well be spurious. Some critics go so far as to argue that democracy and social justice are threatened by the use of analytic methods that are prone to bias in policymaking. Is it correct to lump together all the "formerly incarcerated"? What after all is a "responsible life"? How are such judgments to be reached?

Because public managers operate in spheres of what Terry Moe has called "political rationality" (discussed in chapter 1), values and analytic constructs of necessity play a role in analysis and argument. In a discourse analysis of program performance assessments made by the Office of Management and Budget, Donald Moynihan concluded:

> In contrast to the rational espoused theory of performance budgeting, dialogue theory includes the role of politics and rejects the idea that performance information is objective enough to be uniformly understood in the same way and to prompt similar responses among different actors in the budgetary process. Rather, performance information is used, but the meanings assigned to such data are subjective and will be interpreted and debated among different actors consistent with their values, training, motivations, partisan positions, and cognitive characteristics.[20]

Arguments for action therefore may be based on different interpretations of the same information or "facts," especially when causal relationships are unclear or unspecified.

That need not be a bad thing, however. One task of policymaking and public management is not only to put arguments forward but also to critique the arguments of others to expose their biases, flaws in reasoning, and faulty evidence. Such policy debates, whether conducted among the branches of government—legislators reviewing the arguments of presidents, governors, and department heads or judges reviewing the arguments of plaintiffs and defendants—can lead to much greater enlightenment as to what is at stake in taking a proposed course of action than if debate were based solely on values and beliefs with no attempt by any actors in the process to put forward reasons or evidence of any kind.

Lazarsfeld's criteria for causality provide a helpful frame for identifying a causal relationship (or its absence). Yet James Bradley and Kurt Schaefer argue that a "mechanism" or "conceptual framework" that justifies an expected relationship between a cause and its effects is really needed for understanding such relationships in the social sciences in particular.[21] Such explication of causal mechanisms provides a guide for action. Further, the need for describing such mechanisms is arguably greater still when it is not possible to establish Lazarsfeld's criteria—a very common state of the world in the social sciences, especially in public management, where it can be extremely difficult to identify causal relationships. Thus, the door is opened for the theories and frameworks of the social sciences, which provide an important resource for developing hypotheses about causes and effects—that is, for specifying warrants.

The Importance of Warrants in Argument

What does "thinking analytically" involve? In addition to articulating claims, reasons, evidence, and acknowledgments and responses, thinking analytically involves providing warrants in support of an argument. Warrants are statements that relate a general circumstance to a general inference, and can be stated in the following form: "Whenever X, then Y." [22] Often, reasons and evidence are consistent with many claims; the warrant points the analyst to the claims that are most appropriate, given the reasons and evidence. Put another way, a warrant is a general statement that provides a justification for why *a particular* reason and body of evidence are a basis for making *a particular claim.*[23]

In some cases, a claim does not require an explicit warrant if the underlying warrant is widely accepted or self-evident. In other cases, drawing appropriate conclusions requires articulation of the principles or causes that link the reasons, evidence, and claim. Regardless of whether warrants are made explicit, they play an essential role in argument. As Toulmin put it:

> unless, in any particular field of argument, we are prepared to work with warrants of *some* kind, it will become impossible in that field to subject arguments to rational assessment. The data we cite if a claim is challenged depends on the warrants we are prepared to operate within that field, and the warrants to which we commit ourselves are implicit in the particular steps from data to claims we are prepared to take and to admit.[24]

In private sector management, where the basis for decisions is widely accepted to be the prospect of increased profit, "[o]ften the warrants are only implied: they are clearly understood, because all involved are intimately familiar with the organization's goals and values, which determine the operative warrants for most such arguments." [25] Shared, obvious warrants are less likely to be present in the realm of public management analysis because of the lack of a single unifying goal and because causal links may be difficult or impossible to establish. Specific warrants therefore are important in advancing an argument in the sphere of public management.

To establish warrants that link reasons and evidence to claims, public managers may draw on different sources: opinions or ideologies, experience, authority, general cultural beliefs, methodological/logical grounds, articles of faith, and systems of knowledge and beliefs.[26] As will be discussed in chapter 7, public managers most frequently draw on experiential, normative/ideological, and academic/empirical sources. Although no one type of knowledge or understanding will suffice to comprehend complex situations, some of these sources provide stronger backing for warrants than others. Opinions and ideologies, perhaps faith, are likely to be the most fragile basis for warrants because they tend to be more purely subjective and less confirmable by evidence than the other sources—in the case of faith, by definition, no evidence is available. Warrants with these bases are likely to be contested and provide a weaker justification for linking claims and reasons in any particular context.

CONCEPTS IN ACTION

Explanation of a Specific Warrant

The excerpt below describes an argument that states the specific warrant in the general form of "whenever X, then Y": "When more resources are invested to prevent something but its incidence goes up, those resources have been wasted." After reading the excerpt, consider the fit between the claim, reason, and warrant. Why might an increase in drug smuggling, despite higher budgets to control it, not necessarily indicate that resources were wasted?

Suppose your friend makes this argument:

> Despite Congress's doubling the budget to reduce drug smuggling, the amount of drugs smuggled into this country has risen.$_{reason}$ Clearly, we are wasting our money.$_{claim}$ . . .

To persuade you to accept that reason as supporting that claim, your friend would have to respond with the general principle that explains why it does. His principle would consist of two parts, a general circumstance and a general consequence that reliably follows from it:

> When more resources are invested to prevent something but its incidence goes up,$_{general\ circumstance}$ those resources have been wasted.$_{general\ consequence}$

If you accept the general principle (you might not), then you should accept the same relationship between a *specific instance* of that circumstance and any *specific instance* of that consequence. If you accept that the general consequence follows from the general circumstance, then you should also accept that the specific consequence follows from the specific circumstance. . . .

If the warrant and reason are true and the reason and claim are good instances of the warrant, then the claim must be true. Of course, the warrant will not "work" if you don't accept it as a true general principle.

Source: Wayne C. Booth, Gregory G. Colomb, and Joseph M. Williams, *The Craft of Research,* 2nd ed. (Chicago: University of Chicago Press, 2003), 166–167.

Warrants based on systems of knowledge, including academic/empirical findings, may hold the most promise for public management analysis. That is, the theories and evidence from the social sciences, their potential for bias notwithstanding, are a resource from which warrants can be, or have already been, developed. By the very nature of social science, the theories and hypotheses and resultant warrants are subject to scrutiny and to empirical testing in particular settings. The accumulated knowledge from these processes—resulting in the kinds of theories, concepts, and analytic frameworks discussed throughout this book—are a source of generalizable, verifiable warrants that public managers can use in their arguments to link specific claims with specific reasons in specific circumstances. Drawing on theory and research instead of mere opinion or faith for making an argument increases the appeal to reason of a manager's argument, thereby increasing the likelihood that the analysis is viewed as trustworthy and dispassionate.

Arguments with warrants drawn from systems of knowledge reflect rational analysis. Yet the world of public management is most often one of "political rationality," not "technical rationality," as Moe expresses it.[27] Two factors, political pressures and the fact that so many policymakers are lawyers, incline political actors to make strong, partisan arguments meant to sway public opinion. Such arguments are most often based on warrants rooted in opinion or ideology rather than bodies of knowledge and fairly weighed evidence. As participants in this system of "political rationality," then, public managers' arguments that solely reflect technical rationality may fail to persuade or capture the attention of policymakers, politicians, and interest groups. Indeed, such arguments may fall flat.

It may not always be feasible to make a sound, persuasive argument supported by warrants drawn from the knowledge, theories, and frameworks of the social sciences, that is, one that reflects technical rationality, but having the skills to do so enhances public managers' trustworthiness and effectiveness as purveyors of reliable advice.

Constructing, Conveying, and Critiquing Arguments

To some, the idea that a complete argument contains basic elements—claims, reasons, evidence, warrants, counterarguments, and responses—seems unremarkable, a matter of common sense. Yet one of the main reasons for devoting a whole chapter to the method of argument is that constructing such arguments is *not* second nature to many people. As discussed in the next section, there may be valid reasons that an argument presented in a particular political forum is not complete. But gaining the skills to construct and convey a complete argument (before making an explicit decision of whether to communicate all of the argument's elements) is essential for increasing one's chances of thoroughly understanding a particular situation and the reasons for action (or inaction).

In part, skills of analysis and argument are built by examining the decisions and behaviors of others. This idea underlies the use of **case analysis** in management training for both the public and private sectors. Sources of case materials for public management training include the Kennedy School Case Program, the Electronic Hallway, news accounts, and government reports.[28] A successful case analysis essentially requires constructing an argument.

CONCEPTS IN ACTION

Ideology as Warrant

Managers and other individuals may use ideology to explain or justify actions. Stated differently, warrants—or general principles—based on ideology are used to justify action. In this excerpt, justifications such as "clinical freedom" or "the right to manage" are examples of such warrants.

[I]deology can, and often does, provide the justification for some particular course of action. The justification may be pre- or post-hoc, but it is legitimation none the less. Individuals who say "I did this as a matter of good management practice" are tapping into a wider, socially shared paradigm of approved actions. Like doctors who cite "customary medical practice" they are trying to clothe themselves in the garb of warranted professional procedure. Like "clinical freedom" the "right to manage" is a claim to justified, socially beneficial autonomy. Even when management actions at first sight appear misguided, the actors concerned may seek the shelter of this protected sphere—to cite the textbook tends to be a less compelling defence than worldly success, but it is better than no defence at all.

Source: Christopher Pollitt, *Managerialism and the Public Services: The Anglo-American Experience* (Oxford: Basil Blackwell, 1990), 10.

Take, for example, a list of general questions that can be used with many cases—including those at the end of each chapter in this book—to identify the information needed to construct an argument:

- Who is the main decision maker, and what specific decisions does he or she have to make?
- Who are the other important actors in the case, and what are their objectives?
- What are the principal issues (facts or assumptions) that must be resolved to reach a decision?
- What is the context or environment that the main decision maker and other actors are operating in?
- What alternatives should the decision maker consider, and what are the consequences of each course of action?[29]

To answer almost every one of these questions, the analyst can utilize the method of argument. Often, cases end with an actor facing a specific decision and the ultimate question:

- What would you do in these circumstances, and WHY?

In answer to this question as well, a particular claim must be made, and it should be supported by reasons, evidence, warrants, counterarguments, and responses. The utility of the recommendation, then, rests on the soundness of the analysis and argument.

Because public managers must convey their arguments orally as well as in writing, the use of analysis and argument in a public management course may incorporate practice using the method of argument in class discussion (of cases, news articles, or other material), as well as in memos and other written assignments. For example, two versions of memos might be turned in by students—one clean copy and one that classifies statements in the memo according to their elements of argument. Such explicit mapping of argument encourages students to focus on how they incorporate the method in their own thinking and writing. By reinforcing the method of argument through oral and written communications throughout the course, awareness of the method is raised and students get many opportunities to practice articulating their arguments. A tool for helping students and instructors distinguish the quality of an argument is described in Box 3.1.

Additional resources for reading and analyzing cases, leading case discussions, constructing arguments, writing memos, and more generally conveying arguments in writing are available from various sources, including the Kennedy School Case Program and in the "Teaching Resources" section of the Electronic Hallway.[30]

In addition to practicing the method of argument through one's own oral and written communications, a useful way to learn the method is to analyze and critique arguments made by others. The case at the end of this chapter, for example, asks readers to identify the elements of argument in school chancellor Michelle Rhee's testimony before the city council in Washington, D.C.

The method of argument can also be used to analyze scholarly articles or books. What claims does the author make? What reasons are provided to support these claims? What evidence (data, methods, and findings) is offered? What warrants (theories, frameworks, or other sources) are presented to link the evidence to the claims? Finally, does the author discuss alternative possible interpretations of the evidence, or acknowledge shortcomings of the analysis, and what, if any, response is provided to those potential issues? Using the method of argument to analyze a research article can be a fruitful way to systematically assess the validity of the work. The case at the end of chapter 9, for example, asks readers to analyze the argument made by Carolyn J. Heinrich in an article about performance measurement and management. A published example of argument analysis of a scholarly work is Melvin J. Dubnick's critique of Guy B. Adams and Danny L. Balfour's book *Unmasking Administrative Evil.*[31] Dubnick invokes Toulmin's framework and critiques the book by analyzing its claims, warrants, and qualifiers. Dubnick's article represents an argument to which Adams and Balfour respond.[32]

Box 3.1

RANKING THE STRENGTH OF ARGUMENTS

Arguments may be evaluated using the following ranking scheme, presented from the least to the most appropriate type of argument. This ranking scheme might be used to assess arguments made in the context of a public management course for in-class discussions or assignments or as a part of public management practice either for constructing one's own argument or assessing the arguments of others.

The "No argument" argument

A public manager took particular actions. She should have taken other actions instead.

Problem: No reasons, evidence, warrants, or qualifications are supplied to support the conclusion.

The "Well, of course, but . . . " argument

A public manager took particular actions. She should have acted differently

- for reasons that are obvious in hindsight, such as she had no political support, so she should have mobilized the support she needed; she failed to win over the constituency that ended up defeating her;
- because of principles that, on reflection, always apply, such as always consider the values and feelings of your subordinates.

Problem: Although the argument presents reasons and evidence, it emphasizes hindsight and does not link the evidence and reason to the claim in a way that invokes a general principle in the context of the situation. A warmed-over "counsel of perfection" is conveyed, rather than insight into how to handle complex public management situations.

The "Almost, but not quite" argument

A public manager took particular actions. It would have been better had she taken different actions based on reasoning

- drawn from shrewd observation of the evidence in the case or lessons from personal experience;
- that implies but does not state a more complex theory or concept of general but not universal application. For example, her actions assumed that her subordinates would comply, but they stood to gain more by noncompliance.

Problem: Although the argument presents reasons and evidence, and hints at warrants linking those elements with the claim, the full logic is not articulated and appropriate qualifications are not offered, leaving the argument with holes.

The "I know how to construct an argument" argument

A public manager took particular actions. It would have been better had she taken different actions because this is an example of a theory/framework/model/concept that incorporates cause-effect logic. Appropriate qualifications and acknowledgments and responses are included. The framework is

- used as a source of vocabulary for interpreting the facts in the case;
- used to derive conclusions based on those facts.

Why This Works: The emphasis in these arguments is on applying the logic of analytic models to the facts of cases or real world problems in order to gain nonobvious, nondescriptive insights into how the managerial world works. Theories and frameworks are used to establish warrants, which then drive the linking of evidence, reasons, and claims, noting appropriate qualifications. Counterarguments are acknowledged and responded to.

To summarize, analysis and argument, intellectual skills, and rhetorical skills are fundamental to public management practice. Practicing the methods of argument through oral and written communications, and through examining the work of others, can build and improve these important skills. Armed with a clearly reasoned, complete argument, the public manager must then consider how to convey the argument.

ARGUMENTS IN PRACTICE

A well-crafted argument should contain the four or five key elements discussed in the chapter, but that does not mean that arguments by public officials always do contain these elements. In the realm of public management as it is actually practiced, carefully and completely constructed arguments are relatively rare. Instead, public arguments made by public officials and public managers often lack reasons, evidence, warrants, or qualifications; sometimes even claims are missing. Assertions are made that are not supported by any evidence; evidence may be used selectively to support the particular claim and the reasons to support the claim; warrants may be missing, vague, or faulty; and potential concerns of critics may be mischaracterized or ignored.

Herbert Simon suggests one reason for incomplete arguments. He wrote that humans exhibit bounded rationality—that is, limited capacity to obtain and assess all possibly relevant information.[33] If this is the case, then arguments constructed on such limited information may be limited or incomplete as well.

Beyond this cognitive constraint, however, it is not surprising that incomplete or flawed arguments are relatively common in a democracy of separated powers and political partisanship. Presenting all relevant evidence or data on both sides of an issue may bring charges of inconsistency—of being a "waffler" or a "flip-flopper" or being "two-handed," as in framing arguments in terms of "on the one hand" and "on the other hand." Offering no evidence may bring charges of evasion from opponents; but offering any evidence at all may provide a target for dissection and counterargument. **Qualifications** or acknowledgment of critics' concerns are rarely offered because to do so may be interpreted in the political arena as a sign of weakness. In the light of these risks, the most effective arguments may be incomplete arguments.

Political rationality may help explain why complete arguments are so rare in the public sphere. Another reason may be the constraints of particular settings or forums in which the arguments of public officials and managers are conveyed. Regardless of whether the full scope of an argument is conveyed in a particular forum—and as just discussed, there may be valid reasons, such as a the lack of time, for not doing so—a skilled public manager will have a firm grasp of the relationship between the claims, reasons, evidence, warrants, and counterarguments and responses that support his or her preferred course of action. The skilled public manager will also understand how and where to present an argument.

Arguments are made by public managers and officials at all levels of government about ideas, courses of action, processes, programs, and policies. Some arguments aim to sway or convince internal organizational actors about a position or action, while others aim to sway or convince external actors, such as elected officials, interest groups, newspaper editorial boards, or the general public. Arguments may address topics that range from everyday matters such as the style and format required for proposals for local garbage collection to matters literally of life and death such as whether to mobilize troops for a military intervention or to intervene in a child welfare case.

Regardless of the specific format of an argument or its forum, most arguments made by public managers are aimed toward one of three general purposes. First, the argument may address the need for change or action. Examples include Walker's burning platform argument; appeals from a local school board to the community for a levy increase; analyses by public officials, scholars, and pundits following Hurricane Katrina arguing for FEMA restructuring; or Mayor Daley's argument about the need for a prisoner reentry initiative. Second, the argument may address the *ex post facto* (after the fact) justification or support of a prior decision. Examples include the Bush administration's defense of NSA wiretapping, a child welfare agency's documentation that it followed procedures after a publicized incident involving harm to a child, or, again, Daley's statement. Finally, the argument may address the need to maintain the status quo, such as a defense of the current system of generic drug approval by the FDA.

In making their arguments, public officials use a number of different types of **formats, forums, and media:**

- giving speeches (such as Alberto Gonzales' speech at Georgetown University);
- testifying before legislative bodies (such as Department of Homeland Security Secretary Michael Chertoff appearing before the U.S. Senate Committee on Homeland Security and Government Affairs);[34]
- writing intra- or interoffice memos or e-mail messages (such as an e-mail message from a local FEMA official to FEMA director Mike Brown on August 31, 2005);
- writing position papers, reports, or "white papers" (such as a Environmental Protection Agency white paper on nanotechnology);[35]
- issuing commission reports (such as the one issued by President Bush's Commission to Strengthen Social Security);[36]
- issuing or responding to audit reports (such as an audit of management practices of the Los Angeles Fire Department conducted by the city controller's office);[37]

- addressing public forums (such as those held to discuss a school tax levy increase in a local school district); and
- giving interviews to the media, including newspapers, magazines, TV, radio, Web sites, specialized journals or newsletters (such as Walker's appearance on *60 Minutes*).[38]

An argument about a particular topic may be presented using different media, in different formats and forums. Walker made his burning platform argument in speeches, newsletter or journal articles, and PowerPoint presentations; he spoke to members of Congress, to Rotary Club members in Atlanta, to audiences on college campuses, and to professional associations. The argument is even conveyed in a documentary, I.O.U.S.A., released in August 2008.

A particular forum and format may not be well suited to a full presentation of an argument; this is especially true for media accounts and interviews. The following newspaper story from the *Denver Post* concerns air traffic control staffing at Denver International Airport. The elements of argument are identified in brackets:

> Answering criticism from the air-traffic controllers' union, a Federal Aviation Administration official said Wednesday that three air-traffic facilities in the Denver area have enough controllers to ensure safe flying at Denver International Airport [DIA] and other Colorado airports. [$\text{claim}_{\text{FAA}}$]
>
> Last week, local leaders of the National Air Traffic Controllers Association [NATCA] highlighted "two serious crises facing the aviation system" [$\text{claim}_{\text{NATCA}}$]—an acute staffing shortage [$\text{reason1}_{\text{NATCA}}$] and archaic equipment at local air-traffic facilities. [$\text{reason2}_{\text{NATCA}}$]
>
> According to the union, those facilities include DIA's tower, the terminal radar approach control operation near DIA and one in Longmont that handles high-altitude air traffic for Colorado and surrounding states. [$\text{evidence}_{\text{NATCA}}$]
>
> But Steve Stcynske, acting manager of the FAA radar facility near DIA, said Wednesday that all three air-traffic operations will have enough newly trained controllers to replace those scheduled for retirement. [$\text{claim}_{\text{FAA}}$]
>
> Air-traffic controllers must retire at 56.
>
> To illustrate why current staffing levels are adequate, Stcynske said the number of "operational errors" by controllers has declined 13 percent in the past year while airline traffic has increased by 1 percent in the same period.[39] [$\text{evidence}_{\text{FAA}}$]

The mapping of the elements of argument onto the information available in the article makes it clear that many elements of an argument are missing from this account—both from the FAA's position, and from NATCA's position. No warrants or qualifications are available either for NATCA's or FAA's argument. Further, the article describes an FAA official's response to one, but not both, of the reasons set forth by NATCA leaders. In sum, not enough information is available—at least in this account—to fully assess the arguments of either actor. Yet at least part of the absence of information is due to the medium through which the arguments are being conveyed. Newspapers have limited space, and writers' and editors' decisions will always determine what parts of a manager's arguments are conveyed.

CONCEPTS IN ACTION

Elements of Argument in a News Article

The following article on foster care programs in Missouri illustrates how argument and counterargument are conveyed in a newspaper account. Do the reasons and evidence directly support the claims? What elements of the argument are missing or implied in this account?

State Auditor Claire McCaskill on Thursday accused the state of dragging its feet in finding adoptive homes for thousands of foster children. [claim1$_{\text{Auditor}}$]

Her audit blames several factors, such as poor communication with potential adoptive parents, [reason1$_{\text{Auditor}}$] a lack of collaboration with the courts [reason2$_{\text{Auditor}}$] and problems with computerized records. [reason3$_{\text{Auditor}}$]

"There is nothing more important than finding a good adoptive home for a child who has been abandoned or neglected, and frankly it is what the state ought to do better than anything else," [warrant$_{\text{Auditor}}$] McCaskill said.

The report points to a downturn in adoptions in the past few years. [evidence1$_{\text{Auditor}}$] What the audit does not mention is that the number of adoptions from foster care had previously doubled between the years of 1997 and 2002.

Deb Scott, a spokeswoman for the Department of Social Services [DSS], said the audit "fails to present a full picture of adoption efforts" and the successes the state has had in increasing rates of adoption. [claim$_{\text{DSS}}$]

The increase had been prompted, in part, by new federal standards that seek to move foster children to permanent homes more quickly. [reason$_{\text{DSS}}$] Those new standards helped to speed up adoptions nationwide. [evidence1$_{\text{DSS}}$] Adoptions have since slowed as a backlog of cases have been closed. [evidence2$_{\text{DSS}}$] Many say the children who remain tend to be older and harder to adopt. [evidence3$_{\text{DSS}}$]

McCaskill said Thursday she's aware of that trend [acknowledgment$_{\text{Auditor}}$]. But she said her audit isn't merely about the number of adoptions, but on flaws in the system that could be fixed. [response$_{\text{Auditor}}$]

Chief among her concerns are delays in terminating parental rights so that children can become eligible for adoption. [evidence2$_{\text{Auditor}}$]

Federal policy calls for adoption to take place within 24 months after a child lands in foster care. The current standard calls for states to meet that deadline for at least 32 percent of its foster children each year.

For the past two years, Missouri has met those federal requirements [evidence3$_{\text{Auditor}}$]. McCaskill said the state can do much better. [claim2$_{\text{Auditor}}$]

In a response to the audit, the Department of Social Services points out that most decisions related to adoption are made by the courts, not the state. [evidence3$_{DSS}$] How each judge handles adoption cases varies, with some waiting longer than others to terminate parental rights. [evidence4$_{DSS}$]

State officials say a new foster care law passed last year should help address the problem, calling for stricter timelines for courts as they handle foster care cases. [acknowledgment/response1$_{DSS}$]

Much of the audit criticizes the state's computer system for containing outdated information on the status of foster children. [reason4$_{Auditor}$] In some cases, children were still in the system despite having been adopted. [evidence4$_{Auditor}$] Others who were eligible for adoption were not listed as such. [evidence5$_{Auditor}$]

The state is in the process of rolling out a new computer system that officials say should address those errors. [acknowledgment/response2$_{DSS}$]

Source: Matthew Franck, "State Is Chastised over Foster Adoption Rates," *St. Louis Post-Dispatch,* October 28, 2005, Sec. D.

Additional information on the arguments of the FAA and NATCA can be found by conducting an Internet search to identify other sources with additional pieces or a full account of either side's argument. This example illustrates as least two important points: First, even if a manager's argument is "complete" (in the five-element sense), it may not emerge that way in any particular forum, especially when the manager may not have control over the final version, as with a news story. Second, consumers of arguments must keep in mind that a single source or forum will seldom convey the whole argument and that additional research may be necessary.

ANALYSIS AND ARGUMENT AS MANAGEMENT SKILLS

A proficient public manager is able to make sound arguments and to understand and critique the arguments of others. This means formulating specific, concise claims, citing the reasons and evidence that sustain the claims, selecting and specifying warrants that provide a causal logic for linking the reasons to the claims, and acknowledging and responding to potential objections. Scrupulously noting any qualifications on claims, reasons, evidence, warrants, and responses is also fundamental. Arguments constructed in this way are analytical in that they are based on a careful and dispassionate consideration of the facts and issues in a given case. In effect, any preconceptions are put to the test of examining their consistency with the facts and with alternative explanations for those facts.

Being skilled in the method of argument will increase understanding of the actions, statements, and positions of other actors after the fact (*ex post*) and understanding of a situation prior to action in real time (*ex ante*) as a practicing public manager. With greater familiarity and practice in the method of argument and its successful application in various formats, forums, and media, skills for developing arguments in *ex ante* situations will become stronger. Opportunities to practice applying the method of argument are provided throughout this book.

After a first reading of a case, readers might form opinions supported by reasons, based on their own prior experiences or knowledge or on some facts in the case that strike them as particularly telling or revealing. As noted at the beginning of the chapter, the book is built around two complementary analytical tools: the three dimensions of public management—structure, culture, and craft—described in chapter 2 and the method of argument described in this chapter. This book therefore prompts readers to strengthen their analytical skills by pushing beyond their initial responses after reading cases, analyzing managerial actions of others, or planning their own next steps. After their initial assessments, they can next think about the issue using the heuristic of the three dimensions. And finally, they can ensure that their analysis constitutes a complete and coherent argument by clearly stating claims, reasons, evidence, warrants, and acknowledgments and responses.

The tools of argument and the three-dimensional framework do not guarantee a tidy, formulaic approach for conducting analysis of public management problems. Instead, they can be employed as management analysts develop judgment and skill in synthesizing insights from diverse sources. The examples discussed throughout the book and the cases presented at the end of each chapter are intended to provide opportunities for practicing this full set of skills.

Key Concepts

method of argument
claim
reasons
evidence
warrant
acknowledgment and response
causal relationship
counterfactual
case analysis
qualification
formats, forums, and media

Analysis and Argument: Test Your Understanding

Control of the Washington, D.C., public schools was transferred from the city council to Mayor Adrian Fenty in June 2007. He immediately named Michelle Rhee to be the school system's chancellor. Rhee, thirty-seven years old at the time, was a founder of the New Teacher Project, a nonprofit that encouraged training and employment of high-quality teachers in K–12 schools. She had no previous experience running a large urban school district.

One of Rhee's objectives, described in her *Year 1 Plan,* was to "Create a central office that effectively serves schools." [40] As part of that plan, the mayor submitted to the city council draft legislation for the District of Columbia Education Personnel Reform Amendment Act of 2007. The act would convert nonunion central office staff members to "at-will" employees, grant the mayor authority for reduction-in-force decisions for certain employees, and remove the ability for nonunion central office staff to form collective bargaining units.

Rhee testified before the city council regarding the proposed act on November 2, 2007, and she addressed the issue in a letter to teachers in December.

Read the documents listed below and answer the questions that follow.

Testimony of Michelle Rhee, Chancellor, Meeting of the District of Columbia City Council, http://www.k12.dc.us/chancellor/testimony/11.2Testimony_pdf.pdf, November 2, 2007.

Michelle Rhee, Chancellor. Letter to District of Columbia Public School Teachers, December 2007, http://www.k12.dc.us/chancellor/documents/Letter%20to%20Teachers_December_2007.pdf.

1. Select one argument in Rhee's testimony. Identify the specific claim, reason(s), evidence, warrant(s), and acknowledgments and responses (and note whether any of these elements is missing for a particular argument).
2. Did you find the process of analyzing the argument easy to do? Which elements were most difficult to identify?
3. Does Rhee address the argument you identified in her letter to teachers? If so, are different elements of the argument presented in that forum?

4 Public Management's Backbone: The Rule of Law

It is an article of faith that America is "a government of laws, not of men." This overarching concept of governance was the founders' intent. Public management in America is, and must be, in all of its dimensions, lawful. As Thomas Paine put it, the law is king, the king is not law.[1] It is ironic, however, that the legitimacy of the rule of law in America depends on an unwritten and unenforceable faith in law and legal institutions. Legal scholar Michael Mullane says:

> When you get right down to it, the rule of law only exists because enough of us believe in it and insist that everyone, even the non-believers, behave as if it exists. The minute enough of us stop believing, stop insisting that the law protect us all, and that every single one of us is accountable to the law—in that moment, the rule of law will be gone. So I cling to my belief in the rule of law. It is probably the single greatest achievement of our society. It is our bulwark against both mob rule and the overweening power of the modern state. It is the rule of law that governs us, that protects each one of us when we stand alone against those who disagree with us, or fear us, or do not like us because we are different. It is the strongbox that keeps all our other values safe.[2]

The reason for emphasizing commitment to the rule of law as the *modus operandi* of public management is that the authority and, of equal importance, the legitimacy of public management—the faith placed in it by citizens, elected officials, and judges—is ultimately derived from public managers' sense of responsibility—their accountability—to constitutional principles and institutions: elected legislatures, elected executives, the courts of law that review political and administrative acts for their lawfulness, and the additional institutions and conventions, the checks and balances, authorized by representative and judicial bodies.

This chapter describes how law affects public management. Two examples are presented to set the stage. The first concerns responses to the highly publicized "Reinventing Government" public management reform initiative of President Bill Clinton's administration. (This and other "strategic reforms" are discussed at greater length in chapter 9.) One of its components was inspired by a reform ideology that had been implemented in Great Britain and New Zealand and is still known as New Public Management. The Clinton administration sought to imitate Great Britain's "Next Steps" reform, according to which, mimicking corporate management, individual agencies headed by chief executive officers (CEOs) were created to handle distinct governmental activities on behalf of ministries (equivalent to cabinet-level departments), each within a regulatory framework that included features such as performance requirements and targets. Although they were civil servants, the CEOs' pay was to be based on measured performance, and removal for poor performance was possible in principle. The Clinton administration called its version of such agencies "performance-based organizations" (PBOs).

As public administration scholars Andrew Graham and Alasdair Roberts have shown, America's formal separation of powers meant that "an influential third party—Congress—threatened to complicate negotiations over the content of annual performance agreements." [3] The idea was to have such agreements require the administration to commit to provide specific budgets for the period of years covered by the agreements. But future Congresses cannot be legally bound by the decisions of a sitting Congress, and power can change hands from Congress to Congress. An additional problem was the inclusion of terms restricting the termination of CEOs for other than performance-related reasons. In the U.S. system of governance, Congress "may not limit the ability of the President to remove appointees, unless those appointees exercise quasi-legislative or quasi-judicial functions that require some independence from the administration." [4] The three PBOs that were ultimately created were denied significant flexibilities and were but a pale reflection of the British model. In general, management strategies available to governments without a separation of powers (such as the United Kingdom) or to corporate executives in the private sector are available only in highly attenuated form to public managers in governments with separation of powers.

Another example of how law affects public management is illustrated by the response to the Brady Handgun Violence Prevention Act, signed into law in 1995. The act required the U.S. attorney general to establish a national system for instant background checks on prospective handgun purchasers. It directed the "chief law enforcement officer" (CLEO) of each local jurisdiction—sheriffs, chiefs of police—to conduct such checks and perform related tasks on an interim basis until the national system was in place. The CLEOs of two counties, one in Montana and the other in Arizona, filed separate lawsuits in federal district court. Sheriffs Jay Printz and Richard Mack "refused to run federally-mandated background checks on firearm purchasers, arguing not only that such busywork withdrew vital resources from law-enforcement, but that they were local, not federal employees, and therefore, the federal government had no authority to commandeer their labor." [5]

The U.S. Supreme Court, in its decision in *Printz v. United States* (1997) agreed. Justice Antonin Scalia wrote for the majority:

> We . . . conclude categorically, as we concluded categorically in [an earlier case]: "The Federal Government may not compel the States to enact or administer a federal regulatory program. . . .
>
> [T]he central obligation imposed upon CLEOs by the interim provisions of the Brady Act—the obligation to "make a reasonable effort to ascertain within 5 business days whether receipt or possession [of a handgun] would be in violation of the law, including research in whatever State and local record keeping systems are available and in a national system designated by the Attorney General"—is unconstitutional.[6]

As constitutional scholar John A. Rohr interprets the ruling, Justice Scalia's opinion found fault with the Brady Act not only on grounds of federalism but also on separation of powers grounds. Imposing duties on state officers ignores the constitutional provision that the president is to "take care that the Laws be faithfully executed" and that reliance on state CLEOs is an ineffective, because unreliable, means of doing so. Justice David Souter made a strong dissent, arguing, based on *The Federalist,* that the intention of the framers was to incorporate state executives into the federal scheme, using them as auxiliaries of federal power, in Alexander Hamilton's term.[7]

These examples demonstrate that, even in its highest form, the U.S. Constitution, law shapes and constrains the managerial activities of American governments at all levels. Principled arguments based on that document are invoked to govern the authoritative relations between executives and their agents and, as in *Printz,* the character of the services performed by county sheriffs and all other local CLEOs. In its less-exalted forms, such as statutes, executive orders, and regulations, the rule of law is even more pervasive. Almost no matter requiring managerial discretion lies beyond its actual or potential influence.

Although the concept of the rule of law is pervasive in public management, the necessity of managerial judgment and an active role for managers in policymaking are not thereby extinguished. Managerial discretion has become a fundamental aspect of the rule of law, rather than an exception to it, as Justice Scalia wrote in *Printz.*

> Executive action that has utterly no policymaking component is rare, particularly at an executive level as high as a jurisdiction's chief law enforcement officer. Is it really true that there is no policymaking involved in deciding, for example, what "reasonable efforts" shall be expended to conduct a background check? It may well satisfy the Act for a CLEO to direct that (a) no background checks will be conducted that divert personnel time from pending felony investigations, and (b) no background check will be permitted to consume more than one half hour of an officer's time. But nothing in the Act *requires* a CLEO to be so parsimonious; diverting at least *some* felony investigation time, and permitting at least *some* background checks beyond one half hour would certainly not be *un*reasonable. Is this decision whether to devote maximum "reasonable efforts" or minimum "reasonable efforts" not preeminently a matter of policy? It is

> quite impossible, in short, to draw the Government's proposed line at "no policymaking," and we would have to fall back upon a line of "not too much policymaking." How much is too much is not likely to be answered precisely; and an imprecise barrier against federal intrusion upon state authority is not likely to be an effective one.[8]

As Scalia notes, however, it may be difficult to know where to draw the "no policymaking" line.

The lawmaking and fiscal powers assigned to legislatures and the powers assigned to the courts by Articles I and III of the U.S. Constitution, elaborated since the founding by countless U.S. Supreme Court decisions, result in a hierarchical fiscal and administrative "backbone" that structures American public management. Thus, apart from the powers expressly assigned the executive by Article II (again, as interpreted by courts), managerial judgment in the executive branches of American governments is formally subordinated to the other two branches.

This hierarchical backbone operates even when public managers derive less formal power and influence from the decentralized nature of policy and program administration, from the creation of networks of interdependence among public and private agencies, and from various forms of direct democracy: public consultation, advisory bodies, and power-sharing arrangements with citizens. However empowered by politics, the authenticity of managerial actions is ultimately referable to legislatures and courts. However much a manager's discretionary actions may be oriented toward community values, guided by the policy preferences of superiors, influenced by the interests of particular constituencies, or reflections of conscience, their legitimacy must, when and if challenged, be ratified by duly constituted authority.

This is not to say that legality, no matter how defined, is the only source of legitimacy for managerial conduct. The Constitution, after all, is a means to an end, as its Preamble makes clear: "We the People of the United States, in Order to form a more perfect Union, establish Justice, insure domestic Tranquility, provide for the common defense, promote the general Welfare, and secure the Blessings of Liberty to ourselves and our Posterity, do ordain and establish this Constitution for the United States of America." Legitimacy is conferred by evidence of managerial commitment to forming a more perfect Union, by managerial respect for individual rights, for members of society as citizens, and for obligations and commitments, and by personal qualities of character and integrity that inspire trust. But if the legitimacy of managerial conduct comes into question, no matter how well-intentioned, public managers may be, and often are, called upon to justify their actions before legislative bodies and in court, and legislative approval and the law as interpreted by the judges having jurisdiction will decide matters in dispute.

What, then, is the meaning of the term *rule of law* as an operational aspect of public management? What if the law is silent or ambiguous or incomplete? What is the relationship between the exercise of delegated authority—that is, the authorized discretion to use one's best judgment—and the rule of law? What if laws appear to be in conflict with one another? What if elected executives and legislators disagree on how a law should be interpreted or carried out? Like every other aspect of public management, obedience to the rule of law is no straightforward matter.

Careful study of the detailed examples throughout the discussion below will suggest the extent to which the rule of law infuses the routine activities of public management at all levels of government. As will be discussed, a sufficient test of lawfulness is that the public manager's conduct does not violate clearly established statutory or constitutional rights that a reasonable person in his or her position would have known.[9] A superficial grasp of what lawfulness requires is inadequate for reasonable and responsible public service. Public managers therefore must make the effort to educate themselves about the lawful foundations of the activities for which they are responsible.

This chapter explains how the rule of law constitutes a foundation for all three dimensions of public management: structure, culture, and craft. First discussed are the meaning of the term rule of law, the various sources of law, and the role of federalism in the American constitutional scheme. The clearest manifestation of the rule of law, the system of checks and balances that has its roots in federal and state constitutions and the institutions they authorize, is discussed next, with special attention to those checks and balances that are derived from constitutional principles rather than being part of the Constitution's text. Then, public management is situated within its larger, constitutionally based context by reference to a "logic of governance," an analytic framework that conceptualizes both the interrelationships among the various hierarchical levels of delegated authority and the interrelationships among public management's three dimensions. Finally, the chapter summarizes the practical implications of managing according to the rule of law. The end-of-chapter exercise looks at a lawsuit, *Wyatt v. Stickney,* which examines issues of constitutional rights, budget constraints, role of the courts, separation of powers, and administrative discretion.

WHAT IS THE RULE OF LAW?

Following the Declaration of Independence, the framers of the first state constitutions, and ultimately the federal constitution, insisted upon an assignment of powers to three separate branches of government. One of the best known expressions of the principle behind the rule of law in America was drafted by John Adams for the constitution of the Commonwealth of Massachusetts to provide a rationale for such a **separation of powers:**

> In the government of this commonwealth, the legislative department shall never exercise the executive and judicial powers of either of them: the executive shall never exercise the legislative and judicial powers, or either of them: the judicial shall never exercise the legislative and executive powers, or either of them: *to the end it may be a government of laws and not of men* (emphasis added).[10]

Thus, in the American legal tradition, the rule of law is viewed in the first instance as a protection against tyranny and an overly powerful government.[11] With respect to public management, the **rule of law** means that duly promulgated written principles and policies are the primary basis for the legitimate exercise of administrative authority and therefore are protection against arbitrary, capricious, and nontransparent acts by public managers.

Sources of Law

The Constitution is not the only source of law, but is the most important among five distinct sources: constitutional law, statutory law, administrative law, common law, and international law.

Constitutional law is the body of law that codifies the decisions of the U.S. Supreme Court and of state higher courts of review that define and interpret the meaning and implications of the formal provisions of constitutions.[12] The "political branches" of government, that is, the legislative and executive branches, may, in exercising their authority, make decisions or take actions that are ultimately subject to review and reversal by the U.S. Supreme Court or by equivalent state courts. The body of constitutional law resulting from judicial review carries considerable weight in the decision making of lower courts and the Supreme Court, although earlier decisions are not necessarily immutable, as precedents are sometimes overturned. Consider the far-reaching public management effects of *Brown v. Board of Education* (1954), which overturned *Plessy v. Ferguson* (1896).

The second and most widely recognized source of law is **statutory law.** It is the body of law that codifies the enactments (subject to signature by the executive) of the U.S. Congress and of state and local legislatures. The power to legislate is not unconstrained. All acts of Congress must be presented to the president for approval and are subject to veto (although vetoes may be overridden). Article I of the U.S. Constitution enumerates the legislative powers of Congress and the limitations on those powers. Of special interest is that, according to Article I, Section 7, "All Bills for raising Revenue shall originate in the House of Representatives; but the Senate may propose or concur with Amendments as on other Bills."

The third source of law is **administrative law,** which consists of rulemaking and the adjudication of alleged rules violations by administrators, always pursuant to legislatively authorized purposes, by executive agencies such as the Environmental Protection Agency (EPA) and the Federal Aviation Administration (FAA) and by independent regulatory agencies such as the Federal Trade Commission, the Federal Labor Relations Board, and the Federal Mine Safety and Health Review Commission.[13] Rulemaking—the issuance of regulations to accomplish the agency's purposes—can be both substantive and procedural. Administrative law scholar David Rosenbloom cites the example of the director of the FAA issuing rules concerning child safety aboard airplanes.[14] The failure to issue rules may also be an issue. Ten states sued the EPA for its alleged failure to issue rules on carbon dioxide emissions. Administrative law concerns the procedures for the lawful issuance of such rules and for their application in specific cases, in effect, the rules for issuing and applying rules. Adjudication of alleged rules violations by administrators takes the form of court-like proceedings in which individual petitions for relief are heard and decided by an administrative law judge or a hearing examiner, positions authorized by the Administrative Procedure Act of 1946.

Executive orders or directives issued under constitutional or statutory authority are of considerable importance in administrative law. An executive order is a declaration issued by the president or a governor that has the force of law. Executive orders are usually based on existing statutory authority and require no action by Congress or a state legislature to become effective. At the federal level, executive orders are published in the Federal Register as they are issued and then codified in Statutes at Large and Title 3 of the *Code of Federal Regulations* each year.

The fourth source of law is the body of case law that makes up American **common law.** According to the common law, a citizen may sue another individual or organization for the harms the defendants allegedly have caused and be awarded compensation or damages if a judge or jury agrees with the plaintiff. Under the common law doctrine of sovereign immunity, the state, and those operating on its behalf, may not be sued unless sovereign immunity has been waived or the courts have recognized a specific exception. If the state and its officers cause injury, the individual's usual recourse is to persuade a legislature to specifically authorize compensation for such injury.

Congress and state legislatures have passed various tort claims acts that waive sovereign immunity in certain circumstances, allowing citizens to make claims of negligence against public officials. An alternative—allowing unlimited legal liability—is not regarded as feasible because it would provide incentives for bringing claims and result in the legislature reducing public services and qualified professionals being hesitant to enter public service. The U.S. government, through the Tucker Act of March 3, 1887, has waived its sovereign immunity in specific circumstances, such as lawsuits arising out of contracts to which it, or one of its agencies, is a party. Congress has also passed civil rights acts that allow suits against officers acting under the authority of state law who violate constitutional and statutory rights intentionally or through negligence.

The fifth source of law is **international law** incorporated in duly-ratified treaties and conventions, such as the North American Free Trade Agreement, the U.S.-Canada Agreement on Air Quality, and the Geneva Conventions defining the laws of war. If a treaty and a federal statute are in conflict, the more recent or more specific will typically control. Treaties, moreover, are often implemented by federal statutes. American public management may also be affected by the decisions of regional and international judicial institutions. In May 2006 the European Union's highest court ruled that the EU had overstepped its authority by agreeing to give the United States personal details about airline passengers on flights to America in an effort to fight terrorism. The decision forced the two sides to renegotiate their agreement at a time when European concerns for infringements of civil liberties were rising.

Together, these five sources of law—the Constitution, statutes, administrative orders, case law, and international agreements—create an extensive, complex, and intrusive environment for public management. "Today," says Rosenbloom, "administrative practice is infused with constitutional concerns . . . sometimes in surprising ways." [15]

CONCEPTS IN ACTION

The Rule of Law and Human Rights

The concept of the rule of law is recognized by democracies around the world. The following is an international perspective on the rule of law that summarizes its main institutional expressions, especially in countries where democracy and human rights are less well established.

An independent, impartial judiciary; the presumption of innocence; the right to a fair and public trial without undue delay; a rational and proportionate approach to punishment; a strong and independent legal profession; strict protection of confidential communications between lawyer and client; equality of all before the law; these are all fundamental principles of the Rule of Law. Accordingly, arbitrary arrests; secret trials; indefinite detention without trial; cruel or degrading treatment or punishment; intimidation or corruption in the electoral process; are all unacceptable. The Rule of Law is the foundation of a civilised society. It establishes a transparent process accessible and equal to all. It ensures adherence to principles that both liberate and protect.

Source: International Bar Association, "International Rule of Law Directory," http://www.roldirectory.org/.

Federalism

The United States is a federal republic. It has a system of government in which the authority to legislate and to administer and enforce the laws is distributed among a central government and the governments of the states. The goal of American **federalism** is to ensure that the federal government has sufficient power to act on behalf of national interests while preserving the powers of state governments. The Tenth Amendment clarifies the powers of the states as follows: "The powers not delegated to the United States [the federal government] by the Constitution, nor prohibited by it to the States, are reserved to the States respectively, or to the people." In other words, if neither expressly delegated to the federal government nor denied to the states, power is assumed to belong to the states or to the people.

It is not widely understood that local government in the United States is a creation not of the Constitution but of state legislatures acting under the power reserved to them by the Tenth Amendment. An 1868 decision by an Iowa state court that was subsequently adopted by the U.S. Supreme Court (and is now known as **Dillon's Rule**) states: "Municipal corporations [cities and towns] owe their origin to, and derive their powers and rights wholly from, the legislature. It breathes into them the breath of life, without which they cannot exist. As it [the legislature] creates, so may it destroy. If it may destroy, it may abridge and control." [16] As one would expect, states vary widely in the extent and types of authority granted to their units of local government. To avoid micromanagement by state legislatures, numerous municipalities have obtained what are termed **"home rule charters"** that grant local discretion over all matters not expressly precluded by state statutes or constitutions. Such matters may include public personnel policies or the administration of local property taxes.

In general, as local government expert David R. Berman says, "The various levels of government . . . are tied together by a variety of factors: money, programs, political parties, and the play of interest groups among them." [17] Public interest groups may choose to move the locus of public debate from Congress to state legislatures and have done so on matters such as expanding health coverage for the uninsured and controlling carbon emissions. Business interest groups may choose the federal government over the states, preferring national to state regulation of air quality. They may also to choose to fight their battles in the courts rather than in legislatures, confronting public managers with litigation in addition to partisan legislative politics on the same issues.

The Rule of Law in the States

This book is concerned with public management at all levels of government—federal, state, and local.[18] It is therefore important to understand, as state government scholar G. Alan Tarr has put it, that "despite . . . superficial similarities, state governments are not merely miniature versions of the national government—or at least need not be." [19] The U.S. Constitution does not impose separation-of-powers restrictions on the states, and the states need not follow federal interpretations in crafting the structural provisions of their constitutions. State constitutional traditions and the particular characteristics of the rule of law in the states have evolved over time, vary widely, and may differ in significant ways from those of the federal government.

That said, several aspects of state governance must be noted in the context of the rule of law. When first adopted in the nineteenth century, most state constitutions, while formally recognizing a separation of powers, were unconcerned with the balance of power among the three branches. Power was intentionally concentrated in legislatures. As popular dissatisfaction with corrupt legislatures grew, power was shifted not to elected executives or the courts, but to the people, especially in the form of the direct election of state constitutional officers, such as attorneys general, secretaries of state, and treasurers. Many states amended their constitutions to incorporate forms of direct democracy, such as the initiative, referendum, and recall. As a result, "the three branches of state government differ considerably from their federal counterparts." [20] Most state governments differ from the federal government in not having a unitary executive; many states have "weak" governors, and all have many state administrators who are elected rather than appointed by the governor. Another difference is the power state governors have over their budgets through the line-item veto, which the president does not have.

CONCEPTS IN ACTION

Differences among States

The unique possibilities of the rule of law in the states are illustrated by the powers of the governor of Texas, which are surprisingly limited compared to states with structurally "strong governors." As governor of Texas, George W. Bush's craft emphasized working closely with other constitutional officers and the legislature because he had to.

The plural executive in Texas limits the power of the Governor by distributing power usually associated with a chief executive among many elected political leaders [including the attorney general, the comptroller of public accounts, the commissioner of the General Land Office, the commissioner of Agriculture, the Texas Railroad Commission, and the state Board of Education]. The only executive official appointed by the Governor is the Secretary of State. Other officials are elected independently and do not campaign for office as a unified slate. They do not have to answer to the Governor, nor do they work together as a cabinet in the way that executive officials serve the U.S. President. Party leadership may encourage unity among candidates, but the campaign organizations operate independently of each other. . . . This arrangement produces an executive branch whose officials jealously guard their jurisdiction, their power, and their prerogatives. . . . The Governor is often the nominal head of his or her party in the state, but this does not offset the institutional political base other executives possess. As a result, the executive branch lacks cohesion, with different executives and their agencies often pursuing different goals.

Source: "The Plural Executive," http://texaspolitics.laits.utexas.edu/html/exec/0900.html.

Some states require extraordinary majorities to enact certain legislation, have procedural requirements for the legislative process, or impose substantive prohibitions on legislative action, none of which exist in the U.S. Constitution. One popular state constitutional provision, limiting the frequency and duration of legislative sessions, has a significant bearing on public management. A legislature not in session cannot exercise the same kind of oversight as one, such as the U.S. Congress, which is virtually always in session. Substitute provisions for control, such as the legislative veto and legislative appointment of officials performing executive functions, are adopted instead.

This book includes a great many general statements concerning public management in its three dimensions, but it is important to keep in mind that constitutional and statutory frameworks differ across the states and across localities. The study of public management in a particular state must, therefore, be attentive to its unique governing framework and context.

Intergovernmental Relations

The division of powers among federal, state, and local governments is the basis of a field of study and practice within public management known both as federalism and as **intergovernmental relations.** It can also be called "third-party government" or "indirect government." The logic of governance discussed later in this chapter links not only multiple levels within the federal or state governments but also levels of federal, state, and local governments and Indian tribes. In Figure 1.1 (page 15) the multiple levels of administration within the federal Head Start Program are linked to multiple levels of local government administration of that program. The administration of a program, therefore, may involve all three levels of government as well as agents—grantees, contractors, and subcontractors—within the private sector. Emergency management planning and response to a hurricane typically involves all levels of government and the nonprofit and for-profit sectors.

Hierarchical relations among levels of government have as their purpose the alignment of policy and program priorities. Federal, state, and local governments are hierarchically linked by a variety of structural tools or instruments.[21] These structures include mandates in the form of rules, regulations, or instructions, which may be incorporated in the language of statutes, grants, or contracts that prescribe specific actions or types of action that other levels of government are to take. Different types of mandates may be combined in various ways. Directives accompanied by grants of financial support result in a combined carrot-and-stick relationship. Another type of structure is devolution, by which higher levels of government delegate to lower levels of government the power to take various actions or exercise certain types of responsibility. The granting of home rule charters by state legislatures is a form of devolution, as is the federal deregulation of a program that was formerly highly directive and the substitution of broad-purpose grants for specific categorical grants.

As the Hurricane Katrina example, discussed at length in chapter 1, illustrates, intergovernmental relations are horizontal as well as vertical. Departments and agencies of government at the same level cooperate and coordinate with each other through formal structures such as regional authorities, incident-related communication and coordination arrangements, and programs and projects sponsored by higher levels of government. The patterns of intergovernmental relationships resemble a matrix (or rectangular array) reflecting how the problems that policymakers address cannot be confined to a particular political jurisdiction. Policymakers therefore need to recognize the jurisdictional interdependence of policy problems and public management solutions.

CONCEPTS IN ACTION

How Federalism Works

The State Children's Health Insurance Program (SCHIP) is a typical example of how the concept of federalism illuminates intergovernmental relations. Research has shown that it has increased poor children's access to medical care and changed health care delivery in other ways.

The program was enacted by Congress as "Title XXI of the Social Security Act and is jointly financed by the Federal and State governments and administered by the States. Within broad Federal guidelines, each State determines the design of its program, eligibility groups, benefit packages, payment levels for coverage, and administrative and operating procedures."

States may, for example, expand their Medicaid programs to provide additional coverage for children or create separate SCHIP programs. SCHIP provides a capped amount of funds to States on a matching basis. The Social Security Act authorizes multiple waiver and demonstration authorities to allow states flexibility in operating Medicaid programs and SCHIP programs. Each authority has a distinct purpose, and distinct requirements. Each State, Territory, and the District of Columbia has a coordinator for the SCHIP program—a state-level managerial position required by federal law—who is responsible for the administration of the approved SCHIP state plan. Through Fiscal Year 2007, over ten million children had benefitted from this program.

A study of the impact of SCHIP in New York State found:

> substantial improvements in access and quality of care after enrollment in SCHIP. One possible mechanism to account for these improvements is that the pattern of care changed after enrollment, centering more on the primary care provider or the USC [usual source of care]. After enrolling in SCHIP, children had a greater proportion of all health care visits at their USC, less fragmentation across multiple sources, and a corresponding higher rating of accessibility and quality of primary care. Furthermore, the reduction in unmet needs in the face of relatively stable utilization rates suggests the possibility of more efficient care delivery. Altogether, these findings point to a changing pattern of health care after enrollment in SCHIP, with improved coordination and receipt of primary care, resulting in greater parental ratings of quality.

Sources: U.S. Department of Health and Human Services, http://www.cms.hhs.gov/LowCostHealthInsFamChild/. Quote from the SCHIP impact study is from Peter G. Szilagyi et al., "Improved Access and Quality of Care after Enrollment in the New York State Children's Health Insurance Program (SCHIP)," *Pediatrics* (2004): 113, e395–e404.

Intergovernmental relations are not confined to the structural dimension. Habits of vertical or horizontal cooperation and coordination, or their opposite—secretiveness and refusal to share information or authority—may become institutionalized as cultural values. Within the constraints of structures and organizational cultures, individual managers may employ their craft to transcend their limitations: to promote good communication, maintain the transparency of relationships, and promote the goals of agencies, their policies, and programs, especially when under pressure from policymakers to demonstrate effectiveness or performance. But, as public administration scholar Nicholas Henry notes, how the literally thousands of units of American government relate to one another "is based on broad rules of the game set by the Constitution and court decisions" and thus are a reflection of the rule of law.[22]

CHECKS AND BALANCES

The separation of powers is a protection against the tyranny of an overly powerful government, but it is not the only such protection. Another is the elaborate system of **checks and balances** that limits the encroachment of the branches upon each other.[23] Checks and balances, the legacy of James Madison's role in writing the Constitution, are not formally required or enumerated as such in that document. What the Constitution does is create three branches, each with its own primary functions, and various means by which each of the branches can resist attempts at encroachment by the others.[24] Checks and balances have the effect of not only imposing structures on public managers but also of creating opportunities and challenges for managers practicing their craft within the confines of those structures.

These explicit constitutional provisions may be referred to as "primary" checks and balances because they were given formal expression by the founders. They are distinguished from secondary checks and balances, which are defined and discussed below.

Primary Checks and Balances

The most important of the primary checks and balances are listed in Box 4.1. The influence of these checks and balances on public management practice are shown in the examples that follow.

The first two checks and balances listed in Box 4.1 are illustrated in *Shoemaker v. United States* (1893). The U.S. Supreme Court declared that Congress shares authority with the executive branch over the assignment of administrative responsibilities to executive branch offices: "It cannot be doubted, and it has frequently been the case, that Congress may increase the power and duties of an existing office without thereby rendering it necessary that the incumbent should be again nominated and appointed." For the imposition of new duties on an officer to be valid under *Shoemaker,* two requirements must be met. First, the legislation must confer new duties on "*offices,* . . . [not] on any particular *officer.*" Second, the new duties must be "germane to the offices already held by" the affected officers.[25] Under *Shoemaker,* Congress could transfer the U.S. Coast Guard from the Treasury Department to the Homeland Security Department and modify the responsibilities of senior officials in both departments.

Box 4.1

PRIMARY CHECKS AND BALANCES

- Legislative authority to make all laws governing the execution of powers vested in Congress, the government of the United States, or any department or officer thereof;
- Legislative authority to provide advice and consent on certain executive branch appointments;
- Legislative control of appropriations;
- Requirement that both houses of Congress approve a statute;
- Executive nomination of federal judges (subject to legislative advice and consent);
- Review of administrative actions by the judicial branch;
- Presidential power to veto legislation passed by Congress and congressional power to override such vetoes;
- Provision for legislative impeachment of the president and of federal judges;
- First Amendment endorsement of freedom of the press; and
- Initiative, referendum, and recall provisions of state constitutions.

John Rohr has discussed how Congress delegates authority to—or imposes a duty on—subordinate officers, thereby providing them with independence from the president in specific situations defined by statute. According to Rohr, "This accountability to Congress severs the hierarchical chain of command in the executive branch and exposes the subordinate to the full force of Congress's impressive powers to investigate the public administration and to subject it to the rigors of legislative oversight." [26] These delegations make explicit the fact that executive officers are not simply the president's appointees but are also officers of the law.

Another example of the primary checks and balances is the structure of the National Cancer Institute (NCI), created during the presidency of Richard M. Nixon. The National Cancer Act of 1971 authorized a "war on cancer," and rather than leave it to the administration to decide how to organize this war, Congress decreed that the NCI should have substantial independence to carry out the mission. Instead of creating a new, independent agency, Congress promoted the NCI to bureau status within the Department of Health, Education and Welfare (HEW), and its director was made a presidential appointee and authorized to coordinate the national cancer program. Further, the director was authorized to submit his annual budget request directly to the president without prior review by the National Institutes of Health or HEW. The authorization created a "bypass budget," which is beyond the control of departmental management, an arrangement that exists to this day. The former National Cancer Advisory Council was promoted to the status of a presidentially appointed Cancer Advisory Board, and the President's Cancer Panel was created to oversee implementation and bring delays or barriers to the attention of the president. According to some experts, the early bypass budgets were merely wish lists, but, as budget resources became tighter over the years, it became more of a priority-setting management tool.

The way courts participate in public administration is illustrated by the so-called Shakman decrees. In 1969 a group that included Michael Shakman, an independent candidate for delegate to the 1970 Illinois Constitutional Convention, filed suit against the Democratic Organization of Cook County. He argued that Chicago's long-standing system of political patronage based hiring, firing, promotion, and transfer decisions on political loyalty, which denied independents like himself their legal and constitutional rights to seek and hold public office. The suit also alleged that public resources were spent on partisan political activity.

In 1972 several defendants, including the city of Chicago and its mayor, entered into a negotiated settlement, known as a consent decree, with the plaintiffs to resolve some of their claims. A consent decree commits the agency to remedial action and to improved monitoring and evaluation of agency operations and effectiveness. For the great majority of positions within city government, the 1972 consent decree specifically prohibited the city from "conditioning, basing or knowingly prejudicing or affecting any term or aspect of governmental employment with respect to one who is *at the time already a governmental employee,* upon or because of any political reason or factor." A subsequent consent decree was entered in 1983 that extended these prohibitions to the city's hiring practices as well. The U.S. District Court for the Northern District of Illinois has retained jurisdiction over the case. The court's powers include the power to enforce the consent decrees.

In September 2001 the court held that the city had violated the decree almost eighteen hundred times over a period of nearly a decade. The court then instructed Shakman to file a rule to show cause why the city and its mayor should not be held in contempt of court for those violations. In response to the looming contempt proceedings, the mayor instructed the city's corporation counsel to attempt to vacate the long-standing decree, thereby disabling this check on patronage hiring.

On July 26, 2005, the plaintiffs in the Shakman lawsuit filed an application to hold the city and its mayor in civil contempt for violations of the court orders. On August 2 Judge Wayne R. Andersen appointed Noelle C. Brennan as the court's monitor in an effort to "ensure future compliance" with the Shakman decrees. As part of its appointment order, the court directed Brennan, along with her appointed legal counsel, to study Chicago's "existing employment practices, policies and procedures for non-political hiring, promotion, transfer, discipline and discharge." Further, the court ordered Brennan to propose a "mechanism for ensuring future employment actions [by the city] are in compliance with the Court's previous Orders." During 2006 federal criminal trials proceeded against several city officials accused of engaging in a vast and long-running conspiracy to reward political operatives with city jobs, in defiance of the Shakman decrees.

As these examples show, primary checks and balances reach deeply into public management at all levels of government. They are both an actual and a potential source of restraint on the exercise of managerial discretion and a factor in the balance of power among officials within the executive branch, which can be altered in significant ways by legislatures and judges.

Secondary Checks and Balances

The much larger class of checks and balances at federal and state levels of government may be described as secondary checks and balances because they are created pursuant to the exercise of constitutional authority. They are expressed in statutes or even operate as conventions of governance, that is, as practices that are widely acknowledged even if not given formal written expression anywhere. Four categories of secondary checks and balances are listed in Box 4.2. The original constitutional checks and balances are staples of all civics curriculums, but secondary checks and balances are not usually recognized as such. Because of their pervasive influence, however, they merit further explanation and illustration.

Box 4.2 SECONDARY CHECKS AND BALANCES

Between the branches of government

- Legislative authority to compel executive branch officials to testify under oath concerning their actions;
- Judicial authority to issue and enforce consent decrees and injunctions;
- Government Accountability Office, Congressional Budget Office, and state equivalents;
- Foreign Intelligence Surveillance Act;
- Legislative and legislatively authorized oversight and investigation; and
- "Sunset" laws.

Within the branches of government

- Inspectors general;
- U.S. Office of the Special Counsel;
- Whistleblower and other public employee protections;
- Separation of legislative authorization and appropriation processes;
- Multitiered judiciary;
- Overhead offices (personnel, budget, audit, general counsel); and
- Professional advisory panels, state laboratories.

Outside the branches of government

- Administrative Procedure Act;
- Freedom-of-information, government-in-the-sunshine acts; WTO disclosure rules;
- Office of the IRS Taxpayer Advocate, ombudsmen;
- Laws at all levels of government authorizing "citizens petitions"; and
- "Watchdog" groups organized under federal and state laws as nonprofit organizations.

Other

- National Academy of Sciences/Institute of Medicine;
- Federal False Claims Act;
- Anonymous leaks of information;
- Independent professionals (auditors, actuaries, statisticians, intelligence analysts, scientists); and
- Negotiated and private standard-setting and rulemaking.

The first category of secondary checks and balances adds to the original capabilities of each branch to check the others. It includes the authority of the courts to approve, monitor, and enforce consent decrees in lawsuits in which the government is a defendant. It includes the activities of the Government Accountability Office and the Congressional Budget Office, both of which are agencies of Congress, and their equivalents in some states, to provide audits, analyses, research, and evaluations that often contain alternative perspectives to those of the executive branch on public policy and management issues and, therefore, provide a check on executive branch versions of issues and events. It also includes the authority of legislatures to oversee, monitor, and investigate the activities of public officers and agencies and to authorize independent investigations for these purposes.

Two examples illustrate how this category of secondary checks and balances affects public management. On June 15, 2001, the city of Los Angeles and the Los Angeles Police Department (LAPD) entered into a consent decree with the U.S. Department of Justice. Approved by a U.S. district court judge, the consent decree provides specific guidelines on new policies and procedures to reform the conduct of the LAPD. The police had been charged with making seizures and arrests without probable cause and with serious deficiencies in procedures for training, supervision, and the investigation and discipline of police officers, including failure to identify patterns of at-risk officer behavior and to respond properly to citizen complaints. The police commissioners and the inspector general were said to lack the resources to provide proper oversight. Reforms were to include tighter controls on gang units, strict oversight of the use of force, a shift of responsibility for investigations of misconduct complaints, a sophisticated computerized system to identify potential at-risk behavior, and data collection relative to pedestrian and motor vehicle stops.

Michael Cherkasky and his company, Kroll Inc., were hired as the independent monitor to ensure that consent decree reforms were implemented in an effective and timely manner. Kroll advertises itself as "the world's leading risk consulting company," which "helps clients reduce their exposure to global threats, seize opportunities, and protect employees and assets." [27] Kroll had monitored the consent decree between the Justice Department and Detroit's police department and was commissioned by the governors of Pennsylvania and New Jersey to investigate problems in their state police departments.[28] In addition, Cherkasky was a former chief of investigations for the district attorney's office of New York County.

As of mid-2006, the independent monitor had issued nineteen quarterly reports. To the nineteenth report was appended an eight-page report card. [29] According to the executive summary, "During the quarter ending March 31, 2006, the Monitor examined 45 paragraphs or subparagraphs of the Consent Decree. Of these, the City and the LAPD successfully complied with 33, failed to achieve compliance with 10, and, for reasons stated in the body of this report, the Monitor withheld a determination of compliance with the remaining 2 paragraphs." The primary area of concern was that the LAPD "continues to struggle with the Consent Decree's requirements regarding supervisory oversight of search warrants, and has been non-compliant with several such requirements for the majority of the Consent Decree. Many of the deficiencies in this area were identified by the LAPD's Audit Division in its *Warrant Applications and Supporting Affidavits Audit.*" Although the report card praised "significant accomplishments," it also said an extension of the consent decree was essential.

HOW THE WORLD WORKS

Cross-Checks and Balances

Secondary checks and balances can create complex, even conflicting incentives for the various parties affected by them. As suggested in the following account, a court-approved consent decree might have created a conflict of interest for the defendant, Chief of Police William Bratton. It also created administrative issues that the police department's inspector general found confusing.

William Bratton, former commissioner of the New York City Police Department who was appointed Chief of the Los Angeles Police Department (LAPD) in October 2002, predicted in early 2006 that the court-approved consent decree under which the LAPD was operating with the help of the Kroll International consulting firm would have to be extended beyond its upcoming five-year deadline. Shortly thereafter, Full Disclosure Network, which produces public affairs programming, quoted retired LAPD captain Ken Hillman as follows:

> The problem is that Chief Bratton previously was an Associate with Kroll (International Consultants) and as such he was put in a position to oversee and monitor the implementation of the Federal Consent Decree for LAPD prior to being selected as Chief of Police (LAPD). I don't know if there is really an incentive for Chief Bratton to get out of the Federal Consent Decree because, in turn, if he were to get the Police Department out of the Federal Consent decree, his friends and Associates at Kroll would no longer have a job with the City of Los Angeles.

Former Assistant LAPD Chief Dave Gascon describes how the 300 best and brightest (police employees) were to be taken off the streets to perform (paper work) functions of the Federal Consent Decree. Chief Bratton defends the use of highly trained personnel, including himself in performing the Court mandated functions. LAPD Inspector General Jeffery Eglash describes how under the Federal Consent Decree the auditors are now auditing the auditors and "there are a lot of redundancies in the process."

Source: "Bratton Conflict on LAPD Consent Decree," *Full Disclosure Network,* March 30, 2006, http://www.fulldisclosure.net/Program_Details/VideoBlog26.html.

A series of critical reports by the General Accounting Office, the predecessor of the Government Accountability Office, on the Head Start program illustrates how secondary checks and balances affect the relationships between branches of government. Republican legislators used the reports during appropriations hearings to challenge the effectiveness of Head Start. According to the GAO, "The body of research on current Head Start is insufficient to draw conclusions about the impact of the national program." [30] As a consequence, Section 649(g) of the Head Start Act was amended (P.L. 105-285) to require the Department of Health and Human Services (HHS) to conduct a national analysis of the impact of Head Start. The legislation also charged the secretary to appoint an independent panel of experts to review and make recommendations on the design of a plan for research on the impact of Head Start within one year after the date of enactment of P.L. 105-285 and to advise the secretary regarding the progress of the research. As a result, the Administration of Children and Families initiated the Head Start Impact Study, which employed a rigorous, nationally representative, random assignment design. An interim report to Congress was published in September 2003 and a final report in May 2005.[31]

These examples show how the branches check each other's authority. The courts use consent decrees to establish an ongoing oversight of executive agencies. Congress uses its investigative arm to bring pressure to bear on public managers to implement particular kinds of analyses, perhaps leading to a change in managerial strategies.

A second category of secondary checks and balances operates within the branches of government. Within the executive branch, it includes inspectors general, protections afforded whistleblowers and other employee rights (including the right to sue employers), and offices that perform oversight functions such as budget review and execution, personnel administration, and internal audit. Within the judicial branch, it includes the multiple levels of review that oversee the decisions of trial courts. Within the legislative branch, it includes the separation of the authorization and the appropriations processes and a wide variety of rules that balance competing interests within representative institutions.

For example, a group of pro-environmental employees of the U.S. Forest Service (USFS), who organized themselves as Forest Service Employees for Environmental Ethics, believes the Forest Service is fighting too many fires, thereby endangering firefighters and harming the forest ecology.[32] They filed a lawsuit against their employer requesting that the USFS be enjoined to study its policies concerning fire management, retardant use, and other matters. The USFS responded by noting that (1) people are moving in ever larger numbers into fire-threatened areas, and the agency and its partners in the states are obligated to protect them and their property, and (2) fire fighting has become a big business for which there are many influential political stakeholders, including property owners and fire-fighting agencies and their suppliers.[33]

In a related matter, a longtime USFS biologist sued his superiors over whether their practice of sprucing up old logging roads without an environmental review is legal. The lawsuit alleges that the federal agency is reconstructing so-called "Roads to Nowhere" in Alaska's

Tongass National Forest without analyzing the potential effects on the environment. He contends that the Forest Service is trying to encourage logging by circumventing the law, an allegation the federal agency denies.[34]

Another illustration of secondary checks and balances affecting relationships within branches of government is a case arising in the Los Angeles County district attorney's office. Since 1989 Richard Ceballos had worked in the Pomona branch as a deputy district attorney responsible for managing trial procedures. In February 2000 a defense attorney contacted Ceballos about a pending criminal case, saying that there were inaccuracies in an affidavit used to obtain a critical search warrant. After examining the affidavit and visiting the location it described, Ceballos determined the affidavit did indeed contain serious misrepresentations. He recommended that the case be dismissed. In a lawsuit filed against his employers, Ceballos claimed that as retaliation for disagreeing with his superiors, he was reassigned from his calendar deputy position to a trial deputy position, transferred to another courthouse, and denied a promotion. He argued that his superiors violated his First Amendment rights. The U.S. Supreme Court overturned the circuit court opinion in Ceballos's favor and ruled that Ceballos does not have "whistle-blower protection rights" under the First Amendment.[35]

The ruling turned on a distinction between "citizen speech" and "employee speech." If an employee's speech is found to be "citizen" speech, under the dichotomy the Court had established, these comments would be analyzed under a 1968 Supreme Court precedent that set up a balancing test for whether a public employee's speech is constitutionally protected. Courts weigh the employee's interest in commenting on matters of public concern against the employer's interests as a manager.

> In reaching its conclusion the [Ninth Circuit] court looked to the First Amendment analysis set forth in *Pickering v. Board of Ed. of Township High School Dist. 205, Will Cty.*, 391 U.S. 563 (1968), and *Connick* [v. *Meyers,*] 461 U.S. 138 [1983]. *Connick* instructs courts to begin by considering whether the expressions in question were made by the speaker "as a citizen upon matters of public concern." The Court of Appeals determined that Ceballos' memo, which recited what he thought to be governmental misconduct, was "inherently a matter of public concern." The court did not, however, consider whether the speech was made in Ceballos' capacity as a citizen. Rather, it relied on Circuit precedent rejecting the idea that "a public employee's speech is deprived of First Amendment protection whenever those views are expressed, to government workers or others, pursuant to an employment responsibility." . . .
>
> We hold that when public employees make statements pursuant to their official duties, the employees are not speaking as citizens for First Amendment purposes, and the Constitution does not insulate their communications from employer discipline. . . .
>
> Ceballos did not . . . speak as a citizen by writing a memo that addressed the proper disposition of a pending criminal case. When he went to work and performed the tasks he was paid to perform, Ceballos acted as a government employee. *The fact that his duties sometimes required him to speak or write does not mean his supervisors were prohibited from evaluating his performance.* [Emphasis added.][36]

The first example shows that within the executive branch, employees have the power to check the authority of public managers to pursue their strategies by enlisting the assistance of the courts. The second example further illustrates this point, but shows that in certain instances—although not in this one—employees can claim First Amendment protection for certain communications with their superiors. To an important extent, the law, not managerial prerogative, governs employer-employee relations.

A third category of secondary checks and balances concerns the power of private citizens and groups with respect to the three branches of government. This category includes various transparency measures such as labor relations acts, freedom of information acts, administrative procedure acts, acts authorizing citizens' petitions, and "government in the sunshine" acts, some of which are written into state constitutions. Such measures provide citizens with opportunities to question the exercise of government authority, with the attendant political consequences or even, usually on an ad hoc basis, to share power. This category also includes not-for-profit watchdog groups, which enjoy the privileges of formal not-for-profit status, such as tax exemption and the right to receive tax-exempt contributions. Many of these groups engage in virtually constant surveillance of public agency activity and actively engage in litigation on behalf of their constituencies.

In June 2006, under the authority of the National Labor Relations Act, the National Labor Relations Board (NLRB) asserted jurisdiction over a private company providing passenger and baggage screening services to the Kansas City International Airport on behalf of company employees who wished to join a union. The decision countered a determination by Undersecretary James Loy of the Transportation Security Administration (TSA) that the NLRB lacked jurisdiction because the private employees were involved in protecting national security. Loy had previously denied union rights to the TSA's security screeners, which was within his statutory authority.

Another way that secondary checks and balances operate outside the branches of government is through the Administrative Procedure Act (APA) of the federal government and every state government.[37] (The state acts apply to state agencies but not to local governments.[38]) In general, these acts are intended to ensure that administrative actions "embrace the basic democratic-constitutional values of openness for accountability; representativeness and public participation in policy formulation; reviewability for adherence to the rule of law; procedural due process for the fair treatment of individuals; and rationality when regulating private parties and other entities." [39]

Legal action by advocacy groups is also a form of external secondary checks and balances. Advocacy groups regularly sue state and local departments and agencies that serve populations with specific needs—child protection, corrections, housing, education—or provide services in a nondiscriminatory manner—schools, police departments. The suits often allege that individuals served by these agencies are being denied their constitutional and statutory rights, usually because of mismanagement. These class actions have been termed *institutional reform* or *structural reform* lawsuits because the plaintiffs seek, a among other things, far-reaching changes in agency management and operations. A suit filed by Children's

Rights, Inc. (among others), an organization that engages in extensive litigation on behalf of children (its Web site lists thirteen lawsuits), alleged that the Milwaukee Department of Human Services conducted inadequate investigations of child abuse and neglect, failed to protect children vulnerable to abuse or neglect, failed to provide appropriate care and proper placements for children in their custody, and failed to create and implement appropriate plans to assure their proper care and appropriate placement, thus violating children's rights under state and federal constitutions as well as under various statutes.

Such lawsuits compel public managers to respond to plaintiffs' allegations in court. Judges may well decide that agencies and their managers be closely monitored by outside experts or independent officers appointed by the court. Agencies may be under legally required surveillance for many years or even decades. Even though the state of Alabama had made significant improvements in child welfare services by 2005, a federal district judge declined to end court oversight arising from a suit filed in 1988 because the state had not proved that it could sustain its gains. And the historic *Wyatt v. Stickney* case mandating mental health facility reform, initiated in 1970, was finally terminated in 2003.

In the Milwaukee case, the filing of the lawsuit prompted the state of Wisconsin to take over the management and operation of child welfare services from Milwaukee County and to institute extensive management reforms. State officials then claimed that court intervention was unnecessary. Nevertheless, the final settlement required defendants to, in the court's language, meet specific percentage (of total cases) goals in closing cases in specific ways, meet specific percentage goals in providing specific support services to children and families in their custody, and meet specific standards in organizing and providing casework, such as creating special diagnostic/assessment centers for children over twelve years of age who need further assessment in order to determine the appropriate placement.

The consequences of such suits can be salutary. Often, responsible officials—legislators, elected officials, and agency and overhead managers—will act to correct long-standing problems in agency organization and in relations with supervisory agencies and governors or mayors and their staffs. If the complaints are considered to have merit, officials must negotiate consent decrees with plaintiffs' representatives and the court. In other cases, however, especially those where public management has made responsible efforts to confront the issues raised by the lawsuit, the imposition of remedies by the court following an adversary proceeding may do more harm than good. Such interference can disrupt the orderly development of stable and effective management structures and routines and allow the intrusion of an adversary process dominated by lawyers into the otherwise progressive and competent management and delivery of services.

An interesting example of how citizens gain access to institutions empowered to address their concerns is provided by the National Vaccine Injury Compensation Program (VICP). Created in 1988, the VICP is administered by HHS and the Justice Department. The HHS component of the VICP is located organizationally in the Health Resources and Services Administration, Healthcare Systems Bureau, Division of Vaccine Injury Compensation (DVIC). The DOJ, Civil Division, Torts Branch, Vaccine Litigation represents the secretary of HHS in legal proceedings before the U.S. Court of Federal Claims, also known as the

"Vaccine Court." The court decides which claims will be compensated and affords a no-fault alternative to civil lawsuits for parents who believe their children have been injured by a vaccine. The VICP has been in the news in recent years because a large volume of claims have been filed alleging that vaccines cause autism in children. The CDC (Centers for Disease Control and Prevention) and the American Academy of Pediatrics deny any scientific basis for such a causal relationship. According to legal scholar Stephen Sugarman:

> To win a VICP award, the claimant does not need to prove everything that is required to hold a vaccine maker liable in a product liability lawsuit. But a causal connection must be shown. If medical records show that a child had one of several listed [by HHS] adverse effects within a short period after vaccination, the VICP presumes that it was caused by the vaccine (although the government can seek to prove otherwise). An advisory committee helps to amend the list of adverse effects as the consensus view [within the scientific community] changes with the availability of new studies. If families claim that a vaccine caused an adverse effect that is not on the list [autism is not on the list], the burden of proof rests with them. . . . In the VICP context, proof of causation does not need to be shown to the extent of what some might call scientific certainty. Rather, it suffices to prove causation according to the civil-law standard of "the preponderance of the evidence," showing that causation is "more likely than not." Although proving a mere possibility won't suffice, proof "beyond a reasonable doubt" is not required.[40]

To resolve the large volume of autism claims more expeditiously, in 2002 the VICP announced that some test cases would examine the general causation question, putting aside the question of harm to any particular child. In its 2006 strategic plan, however, the VICP argued, "Relaxed standards for assessing causation of vaccine-related injury could jeopardize the public's trust of, and reliance upon, vaccines as the first line defense against serious infectious diseases. The relaxed standard may lead to more claims being compensated; and therefore, the public may think that vaccines are not safe." [41] In one test case, decided by the Vaccine Court in March 2008, a family claiming that vaccines caused their daughter's autism was awarded compensation.

The ruling was controversial. Critics said the court had turned its back on science. But CDC director Julie Gerberding said, "Let me be very clear that [the] government has made absolutely no statement about indicating that vaccines are a cause of autism. . . . That is a complete mischaracterization of the findings of the case, and a complete mischaracterization of any of the science that we have at our disposal today." [42] The government refused to release the case files, however, so the court's argument was not known.

Because of secondary checks and balances, citizens, whether employed by private firms doing business with the government, affected in one way or another by public management, or as citizens, have access to legal procedures that adjudicate their rights against the potentially arbitrary and capricious exercise of managerial authority. As the VICP example shows, however, attempts to address one set of problems may raise altogether new problems—in the autism case, a polarizing debate over what standards of proof should govern compensation awards to vaccine victims.

A fourth category of secondary checks and balances is the distribution of power and influence among individuals and entities created or allowed to exercise it. This category includes congressional chartering of the National Academy of Sciences and the Institute of Medicine, which are often commissioned by the executive branch and Congress to produce authoritative analysis of controversial public policy issues, such as dietary standards and global warming; the power inherent in the independent professional status of public employees such as actuaries, scientists, physicians, and statisticians; the Federal False Claims Act, which entitles employees of private firms under contract to the government who report deliberate waste of public funds to a share of any funds that are recovered through legal action; government's reliance on what are termed negotiated and private rulemaking and on self-regulation; and the power of individual employees to influence public debate about controversial policies by leaking privileged information, a long-standing practice included in what public administration scholar Rosemary O'Leary has termed "guerrilla government." [43]

Other kinds of secondary checks and balances also affect public management. The National Research Council is part of the National Academies, which include the National Academy of Sciences, National Academy of Engineering, and Institute of Medicine. They are private, nonprofit institutions that provide science, technology, and health policy advice under a congressional charter. The act of incorporation for the National Academy of Sciences, signed by President Lincoln on March 3, 1863, established service to the nation as its dominant purpose. The Research Council was organized by the National Academy of Sciences in 1916 to associate the broad community of science and technology with the academy's purposes of furthering knowledge and advising the federal government.

In 2005 the National Research Council weighed into one of the most intensely controversial of public policy issues by publishing "Guidelines for Human Embryonic Stem [hES] Cell Research." The National Academies developed the guidelines on behalf of the scientific community and without government involvement. Of this project, the two co-chairs wrote:

> As the study of hES cells accelerates worldwide, federal funding for this research area in the United States has been severely limited by ethical controversy. As a consequence, the normal leadership role of the US National Institutes of Health in supporting health-related research and providing the oversight that comes with federal funding has been absent. Investigation of hES cells is being funded increasingly by individual states and by private foundations in the absence of universal rules for conduct of the research. In most states, there are no regulations; in some, the research is illegal, either in whole or in part; and, in others, legislation has explicitly legalized research efforts and even provided public funding. Thus, the research is proceeding actively but under a confusing patchwork of regulations. This situation is particularly inappropriate for an area of investigation that, although offering great promise, raises ethical issues. In response to scientists' concerns about the lack of federal oversight, a committee of the National Research Council and the Institute of Medicine of the National Academies undertook to formulate guidelines for the appropriate conduct of hES cell research. The guidelines were released April 26, 2005, after eight months of deliberations, many meetings and a two-day public workshop.[44]

Information from "guerrillas" in the intelligence community is another form of secondary checks and balances. In response to such information, Rep. Peter Hoekstra, the Republican chair of the House Intelligence Committee, sent a letter to the Republican president of the United States. The final page of this letter is shown in Box 4.3.

Box 4.3

LETTER FROM REP. PETE HOEKSTRA TO PRESIDENT GEORGE W. BUSH

The Honorable George W. Bush
May 18, 2006
Page Four

Finally, Mr. President, but perhaps most importantly, I want to reemphasize that the Administration has the legal responsibility to "fully and currently" inform the House and Senate Intelligence Committees of its intelligence and intelligence-related activities. Although the law gives you and the committees flexibility on how we accomplish that (I have been fully supportive of your concerns in that respect), it is clear that we, the Congress, are to be provided all information about such activities. I have learned of some alleged Intelligence Community activities about which our committee has not been briefed. In the next few days I will be formally requesting information on these activities. If these allegations are true, they may represent a breach of responsibility by the Administration, a violation of law, and, just as importantly, a direct affront to me and the Members of this committee who have so ardently supported efforts to collect information on our enemies. I strongly encourage you to direct all elements of the Intelligence Community to fulfill their legal responsibility to keep the Intelligence Committees fully briefed on their activities. The U.S. Congress simply should not have to play 'Twenty Questions' to get the information that it deserves under our Constitution.

I've shared these thoughts with the Speaker, and he concurs with my concerns. Regrettably, there are other issues that need to be discussed. What I've provided here are the most pressing. Thank you for your consideration of these items.

Sincerely yours,

Pete Hoekstra

Pete

Cc: Steve Hadley
Josh Bolton
John Negroponte

The activities of the United Network for Organ Sharing (UNOS) also illustrate how secondary checks and balances work. Over a fifty-year period, human organ transplantation has become a significant part of medical practice.[45] The Social Security Act Amendments of 1972 extended Medicare coverage to kidney dialysis and transplantation, which led to greater use of the procedure. The need for a coordinated method to match organ donors and recipients soon became apparent. The solution to this regulatory problem devised in the U.S. Senate was to create UNOS, a nonprofit organization, to operate the Organ Procurement and Transplantation Network (OPTN) under the authority of the National Organ Transplant Act of 1984. The HHS secretary is required to approve all rules promulgated by UNOS before they become enforceable as federal rules, but David L. Weimer notes that "the [OPTN] can discipline members who fail to comply. [B]ecause the DHHS has yet to accept formally any OPTN rule through a federal rulemaking process, the OPTN effectively retains responsibility for developing the content of the rules themselves."[46] HHS could revoke this informal delegation if it chose.

CONCEPTS IN ACTION

Private Rulemaking

The concept of "private rulemaking" is a distinctive feature of a government of separated powers and of secondary checks and balances. In cases such as this, the rule of law may authorize the private exercise of public authority.

Private regulation has always had a significant role in U.S. political economy. Many states rely heavily on private organizations in setting the conditions for the certification and licensing of those who wish to practice professions such as law and medicine. Individuals often form organizations to engage in self-regulation in order to weed out firms that attempt to gain market share with low-quality but low-cost products, to head off threats of public regulation, or to establish a defense against legal negligence. Professions such as industrial hygienists and accountants who work within firms often bring norms of practice that constrain managerial discretion to achieve goals that might otherwise be addressed through public regulation.

Source: David L. Weimer, "The Puzzle of Private Rulemaking: Expertise, Flexibility, and Blame Avoidance in U.S. Regulation," *Public Administration Review* 66 (July/August 2006): 574.

A final example of other kinds of secondary checks and balances concerns the actions of the Red Cross following the Abu Ghraib scandal in Iraq. Physicians who cooperated with interrogations of prisoners at Abu Ghraib prison in Iraq were accused by the International Committee of the Red Cross and by members of the medical profession with violating the Geneva Conventions and widely accepted codes of ethics governing medical practice, and with failure to report evidence of prisoner abuse. These violations occurred when physicians provided information on the medical condition of individual prisoners to personnel engaged in interrogations to assist them in designing effective coercive methods. Physicians and psychiatrists were often on hand to monitor the use of these methods through one-way mirrors that concealed their presence.[47] During the same period, lawyers in the judge advocate general's offices of the military services were vigorously contesting detainee interrogation policies they believed were in violation of applicable statutory and international laws and that jeopardized the lives of American military personnel.

These examples show how influence can be exercised both formally and informally through the agency of nongovernmental entities that are able to take advantage of the separation of powers to impose checks on managerial discretion.

Governance without Government?

A constitutional scheme of governance in which the federal and state governments have three branches interrelated through complex webs of checks and balances creates a wide dispersal and sharing of public authority. Many scholars characterize this scheme as polycentric—having many centers of authority and control—and governed by configurations of laws, rules, and practices that create patterns of mutual influence rather than hierarchical influence among those sharing that authority. Some scholars argue that public authority has been moving away from the agencies of government and their managers toward the organizations and institutions of civil society: nonprofit organizations, associations, and networks, religious entities, and for-profit corporations.[48] We are moving, some say, toward **governance without government.**

There can be little doubt that **"third-party government"**—that is, the reliance of governments on lower levels of government and on nongovernmental organizations to perform administrative functions and to deliver services—has increased and that there is a greater degree of interdependence among entities providing public services. It nevertheless remains true that the exercise of public authority has a hierarchical structure—the "backbone" mentioned at the beginning of this chapter—whose authority is the Constitution, linking citizens who possess ultimate sovereign power with those who exercise authority in their name, whether in the public or private sectors. (Figure 1.1, page 15, illustrates the administrative part of this hierarchical structure.) By way of analogy, although the delta of a mighty river might be flat, wide, and a mix of waters from different sources, it is sustained by a main channel whose headwaters and principal tributaries account for its basic character. The same is true for the Constitution and other sources of law, which sustain the U.S. system of government.

A LOGIC OF CONSTITUTIONAL GOVERNANCE

To clarify how public management relates to this overall scheme of governance, it is useful to locate public management and public managers within a rule-of-law-based, Madisonian, and multilevel **logic of governance.** This frame of reference highlights the mutual influences among the values and interests represented in civil society (the sovereign people), the preferences of the political branches (executive and legislative), and the role of legal institutions (the courts, administrative law rulings) on managerial roles and practices and, through them, on governmental performance.

Defining Governance

The term *governance* as used here may be defined as "regimes of laws, rules, judicial decisions, and administrative practices that constrain, prescribe, and enable the provision of publicly supported goods and services" through formal and informal relationships with agents in the public and private sectors.[49] Although other definitions of governance—including other multilevel conceptualizations of governance—abound in the research literature, this particular definition links constitutional institutions with the processes of policymaking, public management, and service delivery and with the politics of government performance.[50] Underlying this definition is recognition that governance involves the means for achieving direction, control, and coordination of individuals and organizations on behalf of collective interests incorporated in public policies.[51]

From the starting point of the rule of law defined by our constitutional scheme, an analytic framework—a "logic of governance"—can be constructed to provide conceptual order to the complex system of checks and balances that characterizes rule-of-law–based public administration and management in the United States. Governance is the resultant of a dynamic process which may be expressed in a set of hierarchical interrelationships, which are visualized in Figure 4.1:

- between citizen preferences and interests expressed politically (a) and decisions by policymakers in the form of enacted legislation or executive directives that have the force of law (b);
- between the concrete expressions of public policy (b) and the formal structures and processes of public (or quasi-public) agencies, which reflect the delegation of authority or responsibility to act to subordinate officials (c);
- between the structures of formal delegation (c) and the decisions and actions of managers operating under these grants of authority (d);
- between the decisions and actions of public managers (d) and the many characteristics of service delivery, including core technologies, primary work tasks, and service transactions with beneficiaries or recipients (e);
- between service delivery (e) and its consequences in the form of outputs, outcomes, or results (f);
- between these consequences (f) and stakeholder assessments of agency or program effectiveness or legitimacy (g); and
- between stakeholder assessments (g) and citizen preferences and interests expressed politically (a).

FIGURE 4.1 **A Constitutional Logic of Governance**

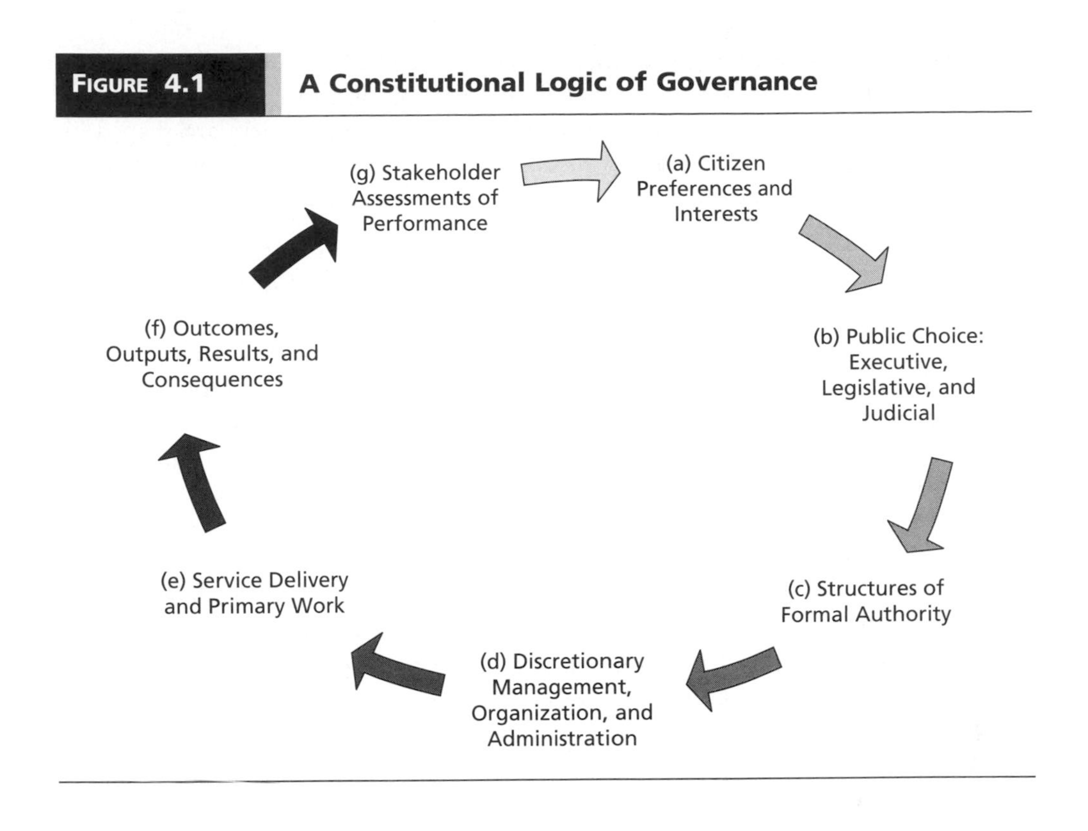

This multilevel or nested logic of governance is related conceptually to the three dimensions of public management discussed in chapter 2. The logic of governance adds to the three-dimensional approach to public management a depiction, in general terms, of the legal and political environment within which public management is embedded and the kinds of activities and processes bearing on public management that are regularly occurring in that environment. This relationship can be understood in terms of the following propositions:

- The first dimension—formally authorized structures and processes—is shaped by the actions of public officials, including legislators, elected executives, public managers, field supervisors, and judges, operating at levels (b), (d), and (e) in the logic of governance, and manifested at these levels as well as at the (c) level;
- the second dimension—organizational cultures and the norms and standards governing organizational behavior and official conduct—is shaped by the exemplary actions and the beliefs and values of public managers, supervisors, functional specialists (such as personnel and budget officers), and service providers operating at levels (d), (e), and (f) in the logic of governance;
- the third dimension—managerial craftsmanship—like the second dimension, is shaped by public managers and others with managerial and supervisory responsibilities at levels (d) and (e) in the logic of governance.

In other words, the actions and decisions taken at multiple levels of governance shape the actual institutions of governance and their interrelationships and, in turn, the actions and decisions of policymakers, public managers, and service providers are shaped by those institutions. Though influence flows in multiple directions, a hierarchical rule-of-law backbone, as noted earlier, structures the levels into a uniquely American system of governance.

The Logic of Governance in Action: Abu Ghraib

The prisoner abuse scandal reveals how actions at the "street level" of government can be linked to hierarchical relationships involving the Constitution, treaties, and other statutes and extending through presidential, departmental, and field level managerial decisions and directives. The behavior of the "few bad apples" at Abu Ghraib and the Guantánamo Bay naval base was arguably derived from, even if it was not clearly mandated by, a series of hierarchical delegations and managerial judgments that made up a nested system of authority, which is laid out in Table 4.1.

The logic of governance enables one to map out the formal and informal interrelationships among different hierarchical levels of political/administrative systems to identify potentially significant causal relationships, in this case, between policy documents promulgated at the top levels of the Bush administration and the actions of street-level personnel in the dead of night far away in the field. A study by Human Rights Watch reached the following conclusion:

> What is clear is that U.S. military personnel at Abu Ghraib felt empowered to abuse the detainees. The brazenness with which the soldiers at the center of the scandal conducted themselves, snapping photographs and flashing the "thumbs-up" sign as they abused prisoners, suggests they felt they had nothing to hide from their superiors. The abuse was so widely known and accepted that a picture of naked detainees forced into a human pyramid was reportedly used as a screen saver on a computer in the interrogation room. . . . According to Maj. Gen. [Antonio] Taguba [who conducted an investigation of prisoner abuse at Abu Ghraib in 2004], "interrogators actively requested that MP guards set physical and mental conditions for favorable interrogation of witnesses." . . . [The] MP Brigade [was] directed to change facility procedures to "set the conditions" for military intelligence interrogations. Taguba cited the testimony of several military police: "One said the orders were 'Loosen this guy up for us. Make sure he has a bad night. Make sure he gets the treatment.' " Another stated that "the prison wing belongs to [Military Intelligence] and it appeared that MI personnel approved the abuse." That MP also noted that "[t]he MI staffs, to my understanding, have been giving [Charles] Graner [an MP in charge of night shifts at Abu Ghraib] compliments on the way he has been handling the MI [detainees]. Example being statements like 'Good job, they're breaking down real fast.' " [52]

TABLE 4.1 Official Actions/Policy and Frontline Responses at Abu Ghraib

Date	Actions/Policy Documents	Frontline Responses
February 7, 2002	President Bush decides that Geneva Conventions will not apply to captives of al Qaeda and the Taliban, who are declared to be "unlawful combatants," not prisoners of war.	Decision opposed by State Department and many military lawyers who feared the undermining of military culture and respect for laws of war.
October 2002	Authorities at Guantánamo Bay request approval of stronger counterinterrogation techniques. Rumsfeld aides respond by canvassing the ideas of officers in Afghanistan and elsewhere.	
December 2002	Rumsfeld approves request from Guantánamo, authorizing nudity, stress positions, dogs (first used in Afghanistan), sensory deprivation, and isolation.	These approved techniques began circulating around the world, especially in Afghanistan, but also in Iraq, where Geneva Conventions *did* apply.
April 16, 2003	Rumsfeld revises his December 2002 guidance, withdrawing certain approvals.	Rumsfeld was urged to do this by military lawyers, especially the Navy general counsel, who had not been consulted in December.
July 2003	The 519th Military Intelligence Battalion transfers from Afghanistan to Iraq; begins drafting its "interrogation rules of engagement."	
July 15, 2003	Joint Task Force 121, formed to search for Saddam's government, issues its interrogation policy.	
August 7 and 27, 2003	The 519th sends draft of its rules, similar to the JTF 121 rules, to 205th Military Intelligence Brigade. Guantánamo Bay commanding officer Gen. Miller arrives in Iraq with Rumsfeld's April policy guidelines, gives them to General Sanchez, commander of U.S. forces in Iraq.	
September 2003	Sanchez's top lawyer Colonel Warren works with 205th to produce interrogation rules drawing on Rumsfeld's	

continues

TABLE 4.1 Official Actions/Policy and Frontline Responses at Abu Ghraib (continued)

Date	Actions/Policy Documents	Frontline Responses
	April memo and Miller's memos from Cuba. The 519th adds some techniques from its August 27 draft. Warren adds techniques not in use at Guantánamo, including use of dogs.	
September 14, 2003	Sanchez notifies his commanding officer at U.S. Central Command (CENTCOM) that he has authorized a dozen interrogation techniques beyond standard Army practice under the Geneva Conventions (and in violation of international law), including five beyond those approved for Guantánamo, using reasoning from Bush's February 7, 2002, memorandum. An exception to this authorization was noted for "enemy prisoners of war," of which there were very few in Iraq; most Iraqi prisoners were "civilian internees."	These techniques went into use by soldiers and contractors who believed they were executing official policy. Sanchez used an outdated 1987 version of the applicable Army Field Manual because the more restrained updated version (in1992) had not been placed on a key Army Web site.
October 12, 2003	Sanchez rescinds his September guidance on instructions from CENTCOM, issues new interrogation policy for Iraq derived mostly from a draft by Warren that provides broader leeway to interrogators.	Policies authorized for Guantánamo Bay, Afghanistan, and Iraq are now thoroughly conflated, and several sets of interrogation rules are in circulation, leading to considerable confusion down the chain of command.
November 2003	Guantánamo Bay commander now in Iraq to head military detainee operations; Army brings several dog teams to Abu Ghraib to be used to "fear up" detainees for productive interrogations.	
February 2004	International Committee of the Red Cross (ICRC) issues its report on abuses of Iraqi prisoners between March and November 2003.	General Taguba's investigation was initiated about then, seemingly in response to the ICRC Report.

Source: Created by Laurence E. Lynn Jr. based on contemporaneous *New York Times* and *Washington Post* reporting, on the "AR 15-6 Investigation of the Abu Ghraib Detention Facility and 205th Military Intelligence Brigade" by Maj. Gen. George R. Fay, August 25, 2004, and on the Schlesinger Report, a 2004 investigation into prisoner abuse at Abu Ghraib prison by former secretary of defense James R. Schlesinger.

MANAGING ACCORDING TO THE RULE OF LAW

Conceptualizing the logic of constitutional governance is one thing. Putting that logic into managerial practice is quite another. Operationally, public management necessarily reflects the tensions inherent in three particular features of the American constitutional scheme. Public managers must live with and respond creatively to the challenges presented by these tensions.[53]

First, the Madisonian interplay of faction and power establishes the political context of public management. Legislatures delegate responsibility and appropriate resources to public organizations and their managers after political deliberations in which compromise is reached among contending individuals, parties, and interests. As the discussion in chapter 1 suggests, it is largely accidental if delegations of authority resulting from partisan debate, negotiation, compromise, or interventions by judges in the form of consent decrees create public agency structures and processes that facilitate technically rational management. However cleverly they attempt to work around obstacles and breach constraints, public managers must play the hands they are dealt by the political and judicial branches of government. Public management cannot be separated from politics, and public managers must actively engage in making discretionary judgments concerning, as Harold D. Lasswell put it, "who gets what, when, how," the essential function of politics.

Second, the separation of powers among the legislative, executive, and judicial branches of governments creates another—perhaps the central—issue for public managers: balancing the legitimate concerns and interests of legislators, elected executives, and judges, who generally compete for control of public administration. Contests between public executives and legislative bodies over the release of information that executives assert is privileged are common, and such contests often spill over into the courts. Tensions between executives and legislators, on the one hand, and both of them and the courts, on the other, are also common and often play out in the confirmation of judicial nominees or in legislative restraints on the authority of the courts.

Third, the ever-evolving farrago of checks and balances looms over managerial discretion. Presidential signing statements that public managers may have had no opportunity to influence, may, without warning, convey restrictions on how they are to use their discretion that neither legislatures nor courts have reviewed or held to be legitimate. Investigations by departmental inspectors general and the GAO, critical reports by watchdog groups, and information made available through leaks or Freedom of Information Act requests may further roil the waters of managerial strategy.

The law in all its forms—constitutional, statutory, administrative, common, and international—is often ambiguous. To make matters more challenging, it is constantly changing. Authorizing statutes and the authoritative language of appropriations acts are regularly amended. Albeit in a more deliberate way, a steady stream of rulings from courts at all levels of the judicial system interprets statutes and adjudicates claims of rights violations, usually with implications for public management.

CONCEPTS IN ACTION

Signing Statements

A controversy has arisen over the role of the executive branch in deciding on the constitutionality of legislation, a tension heightened by President George W. Bush's practice of issuing interpretive "signing statements" when affixing his signature to laws submitted to him by Congress. Bush used these signing statements—a formerly obscure type of secondary checks and balances—to declare his views on the constitutionality of legislation and often his determination not to enforce the provisions of these laws that he deemed unconstitutional. As of May 21, 2008, President Bush had issued 161 signing statements, which challenged 1,167 provisions of law.

By [Phillip J.] Cooper's count [in *By Order of the President: The Use and Abuse of Executive Direct Action*], George W. Bush issued 23 signing statements in 2001; 34 statements in 2002, raising 168 constitutional objections; 27 statements in 2003, raising 142 constitutional challenges, and 23 statements in 2004, raising 175 constitutional criticisms. In total, during his first term Bush raised . . . 505 constitutional challenges to various provisions of legislation that became law. . . . Yet Bush has not vetoed a single bill [he subsequently vetoed 12], notwithstanding all these claims, in his own signing statements, that they are unconstitutional insofar as they relate to him.

Rather than veto laws passed by Congress, Bush is using his signing statements to effectively nullify them as they relate to the executive branch. *These statements, for him, function as directives to executive branch Departments and agencies as to how they are to implement the relevant law.* (emphasis added).

Sources: John W. Dean, "The Problem with Presidential Signing Statements: Their Use and Misuse by the Bush Administration," http://writ.news.findlaw.com/dean/20060113.html. May 21, 2008, statistic from Christopher S. Kelley, personal Web site at Miami University of Ohio, http://www.users.muohio.edu/kelleycs/.

In June 2006 the U.S. Supreme Court issued what many experts regarded as a confused ruling on what constitutes a "wetland" subject to federal protection by the U.S. Army Corps of Engineers under the Clean Water Act. The controlling view, though not the majority view, was that of Justice Anthony Kennedy. He concluded:

> When the Corps seeks to regulate wetlands adjacent to navigable-in-fact waters, it may rely on adjacency to establish its jurisdiction. Absent more specific regulations, how-

> ever, the Corps must establish a significant nexus on a case-by-case basis when it seeks to regulate wetlands based on adjacency to nonnavigable tributaries. Given the potential overbreadth of the Corps' regulations, this showing is necessary to avoid unreasonable applications of the statute. Where an adequate nexus is established for a particular wetland, it may be permissible, as a matter of administrative convenience or necessity, to presume covered status for other comparable wetlands in the region.[54]

In a concurring opinion, Chief Justice John Roberts made a point with respect to the task now confronting public managers in the Corps of Engineers and those engaged in economic development: "It is unfortunate that no opinion commands a majority of the Court on precisely how to read Congress' limits on the reach of the Clean Water Act. Lower courts and regulated entities will now have to feel their way on a case-by-case basis." So will public managers.

Controversies

As if that were not enough, the meaning of the rule of law is controversial within the professional field of public administration and management. Some public administration scholars contend that shortcomings in our constitutional scheme of governance justify a role for public management that rejects strict subordination to the political branches or even to the courts. John Rohr argues that the House of Representatives "presents a serious defect in the Constitution [because] it is at odds with what the founding generation thought representation should be. This defect is serious and perennial." His solution is implementation of a concept called "representative bureaucracy." If measures can be adopted to ensure that public officials are more representative of the American people than the House of Representatives, then "the *administrative state* . . . heals and repairs a defect in the Constitution of the United States." [55] (Representative bureaucracy is discussed further in chapter 8.)

Other experts believe that because of defects in representative institutions, public managers should infuse their actions with specific values, which as often as not reflect a politi cally liberal sensibility. Public managers should, they argue, take it upon themselves to ensure social equity through democratic participation, to listen carefully to the many voices of those affected by policymaking who otherwise might not be heard or who have been ignored by legislative bodies, and to recognize the many different kinds of policy outcomes, both measurable and unmeasurable, that citizens value, not just those given expressed in legislation or budget guidelines.[56] However laudable these values might be, they are a controversial basis for public management because they cannot be derived from the Constitution itself and thus pose dangers to the rule of law. Less-benign values, including those inimical to the Constitution itself, might also be embraced by public managers as credos or touchstones. Acting on their own interpretations, public managers might provide more access to publicly financed services than policymakers intend, or they might deprive individuals of liberty and human rights in ways that have no legitimate legal basis, or they might simply choose to ignore legal mandates that offend them. Adherence to constitutional principles by public managers helps ensure against such unwarranted uses of public authority.

Still other experts would have public managers be aggressively independent of the political branches if conscience and circumstances require it, deciding for themselves, without apology, what the Constitution requires of them. Public management's role, in one such view, "is not to cower before a sovereign legislative assembly or a sovereign elected executive." [57] Managers should regard themselves as trustees for the people, who, alone, are sovereign. Michael Spicer and Larry Terry believe that it is legitimate for public managers "to modify, delay, or resist the directives of political leaders in a lawful manner" if the managers believe faithfulness to constitutional values warrants such nullification of public authority.[58] George Frederickson argues that public managers, using their own judgment, "must resist, thwart, or refuse to implement policy that runs counter to the founding documents or to American regime values." [59] Views such as these imply that public managers should independently exercise the power of constitutional interpretation, a clear encroachment on the prerogatives of the other branches, although rarely acknowledged as such by their proponents.

But constitutional governance has its defenders. In *Madison's Managers: Public Administration and the Constitution,* Anthony Bertelli and Laurence Lynn argue:

> If . . . public managers take it upon themselves . . . to give back to "the people" powers that the framers assigned to the separate [branches], they will almost surely upset the balance of interests struck between Congress and the president, a balance that is, after all, public management's constitutional root, even after judicial review. Public management forswears legitimacy within the separation of powers when it seeks to second-guess and reorient the deliberative results of the political branches and the constitutional reasoning of the judiciary.[60]

In a similar vein, David Rosenbloom has argued that members of Congress have "very broad supervisory authority over federal administration" acting on behalf of their constituents, while judicial review can keep in check executive indiscretion. More specifically, he summarizes the context of public management as follows:

> [The] four key aspects of public administration's constitutional framework [are]: (1) the separation of powers, which places administrative agencies under executive, legislative, and judicial authority; (2) federalism, which affects the relationships between state and federal administrators; (3) individuals' rights in the context of different administrative encounters; and (4) public administrators' liabilities for violating individuals' constitutional rights. Together, these constitutional features define and confine U.S. public administration. They make it clear that although politicians, reformers, and media pundits often call for running government like a business, constitutional law makes the public's business very different from others.[61]

With respect to these controversies over the rule of law, the Supreme Court's constitutional perspective was expressed in its 1997 ruling in *City of Boerne v. Flores:*

> Our national experience teaches that the Constitution is preserved best when each part of the government respects both the Constitution and the proper actions and determinations of the other branches. When the Court has interpreted the Constitution, it has acted within the province of the Judicial Branch, which embraces the duty to say what the law is. *Marbury v. Madison.* When the political branches of the Government act against the background of a judicial interpretation of the Constitution already issued, it must be understood that in later cases and controversies the Court will treat its precedents with the respect due them under settled principles, including stare decisis, and contrary expectations must be disappointed.[62]

Until 1971 federal officials performing discretionary functions enjoyed an absolute immunity from lawsuits seeking civil damages liability. At that point the Supreme Court held that federal narcotics agents had violated a plaintiff's Fourth Amendment rights against unreasonable searches and seizures and were therefore liable for civil damages. The "doctrine of objective reasonableness" was articulated in two Supreme Court cases, *Harlow v. Fitzgerald* and *Anderson v. Creighton.*[63] Yong Lee notes that the "concept of objective reasonableness grew out of the common law of sovereign immunity historically extended to public officials in one form or another" and describes the standard as follows:

> If the officials are found to have acted objectively unreasonably—that is, by violating clearly established statutory or constitutional rights that a reasonable person would know—the courts will have them stand trial for civil damages liability. On the other hand, if the public officials are found to have acted objectively reasonably—that is, even if they violated rights, they did not violate the law (the existing law or legal rules) because the rights in question were not clearly established at the time of the violation—the courts will shield the officials from trial on the grounds of qualified immunity. Stated simply, the theory of the constitutionally reasonable public servant is predicated on whether the public official, if challenged in court, would pass the test of "objective reasonableness."[64]

Thus, one constitutional basis for public management is the **objective reasonableness doctrine,** which states the terms on which a public official may be held to be exempt from civil damages liability—that is, from having to pay their own legal fees and adjudicated damages—when sued for violating a plaintiff's constitutional or statutory rights. (Constitutional accountability is discussed further in chapter 8.) This is not an arcane issue. It was reported in 2006 that CIA officers who engaged in aggressive interrogations of suspected terrorist detainees were purchasing private insurance that would pay their civil judgments and legal expenses if they were sued or charged with criminal wrongdoing and were found to have violated the objective reasonableness doctrine.[65]

The Slate Is Not Clean

Because of the elaborate array of checks and balances on official discretion, the managers of public agencies cannot simply define the scope of their own authority, choose their own goals, and employ whatever organizations, personnel, strategies, and resources they think necessary to achieve their purposes. They cannot, as corporate managers can, freely choose the business they are in, the customers they wish to serve, the goods and services they provide, and the prices, quantities, and qualities of what they produce. To a preponderant extent, those kinds of choices are either made by or are subject to the approval of external authorities, such as elected officials, and are subject to interpretation of statutory and constitutional propriety by the judicial branch, and by internal authorities—such elected officials and their appointees and officials in budget and personnel agencies—with sufficient authority or influence to constrain managerial discretion.

The pervasiveness of law does not mean that lawmakers scrutinize every decision and action, every exercise of discretion, taken by public managers and supervisors. Oversight often occurs "by exception" or if a fire alarm goes off, and courts can rule only on cases and causes brought before them. As Herbert Kaufman has noted, most of the time the legal bases for managerial activities are well in the background or have been institutionalized in accepted agency routines and practices and in taken-for-granted norms and standards of conduct.[66] But the rules, guidelines, applicable statutes, and judicial decrees are never far away, and controversies over their possible violation may erupt unexpectedly and with little warning. The occasional failure by a child welfare worker to conduct a home visit will ordinarily raise no concerns unless that child becomes a high-profile victim of violence. When that happens, the worker's superiors may well find themselves in court answering for the worker's dereliction of duty.

As Kaufman put it, for public managers, "the slate is not clean." [67] What's on the slate? Hundreds of pages of written directives and guidance, in statutes, government-wide regulations, departmental and bureau regulations, opinions and judgments by courts, the Government Accountability Office, the Office of Personnel Management, and legislative hearings and floor debates. Administrative leaders, Kaufman argues on the basis of studying many of them, cannot afford to ignore anything in their environments that bears on their organizations. He notes, perhaps wryly, that you do not actually have to pay attention or even know about most of this stuff, unless you want to introduce changes, in which case you will run into it head on, or unless you are taken by surprise by events beyond your control.

As this book emphasizes, public managers have ample opportunity to exercise their judgment (see the discussion of craft in chapters 2 and 7). The point is that in doing so, they are not free agents, nor have they been assigned the role of deciding on behalf of the people what the Constitution requires or what values shall be reflected in public policy implementation. Administrative law scholar Phillip J. Cooper observes that Alexis de Toqueville's "familiar observation that almost all important political problems in America sooner or later are recast as legal problems" might be brought up to date in the following way: "Sooner or later most important political problems in America are transformed into administrative problems which, in turn, find their way into the courts." [68]

HOW THE WORLD WORKS

Know the Rules

Knowing the precise details of a voluminous code of laws and rules governing official conduct might not seem necessary or even possible—until you unknowingly violate one of them. The implication is clear: Public managers must know the legal basis for their authority, and the basic legal principles that should inform their judgments.

The following testimony occurred during the 1995 trial of O. J. Simpson for the murder of his former wife, Nicole Simpson. A defense attorney is cross-examining a Los Angeles Police Department detective who had initially investigated the crime scene.

Q. Sergeant Rossi, you said that you were familiar with certain parts of the health and safety code? . . .
A. . . . [Y]es, I am familiar with some [sections].
Q. Are you familiar with any portion of the health and safety code that mandate the calling of the coroner in a homicide case?
A. No, I'm not.
Q. Do you, from time to time, review the LAPD manual?
A. Yes, sir.
Q. Do you ever look at Volume 4?
A. Occasionally, yes.
Q. What about Section 238.46 entitled Notification of the Coroner, do you ever look at that?
A. I don't believe I ever looked at that, no. . . .
Q. Do you ever recall reading anything about the mandate to notify the coroner?
A. No.
Q. You don't. Were you, in fact, in charge of this crime scene from your arrival at 1:25 a.m. until 2:10 when Detective Philips showed up?
A. Yes, I was. . . .
Q. Now, did you, during that 45-minute period, have a legal duty to call the coroner?
A. Not as far as I know, no.
Q. Did you know it was a misdemeanor to fail to call the coroner, Sergeant?
A. I don't believe so, sir.

Even presumptively conscientious and competent public officials, and their superiors, can be made to look dangerously inept by a lawyer or legislator intent on tripping them up with an obscure but binding rule.

Source: "The Trial Transcripts," http://edition.cnn.com/US/OJ/trial/, February 15, 1995.

In summary, managing according to the rule of law requires public managers to have a well-developed ethic of accountability to the institutions that define the rule of law. Because of the importance of the concept of accountability for public management, chapter 8 is devoted to giving it further definition and discussing its implications with respect to each of public management's three dimensions.

Key Concepts

separation of powers
rule of law
constitutional law
statutory law
administrative law
executive orders
common law
international law
federalism
Dillon's Rule
home rule charters
intergovernmental relations
checks and balances
governance without government
third-party government
logic of governance
objective reasonableness doctrine

Analysis and Argument: Test Your Understanding

In the case known as *Wyatt v. Stickney* (U.S. District Court Alabama, 325 F. Supp. 781, decided March 12, 1971), the guardians of some patients confined at a state mental hospital and a number of hospital employees brought a class action lawsuit in behalf of patients who were involuntarily committed through noncriminal procedures for treatment purposes. The patients therefore retained a constitutional right to receive individual treatment that would give them a realistic opportunity to be cured and improve their mental condition. Budget cuts had caused many employees to be terminated, which led to staffing shortages that allegedly impeded the quality of treatment.

U.S. District Court judge Frank Johnson found that Bryce State Hospital, named in the suit, and others had treatment programs that were scientifically and medically inadequate and deprived patients of their constitutional rights. The court said that lack of adequate standards or facilities cannot justify the failure to provide suitable treatment. The court initially reserved ruling to afford state officials opportunity to promulgate and implement proper standards. If the Department of Mental Health failed to fully implement an adequate treatment program within six months, the court would appoint a panel of experts to determine what standards would be required by making a full inspection of the institution and studying treatment practices and programs.

The case raises questions of constitutional rights, budget constraints, the role of the courts, separation of powers, and administrative discretion: Are the courts protecting rights or engaging in policymaking? Does the court have the right to require expenditures (which implicitly requires raising them from some source)? How much latitude should administrators have in designing programs? Do courts have the expertise to be managers?

Read the text of the decision below and answer the following questions.[69]

1. Who are the plaintiffs? What were their claims? What reasons and evidence do they put forward in support of their claims? Are warrants (implicit or explicit) evident in their argument?
2. What aspects of structure at Bryce Hospital are described? Compare the type and number of different job positions before and after staff cuts, the types of patients served, and the reorganization efforts prior to the judge's decision.
3. What aspects of culture or managerial craft at Bryce Hospital or in the state's mental health system more generally are explicitly stated or implied?
4. What does Judge Johnson decide? What reasons and evidence does he cite?
5. If you were the director of Bryce Hospital, how would you react to the court's decision? In answering this question, use the method of argument discussed in chapter 3: Clearly state your claims, reasons, evidence, warrants, and acknowledgments and responses. Would your argument be different if instead you viewed this question from the position of the commissioner of Alabama's Department of Mental Health? From the position of the governor of Alabama?
6. In your view, did Judge Johnson make the appropriate decision? Use the method of argument to develop your answer to this question.

Ricky WYATT, by and through his Aunt and legal guardian Mrs. W. C. Rawlins, Jr., et al., Plaintiffs, v. Dr. Stonewall B. STICKNEY, as Commissioner of Mental Health and the State of Alabama Mental Health Officer, et al., Defendants

Civ. A. No. 3195-N
United States District Court for the Middle District
of Alabama, Northern Division
325 F. Supp. 781; 1971 U.S. Dist. LEXIS 14217

March 12, 1971

PROCEDURAL POSTURE: Plaintiff class representatives, who were members of a class of guardians of patients confined to a mental health facility, sought injunctive relief against defendants, state government officials and agencies, by way of an order of reference [a court order appointing a referee to hear and recommend action on specified issues]. The representatives sought a determination of the adequacy of the mental treatment used and that would have been used in effectuating the right to treatment for those who were incarcerated at the facility.

OVERVIEW: In an effort to allegedly provide better treatment for patients confined to a mental health facility, defendant department of mental health terminated a number of the facility's employees as part of an effort to reorganize into a unit-team system of mental health care service delivery. The class representatives filed a motion seeking an order of reference so that there would have been an authoritative determination of standards of the adequacy of the mental treatment used and that would have been used under the reorganization. Defendants argued that they should have been given the opportunity to set standards and to make evaluations for submission to the court prior to the court's appointing masters to perform that task. The court reserved ruling upon the representatives' motion for an order of reference. The court held that defendants' failure to fully implement, within a limited time, a treatment program, which would give each of the treatable patients an opportunity to be cured or to improve his condition, would necessitate the appointment of a panel of mental health experts to determine what standards would be required to furnish adequate treatment to the facility's patients.

OUTCOME: The court reserved ruling on the class representatives' motion for an order of reference, which would have determined the adequacy of the treatment and future treatment of patients at the mental health facility. The court gave defendants a limited time to implement a treatment plan and failure to do so would result in the appointment of a panel to determine what standards would be required to furnish adequate treatment to the facility's patients.

JUDGES: [**1] Johnson, Chief Judge.

OPINION BY: JOHNSON

Opinion

[*782] ORDER
JOHNSON, Chief Judge.

This is a class action that was initiated by guardians of patients confined at Bryce Hospital, Tuscaloosa, Alabama, and by certain employees of the Alabama Mental Health Board who are assigned to Bryce Hospital. The plaintiffs sue on behalf of themselves and on behalf of other members of their respective classes.[70]

The defendants are the commissioner and the deputy commissioner of the Department of Mental Health of the State of Alabama, the members of the Alabama Mental Health Board, the Governor of the State of Alabama, and the probate judge of Montgomery County, Alabama, as representative of the other judges of probate in the State of Alabama.

The case is now submitted upon plaintiffs' motion for a preliminary injunction, the [**2] opposition of the defendants thereto, and the testimony taken in connection with the hearing on plaintiffs' motion.

The Alabama Mental Health Board is a public corporation created by the State of Alabama through legislation codified at Title 22, Sections 311-336, Alabama Code (Supplement 1969). This board is responsible for the administration of all State mental health facilities and treatment centers, including Bryce Hospital, Tuscaloosa, Alabama. When not in session, the Alabama Mental

Health Board acts through its chief administrative officer whose title is State Mental Health Officer. This position is presently held by Dr. Stonewall B. Stickney.[71]

[**3] Bryce Hospital is located in Tuscaloosa, Alabama, and is a part of the mental health service delivery system for the State of Alabama. Bryce Hospital has approximately 5,000 patients, the majority of whom are involuntarily committed through civil proceedings by the various probate judges in Alabama. Approximately 1,600 employees were assigned to various duties at the Bryce Hospital facility when this case was heard on plaintiffs' motion for a preliminary injunction.

During October 1970, the Alabama Mental Health Board and the administration of the Department of Mental Health terminated 99 of these employees. These terminations were made [*783] due to budgetary considerations and, according to the evidence, were necessary to bring the expenditures at Bryce Hospital within the framework of available resources. This budget cut at Bryce Hospital was allegedly necessary because of a reduction in the tax revenues available to the Department of Mental Health of the State of Alabama, and also because an adjustment in the pay periods for personnel which had been directed by the Alabama legislature would require additional expenditures. The employees who were terminated included [**4] 41 persons who were assigned to duties such as food service, maintenance, typing, and other functional duties not involving direct patient care in the hospital therapeutic programs. Twenty-six persons were discharged who were involved in patient activity and recreational programs. These workers were involved in planning social and other types of recreational programs for the patient population. The remaining 32 employees who were discharged included 9 in the department of psychology, 11 in the social service department, with varying degrees of educational background and experience, three registered nurses, two physicians, one dentist and six dental aides. After the termination of these employees, there remained at Bryce Hospital 17 physicians, approximately 850 psychiatric aides, 21 registered nurses, 12 patient activity workers, and 12 psychologists with varying academic qualifications and experience, together with 13 social service workers. Of the employees remaining whose duties involved direct patient care in the hospital therapeutic programs, there are only one Ph. D. clinical psychologist, three medical doctors with some psychiatric training (including one board eligible [**5] but no board-certified psychiatrist) and two M.S.W. social workers.

The Alabama Department of Mental Health, during the last two and one-half years, has been engaged in rather extensive reorganization. This reorganizational effort, according to testimony, is designed to render a more efficient and effective delivery of treatment to patients at Bryce Hospital and in the other mental hospitals[72] within the Alabama Mental Health system. A part of the organizational effort was a transition from a departmental system of organization at Bryce Hospital to the unit-team system of delivery of mental health services and treatment to patients at Bryce Hospital. The unit-team system, as it is termed, divides the State of Alabama into contiguous geographical county units, with mentally ill patients from each such geographical area being assigned to a particular unit within the hospital. This geographical distribution is divided between Searcy and Bryce Hospitals, with Searcy accommodating the counties in the southerly part of the State and Bryce in the remainder of the State. Approximately ten units are ultimately planned for the Bryce facility. The unit is to be headed by a team leader [**6] who will normally be a professional. It is proposed that the units contain such professionals as physicians, psychologists, and social workers, as well as psychiatric aides and nurses. The patients within the unit are to receive individual attention from such hospital personnel according to their needs. This Court cannot now say upon the evidence that has been presented that the decision of the Alabama Department of Mental Health to adopt the unit-team treatment delivery approach was an improper exercise of medical and professional judgment. The evidence is clear that the unit-team approach is a scientifically recognized and acceptable method of delivering treatment to mental health patients. It seems to be a nationally recognized method for the improvement of the delivery of therapeutic services to patients in mental hospitals. This Court is unable at this time to evaluate the therapeutic effectiveness of the unit-team delivery approach at Bryce Hospital. This [*784] is true due to the fact that at the time of the hearing upon plaintiffs' motion for a preliminary injunction the transition had only just been completed, but not fully implemented.

[**7] Included in the Bryce Hospital patient population are between 1,500 and 1,600 geriatric patients who are provided custodial care but no treatment. The evidence is without dispute that these patients are not properly confined at Bryce Hospital since these geriatric patients cannot benefit from any psychiatric treatment or are not mentally ill. Also included in the Bryce patient population are approximately 1,000 mental retardates, most of whom receive only custodial care without any psychiatric treatment. Thus, the evidence reflects that there is considerable confusion regarding the primary mission and function of Bryce Hospital since certain nonpsychotic geriatric patients and the mental retardates, and perhaps other nonmentally ill persons, have been and remain committed there for a variety of reasons.

The evidence further reflects that Alabama ranks fiftieth among all the states in the Union in per-patient expenditures per day.[73] This Court must, and does, find from the evidence that the programs of treatment in use at Bryce Hospital prior to the reorganization that has resulted in the unit-team approach were scientifically and medically inadequate. These programs of treatment [**8] failed to conform to any known minimums established for providing treatment for the mentally ill.

The patients at Bryce Hospital, for the most part, were involuntarily committed through noncriminal procedures and without the constitutional protections that are afforded defendants in criminal proceedings. [HN1] When patients are so committed for treatment purposes they unquestionably have a constitutional right to receive such individual treatment as will give each of them a realistic opportunity to be cured or to improve his or her mental condition. *Rouse v. Cameron,* 125 U.S. App. D.C. [**9] 366, 373 F.2d 451; *Covington v. Harris,* 136 U.S. App. D.C. 35, 419 F.2d 617. Adequate and effective treatment is constitutionally required because, absent treatment, the hospital is transformed "into a penitentiary where one could be held indefinitely for no convicted offense." *Ragsdale v. Overholser,* 108 U.S. App. D.C. 308, 281 F.2d 943, 950 (1960). [HN2] The purpose of involuntary hospitalization for treatment purposes is *treatment* and not mere custodial care or punishment. This is the only justification, from a constitutional standpoint, that allows civil commitments to mental institutions such as Bryce. According to the evidence in this case, the failure of Bryce Hospital to supply adequate treatment is due to a lack of operating funds. [HN3] The failure to provide suitable and adequate treatment to the mentally ill cannot be justified by lack of staff or facilities. *Rouse v. Cameron,* supra. In *Rouse* the Court stated:

> We are aware that shortage of psychiatric personnel is a most serious problem today in the care of the mentally ill. In the opinion of the American Psychiatric Association no tax-supported hospital in the United States can be considered adequately staffed. We [**10] also recognize that shortage cannot be remedied immediately. But indefinite delay cannot be approved. "The rights here asserted are * * * *present* rights * * * and, unless there is an overwhelming compelling reason, they are to be promptly fulfilled." *Watson v. City of Memphis,* 373 U.S. 526, 533, [83 S. Ct. 1314, 1318, 10 L. Ed. 2d 529] (1963). (Emphasis in original.)

[*785] There can be no legal (or moral) justification for the State of Alabama's failing to afford treatment—and adequate treatment from a medical standpoint—to the several thousand patients who have been civilly committed to Bryce for treatment purposes. [HN4] To deprive any citizen of his or her liberty upon the altruistic theory that the confinement is for humane therapeutic reasons and then fail to provide adequate treatment violates the very fundamentals of due process.

As stated, this Court cannot at this time make any finding with regard to whether the unit-team system approach or the departmental approach is a better treatment delivery mechanism for Bryce Hospital. Nor can this Court at this time make any finding regarding the "adequacy" of the treatment to be given under the unit-team approach. [**11] It may very well be that when the unit-team approach is implemented in the Bryce facility the patients committed there will be receiving such individual treatment as will give each of them a realistic opportunity to be cured or to improve his mental condition. On the other hand, it may be that the unit-team approach will not provide such treatment.

The plaintiffs by formal motion ask this Court for an order of reference in order that there may be an authoritative determination of standards of the adequacy of the mental treatment now used and to be used in effectuating the right to treatment for those who are incarcerated in the Bryce facility. The defendants oppose this Court's making such an order of reference at this time, arguing that it is only proper that the defendants be allowed the opportunity to set standards and to make evaluations for submission to the Court prior to the time this Court appoints masters to perform this task. This Court has concluded that it will, for the time being, reserve ruling upon plaintiffs' motion for an order of reference. The reservation upon plaintiffs' motion for an order of reference will be *for a limited time* so as to afford the defendants [**12] an opportunity to promulgate and implement proper standards for the adequate mental care of the patients in the Bryce Hospital facility and in order to allow the defendants a reasonable time to implement fully the unit-team approach and to measure the effectiveness of the unit-team therapeutic treatment programs at the Bryce facility. This Court recognizes that this is a matter which will take thorough study and will require professional judgment and evaluation. The evidence reflects that the defendant Dr. Stonewall B. Stickney is, if he is afforded adequate funds for staffing and facilities, qualified to study, to evaluate, to institute, and to implement fully appropriate mental health treatment programs. A failure on the part of the defendants to implement fully, within six months from the date of this order, a treatment program so as to give each of the treatable patients committed to Bryce facility a realistic opportunity to be cured or to improve his or her mental condition, will necessitate this Court's appointing a panel of experts in the area of mental health to determine what objective and subjective hospital standards will be required to furnish adequate treatment to the [**13] treatable mentally ill in the Bryce facility. This will include an order requiring a full inspection of the existing facilities, a study of the operational and treatment practices and programs, and recommendations that will enable this Court to determine what will be necessary in order to render the Bryce facilities a mental health unit providing adequate and effective treatment, in a constitutional sense, for the patients who have been involuntarily committed and are confined there.

Accordingly, it is the order, judgment and decree of this Court that the defendants, within ninety days from the date hereof, prepare and file with this Court:

a. A precise definition of the mission and functions of Bryce Hospital;
b. A specific plan whereby appropriate and adequate treatment will be provided to the patients at Bryce Hospital [*786] who, from a medical standpoint, may be responsive to mental health treatment;
c. A report reflecting in detail the progress on the implementation of the unit-team approach in the Bryce facility. This report should reflect the number of unit teams, the number of patients in each unit, a breakdown of professionals assigned to each unit by discipline, [**14] and the number of patients in each unit who are receiving individual attention from some member of the professional disciplines and how often this treatment is accorded.

In this connection, records are to be maintained detailing the names of the patients entitled to receive—from a medical standpoint—psychiatric care and treatment, and the type and extent of the treatment being administered. Such reports must be made available to plaintiffs' attorneys and to the attorneys of any other parties who may appear in this case as amicus.

It is further ordered that the United States of America, acting through the United States Department of Justice and other appropriate officials such as the officials of the United States Department of Health, Education and Welfare, be and it is hereby requested and invited to appear in this cause as amicus for the purpose of assisting this Court in evaluating the treatment programs at the Bryce Hospital facility and in assisting the defendants in meeting the subjective standards of the United States Department of Health, Education and Welfare as said standards pertain to adequate treatment, personnel, space, equipment and facilities. The Department [**15] of Health, Education and Welfare and the United States Public Health Service are also requested and invited to participate, through the United States Department of Justice, as amicus, in order to assist the defendants in qualifying for Social Security benefits for the approximately 1,500 to 1,600 geriatric patients who are presently housed at Bryce Hospital for custodial purposes; this invitation to these agencies is also for the purpose of rendering assistance to the defendants in formulating and implementing a feasible plan that will benefit each of these geriatric patients by his or her becoming appropriately situated in some type facility other than a facility for the treatment of the mentally ill.

It is further ordered that ruling on plaintiffs' motion for an order of reference be and the same is hereby reserved.

This Court specifically retains jurisdiction of this case.

5 Public Management: The Structural Dimension

The central role that structural factors played in Hurricane Katrina preparation and response and in the space shuttle *Columbia* accident were described in chapters 1 and 2. As emphasized in those discussions, a one-dimensional perspective is seldom adequate for a complete analysis of the challenges and opportunities facing public managers. It is also true that skill in multidimensional analysis requires building in-depth appreciation for each separate dimension. Accordingly, this chapter and the next two focus on each dimension in turn. The structural dimension, the subject here, describes the formal and lawful delegations of specific responsibilities to designated organizations and officials. Such delegations are the principal form of leverage that policymakers have over public management. They may take the form either of constraints on the decisions or activities of actors to whom authority has been delegated or as authority that directs and enables actors to exercise discretion in pursuing public policy objectives.

Structures are defined in the provisions of authorizing statutes; in approved legislative budgets; in executive orders, regulations, and rules that have the force of law; in decisions and directives by executives and managers within their spheres of authority; and in the decisions, injunctions, and consent decrees issued by courts. Delegated responsibilities and authorities may include creating additional administrative structures; establishing planning, decision-making, and communication processes; prescribing specific standards for the performance of functions and tasks; and allocating specific levels of personnel and budgetary resources to agency offices and activities together with rules and guidelines for their use.

The following article describes a structural change—the reorganization of the former Immigration and Naturalization Service (INS) and the Customs Service into a new agency, Immigration and Customs Enforcement (ICE), located in the Department of Homeland Security (DHS)—that enabled public managers to expand an investigative operation beyond what it otherwise would have covered:

> Two years ago, investigators with the old Immigration and Naturalization Service in Albany, N.Y., began looking into reports that several Chinese restaurants in upstate New York were harboring illegal immigrants who were allegedly working in the kitchens. It hardly seemed an unusual case—the restaurant industry long has been known for its reliance on and exploitation of undocumented immigrant labor.
>
> Then the case took an unexpected turn. INS was abolished. The agency's investigators were partnered with Customs Service investigators in the bureaucratic equivalent of a shotgun marriage, one of many organizational twists that occurred when the Homeland Security Department was established in March 2003.
>
> The unholy union of immigration and customs investigators resulted in the Immigration and Customs Enforcement agency, known as ICE, which is part of Homeland Security's sprawling Border and Transportation Security bureau. In an agency where consensus can be hard to find, all parties seem to agree that the ICE merger was no love match. The divide ran deep, ranging from differences in cultures and investigation methods to training, databases, and contacts with state and local law enforcement organizations. Not surprisingly, the move into a new organization caused plenty of heartburn for everyone.
>
> Nonetheless, the New York immigration investigation continued, but, like the new agency, with a twist. Jack McQuade, the resident agent in charge of the ICE office in Albany, says agents continued to pursue the case. But under orders from Peter Smith, the ICE agent in charge of the Buffalo regional office—which oversees the Albany office—the inquiry was expanded to include money-laundering.
>
> McQuade, formerly a Customs agent, says it made sense to draw on the expertise of both agencies. "I told a [former] Customs agent, 'You're going to work an immigration case, but you're going to work it from a money-laundering perspective. We are going to go after these individuals' assets.' This would definitely not have occurred if this had remained strictly an immigration issue."
>
> The ICE agents conducted surveillance in New York City, where they discovered that restaurant owners upstate were operating a tour bus to pick up illegal immigrants in Chinatown, Brooklyn and Queens, and transport them to the Albany area. For months, investigators followed a trail that eventually led to a human smuggling ring holding at least several dozen illegal immigrants essentially enslaved as indentured servants and more than 40 illicit bank accounts. Along the way the Internal Revenue Service joined in, to pursue tax evasion charges, with investigators from the Labor Department, the U.S. attorney for the northern district of New York, the New York State Police and a number of local police departments.
>
> Last November, ICE executed search warrants on several restaurants and homes, arrested ringleaders, and seized 11 vehicles and nearly $4 million in cash, real estate and other assets. The probe remains open as investigators continue to pore through cartons of seized documents.

> "This is a perfect example showing how you can really hurt a criminal organization when you draw on expertise from both former Customs and former INS," says Smith. "The legacy immigration people knew exactly what to look for, what documents to get, what surveillance to do, what we needed to charge these people with, with regard to human trafficking. Then you come in with the legacy Customs powers. The legacy Customs people see that not only do we have a great immigration case, but we can now go after this group and their assets."
>
> Adds McQuade: "This would not have happened had the decision not been made to work it from both angles. It's a good example of what you can do if you work together, and if you elicit the assistance of local police agencies." [1]

After the ICE reorganization, managers Peter Smith and Jack McQuade had the authority to decide on a matter that might have been dealt with quite differently in the past. As separate entities, the INS and Customs Service might not have garnered the resources or followed the same path. The case might have fallen between the cracks or been a source of conflict needing to be resolved at a higher level. Structural reorganization enabled a more successful kind of operation to occur.

This chapter explores the structural dimension in the context of specific frameworks, theories, and concepts that facilitate a more analytical approach for understanding how structures shape the incentives, decisions, and actions of managers and frontline employees. Public managers deal with such issues whether they operate within structures that are outside their power to change or they have the authority to choose new structural arrangements or to change existing ones.

The types of structures described in this chapter are not restricted to those typically equated with the term *structure* in other public management texts, which often limit the meaning to internal organizational matters.[2] Some of those topics—job positions, tasks and technology, budgets, and human resource policies—are discussed here, but the chapter also conveys broader structural concerns for public managers. The chapter explores contracts and contracting out at some length, as well as government-sponsored enterprises and nonprofit organizations. The goal is not to provide an exhaustive list of all possible internal or external structures that are relevant to public management practice; rather, it is to convey a broad appreciation for how structure influences managerial strategies and actions as both cause and effect.

The chapter therefore explores how structure affects and interacts with the practice of public management. First, the meanings of structure are discussed, and the distinction between constraining and enabling structures is elaborated upon. Next, the evolution of the structural perspective is described. The final section discusses political rationality and its influence on structural realities faced by public managers. The end-of-chapter exercise deals with a reorganization of state social services and welfare departments, mandated by a state legislature. Readers are asked to consider whether the structural reforms are likely to lead to the changes in outcomes the legislature had hoped for.

WHAT IS STRUCTURE?

A principal source of insights into structure is organization theory. James D. Thompson's view of structure, for example, focuses on internal organizational structure, where the "major components of a complex organization . . . are further segmented, or departmentalized, and connections are established within and between departments," leading to "internal differentiation and patterning of relationships."[3] Derek S. Pugh and his colleagues define and operationalize the dimensions of organization structure as specialization, standardization, formalization, centralization, and configuration.[4] W. Richard Scott also focuses on internal organizational structure, such as those elements "defining the division of labor—structural differentiation, including occupational and role specialization, departmentalization, and multidivisional forms—and those relating to coordination and control of work—formalization, hierarchy, centralization, and various structures for facilitating lateral information flows."[5]

Lee G. Bolman and Terrence E. Deal expand the concept of structure somewhat by defining it as "a blueprint for the pattern of expectations and exchanges among internal players (executives, managers, employees) and external constituencies (such as customers and clients). . . . [S]tructural form both enhances and constrains what organizations can accomplish."[6] They point to two primary classes of structures used to coordinate the actions of organizational participants: vertical coordination (rules, policies, authority, and planning and control systems), and horizontal coordination (meetings, task forces, networks, and matrix structures, which combine vertical and horizontal orientations). Bolman and Deal's distinction between vertical and horizontal aspects are echoed in Morten Egeberg's definition of key structural components: organizational size, vertical specialization (or hierarchy), and horizontal specialization ("how different issues and policy areas, for example transport and environmental protection, are supposed to be linked together or de-coupled from each other").[7]

Another approach to defining structure does not attempt to define it as necessarily internal or external to an organization, but to identify its characteristic elements. Elinor Ostrom's definition of "rules" refers to "prescriptions commonly known and used by a set of participants to order repetitive, interdependent relationships" and to identify "which actions (or states of the world) are *required, prohibited,* or *permitted.*"[8] Ostrom elaborates:

> Rules are the result of implicit or explicit efforts by a set of individuals to achieve order and predictability within defined situations by: (1) creating positions . . . ; (2) stating how participants enter or leave positions; (3) stating which actions participants in these positions are required, permitted, or forbidden to take; and (4) stating which outcome participants are required, permitted, or forbidden to affect.[9]

To consider the scope of the structural dimension in public management, this text incorporates elements of these different views but overlays them with a concern unique to public organizations for which, as discussed in chapter 4, the rule of law forms the backbone. Structure is therefore defined as *formal and lawful delegations of authority and specific responsibility to designated officials and organizations to take action on behalf of policy and program objectives.* This definition is broader than those of Thompson or Scott because it does not restrict attention to internal organizational structure. This expanded definition includes the tools of government action, that is, structural policy features such as contracting, grants, fees and charges, and vouchers, which governance scholar Lester M. Salamon has identified.[10] The structural dimension does not, however, encompass informal or shared understandings about relationships between actors or about ways of working. Such understandings are included in Ostrom's conception of a "rule," but in the three-dimensional framework considered here, they are considered to be aspects of organizational culture (discussed in chapter 6).

Formal and lawfully authorized delegations of authority and specific responsibility may create structures that either constrain or enable the actions of public managers. **Constraining structures** direct or deny specific activities, consistent with Ostrom's "required" or "prohibited" characteristics; **enabling structures** allow the exercise of discretion, consistent with Ostrom's "permitted" characteristic.

Further, enabling and constraining structures may emanate from sources of authority that are either external or internal to the organization. Considering the organization as the unit of analysis, when the authorizing of formal authority is external to the organization, specifications of structure are said to be externally authorized (operating primarily at the "b" and "c" levels in the logic of governance described in chapter 4). A legislative directive to an executive branch agency is an externally authorized formal authority. When the authorizing of formal authority is internal to the organization, specifications of structure are said to be internally authorized (operating primarily at the "d" level of the logic of governance). An example is a cabinet secretary's restructuring of reporting lines or job responsibilities for agency staff. Internally authorized formal authority is necessary because, operating within the confines or allowances of externally authorized structures, managers of public organizations are faced with the necessity and opportunity to impose additional order on their organizations' operations.

Structures can therefore be classified using a two-by-two categorization whose first dimension describes the type of structure—constraining or enabling—and the second describes the source of formal authority that authorizes the structure—external or internal to the organization. This categorization is shown in Table 5.1.

Mandates, restrictions, conditions, and other boundary-setting directives on organizations or their public managers are examples of broad constraining structures—the first row of the table. These constraints include specific rules and procedures including **red tape** or "rules, regulations, and procedures that remain in force and entail a compliance burden but do not advance the legitimate purposes the rules were intended to serve."[11] They also include decision-making and communication processes; standards, criteria, and organization for the performance of jobs, functions, programs, and tasks; required reporting lines of authority or accountability; budgets; payment or reimbursement formulas; and civil service rules.

TABLE 5.1 Enabling and Constraining Structures

Type of Structure	Source of Formal Authority in Relation to the Organization: *External*	*Internal*
Constraining	Required use of performance incentives by legislation (e.g., Workforce Investment Act)	Job descriptions defined by managers
		Details of performance incentives developed by managers and staff
	Required reporting lines of authority, detailed in legislation or external executive agency/authority (e.g., process for Bush administration's Program Assessment Rating Tool)	Centers for Medicare & Medicaid Services regulations for physician reimbursement
Enabling	Tenth Amendment to U.S. Constitution	Forest Service rule regarding National Forest System Land Management Planning
	Congressional creation of executive departments	Managers' delegations to subordinates for figuring out how to perform specific tasks

A constraining structure found in the U.S. Constitution, Article II, Section 2, states, "[The president] shall have Power, by and with the Advice and Consent of the Senate, to make Treaties, provided two thirds of the Senators present concur." The Homeland Security Act describes a constraining structure when it defines jurisdiction: "Except as specifically provided by law with respect to entities transferred to the Department under this Act, primary responsibility for investigating and prosecuting acts of terrorism shall be vested not in the Department, but rather in Federal, State, and local law enforcement agencies with jurisdiction over the acts in question." A regulation that imposes a constraining structure is the reimbursement formula for physicians who care for patients covered by Medicare. The Centers for Medicare & Medicaid Services in the Department of Health and Human Services issues these regulations.

> [A]s discussed in section IV.D of this final rule with comment period, due to the need to meet the budget neutrality (BN) provisions of 1848(c)(2)(B)(ii), we are applying a BN adjustor to the work RVUs in order to calculate payment for a service. Therefore, payment for services will now be calculated as follows: Payment = [(RVU work × BN adjustor × GPCI work) + (RVU PE × GPCI PE)+ (RVU malpractice × GPCI malpractice)] × CF.)[12]

In this formula, RVU stands for "relative value unit," BN for "budget neutrality," GPCI for "geographic practice cost index," PE for "practice expense," and CF for "conversion factor." The explicit formula provided in this regulation removes discretion regarding the reimbursement amount for services; reimbursement is defined exactly as stated in the regulation and thus constitutes a constraining structure.

Enabling structures, shown in the second row of Table 5.1, are formal delegations of authority that explicitly or implicitly allow discretion on the part of designated officials or organizations. Public managers' discretionary actions either create structures or infuse an existing structure with distinction and meaning (though these structures may not be wholly determined by managerial actors).

Enabling structures, like constraining structures, are communicated through provisions of authorizing statutes or executive orders, regulations, or rules. The Constitution contains many enabling structures, such as "The executive Power shall be vested in a President of the United States of America." The Tenth Amendment is also an enabling structure: "The powers not delegated to the United States by the Constitution, nor prohibited by it to the States, are reserved to the States respectively, or to the people." The section of the Homeland Security Act of 2002 that states, "The Secretary is the head of the Department and shall have direction, authority, and control over it" is an enabling structure, as is the following portion of a rule issued by the Forest Service:

> In this final rule, guidelines are described as "information and guidance for project and activity decisionmaking." Guidelines will not contain final decisions approving activities and uses. A Responsible Official has the discretion to act within the range of guidelines, as well as the latitude to depart from guidelines when circumstances warrant it. In the latter case, the Responsible Official should document the rationale for taking such exception to guidelines.[13]

In each of these examples, authority to act is formally granted to a particular actor—the president, the secretary of DHS, the states, and the Forest Service's Responsible Official, respectively—but specific actions or decisions are neither directed nor denied within these broad grants of authority. Thus, they constitute enabling structures.

To summarize, the structural dimension of public management refers to formal and lawful delegations of authority and specific responsibility to designated officials and organizations to take action on behalf of policy and program objectives. Whether this formal authority is delegated from sources external or internal to the organization, it may either constrain the actions and decisions of public managers or enable their exercise of discretion within defined limits. An awareness and appreciation of these sources of formal authority, and their resultant effects on options and choices for actors in managerial roles, is fundamental for the responsible practice of public management.

CONCEPTS IN ACTION

Performance Incentives as Constraining Structures

Details of program performance standards and incentive payments are constraining structures because they specify the exact terms or goals that organizations must meet to receive awards or penalties. They may be externally or internally authorized, depending on the point at which the specific standards or incentives are set. If set by legislation or if set by a state agency and applied to local contractors, they are externally authorized. If set by a state agency and applied to implementing offices in the agency's internal hierarchy, they are internally authorized. The following excerpt from a Workforce Investment Field Instruction memo for the state of Maryland is an example of a performance incentive policy.

The State has established the following specific incentive policy for PY2006, based on the recommendation of the performance workgroup and input from the local workforce investment system:

- Maryland applied for and was granted a waiver that allows for the implementation of Common Measures effective July 1, 2006.
- Local areas will be held to the State's negotiated performance standards, with the exception of the two Average Earnings measures. The State will implement a local adjustment methodology for the Average Earnings measures, based on an analysis of actual WIA participant wage averages for the previous four years. (Attachment B)
- Incentive payouts will be calculated on three factors: relative % share of allocation for those areas qualifying for incentives, meeting each of 6 performance measures, and the following weights applied to each measure:
  - 20% Entered Employment—Adult
  - 20% Entered Employment—Dislocated Worker
  - 15% Employment Retention—Adult
  - 15% Employment Retention—Dislocated Worker
  - 20% Youth Placement in Employment or Education
  - 10% Youth Attainment of Degree or Certificate.

Source: Maryland Department of Labor, Licensing and Regulation, "Workforce Investment Field Instruction (WIFI) # 07-06," December 21, 2006, http://www.dllr.state.md.us/employment/wifi/wifi7-06.doc.

EVOLUTION OF THE STRUCTURAL PERSPECTIVE

That public management involves the interrelated elements of formal delegation of authority, as well as external control over the exercise of delegated authority, accounts for the emergence of concern early in the twentieth century for the structures and processes of government. As legal scholar Ernest Freund put it in a 1915 article, "The Substitution of Rule for Discretion in Administrative Law," "Increased administrative powers call for increased safeguards against their abuses, and as long as there is the possibility of official error, partiality or excess of zeal, the protection of private right is as important an object as the effectuation of some governmental policy." [14] The evolution of the structural perspective is fundamentally a story of the competition among the branches of government for control of administration.[15]

The story begins in the private sector. As the size and diversification of business organizations increased in the latter decades of the nineteenth century, so too did concern "for appropriate organizational forms and for internal management techniques to substitute for the personal contacts and incentives that had been effective in the days of smaller, owner-administered business units." [16] The early emphasis on centralized, functionally organized management structures went hand-in-hand with the professionalization of business management, the emergence of general management, and concern for the control of labor and other costs.

Similar trends were apparent in federal, state, and municipal governments. Political scientists Jack H. Knott and Gary J. Miller recall Woodrow Wilson's 1887 argument that all governments can and should have a "strong structural likeness." [17] Progressive reformers and policymakers, taking cues both from American business and from European administrative systems, became attentive to the structures and processes of the new public bureaus and agencies created to meet the needs of an organizing and industrializing society, and they strove to define and refine that structural likeness. In effect, business and government were becoming bureaucratic in the manner of their European counterparts.

The business-government analogy fit those times: The rapid growth of business along with a generally laissez-faire attitude toward private enterprise and the distrust of government encoded in American DNA strongly implied that government, to the extent that it was necessary, should at least be businesslike. This managerial/structural ideology was particularly evident in municipal government, where the goal of efficient administration, accomplished through the separation of politics and administration carried out by neutrally competent administration became a kind of orthodoxy, widely enacted in the structures and processes of the city manager form of local government.

According to Bolman and Deal, the structural perspective has two main intellectual roots.[18] One is the scientific management movement associated with the work of Frederick W. Taylor, an industrial engineer who pioneered the use of measurement and analysis to identify the "one best way" of organizing the production of goods and services.[19] The work of Taylor, French industrialist Henri Fayol, Lyndall F. Urwick, and Luther H. Gulick led to the formulation of principles on specialization, span of control, authority, and delegation of responsibility. Perhaps the most famous expression of the structural perspective is Gulick's 1937 essay, "Notes on the Theory of Organization," prepared for President Franklin Roosevelt's Committee on Administrative Management. The committee's report, known as the Brownlow Report after its chair Louis Brownlow, was issued that year; it is further discussed in chapter 9.[20]

The second source of the structural perspective, in Bolman and Deal's view, is the work of Max Weber and other theorists of bureaucracy. Although Weber's work was not widely known in America until English translations became available after World War II, bureaucracy as an ideal structure was influential early in the formation of the American administrative state.[21] Bureaucratic principles emphasized the rationally defined division of labor, hierarchy, formal rules, separation of personnel from property rights, the technical qualifications of personnel, and employment as a career. The study of bureaucracy became popular among American social scientists, and Weberian bureaucracy became the "structural likeness" that reformers aspired to.

The structural perspective was supplemented by other theories of organization, as scholars and practitioners began to recognize the limitations of a strictly structural perspective for understanding the problems of public and private organizations. A human relations movement that focused on the interrelationships between organizations and the human needs and aspirations of their employees grew in influence in the 1930s. Schuyler T. Wallace's 1941 book, *Federal Departmentalization: A Critique of Theories of Organization,* challenged the kind of thinking represented in the Brownlow Report. Wallace argued that organizations cannot be designed by rote application of abstract principles. Beginning in the 1960s, scholars began to investigate the phenomenon of bureaucratic politics and its influence on organizational behavior and performance.

Because it is so closely associated with the separation of powers, the structural perspective continues to exert an exceptionally strong influence on policymakers concerned with controlling and improving governmental performance. Executive policymakers have often sought to expand their authority to reorganize government agencies and activities. President George W. Bush's administration sought greatly strengthened reorganization authority in its proposed Government Reorganization and Program Performance Improvement Act of 2005, which was introduced in Congress but never moved out of committee. Congress zealously protects its authority over the organization of government in order to retain control over the deployment of administrative resources in behalf of the policies it has authorized. Indeed, legislative micromanagement of government structures and processes remains one of the most frequently used tools of governance. Structural reforms initiated by Congress include the creation of the Department of Homeland Security and the Directorate of National Intelligence. At the state level, legislative initiatives include specification of educational financial aid formulas, such as the CalGrant program in California, and criminal justice policies, such as the Connecticut law requiring monthly reporting to municipalities of arrest warrants for probation violations.

CONCEPTS IN ACTION

An Argument for Restructuring to Create the EPA

On July 9, 1970, President Richard M. Nixon sent to Congress a message on the need to restructure the federal government's environmental programs by creating one new entity, the Environmental Protection Agency. His message conveyed his argument for favoring this structural solution to the issues he identifies.

As no disjointed array of separate programs can, the EPA would be able—in concert with the States—to set and enforce standards for air and water quality and for individual pollutants. This consolidation of pollution control authorities would help assure that we do not create new environmental problems in the process of controlling existing ones. Industries seeking to minimize the adverse impact of their activities on the environment would be assured of consistent standards covering the full range of their waste disposal problems. As the States develop and expand their own pollution control programs, they would be able to look to one agency to support their efforts with financial and technical assistance and training.

In proposing . . . a separate new agency, I am making an exception to one of my own principles: . . . additional new independent agencies normally should not be created. . . . [H]owever, the arguments against [the status quo] are compelling.

[E]ach [existing] department also has its own primary mission . . . which necessarily affects its own view of environmental questions. . . . [I]f the critical standard-setting functions were centralized within any one existing department, it would require that department constantly to make decisions affecting other departments. . . . Because environmental protection cuts across so many jurisdictions, and because arresting environmental deterioration is of great importance to the quality of life in our country and the world, I believe that in this case a strong, independent agency is needed.

Source: Title 42, Chapter 5, §4321, Pub. L. 91–190, §2, Jan. 1, 1970, 83 Stat. 852.

Striking the right balance between capacity and control remains a controversial aspect of public management, however, and the failure to do so often defeats efforts to achieve public management reform (see chapter 9). As Donald F. Kettl has expressed it, tensions continue to exist between "making managers manage," that is, imposing controls over managerial discretion, and "letting managers manage," that is, holding public managers accountable for their performance rather than for their compliance with formal rules and procedures. These two strategies, Kettl notes, "require culture shifts in opposite directions," a reality not always fully appreciated by advocates of public management reform.[22]

PROMINENT CONSTRAINING STRUCTURES

Constraining structures define managerial realities in two ways. First, they may control the options or actions of public managers, and, second, they may provide managers with potentially powerful tools to control the options or actions of actors over whom the managers themselves have authority. Because of the broad scope of constraining structures, as noted earlier, it is not feasible to discuss all those pertinent for managerial practice. Rather than discuss topics that are available in more specialized texts, this section's approach is to present several examples of constraining structures—positions and tasks, budgets, personnel policies, contracts, and networks—along with illustrations of theories, concepts, frameworks, and ideas that provide insight into analyzing their implications for public management.

Positions and Tasks

One major constraining structure is that of the job positions, tasks, and reporting relationships in an organization. Job positions and their relationship to each other are often conveyed in an organization chart, which represents the formal and usually hierarchical structure of work in an organization. Figure 1.1 (page 15) showed the managerial hierarchy of the Head Start program at the national, regional, and local levels. Figure 5.1 is the organization chart of a particular Head Start program, run by Southern Illinois University Edwardsville (SIUE).

Line positions—the home visitors, nurses, and teachers—deliver services or are otherwise directly involved in implementation or production of the organization's output. **Staff positions,** such as the assistant to the program director for budgets and administration, provide administrative support for the line positions but are not directly involved in the implementation of the organization's programs or policies, in this case the education and care of children.

Paul C. Light has documented the trend within federal agencies of "thickening government," by which he means increasing both the height and width of managerial positions in the hierarchy or the number of managerial positions between the frontline positions providing services, such as a Head Start teacher, and the top management position, the secretary of Health and Human Services. Light also notes the number of particular types of positions available.[23] Using information from the *Federal Yellow Book* directory, Light reports that federal managerial positions grew in height from seventeen managerial titles in 1960, including secretary, under secretary, assistant secretary, and deputy assistant secretary, to sixty-four in 2004, adding to the positions just listed principal associate deputy secretary, principal assistant deputy undersecretary, and chief of staff to the assistant assistant secretary, though not all positions were found in all federal agencies.[24] Width of the hierarchy has also grown, from 451 senior executives in 1960 to 2,592 in 2004. (These positions include political appointees

FIGURE 5.1 Organization Chart for Head Start Program Run by Southern Illinois University Edwardsville

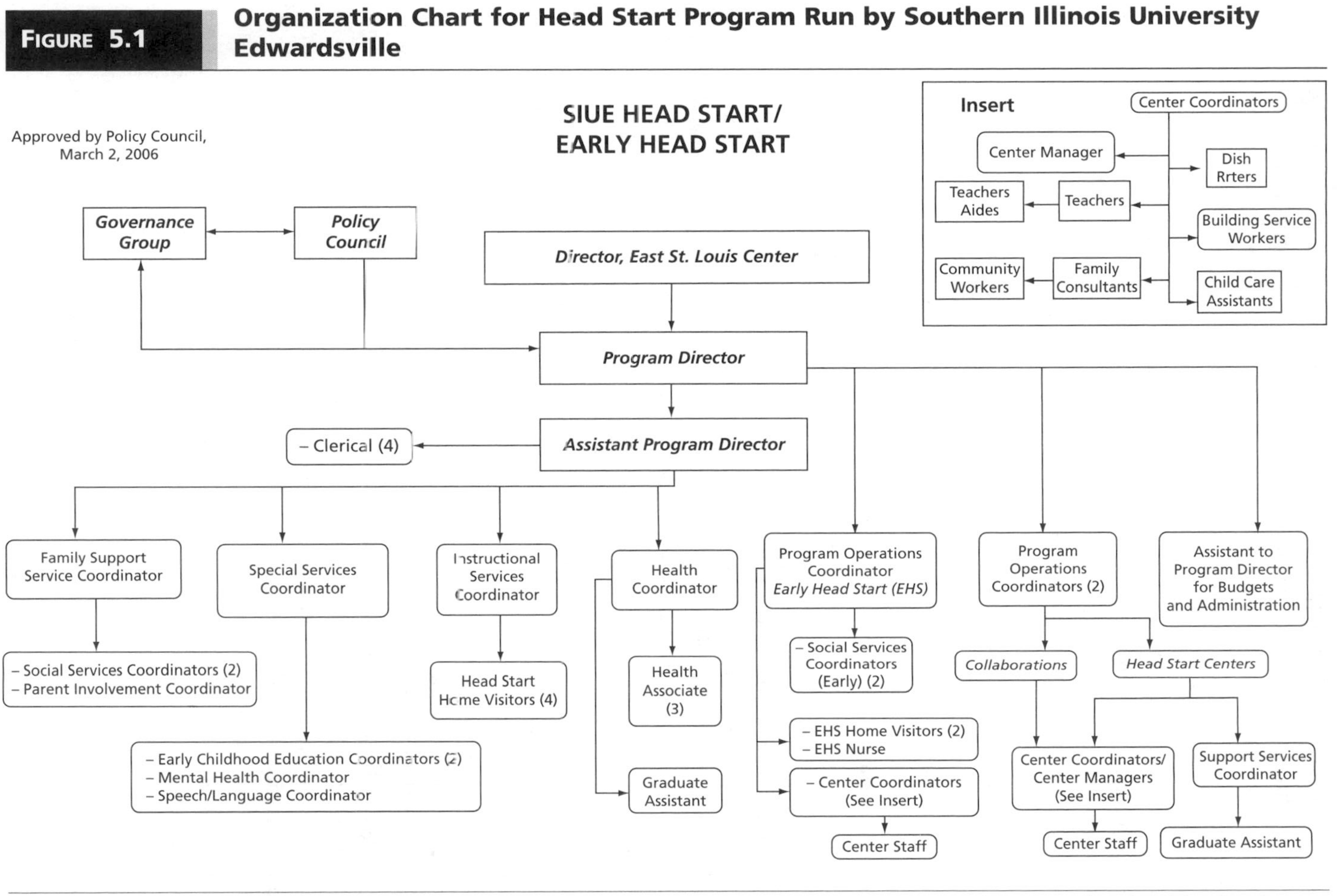

Source: SIUE Head Start/Early Head Start Policies and Procedures Manual, "Introduction," September 21, 2006, p. 27; http://www.siue.edu/eslc/headstart/resources.shtml#plan. Accessed January 28, 2008.

as well as career staff.) In Light's view, four explanations account for these trends: "(1) an ever-expanding federal agenda, (2) the use of promotions in lieu of pay increases as a reward for senior career executives, (3) the effort to control the federal bureaucracy through ever denser networks of political appointees, and (4) the creation of new titles such as the chief information officer and inspector general by Congress." [25]

Certain positions by definition have power over others. In the SIUE Head Start program, the organization chart indicates that the assistant program director has power over the health coordinator, but not over the EHS (Early Head Start) nurse. Positions in and of themselves impart power, as Scott explains, because:

> Differences in power are built into the design of the technologies or into the definition of relations among positions, and these power differences are normatively justified. . . . [T]hose with structural power do not need to mobilize resources in order to have their interests taken into account. It is automatically assumed that they are "entitled" to be represented in any matter affecting their interests. By contrast, interests that are not structured have to become mobilized if they are to be heard.[26]

Positions therefore are structural features that directly affect working relationships within the organization. If an organization chart provides a reasonably accurate depiction of the interdependence of relationships within an organization—that is, the positions are highly interdependent and their formal structures determine or closely correspond with how work actually gets done in the organization—the organization is said to be **tightly coupled.** If, on the other hand, the organization chart does not provide an accurate depiction of how work is actually accomplished—that is, the positions have low interdependence and the formal structure and actual activity are not closely linked—the organization is said to be **loosely coupled.** (Public schools are the quintessential loosely coupled organizations.) As is discussed in chapter 6, in loosely coupled organizations, formal structure primarily serves as the "myth and ceremony" rather than the hard reality of organizational life.[27]

Whether tightly or loosely coupled, an organization's structure, through its definition of positions and their relationships to each other, is likely to affect how its work is done and what kinds of decisions are made and how. Political scientist Thomas H. Hammond and sociologist Charles B. Perrow provide two frameworks that can be used to analyze the roles and importance of positions and tasks in an organization.

For the first framework, Hammond argues that because a bureaucratic structure "influences which options are to be compared, in what sequence, and by whom, *a particular organizational structure is, in effect, the organization's agenda,*" that is, the matters to be considered and acted upon by the organization.[28] His model addresses two types of tasks and generates a number of predictions for each: the flow of advice upward through the organization (**advisory tasks**) and the resolution of operational conflicts (**operating tasks**). Hammond develops propositions in regard to advisory tasks: "The organizational structure can influence what options the director has available for choice, and thus can influence what choices the director makes." And, "Different structures may convert the same raw data into different kinds of official organizational beliefs." [29]

Hammond then turns to operating tasks, which, he argues, are fundamental to decision making in bureaucracies:

> When there are conflicts among field officials doing some work, a low-level supervisor will often settle the dispute on the spot so the work can proceed. The director may never even discover that some informal "policy" has thereby been adopted or, perhaps even worse, that some "official" policy is being contravened. . . .
>
> [T]he organizational structure will determine which of these conflicts rise to the director for resolution and which do not. What the director knows about his organization, and thus what kinds of issues he has influence over, will be a function of the structure. If we think of structures as agendas affecting who makes what choices from among what options, these agendas may be even more important for operating tasks than for advisory tasks because they will keep high-level officials *from being involved at all* in some kinds of issues.[30]

Hammond points to **uncertainty absorption,** which occurs when preferences are communicated upward, that is, staff claims from a body of evidence, but not the evidence itself, are communicated to hierarchical superiors. Managers may have difficulty judging the quality—the validity, consistency, or correctness—of the recommendations they receive. A perennial example of uncertainty absorption is the president's daily brief (PDB), a daily intelligence report for which the director of national intelligence is responsible. In the PDB, claims—not detailed evidence—tend to be reported, and the claims depend in turn upon the coordination of intelligence across a number of sources, which usually means they incorporate compromises and gloss over doubts or disagreements.

Reflecting on the numerous propositions, Hammond develops some conjectures: There is some structure that will generate any outcome; some structures will generate outcomes that no one prefers; manipulating outcomes is easier in a bureaucracy than in a legislature because majority voting is not involved; and "it is impossible to design a 'neutral' structure, that is, a structure that does not influence the choices that are made via the structure." [31] In other words, structure always influences outcomes.

The propositions from Hammond's model can be illustrated with findings from the investigation of the space shuttle *Columbia* accident. The accident report suggested that NASA administrator Sean O'Keefe did not know about concerns at lower levels of the organization regarding the dangers to the orbiter while it was in flight. One implication of Hammond's analysis is that some structure exists that would have pushed the NASA engineers' anxieties up to higher levels, perhaps all the way to O'Keefe, in a timely fashion. As argued in chapter 2, the causes of the *Columbia* accident were almost certainly multidimensional, not only structural. Hammond's framework provides a specific explanation—a warrant—for understanding the role that structure in particular might have played in this situation.

The second framework that focuses on the positions and tasks in an organization is based on the work of Perrow. He argues that work processes (or technologies) may be divided into two dimensions: the frequency with which exceptions arise and the degree to which these exceptions are analyzable, that is, whether rational investigation and intervention can address and correct these exceptions.[32] At one end of the spectrum are routine technologies, characterized by few exceptions that are easily analyzable, such as administrative support jobs that require checking completed forms or making copies. At the other end of the spectrum are nonroutine technologies, characterized by many exceptions that are difficult to analyze, such as research and development activities. In between are technologies with combinations of the two characteristics: craft technologies that have few exceptions that are nevertheless difficult to analyze, such as budget analysis; and engineering technologies with many exceptions that are nevertheless relatively easy to analyze, such as auditing review. Perrow argues that important implications for management and supervision of activities can be gleaned from the type of technology employed. Routine tasks can be managed with more rules and less coordination and communication, but less-routine tasks must be managed with fewer rules, a greater amount of communication and coordination, and therefore, more decentralization of authority.

Prosecution of crimes is an administrative technology that might be considered nonroutine, with processes that are not easily standardized. Criminal prosecutions tend to be decentralized, with local prosecutors deciding on the strategies for each case. In 2003, when John D. Ashcroft was the U.S. attorney general, he sought to change the basic technology of prosecutions by directing federal prosecutors to seek the most serious provable charges in almost all cases to reduce the amount of plea bargaining.[33] This directive was intended to introduce more routine into prosecutions, subject to standards promulgated from the central office. Exceptions to the policy would require approval from higher levels in the Justice Department. Critics charged that Ashcroft was taking away from local prosecutors the discretion they needed to do their jobs. A *New York Times* story described the likely behavioral responses to the new policy:

> [A]lmost no one expects strict enforcement of the directive. Instead, if history is any guide, local prosecutors will retain substantial flexibility but will exercise it quietly and early, before rather than after charges are filed. . . .
>
> Allowing prosecutors to decide on which crimes are "readily provable" also gives them great discretion. And several prosecutors said they doubted that officials in Washington would have a way to enforce the policy in far-flung districts.[34]

Ashcroft's reform sought to fundamentally change the administrative technology of criminal prosecutions by imposing a constraining structure on local prosecutors. Yet in one sense, this directive could not change the fundamental nature of the prosecutorial task or the amount of discretion involved in its exercise, because discretion was merely shifted to an earlier stage in the process. (Ashcroft's management strategy is discussed further in chapter 7.)

HOW THE WORLD WORKS

Manipulating Criminal Sentences

The following analysis of plea bargaining suggests that a good argument might be made for Attorney General John Ashcroft's policy of eliminating variation in the practice across U.S. attorney's offices. It might also be used as an argument against that policy. As noted throughout this book, managerial discretion is inevitable.

[I]f a defendant actually sold five kilograms of cocaine but is found for sentencing purposes to have sold only four, his sentencing range will be 8 to 10 years instead of 10 to 12. This reduction can be accomplished if the prosecutor stipulates, as part of a plea agreement, to less cocaine than he could prove, or if the judge finds that, despite evidence of five kilos, only four have been proven. . . . [T]he length of the average federal drug sentence has been declining since the early 1990s, largely as a result of choices made by both prosecutors and judges during plea bargaining and sentencing. And sentence manipulation is not confined to drug cases.

Source: Frank O. Bowman III, "When Sentences Don't Make Sense," *Washington Post,* August 15, 2003.

This section has focused on particular positions, tasks, and technologies that carry out the work of an organization. Managers who either are operating within already-defined structures with particular positions or types of tasks, or who have control over how to define those positions, need to be aware of the various implications for how work is done and how it can (or cannot) be managed effectively. Two additional concepts for considering the importance and implications of positions in an organization—street-level bureaucracy and management capacity—are discussed next.

Street-Level Bureaucracy

Street-level bureaucrats are the people who implement policies or deliver services at the front lines, where public employees and their agents directly engage citizens.[35] They are local prosecutors, teachers, welfare caseworkers, prison guards, police officers, forest rangers, customs officials, and agricultural extension agents. Their work is controversial because it directly affects people, and their competence and judgment literally may have life and death significance. Many such workers, moreover, perform labor-intensive services. Modern technology, such as radar guns for police to catch speeders or computerized systems for tracking welfare cases, may help them be more productive, but cannot eliminate the position or what the workers do.[36]

Awareness of the position of street-level bureaucrats and how they perform their jobs is important for managers, because the priorities of managers and street-level bureaucrats are likely to differ. Political scientist Michael Lipsky argues that managers tend to be oriented toward high-level organizational and policy goals, while frontline workers tend to be client oriented; managers want cooperation with higher-level objectives and accountability (on which the manager's own success may depend), while frontline workers want support, resources, and freedom from undue interference.[37] Each depends on the other, but tensions are inevitable, and breakdowns in relationships are common. Ashcroft's prosecutorial reforms were a direct managerial attempt to limit local prosecutors' discretion, with the reasoning that "[d]efendants shouldn't receive different sentences depending on which assistant prosecutor they happen to get." [38] Yet as described above, the reform merely shifted the locus of discretion exercised by these street-level bureaucrats.

Agricultural inspection officers are also street-level bureaucrats.[39] Before they became part of the Customs and Border Protection (CBP) agency of DHS, these officers were part of the Plant Protection and Quarantine Agency in the Agriculture Department. Their job is to implement the Plant Protection Act, which is designed to keep pests and illegal or diseased plants from entering the United States. The act empowers this agency to impose civil penalties on violators of the law if, first, the person "made a negative declaration (oral or written) to the primary inspector," that is, lied about trying to bring in illegal plants, and, second, "if the primary declaration was negative, the person must have been given an opportunity to amend that declaration," that is, given a chance to tell the truth.[40]

Prior to the structural reform that created the CBP in Homeland Security, an officer from either INS or U.S. Customs (USC) obtained the initial declaration. If that officer was suspicious, the person would be sent to a second inspector, an agriculture officer, for a more thorough review. If appropriate, the second officer would administer the second criterion, asking for an amended declaration. A civil penalty could be imposed on someone trying to smuggle illegal plants into the country only if both officers, in sequence, did their jobs.

With the creation of DHS, terrorism deterrence became the chief mission of border protection. The primary inspector from INS or USC now asks a person "in general terms" what he or she is bringing into the country; if the response raises suspicion, the primary inspector may pursue the second criterion and may search the vehicle, instead of automatically bringing in an agricultural officer. Because primary inspectors now have discretion over whether to refer someone to a secondary inspector, some vehicles are released without further referral to an agricultural officer. The result, according to one agricultural inspection officer, is that protecting agriculture has a lower priority than it did before the structural reorganization of DHS, and smugglers know this.[41] This example points to the influence of structural arrangements on discretion and the locus of control, the importance of discretion, the potential disconnect between the interests of street-level bureaucrats and their hierarchical superiors, and the challenges of managing in organizations that include street-level bureaucrat positions.

Street-level bureaucrats' judgments are indispensable to quality service and to individualized justice that can reflect the unique aspects of each situation or individual. Human services clients expect that the workers serving them have discretion and the power to address their particular problems. The values, motives, and incentives facing frontline workers are likely to shape their judgments. One implication is that street-level bureaucrats who work for private sector organizations (for-profit or nonprofit)—a growing trend in social services—may exercise judgment in ways fundamentally different from employees of public organizations.[42] Managing in organizations involving street-level bureaucrats, no matter which sector employs them, is likely to involve structure as well as aspects of organizational culture and craft, discussed in chapters 6 and 7.

Management Capacity

As mentioned above, positions in an organization can be classified as either line or staff positions—that is, as positions that are directly involved in delivering the program or services of an organization or positions that provide administrative support for those activities. Public administration scholars Patricia W. Ingraham and Amy Kneedler Donahue focus on the importance of having adequate resources and capacity for staff positions, arguing that these "[administrative functions] support all of the other managerial work of government more directly related to running programs."[43] They argue that assuring such administrative or **management capacity** is a necessary condition for managing and achieving effective policy implementation. Four core management systems make up this administrative capacity: financial management, human resources management, information technology management, and capital management.[44]

Yet, having capacity in place in each of these four areas is not in itself sufficient to ensure high performance. In addition, the decisions managers make about the deployment of these resources are consequential. Effective utilization of the four core management systems depends in turn on four "levers" to make them work: the character of a government's management systems; the level and nature of leadership emphasis; the degree of integration and alignment across its management systems; and the extent to which it manages for results.[45]

These levers reflect the efforts of public managers to mobilize core management systems in behalf of good performance. Focusing on the staff positions represented in the core management systems, the framework emphasized that effective management depends not only on the existence of the positions, but also on their realization through the four levers. Elements of the core management systems interact with other structural features of the levers (the character of the systems, the degree of integration/alignment, and a managing-for-results emphasis), as well as with craft aspects (leadership emphasis). In this view, managing the structures of organizations has direct consequences for the capacity for effective management. As will be discussed in chapter 8, the Government Performance Project has used this management capacity framework to rate the efforts of states and localities, assessing their capacity for program implementation.[46]

The ideas discussed in this section provide insight into the managerial implications associated with constraining structures of job positions, tasks, and reporting relationships. The next section turns to budgets—another significant constraining structure.

Budgets

By allotting financial resources to programs, projects, initiatives, and functions, **budgets** are constraining structures that convey priorities of budget makers in the form of resource constraints and rules for their use. In the words of Aaron Wildavsky, a budget is "a series of goals with price tags attached." [47]

Information on the processes, politics, and history of budgeting at federal, state, and local levels is vast. Many excellent resources provide rich detail on these topics, including preparation of executive budgets, legislative authorization and appropriation procedures, budget execution, and financial and performance audits.[48] The goal of this section is to stress that although budgets are constraining structures for public managers, the characteristics of many budget processes mean that budgets can also be enabling structures. Managers may be able to help define and shape their budgets and, in turn, their programmatic priorities.

The question of whether public managers have control over their budgets and, if so, what their interests and preferences are, is raised in the theories of William A. Niskanen Jr. and Patrick Dunleavy. Employing a rational choice perspective, Niskanen argues that self-interested public agency officials want to increase their own power and prestige.[49] The path to greater power, Niskanen argues, is through larger budgets. The model of the "budget-maximizing bureaucrat" is the primary rational choice view of public managers, consistent with stereotypes of self-serving, inefficient bureaucrats whose budgets are always inadequate for good performance. From a structural perspective, the model's implication is that policymakers and public managers influence a primary structure under which governments and their agents operate: their budgets.[50]

In contrast to Niskanen's monolithic view, Dunleavy has developed a model of the "bureau-shaping" bureaucrat.[51] Dunleavy argues that public officials do not have a uniform interest in maximizing their budgets. Because of the collective action problems that exist within agencies, if the costs to an individual official of effort to secure a larger budget, which will be enjoyed by the agency as a whole, are greater than the expected value of that larger budget to the official, then the official has an incentive to free ride on the efforts of other officials, letting them work for budget increases. Individual officials will expend effort only when the expected benefit accruing to them personally exceeds the cost of their effort; they will pursue goals that have a net payoff greater than the payoff from doing something else. Dunleavy points out that the results of such calculations are likely to vary depending on an official's hierarchical rank in the organization and the type of agency in which the official works, which is discussed in chapter 1.

Dunleavy argues that rather than seeking larger budgets, senior officials are more likely to pursue work-related benefits that preserve or enhance their standing or future opportunities: They want satisfying work, a congenial work environment, and a balance of intrinsic (personal) and extrinsic (economic) rewards that include status, prestige, patronage, and influence. The consequence is that "[r]ational officials want to work in small, elite, collegial bureaus close to political power centers. They do not want to head up heavily staffed, large budget but routine, conflictual, and low-status agencies." [52] The implication of Dunleavy's model for public managers is that they are drawn to bureau-shaping strategies that include structural aspects such as major internal reorganizations, transformation of internal work practices, competition with other bureaus, contracting out (provision by government but production by the private sector or other governmental entities, discussed later in this chapter), and load-shedding (encouraging provision and production by the private sector).

Discussing the popular proposition that public managers uniformly seek to maximize their budgets, Laurence E. Lynn Jr. argues that their motives are more complex. What managers want more than larger budgets is control over discretionary resources within a given budget.[53] But, he continues,

> few bureaucrats—whether career officials or appointed executives—believe that appropriations are adequate to produce the levels of output that are mandated by authorizing statutes or that are required if the bureau is to fulfill its mission. Most bureaucrats [especially those in what Dunleavy calls "delivery agencies"] regularly seek to demonstrate to sponsors the existence of unmet needs, deficiencies in the quality of output, inadequate enforcement, insufficient outreach, and the like.[54]

In state and local agencies, in contrast, "it is not unusual for officials to seek reputations for maintaining control over spending, eliminating waste, fraud, and abuse from budgets and for achieving gains in efficiency that save money." [55]

This section highlights the motives and opportunities public managers might have to influence the fiscal situation of their organizations, which constitutes a prominent constraining structure. In addition to fiscal capital, human capital and resources may also be shaped by constraining structures.

Personnel Policies

A third major constraining structure is the **personnel policies** governing how to hire, compensate, reward, train, promote, discipline, or terminate employees in public organizations.[56] First instituted in the United States in the late 1800s, the federal civil service system—whose statutory basis is in Title 5 of the U.S. Code—was designed to reward merit, not political loyalty, and therefore to protect employees from reprisals or arbitrary decisions by political officials. Additional sources of such protections are the provisions of standard labor contracts negotiated through collective bargaining with public employee unions.

The federal civil service system and the personnel systems of other governments (states, cities, counties, school districts), are, as Patricia Ingraham notes, "often built upon both legal and bureaucratic rules and processes, [and] they are rather Byzantine structures and systems, involving many pages of rules and regulations, multiple processes for consultation and appeal (for employees), and substantial separation from political and other external authority." [57] Personnel systems, together with the provisions of collective bargaining agreements, have been largely defined by their structural features rather than by their role in supporting government performance, and a standard complaint of public managers is that these systems prevent them from managing effectively.

In recent years, as pressures for greater government efficiency and performance have mounted, the management of people has been more commonly referred to as "human resource management" or "human capital management." These terms reflect a shift in emphasis from a primarily rule-based approach of managing employees to an approach that "lets managers manage" and therefore requires the kind of three-dimensional management that is discussed in chapter 10. Reforms to personnel systems have introduced flexibility, managerial discretion, decentralization of authority over personnel matters, and performance-based pay.[58]

Performance-based pay reforms encompass "a broad spectrum of compensation systems that can be clustered under two general categories: merit pay plans and variable pay plans, which include both individual and group incentive plans." [59] These systems are based on the idea that monetary incentives prompt greater employee effort and higher performance and productivity. The effectiveness of these systems has been a matter of debate. Proponents argue that such systems are an improvement on tenure-based pay systems because they provide employees with explicit and meaningful incentives and feedback and ultimately improve organizational performance.[60] Yet pay for performance may be effective only when certain conditions are met relating to the structure of work, the culture of the organization, and the nature of the external environment.[61] When the work task is well defined and its successful performance is observable and easily measured, and when employee motives are driven by absolute levels of income, not relative to others in the organization, pay for performance may be effective.

To avoid the structural constraints imposed by personnel systems, public policymakers and managers have turned to the contracting out of public service delivery and of planning and management functions (discussed further below) and to reliance on part-time workers and "independent contractors," who are not governed by the full panoply of personnel rules or eligible for a full range of benefits.

By eroding the significance of the protection principle, all such measures pose a threat to public employees' morale and their commitment to the values of public service (see chapters 6 and 9). What is gained in managerial flexibility may, therefore, come at the cost of lower employee quality and dedication to agency missions. Opposing these trends are not only many public employees and their unions but also legislators who represent these employees and who tend to favor employee rights and protections and the continued necessity of rules constraining managerial discretion.

CONCEPTS IN ACTION

Merit Pay in Public Schools

Linking the pay of public school teachers to the performance of their students has often encountered opposition from teachers' unions. Yet such pay-for-performance proposals continue to surface, such as the reauthorization of the federal No Child Left Behind Act, in John Edwards's 2008 presidential campaign platform, and in local initiatives.

For years, the unionized teaching profession opposed few ideas more vehemently than merit pay, but those objections appear to be eroding as school districts in dozens of states experiment with plans that compensate teachers partly based on classroom performance.

Here in Minneapolis, for instance, the teachers' union is cooperating with Minnesota's Republican governor on a plan in which teachers in some schools work with mentors to improve their instruction and get bonuses for raising student achievement.

. . . A consensus is building across the political spectrum that rewarding teachers with bonuses or raises for improving student achievement, working in lower income schools or teaching subjects that are hard to staff can energize veteran teachers and attract bright rookies to the profession.

. . . Merit pay, or compensating teachers for classroom performance rather than their years on the job and coursework completed, found some support in the 1980s among policy makers and school administrators, who saw it as a way to encourage good teachers to work harder and to weed out the bad ones. But teachers saw it as a gimmick used by principals to reward cronies based on favoritism.

How thoroughly unions will embrace merit pay remains unclear, said Chester E. Finn Jr., an education scholar who served in the Reagan administration. In some cities where unions have agreed to participate in merit pay programs, they have consented only after reshaping the programs so thoroughly that student achievement is one of many factors by which teachers are judged, reducing the programs' effectiveness, Mr. Finn said.

The rewards teachers receive for outstanding performance range from a few hundred dollars to $10,000 or more in a few districts. . . .

The positions of the two national teachers' unions diverge on merit pay. The National Education Association, the larger of the two, has adopted a resolution that labels merit pay, or any other pay system based on an evaluation of teachers' performance, as "inappropriate."

The American Federation of Teachers says it opposes plans that allow administrators alone to decide which teachers get extra money or that pay individual teachers based solely on how students perform on standardized test scores, which they consider unreliable. But it encourages efforts to raise teaching quality and has endorsed arrangements that reward teams of teachers whose students show outstanding achievement growth.

Source: Sam Dillon, "Long Reviled, Merit Pay Gains Among Teachers," *New York Times,* June 18, 2007.

Contracts

Contracts are a fourth major type of constraining structure. A **contracts** is a compact or agreement between actors with mutual interests that "encourage the sort of actions each is to take, any payments that might flow from one to another, the rules and procedures they will use to decide matters in the future, and the behavior that each might expect from the others." [62] A successful contract is one that ensures full reciprocity between the contracting parties in the sense that each receives exactly what it expects to receive.

Contracts may be classified as either complete or incomplete. A **complete contract** covers all conceivable circumstances of interest to both parties, spelling out every relevant situation and resulting action that the implementer is to take. An **incomplete contract** does not (usually because it cannot) anticipate all conceivable circumstances that might arise. A solution to this problem is the relational contract. It frames a relationship without formalizing all aspects of it, perhaps supplemented by implicit contracts, which express shared expectations and depend for their reliable execution on an element of trust.

All of government involves contracts in the sense that such agreements (formal or informal, explicit or implicit) exist at many levels, involving interorganizational and intraorganizational relationships. They exist between citizens and elected officials, between elected officials and appointed officials and agency permanent staff, between managers and frontline workers in public organizations; and between public organizations and contractors in the public or private sectors. In each of these relationships, the "contractor" is "under contract" to meet the expectations of a superior.

This chapter next reviews theories and frameworks for analyzing and designing contracts: these include the principal-agent model and transaction cost theory. Next, because of its heavy use, the process of contracting out is discussed in some detail, including decisions of whether and what to contract out (the "make or buy decision") as well as contract design and management.

The Principal-Agent Model

Within the types of contractual relationships described above, **principal-agent relationships** exist.[63] The basic characteristics of principal-agent relationships can be described as follows: A hierarchical superior (the principal) aims to achieve a particular output or outcome but must rely on another party (the agent) for implementation. Both principal and agent are assumed to be rational and inclined to act in ways consistent with their own best interests.

The relationship is further characterized by at least two types of information asymmetry, or differences in information between the two parties. The first type, **adverse selection,** refers to the differences in preferences, beliefs, or knowledge on the part of principal and agent that are present *ex ante* or prior to entering into the contract agreement. The second type, **moral hazard,** refers to the actions the agent takes *ex post,* after entering into the contract agreement.[64] Therefore, the principal and agent potentially have different levels of knowledge about preferences, actions, and outcomes of the agent. The principal's goal is to design a contract with incentives that induce the agent to pursue the principal's objectives in the presence of these information asymmetries, that is, to design a contract involving incentives and monitoring that "in mitigating the informational asymmetries and structuring rewards, prompts the agent to behave as the principal himself would under whatever conditions might prevail." [65] Terry Moe emphasizes the central importance of moral hazard and adverse selection in any situation involving hierarchy or contracts:

> As theoretical concepts, they are particularly valuable for understanding situations in which one party seeks to control the behavior of another, or, more generally, to achieve certain outcomes . . . by relying on structuring the behavior of various other actors. These, of course, are the essence of organizational analysis, whether the substance has to do with decentralization, division of labor, formal rules, structure, communication, or ownership vs. control: all are reflections of efforts to control the productive efforts of organization members—and all, because of information asymmetries, are shaped by moral hazard and adverse selection.[66]

The potential severity of problems between principal and agent is a directly related to the degree of information asymmetry. Because they have relatively high levels of discretion and autonomy from organizational authority (increasing the risk of moral hazard), and because their interests and preferences differ from those of managers (adverse selection), street-level bureaucrats often represent conspicuous examples of the principal-agent problem. The efforts of social workers and police officers, for example, are difficult for managers to observe and evaluate, and these working professionals may have different values than their managers.

Regardless of the specific setting, principal-agent problems exist because the principal and agent cannot fully describe and agree in advance on the actions to be taken in every conceivable situation. Although structures such as rules, agreements, regulations, or contracts may be defined and imposed *ex ante* to control the behavior of agents, it simply is not possible to know the preferences of the agent or to conceive of every problematic situation that might arise on which agreement in advance would be helpful. *Ex ante* agreements also do not ensure full compliance because of the moral hazard problem; even with a specification covering a particular contingency, the principal may not be able to tell whether the agent abides by its terms: Did the social worker really make every effort desired by management to encourage a client to find work? As chapter 8 discusses, performance measurement and management attempt to reduce information asymmetries between principals and agents and to lessen the severity of principal-agent problems. Yet the managerial challenge in these relationships of aligning interests remains. Ideally, it will be in the agent's interest to pursue the outcomes that the principal desires and to make the desired level of effort, with as few structural constraints as possible. The cultural and craft aspects of management may be effective in aligning interests and ensuring compliance in principal-agent relationships.

Ashcroft's proposed restrictions on plea bargaining illustrate the principal-agent relationships of that administrative technology. Ashcroft (the principal) aimed to control the actions of line prosecutors (the agents) by restricting their discretion in negotiating plea bargains to ensure what the Justice Department saw as consistent treatment for the same types of offenses. Yet line prosecutors' interests are not aligned with those of senior officials in the Justice Department. Because of the information asymmetries between them, monitoring the policy is extremely difficult. A mandate such as Ashcroft's, even one accompanied by training, on-site visits, and threats of negative evaluations, cannot fully align the interests of prosecutors and the central office or entirely overcome the information asymmetries.

Extensions to the basic principal-agent problem provide further useful frames of reference for managerial analysis. One type of extension is the moral hazard problem that arises when an agent is involved in multiple activities or tasks and faces the decision of how to divide work effort among them. A caseworker in a welfare-to-work office may be responsible for client intake and assessment, for assigning clients to education or work activities, for monitoring clients in these activities, for developing job contacts, and for other activities. Agents have incentives to devote more effort to tasks that are measurable and that supervisors can observe more easily and to devote less effort to tasks that are unmeasured or unobserved. Managers may find it easier to assess the number of job contacts that a caseworker has developed but more difficult to assess the caseworker's success in client intake.[67] In this situation, the caseworker has greater incentive to devote effort to the former task than to the latter. Economists Bengt Holmstrom and Paul Milgrom point out that in **multitask situations,**

> incentives for tasks can be provided in two ways: either the task itself can be rewarded or the marginal opportunity cost for the task can be lowered by removing or reducing the incentives on competing tasks. Constraints are substitutes for performance incentives and are extensively used when it is hard to assess the performance of the agent.[68]

The implication for managers who can affect how jobs are designed—that is, what tasks are included in a particular position—is that tasks that are relatively easier to observe and measure should be assigned to different jobs than those tasks that are more difficult to measure. In this way, constraints—structures through job position definition—may be effective for directing the work of agents in those jobs toward managerial or organizational goals, even when performance is not formally measured. Another model implication that can be useful for managers is that "the desirability of providing incentives for any one activity decreases with the difficulty of measuring performance in any other activities that make competing demands on the agent's time and attention." [69] Stated differently, if an agent's work requires many different tasks but performance on some is much more easily measured than on others, then it is not advisable to provide strong incentives for those more easily measured tasks. Doing so likely means that the agent's efforts on the remaining difficult-to-measure tasks will be diminished.

A second type of extension to the basic principal-agent framework is the **common agency** model, which may involve both moral hazard and adverse selection.[70] Here, an agent has multiple principals, each of whom offers specific incentives for the agent to align with the principals' interests. In theory, this situation can lead to an efficient aggregation of the principals' varying interests, with important implications for public management. If the principals are, for example, organized interest groups, they can offer valuable political support to the agent—perhaps an executive agency—by lobbying legislators for higher appropriations or providing favorable publicity for agency programs and activities. As the bureau-shaping discussion above suggests, the agent may have interests of its own that differ from those of the principals. In such circumstances, public managers become engaged in balancing competing internal and external interests to achieve a result that no one has an incentive to overturn. The general result is that policy change tends to be incremental, the process itself serving as a constraint on bold departures from the status quo.[71]

Transaction Costs

The **transaction costs** associated with exchanges and interactions between actors are another concept that managers can use to analyze contractual relationships.[72] Transaction cost theory has been used to examine the making of economic policy, antitrust rules, local governments' decisions on whether to contract out the production or provision of goods or services to other public or private sector entities, and the relative efficiency of private versus public sector provision of mental health services.[73] The general point is that it may be cheaper and easier to organize transactions one way rather than another.

With the transaction as the unit of analysis, transaction cost theory holds that in any exchange, costs—of money, time, or opportunity—are incurred to gain information, bargain, monitor, and enforce agreements between actors. An analysis based on transaction cost theory focuses on three main characteristics of the transaction: its frequency (how often the transaction take place), uncertainty (the predictability of the production process and other factors affecting either party to the transaction over the time period of the transaction), and **asset specificity** (the degree to which assets, both physical and human, are uniquely suited to a particular transaction and cannot be easily converted to other uses). Asset specificity is important because specialized investments may be difficult to convert to other needs. Investing in a specialized facility may create a dependency on continued support because that facility can perform no other kind of work.

Transaction cost analysis uses information about transactions' frequency, uncertainty, and asset specificity to identify structures—typically, markets or hierarchies—that are consistent with achieving the lowest transaction costs. Transactions that are infrequent, have low uncertainty, and have low asset specificity tend to incur lower transaction costs and are best conducted through markets, while transactions that are frequent, uncertain, and have high asset specificity tend to be more costly, and these costs might be minimized by conducting the transaction "in-house," rather than in the market.

The acquisition of standard office computers for a particular government office would tend to have low transaction costs because their purchase occurs relatively rarely, the technology or the time needed to produce and deliver them is fairly predictable, and neither the computers nor the resources used to produce them are uniquely suited for that particular transaction or ultimate office destination. Therefore, the preferred way to provide computers for an office would be through the market. In contrast, the design of a complex new weapon system to meet specialized military requirements, because it is a one-time undertaking that is fraught with uncertainty and requires unique capabilities, might be better done by an in-house research and development organization rather than by a contractor.

Both the principal-agent model and transaction cost theory can be useful in analyzing what kinds of structural arrangements might be most appropriate to accomplishing the work of an organization. Many such structures may be imposed by policymakers, but public managers, especially at senior levels, generally have the latitude to make at least some of these choices, especially those involving contracting out, the subject of the next section.

Contracting Out

What functions will government serve, what services will it provide, what will it pay for? A decision to turn over a function or activity to a lower level of government is known as devolution or decentralization. The opposite phenomenon, assuming a responsibility formerly exercised by lower levels of government, is centralization. A decision to turn an existing function or activity over to the private sector—that is, to get out of a particular "business" or mission, is termed **privatization.** If government provides funding for, but does not produce a good or service (perhaps as a result of a transaction cost analysis), the resulting use of a third-party for the production is termed **contracting out.**[74]

In some instances, mandates to contract out may be given by authorities external to the organization, such as laws, regulation, or other guidance from policymakers. In other instances, the decision to contract out lies with an individual manager within the organization. Whether a public manager is making the decision to contract out in the first place or specifying terms for a contract, understanding the benefits and trade-offs of the make-or-buy decision in particular circumstances can help a manager think analytically about the problems and potential solutions at hand.

Governments may contract out the production of goods or services through arrangements with private sector entities, either for-profit or not-for-profit. Government contracts with private parties date back to the nineteenth century and have been relied on intermittently ever since. In the late nineteenth century a sophisticated awareness of the issues affecting public use of private charity had developed in the social work profession.[75] State and local governments "subsidized" service provision by private organizations.

Relationships between public and private sectors grew as government increased in size and in the reach of its responsibilities. Contracting out in social services began in earnest during the Kennedy and Johnson presidencies, in which there was not only a great expansion in the range of government supports for social services but also a strong emphasis on partnerships and cooperation with the private sector, especially the nonprofit sector. (See chapter 9 for further discussion of the movement toward third-party government.) The trend toward financing privately provided services was given further impetus by the deinstitutionalization of state hospitals, state training schools, and public juvenile detention centers in favor of community-based counseling, training, and residential services.

The process of contracting out involves deciding whether and what goods or services to keep in-house and which should be contracted out. If contracting out is decided upon, the terms of the contract must be determined or negotiated, managed, and the contractor's performance must be monitored.

The first step in the process—deciding whether to keep production in-house or to contract it out—is referred to as the **make or buy decision.** At least four separate but related frameworks provide insight into the make or buy decision for public managers: the transaction costs in the relationship, whether the activity is "inherently governmental," the presence or absence of market failures, and the extent and consequences of incomplete contracts.

Transaction costs are one framework for considering the make or buy decision. Trevor L. Brown and Matthew Potoski draw on transaction cost theory (as well as on institutional theory) to specify hypotheses regarding local governments' decisions to make or buy more than sixty types of services, such as data processing, treatment for drug and alcohol dependence, running correctional facilities, and sewage collection and treatment.[76] They hypothesize that governments will produce a service in-house if it is characterized by high asset specificity (though high fixed costs may lead to contracting out for services that are highly asset specific). Producing in-house would protect the government from exploitation by opportunistic monopoly providers. Another hypothesis suggests that competitive markets for services lead to lower transaction costs and lower inefficiencies because of the information about quality, quantity, and price revealed through the bidding process. When markets for services are competitive, governments tend to contract out more.

Drawing on principal-agent theory as well, Brown and Potoski hypothesize that when governments do contract out services that are highly asset specific, whose outcomes are difficult to measure, or that exist in noncompetitive markets, they will more likely contract with other governments or use joint contracting. As they explain joint contracting, a government "contracts with an external vendor while retaining a portion of the service production in-house or contracts simultaneously with several vendors for the same service." [77] Using data from the International City/County Management Association, the researchers find support for each of these hypotheses.

Competitive markets—the availability of several potential suppliers who compete on the basis of price as well as quality—are often essential to successful contracting relationships. When competition is absent, public and private sector entities may become dependent on each other, and government becomes vulnerable to manipulation and exploitation by the monopolist contractor. The supply of body armor for troops in Iraq is one case in which a limited number of suppliers caused difficulties. The Pentagon was widely criticized for failing to provide adequate body armor to the troops in Iraq. A design challenge was to keep the armor as light as possible, but the private contractors who were producing vests with innovative new materials were part of "a cottage industry of small armor makers with limited production capacity. In addition, each company must independently come up with its own design for the plates, which then undergo military testing." [78] Because the military services are often unable to secure the rights to use the designs from these small contractors, successful designs cannot be contracted out to other manufacturers. This example shows how the lack of competition hindered the large-scale production of this needed equipment and the exposure of the military for relying on a few small-scale suppliers.

A second framework for considering the make or buy decision for public organizations is whether the good, service, or activity in question is **inherently governmental.** Circular A-76, issued by the Office of Management and Budget (OMB), provides guidance to federal agencies regarding contracting out and defines inherently governmental activities. The OMB requires each agency to make lists available to the public of inherently governmental activities as well as commercial activities.[79]

Although Circular A-76 provides guidance on the definition of inherently governmental activities, determination of such activities remains subjective and fluid. In December 2000 President Clinton signed Executive Order 13180, the preamble of which parenthetically referred to the provision of air traffic services as "an inherently governmental function." [80] Less than two years later, in June 2002, President Bush signed Executive Order 13264, which amended that language by stating, " 'The first sentence of [Executive Order 13180] is amended by deleting "an inherently governmental function.' " [81] A commentary from the Reason Foundation, a libertarian think tank, argued:

> Most aviation experts agree that [air traffic control] is a high-tech service business, which can be provided either by government or by commercial entities—always operating under stringent governmental safety regulation. It's the safety regulation that most would agree is inherently governmental. . . . One of the reasons President Bush issued his June order was to protect the legal status of the FAA's long-standing program of contracting out the operation of over 200 control towers at smaller airports.[82]

Specification of the inherently governmental nature in this example changed over time and affected whether services would actually be contracted out.

Circular A-76 provides some guidance regarding the make-or-buy decision, but it does not, as public administration law scholars David H. Rosenbloom and Suzanne J. Piotrowski point out, provide similar guidance or requirements for private sector contractors to adhere to constitutional or administrative law norms. In fact, they write, "Public officials and administrators have largely ceded the process of outsourcing constitutional and administrative law norms to the federal and state judiciaries." [83]

Market failures are a third framework for considering the make-or-buy decision for public organizations. As discussed in chapter 1, market failures result when a free market produces inefficient resource allocations. The main concepts include externalities, distributional concerns, and information problems. The presence or absence of these problems for a particular good or service indicates different types of optimal involvement by the public sector. When a particular good or service such as garbage collection exhibits no externalities, no agency problems, no distributional concerns, and output quality that is observable, the optimal arrangement is for the private sector to both own and manage it (with regulation from the government). At the opposite end of the spectrum, for a good or service, such as foster care for children, that is characterized by the presence of externalities, distributional concerns, agency problems, and unobservable quality, the optimal decision is likely, though not necessarily, to be for the public sector to own and manage it

RULE OF LAW

Inherently Governmental Activities

The Office of Management and Budget issues Circular A-76, which provides guidance for the make or buy decision by describing characteristics of inherently governmental activities. Following is an excerpt from this circular.

B. CATEGORIZING ACTIVITIES PERFORMED BY GOVERNMENT PERSONNEL AS INHERENTLY GOVERNMENTAL OR COMMERCIAL.

1. Inherently Governmental Activities. The CSO [competitive sourcing official] shall justify, in writing, any designation of government personnel performing inherently governmental activities. The justification shall be made available to OMB and the public upon request. An agency shall base inherently governmental justifications on the following criteria:

a. An inherently governmental activity is an activity that is so intimately related to the public interest as to mandate performance by government personnel. These activities require the exercise of substantial discretion in applying government authority and/or in making decisions for the government. Inherently governmental activities normally fall into two categories: the exercise of sovereign government authority or the establishment of procedures and processes related to the oversight of monetary transactions or entitlements. An inherently governmental activity involves:

(1) Binding the United States to take or not to take some action by contract, policy, regulation, authorization, order, or otherwise;

(2) Determining, protecting, and advancing economic, political, territorial, property, or other interests by military or diplomatic action, civil or criminal judicial proceedings, contract management, or otherwise;

(3) Significantly affecting the life, liberty, or property of private persons; or

(4) Exerting ultimate control over the acquisition, use, or disposition of United States property (real or personal, tangible or intangible), including establishing policies or procedures for the collection, control, or disbursement of appropriated and other federal funds.

b. While inherently governmental activities require the exercise of substantial discretion, not every exercise of discretion is evidence that an activity is inherently governmental. Rather, the use of discretion shall be deemed inherently governmental if it commits the government to a course of action when two or more alternative courses of action exist and decision making is not already limited or guided by existing policies, procedures, directions, orders, and other guidance that (1) identify specified ranges of acceptable decisions or conduct and (2) subject the discretionary authority to final approval or regular oversight by agency officials.

Source: Executive Office of the President, Office of Management and Budget, "Circular No. A-76 (Revised)," A-2–A-3, May 29, 2003, http://www.whitehouse.gov/omb/circulars/a076/a76_rev2003.pdf.

and not contract it out. Different combinations of market failures imply different optimal arrangements for ownership and management, summarized by economist Rebecca M. Blank and shown in Table 5.2.

Finally, a fourth framework for considering the make or buy decision, which is based in incomplete contracts, focuses on quality issues. Economists Oliver S. D. Hart, Andrei Shleifer, and Robert W. Vishny focus on a private sector supplier's incentives to implement cost-reducing or quality-enhancing innovations that were not addressed in the initial contract between government and the supplier.[84] Because these innovations were not foreseen or specified in the contract *ex ante*, this situation is an example of an incomplete contract.

Hart, Shleifer, and Vishny have developed a formal model to show the trade-offs of the make-or-buy decision. In their model, the government derives a benefit of observable but unverifiable quality from the produced good. The private sector producer will implement innovations during the contract period that will reduce its costs, but will wait until contract renegotiation to bargain over innovations that can increase quality because these kinds of innovations will raise the producer's costs during the contract term. Under these circumstances, results from the model indicate that costs are always lower when governments contract out instead of producing in-house, even though "the private contractor's incentive to engage in cost reduction is typically *too* strong since he ignores the adverse impact on quality." [85] The model further indicates that quality may be higher or lower in private production compared with in-house government production.

TABLE 5.2 Models of Public/Private Interaction by Type of Market Failure

	Externalities	Distributional Concerns	Agency Problems	Unobservable Output Quality
1. Private sector owns and manages, with regulation	Yes	No	No	No
2. Private sector owns and manages, with regulation and vouchers	Yes	Yes	No	No
3. Public sector owns/private sector manages	Yes	Yes	Yes	No
4. Public sector owns and manages	Yes	Yes	Yes	Yes

Source: Rebecca M. Blank, "When Can Public Policy Makers Rely on Private Markets? The Effective Provision of Social Services," *The Economic Journal* 110 (March 2000): table 1, C40.

After considering the implications of their model for different types of services, the authors conclude that

> the case for in-house provision is very strong in such services as the conduct of foreign policy and maintenance of police and armed forces, but can also be made reasonably persuasively for prisons. In contrast, the case for privatization is strong in such activities as garbage collection and weapons production, but can also be made reasonably persuasively for schools. In some other services, such as provision of health care, an analysis of the efficiency of alternative arrangements . . . requires a much more detailed model of competition, contracts, and regulation.[86]

Later in this chapter, an extension to the Hart, Shleifer, and Vishny model addresses the issue of health care, focusing on how a private sector producer that has nonprofit status may affect the make-or-buy decision in this area.

Quality problems have been observed in the Medicare program, for example, which outsources many of its enforcement activities to private contractors who often overlook or ignore quality issues. Medicare reimburses costs according to procedure, test, physician encounter, or length of stay, with virtually no consideration being given to the quality of care provided. An in-depth investigation of the Medicare program by the *Washington Post* found:

> a pervasive problem that costs the federal insurance program billions of dollars a year while rewarding doctors, hospitals and health plans for bad medicine. In Medicare's upside-down reimbursement system, hospitals and doctors who order unnecessary tests, provide poor care or even injure patients often receive higher payments than those who provide efficient, high-quality medicine.[87]

Public managers can use these four frameworks to analyze the benefits and trade-offs of either producing in-house or contracting out for different kinds of goods and services. Once a decision has been made to contract out—to "buy"—public managers must deal with further structural issues likely to arise within their scope of authority—oversight of the design, management, and implementation of the contract. As noted, contracts are characterized by principal-agent problems of information asymmetries and divergent interests between principals (the government) and agents (the contractor). Contract specifications may also be affected by the transaction cost characteristics of the relationships: Asset specificity, uncertainty, and frequency of interaction may all affect how contracts are specified and managed.[88]

Crucial to understanding the dynamics of contracting is exposure of either or both parties to the risk that their expectations will not be met due to factors that are beyond their control. If expectations are not met, then the question of compensation arises: Who bears the costs of disappointed expectations? Contracting parties typically do not want to bear any costly risks; they are risk averse. If risks are inherent in the situation simply because it is impossible to spell out in advance all possible contingencies, then a contracting party will make every effort to shift the risk onto the other party, minimizing its own exposure.

With a **cost-plus-fixed-fee contract,** in which the contractor agent receives reimbursement for all costs plus a fee or profit, the contractor assumes none of the risks. If risks are quantifiable, then it may be possible to take out insurance against them because their costs can be accurately estimated. A seller of a product may offer such insurance in the form of a service agreement or a warranty so that the buyer bears no costly risk. Or the buyer may purchase insurance against risks that are beyond either party's control.

The issue of risk underlies contracting for outputs or outcomes, where concern focuses on measurability as well as on risk sharing. For activities such as issuing drivers' licenses, contracting for outputs or for outcomes may be identical. For activities such as welfare-to-work casework, however, the issues involved with contracting for outputs or outcomes may diverge considerably. It may be difficult to attribute an improvement in recipients' ultimate well-being to a program output (such as number of hours of job training completed). Causal relationships between program and outcome are difficult to establish because many other personal, organizational, and environmental factors might have led to the outcome. Agents therefore prefer to contract for outputs rather than for outcomes, because outputs are more predictable and in the agent's control. If agents must contract for outcomes, they want to minimize their exposure to risk if outcomes do not occur because of factors beyond their control.

Consider a policy whose goal is to achieve favorable outcomes for a particular clientele such as the profoundly disabled. The policy goal of improved functioning can be considered an outcome. In one scenario, a **fee-for-service contract** might establish a fee schedule for contractor-produced outputs thought to be related to a favorable outcome. Yet from the contractor's or agent's point of view, the best arrangement is a cost-plus contract that reimburses whatever costs are incurred in producing the outputs, and the contractor is paid whether or not any useful outputs or outcomes are produced. In this arrangement, the contractor bears no risk if outputs or outcomes are not achieved; all risks are borne by the principal (the government) if the program does not work as intended or hoped.

In another scenario, a performance contract might establish a fee schedule for contractor-produced outcomes. The fee might be a flat rate based on a calculated average cost of achieving these kinds of outcomes or a rate that represents what the government is willing to pay or thinks the outcome is worth. Because the contractor is not paid more if costs exceed the agreed-upon rate, and is not paid at all if outcomes are not achieved, regardless how much time, effort, and money the contractor spent trying to produce the outcome, the contractor bears full risk while the government bears no risk at all, except criticism for choosing a method of implementation that produces no results.

CONCEPTS IN ACTION

Cost-Plus-Fixed-Fee Contracts and Excessive Spending

At a Senate Defense Appropriations Subcommittee hearing on contracting abuses in Iraq and Afghanistan, specific mention was made of abuses arising from a cost-plus-fixed-fee contract in which the contractor had no incentive to control costs.

Sen. Byron Dorgan, D-N.D. . . . cit[ed] a specific case of apparent excessive spending and an incident of contractor performance that could have endangered the health of U.S. personnel. Dorgan said a lower-level employee of KBR, which has received hundreds of billions of dollars in contracts for services in Iraq, told him that he had been ordered to put the company's logo on towels being furnished to troops, even though it could triple the cost. The unnamed employee said he was told the price did not matter because "it was a cost-plus contract," Dorgan said, waving a white towel embossed with a large KBR emblem.

Source: Otto Kreisher, "Appropriators Skewer Army over Contracting Abuse, Care," *CongressDailyPM,* February 27, 2008.

The types of relationships among government principals and private sector agents that have emerged through contract relationships have been characterized by public administration scholar Donald F. Kettl as falling into three categories.[89] First, convergence of interests has occurred in less-competitive markets with greater degrees of interdependence between buyer and seller (principal and agent). Examples include weapons manufacturers and many specialized human service providers. Second, the line between principal and agent has eroded, making it difficult to tell which actors are responsible or liable. An example is the civilian contractors engaged in intelligence activities at Abu Ghraib. Third, tightly coupled arrangements have arisen with a limited number of sellers or with asset specificity. Examples abound at NASA and became manifest in the two major shuttle accidents. Complementary to Kettl's analysis, one can also observe divergent interests, common in social services contracting, where the government seeks standardization while contractors—often nonprofit organizations—seek to preserve independence or uniqueness.

Kettl also argues that when serious market imperfections are present, government's authority becomes more important in overcoming agency problems, but exercising it becomes more problematic. He cites the *Challenger* accident, where the government exercised its authority and overrode its contractor, with disastrous consequences. Building from a principal-agent framework, Kettl describes a "smart buyer" framework for government that requires it to know what to buy, from whom to buy it, and what has been bought.

Phillip J. Cooper has argued that public sector contract administration is unique in that it is "at the intersection of the vertical, authority-based model of government action and the horizontal model designed to function on the basis of negotiation in business dealings." [90] It involves government contract administrators in the world of competitive politics, with all of its tendencies toward political rationality and technical irrationality, and the world of competitive markets, with all of the potential benefits and costs of the profit motive and technical rationality. He warns that contract administration may degenerate into operations resembling police patrols, featuring procedural audits instead of smart-buyer management. Instead, Cooper argues, public sector principals should foster relationships with contractors in order to deal with contracts' inherent incompleteness, although he is fully aware of the tensions associated with trying to do so.

Both Cooper and Steven J. Kelman emphasize the importance of assuring that governments build and maintain the human resource capacity to manage contracts.[91] Kelman argues that ensuring "strategic contracting management" capacity, which encompasses business strategy, source selection, and contract administration, is essential for public organizations. Contrasted with "a traditional view that regards contracting as a subsidiary administration function that rightly receives little attention from senior agency leadership," Kelman says, "strategic contracting management needs to become a central concern of senior agency political and career executives, like other organizational core competencies." [92]

The propensity for governments to contract out the production of goods and services has resulted in its own form of associated structures, referred to as "government by proxy," "third party government," and the "hollow state." [93] (These trends are discussed further in chapter 9.) H. Brinton Milward and Keith G. Provan describe the **hollow state** as:

> any joint production situation where a governmental agency relies on others (firms, nonprofits, or other government agencies) to jointly deliver public services. Carried to extreme, it refers to a government that as a matter of public policy has chosen to contract out all its production capability to third parties, perhaps retaining only a systems integration function that is responsible for negotiating, monitoring, and evaluating contracts. . . . [W]hile hollowness varies from case to case, the central task of the hollow state does not—that is to arrange networks rather than to carry out the traditional task of government, which is to manage hierarchies.[94]

CONCEPTS IN ACTION

Switching from Buying to Making

The excerpt below describes a decision by the U.S. Coast Guard to keep acquisition of a patrol boat in-house instead of continuing to contract out its acquisition, a switch from "buying" to "making." As noted, previous problems with management of the contract—"over-reliance on the service's commercial contractors"—and a more recent improvement of in-house capability for running the acquisition program were reasons for the return to in-house acquisition.

"I just signed a decision memorandum approving the termination of the current FRC-B acquisition with Integrated Coast Guard Systems, and we are reassigning that to the Coast Guard Office of Acquisition," Coast Guard Commandant Adm. Thad Allen told reporters at a press conference March 14.

The FRC-B is an alternative Fast Response Cutter that the Coast Guard needs to quickly replace its aging 110-foot patrol boats. The service intends to buy at least 12 FRC-Bs.

The decision marks the first major change in the Deepwater program, a 25-year, $24 billion effort to upgrade and replace many of the service's ships, aircraft and systems. Under a 2002 contract, Integrated Coast Guard Systems (ICGS), co-managed by Lockheed Martin and Northrop Grumman, previously has handled all Deepwater acquisition and development efforts.

But the Coast Guard has come under fire from Capitol Hill and government analysts for its management of the effort—the largest acquisition program ever for the 40,000-member service. One of the chief complaints has been the perception of over-reliance on the service's commercial contractors. . . .

[Rear Adm. Gary Blore, head of the Deepwater program] noted that the service is much more able to handle the acquisition than it was when the Deepwater contract was first awarded.

"When Deepwater started, it had 75 government personnel assigned to it," Blore said. "And we have upwards of 103 government personnel now and a good number of support contractors on the technical side. So the Coast Guard has become a lot more self-sufficient than it was at the start of the Deepwater program. I think we're ready to tackle this. I know we're ready to tackle this."

Blore added that the program strikes at the core of Coast Guard competency.

"We are the patrol-boat experts in the United States. We are the patrol-boat experts pretty much worldwide. We really understand this market. We've already researched what's out there."

Source: Patricia Kime and Christopher P. Cavas, "U.S. Coast Guard Takes Control of Patrol Boat Program: Ends Contract with Lockheed Martin, Northrop Grumman," defensenews.com, March 15, 2007, http://defensenews.com/story.php?F=2624965&C=navwar.

In an effort to determine the extent of the hollow state, Paul Light sought to measure the "true size of government" at the federal level, taking into account not only civil service, military, and postal service workers, but also the number of contractors and grantees.[95] Light provides an interesting quantitative picture of the American administrative system, finding that while the total number of federal civil servants declined by more than 45,000 between 1999 and 2002, the total number of contractors and grantees grew by more than 1 million.[96]

Milward and Provan identified a number of problems with the hollowing out of the state: loss of managerial control over agents, loss of political control to organized contractor interests, substitution of self-interest for the public interest in service delivery, weakened or confused accountability to citizens and legislatures, lower service quality, creation of organizations dependent on public funds, and goal displacement in nonprofit sector.[97]

Whatever one's view of the policy issue, third-party government has important implications for public management. As Richard Elmore has put it, "Managing indirect relations—on either end—requires an understanding of differences in incentive structures and modes of operation among different types of organizations and also of the mechanisms of influence other than direct controls. Indirect management requires a range of skills far wider than those necessary for more conventional superior-subordinate relationships." [98] Meeting the challenges of managing contracts may be (or perhaps can only be) met with structural solutions, although, as indicated, the craft and cultural dimensions may also be necessary for effective results.

Whether contracts are imposed on managers as constraining structures, or are available to managers through enabling structures, an appreciation of the structural dimension of public management necessarily must include understanding the incentives and various issues that arise with contracts. The hollow state, decentralized service delivery, and the multifaceted issues and actors involved in a particular public policy arena raise the need for structures that can coordinate service provision across a number of actors and providers. The definition and management of those structures are of increasing interest in public management and are examined in the next section.[99]

Networks

Network governance is a way of coordinating largely autonomous actors without either markets or hierarchies.[100] It includes arrangements that promote voluntary self-enforcement and cooperation even when self-interest might call for defection, noncooperation, or opportunism.[101] Laurence J. O'Toole Jr. has defined networks as "structures of interdependence, involving multiple organizations or parts thereof, where one unit is not merely the formal subordinate of the others in some hierarchical arrangement," where "[t]he institutional glue congealing networked ties may include authority bonds, exchange relations, and coalitions based on common interest, all within a single multiunit structure." [102]

CONCEPTS IN ACTION

Collaboration among Public and Private Organizations

The Family and Community Trust in Missouri is an example of a complex network of stakeholders and providers, created by the state's governor. The following description is from the trust's Web site.

In November 1993, Governor [Mel] Carnahan established the Family Investment Trust as a state-level entity. The name of the organization was changed to Family and Community Trust by executive order of Governor Bob Holden on April 2, 2001. The Family and Community Trust's charge is to provide leadership in collaboration with Caring Communities Community Partnerships to measurably improve the condition of Missouri's families, children, individuals, and communities; and to encourage collaboration among public and private community entities to build and strengthen comprehensive community-based support systems.

By developing community-based supports and services, the aim is to enhance the well-being of children, which is inseparable from the well-being of their families and the stability and economic viability of the communities where they live. . . .

THE FAMILY AND COMMUNITY TRUST

The Family and Community Trust was established through Executive Order. The board of directors is composed of the directors of the state agency partners and eight civic and business leaders. The board sets the macro-strategy for the system reform effort, builds leadership in state agencies and communities, measures progress, and keeps the focus on the vision. Family and Community Trust helps state agencies and communities through sustained technical support, conferences, trainings, and resource materials.

COMMUNITIES

Caring Communities Partnerships bring together stakeholders to shape priorities for children and families. In 1995, the state departments invited seven communities to partner with them to improve results for children and families. Four additional communities became Caring Communities Partnerships in 1996, three more in 1997, and four more in 1998. In June 1999, there are eighteen Caring Communities Partnerships with 103 Caring Communities sites across Missouri. Other communities, called Caring Communities Collaboratives, are preparing to become Caring Communities Partnerships. New Caring Communities Partnerships will establish additional Caring Communities sites.

On the neighborhood level, a Caring Communities site council is the broadly representative decision-making body. It partners with Caring Community Partnerships to plan, develop, finance, and monitor to achieve the Core Results. The Caring Communities council works in partnership with the Community Partnership which serves as the parent board and shares in the accountability for improved results.

STATE AGENCY PARTNERS

The departments of Corrections, Economic Development, Elementary and Secondary Education, Health, Labor and Industrial Relations, Mental Health, Public Safety and Social Services are partnering in the system reform initiative. They established a cross-agency structure to work together to measurably improve the condition of Missouri's families and their children, to establish greater collaboration among human service agencies, and to implement the broad-based systems reform initiative.

This structure includes the interagency groups of directors, deputy directors, Results Subgroup, Finance Subgroup, Capacity Building Subgroup, and Caring Communities coordinators.

Source: The Family and Community Trust, http://www.mofact.org.

Provan and Milward describe the idea of a network as structure in their study of a network of mental health service providers.[103] They argue that coordination among network actors is costly, both in terms of transaction costs and in terms of dependency on other organizations, which restricts flexibility, and that numerous conflicts among goals and notions of effectiveness are likely. Provan and Milward point to the importance of "network administrative organizations"—a structural feature—to govern coordination, goal selection, and the monitoring of efficiency and effectiveness. But the challenges to governance are intense because each action or decision may not be in the best interests of every party involved in the network—communities, organizations, clients/customers. Therefore, tradeoffs are needed, and if organizations see the tradeoffs as contrary to their interests, the network will fall apart or come to be dominated by the most powerful members.

Relying solely on informal coordination to organize network or collaborative members is unrealistic, leading to the idea that these arrangements themselves need to be actively managed. Such management may involve structural as well as cultural dimensions of public management. Ann Marie Thompson and James L. Perry point to five aspects of collaborative process: governance, administration, organizational autonomy, mutuality, and norms.[104] They argue that active management of these aspects of the collaboration is necessary for it to be effective, that is, to address the challenges involved in managing multiple network participants and coordinating service provision. Managing collaborations and designing governance mechanisms to ensure their success requires, among other things, attention to the motives behind each participant in the collaboration or network, the organizational structures and operating technologies of each participant in the network, the types of resource exchanges involved, and the degree of discretion for participants in each organization.[105]

Robert Agranoff and Michael McGuire seek to inform the practice of network management by examining the empirical literature and identifying areas in need of greater study, which they label "the big questions." The issues they raise include managerial functions and roles, trust, flexibility, accountability, and productivity. For example, they ask: "What are the critical functional equivalents to traditional management processes? Is there a[n] . . . equivalent set of tasks that replaces the standard planning, organizing, and so forth?" "How do networks provide flexibility beyond rapid adaptation or procedural accommodation?" [106]

This section has discussed a number of prominent constraining structures—positions and tasks, budgets, personnel policies, contracts, and networks—that may control managerial options or that public managers might use to control the actions of their agents. As emphasized, many other constraining structures exist. Those discussed here—along with theories, concepts, frameworks, and ideas that provide insight into analyzing their implications for public management—are general features of government and illustrate the importance of constraining structures in shaping managerial realities.

ORGANIZATIONAL FORM

Organizational form, or ownership, is a fundamental structural characteristic that may determine particular types of preferences, activities, or incentives; that is, whether an organization is public, private for-profit, or private nonprofit may be a predictor of its behavior and performance. Nonprofits are private sector organizations that are prohibited by law from distributing profits to any group of stakeholders (a characteristic feature of these organizations known as the nondistribution constraint). As discussed in chapter 1, public sector and private sector management share some similarities, but are also characterized by important differences.

This section first discusses quasi-public organizations, which have the characteristics of both public and private sector organizations, and, second, nonprofit organizations. Because organizational form can influence both the internal and external environments of managers who work in them, as well as managers in public sector organizations who interact with them, this section devotes considerable attention to the structural characteristic of the nonprofit organizational form.

Quangos and Government-Sponsored Enterprises

The quasi-autonomous nongovernmental organization, or **quango,** is a structural form that falls in the middle of the "publicness" spectrum, neither fully public nor fully private. This form is widespread in the United Kingdom and Australia, among other countries. Australia and Germany have relied on quangos regulated by government to control national and international air traffic; the United States also relies on quangos for air traffic control, but only at small airports.

Policymakers have specific reasons for preferring such organizations over direct government production of such services. Sandra Van Thiel describes these reasons in what she calls "practitioner theory." [107] In Van Thiel's view, policymakers say that organizational arrangements that seem more like corporations (because of their financial motives) and less like public bureaucracies are apt to be more efficient and effective, closer to their customers, more flexible, more responsive, and less entangled in red tape.

Special districts are one form of this type of organization widely used at state and local levels. As explained by Thomas H. Stanton and Ronald C. Moe, "literally thousands of government authorities and enterprises, especially in areas of transportation, power production, and finance" have been created, often as corporations. Stanton and Moe further point out that such organizations "are supposed to be financially self-sustaining from revenues that they derive from operations. Often state governments establish these organizations as a way to avoid state constitutional limitations on borrowing." [108]

In addition to government corporations, **government-sponsored enterprises** (GSEs) are examples of quangos. Government corporations at the federal level include the U.S. Postal Service, Amtrak, and the Tennessee Valley Authority. Examples of GSEs—privately owned corporations—include the Federal National Mortgage Association (Fannie Mae), the Federal Home Loan Mortgage Corporation (Freddie Mac), the Federal Home Loan Bank System, and the Student Loan Marketing Association (Sallie Mae). Congress created GSEs to reduce the costs of borrowing for certain types of purposes such as housing and education.

The question of the public assumption of the financial risk associated with loans made by GSEs, especially by Fannie and Freddie, has been of interest in recent years. Regulatory oversight of Fannie and Freddie has been the responsibility of the Department of Housing and Urban Development, specifically, the Office of Federal Housing Enterprise Oversight, an entity whose operating funds are provided by the two corporations it regulates. Following a series of accounting problems and reports questioning the extent to which these GSEs actually do reduce the costs of borrowing for homeowners, calls for regulatory reform of Fannie and Freddie increased. In September 2008 the Bush administration ousted the chief executive officers of Fannie and Freddie and placed the organizations under public conservatorship with management control by the Federal Housing Finance Agency, a new federal regulator. Treasury Secretary Henry Paulson Jr. attributed the need for the move "primarily to the inherent conflict and flawed business model embedded in the GSE structure, and to the ongoing housing correction." [109] The Bush administration instituted other measures to help shore up the institutions, but many of the details affecting the future of Fannie and Freddie were left to future administrations. Paulson highlighted the political, policy, and structural issues raised by the decisions that would be faced:

CONCEPTS IN ACTION

The Structure of Amtrak

Amtrak is a private for-profit corporation that receives considerable federal subsidies. The following excerpt from a Government Accountability Office (GAO) report on Amtrak's management and performance illustrates the structural features that define and shape how Amtrak operates and focuses on the structural initiatives by its president to improve performance.

Amtrak, although federally established and unable to operate without substantial federal subsidies to remain solvent, is not a government agency, but rather a private, for-profit corporation. . . . Its financial condition remains precarious, and, according to Amtrak's management, the corporation will require billions of dollars to improve infrastructure for operation of the nationwide intercity passenger rail service.

Amtrak's financial struggles have led to numerous changes in corporate direction and organizational structure. Amtrak has also been influenced by requirements in the Amtrak Reform and Accountability Act of 1997 that it become operationally self-sufficient by 2002—a goal Amtrak did not meet. In 2002, under the direction of a new president, Amtrak established a more centralized, functional organization; adopted a new approach to management; and stated its intent to focus on financial stability and achieving a "state of good repair." . . . As a centerpiece for these changes, Amtrak's president adopted a multipronged management approach that is based on the following five tools—all of which were designed to instill a sense of discipline to company operations:

- department goals that are to be a basis for Amtrak's budget;
- defined organization charts that identify a clear chain of command and are to be used to control labor costs;
- a capital program of specific projects and production targets needed to stabilize the railroad;
- a zero-based operating budget with a focus on maintaining or reducing the budget; and
- monthly performance reports, which are to be Amtrak's primary tool for reporting on company performance results, internally and externally.

In April 2005, as GAO's report was being prepared, Amtrak's management and its board of directors released a proposed set of strategic reform initiatives—containing, among other things, a new vision statement—that would substantially change how the corporation operates. Among other things, this proposal would give states a larger role in deciding what services to offer and introduces greater potential for competition in providing intercity passenger rail service. The future of this proposal is largely unknown, and implementation will require both legislative changes (such as the federal government either assuming annual debt service payments or eliminating Amtrak's debt burden as well as removing Amtrak from the railroad retirement system) and extensive changes internally within Amtrak.

Source: U.S. Government Accountability Office, "Amtrak Management: Systemic Problems Require Actions to Improve Efficiency, Effectiveness, and Accountability (GAO-08-148)," October 2005, http://www.gao.gov/new.items/d06145.pdf.

> Because the GSEs are Congressionally-chartered, only Congress can address the inherent conflict of attempting to serve both shareholders and a public mission. The new Congress and the next Administration must decide what role government in general, and these entities in particular, should play in the housing market. There is a consensus today that these enterprises pose a systemic risk and they cannot continue in their current form. Government support needs to be either explicit or non-existent, and structured to resolve the conflict between public and private purposes. And policymakers must address the issue of systemic risk. I recognize that there are strong differences of opinion over the role of government in supporting housing, but under any course policymakers choose, there are ways to structure these entities in order to address market stability in the transition and limit systemic risk and conflict of purposes for the long-term. We will make a grave error if we don't use this time out to permanently address the structural issues presented by the GSEs.[110]

Nonprofit Organizations

Nonprofit organizations can be viewed as a type of tool for organizing collective action, used instead of or in addition to direct government.[111] This section focuses on the nonprofit organizational form, reviewing the rationales for its existence, managerial incentives, and costs compared to other forms.

Rationales

A number of rationales have been proposed to explain the formation and existence of the nonprofit organizational form. Burton Weisbrod developed an explanation based on the theory of public goods (discussed in chapter 1); he argued that government and for-profit firms will underprovide such goods.[112] Because of the public choice mechanism of majority rule, governments will underprovide public goods when provision is favored only by a minority or when provision is favored by a majority whose members choose to conceal their preferences and free ride on the efforts of others. For-profit firms will underprovide public goods if it is not feasible to collect fees or charges that cover their costs from free riders. Even if private firms supply goods with collective characteristics, Weisbrod says, these goods may not be what consumers prefer. For example, a for-profit clinic may not adequately serve the medical needs of the poor.

Given that both government and for-profit firms undersupply goods with public goods characteristics, "a class of voluntary organizations will come into existence as *extragovernmental providers of collective consumption goods.*"[113] Indeed, as is the case with education, medical care, nursing homes, and rehabilitation services, public and private provision may exist side by side, each sector providing somewhat different services. Weisbrod's theory does not, however, address whether and how free riding behavior will be overcome in the provision of collective consumption goods by nonprofits or why government might prefer to subsidize nonprofits instead of for-profits as suppliers of collective goods.

Other scholars attempt to answer these questions. Henry Hansmann has developed a theory of nonprofits, based on contract failure, that provides a broader explanation for why governments might prefer nonprofits to for-profits for producing human services. As discussed in the section on incomplete contracts, for-profit producers have incentives to increase profit by raising prices or cutting costs if a good or service is of unknown or difficult-to-verify quality. Such a situation characterizes many human services. Nonprofits have no such incentives, Hansmann argues, because of the **nondistribution constraint,** part of the legal framework that defines the nonprofit form, which prohibits managers or others associated with the organization from obtaining a share of revenues that exceed costs. In nonprofits, then,

> the discipline of the market is supplemented by the additional protection given the consumer by another, broader "contract," the organization's legal commitment to devote its entire earnings to the production of services. As a result of this institutional constraint, it is less imperative for the consumer either to shop around first or to enforce rigorously the contract he makes.[114]

Hansmann's theory of nonprofits proposes a structural solution—the creation of the nonprofit organizational form as a guarantee of quality and trustworthiness—to address contract failure problems faced by consumers. A situation where the purchaser of the service is not the same as the consumer of that service is a straightforward application of the theory. The "purchaser" might be a state government that contracts with a local nonprofit organization to provide foster care placement and monitoring services. The "consumer," the child in foster care, uses but does not buy the services she receives.

Another application of Hansmann's theory explains why nonprofits will be suppliers of goods with public good characteristics. Weisbrod had argued that free riding leads to underprovision of public goods by government and for-profits, creating a role for nonprofits. Contract failure explains why nonprofits would provide public goods, making Weisbrod's theory for collective goods provision "simply . . . a special case of the more general contract failure theory." In the public goods case, the contract failure problem still arises, even in the absence of free riding: "The latter is concerned with the lack of incentive to contribute to the cost of a public good, while the former is concerned with the inability to control the use to which a contribution is put once it is made." [115]

Edward L. Glaeser and Andrei Shleifer also use the concept of incomplete contracts to account for nonprofit entrepreneurship (or formation). In circumstances where high-powered incentives (complete contracts) cannot ensure against inefficient behavior and especially stinting on quality, "[c]ommitment to non-profit status softens these incentives, and thus reassures [customers, donors, volunteers and employees] that quality will be higher" [116] This theory depends neither on altruism nor on information asymmetries between nonprofit officers and donors. The argument is that nonprofit status attracts entrepreneurs who have a restrained taste for perquisites and income per se by providing an incentive, in the form of the benefits of nonprofit status, to produce those kinds of goods and services for which mission orientation and quality are important considerations.

Lester Salamon proposes another rationale for the nonprofit form, making the argument that nonprofit organizations, not governments, respond to market failures and are the natural "first" provider of collective goods.[117] As with markets and governments, however, nonprofits, too, are vulnerable to particular kinds of failure.

Specifically, Salamon cites four failures of the nonprofit, or voluntary sector. First, "philanthropic insufficiency" occurs, partly due to free rider problems, because nonprofits cannot attract enough resources to fully meet demands for what they provide. Second, "philanthropic particularism" occurs because nonprofits may choose to serve some needs or provide some services—for example, to those of a certain religion or ethnicity—but not others, and some services may be duplicated. Third, "philanthropic paternalism" occurs because the benefactors of nonprofits will influence distribution of resources and emphases for funding, with no guarantee that equitable distribution occurs; board members and donors may not reflect community values. Finally, "philanthropic amateurism" occurs because delivery of services by nonprofits may involve well-meaning but unskilled staff or service technologies that do not correspond with professional or scientific standards or best practices. Because they are unable on their own to overcome collective action problems, the public sector may step in to supplement nonprofit provision and co-opt nonprofit organizations into serving larger public purposes.

Avner Ben-Ner and Theresa Van Hoomissen attempt a more complete specification of the motivations for both the demand for and supply of nonprofit organizations:

> A nonprofit organization will be formed only if a group of interested stakeholders (individuals or organizations) has the ability to exercise control over the organization. Stakeholder control is a *sine qua non* for the existence of nonprofit organizations, because it avails the trust required for patronizing the organization, revealing demand to it, and making donations to it.[118]

Actual control is exercised by the demand-side stakeholders, who, in choosing to create non-profit firms, renounce the creation of ownership shares in favor of personal control using the nondistribution constraint to ameliorate agency problems between donors and managers.[119]

Preferences of Nonprofit Managers

Whatever the reason for the existence of nonprofits, both formal models and empirical evidence indicate that the nonprofit form provides a signal about the values and motives of nonprofit managers.[120] Susan Rose-Ackerman argues that "organization form, per se, may not serve an important signaling function for patrons. It may only be an indication that certain kinds of entrepreneurs and managers find the nonprofit form desirable." [121]

Dennis R. Young also suggests that screening of personalities and goals may underlie an entrepreneur's choice to organize as a for-profit or nonprofit. In particular, even though variation exists across for-profit and nonprofit organizations, he argues from case study evidence that "income seekers" and "independents" are drawn to the for-profit sector, while "believers," "conservers," "poets," "searchers," and "professionals" are more likely drawn to the nonprofit sector.[122]

Yet Steven Smith and Michael Lipksy argue that the administrative requirements of managing government contracts require professional skills and administrative expertise that some traditional nonprofit leaders may not have.[123] Professional managers of nonprofits that rely heavily on government contracts may have preferences that more closely mirror those of for-profit organizations than those of nonprofits with traditional community or public service roots.

Cost Control

Managerial preferences may be critical because monitoring and incentive problems may lead to difficulty in enforcing the nondistribution constraint. Cross-subsidization—using revenues from "profitable" activities such as art museum shops, to subsidize "unprofitable" activities such as art programs for low-income neighborhoods and groups—may occur and may be inconsistent with the intentions of donors who favor art acquisitions or consumers who favor low entry fees, and managers may be opportunistic and take advantage of the trust that donors and clients place in them.[124] The nondistribution constraint means that nonprofits do not have strong incentives to minimize costs, which theory predicts would lead to excessively costly services to and overspending on perquisites, such as office amenities, leased vehicles, and expensive information technology, or inflated salaries by nonprofit managers.[125]

One review of the literature in human services, however, found no clear evidence that nonprofits were markedly different from for-profits in terms of cost minimization, concluding that "concerns about the operating inefficiency imposed upon the human services through their heavy reliance on nonprofit firms, while not entirely misplaced, are easily exaggerated." [126] In contrast to that view, a 2004 report indicates that confidence in the nonprofit sector is declining amid a belief that these organizations operate inefficiently.[127]

Such a decline in confidence, if real, should worry nonprofit managers and their boards. Laurence Lynn and Steven Smith describe the reliance on the legal roots of the nonprofit organizational form and their resulting vulnerability:

> The American nonprofit sector is a creature of the policies formalized in federal, state and local statutes and regulations regarding incorporation, exemption from corporate taxation and various regulations and the tax treatment of charitable donations. . . . As agents of public policy, nonprofit organizations are in principle accountable to legislatures, tax authorities, and various interest groups who comprise their stakeholders and they are thus vulnerable to the withdrawal of the privileges that substantially enable their existence.[128]

They argue that nonprofits must address these concerns through governance reforms and articulation of fiduciary norms.

The Nonprofit Form and Contracting Out

To illustrate the structural implications for public management of different organizational forms, this section describes a model, developed by Karen Eggleston and Richard Zeckhauser, that shows how it can be technically (if not necessarily politically) rational for government to take advantage of the strengths and weaknesses of different ownership forms in the health care market.[129] All three ownership forms—public, private for-profit (investor-owned), and private nonprofit—provide health care through hospitals. Government plays a role in distributing access to health care through its tax and expenditure policies, although health care has limited public goods characteristics. Certain kinds of health care services, such as immunizations, do provide community benefits, however. Health care delivery has noncontractible uncertainties, such as the extent and nature of quality improvement and the emphasis on cost control, meaning that contracts for health care are necessarily incomplete. Cost control, moreover, may come at the expense of service quality.

Eggelston and Zeckhauser's model builds on the incomplete contracts framework of Hart, Shleifer, and Vishny and assumes it is not possible to fully specify and contract for treatment costs, innovations, or quality of care above some minimum. Further, the model assumes that the three different ownership forms are equally productive, meaning that they can treat a given condition equally effectively, and have equal preferences between cost (or efficiency) and quality. While oversimplified, these assumptions provide a baseline for examining the different incentives across the three sectors.

In the case of a government-owned facility, Eggleston and Zeckhauser find that the provider would deliver the minimum acceptable quantity and quality of care unless payments could be renegotiated from time to time and the provider could count on sharing in the benefits of cost control and quality improvement, although the share may be low because of government compensation constraints. Here, incentives exist to pursue innovations that increase patient benefits.

In an investor-owned facility, the owner has property rights over the benefits of cost reduction and has a strong incentive to pursue cost controls. These controls may be pursued even at the expense of treatment quality unless the provider can renegotiate the reimbursement rates to cover the costs of quality-enhancing innovation. Still, the result may not be high levels of innovation. "Even with identical preferences, public and private providers will make different investment choices because they have different claims on the returns from those investments." [130] If aggressive cost control has adverse side effects on the quality of patient care, the implication is that government ownership is preferred.

> Whether in-house provision is preferable to contracting out to a for-profit provider will depend on several issues: the characteristics of the health services in question, the ability to specify desired quality and treatment intensity in the contract, and the availability of complementary purchasing strategies (such as allowing patient choice of provider to motivate investment in quality enhancement).[131]

In the case of nonprofits, the providers have incentives to maximize their surplus and redirect it back into perks or into mission-related activity. For this reason, nonprofits may be more motivated by altruism toward patients (which may or may not be desirable) and less motivated by cost control possibilities unless the organization is operating in a competitive environment. Among nonprofit providers, quality may actually be overemphasized, resulting in expenditures on state-of-the-art equipment or patient amenities that are not socially optimal.

Eggleston and Zeckhauser also discuss structural features of contracts for health care. For example, a prepaid capitation agreement has different implications than a fee-for-service contract, which entails higher costs, especially in the case of for-profit providers. If quality is multidimensional, providers have an incentive to emphasize those dimensions that patients are likely to notice. When patients are heterogeneous, incentives are present for patient selection or creamskimming (see chapter 8). Payers may use risk adjustment to weaken these incentives. If the budget constraint is soft—that is, if providers are likely to be bailed out of financial difficulties—then budgets are likely to grow.

Eggleston and Zeckhauser's analysis is one example of how the structural dimension—specifically, ownership type and contractual terms—provides insight into the comparative advantage of different sectors in supplying health care.

STRUCTURES AND POLITICAL RATIONALITY

Structure—in all of its varied meanings and forms—provides the framework for the work of organizations. Yet, as discussed in chapter 1, Terry Moe has argued that the structures of public organizations reflect political rationality more than technical rationality.[132]

For example, a controversial issue in health care administration is the rationing of scarce medical resources: Who should be treated, and how, and who should be assigned a lower priority and given less intensive treatment or not treated at all? In other words, what structures guide the provision of health care? Ideally, sufficient resources would be available so that rationing would not be necessary and every person in need of care would receive it. Yet the reality is that difficult choices must be made, and rationing of some kind is necessary. Who should make these decisions? What would a technically rational solution look like?[133]

The state of Oregon approaches a technical ideal, but only for those eligible for Medicaid. Under a waiver from the federal government, Oregon developed the Prioritized List of Integrated Health Services, which assigns a priority to every condition and treatment.[134] In general, however, no formal rationing policy or system and no universal health insurance exist in the United States. Instead, rationing decisions are pushed down to street-level bureaucrats: "The people who make these [rationing] decisions are harried doctors, Medicaid functionaries, hospital administrators, insurance workers, and nurses. These are the gatekeepers of the American health-care system, the ones forced to say 'no' to certain demands for treatment." [135]

This state of affairs reflects years of political bargaining among the health care system's stakeholders and advocates for and opponents of various kinds of reforms. The resulting "nonsystem" raises questions: Are the actors making rationing decisions the "right" actors to be doing so, and are they using criteria that most citizens would regard as legitimate? Does the fact that health care is rationed by street-level bureaucrats and not by a higher-level structure—producing inconsistent, nonstandardized decisions—mean that health care financing should be reformed to locate the management of the rationing process in different hands, charged with producing more equitable results?

Another example of how political rationality intersects with technical rationality is prescription drug reimbursement by Medicare. These decisions are partly governed by standards set by the federal government and partly by some two dozen government-contracted private insurers who handle physician and hospital claims for groups of states and are empowered to establish local rules for drug coverage. This arrangement grew out of a bargain struck between the federal government and the American Medical Association, which opposed any kind of nationalization of health care. The result is more than nine thousand local medical review policies.[136] But practitioners and advocates often do not know what the policies are and, further, are not allowed to provide feedback on the policies before they are promulgated.

The history and use of Xigris, a drug manufactured by Eli Lilly, also illustrates how political rationality interacts with technical rationality in creating structures to deliver services.[137] Xigris is used to treat severe sepsis (systemic inflammatory response syndrome, or SIRS, in response to infection), which kills about 250,000 people a year. The drug costs more than $6,000 per dose, but it saves lives, according to its supporters. Contrary to Lilly's expectations, the drug's adoption rates were low. Doctors and hospital pharmacists resisted its cost and doubted its effectiveness compared with cheaper alternatives. To overcome this resistance, Lilly mounted a campaign that focused on structural changes that would benefit them. First, they encouraged state legislators to introduce legislation designed to promote the drug's use by mandating that sepsis cases be tracked by hospitals and reported to the state government. Second, they successfully won a new federal diagnostic code for severe sepsis, so hospitals would begin reporting how many patients they see who have the condition and might be eligible to receive the drug. Finally, they successfully petitioned the Centers for Medicare & Medicaid Services for "new technology" status for Xigris, winning a special dispensation for 50 percent reimbursement from the federal government, up to $3,400. It was the first time such approval has been given. In most cases, hospitals are reimbursed for the cost of treating a disease or condition rather than for the cost of a specific drug.

Yet another example of how political rationality creates technically irrational solutions is the effort to collect small tax debts ($25,000 or less), which has been contracted out to private debt collection companies. IRS officials admit that it is more expensive to collect tax debts this way than to do it with IRS employees—22 to 24 cents on the dollar with contractors compared to 3 cents on the dollar—but that Congress forced their hand by refusing to let them hire more revenue officers. Critics say that using private debt collectors exposes taxpayers to scam artists and fraud or to abusive collection techniques, although some of these problems can be forestalled. Further, private collectors have no incentive to counsel taxpayers on how to minimize their indebtedness by avoiding penalties.

Speaking of public education, John Chubb and Terry Moe argue that the combination of politics and structure is actually harmful.[138] They contend that public schools (democratically controlled bureaucracies) perform less well than private schools (market-controlled bureaucracies) and that wherever possible, market control should be substituted for political control.

Chubb and Moe point out that many different interests compete for public authority, because its coercive use, such as requiring students to attend neighborhood schools, is so valuable. Winners of this political struggle are able to impose their priorities on the losers. In general, interests represented at federal, state, and local levels of government are all determined to restrict the discretion of parents, principals, and teachers to make choices that are offensive to those interests. The result is a rather elaborate public school bureaucracy. Chubb and Moe observe that such a bureaucracy is the only apparent way of ensuring that the public interest (or those interests that win the political struggle) is reflected in what schools do.

Probably the least powerful competitors for influence in this structure are parents and students. They have some power through their choices of where to live: Parents shop for good school districts and bring their tax payments with them. But "democracy cannot remedy the mismatch between what parents and students want and what the public schools provide." [139] In contrast, private authority is competitive and "radically decentralized," mainly in the hands of parents. In the private market, an individual school offers its "product" to parents and students, who are free to take it or find it elsewhere; the result is that schools are heavily shaped by parental choice. Chubb and Moe argue that such a system is preferable to the traditional system of public schools.

The structures described in this section reflect the political rationality of the processes that produced them. Not all structures reflect political rationality so directly. Yet regardless of the degree of political or technical rationality of various structural arrangements, structures are a fact of public organizational life. The theories and ideas described in this chapter start from the premise that structures affect organizational functioning and performance—a point about which almost all participants in organizations would agree.

Because structures are expressions of formal authority—whether externally or internally imposed, enabling or constraining, politically or technically rational—that shape the public manager's operating environment, the roles and capacities of the organization's managers, and the ways that the manager and the organization interact with external actors, it is imperative that public managers attend to the structural dimensions of their environments. The theories, concepts, arguments, and examples presented throughout this chapter illustrate aspects of the structural dimension that can be understood and analyzed.

Key Concepts

constraining structures
enabling structures
red tape
line positions
staff positions
tightly coupled
loosely coupled
advisory tasks
operating tasks
uncertainty absorption
street-level bureaucrats
management capacity
budgets
personnel policies
performance-based pay
contract
complete contract
incomplete contract
principal-agent relationships
adverse selection
moral hazard
multitask situations
common agency
transaction costs
asset specificity
privatization
contracting out
make or buy decision
inherently governmental
cost-plus-fixed-fee contract
fee-for-service contract
hollow state
network governance
organizational form
quango
government-sponsored enterprises
nonprofit organizations
nondistribution constraint

Analysis and Argument: Test Your Understanding

Read the teaching case: "Preventing Child Abuse: The Challenge for the State Department of Social Services," available through the Electronic Hallway, https://hallway.org/index.php.

The case involves a legislatively mandated reorganization of the Secretariat of Human Resources, creating the Department of Social Services to assume the social service responsibilities of the Department of Welfare. The legislature evidently believed that "structure mattered," that is, that the reorganization would somehow reduce the risk to children who are actually or potentially under state supervision or in state custody.

After reading the case, consider the questions below regarding possible relationships between the structural dimension, employee behavior, and overall agency performance. These questions incorporate those raised in chapter 3. They also ask the reader to practice using the method of argument. (A teaching note, written by Jon Brock, is also available to instructors on the Electronic Hallway site.)

1. What issues must Bradley Patton resolve at the end of the case?
2. Focus on the legislatively mandated structural reorganization that Patton is faced with:
   a. Why would elected officials want to create a separate department responsible for social services rather than having both social services and assistance payments be equal divisions of the Department of Welfare?
   b. Is this reorganization a solution to the child safety problem? If it is a solution, why? If it is not a solution, why not? Make an argument (claims, reasons, evidence, warrants, acknowledgments and responses) to support your position.
3. With regard to the issues you identified in question 1, what should Patton do now, and why? For each decision Patton faces, make a complete argument to support your recommendation.

6 Public Management: The Cultural Dimension

The cultural dimension of public management was introduced in chapters 1 and 2 through descriptions of the preparation for and response to Hurricane Katrina and the contributing factors to the space shuttle *Columbia* accident. In the Katrina case, institutionalized values reflecting turf protection inhibited effective response and coordination among organizations and individual responders, while those reflecting the exercise of responsible professional judgment were instrumental in alleviating suffering and saving lives. In the *Columbia* case, institutionalized values were reflected by shuttle program managers who subordinated safety to maintenance of flight schedules and budgets, by the reluctance of NASA employees to speak up forcefully in opposition to those values, and by the acceptance of risks to flight safety from debris strikes as normal and acceptable.

The Katrina and *Columbia* incidents illustrate why analyzing the success or failure of a particular situation by utilizing one framework or concept, or even a broad dimension such as structure, is seldom adequate. Instead, to analyze and respond appropriately to the distinctive challenges of public management requires a multidimensional analysis incorporating structure, culture, and craft. As a step toward building the capacity for multidimensional analysis, this chapter focuses on the cultural dimension of public management.

Public managers must contend not only with structures of formal authority (discussed in chapter 5), but also with the informal, or cultural, aspects of their organizations. In this text, these cultural aspects encompass shared norms and understandings as to what the work of the organization is or should be, and how it is or should be accomplished. Organizational cultures also include the values, ethics, and motives of individual participants in the organization: frontline employees, professionals, and managers. Because these cultural aspects are likely to have developed over time, they may be firmly entrenched as facts of organizational life.

Such informal aspects can be highly consequential, as observed in the Katrina and *Columbia* incidents and illustrated by this excerpt from NASA's Columbia Accident Investigation Board (CAIB) report.

> The human space flight culture within NASA originated in the Cold War environment. The space agency itself was created in 1958 as a response to the Soviet launch of Sputnik, the first artificial Earth satellite. In 1961, President John F. Kennedy charged the new space agency with the task of reaching the moon before the end of the decade, and asked Congress and the American people to commit the immense resources for doing so, even though at the time NASA had only accumulated 15 minutes of human space flight experience. With its efforts linked to U.S.-Soviet competition for global leadership, there was a sense in the NASA workforce that the agency was engaged in a historic struggle central to the nation's agenda.
>
> The Apollo era created at NASA an exceptional "can-do" culture marked by tenacity in the face of seemingly impossible challenges. This culture valued the interaction among research and testing, hands-on engineering experience, and a dependence on the exceptional quality of its workforce and leadership that provided in-house technical capability to oversee the work of contractors. The culture also accepted risk and failure as inevitable aspects of operating in space, even as it held as its highest value attention to detail in order to lower the chances of failure.
>
> The dramatic Apollo 11 lunar landing in July 1969 fixed NASA's achievements in the national consciousness, and in history. However, the numerous accolades in the wake of the moon landing also helped reinforce the NASA staff's faith in their organizational culture. Apollo successes created the powerful image of the space agency as a "perfect place," as "the best organization that human beings could create to accomplish selected goals." . . . During Apollo, NASA was in many respects a highly successful organization capable of achieving seemingly impossible feats. The continuing image of NASA as a "perfect place" in the years after Apollo left NASA employees unable to recognize that NASA never had been, and still was not, perfect, nor was it as symbolically important in the continuing Cold War struggle as it had been for its first decade of existence. NASA personnel maintained a vision of their agency that was rooted in the glories of an earlier time, even as the world, and thus the context within which the space agency operated, changed around them.
>
> As a result, NASA's human space flight culture never fully adapted to the Space Shuttle Program, with its goal of routine access to space rather than further exploration beyond low-Earth orbit. The Apollo-era organizational culture came to be in tension with the more bureaucratic space agency of the 1970s, whose focus turned from designing new spacecraft at any expense to repetitively flying a reusable vehicle on an ever-tightening budget. This trend toward bureaucracy and the associated increased reliance on contracting necessitated more effective communications and more extensive safety oversight processes than had been in place during the Apollo era, but the Rogers Commission found that such features were lacking.
>
> In the aftermath of the Challenger accident, these contradictory forces prompted a resistance to externally imposed changes and an attempt to maintain the internal belief that NASA was still a "perfect place," alone in its ability to execute a program of human

> space flight. Within NASA centers, as Human Space Flight Program managers strove to maintain their view of the organization, they lost their ability to accept criticism, leading them to reject the recommendations of many boards and blue-ribbon panels, the Rogers Commission among them.
>
> External criticism and doubt, rather than spurring NASA to change for the better, instead reinforced the will to "impose the party line vision on the environment, not to reconsider it," according to one authority on organizational behavior. This in turn led to "flawed decision making, self deception, introversion and a diminished curiosity about the world outside the perfect place." . . . The NASA human space flight culture the Board found during its investigation manifested many of these characteristics, in particular a self-confidence about NASA possessing unique knowledge about how to safely launch people into space . . . the Board views this cultural resistance as a fundamental impediment to NASA's effective organizational performance.[1]

As the CAIB emphasizes, at least part of NASA's early successes were associated with its "can-do" organizational culture, showing how the informal aspects of organizations can prove to be a source of stability, motivation, and reliability. Such stable cultures can provide continuity and an insulating buffer in the face of ill-conceived or politically motivated attempts to impose change that might go undetected by existing structures for oversight and approval. Yet, as illustrated by the problems with the space shuttle program, especially the *Challenger* and *Columbia* disasters and their aftermath, resistance to change may have a downside, as it may present obstacles to implementing necessary structural changes such as oversight reforms and the realignment of agency priorities.

Entrenched informal aspects of organizations are no less constraints on a manager's activity than are structural constraints incorporated in formal authority. To the extent that formal and informal characteristics—that is, structure and culture—are "given" or unchangeable (or changeable only at great cost), managers are "creatures" of their organizational environments, as discussed in chapter 1. Yet in some circumstances, managers may be able to act as "creators" to influence formal or informal aspects of their organizations. This chapter is concerned with the informal aspects of public organizations that managers confront; it also considers the opportunities and strategies that might be available to managers in their roles as creators.

The chapter further defines the cultural dimension, including specific definitions of the construct of organizational culture, and then traces the evolution of culture as a recognized component of the internal environments of public organizations. Next, it discusses the building blocks of culture, focusing on individual-level factors such as values, professionalization, ethics, and motives, as well as on trust and reputation, which characterize both individuals and organizations. The chapter then examines how structure and culture interact, including how each exerts influence on and shapes the other. Finally, interactions of craft and culture are reviewed, followed by a short case study of how culture matters in theory and in practice, specifically discussing pay for performance in public organizations. The end-of-chapter exercise concerns revelations of ethical lapses and other problems in a transit agency and raises again the interactions of structure and culture in this particular organizational context.

WHAT IS CULTURE?

Culture—the informal aspects of organizations—are the values, beliefs, ethics, and motives of individual participants in addition to the shared norms and understandings that broadly characterize the organization or its subunits.

Thus defined, the cultural dimension of public management encompasses but is not limited to **organizational culture,** which has a unique meaning and extensive literature of its own.[2] Organizational culture, widely acknowledged to be a fact of organizational life, refers broadly to "the tribal aspect of contemporary organizations," "the way we do things around here," or the "persistent, patterned way of thinking about the central tasks of and human relationships within an organization." [3] Social psychologist Edgar H. Schein defines organizational culture as "a pattern of shared basic assumptions that the group learned as it solved its problems of external adaptation and internal integration, that has worked well enough to be considered valid and, therefore, to be taught to new members as the correct way to perceive, think, and feel in relation to those problems." [4] Another definition of organizational culture is from Harrison M. Trice and Janice M. Beyer, who say it includes two aspects: "(1) substance, which consists of shared systems of beliefs, values, and norms, and (2) forms, which are observable ways that members of a culture express cultural ideas." [5]

Organizations are unlikely to have just a single overarching culture. Instead, multiple cultures or subcultures are often present. Trice and Beyer review the different bases for these subcultures: occupations, informal groups (friends and coalitions), and formal groups (technology and work flows, departments, line and staff distinctions, and hierarchical differences) within the organization, as well as managerial cultures or demographic groups that transcend organizational boundaries.

Organizational cultures are the shared experiences resulting from both low- and high-profile successes and failures, patterns of conduct, and self-regulating practices. They may be tacit or explicit, shaping the ingrained views and habitual behaviors of workers at all levels of the organization—field-level workers, middle managers, and senior career officials. Culture can infuse employees with beliefs and values that enhance the organization's reputation for reliability and competent service, integrity, and performance, or it can produce a set of dysfunctional and unproductive responses that harm the organization's reputation.

Another way of describing organizational culture is that it reflects **institutionalized values,** where institutionalization is the process by which the members of an organization "acquire values that go beyond the technical requirements of organizational tasks" or "the emergence of orderly, stable, socially integrating patterns out of unstable, loosely organized, or narrowly technical activities." [6] Indeed, James G. March and Johan P. Olsen define *institutions* as "the beliefs, paradigms, codes, cultures, and knowledge that support rules and routines," and they argue that organizational participants seek to act in ways consistent with their institutional environment.[7] Therefore, institutionalized values—or organizational cultures—provide a unifying source of meaning and purpose that formal structures of authority and assignments of responsibility cannot alone provide.

CONCEPTS IN ACTION

Blending Multiple Cultures at the Department of Homeland Security

In January 2007 the Culture Task Force (CTF) of the Department of Homeland Security Advisory Council issued its report with recommendations for "creating and sustaining an energetic, dedicated, and empowering mission-focused organization." Its fourth recommendation addressed the issue of multiple cultures in the department and proposed a structural solution to a problem it identified concerning them.

The CTF believes that given the diversity, history and strong culture of many of its component organizations, there can be no hierarchically imposed "single culture" within the Department. We do, however, believe that an overarching and blended culture can be developed that is based on threads of common values, goals, and focus of mission among DHS Headquarters and its component organizations. The CTF recommends that the Secretary appoint a senior career/general schedule homeland security employee reporting to the Secretary to assist/support the Secretary in the continuous development and sustainment of the overarching/blended culture within the Department. With the support and direction of the Secretary and supported by staff from all DHS components, this leader will help develop the Secretary's overarching cultural vision and the strategic goals required to create the desired diverse but mission focused Homeland Security culture. This individual will also provide staff support for monitoring, testing, and supporting the continuous improvement of that culture with ultimate emphasis upon the readiness and the spirit de corps of the "troops in the field."

Source: Homeland Security Advisory Council, "Report of the Culture Task Force," January 2007, http://www.dhs.gov/xlibrary/assets/hsac-culture-010107.pdf.

Yet if the institutionalized aspects were thought to wholly constitute the informal organization in public organizations, an important part of the picture would be missing. The history of public administration and management places a special emphasis on individual responsibility (an "inner check" in the words of John M. Gaus), and more recent theories and empirical work point to the potential importance of particular motives for individuals who serve in public organizations. These and other individual characteristics are likely to be an important part of the informal organization that public managers will face, and this text considers them part of the cultural dimension of public management.

To summarize, culture constitutes the shared norms, values, and understandings that provide meaning, purpose, and motivation to individuals in their roles as employees of an organizational unit, as well as the values, ethics, and motives unique to individuals in their own right. In terms of the logic of governance described in chapter 4, page 117, culture operates primarily at the levels of management (Figure 4.1, level d) through the discretionary use of structures, tools, and values and strategies; and service delivery (level e) through factors such as employees' beliefs and values that affect how the work of the organization is accomplished by frontline employees. The cultural dimension is fundamental to an organization's capacity to carry out its lawful responsibilities.

CULTURE IN HISTORICAL PERSPECTIVE

The ideas incorporated into the concept of culture have long been of interest to those who study public administration and management.[8] The earliest concern for what we now call culture in public administration and management was about professional rather than agency or organizational values. The concern was for those values that motivate and ensure the legitimacy of unelected "bureaucrats" who may have job protection under a merit system and, therefore, be resistant to formal accountability. Based on European examples, Americans were suspicious of the antidemocratic values that they regarded as endemic to bureaucratic government.

The antidote, in the view of those who were promoting "the new public administration," was an ingrained sense of responsibility to democratic institutions on the part of public officials. Woodrow Wilson argued in 1887 that Americans need not fear professional administration of public affairs if they can rely on public administrators to exhibit responsible conduct—accountability to citizens and their representatives.[9] The notion that a sense of responsibility is the foundational public service value is a theme that ran continuously through public administration literature during the ensuing six decades.

Anticipating the later emergence of the concept of "informal organization," John Dickinson argued in 1927 that, although law narrows the possible range of governmental action to make it more predictable and controllable, laying down a rule for everything public officials must do is impossible. But, he said, the control of necessary discretion requires some entity other than law. That entity has been found "in political responsibility of government to the governed." [10] In a broadly comparative analysis, John Gaus argued in 1936 that in "the new administration" responsibility is an evolving concept and currently multidimensional: not only political and constitutional but also professional, which ensures an "inner check" on official conduct.[11]

The notion of an "inner check" created an axis of tension concerning the question of how to reconcile administrative discretion with responsibility to democratic values.[12] This tension was manifest in the 1940 debate between political scientists Herman Finer and Carl

Friedrich over the sources of administrative responsibility. Finer argued that responsible administration in a democracy can be ensured only through external control, as under the Interstate Commerce Act: "The servants of the public are not to decide their own course; they are to be responsible to the elected representatives of the public, and these are to determine the course of action of the public servants *to the most minute degree that is technically feasible*" (emphasis added).[13] Friedrich, in contrast (and echoing Dickinson), took a dim view of the ability of courts and legislatures to control administration.[14] He argued that any movement toward democratic responsibility requires that officials have the right orientation toward their work. The checks on abuse of administrative discretion are, in Friedrich's view, expertise and professionalism: the administrators' preferences and values and, in particular their fidelity to democratic accountability. Chapter 8 returns to these ideas in a broader discussion of accountability; here, the main idea is that informal norms expressed through individual values have been a concern in public administration for some time.

The appropriateness of intrinsic motivation and self-control by public managers, a recurring issue since the Friedrich-Finer debate, is reflected in later discussions of administrative values. John Rohr argued, "Administrators should use their discretionary power in order to maintain the constitutional balance of powers in support of individual rights." [15] Robert B. Denhardt urged that public managers commit themselves to "values that relate to the concept of freedom, justice, and the public interest." [16] And H. George Frederickson asserted that public managers "must resist, thwart, or refuse to implement policy that runs counter to the founding documents or to American regime values." [17]

The publication in 1938 of Chester I. Barnard's *The Functions of the Executive* established an organizational context in which to consider how the values and ingrained norms of workers influence organizational behavior.[18] In their report on the famous Hawthorne studies (of worker motivation at a manufacturing plant), Fritz Roethlisberger and William J. Dickson described how the informal norms of workers, the "informal organization," could frustrate the achievement of management's goals.[19] Herbert A. Simon incorporated the notion of an informal organization in tension with the formal structure into public administration doctrine. In *Administrative Behavior: A Study of Decision-Making Processes in Administrative Organizations,* Simon defines "informal organization" as "interpersonal relationships in the organization that affect decisions within it but either are omitted from the formal [organization chart] or are not consistent with that scheme." Formal and informal organizations are interrelated, Simon suggested. Because it cannot govern behavior in detail, the formal organization requires an informal organization to supplement it. The function of the formal organization, in turn, is to prevent the informal organization from becoming dysfunctional and to encourage "attitudes of cooperation within the formal structure." [20]

Beginning in the 1950s the term *organizational culture* began to appear regularly in academic journals such as *Administrative Science Quarterly* and *Public Administration Review.* One concern, for example, was the extent to which individuals with particular civic values, such as those who recognized "no patterned authority," could be socialized into the acceptance of bureaucratic values. In his 1968 study of an antipoverty agency in southern Appalachia,

Robert Denhardt argued that socialization was "an essential element of organizational maintenance." [21] He found that with respect to deference to authority, the organizational culture can, as an agent of resocialization, overcome even the influence of the local area's civic culture, while integrating local values into the work of the organization.

The concept of organizational culture matured as a subject of academic investigation in the 1980s; as Schein said in 1988, "Organizational culture as a concept has a fairly recent origin." [22] Schein sees its origins in social psychological studies of group norms and organizational climate. But, in their 1985 survey article "Organizational Culture," William Ouchi and Alan Wilkins argue that "[t]hough anthropology and cognitive psychology have made significant contributions to this new field, the study of organizational culture may be seen as a return to some of the most basic concerns about the nature of organizations and the appropriate methods for analyzing them" by sociologists.[23] As an academic interest, say Ouchi and Wilkins, the study of culture was eclipsing the study of formal structure, organizational environments, and bureaucracy.

The concept of culture moved beyond the academic realm with the publication of widely read books such as Thomas Peters and Robert Waterman's *In Search of Excellence* and Terrence Deal and Allan Kennedy's *Corporate Cultures: The Rites and Rituals of Corporate Life*.[24] With the publication of the first edition of *Organizational Culture and Leadership* in 1985, Schein gave definitive intellectual shape to the concept and formally linked it to the subject of leadership, the roots of which were in studies of leadership training in the 1940s. The fields of business and public administration, increasingly faced with issues concerning organizational competitiveness, performance, and adaptability to change, began incorporating the concept of culture into their analytic toolkits. The emergence of the organizational culture concept came about through efforts to understand the reasons for performance differences, as Schein described:

> What has really thrust the concept into the forefront is the recent emphasis on trying to explain why U.S. companies do not perform as well as some of their counterpart companies in other societies, notably Japan. In observing the differences, it has been noted that national culture is not a sufficient explanation. One needs concepts that permit one to differentiate between organizations within a society, especially in relation to different levels of effectiveness, and, for this purpose, organizational culture has served well.[25]

INDIVIDUAL CHARACTERISTICS AND BUILDING BLOCKS OF CULTURE

The shared understandings constituting an organization's culture are developed over time and through repeated interactions among the participants. Although culture is an organizational-level construct, its elemental features derive from both individual- and group-level characteristics. In other words, the unit of analysis may be either the individual (consistent with the above discussion regarding professional and responsible administration) or the organization (consistent with the more recent focus at the organization level).

The values, professional judgments, ethics, and motives of individuals in organizations, discussed next, are of concern to public managers because they contribute to the organization's cultures and may also exert independent effects on the organization and its functioning. Trust and reputation, which can be viewed as both individual- and organizational-level constructs, also contribute to understanding the cultures of public organizations, even though they are not typically included in writings on organizational culture. An understanding of these aspects is important to public managers for two reasons: first, because these factors may influence the decisions and behaviors of individuals in the organization over whom the manager has control and, second, because these factors may influence the decisions and behaviors of managers themselves. Both contribute to the culture of the organization and both potentially influence the ability or inability to exercise managerial craft.

Values

Individual participants in organizations bring with them intrinsic **values,** or "complex and broad-based assessment[s] of an object or set of objects . . . characterized by both cognitive and emotive elements, arrived at after some deliberation . . . [B]ecause and, because a value is part of the individual's definition of self, it is not easily changed and it has the potential to elicit action." [26] Dwight Waldo emphasized the importance and inevitability of the role of values in democratic administration, arguing that even public administrators' decisions regarding efficiency, often regarded as a technical matter, were value laden: "[T]here is no realm of 'factual' decisions from which values are excluded. To decide is to choose between alternatives; to choose between alternatives is to introduce values." [27]

Values observed for different types of interactions relating to public organizations were recently inventoried by Torben Beck Jørgensen and Barry Bozeman.[28] They examined more than 230 research articles that looked at public values and were published in public administration journals from 1990 to 2003. They identified seventy-two unique public values (Table 6.1).

Jørgensen and Bozeman argue that public values are "analogous to the principles of common value—an ambiguous but potentially viable set of criteria for action and accountability." [29] They emphasize that public values are not solely reflected by government organizations, but instead are associated with political authority. This idea links to Bozeman's work on "degrees of publicness," discussed in chapter 1, which locates public and private sector organizations along a continuum of authority from economic to political.[30]

Values or preferences are one factor (though not the only one) in what Jon Elster calls local justice—decisions regarding the allocation of scarce resources such as college admissions, kidney transplants, military service, or immigration. For example, staff in welfare-to-work offices can exercise discretion and steer clients to particular activities such as basic education or job training. Within their scope of discretion, judges may require or allow participation in rehabilitation. Or, in determining whom to treat and how, norms of thoroughness and compassion

Table 6.1 Values Found in Recent Public Administration Literature

Value Category	Value Set
Public sector's contribution to society	Common good (public interest, social cohesion) Altruism (human dignity) Sustainability (voice of the future) Regime dignity (regime stability)
Transformation of interests to decisions	Majority rule (democracy, will of the people, collective choice) User democracy (local governance, citizen involvement) Protection of minorities (protection of individual rights)
Relationship between public administrators and politicians	Political loyalty (accountability, responsiveness)
Relationship between public administrators and their environment	Openness-secrecy (responsiveness, listening to public opinion) Advocacy-neutrality (compromise, balancing of interests) Competitiveness-cooperativeness (stakeholder or shareholder value)
Intraorganizational aspects of public administration	Robustness (adaptability, stability, reliability, timeliness) Innovation (enthusiasm, risk-readiness) Productivity (effectiveness, parsimony, business-like approach) Self-development of employees (good working environment)
Behavior of public-sector employees	Accountability (professionalism, honesty, moral standards, ethical consciousness, integrity)
Relationship between public administration and the citizens	Legality (protection of rights of the individual, equal treatment, rule of law, justice) Equity (reasonableness, fairness, professionalism) Dialogue (responsiveness, user democracy, citizen involvement, citizen's self-development) User orientation (timeliness, friendliness)

Source: Adapted from Torben Beck Jørgensen and Barry Bozeman, "Public Values: An Inventory," *Administration & Society* 39, no. 3 (2007): table 1, 360–361.

may guide a physician's decision instead of the economic incentives governing medical practice. Such decisions reflect local justice and are influenced by a number of factors including structures, politics, incentives, public opinion, and information.[31] They also reflect professional norms.

RULE OF LAW

Changing Values to Stop Racial Profiling

Racial profiling during traffic stops by state troopers in New Jersey, reflecting a culture of racial bias in the organization, was described in chapter 2. As a result of the particular incident described, the courts placed the New Jersey State Police under a consent decree that required federal supervision of their operations. As the excerpt below describes, this formal legal process was apparently successful in changing the culture of the state police, bringing about changes in the values (as described by Torben Beck Jørgensen and Barry Bozeman) that characterize the behavior of public employees toward citizens and the relationship between public administration and citizens.

Eight years after New Jersey acknowledged that troopers were focusing on black and Hispanic drivers at traffic stops, federal monitors said on Wednesday that the New Jersey State Police had made so much progress in its attempts to eliminate racial profiling that it no longer needed federal supervision.

The monitors concluded in a report that in periodic reviews during the past eight years, the police had shown significant improvement in procedures and training.

In a consent decree signed in 1999, the state agreed to allow the federal Department of Justice to oversee how traffic stops were conducted, along with other State Police activities.

Stating that "compliance requirements in all areas are now at 100 percent levels," the report said that "it appears the ultimate goal has been attained."

"Ample evidence exists to suggest that the agency has become self-monitoring and self-correcting to a degree not often observed in American law enforcement," the report added. . . .

If federal supervision is waived, New Jersey would be able to formally move beyond a troubling era in which the delicate topics of race, politics and the police often collided. And now, given the recent directive on illegal immigration by Attorney General Anne Milgram that requires all law enforcement agencies to ask people who are arrested their immigration status, the lessons learned from racial profiling are more important than ever, said Capt. Al Della Fave, a spokesman for the State Police. . . .

"In effect, the New Jersey State Police have taken the [Management Awareness and Personnel Performance System, or Mapps] system beyond the requirements of the consent decree, using it for more than a tracking and control device for motor vehicle stops, use of force and complaints, and instead using it to identify systemic organizational issues and to craft solutions to those issues before they negatively impact the organization in any significant way," the report concluded.

Source: David W. Chen, "New Jersey Police Win Praise for Efforts to End Profiling," *New York Times,* September 6, 2007.

Professionals and Professional Training

Through their education and training, individuals may develop strong identification with professional values and norms that can transcend the cultures or norms of specific organizational contexts. These values and norms shape behavior and decisions (as in the Rule of Law box, page 199), and at a fundamental level they shape the professional's basic analytical reasoning processes. Lawyers tend to use "analogical reasoning and formal, inductive logic applied to the essential facts of a case." Medical doctors tend to employ "a highly compressed version of the formal logic of deductive science in which facts are examined in the light of pre-formed hypotheses as to what they might mean." Business and public administrators tend to reason in ways that are "experiential and associative, involving pattern recognition and intuition." [32] Policy analysts combine the analytically rigorous reasoning processes of law or medicine with the more experiential reasoning processes of business or public administrators. (Note that one of the goals of this book is to encourage analysis and argument by public managers that incorporate theory, analytic frameworks, *and* experience.)

Professionals may also influence the cultures of organizations directly through their decisions that affect structure and service technology. As Richard Scott observes,

> More so than other types of collective actors, the professions exercise control by defining social reality—by devising ontological frameworks, proposing distinctions, creating typifications, and fabricating principles or guidelines for action. They define the nature of many problems—from physical illness to economic degrees—monopolizing diagnostic techniques as well as treatment regimes. They underwrite the legitimacy of providers as well as practices.[33]

James Q. Wilson contrasts the experiences of the U.S. Forest Service, in which forestry professionals influenced the definition of the work of the organization to be the "scientific management of forests in order to produce a sustained yield of timber and other natural resources" and the U.S. National Park Service, which never encouraged an analogous professional "park ranger." [34] The result is that the main focus of Park Service rangers is on the protection and management of visitors, not on the physical aspects of the parks.

Structural reorganization that empowers a particular professional group may change decision-making processes and the balance of power in an organization. Marc Allen Eisner and Kenneth J. Meier analyzed the effects of an initiative by an assistant attorney general in the Department of Justice to increase the staff of Ph.D. economists and assign them more central roles in the selection of antitrust cases, which previously had been dominated by legal staff.[35] Eisner and Meier were interested in whether this change would affect the types of antitrust cases—price fixing, mergers, or monopoly—the agency pursued. They found that "the economists' professional norms and values (as embodied in the dominant school of economic thought) came to play a central role in the definition of antitrust policy. The interplay of bureaucratic evolution and critical shifts in the economics discipline provided the basis for change in antitrust." [36] The authors noted that mandatory training in economics and industrial organization was conducted and cases were pursued only if an economic analysis supported them.

Changes in organizational priorities and cultures also have occurred in other policy and organization settings as a result of professionals' involvement. The increased presence in social service organizations of managers with MBA degrees has resulted in tensions as their emphasis on the bottom line clashes with the more traditional social service values of line staff. And policy analysts won "a place at the decision table" [37] beginning in the 1960s and 1970s for their contributions of evidence-based, rigorous analysis.[38] Alice Rivlin observed that "analysts have probably done more to reveal how difficult the problems and choices are than to make the decisions easier," [39] shifting both the way work is done and the organizational culture. In a study of policy analysts at the Department of Energy, Martha Feldman concluded that although the reports and information the policy analysts produced had little direct effect on decision making, their activities "affect[ed] the definition of problems and the composition of participants in the problem-solving process" and therefore their work was an important, if indirect, part of the decision-making process.[40]

Ethics

Ethics are "rules of conduct and behavior . . . which relate to questions of right or wrong, good and evil." [41] Because "[a]dministrators and employees . . . have considerable freedom to decide matters on the basis of their own ethical promptings," [42] the ethics of individuals in organizations also contribute to the cultural dimension.[43] Frederickson argues that because public administrators operate within particular contexts defined by rules, budgets, and enabling legislation, they practice "bounded ethics," "generally accept[ing] the agency's purposes and policies, and practic[ing] ethics within those bounds." [44] Whistleblowing or the leaking of information may reflect what employees regard as ethical behavior because they are revealing misconduct within their organizations. As discussed in chapters 4 and 8, legal protections are in place to shield whistleblowers (those who observe and report an incident of illegal or wasteful activity involving their agency) from reprisals for their revelations, although enforcement of such protections by the Justice Department is not always zealous.

Special offices or committees in the federal executive, legislative, and judicial branches and in states and localities provide ethics guidance and clearinghouses for ethics-related information. The mission of the Office of Government Ethics (OGE), a federal executive branch agency, is to ensure integrity in decision making in public organizations and to "prevent conflicts of interest on the part of Government employees, and to resolve those conflicts of interest that do occur. In partnership with executive branch agencies and departments, OGE fosters high ethical standards for employees and strengthens the public's confidence that the Government's business is conducted with impartiality and integrity." [45] The agency is concerned with conflicts of interest (including bribery), financial disclosure requirements, procurement and contracting, gifts and travel, employment (including nepotism), use of government property, and political activities. Each agency has a designated ethics official who works with the OGE on these and other issues. One of the OGE's functions is to provide guidance and justification for completion of financial disclosure forms by certain public employees, as required by the Ethics in Government Act of 1978:

> Although a financial disclosure report sometimes reveals a violation of law or regulation, the primary purpose of disclosure is to assist agencies in identifying *potential* conflicts of interest between a filer's official duties and her private financial interests and affiliations. Once a reviewing official identifies a potential conflict of interest and consults with the filer's supervisor as necessary, several remedies are available to avoid an actual or apparent violation of Federal ethics laws and regulations.[46]

Although procedural and legal requirements such as those administered by the OGE provide structural safeguards, managers also can encourage an "ethical climate" by clearly specifying ethical standards (for an example, see Box 6.1), providing training, and conveying clear rules and expectations about appropriate behaviors and consequences of wrongdoing.[47] Yet Christopher Pollitt has observed that simply posting a code of ethics is insufficient for ensuring ethical behavior because "rascals will be rascals, and the existence and vigorous use of disciplinary procedures are likely to be a much more important curb on their activities than codes of ethics." [48]

Box 6.1

AMERICAN SOCIETY FOR PUBLIC ADMINISTRATION'S CODE OF ETHICS

I. Serve the Public Interest

Serve the public, beyond serving oneself. ASPA members are committed to:

1. Exercise discretionary authority to promote the public interest.
2. Oppose all forms of discrimination and harassment, and promote affirmative action.
3. Recognize and support the public's right to know the public's business.
4. Involve citizens in policy decision making.
5. Exercise compassion, benevolence, fairness, and optimism.
6. Respond to the public in ways that are complete, clear, and easy to understand.
7. Assist citizens in their dealings with government.
8. Be prepared to make decisions that may not be popular.

II. Respect the Constitution and the Law

Respect, support, and study government constitutions and laws that define responsibilities of public agencies, employees, and all citizens. ASPA members are committed to:

1. Understand and apply legislation and regulations relevant to their professional role.
2. Work to improve and change laws and policies that are counterproductive or obsolete.
3. Eliminate unlawful discrimination.
4. Prevent all forms of mismanagement of public funds by establishing and maintaining strong fiscal and management controls, and by supporting audits and investigative activities.
5. Respect and protect privileged information.
6. Encourage and facilitate legitimate dissent activities in government and protect the whistle-blowing rights of public employees.
7. Promote constitutional principles of equality, fairness, representativeness, responsiveness, and due process in protecting citizens' rights.

III. Demonstrate Personal Integrity

Demonstrate the highest standards in all activities to inspire public confidence and trust in public service. ASPA members are committed to:

1. Maintain truthfulness and honesty and to not compromise them for advancement, honor, or personal gain.
2. Ensure that others receive credit for their work and contributions.
3. Zealously guard against conflict of interest or its appearance: e.g., nepotism, improper outside employment, misuse of public resources, or the acceptance of gifts.
4. Respect superiors, subordinates, colleagues, and the public.
5. Take responsibility for their own errors.
6. Conduct official acts without partisanship.

IV. Promote Ethical Organizations

Strengthen organizational capabilities to apply ethics, efficiency, and effectiveness in serving the public. ASPA members are committed to:

1. Enhance organizational capacity for open communication, creativity, and dedication.
2. Subordinate institutional loyalties to the public good.
3. Establish procedures that promote ethical behavior and hold individuals and organizations accountable for their conduct.
4. Provide organization members with an administrative means for dissent, assurance of due process, and safeguards against reprisal.
5. Promote merit principles that protect against arbitrary and capricious actions.
6. Promote organizational accountability through appropriate controls and procedures.
7. Encourage organizations to adopt, distribute, and periodically review a code of ethics as a living document.

V. Strive for Professional Excellence

Strengthen individual capabilities and encourage the professional development of others. ASPA members are committed to:

1. Provide support and encouragement to upgrade competence.
2. Accept as a personal duty the responsibility to keep up to date on emerging issues and potential problems.
3. Encourage others, throughout their careers, to participate in professional activities and associations.
4. Allocate time to meet with students and provide a bridge between classroom studies and the realities of public service.

Source: American Society for Public Administration, http://www.aspanet.org/scriptcontent/index_codeofethics.cfm.

CONCEPTS IN ACTION

Encyclopedia of Ethical Failure

Stephen Epstein, director of the Standards of Conduct Office at the Pentagon, compiles the "Encyclopedia of Ethical Failure." The introduction states that the "goal is to provide [Department of Defense] personnel with real examples of Federal employees who have intentionally or unwittingly violated the standards of conduct." Violations are organized in section by type, including abuse of position, financial disclosure violations, misuse of government resources and personnel, and time and attendance violations. In the excerpt below, reporter Jonathan Karp discusses Epstein's work. The encyclopedia is publicly available at: http://www.dod.mil/dodgc/defense_ethics/.

Government workers who are caught misbehaving often are suspended, fired or prosecuted for their misdeeds. Then, when all that is done, they face one last humiliation—a virtual dressing down at the hands of Pentagon lawyer Stephen Epstein. . . .

Take the case of the Customs and Border Protection officer who landed a government helicopter on his daughter's grade-school playground: Despite having a supervisor's ill-considered clearance to fly there, Mr. Epstein writes, the officer was fired for misusing government property. When one Army base official was caught funneling bogus business to himself and to his girlfriend's daughter, Mr. Epstein ran the item under the headline, "One Happy Family Spends Time Together in Jail."

With so much federal money sloshing around thanks to record defense spending, Mr. Epstein hopes to drive home the importance of ethics by publicizing wrongdoers. It's "like public executions," he says. "We try to write the entries with a sense of humor, but the message is clear that this behavior is ruinous." . . .

As a top Pentagon ethics official, the understated Mr. Epstein oversees an office that advises on workplace behavior, trains senior bureaucrats individually in one-hour sessions once a year, and counsels officials seeking work in the private sector. . . .

Mr. Epstein combs through the press, legal records and internal government investigation reports for material, distilling most entries to a few paragraphs. Many of the entries are straightforward, but he often finds humor in the missteps. Two Veterans Affairs bureaucrats were charged with overbilling the government and receiving kickbacks from a supplier. "The product?" Mr. Epstein dryly notes: "Red tape." It was more than 100,000 rolls of a special type used to prevent tampering with prescription-drug orders. . . .

Patrick Carney, assistant general counsel for ethics at the Federal Communications Commission, draws on the Encyclopedia for training and encourages his staff to read the document online because the "bite-size examples are more entertaining than reading the statutes" themselves, he says. In quarterly internal FCC "Ethicsgram" newsletters, Mr. Carney includes items from the Encyclopedia. "Everyone around town is looking for ways to get the word out on ethics, and Steve's material is often used," he says.

Source: Jonathan Karp, "At the Pentagon, an 'Encyclopedia of Ethical Failure.' " *Wall Street Journal,* May 14, 2007.

Motives

Individuals' ethics and values in turn influence motives—"psychological constructs used to answer the question '*why* did she/he/they do that?' "[49] For example, the fundamental motive underlying rational choice theories and frameworks such as the principal-agent model and transaction cost theory (see chapter 5) is self-interest: Individuals act in ways that further their own interests.[50]

At the opposite end of the spectrum, stewardship theory asserts that individuals are motivated not by self-interest, but by a desire to serve the collective so that their interests are aligned with the organization and its leaders.[51] Although potentially useful for understanding the motives of public sector employees, the theory has been tested almost exclusively in private sector organizations.[52]

One example that seems consistent with stewardship theory (but does not invoke it explicitly) is John D. DiIulio Jr.'s case study of the Federal Bureau of Prisons (BOP). He argues that rational choice models do not sufficiently characterize the motives of many participants in public organizations. Instead, DiIulio suggests an alternative model of "principled agents" "who do not shirk, subvert, or steal on the job even when the pecuniary and other tangible incentives to refrain from these behaviors are weak or nonexistent."[53] DiIulio develops this model based on observations of the behaviors and motives of BOP guards and managers and argues:

> [R]ational choice theorists of bureaucracy underestimate the propensity of people to redefine their self-interest in terms of the preferences of leaders they respect, the well-being of co-workers they care about, and the survival and reputation of organizations they labor for. It may well be true that under most conditions, most bureaucrats, especially within government, follow narrow definitions of self-interest. But that is neither the whole story nor the most important part of the story of what public servants . . . do on a day-to-day basis. Even in the bowels of government agencies, there is more self-sacrifice, and less self-interest, than rational choice theory allows.[54]

In their theory of **public service motivation** (PSM), James L. Perry and Lois Recascino Wise propose a related framework for understanding motivation of employees in public organizations.[55] Drawing on work by Anthony Downs, Luther Gulick, Frederick Mosher, H. George Frederickson, and others, Perry and Wise argue that a unique PSM has three bases. The first is rational motives, reflecting an individual's personal interest or commitment to a particular program, desire to participate in the policy process, which can be exciting and personally fulfilling, and use of his or her public service position for advocacy for a favored position or group (a motive related to the representative bureaucracy literature, discussed in chapter 8). The second is norm-based motives which reflect an individual's interest in social equity, a sense of loyalty or duty to government itself, and a desire to serve the public interest. Finally, affective motives form a third base for PSM, reflecting specific convictions about the particular program an individual works in, as well as a "patriotism of benevolence"—a construct described by Frederickson and David K. Hart meaning "an extensive love of all people within our political boundaries and the imperative that they must be protected in all of the basic rights granted to them by the enabling documents." [56]

Empirical studies of the PSM framework have found some support for it. Studies suggest that PSM is positively related to organizational commitment; that whistleblowers exhibit higher levels of PSM than "inactive observers" (those who observe but do not report illegal activity); that PSM is positively associated with higher levels of job satisfaction, performance, and intention to remain in public service; that PSM is positively related to employees viewing their jobs as important and, in turn, to work effort; and that PSM is positively related to interpersonal citizenship ("helping behavior directed at coworkers") in public organizations.[57] Not all studies have found positive effects of PSM, however. These inconsistent findings may be the result of a mediating influence: Bradley E. Wright and Sanjay K. Pandey find that the relationships between PSM and job satisfaction is "mediated by the extent to which the employee perceives that his or her values are congruent with those of the public sector organization." [58]

As this chapter will discuss, awareness of the motives of employees (to the extent they are observable) may be important for public sector managers in situations such as managing change or in personnel recruitment and selection.[59]

Trust and Reputation

Another building block of the culture dimension is the development and presence of **trust:** "the willingness of a party to be vulnerable to the actions of another party based on the expectation that the other will perform a particular action important to the trustor, irrespective of the ability to monitor or control that other party." [60] Trust forms the basis for cooperation and repeated interactions over time.[61] It is thought to facilitate interactions when actors are vulnerable to the opportunistic actions of others, when a situation poses risks of unpredictable action, and when stable expectations about the behavior of other actors can be developed.[62] Yet whether these characteristics are antecedents to trust, or whether trust enables these characteristics to develop is a matter of some debate.

Individuals with strong public service values create reputations for reliability and integrity for their organizations. This development is important because trust between organizations and their principals, especially in the context of service provider agreements, is of considerable interest as public managers operate in their external environments—for example, in promoting cooperation among providers and other actors in mental health networks, interlocal networks of service providers, and environmental issues.[63] Because organizations in a network are likely to exhibit different cultures (and subcultures), additional uncertainty is introduced into these relationships.[64]

The construct of trust is closely related to that of **reputation,** which provides a signal regarding future behaviors by individuals or organizations in the face of unforeseen circumstances.[65] Because "reputation . . . allows predictability in an uncertain world," political actors may take reputation into account when designing bureaucratic structures.[66] For example, Treasury Department officials in the George W. Bush administration wanted to shift oversight of the Federal National Mortgage Association (Fannie Mae) away from the Department of Housing and Urban Development (HUD)—which had a reputation in Treasury for lax oversight—to the Treasury Department where they would have greater control. Congress, however, resisted the proposal; concerned legislators seemed to trust HUD oversight more than what they anticipated from Treasury. This classical political conflict, which stalled regulatory reform, may have contributed to the 2008 financial crisis which led to the federal government's takeover of Fannie and Freddie.

In the world of policymaking (and in the world of public management, as this text argues), a reputation for **neutral competence** can be valuable because it connotes the ability to use "appropriate methods for assessing problems and predicting the consequences of policy alternatives as well as neutrality in choosing and arguing for the social values that provide a basis for comparison of the alternatives." The Government Accountability Office (GAO) and the Congressional Budget Office (CBO) are legislative branch organizations that have reputations for contributing "skillful, neutral, and nonpartisan analysis to the public discourse on policy issues."[67] Resources for the Future, the RAND Corporation, and MDRC are examples of independent organizations (discussed further in chapter 7) with such reputations. Neutral competence reflects the skills and reputation of organizational members as well as the structure of the organization itself. In part because of the professionals employed by them, independent organizations such as the CBO can more easily establish a reputation for neutral competence than, for example, the office of the Assistant Secretary for Planning and Evaluation (ASPE) in the Department of Health and Human Services (HHS), even though within HHS, ASPE is viewed as having greater neutral competence than analysts in the program bureaus of the department.

The building blocks of culture discussed in this section—values, professions, ethics, and motives of individual participants as well as trust and reputation of individuals and the organization as a whole—contribute to the culture of an organization and its institutionalized norms. The cultural dimension interacts with the structural and craft dimensions of public management, sometimes in complex ways, as discussed in the following sections.

CONCEPTS IN ACTION

Neutral Competence at the Congressional Budget Office

The Congressional Budget Office (CBO) was led from 2003 to 2005 by Douglas Holtz-Eakin, who served as chief economist of President George W. Bush's Council of Economic Advisors from 2001 to 2002 and as a senior policy adviser for John McCain's presidential campaign in 2008. Holtz-Eakin maintained and fostered the CBO's reputation for neutral competence (of which nonpartisan analysis is one aspect) during his term as director. The excerpt below is from the *New York Times* on the occasion of Holtz-Eakin's retirement.

As director of the Congressional Budget Office, Douglas Holtz-Eakin has been Congress's top economist, handpicked by the Republican leadership. Recently, he had some advice for lawmakers—mostly Republicans—who insist that more tax cuts will foster economic growth and raise tax revenue: "Don't even think about it."

The occasion was the release of the agency's long-term outlook, which shows huge unending deficits. "You can't grow yourself out of this problem," said Mr. Holtz-Eakin. "It's just too big."

That's startlingly straight talk, given that Republicans are determined to pass tens of billions in unpaid-for tax cuts come January. But it is typical of Mr. Holtz-Eakin, who is retiring this week after three years as the director. In those years, he has delivered nonpartisan, data-driven research on some of the most controversial issues.

Often, what Mr. Holtz-Eakin said wasn't what his bosses wanted to hear. He went on record in 2003 saying that President Bush's tax and spending plans would do little or nothing for long-term economic growth. One report issued under his leadership showed that Mr. Bush's tax cuts heavily favored the wealthiest Americans. Another debunked the politically potent but false contention that the estate tax hurts farmers.

By going where the facts and figures led, Mr. Holtz-Eakin also protected his agency, which may be the last bastion of neutral government analysis in Washington. To succeed him, Congressional leaders need a top economist who has a reputation to protect and is a superb number cruncher, fluent communicator of complex issues and good manager.

That is a lot to ask. But, after all, they picked Mr. Holtz-Eakin in 2003.

Source: "The Right Stuff," *New York Times,* December 27, 2005, Sec. A.

STRUCTURE AND CULTURE

The symbiosis between the formal and informal organization—between structure and culture—that Herbert Simon described introduces a number of interesting challenges for public managers. The linkages are numerous and complex. This section aims to raise awareness of the possibility of these linkages and their importance through examples where culture has mediated the effects of structure on outcomes, where culture has affected the implementation of new structures, where new structures have influenced existing cultures, how characteristics of cultures might differ in loosely and tightly coupled organizations, and how interactions of culture and structure can affect whether and how organizations "learn."

Carolyn Ban's study of U.S. federal agencies illustrates the mediating effect of culture. Even when faced with similar structural constraints, managers' responses ranged from adhering strictly to the constraints to finding ways to work around them through informal channels.[68] Ban attributed these strategy differences in part to differences in organizational cultures (although, as discussed in chapter 7, they might also reflect differences in individual managers). This insight was investigated further by Sanjay K. Pandey, David H. Coursey, and Donald P. Moynihan, who sought to test whether culture might mediate the relationship between red tape (a structural constraint) and organizational effectiveness.[69] The authors found that culture played such a role, explaining their finding and its implication for public managers as follows:

> [T]wo organizations with the same level of red tape might see their effectiveness suffer, but the organization with a culture more attuned to coping with and working around red tape is likely to experience smaller performance declines. The implication is that in public organizations in which the reduction of red tape is often, at best, difficult to achieve, fostering cultures that promote adaptive responses to red tape may mitigate the negative aspects of burdensome rules and procedures.[70]

Structural Change and Culture

Structural changes—introduction of new formal delegations of authority or revision of existing ones—by authorities external or internal to the organization may interact with culture in complex ways. A full discussion of the theories, mechanisms, and development of this literature is beyond the scope of this book.[71] So the goal here is to provide some concrete examples of three types of cases: (1) where culture affects the implementation of new structures or mediates the effects of those new structures on outputs or outcomes; (2) where structural changes affect culture; and (3) where both types of effects seem to be operating simultaneously.

The creation of the U.S. Department of Energy in 1977 illustrates culture influencing structural change and its effectiveness. When responsibilities in areas as disparate as nuclear weapons and energy conservation were brought together under the new department's umbrella, organizational cultures unique to each program clashed, affecting the success of the reorganization and the performance of the department.[72] History seemed to repeat itself when the Department of Homeland Security (DHS) was formed. Culture clashes and turf wars erupted as twenty-two organizations, including the Federal Emergency Management Agency, the Coast Guard, and the Secret Service were brought under one big organizational tent. Chapter 5 featured a story about combining the former Immigration and Naturalization Service (INS) and the Customs Service to create the new Immigration and Customs Enforcement (ICE) bureau in DHS. A GAO report indicated that "[t]he integration of INS and Customs investigators into a single investigative program has involved the blending of two vastly different workforces, each with its own culture, policies, procedures, and mission priorities"; that blending resulted in "no love match," as the article excerpted in chapter 5, page 136, put it. Because of the different cultures within ICE, managers faced "a greater challenge in creating a unified bureau." [73] Although they introduced challenges, the new structural arrangements were not completely crippled by the cultural clashes between the two former agencies; in at least one instance, the structural reorganization led to a more successful kind of operation.

Jane E. Fountain's book, *Building the Virtual State* offers another example of culture influencing the implementation of structural changes.[74] Fountain focuses on a particular type of structural change: technology adoption by public organizations, such as the use of Web sites, internal agency networks, or cross-agency networks or systems. She argues that the enactment of such "objective" technologies (the actual physical technology of hardware or software) is not at all a linear, rational process that is identical across organizations. Instead, the precise path technology enactment takes is indeterminate due to the cultural, political, cognitive, and legal environments in which organizations operate.

The intention to use alternative dispute resolution (ADR) in the Environmental Protection Agency (EPA) is another illustration of culture influencing the implementation of structural changes and their intended effects. In 2000 the EPA announced its intention to increase the use of ADR, a structural mechanism already in use, to resolve disputes involving the agency. In their analysis of past use of ADR, Rosemary O'Leary and Susan Summers Raines found that the EPA's organizational culture was not supportive of ADR and was likely to impede its expanded use. Lack of support was reflected in managers' comments, such as "EPA sees itself as the most important party to the negotiation," and "The EPA has a strong tradition of being cautious, particularly in policy development. Issues must go up and down a chain of command." [75] Such comments indicate that it would be no small task to overcome the entrenched views of EPA employees to promote greater use of ADRs.

The direction of influence may run in the other direction as well; that is, structural changes may affect culture, as the organization adjusts to incorporate new ways of organizing work or new accountability requirements. In the mid-1970s the Social Security Administration (SSA) was tasked with administering the Supplemental Security Income (SSI) program; and in the early 1980s with performing reviews of eligibility for recipients of disability insurance. As Martha Derthick details, the implementation of these programs was characterized by many errors in SSI payment processing and in disability eligibility determination. She found that the agency's culture suffered as a result:

> In both instances [SSA] was left with responsibility for a fragmented, decentralized program over which it had lost its customary share of policy control. To the extent that uniform policies and practices were sacrificed (to the states in SSI, to the courts in the disability review), so was the essential character of the SSA as a national agency. Relations with employees and state agents were impaired as a consequence of their having been assigned demoralizing tasks. . . .
>
> Finally, the agency suffered a loss of prestige and self-confidence. Historically, it had had an exceptional degree of pride. It was the Marine Corps of the domestic civil service—elite and invincible. . . . SSI and the disability review therefore came as rude shocks, both from the evidence that the agency was not as good as it thought it was (however good nonetheless) and from the brutal criticism by Congress, press, and the courts. Whether or not pride was lost, a sense of invulnerability certainly was. After 1974, the agency wore a wounded air.[76]

Nonprofit social service organizations that provide services under contract also illustrate how structural change can affect internal cultures. The increased "marketization" of nonprofits has led to a kind of business professionalization and emphases on the values reflected by those professionals, introducing interests beyond those of the nonprofit's mission: "Rather than focus on responding to the organization's founding commitments, executives now grapple with organizational survival and professional career advancement." [77]

Finally, the direction of influence may run both ways: Culture may affect the implementation and effectiveness of structural change, and structural change may affect culture. Barbara S. Romzek and Jocelyn M. Johnston found that the organizational cultures of the Area Agencies on Aging (AAAs), nonprofits that provided contracted case management services for Medicaid in Kansas, exhibited direct influence on implementation. Although the relationships between the AAAs (the agent) and the state departments of Social and Rehabilitation Services and Aging (the principals) were aided by a shared "culture of service," "these shared values have not offset other tensions created by the differences in administrative culture and policy role." In addition, the structural changes influenced culture in the AAAs, reflecting the challenges they faced in implementing the policy. Because the contract essentially called for the AAAs to "expand their role beyond advocacy to encompass service delivery," their cultures were affected by structural changes such as more reliance on field offices, a different mix of professionals, and different divisions of labor.[78]

The examples in this section illustrate the interactions between structural change and culture. The interactions are likely to be complex and perhaps unpredictable or indeterminate. What seems clear is that structural change seldom consists only of a "technical" or rational implementation process. Managers who anticipate this fact may be prepared to exercise their managerial craft by influencing the specific forms of structural changes (to the extent possible) so they are more congruent with their organizational cultures or by attempts to influence cultures following a structural change. These craft aspects are discussed later in this chapter and in chapter 7.

CONCEPTS IN ACTION

The Need for Cultural Change at DOE Weapons Laboratories

President Bill Clinton asked a special investigative panel of the President's Foreign Intelligence Advisory Board to examine issues of security in the Department of Energy's laboratories that design nuclear weapons. The panel reported that structural reforms proposed by Energy Secretary Bill Richardson were necessary but not sufficient to address the lax attitudes toward security in the labs. Instead, the panel concluded, fundamental changes in culture and employee attitudes and behaviors were essential.

[T]he Department of Energy is incapable of reforming itself—bureaucratically and culturally—in a lasting way, even under an activist Secretary.

The panel has found that DOE and the weapons laboratories have a deeply rooted culture of low regard for and, at times, hostility to security issues, which has continually frustrated the efforts of its internal and external critics, notably the GAO and the House Energy and Commerce Committee. Therefore, a reshuffling of offices and lines of accountability may be a necessary step toward meaningful reform, but it almost certainly will not be sufficient.

Even if every aspect of the ongoing structural reforms is fully implemented, the most powerful guarantor of security at the nation's weapons laboratories will not be laws, regulations, or management charts. It will be the attitudes and behavior of the men and women who are responsible for the operation of the labs each day. These will not change overnight, and they are likely to change only in a different cultural environment—one that values security as a vital and integral part of day-to-day activities and believes it can coexist with great science.

Source: Special Investigative Panel, President's Foreign Intelligence Advisory Board, "Science at Its Best, Security at Its Worst: A Report on the Security Problems at the U.S. Department of Energy," June 1999, http://www.fas.org/sgp/library/pfiab/foreword.html.

Culture in Loosely and Tightly Coupled Organizations

In loosely coupled organizations (such as public schools) the formal organizational structure tends not to reflect the actual activities of its participants (see chapter 5).[79] Instead, structures such as organization charts may shape organizational culture by providing "myth and ceremony." John Meyer and Brian Rowan illustrate the central role that culture, through myth and ceremony, plays in this kind of organization:

> Activities are performed beyond the purview of managers. In particular, organizations actively encourage professionalism, and activities are delegated to professionals.
>
> Goals are made ambiguous or vacuous, and categorical ends are substituted for technical ends. Hospitals treat, not cure patients. Schools produce students, not learning. In fact, data on technical performance are eliminated or rendered invisible. Hospitals try to ignore information on cure rates, public services avoid data about effectiveness, and schools deemphasize measures of achievement.
>
> Integration is avoided, program implementation is neglected, and inspection and evaluation are ceremonialized.
>
> Human relations are made very important. The organization cannot formally coordinate activities because its formal rules, if applied, would generate inconsistencies. Therefore individuals are left to work out technical interdependencies informally. The ability to coordinate things in violation of the rules—that is, to get along with other people—is highly valued.[80]

In tightly coupled organizations, structure is meaningful in that it reflects how work gets done. Although myth and ceremony aspects of structure may exist, different kinds of culture are manifested in tightly coupled organizations. Prominent examples are **high-reliability organizations** (HROs) that perform activities such as nuclear power generation, air traffic control, or airport security, in which mistakes or operating failures would have disastrous consequences.[81]

Todd R. LaPorte and colleagues have examined HROs, guided by a conceptual logic that takes into account organizational culture as well as the formal structures and interdependencies of the organizational communication and decision-making processes among senior officials. They find that HROs tend to have a strong norm of "mission accomplishment," that is, error-free operation, integrated with a "safety culture" or "culture of reliability" that provides guidance for action when unforeseen circumstances arise that are not covered by detailed standard operating procedures. Because the formal rules and incentives are insufficient to cover all contingencies, operating effectiveness "requires a more fully engaged person responding to the norms of individual and group relations that grow out of the particular demands and rewards of the hazardous systems involved." [82] They identify common norms: operator "élan," characterized by competitiveness and a "prideful wariness"; an expectation of autonomy and responsibility; and tensions between those who develop the complex systems involved (the engineers) and those who operate them. Together, these norms constitute the "dominant workways and attitudes about appropriate behaviour at the operating levels" that "give a sense of the strength of the affective nature of HRO operations and provide the basis for the expressive authority and identitive compliance norms that enable the close cooperation necessary" in these organizations.[83]

Understanding the role that culture plays in HROs provides a useful device for analyzing reliability not only for "error adverse" organizations such as nuclear power plants, but also for a broader class of "error tolerant" organizations that are performing "impossible jobs." [84] Can child protection agencies, which are typically plagued with management problems, ever become high-reliability organizations?

CONCEPTS IN ACTION

Teams and Culture in a High-Reliability Organization

A National Academies report examined the human factors associated with the air traffic control system—a high-reliability organization. In this excerpt, the report emphasizes the importance of teams in the organizational culture of air traffic control, highlighting potential structural breakdowns as well as remedies, the role of teamwork and its incorporation into the culture for responding to breakdowns that inevitably occur, and the importance of visible and continuing support from managers to foster these processes.

Teamwork, reflected in verbal communication among controllers and their supervisors and between controllers and flight crews, is likely to be a critical component of air traffic control for the foreseeable future. As in other technological endeavors, a high percentage of operational errors involves breakdowns in communications, coordination, and group decision making. Crew resource management training has proved to be effective in improving team coordination in flight crews and is being mandated on a worldwide basis. Similar training for air traffic controllers and their supervisors and trainers has the potential to provide similar enhancement of teamwork. This potential will only be realized if the necessary commitment by and support from FAA management becomes evident.

The automation of components of the air traffic system may influence team interactions and can, in some circumstances, have a negative effect on teamwork and the ability of controllers to maintain situation awareness. The panel has identified a number of approaches to improving team coordination and communication in the air traffic control system:

1. Making team issues a part of the organizational culture of the air traffic system by defining the nature of team coordination as part of the organization's task description. It is important to include evaluation of team as well as individual skills as part of performance assessment.
2. Focusing on team as well as individual factors in the investigation of operational errors in the air traffic control system.
3. Make team training a centrally funded program required at all air traffic control facilities.

Source: Christopher D. Wickens et al., *Flight to the Future: Human Factors in Air Traffic Control* (Washington, D.C.: National Academies Press, 1997), 150.

Organizational culture therefore influences behavior and the nature of work in both loosely and tightly coupled organizations. Myths, ceremonies, norms, and values work together with the formal structure to define and shape the organization's work.

Organizational Learning

Two related concepts—organizational learning and the learning organization—have attracted considerable attention from scholars, especially those in business administration.[85] Many definitions and emphases of **organizational learning** are found in the literature; they reflect various cultural, cognitive, and/or behavioral aspects of learning and focus on changes in cognition, in potential behavior, or in actual behavior.[86] Some accounts focus on individual learning as a step toward organizational learning, and others examine change at the organizational level. In one view, "Although organizational learning occurs through individuals, it would be a mistake to conclude that organizational learning is nothing but the cumulative result of their members' learning." [87]

One definition of organization learning, offered by Chris Argyris and Donald A. Schön is "the detection and correction of error." They further distinguish "single-loop learning" in which "individuals respond to error by modifying strategies and assumptions within constant organizational norms" and "double-loop learning" in which "response to detected error takes the form of joint inquiry into organizational norms themselves, so as to resolve their inconsistency and make the new norms more effectively realizable." [88]

The elements of culture and structure as part of organizational learning are evidenced in the concept of organizational learning offered by Barbara Levitt and James G. March. They describe organizational learning as "encoding inferences from history into routines that guide behavior" where "routines" are "the forms, rules, procedures, conventions, strategies, and technologies around which organizations are constructed and through which they operate . . . [plus] the structure of beliefs, frameworks, paradigms, codes, cultures, and knowledge that buttress, elaborate, and contradict the formal routines." [89]

Management scholar Eric Tsang notes that the literature on organizational learning is sharply divided into normative and prescriptive studies that focus on how organizations *should* learn and the analytical and empirical studies that focus on how organization actually *do* learn.[90] Characteristic of the former is organizational behavior scholar Swee Goh's identification of the strategic architecture of a learning organization. All organizations can learn, he argues, if they develop five core building blocks: clarity and support for mission and vision, shared leadership and involvement, a culture that encourages experimentation, ability to transfer knowledge across organizational boundaries, and teamwork and cooperation. The foundations for this architecture, Goh says, must consist of an effective organizational design and appropriate employee skills and competencies to execute that design.[91]

Organizational learning would, by Goh's standards, seem to require that the organization not only have a technically rational design but also that it be able to engage external and internal constituencies on its own terms, presuming considerable autonomy on the part of agency managers and considerable stability or longevity of the officials associated with the effort. It is immediately apparent that such conditions are rare in a regime governed by an ongoing process of political competition and penetrated deeply by patronage and the turnover associated with regular elections.

An example of the analytical and empirical approach to organizational learning is Baiyin Yang, Karen Watkins, and Victoria Marsick's model that incorporates three structural elements (connecting the organization to its environment, establishing systems to capture and share learning, and providing strategic leadership for learning) and four human elements (creation of continuous learning opportunities, promotion of inquiry and dialogue, encouragement of collaboration and team learning, and empowerment of people toward a collective vision).[92] The authors argue that relationships among these elements lead to gains in organizational knowledge and increases in organizational performance.

Because the prerequisites for organizational learning often do not fit the contexts in which public organizations operate, the concept has not penetrated American public management thinking to an appreciable degree. Well-known textbooks and handbooks concerned with public management hardly mention organizational learning. Among the exceptions, Julianne Mahler specifically examined the influence of culture on learning in public organizations. She argues from case evidence that "learning by agency actors depends not only on the collection and retrieval of output data and other kinds of information, [but] it also depends on the culture of beliefs, norms, and professional identities that provides the context of meaning for this information." [93] Other research has examined learning in the context of performance management and crisis management and response.[94]

The concept of organization learning is hardly universally popular even on its home ground in the private sector. "[T]here are severe limitations to organizational learning as an instrument of intelligence," argue Levitt and March. "The same processes that yield experiential wisdom produce superstitious learning, competency traps, and erroneous inferences" stemming partly from "inadequacies of human cognitive habits, partly from features of organizations, partly from the characteristics of the structure of experience." [95]

Learning is an appealing and apparently sensible paradigm, however, and managers are in positions to promote it at an organizational level by, for example, institutionalizing planning and evaluation practices, advisory groups, and in-house analytic processes and personnel.[96]

As this section has illustrated, aspects of structure, culture, and their interactions may present managers with the "givens" of their internal environments and place them in roles as creatures who respond to and operate within these constraints. Or these aspects may present opportunities for managers to act as creators to shape structure, culture, and perhaps their interactions. The next section turns specifically to the possibilities of managerial craft in shaping culture.

CRAFT AND CULTURE

When managers are able to influence the cultures of their organizations, they are exercising their roles as creators. Doing so is unlikely to be straightforward, quick, or easy; rather, it requires concerted and sustained efforts. "Political scientists, sociologists, and anthropologists alike acknowledge the power of culture in determining organizational behavior but believe that culture is highly resistant to the change efforts of leaders," observes Anne Khademian.[97] The political context is one likely reason for this resistance in public organizations. Many police departments and public schools, for example, exhibit cultures that seem quite resistant to determined efforts to change them.

But even resistant cultures may be susceptible to change under fortuitous leadership and the right combination of circumstances. In *The Functions of the Executive,* Barnard argued that a primary task of the organization's leader is to create and shape a culture that can unify the employees and improve organizational performance.[98] Schein distinguishes leaders from managers based on their propensities to be creators or creatures: "Leaders create and change cultures, while managers and administrators live within them." [99] DiIulio emphasizes the importance of the leadership role of managers in affecting culture: "It is organizational leaders who either set or do not set in motion the organizational socialization processes that transcend principal-agent problems by nurturing a culture of principled agents." [100]

One way managers may try to influence culture is through defining the organization's **mission.** By shaping shared values and norms, a sense of mission can motivate employees and frame their understanding of their work in the organization.[101] Instead of leaving culture to be formed by "the chance operation of predispositions, professional norms, interest-group pressures, or situational imperatives," managers should actively focus on shaping an organization's mission, argues James Q. Wilson.[102] He acknowledges the difficulty of doing so, however, because of the multiple goals of public organizations, their many structural constraints (legal and political), and that defining a mission typically occurs only when an organization is first formed. Yet an empirical analysis of mission statements in public schools found that "[m]issions are fluid, open to interpretation, multilayered, and contested," suggesting that managers may in fact be in a position to influence them and, it follows (if mission statements matter in this regard), to influence the organization's culture.[103]

Another way that managers may influence culture is through what Khademian calls broad, "relentless" attention to internal roots of culture and their link to organizational commitments, as well as to external political principals and stakeholders. She argues that structures and task requirements create frameworks for "commitments," a term adopted from Philip Selznick's work and defined as the "common understandings held by people working together in an organization or program" that form the "roots" of organizational culture, and in turn define how the work of the agency is done. Khademian acknowledges the difficult task that managers face in changing culture and points out that a manager or leader of an organization cannot simply change culture by fiat.[104] Only when a manager works with the roots of an organization's culture and its commitments, argues Khademian, can cultural change be possible. She provides guidance for identifying roots of culture in public organizations by examining three primary areas: tasks, resources and personnel, and the organization's external environment. Analysis of the roots of culture might focus on specifics such as understanding the educational backgrounds and work experiences of employees; identifying the language used to describe how work is done, how customers or clientele are referred to, and how political superiors and stakeholders are described; and identifying the formal structures of authority.[105]

To appreciate Khademian's framework, consider the experiences of the Internal Revenue Service (IRS) with implementing information technology (IT) modernization. Barry Bozeman studied this process and writes that IRS culture is characterized by risk aversion, insularity, and mistrustfulness, all which have led to some spectacular organizational failures in its IT modernization.[106] The IRS is charged with processing an enormous volume of different kinds of tax returns, dealing with a wide variety of filing formats, and adapting to changes in tax laws every year. IRS employees are mostly "lifers" who have been through turbulence and survived. In addition, tensions are evident between headquarters and field staff. The external environment of the IRS is strongly top-down, with the organization subject to a high level of involvement in its affairs by the Office of Management and Budget, the GAO, Congress, and even the National Academy of Sciences.

These roots of culture result in IRS employee commitments to getting the job done without complaining, to suppressing dissent, to hiding or suppressing bad news, and to protecting turf and boundaries. Bozeman reports that IT modernization is occurring at the IRS, but it is focused on incremental and manageable projects, not on fundamental restructuring of agency-wide systems. This picture suggests that the IRS as an institution is changing very slowly if at all because no one has been able to change the roots of its culture.

Making explicit links to an employee's public service motivation may be another way of tapping into cultural roots and commitments of public organizations. Managers may be able to practice "values management" by focusing on the individual worker, job, workplace, organization, and society levels.[107] Doing so, say Laurie E. Paarlberg, James Perry, and Annie Hondeghem, extends the strategies for harnessing public service motivation "beyond the formal human resource management system to look at social systems of leadership, culture, and interpersonal relationships that shape people and their attitudes and behaviors." [108] They glean specific "tactics" from the literature that managers can use at each of the five levels of analysis they identify: at the individual level, "provide formal and informal opportunities for newcomers to learn about organizational values and expectations for employee behavior that reflect public service values"; at the job level, "interpret broad public service missions in terms of clear and meaningful work expectations"; at the workplace level, "create and maintain incentives that align organizational mission and employee predispositions"; at the organization level, "articulate and symbolize organization mission and vision in ways that connect with employees' zone of existing public service values"; and at the society level, "advocate for and provide opportunities for pre-service experiences." [109] Echoing these themes (although not invoking public service motivation) in his study of the Bureau of Prisons and related work, DiIulio argued,

> the importance of leadership in government has less to do with cultivating outside constituency groups, fine-tuning pay scales, or refereeing intra- or interbureaucratic battles, and more to do with establishing social and moral reward systems that make it possible for government agencies to tap the creativity, sense of duty, and public-spiritedness of their workers.[110]

HOW THE WORLD WORKS

An Attempt to Steer Culture at the IRS

Mark Everson, commissioner of the Internal Revenue Service, attempted to influence the agency's culture by providing a forceful statement of "what the IRS believes" or what he thought the culture *ought* to be. The question, however, is how many IRS employees shared Everson's beliefs about the value of private sector expertise to IRS operations and how many were persuaded by his statement to accept this value. As is discussed in chapter 7, a commissioner's ideology is unlikely to transform an agency's culture without a considerable, time-consuming effort. Everson served as IRS Commissioner for four years of a five-year term.

The IRS believes that private industry, given its established expertise and experience in the field of electronic tax preparation, has a proven track record in providing the best technology and services available. Rather than entering the tax software business, IRS' partnership with private industry: (1) provides taxpayers with high quality services by using the existing private sector expertise; (2) maximizes consumer choice; (3) promotes competition within the marketplace; and (4) meets these objectives at the least cost to taxpayers.

Source: Mark W. Everson, IRS Commissioner, House Committee on Ways and Means Subcommittee on Oversight, April 6, 2006.

A manager who seeks to change the culture of his or her organization—whether by redefining the mission or by attention to the culture's building blocks, roots, and organizational commitments—faces a difficult task. Indeed, Trice and Beyer offer a list of "mistaken assumptions" about culture that a "naïve" manager might make:

- that [managers] can unilaterally decide what the culture of their firm should and will be,
- that a single homogenous culture can be easily created,
- that having such a culture is largely positive and functional, and
- that culture arises from what managers say rather than what they do.[111]

Given structural constraints (emanating from formal authority both internal and external to the organization), and ingrained and perhaps resistant values and motives of organizational members, changing the fundamental culture of an organization undoubtedly takes time and concerted, "relentless" effort. Yet managerial influence over culture is in fact possible and can have important consequences for how an organization and its employees go about their work.

CONCEPTS IN ACTION

Managers' Efforts to Instill a New Culture of Caution and Dissent

The December 2007 National Intelligence Estimate (NIE) revealed new assessments regarding the nuclear threat from Iran, but it also acknowledged some uncertainty regarding the analysis. That such an NIE could be written was due in large part to the craft of the director of National Intelligence, Mike McConnell, and his deputies, Thomas Fingar and Donald M. Kerr, particularly their efforts to change the culture that surrounded the development of the NIEs and to allow for dissent and qualifications to the analysis. The *Washington Post* reported on McConnell's directives.

Drawing lessons from the intelligence debacle over supposed Iraqi weapons of mass destruction, Director of National Intelligence Mike McConnell required agencies to consult more sources and to say to a larger intelligence community audience precisely what they know and how they know it—and to acknowledge, to a degree previously unheard of, what they do not know. . . .

Former and current intelligence officials say the new NIE reflects new analytical methods ordered by McConnell—who took the DNI job in January—and his deputies, including Thomas Fingar, a former head of the State Department's intelligence agency, and Donald M. Kerr, a former director of the Los Alamos National Laboratory and an expert on nuclear weapons technology.

Besides requiring greater transparency about the sources of intelligence, McConnell and his colleagues have compelled analysts working on major estimates to challenge existing assumptions when new information does not fit, according to former and current U.S. officials familiar with the policies. . . .

McConnell said his objective in preparing the Iran estimate was "to present the clinical evidence and let it stand on its own merits with its own qualification," meaning that it would contain dissent. "There are always disagreements on every National Intelligence Estimate," he said.

He and other officials jettisoned a requirement that each conclusion in an NIE reflect a consensus view of the intelligence community—a requirement that in the past yielded "lowest-common-denominator judgments," said one senior intelligence official familiar with the reforms.

"We demolished democracy" by no longer reflecting just a majority opinion, "because we felt we should not be determining the credibility of analytic arguments by a raising of hands," the official said. Some analysts, for example, were not "highly confident" that Iran has not restarted its nuclear program, a result reflected in the classified report. Other analysts said Iran was further away from attaining a nuclear weapons capability than the majority said.

Source: Joby Warrick and Walter Pincus, "Lessons of Iraq Aided Intelligence on Iran: Officials Cite New Caution and a Surge in Spying," *Washington Post,* December 5, 2007, Sec. A.

CULTURE MATTERS: PAY FOR PERFORMANCE IN PUBLIC ORGANIZATIONS

This chapter has considered how culture affects public organizations. In particular, it has reviewed some building blocks of culture such as individual values, ethics, motives, professional values, trust, and reputation. It has also looked at how culture and structure interact and whether and how managers may influence organizational culture. But culture cannot be the entire explanation for the behavior of public organizations. In fact, a problem with focusing solely on organizational culture, "that is, to the subjective states of organization members—[is] that one loses sight of the objective conditions of organizational participation." [112] Nevertheless, as this chapter has attempted to describe, organizational culture can shape the meaning and work of public organizations in significant ways. This section considers the role that culture might play in the implementation of structural reforms that link pay to performance for employees of public organizations.

As discussed in chapter 5, pay-for-performance systems are based on the idea that monetary incentives will prompt greater employee effort and therefore higher performance and productivity. Pay for performance is a structural tool that characterizes employee compensation. Viewed through a cultural lens, pay for performance may serve as "myth and ceremony" as well: "When organization goals are most difficult to define and job performance is thus difficult to evaluate against some agreed-upon criteria, organizations feel compelled to adopt more formal, precise evaluations in order to assure their constituents that they are operating rationally and efficiently." [113]

The suitability of pay for performance likely depends in no small part on structural elements of the job: how specific tasks or accomplishments are rewarded. Yet the cultural dimension almost certainly matters as well. Two related conceptual tools for thinking about the cultural issues that arise with performance pay are the gift exchange and the public-service bargain.

Economist George A. Akerlof develops the idea of employee compensation as a gift exchange, meaning that the exchange of labor for wages is based partially on norms of behavior that are determined by the employment relationship itself. He argues that employees develop sentiments for their fellow employees and for the organization for which they work. In addition, the norms of behavior are based on a comparison of one's own situation with that of other persons in the organization, leading to norms of "fairness" and fair treatment, so that these norms tend to be relative, not absolute. Basing his claims on empirical evidence and formal modeling, Akerlof shows that the optimal labor contract may not set wages at the minimum acceptable level because just as part of worker effort is a gift, so too is part of wages. [114]

By introducing arrangements where labor contracts are governed by market-determined wages for individuals of different capabilities and skills and where wage increases are governed by measured performance, the relevance of public service values to work in public organizations may be undermined. Pay-for-performance reforms may mute or threaten the traditional gift exchange in public organizations, where employees may be motivated at least in part by public service values and where norms of fair treatment expressed through the traditional pay system have evolved.

Akerlof's gift exchange concept is related to Christopher Hood's description of public service bargains, or "reciprocal exchange relationships between public servants and other actors in a political system." [115] Hood argues that public sector reforms often involve essential changes in the nature of a public service bargain. The employment relationship for public sector employees traditionally has been characterized by the public service bargain constituted by the various provisions of the merit systems at federal, state, and local levels of government. Pay for performance therefore represents a fundamentally different kind of relationship between public employees and other actors.

In particular, Hood is concerned with the greater use of the "thermostatic control" model of a public service bargain. In this model, heads of government agencies are given outputs to achieve and considerable latitude in choosing ways to achieve them. Output measurements are obtained, and rewards or sanctions are meted out accordingly: rewards if desired output is exceeded, sanctions or penalties if output falls short of desired output. The No Child Left Behind Act (discussed further in chapter 8) is a well-known example of a thermostatic control mechanism.

In this kind of public service bargain, policymakers give up what many critics regard as the self-defeating practice of assigning impossible jobs to agencies and then holding them responsible when these jobs are not done well. Policymakers also give up the practice of controlling executive agencies by ordering what they do or what they spend rather than what they accomplish. Public employees agree to devote their creative efforts and energies toward accomplishing the highest outputs achievable with the resources appropriated to them. Therefore, the public service bargain, or gift exchange, implied by such reforms, is characterized as follows: "Public managers accept career risk and personal blame in exchange for some decision autonomy and—in most versions—pay and perks at a managerial level, while politicians undertake to steer managers only by transparent and achievable preset objectives in exchange for avoidance of formal blame for operational failures." [116]

Recent pay-for-performance reforms in public sector organizations therefore represent a fundamental shift in the public service bargain and in the gift exchange that has characterized compensation for public employees. Donald Moynihan has cautioned, however, that reforms such as pay for performance may stamp out benefits from public service motivation in two ways: "(1) through a selection effect, by attracting and retaining those with primarily extrinsic motivations; and (2) through an incentive effect, by crowding out intrinsic motivations." [117] This issue will be raised again in the case discussion in chapter 9. Whether public service values as a motivating factor influence the successful implementation of such systems (including the response of employees to the incentives that are introduced), and whether the organizational cultures of different public organizations can accommodate and adapt to the changing public service bargains and gift exchanges represented by pay for performance, remains to be seen.

In their roles as both creatures and creators operating in environments shaped by political rationality, effective public managers practice three-dimensional management. As a further step for building skills to do so, this chapter has focused specifically on the cultural dimension of public management. The ideas, frameworks, and theories offered here have illustrated how this dimension, reflecting both individual and organizational influences on the informal organization, can be understood and analyzed in terms of more effective public managerial roles as either creature or creator.

Key Concepts

organizational culture
institutionalized values
values
professionals
ethics
public service motivation
trust
reputation
neutral competence
high-reliability organizations
organizational learning
mission

Analysis and Argument: Test Your Understanding

The teaching case, "Express Transit Maintenance Division," is available through the Electronic Hallway, https://hallway.org/index.php. It involves revelations of maintenance problems and ethical lapses at Express, a local transit agency, and the responses of its executive director, Martin Jiles, to these revelations.

After reading the case, consider the questions below regarding possible relationships between bureaucratic structures, employee behavior, and overall agency performance. These questions incorporate those raised in chapter 3 and ask you to practice using the method of argument to frame your responses. (*Note:* A usage note with additional questions and comments, written by J. Patrick Dobel, is also available to instructors on the Electronic Hallway site.)

1. What specific decisions does Martin Jiles face at the end of this case?
2. What are the "roots" of culture and the organizational commitments in the Transit Maintenance Division at Express? Use the method of argument (claims, reasons, evidence, warrants, and acknowledgments and responses) to build your response to this question.
3. What dimensions of structure are important for understanding the work of the Transit Maintenance Division? How, if at all, do the structural and cultural dimensions interact? Make arguments to support your answer.
4. What public service values, ethics, and motives are evident among employees at Express? Make an argument to support your answer.
5. Is it possible for Martin Jiles to change the culture of Express and its Transit Maintenance Division? If so, why and how can he do so? If not, why not? Make an argument to support your answer.
6. What specific actions or decisions should Jiles take next, in what order, and why? Make complete arguments to support your recommendations.

7 Public Management: The Craft Dimension

Public managers are not merely creatures of structure and culture, not merely role players following scripts written by legislators, elected executives, budget officers, or departmental lawyers. As chapter 1 argues, they are creators as well—contributors to government performance as individuals in their own right. They may actively influence the design of structures by participating in the drafting of legislation, executive orders, and regulations. In performing managerial functions and exercising responsibilities assigned to them by law, they may discover and implement innovative ways to overcome or mitigate constraints. They may reorient organizational cultures by exemplifying and rewarding goal-oriented behavior. They may make interpretations and judgments, resolve conflicts, define priorities, and represent their organizations in numerous forums so as to enhance reputation and trust.

How do public managers as individuals make a difference in government? Are certain managerial attributes or skills more important to success than others? How do public managers enhance their own effectiveness? How important to good performance is managerial craft? To set the stage for addressing these questions, consider the following two examples of public managers attempting to succeed within a given institutional and organizational context.

Dr. Thomas L. Garthwaite became director and chief medical officer of the Los Angeles County Board of Health Services on February 1, 2002.[1] The fifty-five-year-old Garthwaite had formerly managed the health care system of the Department of Veterans Affairs (with a budget of nearly $20 billion and 180,000 employees) and served as the department's under secretary for health, culminating a twenty-seven-year career in that agency. Regarded as a thoughtful and analytical public manager, he was widely credited with continuing to improve the effectiveness, efficiency, safety, and quality of health care for veterans by emphasizing outpatient services, modernizing information systems, and managing for performance.

In L.A. County, Garthwaite inherited escalating budget deficits while serving a disproportionately uninsured population. He proposed to address financial and service delivery issues through consolidating services, reducing inpatient beds, and closing clinics. "[P]erformance management and performance measurement are critical for any organization because they force you to have a conversation about the goals of the organization and they allow you the opportunity to chart your progress toward those goals," he said. "As you make progress toward those goals, it gives people who work in the system a tremendous amount of pride to see that the work is making a difference." Health care advocates and labor unions were immediately critical of his proposals. Comparing politics in Washington, D.C., and Los Angeles, Garthwaite said: "Here, it's a little more in your face. You have the Board of Supervisors that you see on a regular basis, and the press takes a lot of interest."

On November 29, 2005, Garthwaite, described in media accounts as "embattled," resigned. His efforts to reform health services had made him a lightning rod for criticism by the L.A. County board of supervisors, whose elected members oversee county departments. Garthwaite's resignation occurred as the long-troubled Martin Luther King/Drew Medical Center, a county facility, was threatened with losing its accreditation as a result of soon-to-be publicized inspections by accrediting bodies, including the U.S. Centers for Medicare & Medicaid Services.

The continuing problems at the King/Drew Center, located in Willowbrook, which is south of Watts, were a particular sore point with supervisors and other critics of county health services. In March 2004 federal health inspectors found that staff withheld medications and administered the wrong drugs or dosages even as inspectors watched. On November 1 management of hospital operations was assumed by Navigant Consulting, following its completion of a voluminous report documenting system breakdowns. One problem Navigant cited was anesthesiologists' failure to respond to Code Blue emergencies. (The anesthesiologists contended that Navigant had not distributed the pagers that would alert them to the Code Blues.) In December the *Los Angeles Times* identified numerous failures by hospital officials to inform patients and their families of serious lapses in care that doctors knew about. In March 2005, three patients died because of medical errors by hospital staff, including physician trainees, despite assurances by county officials and hospital administrators that employees had been rigorously retrained and made subject to new policies.

Supervisors then appointed an advisory board to help save the beleaguered hospital, a move that Navigant had recommended. Following several months of contentious meetings, supervisors and Garthwaite criticized the advisory board for conflicts of interest and failing to focus on management issues, recommending that it be reduced in size. Garthwaite rescinded a proposal to shut down the obstetrics, neonatal, and pediatrics units after he learned from state officials that such a move would jeopardize nearly $30 million in government aid to the hospital. Supervisors criticized Garthwaite for a delay in informing them of this jeopardy.

There is a postscript to Garthwaite's story. In August 2007 the renamed Martin Luther King Jr.-Harbor Hospital shut down completely. Early in the month, the federal government withdrew $200 million in financial support following a scathing report on hospital operations by federal inspectors, who found that the hospital had no quality improvement plan.[2] Apparently, no one could fix what ailed this much-needed but beleaguered institution.

The second example concerns Dan Tangherlini, who received a master's degree in public policy from the University of Chicago and an MBA from the Wharton School at the University of Pennsylvania. At thirty-nine, he was appointed city administrator and deputy mayor of the District of Columbia after Adrian Fenty became mayor in January 2007.[3] Tangherlini began his public service as a presidential management intern, served in several staff positions, and oversaw the District's transportation department for six years. He became interim general manager of the Washington Metro system, which operates the subway and bus systems serving residents of the District, Northern Virginia, and nearby Maryland. He was a candidate for permanent appointment to that position, although he had initially been denied it because Virginia representatives on the Metro board were concerned that Tangherlini, as a District resident, might pay too little attention to the interests of their area.

Described in a *Washington Post* account as "easygoing and approachable, with a self-deprecating sense of humor," Tangherlini "seemed to be the tonic Metro needed. "He dropped in at rail yards and bus garages and showed up for track work, parking garage groundbreakings and the bus 'roadeo' competition." He put more light in subway stations, credit card readers in parking facilities, and express lanes at fare gates for those with SmarTrip passes. He linked managers' performance to train and bus performance, stressing customer satisfaction as the ultimate performance measure. He increased the size of internship programs for hard-to-find skill positions. "He [has] a personality that people like to work for," said a former deputy mayor and former city administrator. "He is willing to make decisions and be held accountable for them."

In raising Metro employee expectations, however, Tangherlini was not always able to fulfill them. The *Post* said, "Bus driver Don Folden was overjoyed when Tangherlini rode his route one day . . . but unhappy that Tangherlini did not move faster to get rid of incompetent supervisors." But critics were outnumbered. "He shows concern for the little people," said a station manager. "He's real, not like someone coming out to get votes. And he has great ideas."

Tangherlini said of his new job that he and the mayor planned "to focus on specific outcomes, so people can see tangible results and we can hold agencies accountable." He holds meetings in Starbucks, where good coffee is near at hand, and communicates constantly with the mayor on his BlackBerry. "I like to serve. I like to make a difference. I like to produce results that can improve people's lives. If it was all about the paycheck, I'd go to work for a bank." "Truth told," warned one observer, "Tangherlini . . . comes with the same challenges as his boss. He doesn't know the finer details of the internal decay [of D.C. government]; hasn't developed a comprehensive municipal budget; and hasn't run a bureaucracy of the city's complexity."

By spring 2008 Tangherlini was in the middle of conflicts between the mayor and city council members over the District budget. Council members complained that the narrative descriptions that former mayor Anthony A. Williams used in his budget submission had been replaced by tables of numbers showing shifts in spending but providing little or no explanation. "This is the most opaque budget I've ever seen. . . . The information is scant. It's difficult," Council chairman Vincent C. Gray said at a public hearing. "I've begun to lose faith in [the administration's] ability to provide us information. . . . Every committee has struggled to make informed decisions." [4]

Recognition of the significance of the personal qualities and skills of public managers in difficult political environments introduces additional considerations into the study and practice of public management. It is important to understand:

- how managers differ in temperament, learning, and problem-solving style or what may be termed "managerial type";
- the psychological and emotional factors that influence managerial rationality and how managers deliberate and respond as decision makers to the challenges and opportunities they face;
- how public managers might inform themselves and acquire the knowledge they seek to do their work effectively;
- the perspectives, points of view, or frames of reference that public managers might use to give strategic coherence to how they approach their work; that is, how public managers might make sense of what they are doing in order to do it more effectively; and, in the light of the foregoing considerations,
- the meaning and contributions of leadership as an aspect of public management craft.

This enumeration focuses on the cognitive and strategic aspects of managerial craft. Other craft aspects, largely operational in nature, are not discussed here. Such matters include working with the media; recruiting, supervising, and evaluating subordinates; interacting with interest groups and legislative committees; promoting teamwork; and working with political superiors and peers. (The references cited in endnote 17 focus on these aspects of managerial craft.)

Following a discussion of the meaning of craft and the historical evolution of the craft perspective, the topics listed above are discussed—managerial type, deliberation and decision making, how managers can learn, strategic management, and leadership. The chapter concludes with a discussion of how public management craftsmanship matters, for good or for ill, and offers two examples of managerial craft in action and how craft affects government performance. The end-of-chapter exercise asks readers to analyze the managerial craft of John Ashcroft, who served as the U.S. attorney general from 2001 to 2005. (Ashcroft's initiative to standardize plea bargaining practices in the offices of U.S. attorneys nationwide was discussed in chapter 5 as an example of a structural reform.)

WHAT IS CRAFT?

Thomas Garthwaite and Dan Tangherlini have displayed considerable expertise and skill as public managers over the course of their careers. They used their discretion with discernment and awareness of their contexts. Garthwaite was initially rewarded with leadership of the nation's largest public medical care system, where he continued to strengthen its growing reputation for the efficient delivery of quality care. The L.A. County public health care system presented an altogether different set of challenges, however, owing to budget constraints, intractable problems in street-level service delivery, and micromanagement by elected officials who had conflicting agendas and no apparent inclination to defer to Garthwaite's expertise.

Thanks to his common touch, engaging and self-effacing personality, and technocratic instincts, Tangherlini moved steadily upward toward greater responsibility and, although he was still quite young, he was appointed to an important, highly visible but exposed public management position. It became evident that he, too, would be subject to intense, partisan scrutiny by elected officials who were disinclined to be in awe of his reputation. As a local reporter noted: "The radical changes required in the District will not happen swiftly, or magically—even with [Fenty's] ace assistant Dan Tangherlini."[5] Sure enough, Tangherlini soon found himself embroiled in political conflict associated with implementing an ambitious mayor's agenda.

The Garthwaite and Tangherlini stories illustrate the kinds of personal challenges involved in surmounting the obstacles to effectiveness that make public management distinctive. *Managerial craft may be defined as responses by individual public managers to the challenges and opportunities inherent in their positions.* More simply, craft means "skilled practice."[6] The personal characteristics and individual actions that a particular manager brings to a situation are a reflection of his or her craft. A public manager's success in devising creative responses to situations demonstrates the ability to identify and exploit a given position's opportunities within the constraints imposed by that position's political and organizational contexts. The absence of managerial creativity or a tendency to make poor judgments is also an example of managerial craft, but this kind can have adverse consequences, contributing to policy failures or to an agency's reputation for incompetence. And, as this chapter discusses, a particular public manager may perform well under one set of circumstances and poorly in other situations.

There are grounds for optimism concerning the general prospects for success in managerial craft. As Herbert Kaufman notes:

> "[A]lthough the confines of leadership are indeed binding, they are not necessarily paralyzing. . . . [E]ven leaders who recognize the limits on what they can accomplish during their terms of office are inclined, especially if they are the spirited, driving persons the system tends to select, to use all their powers for whatever effect they can have. . . . To toil at making a small difference, then, is not inevitably an exercise in futility. . . . Pragmatists confronted by constraints do what they can within the constraints.[7]

For good or for ill—and numerous instances of both abound—the men and women who manage government agencies, programs, and activities make a difference; often it's positive.

It is important to keep in mind that how public managers go about defining and pursuing their responsibilities and opportunities within given contexts are, as chapters 5 and 6 suggested, necessarily influenced by the structures and processes of formal authority within which they must work and by the professional and personal standards, norms, and values that may have become institutionalized within frameworks of formal, legal authority. Although public managers are both creatures and creators, considerations of structure and culture may limit or modify the scope for creative craftsmanship or, depending on circumstances, influence how craftsmanship is applied. Indeed, relieving constraints and changing cultures through political entrepreneurship and leadership may become managerial priorities. Because of their importance, the interactions between managerial craft and both structure and culture are discussed at length in chapter 10.

In general, the need for managerial craft has four principal sources, emanating explicitly or implicitly from enabling structures: (1) when an enacting coalition has explicitly delegated the "figuring out" of appropriate action to executive agencies and their managers; (2) when ambiguity exists in the mandate (intended or unintended), so that it is necessary for managers to figure out what actions to take; (3) when fulfilling legislative or administrative objectives requires judgment in applying rules and standards to particular situations; and, as just noted, (4) when public managers decide to change the "givens" of structure and culture to fulfill their goals. Because explicit or implicit delegations are inevitable, managerial craft is almost always a necessity and, therefore, managerial behavior is almost always a factor in government performance. But how much of a factor, under what circumstances, and compared to what are usually difficult to determine.

CONCEPTS IN ACTION

Paul Wolfowitz's Craftsmanship

In spring 2007 Paul Wolfowitz, president of the World Bank, came under heavy criticism from inside and outside the bank for special treatment received by his long-time companion, a bank employee. He was also criticized for an approach to managing that alienated many of those on whom he depended for his own effectiveness. Wolfowitz's multiple failures of managerial craftsmanship impaired the bank's performance and ultimately cost him his job. *New York Times* columnist David Brooks assessed the situation as follows.

Wolfowitz came to the bank with the heavy baggage of [having been an architect of the Iraq war]. Nevertheless, most of the (left-leaning) employees were open to him, and even saw ways his background could help him solve the bank's problems. Furthermore . . . the bank is staffed by people who are criticized from all directions and are desperate for approval and support. Wolfowitz had an opportunity to be their champion, but he forfeited that opportunity by being aloof. . . . [H]e entered a treacherous swirl of political, institutional and personal currents and navigated them poorly. Having failed to woo the open-minded people at the bank, it was inevitable they'd be out to get him.

Source: David Brooks, "Wolfowitz's Big Mistake," *New York Times,* May 3, 2007, Sec. A.

In terms of the logic of governance, discussed in chapter 4, managerial craft is practiced primarily at the (d) level of governance, where public managers, having been enabled and constrained by formal authority, use their discretion and judgment to interpret their roles, establish their priorities, and provide direction to the activities for which they are accountable.

EVOLUTION OF THE CRAFT PERSPECTIVE

The earliest conceptualizations of the public manager's job were essentially prescriptive, emphasizing the democratically responsible exercise of administrative authority by public administrators obedient to statutory and judicial guidance. As mentioned in chapter 1, the most complete and best-known answer to the question, "What do public managers do?" was Luther Gulick's famous "POSDCORB," which stands for planning, organizing, staffing, directing, coordinating, reporting, and budgeting.[8] Public managers were conceived as performing the basic functions of management within the framework of legal authority: managerial craft was neither possible or desirable. Roscoe C. Martin noted that although public administration had by 1940 become virtually synonymous with public management, little consideration was given to what he called the "nature of the craft," that is, of managerial skill.[9]

An intellectual development of seminal importance to the emergence of a more craft-oriented or behavioral view of public management was the appearance in 1938 of Chester Barnard's *The Functions of the Executive,* which laid the groundwork for new perspectives on the responsibilities of managers. As Frederick Mosher wrote, Barnard "defined administrative responsibility as primarily a moral question or, more specifically, as the resolution of competing and conflicting codes, legal, technical, personal, professional, and organizational, in the reaching of individual decisions." [10]

In addition to influencing future Nobel Laureate Herbert A. Simon's path-breaking book, *Administrative Behavior,* Barnard clearly influenced John Millett, whose 1954 book, *Management in the Public Service,* is an early exemplar of the craft perspective. Wrote Millett:

> The challenge to any administrator is to overcome obstacles, to understand and master problems, to use imagination and insight in devising new goals of public service. No able administrator can be content to be simply a good caretaker. He seeks rather to review the ends of organized effort and to advance the goals of administrative endeavor toward better public service.[11]

Millett continued in a manner prefiguring ideas that became popular two decades later:

> In a democratic society this questing [by public managers] is not guided solely by the administrator's own personal sense of desirable social ends. The administrator must convince others as well. He must work with interest groups, with legislators, with chief executives, and with the personnel of his own agency to convince them all that a particular line of policy or program is desirable.[12]

CONCEPTS IN ACTION

Gordon Chase's Craftsmanship

The idea that individual public managers can make a difference by demonstrating creative craftsmanship is exemplified by the reputation earned by the late Gordon Chase, formerly a public manager in New York City and the Commonwealth of Massachusetts. The consistency of Chase's craftsmanship, and his honesty and integrity, earned him a reputation as a public manager for all seasons.

Of Chase, former Massachusetts governor and Democratic presidential candidate Michael Dukakis said: "[A]ll who ever worked for [Chase] have told me the same thing—that he was the best boss they ever worked for. He touched them; lifted their sights; inspired them to do more than they ever thought possible. Nothing was impossible as far as Gordon was concerned."

Chase himself put it this way:

No one can predict with certainty what will make a good public manager. No single combination of education, experience, personality, and talent will make the same person a great commissioner of welfare for New York City and a smashing water and sewer director in Seattle. Each state, city, county, and township has a unique set of political, social, and economic challenges to which an aspiring public manager must adapt. But . . . there are predictable problems, dilemmas, conflicts, and confrontations that are sure to occur at some point, to some degree, in every public manager's life. . . . Stay honest, be smart, and care—the public will be the better for it.

Source: Gordon Chase and Elizabeth C. Reveal, *How to Manage in the Public Sector* (New York: Random House, 1983), 20, 178, 179.

The behavioral approaches to public management have tended to emphasize a concern for choices, decisions, and outcomes; for the political skill needed to perform effectively in specific managerial positions; and for the psychological and emotional demands of managing in the public sector. Moreover, by emphasizing the strategic political role of public managers within given political and institutional settings, these newer conceptions have been concerned with the immediate, pragmatic concerns of managers at executive levels of government organizations more than with the broader role of management in our constitutional scheme of governance. As public management expert Robert Behn put it, "Any emphasis on the perspective of practicing public managers will have a short run focus." [13] A lower priority is placed on the manager's participation in developing and sustaining institutional capacity, molding organizational cultures, adhering to durable democratic values—that is, to public management as an institution—and on management at middle and lower levels of administration, where the politics of public management are more internal than external.

Recent literature on the craft perspective tends to be based on the study and analysis of particular cases of managerial experience.[14] As Graham T. Allison noted in a seminal article, "The effort to develop public management as a field of knowledge should start from problems faced by practicing public managers." [15] The focus of such study is on what managers did or should do in specific settings. Critics view this approach as representing an "ongoing effort to create a new 'myth' for public management. . . . [B]y emphasizing a political and activist orientation—heroes and entrepreneurs became the stock and trade of its case studies" at the expense of institutions.[16] Among the numerous examples of this genre are Kenneth Ashworth's *Caught Between the Dog and the Fireplug, or How to Survive in Public Service,* Steven Cohen and William Eimicke's *The Effective Public Manager,* Philip Heymann's *The Politics of Public Management,* Robert Reich's *Public Management in a Democratic Society,* Behn's *Leadership Counts,* and Mark Moore's *Creating Public Value.*[17]

Anxious to inspire public officials with the conviction that "management counts" and with an entrepreneurial, proactive spirit, the craft literature has turned heavily to prescription. The best of this literature—for example, Norma Riccucci's *Unsung Heroes,* Paul Light's *Sustaining Innovation,* and Eugene Bardach's *Getting Agencies to Work Together*—represents a thoughtful appreciation of the existential challenges of public management at all levels of government and in the nonprofit sector and an attempt to deduce best or smart practices from closely analyzed cases.[18] Other contributions, such as Cohen and Eimicke's *The New Effective Public Manager* and Richard Haass's *The Bureaucratic Entrepreneur,* are explicitly didactic and feature numerous prescriptions and principles based on the experiences and reflections of effective practitioners, including the authors themselves.[19]

Within this genre of literature, many craft-oriented public management scholars have, as noted, generally disregarded or overlooked the structural and cultural dimensions of public management, concerning themselves with the temperamental and psychological capacities of managers to confront the multiple pressures under which they pursue their goals. This approach leads to a highly reductive view of public management that recalls an earlier preoccupation, discussed below, with the traits and personalities of leaders and managers. Successful managers are characterized as enterprising or entrepreneurial, inclined to take risks, purposeful, imaginative and intuitive, and disposed to act rather than reflect. Moore puts it this way: "[C]ool, inner concentration, in the end, can and should guide the calculations of those who would lead public organizations. It describes the 'managerial temperament' that is appropriate for those who would lead organizations that work for a divided and uncertain society. . . . [I]deas and techniques . . . can be no substitute for good character and experience. But, with luck, they might help to extend the limits of one's character and experience." [20]

Other craft-oriented public management experts emphasize simple, generic processes—establishing and reiterating clear goals, managing by "walking around" or by "groping along"—or adhering to unexceptionable principles—develop and focus on a narrow agenda, pay attention to people, and the like. Says Behn: "Most management concepts are simple, and, to have any impact these simple management ideas must be expressible in some pithy phrase." [21] But their simplicity can be deceptive. After citing five unimpeachable principles for achieving influence as a manager—such as look for opportunities to act, be careful—Haass asserts: "Being effective is that simple—and that complicated." [22]

The oversimplifications of many of its proponents should not discredit the importance of managerial craft as a basic dimension of public management. The behavioral and intellectual challenges that any good manager must take into account can be a significant factor in the determination of government performance. There are, as well, what Barnard called the "non-logical" aspects of managerial behavior that account for timely (or untimely) reactions, intuitive insights (or mistaken perceptions), and, ultimately, good (or bad) judgment.

From a craft perspective, some public managers are likely to be better than others in particular circumstances with their unique challenges, though they may not necessarily excel in all circumstances. Thomas Garthwaite's skills in meeting the demands of managing in the Veterans Health Administration were clearly less suited to the much different political and managerial environment of L.A. County. Rigorous empirical research on contributions of managerial craft to governmental performance is relatively scant, but it is reasonable to assume that public management will be better to the extent that public managers are masters of their craft.

TYPECASTING MANAGERS

From the popular literature on managerial effectiveness in public and private sectors, it is possible to conclude that good managers resemble each other in definable ways, such as decisiveness, goal-setting, empathy, tolerance for ambiguity, and clarity of purpose.[23] Yet, as the Garthwaite and Tangherlini stories suggest, and as the serious study of managerial personality and learning styles has revealed, individuals in managerial roles differ significantly in their temperaments and therefore in how they practice their craft. One can readily distinguish between a delegator and a micromanager. Moreover, individuals of quite different temperaments and "skill sets" can be effective managers, although not necessarily equally effective in the same roles. Evidence suggests that effective management results from a good fit between the particular demands of a management position and the particular characteristics of the manager who holds it. The next section discusses typical differences among public managers and the implications of these differences for managerial performance.

Assessing Managerial Type

There are many ways of characterizing differences among individuals in how they approach deliberation and decision making, thinking and learning, problem solving, and leadership.

They are variously based on individuals' emotions, values and attitudes, behaviors in particular situations, and preferences for information processing and analysis. Some are normative; they prescribe how managers *should* think and act to be effective, and they tend toward idealizing particular types or styles of management. Others are experiential or empirical; they depict how managers *do* think and act based on observing or questioning them, and they tend toward identifying the strengths and weaknesses of different styles or types of management in given situations.

One of the most comprehensive attempts to relate differences in "personality" to behavior in real-life situations, and to identify distinct **managerial types,** is associated with applications of Carl Jung's theory of psychological types. Applying Jung's ideas, two psychologists created an instrument called the Myers-Briggs Type Indicator (MBTI).[24] Based on responses to a lengthy questionnaire, the MBTI reports on individuals' preferred ways of apprehending the world—how they perceive reality—and of reacting to issues that arise in their perceived world—how they make judgments or decisions.[25] The MBTI instrument is widely used in executive training, counseling, and social science research. Among its advantages over other instruments that assess individual types or styles is that it is nonjudgmental concerning whether a particular type, style, or preference is inherently "good" or "bad."

The first two preferences can be summarized as follows:

- Individuals choose one of the two contrasting ways of perceiving or becoming aware of the world about them: *sensing* (S), by which they become aware of things directly through sensory experience, or *intuition* (N), by which subconscious processes are relied upon to construct what the individual regards as the real world.
- Individuals also choose one of the two distinct ways of judging or reaching conclusions about perceived reality: *thinking* (T), by which logical, analytical processes are used to produce conclusions, or *feeling* (F), by which conclusions are reached by bestowing on things a personal, subjective value.

Each of the four possible combinations of preferences—ST, SF, NT, and NF—produces "a different kind of personality, characterized by the interests, values, needs, habits of mind, and surface traits that naturally result from" each combination.[26] A reasonable presumption, moreover, is that people are more comfortable with colleagues whose modes of perception and judgment are similar to their own than they are with colleagues whose preferences are sharply different from theirs. Indeed, destructive conflict often develops between individuals of different types. A sensing individual may become highly impatient with the apparent propensity of an intuitive individual to "ignore the facts"; the intuitive individual, in turn, may scorn the sensing type's "lack of imagination." As a result, sensing and intuitive people may have great difficulty understanding and working with each other. A corollary, however, is that a manager, especially one with strong preferences, may benefit from having diverse types on a management team, as different preferences complement one another in addressing complex challenges.

The theory is considerably broadened by the addition of two additional preferences that contribute to basic differences in personality:

- Individuals differ in their relative interest in their "outer" and "inner" worlds: *introverts* (I) are oriented mainly to private processing of reality and may be "hard to know," whereas *extraverts* (E) are more public in their learning and deciding, more engaging and transparent.
- Individuals differ in their relative preferences for perceiving and judging: *perceiving* (P) individuals prefer widening their grasp of reality, whereas *judging* (J) individuals prefer the process of evaluating, reaching conclusions, and deciding, even if they do not have all the information that might be desirable or available.

Individuals' temperaments can be postulated as a manifestation of these four preferences, which they have come to rely on over the course of their lives as the basis for intentional behavior.

The different combinations of these four preferences produce sixteen possible personality types, each of which is associated with a particular pattern of behavior in given situations. Evidence suggests that for the United States, 55 percent to 60 percent of all people are extraverts and that roughly 60 percent prefer sensing and judgment to intuition and perception. Moreover, although all types appear in managerial samples, most managers are both Ts and Js and, therefore, logical or rational decision makers.[27] When the other traits are added, the resulting managerial types can be described as follows:

- *ISTJ* (introverted, sensing, thinking, and judging) managers tend to be serious and quiet, earning success by concentration and thoroughness. They are practical, orderly, matter-of-fact, logical, realistic, and dependable. They make up their minds as to what should be accomplished and work toward it steadily, regardless of distractions or controversies.
- *ENTJ* (extraverted, intuitive, thinking, and judging) managers tend to be hearty, frank, decisive, and leaders in activities. They like to draw others out, asking questions, engaging in discussion and debate. They are usually good at anything requiring reasoning and intelligent talk, such as team-oriented planning and public testimony.
- *INTJ* (introverted, intuitive, thinking, and judging) managers tend to be original and determined, especially when their own interests and beliefs are engaged. They are apt to come across as skeptical, stubborn, and driven. In fields that appeal to them, they have great ability to organize a job and carry it through with or without help. They may be less inclined to deliberate, compromise, or promote teamwork.
- *ESTJ* (extraverted, sensing, thinking, and judging) managers are practical and realistic, down-to-earth, with a natural instinct for organization and administration. They will probe for the facts, for what their teams know, and will be impatient with abstractions and speculation.

An appreciation for differences in types among public managers supports the view that individuals differ in fundamental ways; that these differences have significant implications for managerial performance; that individuals gravitate toward problems, tasks, and situations that allow them to exploit their strengths, and instinctively avoid situations that might put them in a bad light. Effective public managers know the strengths and weaknesses of their own deliberation and decision-making processes and are able to evaluate the strengths and weaknesses of how individuals of different types deliberate and make decisions, using these insights to manage more effectively.

An *ESTP* may perform far less successfully than an *INTJ* in situations requiring conceptual mastery and intellectual concentration. An *INTP* placed in a position that calls for establishing rapport with diverse constituencies and quick, intuitive reactions is likely to do less well than an *ENTJ*. The nature of the fit between personalities and circumstances is of considerable significance in explaining the variations in managerial performance observed in the public sector. An individual of average abilities may perform better in a position for which he or she is well suited than a highly talented individual in the wrong job.

William L. Gardner and Mark J. Martinko report that the prevalence of intuitive (N) managers increases at higher levels in an organization.

> One would expect creative, imaginative and cognitively complex managers to be well-suited for executive positions. Further, these attributes enable Ns to be especially adept at strategic planning. . . . Hence, the prevalence of Ns among top managers is consistent with the notion that they excel in positions that require strategic management skills.[28]

An instructive example of the application of the general idea of managerial type is Yves Gagnon's study of managerial decision making on the adoption of new technologies.[29] Gagnon surveyed a sample of experienced public officials who reported that they had decided to adopt new technologies. Respondents answered seventy-nine questions posed by the researchers concerning who they were, what they did, and what happened as a result.

Gagnon was able to establish that these managers differed from each other along some dimensions predicted by theory. Specifically, their self-identified characteristics and behaviors placed them along a continuum from "administrator/trustee" to "entrepreneur/promoter." It is noteworthy that the sample had approximately equal numbers of each basic type. Also of interest are the results of correlation analyses. The managers who tended to behave in an entrepreneurial way paid less attention to what Gagnon calls "social consideration," which might be interpreted as "organizational culture." The entrepreneurial types seemed to want to press ahead forcefully and override the culture. The administrative/managerial types, in contrast, paid attention to social considerations while introducing new technologies.

It turned out that social consideration was positively associated with the success of these new technology projects. The success in this particular type of organizational change tended to be associated with managers who adopted deliberate, culturally sensitive, longer-term plans. In short, in enacting new technologies, the individual public manager must establish contact with institutionalized values; the more successful change agents are those who instinctively do so, that is, those whose preferences incline them toward considering the social implications of technology.

Do Some People Make Better Managers than Others?

Despite the wide varieties of behaviors exhibited by individuals of differing types, the implication in much of the prescriptive, best-practices literature on public management is that, within the constraints imposed by formal authority and organizational cultures, the effectiveness of public managers is proportional to the quality or appropriateness of their personality, skills, and motivations. In this view, there *is* such a thing as a managerial personality, or character, or temperament, or persona, or skill set that enables those who possess it to outperform those who are less well endowed no matter what the context in which they are working.[30] Certain types of people, in this view, will always do better than others, no matter what the challenge. This impression is reinforced by writers who claim to have identified the correlates of business, military, and political success, and by the popularity of well-known leaders as motivational speakers, such as Rudolph Giuliani, former New York City mayor and hero of 9/11; Jack Welch, former CEO of General Electric Corporation; and Gen. Norman Schwarzkopf, the commander of the 1991 expulsion of Iraq from Kuwait. These individuals often write about "how I did it and how you can do it, too."

To investigate this idea of the ideal manager, Jameson W. Doig, Erwin C. Hargrove, and a team of colleagues studied the accomplishments of a dozen individuals "whose careers at managerial levels were linked to innovative ideas and to efforts to carry these ideas into effect, often attended by some risk to their organizations and to their own careers," individuals widely considered to be effective leaders. Although all had achieved conspicuous success at some point in their lives, the puzzle was that all had also experienced reverses, failures, or mixed results that, for some of them, outweighed the successes. The lead authors reached two conclusions: "Achievement is favored by a good match of individual skill and the organizational task attempted"; and "The favorable match of skill to task must be reinforced by favorable historical conditions if there is to be significant achievement." [31] Achievement, in other words, is contextual as much as it is personal. Individuals who have succeeded in one endeavor cannot simply will success in all their endeavors. (The work of Doig and Hargrove is discussed further below.)

Laurence E. Lynn Jr. reached a similar conclusion in his study of five federal government managers appointed by President Ronald Reagan.[32] Viewing success in changing agency operations as a reflection of the combined effects of a manager's personality, skills and temperament, strategy, and the extent and nature of the constraints on managerial discretion, Lynn concluded that a public manager's strategies are more important to success than their personalities and skill sets; managers may be personable and able supervisors but still misread the political context and, therefore, doom their efforts at change. The degree of success, however, will probably reflect how easy or hard it is to bring about change, that is, on how binding are the constraints on managerial discretion. Well-liked and respected managers—Thomas Garthwaite is a good example—may achieve little in a given position if they choose the wrong strategies or prove unable, perhaps through no defect in their personal characteristics and skills, to overcome obstacles to success.

DELIBERATION AND DECISION MAKING

Whatever their type, public managers engage in many different kinds of activity: reading reports, testifying before legislative committees, making speeches and presentations, conducting and participating in meetings, visiting field offices, attending conferences, and supervising and responding to staff members and their needs and concerns. Although the particular mix of activities varies by the nature of the policies and programs being managed and by the manager's hierarchical position and responsibilities—consider the variety of managerial roles within the Head Start program depicted in chapter 1—all public managers must allocate their scarce and valuable time and attention across diverse kinds of activities. Maintaining a reasonable balance is essential.

Integrating and balancing the various aspects of craftsmanship are the processes of deliberation and decision making. As noted in chapter 5, decision making is an organizational/structural activity, a matter of procedures and protocols and due process, prescribed by law or established by public managers themselves. It is, as well, a personal activity, a manifestation of public managers' intellectual and emotional capacities and inclinations, of their temperaments and styles—in short, of their managerial personalities or types. Of particular importance, **deliberation and decision making** are foundations for preparing the kinds of persuasive arguments that, as chapter 3 made clear, are at the heart of public management as a political craft.

A decision may be defined as "a conclusion or resolution reached after consideration" or deliberation. Decision making need not be an event, nor does it necessarily follow a formal, explicit process; rather, a decision may evolve over time through a series of tentative steps and vaguely defined, deliberative activities. Moreover, a decision not to do something, to continue the status quo, is as much a decision as one to take a specific action to change the status quo. This is not to say that public managers spend most of their time making decisions. Their days are consumed with meeting, talking, listening, questioning, reading, reflecting, and observing—steps in the learning and deliberation processes that lead to decision making. Decisions are the means whereby such processes are transformed into organizational purpose and achievement. Actual decisions on issues of policy, program, and organization may be infrequent and even spontaneous. Decisiveness appropriate to the context is a fundamental component of a public manager's skill set.

The deliberation and decision-making processes by which public managers formulate strategies, confront obstacles, solve problems, and develop arguments in support of their proposals and actions are likely to be influenced by psychological and emotional factors other than cognitive capacity and the ability and inclination, which are essential in American political culture, to appear reasonable and act logically in the light of the facts. Because these factors are reflections of a manager's personality or type, the fit between the manager and the circumstances not only of a particular managerial role but also of the kinds of task demands, or even of particular events such as a crisis, may or may not produce the craftsmanship needed for fully effective performance. Simon wrote, "Of all the knowledge, attitudes, and values stored in a human memory, only a very small fraction are evoked in a given concrete situation." [33] Placing different kinds of people in a given role is likely to lead to different kinds of role behavior: Whether a social worker is a mother, of the same race or age as a client, formerly on welfare herself, professionally educated, or an ideological liberal or conservative may well have a bearing on how she responds to the individuals she serves.

Managers as Rational Actors

A popular theory of choice holds that individuals—citizens, policymakers, public managers, street-level bureaucrats—are intendedly rational; that is, they pursue their goals and interests in ways that are efficient in the use of scarce resources of time, attention, and money to maximize goal attainment. All other things being equal, rational individuals weigh the costs and benefits of alternative ways of pursuing their goals and make decisions that are consistent and transparent in the light of that analysis. Its proponents argue that **rationality** explains a great deal of human behavior, especially behavior in the world of public affairs, where the pressures to be both efficient and effective in pursuing public policy objectives with the taxpayers' money are naturally strong and where punishment for careless and preventable waste may be severe.

In a managerial context, the demands of rationality are not unrealistic or "academic"; instead, rationality has a common sense motivation and interpretation. It "has something to do with thinking, reason, and reasoning processes. An action seems rational if it is agreeable to reason: if it is not absurd, preposterous, extravagant, or foolish, but rather intelligent, sensible, self-conscious, deliberate, and calculated." [34] Or, as John M. Pfiffner put it, the managerial decision maker "saves face by supporting his decision with reasons which possess face validity" (a caution that brings to mind the need for managers to support their decisions with solid arguments, as discussed in chapter 3). Looked at this way, says Pfiffner, rationality as logical, common sense reasoning and persuasive argument is even more demanding than narrower scientific or engineering notions of rationality in that "it takes into consideration a greater variety of data." [35] These data include the kinds of intuitive, anecdotal, and experiential information that are accumulated during human learning processes.

Rationality has explicit motivations within the U.S. constitutional scheme. In political contests between the executive and the legislature, the transparent reasonableness of a political strategy confers an advantage on its proponents.[36] When decision making in either branch lacks transparency, justified suspicions arise that the process that produced the decision is not to be trusted. With the maturing of administrative law, the demonstrable rationality of managerial decisions has become an important criterion for judicial determinations concerning whether or not deference to administrative actions is warranted.

CONCEPTS IN ACTION

A Reasonable Argument for an Endangered Species Listing

On May 14, 2008, Secretary of the Interior Dirk Kempthorne announced that the polar bear had been listed as a "threatened species," that is, likely to become endangered in the foreseeable future, as defined by the Endangered Species Act. He explained the logic of his decision in a statement announcing it and included graphic images based on satellite photography of the shrinking of the Arctic ice cap, which provides habitat for polar bears. The secretary's concise logic, for which he claimed the authority of the department's scientists, provided a transparent justification for a decision that has face validity—it is apparently reasonable.

In taking these actions, I accept the recommendations of the Assistant Secretary for Fish and Wildlife and Parks, Lyle Laverty, and the Director of the U.S. Fish and Wildlife Service, Dale Hall. I also relied upon scientific analysis from the Director of the U.S. Geological Survey, Dr. Mark Myers, and his team of scientists. . . . Today's decision is based on three findings. First, sea ice is vital to polar bear survival. Second, the polar bear's sea-ice habitat has dramatically melted in recent decades. Third, computer models suggest sea ice is likely to further recede in the future. Because polar bears are vulnerable to this loss of habitat, they are, in my judgment, likely to become endangered in the foreseeable future—in this case 45 years. . . . Although the population of bears has grown from a low of about 12,000 in the late 1960's to approximately 25,000 today, our scientists advise me that computer modeling projects a significant population decline by the year 2050. This, in my judgment, makes the polar bear a threatened species. . . . I have also accepted these professionals' best scientific and legal judgments that the loss of sea ice, *not* oil and gas development or subsistence activities, are the reason the polar bear is threatened.

Source: "Remarks by Secretary Kempthorne Press Conference on Polar Bear Listing," May 14, 2008, http://www.doi.gov/secretary/speeches/081405_speech.html.

Alternatives to Rationality

It is apparent, however, and also intuitively obvious that individuals, including public managers, are not always or even usually rational or reasonable in their information processing, although it would be a good thing if they were. Social and behavioral scientists have identified numerous ways in which individuals depart systematically from the strict assumptions of rationality in information processing and problem solving. A rational explanation for a decision might conceal underlying nonrational motivations. Public managers should be aware of these frequently encountered possibilities for three reasons: (1) to increase self-awareness of their own deliberation and decision-making processes; (2) to sharpen their ability to evaluate the arguments of those who advise or attempt to influence them; and (3) to sharpen their ability to critique and react to criticisms by their external constituencies, stakeholders, and service recipients—an important step in constructing arguments to support their decisions.

The following discussion of departures from strict rationality includes situations commonly encountered in public affairs.

Bounded Rationality

Most commonly attributed to Herbert Simon, the concept of **bounded rationality** acknowledges that individuals are typically limited in how well they solve complex problems—in how much effort they make to search for, store, retrieve, and analyze information. They are apt to resort to various shortcuts that reduce stress and increase their confidence in the choices they make, relying, perhaps, on "conventional wisdom," rules of thumb, cues from those thought to be expert or well-informed, or principles of appropriateness, duty, or loyalty.[37]

The reason that such simplified choice making is not considered simply irrational is that there is a kind of rationality in resorting to shortcuts that ease the practical, cognitive, and emotional burdens of decision making. If individuals depart from strict rationality—identifying *all* alternatives, collecting *all* relevant information, weighing *all* uncertainties—they do so for rational reasons: Search and analysis costs are too high to justify an exhaustive analysis. A good decision is one that is good *enough,* one in which the decision maker has confidence. Expending significant additional resources of time and effort that improve the quality of decisions by only a little is hardly reasonable. Instead of "optimizing," decision makers may prefer "satisficing," or settling for an adequate solution to a problem given the costs of doing more.

Bounded rationality may be just as unreasonable, however. Policymakers and public managers also reduce the stresses and uncertainties of decision making by ruling out choices that violate long-held assumptions and beliefs that might well be wrong or have become outdated. Intelligence analysts who had become convinced that Saddam Hussein's Iraq had weapons of mass destruction ignored conflicting evidence provided by defectors, many of whom said the weapons had been destroyed and production halted. The response to the threat posed by al Qaeda prior to the September 11, 2001, attacks may have lacked urgency because many policymakers assumed that states such as China, Iran, Libya, and Iraq posed more significant threats to U.S. interests and security than did threats from stateless terror groups.

Policy making and management concerning health policy confront the issue of bounded rationality in a fundamental way. Proponents of consumer-driven health care argue that the nation's health care system would be more efficient if everyone shopped more carefully and considered a wider range of choices in the light of evidence concerning the costs and benefits of alternative insurance plans, providers, treatments, medications, and hospitals. But consumers of medical care, especially if they are ill, may feel incompetent to make choices on matters in which they are not experts and may be inclined, perhaps out of fear of making a bad choice, to trust their physician's recommendations, to accept the advice of family members or others who have had similar ailments, or to trust what they might have read or heard in various media.

In the end, then, health care choices may be more emotional than strictly rational. Even physicians, out of habit or inertia or reliance on their own intuition and experience, may fail to accept evidence concerning what appears to be "best practices," in whether to use minimal or invasive treatments, when to be cautious rather than acting quickly, and what medications to use. Forcing citizens to confront a wider array of choices and to appraise large amounts of specialized information may lead not to more efficient consumption of health care but to an even greater reliance on unreliable sources of advice. More choices and more demands on information processing may lead to confusion and stress.[38]

Prospect Theory

Psychologists Amos Tversky and Daniel Kahneman reject the version of rational choice theory known as expected utility theory, which makes strong assumptions concerning decision quality, because it does not provide a plausible account of how a great many decisions are actually made.[39] According to Kahneman and Tversky, individuals are irrational, but not randomly so. They are irrational in systematic ways.

Kahneman and Tversky's fundamental claim, termed **"prospect theory,"** is that decisions depend on the way that the prospective consequences of decisions, or prospects, are "framed," that is, presented or described. Prospects may be viewed as positive or negative deviations from a neutral reference point or starting point, which is often the status quo. "Above" such a point—when prospects involve possible gains—individuals tend to be risk averse. They tend to prefer a sure gain to the risky prospect of a much larger gain or else losing what they have. "Below" such a point—when prospects involve possible losses—individuals tend to take more risks, preferring the risky prospect of no losses, but possibly a much larger loss, to the sure prospect of a specific loss.

Evidence that the way prospects are framed changes the decisions people make violates a fundamental postulate of expected utility theory: the invariance of decisions to the particular ways in which choices are presented or described. This behavior would not occur if decision makers systematically "saw through" the presentation to the underlying values at stake; for example, if they aggregated concurrent prospects of gains and losses or if they reduced such prospects to a common unit of assessment. But quite often they do not do these things because it requires more cognitive skill than they typically possess and is more costly in time and effort.

These **framing effects** can be especially poignant in decision making on medical treatment. Describing a patient's chances in terms of likelihood of living instead of the risk of dying will affect a patient's decisions on treatment.[40] In one study, 44 percent of patients chose a specific course of therapy when risks were presented as the reduced chances of dying, but only 18 percent did so when outcomes were expressed as increased the chances of living.[41] Other factors that have been shown to influence choices include the amount of data; the vividness of the presentation (real versus abstract); whether outcomes are expressed as numbers, graphs, or narratives; whether harms are presented as absolute risks or relative risks; and the use of lay language versus medical terminology.[42]

CONCEPTS IN ACTION

Framing Prospects for the Iraq War

The idea that decision makers may take more risks if prospects are framed as avoiding losses found its way into the debate over President George W. Bush's controversial 2007 decision to "surge" troop levels in Iraq. In the following excerpt written by Princeton University economist and *New York Times* columnist Paul Krugman, the argument is made that the Bush administration was framing the prospects of the surge in terms of the increased possibility of additional lives saved rather than the reduced possibility of continuing loss of life. The administration wanted the public to see the issue that way, too, and stay at the Iraq table rather than "walking away." The result of the surge was a substantial increase in "lives saved," that is, a substantial reduction in "lives lost" relative to the reference point: the pre-surge casualty levels.

The only real question about the planned "surge" in Iraq—which is better described as a Vietnam-style escalation—is whether its proponents are cynical or delusional.

Senator Joseph Biden, chairman of the Senate Foreign Relations Committee, thinks they're cynical. He recently told the *Washington Post* that administration officials are simply running out the clock, so that the next president will be "the guy landing helicopters inside the Green Zone, taking people off the roof."

Daniel Kahneman, who won the Nobel Memorial Prize in Economic Science for his research on irrationality in decision-making, thinks they're delusional. Mr. Kahneman and Jonathan Renshon recently argued in *Foreign Policy* magazine that the administration's unwillingness to face reality in Iraq reflects a basic human aversion to cutting one's losses—the same instinct that makes gamblers stay at the table, hoping to break even.

Source: Paul Krugman, "Quagmire of the Vanities," *New York Times,* January 8, 2007.

Cognitive Dissonance

In 1957 psychologist Leon Festinger formulated the concept of **cognitive dissonance.**[43] Cognitive dissonance is a state that individuals reach when they have a conflict of cognitions, defined as mental acquisitions of knowledge through thought, experience, or the senses. A person in a state of cognitive dissonance will tend to seek consonance.

CONCEPTS IN ACTION

Cognitive Dissonance at NASA

The idea that cognitive dissonance is often arbitrarily resolved was reflected in a *New York Times* report on the National Aeronautics and Space Administration's relaunching the space shuttle following the *Columbia* accident. The dissonance—maintaining flight schedules requires taking risks, but doing so might lead to another accident—was resolved by ignoring, or "accepting," the risks.

On Wednesday, barring weather delays or a mechanical problem, NASA's long wait will end, and the space shuttle Discovery will roar toward orbit once again. The launching comes two and a half years after the loss of the shuttle Columbia and its crew of seven astronauts. Since then, the National Aeronautics and Space Administration has struggled on the one hand to reduce risks like that of the falling debris that doomed the Columbia, and on the other to accept the risks it cannot eliminate.

The agency's administrator, Michael D. Griffin, recently told NASA employees "this is a very risky venture," but says it is time to fly again. And outside experts who studied the Columbia disaster agree, giving an even greater impression of cognitive dissonance. "We think that there is no reason they shouldn't fly," Harold W. Gehman Jr., the retired admiral who headed the board investigating the Columbia accident, said in a recent conference call with reporters.

NASA, Admiral Gehman said, has made great strides in meeting his board's safety recommendations. The space agency has significantly reduced the overall risk that falling foam will lead to disaster again, he said, even though a NASA panel that monitored the agency's progress in meeting those goals found that it had fallen short in three areas, including the prevention of all launching debris and the ability to repair damage in space. "I'm sure that this next flight will be safer than the previous ones," Admiral Gehman said. But he added, "By any measure of 'safe,' this is not safe."

Source: John Schwartz, "Facing and Embracing Risk as Return to Space Nears," *New York Times,* July 10, 2005.

Festinger proposed that cognitive dissonance is a psychological tension similar to hunger and thirst and that people seek to resolve this tension as a matter of urgency. There are various ways to achieve this. One way is to promptly reevaluate all prior beliefs. But this process is expensive. Changing a cognition entails some discomfort: a person undergoing this process has to reflect and admit to himself that he has been wrong or that his knowledge is no longer relevant. Therefore, rather than adapt to a new cognition, he may eliminate the conflict by denying its validity. A common term for this is "being in denial." Or he might take the further step of refusing to recognize the validity of all dissonant cognitions, systematically screening them out, perhaps by never listening to a particular adviser or reading a particular publication or source.

Obviously a person feels better when not suffering from cognitive dissonance. But the price of comfort may be refusing to see important realities and making bad decisions as a result. For example, one cognition may be that terrorist threats are sponsored by states such as Iraq (under Saddam Hussein), Syria, and Iran. Another is that a serious breach of security has been caused by an apparently independent, non–state-sponsored entity such as al Qaeda. Consonance may be obtained by insisting that the activities of terrorist cells and networks are in reality sustained by state sponsors, who then become the targets of threats, sanctions, or invasion, even if evidence for this argument is weak.

Groupthink

Based on his study of public policy fiascos—including President Truman's decision to escalate the war against North Korea despite the very real threat of Chinese intervention and President Kennedy's invasion of Cuba at the Bay of Pigs despite evidence that it would not provoke an uprising against Fidel Castro—Irving Janis coined the term **groupthink,** which "refers to a deterioration of mental efficiency, reality testing, and moral judgment that results from in-group pressures." [44] The term often surfaces in discussions of public policy and management decisions that have not turned out well.[45]

Two well-known examples of groupthink occurred at NASA: the decision to launch the *Challenger* space shuttle, which exploded shortly after launch, killing the crew; and management reactions to the damage to the *Columbia* space shuttle that eventually caused its destruction on re-entry, also killing the crew. In both instances, an inner circle of decision makers—those who decided whether to launch—screened out people and evidence that contradicted the view on which they had reached concurrence, and their consensus seemed to be invulnerable to any kind of dissent or analysis of alternative views. Deliberations leading to the decision to attack and occupy Iraq in 2003 are often regarded as having been affected by groupthink. Secretary of State Colin L. Powell, who frequently dissented from the White House consensus, found himself excluded from high-level meetings on matters directly affecting his department and the conduct of foreign policy presumably because he was disruptive of group consensus.

CONCEPTS IN ACTION

Groupthink at the CIA

The term "groupthink" has become a popular explanation for all kinds of public policy decisions that become widely perceived as failures. It is even used to characterize entire organizations, as in the following case for the Central Intelligence Agency (CIA). Recall the Concepts in Action box in chapter 6 (page 220) that described an effort to transform the culture of the National Intelligence Estimate to allow for dissent and qualifications in the analysis.

"Group think grinds top-secret papers into intellectual pulp," said Angelo Codevilla, a former senior staff member of the Senate intelligence committee. "Our intelligence community thinks in herds: Stay close. Don't get out ahead. Don't be thought of as crazy," he said. "There is a tremendous lack of diversity of mind. The most typical phrase in an intelligence estimate is 'We believe' the corporate belief, the official view, calibrated to satisfy—not 'I think.' "

Source: Tim Weiner, "Naivete at the C.I.A.; Every Nation's Just Another U.S.," *New York Times,* June 7, 1998.

Groupthink has a number of symptoms, including the propensity of members of the group to overestimate the importance and morality of the group, the tendency to offer rationalizations rather than reasons for members' preferred solutions, self-imposed censorship and subtle pressures to ward off threats to group solidarity, and preserving the illusion of unanimity. Groups especially vulnerable to groupthink are those that are cohesive, screened from outside scrutiny, and led by leaders who enforce conformity. The purpose is to reduce the stresses and uncertainties of decision making. The psychological props and ploys that individuals employ in stressful circumstances are reinforced by the concurrence-seeking behavior of the group.

Victims of groupthink fail to analyze relevant alternatives, are biased in assembling and assessing evidence, seek little outside help or advice, fail to reexamine premature agreements or preferences, and neglect implementation problems and contingency plans. They seek unanimity and conformity and actively discourage threats to achieving them. Pressures to conform are likely to lead to an implicit bargaining in which dissidents are coerced into silence, perhaps under the implied threat of expulsion from the group.

Other Psychological Biases

Psychologists have confirmed the existence of a wide variety of **psychological biases** in decision making.[46] Among them are several of importance to the craftsmanship of public managers.

First, in what psychologists call "hindsight bias," people tend to claim that, after an event happens, they knew all along that it would happen, a tendency confirmed by experimental evidence. In other words, after the fact, people assign a higher probability to the event than they did before it happened, a form of retrospective overconfidence. "Liberals' assertion that they 'knew all along' that the war in Iraq would go badly are guilty of the hindsight bias," according to psychologist Hal Arkes.[47]

CONCEPTS IN ACTION

Hindsight Bias on No Child Left Behind

In mid-2007 President George W. Bush urged Congress to reauthorize the No Child Left Behind Act, a signature achievement of his administration. The legislation required public schools to show progress in the test scores of all groups of students. Unexpected opposition arose from officials formerly associated with creating and administering the act, who might have been exhibiting hindsight bias.

Bush might have expected that Eugene W. Hickok, a relative of the legendary frontier lawman Wild Bill Hickok and the original sheriff of No Child Left Behind, would support his drive for renewal. As the No. 2 Education Department official in Bush's first term, Hickok wrangled states and schools into compliance with the law so forcefully that foes called him "Wild Gene."

But Hickok, who is now urging Congress to revamp the initiative, said in a recent interview that he always harbored serious doubts about the federal government's expanding reach into the classroom.

"I had these second thoughts in the back of my mind the whole time," said Hickok, a former deputy education secretary. "I believe it was a necessary step at the time, but now that it has been in place for a while, it's important to step back and see if there are other ways to solve the problem."

Source: Amit R. Paley, "Ex-Aides Break With Bush on 'No Child,' " *Washington Post,* June 25, 2007, Sec. A.

Second, neuroscientists postulate that people gradually become immune to repeated warnings of danger or threat, thus attenuating their vigilance.[48] A related psychological phenomenon, also confirmed by experimental evidence, is called "inattentional blindness" by psychologist Brian Scholl, who argues that "attending to things is not without cost, so you can't attend to everything." [49] Therefore, repeated warnings to be on the lookout for unattended backpacks might displace your attention from other clues, such as inappropriate clothing or behavior, and gradually become ineffective as well.

Third, psychologist Eldar Shafir argues on the basis of experimental evidence that when people are asked to choose whom to accept for a role or assignment, they tend to look for positive features in the candidates.[50] When asked whom to reject, they look for negative features as a basis for rejection. This insight is a justification for political candidates running negative campaign ads about their opponents. The mudslinging tends to provide a reason to reject some candidates and increase the attractiveness of the candidates who may have no conspicuous negative qualities—and perhaps no conspicuous positive qualities either.

Fourth, a frequent characteristic of public deliberations is conflicting recollections concerning the same events. Former National Security Council staff member Richard Clarke and former National Security Adviser Condoleezza Rice had different memories of her reactions to his warnings concerning the dangers posed by al Qaeda prior to the September 11 attacks. The issue may not be "who is telling the truth," but a reflection of common memory errors. Memories tend to fade over time, especially of specific details of an experience. Details are often attributed to the wrong source, and recollections of past attitudes are based on current attitudes.[51] Over time, memory shifts from recounting the past to reconstructing a version of it based on general knowledge and beliefs.

Fifth, decision makers honestly may not realize how easily and often their objectivity is compromised by, for example, receiving remuneration or honoraria even if there are "no strings attached." People who recognize that others may engage in self-deception or biased thinking may not accept that they themselves may also do so. But, according to psychologist Daniel Gilbert, "Research shows that while people underestimate the influence of self-interest on their own judgments and decisions, they overestimate its influence on others. . . . [P]eople act in their own interests, but . . . their interests include ideals of fairness, prudence and generosity." Gilbert's lesson: "Because the brain cannot see itself fooling itself, the only reliable method for avoiding bias is to avoid the situations that produce it," such as potentially compromising compensation or honoraria.[52] Avoiding even the appearance of a conflict of interest is psychologically sound.

Sixth, experiments have shown that individuals are inclined to view their own statements and actions as "caused" by someone else's statements and actions, whereas the possible causes of others' statements and actions are overlooked. Partisan conflicts therefore are usually initiated by the other side. Further, according to Gilbert, "hitting back," and hitting back harder than one was hit in the first place, tend to be regarded as justifiable because the initiator is at fault, not the retaliator.[53]

The foregoing enumeration is not a complete account of psychological biases affecting perception, deliberation, and decision making. Other factors, described in the decision-making literature, that can impede problem solving and decision making include defensive avoidance (procrastination or failure to address the task caused by a sense of hopelessness, perhaps due to cognitive dissonance); hypervigilance (a tendency to overreact in given situations or to "invent" problems); cognitive bolstering (overemphasis on facts or opinions that support one's inclinations); escalation of commitment (a high initial investment in an individual, contract, or course of action that leads to even greater commitments regardless of performance); stereotyping, projection, and "halo error" (biased perceptions of individuals that distort accurate evaluation of their capacities or performance); and social loafing or free riding (a tendency to make less effort when working as part of a group than when working alone). The political expectation of reasonableness on the part of policy makers and public managers may well be disappointed when circumstances create stress, confusion, fear, self-interest, or other factors that can be sources of bias.

Even those processes of deliberation and decision making thought to be reasonably constructive can be distorted. For example, brainstorming is widely regarded as a way to elicit good ideas. According to psychologist Paul B. Paulus, however, "There are so many things people do in management because they think it's good, but there's no evidence for it. Teamwork is a good example. Brainstorming is another." [54] It is too seldom acknowledged, he argues, that group brainstorming enables all kinds of self-serving or intimidating behavior by participants, the triumph of bad ideas over good ones, the displacement of blame, confirmation of obvious or lowest-common-denominator ideas, and punishment of those who appear uncooperative.

At the level of the organization, these distortions can be of great consequence. Michael Cohen, James March, and Johan Olsen point out that an organization is a structure made up of diverse "streams": choices looking for problems, issues and feelings looking for situations in which they might be expressed, solutions looking for problems to which they might be the answer, and decision makers looking for work.[55] Ordinary forums for deliberation and decision making provide opportunities for these various streams to come together. To use the authors' infelicitous term, these forums become "garbage cans" into which participants dump their particular issues, concerns, and objectives, and a wide variety of decisions can emerge from the mix. The process that results may be anything but reasonable in a conventional sense, and decision makers may be hard-pressed to construct reasonable arguments and justifications after the fact. The difficulties are compounded when participation is fluid, individual styles and personalities differ, problems are ambiguous, and technologies are unclear.

Craftsmanship and Rationality

With so many possibilities for unreasonableness to distort deliberation and decision making, public managers must be prepared to prevent them or to minimize their adverse effects.

Janis identified methods for overcoming groupthink. One is for the group convener to withhold judgment until a full airing of members' views has taken place. Another is for a preselected individual to be assigned the role of devil's advocate: This person challenges any suggestion presented, which encourages other participants to justify their ideas and to point out flaws in others' thinking and reduces the stigma associated with being the first to dissent. Finally, anonymous or private feedback can be a useful remedy for groupthink; negative or dissenting views can be offered with no individual being seen to do so. This technique preserves the social solidarity of the group, as each member has plausible deniability that he or she disrupted group cohesion. Other solutions include dividing members into subgroups to consider particularly vexing issues, discussing any differences in their views and recommendations, drawing on outside experts, and scheduling subsequent meetings at which dissent is invited.

Jane Addams said, "The cure for the ills of democracy is more democracy." [56] And the cure for the ills of unreasonableness in deliberation and decision making is more reasonableness, which can result from managerial privileging of arguments supported by reasons, evidence, and qualifications; by setting the example; and by creating processes, such as those just enumerated, that reward reasonable deliberation. A more fundamental type of intervention is termed by psychologists Chris Argyris and Donald Schön "double-loop learning" because it requires examining not only the reasonableness of arguments but also what is out of sight: the values, attitudes, and assumptions that lie behind and motivate such arguments.[57] Managerial emphasis on introspective deliberation may over time promote the emergence of the kind of learning organization discussed in chapter 6.

HOW PUBLIC MANAGERS CAN LEARN

Few public managers assume their responsibilities in full possession of all they need to know to do their jobs well.[58] Even familiarity with the formal structures and processes and with the institutionalized values of their organizations, as might be acquired in subordinate positions, will not fully prepare an incoming public manager for the specific contexts of higher-level or more wide-ranging responsibilities. Garthwaite had to learn about the specific health care delivery structures, institutions, and politics of L.A. County. Tangherlini had to learn to view his city from the broader and more complex perspective of the mayor's office than could be acquired in positions dealing with a specific function of local government such as transportation.

This chapter has provided insights into how a manager's type or learning style affects the kinds of information and analysis he or she prefers during the course of deliberation and decision making. In a given situation, some managers may appear to be "quick studies," and others may seem to have a relatively flat learning curve; some search for facts, and others assemble ideas and seek vision. The next section considers various general sources of information and analysis that managers of any type might draw on.

Best Practices

Best practices refers to those processes, strategies, and techniques that have been shown through various methods of analysis to contribute to the success of a manager, an activity, a program, or an organization. To some scholars and practitioners, the term is synonymous with the craft perspective. Such practices are heavily oriented toward managerial behavior rather than toward structural or institutional/cultural considerations.

A common method for identifying best practices is to study in detail the practices of managers and organizations that are widely considered to be successful, discover potential cause-and-effect relationships revealed by the case studies, and (1) establish the practices that seemed to account for success or effectiveness as well as their consequences in given contexts as an ideal against which to compare one's own practices and accomplishments, or (2) distill general principles of effective managerial practice that seem to apply in a wide range of contexts.[59]

The concept of a best practice has roots in the scientific management movement that was inspired by the research of Frederick W. Taylor early in the twentieth century. "Among the various methods and implements used in each element of each trade," Taylor said, "there is always one method and one implement which is quicker and better than any of the rest," a perspective that came to be known as the "one best way." [60] The identification of best practices in public management, however, has depended less on scientific analysis of operational data—Taylor is famous for his time-and-motion studies of factory workers—than on the close analysis of specific cases, on inferences drawn from experiential information, and on the codification of richly textured folk wisdom.

The popularity of "principles of administration" came under sharp criticism in the late 1940s. Such principles are no more than proverbs, insisted Herbert Simon. "For almost every principle one can find an equally plausible and acceptable contradictory principle. . . . What is needed now is empirical research and experimentation to determine the relative desirability of alternative administrative arrangements." [61] Nevertheless, research that distills managerial principles from personal experiences and case analyses has continued to be one of the most popular genres in the field, both in academic publications, in the prescriptive management literature of consultancies, and in government reports such as those of the Government Accountability Office (GAO). Examples of this literary genre were cited earlier in this chapter. One is a publication titled *Excellence in Managing,* by Harry P. Hatry and several coauthors, which advertises itself as follows:

> An easy-to-use, practical guide to more than 125 actions that will improve management and leadership, this book is particularly responsive to public-sector needs. The authors interviewed personnel, their clients, and elected officials from 18 community development agencies across the country to find out what does and does not work for them. The book is a quick reference tool for managers and their staffs at all levels. The foreword is written by Tom Peters, coauthor of *In Search of Excellence.* Awarded a Certificate of Merit for distinguished research by the Governmental Research Association in 1992.[62]

This largely unhistorical, "institutions-are-given" approach to public management drew criticism from traditional public administration scholars and other social scientists for its lack of rigor and concern for democratic values. The research on which the identification of best practices is based is controversial because "[c]ases are subject to a wide variety of selection and interpretation biases. Drawing on specific cases, a clever rhetorician can not only confirm the infinite complexity of the world but also can find support for almost any plausible conjecture about that world," [63] echoing Simon's critique.

The intuitive appeal of lessons drawn from actual experience accounts for the popularity among practitioners of this source of managerial knowledge. Best practices eventually caught the wave of popularity initiated by the success of the "Japanese management" movement and of Thomas Peters and Robert Waterman's *In Search of Excellence: Lessons from America's Best-Run Companies.*[64] The latter book's no-nonsense principles—a bias for action, close to the customer, productivity through people, simple form, lean staff—inspired numerous public sector–oriented imitators motivated to arrest government's declining popularity following the Nixon-era Watergate scandal, the economic crises of the 1970s, and what many regarded as the ineffectual presidency of Jimmy Carter.

The GAO has published extensively on best practices.[65] Its "Selected Initial Implementation Approaches to Manage Senior Executive Performance that May Be Helpful to Other Agencies" included:

> **Provide Useful Data.** The agencies disaggregated data from agency-wide customer and employee surveys. In addition, the Bureau of Land Management and Veterans Benefits Administration provide senior executives with objective data through real-time data systems so that executives can track their individual progress against organizational goals.
>
> **Require Follow-up Action.** The Internal Revenue Service requires senior executives to develop action plans to follow up on customer and employee issues identified through agency-wide surveys. The Federal Highway Administration requires executives to use 360-degree feedback instruments to solicit employee views on their leadership skills and then incorporate action items into their performance plans for the next fiscal year.
>
> **Make Meaningful Distinctions in Performance.** The agencies are working at making distinctions in senior executive performance. To recognize varying levels of significance and complexity among executive performance, the Internal Revenue Service established an executive compensation plan that assigns executives to bonus levels with corresponding bonus ranges based on levels of responsibilities and commitments.[66]

The National Governors Association has created a Center for Best Practices, a consulting service for governors and their principal staff, enabling them to

> quickly learn about what works, what doesn't, and what lessons can be learned from other governors grappling with the same problems; obtain assistance in designing and implementing new programs or in making current programs more effective; receive up-to-date, comprehensive information about what is happening in other state capitals and in Washington, D.C., so governors are aware of cutting edge policies; and learn about emerging national trends and their implications for states so governors can prepare to meet future demands.[67]

In 1991 the International City Management Association promulgated a comprehensive set of best practices for effective local government management. These practices address issues such as staff development; policy facilitation; functional and operational expertise and planning; citizen service; performance measurement/management and quality assurance; initiative, risk taking, vision, creativity, and innovation; technological literacy; democratic advocacy and citizen participation; diversity; functional specializations such as budgeting; presentation skills; and integrity.

Finally, best-practice sites for other policy-specific areas include the National Alliance to End Homelessness, which disseminates best practices in the form of "Ten Essentials for an effective permanent solution to prevent and end homelessness"; the United Nations, which maintains a Peacekeeping Best Practices Section to assist in the planning, conduct, management, and support of peacekeeping operations by learning from experience, problem solving, and transferring best practices in United Nations peacekeeping; and the Finance Center, a nonprofit organization whose activities include making available a database of information concerning "promising practices" for programs serving children, youth, and families.[68]

Paradigms and Ideologies

Public managers may bring to their responsibilities not only their type—preferred ways of learning and making decisions—but also settled beliefs about how the world works, about the causes and appropriate remedies for problems that can be expected to arise. Their decisions may be guided by these taken-for-granted beliefs and presumptions about the issues they face.

In his book *The Structure of Scientific Revolutions,* Thomas Kuhn defines a scientific paradigm as general agreement among members of a scientific community as to what is to be observed and scrutinized; the kind of questions that are supposed to be asked and probed for answers in relation to this subject; how these questions are to be put; and how the results of scientific investigations should be interpreted.[69] Kuhn argued that scientific truth-seeking and beliefs become cultural: It is what we do and what we think. A dominant paradigm can change, but only after a buildup of contrary evidence raising questions that can no longer be ignored.

The term **"paradigm"** has come into more general use (or misuse) to refer to assumptions, concepts, values, and practices that constitute a specific way of viewing reality for the group or community that shares them. It is common to refer to a "bureaucratic paradigm," a way of thinking that views hierarchical organizations governed by statutes, rules, and formal procedures—traditional departments, commissions, and bureaus—as the preferred means for implementing public policies. Paradigms such as this one provide a framework for decision making and action. Some of President George H. W. Bush's advisers, for example, promoted what they called the New Paradigm: programs such as vouchers and empowerment zones that promoted individual choice and decentralized government.

The terms "mindset," "worldview," and **"ideology"** have very similar meanings that apply to smaller- and larger-scale examples of disciplined, paradigmatic thought. All these psychosocial phenomena can be categorized as closed systems of thought, resistant to criticism and debate, in contrast to the kind of "open system" that is promoted by double-loop learning, mentioned above. "A closed system of thought occurs when any framework of knowledge tries to ask and answer all questions concerning values and standards within its own boundaries. Such a system typically leads to the rejection of any knowledge that is outside those boundaries. So another name for a closed system is an ideology." [70]

Connections can be drawn between cultural explanations of decision making, such as paradigms, and psychological or psychosocial explanations, in which culture becomes internalized by individuals. Individuals from outside the organization who assume a managerial position may discover a prevailing paradigm, ideology, or mindset and, either consciously or unconsciously, incorporate it into or embrace it as their own world view without sufficient reflection. (Such a phenomenon was said to have been labeled "going native" by adviser to President Nixon John Ehrlichman, who complained that politically appointed cabinet officials became advocates for their departments' views and values rather than for the views of the president.)

Managerial learning may be guided or framed, consciously or unconsciously, by ideologies, values, or other essentially closed systems of thought. The manager's preferred system of thought may be based on abstract principles or on sensory experience, on logical deduction or empathy and emotion. Some scholars have argued that management itself, that is, the belief that good management is essential to good government, is an ideology or paradigm. Henry Mintzberg talks about a managerialist ideology based on several premises or assumptions: Particular activities can be isolated, both from one another and from direct authority; performance can be fully and properly evaluated by objective measures; and activities can be entrusted to autonomous professional managers held responsible for performance.[71] A fourth element might be added to that kind of managerialist ideology: If the above assumptions are not fulfilled by a program or policy, then the government *should not be doing it.* This view turns on its head the familiar proposition that government does what the private sector cannot or will not do.

In her book *Challenging the Performance Movement: Accountability, Complexity, and Democratic Values,* Beryl Radin identifies what she regards as the mindset, or ideology, underlying advocacy of performance measurement and management (discussed further in chapter 8). Such advocacy, she argues, is based on the following assumptions: (1) goals can be defined clearly and set firmly as the basis for the performance measurement process; (2) goals are specific and the responsibility of definable actors; (3) outcomes can be specified independently of inputs, processes, and outputs; (4) outcomes can be quantified and measured; (5) outcomes are controllable and susceptible to external timing; (6) data are available, clear, and accurate; and (7) results of the performance measurement can be delivered to an actor with authority to respond to the results.[72] In other words, public managers attempting to institute performance measurement and management proceed on the basis of a prior, often unsubstantiated belief that such an effort will succeed, rather than on the basis of evidence, obtained through careful analysis, that the circumstances necessary for success are in fact present.

CONCEPTS IN ACTION

Ideological Rigidity

A distinction is often drawn between those public officials who are regarded as "pragmatic" and those who are regarded as "ideologues" (or, if you are an ideologue, as principled leaders or idealists). *New York Times* columnist David Brooks suggests how ideological rigidity can lead to a failure to grasp new realities.

Back in the 1970s, when Reaganism became popular, top tax rates were in the 70s, growth was stagnant and inflation was high. Federal regulation stifled competition. Government welfare policies enabled a culture of dependency. Socialism was still a coherent creed, and many believed the capitalist world was headed toward a Swedish welfare model.

In short, in the 1970s, normal, nonideological people were right to think that their future prospects might be dimmed by a stultifying state. People were right to believe that government was undermining personal responsibility. People were right to have what Tyler Cowen, in a brilliant essay in *Cato Unbound,* calls the "liberty vs. power" paradigm burned into their minds—the idea that big government means less personal liberty.

But today, many of those old problems have receded or been addressed. Today the big threats to people's future prospects come from complex, decentralized phenomena: Islamic extremism, failed states, global competition, global warming, nuclear proliferation, a skills-based economy, economic and social segmentation.

Normal, nonideological people are less concerned about the threat to their freedom from an overweening state than from the threats posed by these amorphous yet pervasive phenomena. The "liberty vs. power" paradigm is less germane. It's been replaced in the public consciousness with a "security leads to freedom" paradigm. People with a secure base are more free to take risks and explore the possibilities of their world.

People with secure health care can switch jobs more easily. People who feel free from terror can live their lives more loosely. People who come from stable homes and pass through engaged schools are free to choose from a wider range of opportunities.

Source: David Brooks, "No U-Turns," *New York Times,* March 29, 2007.

A different ideology motivating public management reform is based on the belief that direct democracy, that is, citizen participation in all matters affecting them, ought to guide the conduct of public management. Peter and Linda deLeon urge that public managers adopt as a core value the promotion of what they call the democratic ethos at all stages and at all levels of policymaking and management.[73] Their assumption is that citizens only need empowering to become fully proficient at enacting their own and society's best interests. Moreover, this principle of empowerment should be extended to the employees of public agencies; they, too, should be consulted at every stage and level of policymaking and implementation. This consultation should, the deLeons insist, be authentic, not a cynical attempt to make citizens believe they have an influence they do not in fact have.

Scientific Research

Researchers from a wide variety of disciplines, fields, and subfields have systematically studied many of the specific issues and decisions in which public managers participate. Drawing on insights from this research can enlighten public management practice in significant ways. In the United States, the United Kingdom, and elsewhere, interest is growing in evidence-based policy and practice (discussed below), not only in health and medicine, where the idea originated, but also in many other areas of public policy and management.

Science and Government

From a broad historical perspective, science and public administration have long been regarded as in symbiotic relationship to each other. Political scientist Lisa Anderson writes:

> While in absolutist France, . . . politics and administration were considered state monopolies, not to be subject to intellectual inquiry or speculation, for Americans, science seemed to support the cause of liberalism, by breaking the yoke of tradition, questioning authority, and celebrating the individual. . . . Liberalism in turn supported the pursuit of science; freedom of belief, assembly, and association were important prerequisites to unfettered inquiry.[74]

In the 1960s a systematic way of incorporating scientific evidence into public policymaking and management, called the Planning-Programming-Budgeting System, became fashionable following its highly publicized adoption by Secretary of Defense Robert S. McNamara. (Impressed with McNamara's managerialist approach, President Lyndon Johnson mandated its use by all federal agencies. Richard Nixon rescinded the mandate several years later.) At the heart of this management system was a benefit-cost–oriented paradigm that came to be known as **policy analysis.** Political scientist Aaron Wildavsky described "the art of policy analysis" as follows.

> Policy analysis must create problems that decision-makers are able to handle with the variables under their control and in the time available . . . by specifying a desired relationship between manipulable means and obtainable objectives. . . . Unlike social science, policy analysis must be prescriptive; arguments about correct policy, which deal with the future, cannot help but be willful and therefore political.[75]

The number of policy analysts in government grew rapidly, and analytic tools such as policy planning, program development, and program evaluation—whether done "in-house" or by consultants—are now considered to be essential elements in the management of public agencies.

Brookings Institution political scientist James L. Sundquist coined the term "research broker" to describe the role of packaging and retailing to policymakers the intellectual products of the research community by policy analysts. His premise was that knowledge potentially useful to policymakers is often available in the research community but is inaccessible to or unrecognizable by them. Policymaking therefore is often less thoughtful and well informed than it might be. By identifying, assembling, and translating potentially relevant bits of knowledge into intelligence pertinent to the immediate needs of policymakers, research brokers perform an essential role in rationalizing policymaking. Research brokerage was a largely insider role that, in Sundquist's view, was greatly in need of strengthening.[76]

These research brokers were not mere technocrats. In *A Government of Strangers,* Hugh Heclo labeled them "reformers." Heclo observed, "Such analysts are often the agency head's only institutional resource for thinking about substantive policy without commitments to the constituents, jurisdictions, and self-interests of existing programs." He added that "their most enduring problem is one of attracting political customers to use their analysis while maintaining constructive relations and access with the program offices being analyzed." [77]

It is not surprising that preparation for careers in public affairs at undergraduate and graduate levels has come to include as a matter of course an emphasis on "social inquiry"—on social science concepts and their applications to public policy and management, on methods of data and policy analysis, and on the uses of research in planning and decision making. The idea is to ensure that policymakers and public managers at all levels of government can be intelligent consumers of scientific research findings.[78]

Science or Scientism?

Controversies over the relevance of science as a source of knowledge for public management have increased in recent years, especially when the policies concern changing human behavior and improving individual, organizational, community, and social life. This is true even when it comes to managing public policies with significant scientific content, where it might seem that a grasp of the relevant science and its applications would be *sine qua non* to effective public management. In general, sharp tensions have arisen between science and public administration.

Far from being viewed as a matter of bringing scientific truth into the realms of power through the institutions of policy analysis and research brokers, the relationship of science to policymaking has become a matter of evaluating multifarious claims to possession of scientific truth, to arguments over what constitutes scientific "proof," and to the very meaning and moral claims of scientific truth itself. This new attitude toward science is strikingly evident when it comes to issues that involve powerful ideological disagreements, such as stem-cell research and global warming, where arguments over the science may obscure underlying ideological conflicts. But controversies arise in less morally charged issues as well. Says Lawrence Sherman, a great many *scholars* believe that

> Too much social science evidence may mislead policy with statistically biased conclusions due to weak research designs, and too little science evidence is presented in a way that allows government to assess the risk of bias. The two problems are related: If governments cannot rely on social science evidence as unbiased, they have less reason to invest in producing more evidence.[79]

Some critics view science or, in the critics' view, "scientism," as an ideology in itself. They claim that scientific researchers are not free of ideological bias: In what they choose to study, which findings are regarded as worth communicating, and the reasons offered in support of policy choices, researchers do not reflect objectivity toward the world so much as a penchant for selectively chosen findings that produce an ideological fit between research and the policy preferences of researchers. Steven Miller and Marcel Fredericks argue, "We are not suggesting, in some simplistic fashion, that ideological commitments or preferences are always working as 'biasing-filters,' but only that they are an often overlooked factor in *explaining* how social policies are formulated, implemented and evaluated given social science research findings." [80]

According to reporting in the *Wall Street Journal,* for twenty years research into Alzheimer's disease has been dominated by the idea that the cause is the accumulation of sticky plaques made of beta-amyloid.[81] Researchers who wish to explore alternative explanations of the disease encounter difficulties in getting financial support and publishing their findings in prestigious journals. Experimental drugs and vaccines under test are typically based on the amyloid hypothesis, even though the possibility of alternative explanations has respectable scientific support. Amyloid plaques are, scientists have shown, found in normal brains, and amyloid only weakly correlates with differences in Alzheimer's brains.

The science of secondhand smoke is another example. In July 2006 the U.S. surgeon general was quoted as saying "there is no risk-free level of secondhand smoke exposure" and "breathing secondhand smoke for even a short time can damage cells and set the cancer process in motion." [82] The scientific problem is that "instant exposures" to secondhand smoke cannot practically be cumulated over time to derive an individual's lifetime exposure. Instead, individuals who had been exposed to secondhand smoke were asked to recall and describe those exposures, producing information that is unreliable at best. Advocates of smoking bans give short shrift to such difficulties, however, and science is said to justify policies when, in fact, it does no such thing.

The discussion in this section cautions public managers that to the extent they rely on scientific evidence, they should be aware of the potential biases involved in the general approach to the research and, as always, with regard to any specific findings that are produced.

Evidence-Based Policy and Practice

"[T]here is a growing nonpartisan interest," asserts Lawrence Sherman from the perspective of the research community, "*across the range of ideologies,* in gaining better evidence about achieving results in the public sector." He continues: "There may even be more openness to accepting the idea that much of the research we do have is biased and that standards of research must be raised." [83]

In 2001 a nonprofit organization called the Council for Excellence in Government created the Coalition for Evidence-Based Policy, itself a nonprofit, nonpartisan organization. Its mission was to promote government policymaking based on rigorous evidence of program effectiveness, and to that end the coalition established the Evidence-Based Policy Help Desk.[84] Grounded initially in medical practice, the **evidence-based policy and practice** movement has broadened its scope to include public policy more generally and performance management (discussed at length in chapter 8) in particular.[85] Although the term "rigorous evidence" is often considered to mean random-assignment, controlled experiments, many experts advocate models that include specialized knowledge and a broad array of methods for evaluating public programs and building a foundation of knowledge on which public managers may draw.

A cautionary note is warranted, however, especially in areas of public policy for which precise understandings of causal relationships are difficult to obtain. Carolyn J. Heinrich argues that " 'high stakes' performance management systems need to incorporate ample buffers for errors and imprecision in data collection and analysis and allow time for careful case reviews before sanctions are applied or bonuses awarded." [86] The problem is even more general:

> Public policy responses to evidence can be impressive, such as the growing restrictions on cigarette smoking in public places based on observations of nicotine absorption from sidestream smoke. But these highly publicized decisions may be the exception to a more general problem of ignorance about, and failure to act upon, a wide array of evidence affecting the daily workings of government.[87]

An example of Americans' faith in science as a source of knowledge for governing and of the movement toward evidence-based practice is President George W. Bush's major education reform initiative, the No Child Left Behind Act of 2003. The act is best known for requiring states to conduct high-stakes testing of virtually all students to determine their academic progress and to intervene where schools fail to show progress. Although not as well publicized, but arguably more significant, is the act's goal to bring facts and evidence to bear on the subjective issues relating to education policy and practice and promote teaching methods backed by "scientifically based research" instead of instinct and ideology. The phrase "scientifically based" research appears more than one hundred times in the act's text. To assist educators, the U.S. Department of Education's Institute of Education Sciences, whose mission is to provide rigorous evidence on which to base education practice, created the What Works Clearinghouse. Among other things, the clearinghouse offers an "intervention rating scheme" that educators are encouraged to use in evaluating the scientific quality of any particular study of "what works." [88]

RULE OF LAW

The Education Sciences Reform Act

The Education Sciences Reform Act of 2002 established within the U.S. Department of Education, the Institute of Education Sciences (IES). The mission of the IES is to provide rigorous evidence on which to ground education practice and policy.

According to the Act, SCIENTIFICALLY VALID EDUCATION EVALUATION means an evaluation that—

(A) adheres to the highest possible standards of quality with respect to research design and statistical analysis;
(B) provides an adequate description of the programs evaluated and, to the extent possible, examines the relationship between program implementation and program impacts;
(C) provides an analysis of the results achieved by the program with respect to its projected effects;
(D) employs experimental designs using random assignment, when feasible, and other research methodologies that allow for the strongest possible causal inferences when random assignment is not feasible; and
(E) may study program implementation through a combination of scientifically valid and reliable methods.

(20) SCIENTIFICALLY VALID RESEARCH.—The term "scientifically valid research" includes applied research, basic research, and field-initiated research in which the rationale, design, and interpretation are soundly developed in accordance with scientifically based research standards.

Source: Education Sciences Reform Act of 2002, H.R. 3801, 107th Cong., 20 U.S.C. 9501, P.L. 107-279.

As the idea of an "intervention rating scheme" suggests, the evidence-based practice and evidence-led policy movements inevitably raise issues concerning what constitutes scientifically valid evidence. As noted above, many scholars regard random-assignment experiments as the gold standard for high-quality research. In these experiments some subjects—individuals, groups, or organizations—are randomly assigned either to receive a treatment (or intervention) or to be part of a control group that does not receive the treatment (but depending on the study design may receive alternative treatments). The effects of the treatment in relation to the counterfactual represented by the control group can then be identified. The view that random-assignment experiments are the only valid way to understand the effects of a treatment is challenged by those who argue that econometric and other statistical techniques can control the bias that threatens the validity of studies based on nonexperimental, or observational, data, with the added advantage that a much wider range of topics can be studied using such methods. The disconcerting fact seems to be that the two approaches produce different findings when evaluating the same policies and programs.[89]

What to do? In 1982 a group of researchers published a book that continues to put the matter of choosing methods in broad, issue-oriented perspective. In *Data for Decisions: Information Strategies for Policymakers,* the authors identify three issues that arise in the course of the deliberation and decision making associated with policy and public management: identifying cause and effect relationships, measuring the status quo, and predicting the future. They discuss methods that are appropriate for each type of issue, indicating their strengths and weaknesses and providing examples of their appropriate use. Their goal is to provide an accessible guide for public officials and their staffs who wish to be informed consumers and, where their responsibilities call for it, sponsors of scientific research to inform their decision making.[90] European researcher Bent Flyvbjerg argues that "[g]ood social science is problem driven and not methodology driven in the sense that it employs those methods that for a given problem, best help answer the research questions at hand."[91]

Of experiments, the authors of *Data for Decisions* conclude, "The well-conducted controlled trial is the most definitive method of investigating causal relationships both in the laboratory and in the field" and is far less risky in identifying causality than observational studies, although, as others have pointed out, even experiments are not free of threats to their validity. For measuring the status quo, they separately discuss sample surveys, longitudinal and panel studies, case studies, management records, and official statistics. Of case studies, which often are the foundation for best practices, the authors say, "The method has severe biases in even the best of hands because of problems of values, slant, omission, and emphasis." For predicting the future, the authors discuss simulations, forecasting, mathematical modeling, and what they call "introspection and advice," which, they suggest, may be better than nothing if a more effective method is unavailable.

Institutions Providing Analysis and Expertise

As the complexities of government have increased, policymakers and public managers have come to rely on **think tanks,** such as the Brookings Institution, the Heritage Foundation, the Center for Budget and Policy Priorities (CBPP), and the American Enterprise Institute (AEI); nonprofit and for-profit contract research organizations, such as Abt Associates, MDRC, and Mathematica Policy Research (MPR); and management consultancies, such as Booz Allen Hamilton, and Accenture to provide ideas, expertise, and analysis that public agencies may be unable to produce in-house.[92] Some think tanks, such as Brookings, date back to the 1920s, but their participation and influence began to grow in the 1960s and 1970s and accelerated as government began to outsource numerous functions formerly thought to be inherently governmental, including policy development and planning. Now governments at all levels, including small towns, regularly hire outside consultants to assist with matters such as reorganizations, systems designs, land use planning, policy advice, and opinion surveys.

The expanding role of these types of organizations has drawn both praise and condemnation. Think tanks have been lauded for stimulating the "marketplace of ideas" that is essential to democratic self-government. In contrast, the 1976 book *The Shadow Government: The Government's Multi-Billion-Dollar Giveaway of its Decision-Making Powers to Private Management Consultants, "Experts," and Think Tanks,* viewed these developments in alarmist terms.[93] More recently, worries have arisen over the extent to which political polarization and the rise of partisan advocacy groups has compromised the independence of such advisory organizations. Their work at times becomes fodder in various policy conflicts, and their experts and conclusions make the news when they are cited in the course of policy debates. Balanced analysis can become a casualty of such conflicts.[94]

HOW THE WORLD WORKS

Think Tank Town

In a feature titled "Think Tank Town," washingtonpost.com edits and publishes columns submitted by twelve prominent think tanks on a rotating basis every other weekday. These think tanks cover the political spectrum from liberal through centrist to conservative. Each think tank is free to choose its writers and the topics it believes are most important and timely. The participating organizations are: American Enterprise Institute, Carnegie Endowment for International Peace, Cato Institute, Center for American Progress, Center for Strategic and International Studies, Council on Foreign Relations, Heritage Foundation, Hudson Institute, Manhattan Institute, New America Foundation, and RAND Corporation.

Source: "Think Tank Town," washingtonpost.com, http://blog.washingtonpost.com/thinktanktown/.

The following are examples of commentary or research conducted by MPR, AEI, CBPP, and the Heritage Foundation, respectively. They illustrate how findings are publicized.

> Students who participated in sexual abstinence programs were just as likely to have sex as those who did not, according to a study ordered by Congress. Also, those who attended one of the four abstinence classes reviewed reported having similar numbers of sexual partners as those who did not attend the classes. And they first had sex about the same age as other students—14.9 years, according to Mathematica Policy Research Inc.[95]

> Expert advisers to the government who receive money from a drug or device maker would be barred for the first time from voting on whether to approve that company's products under new rules announced Wednesday for the F.D.A.'s powerful advisory committees. . . . Some conservatives were not happy with the new rule. "There are going to be more good people who can't get over the hurdles, and I don't think that's a good thing," said Jack Calfee, a resident scholar at the American Enterprise Institute.[96]

> An obscure provision in last February's Deficit Reduction Act required U.S. citizens to prove their identities and citizenship to qualify for Medicaid. As health officials in Maryland, we see this new policy as a serious threat to public health. . . . According to experts we consulted at the Center for Budget and Policy Priorities in the District, from 1 million to 2 million qualified Americans could lose coverage this year because they will not be able to produce the needed documents in time to sign up for another year of coverage. And while some states are stepping in to pay for care until documents are found, many others are not.[97]

> Wade Horn, the Bush administration's point man for welfare reform, Head Start and abstinence education, resigned Monday as assistant secretary for children and families. In the Department of Health and Human Services, Horn oversaw a $46 billion budget and 65 programs that serve vulnerable children and families. He is best known for his work on issues embraced by social conservatives, such as more money for faith-based groups and organizations that work to help couples improve their marriage. . . . Robert Rector, a senior fellow at the Heritage Foundation, a conservative think tank, said Horn tackled the most important social issue in the United States while others ignored it—the decline of the institution of marriage.[98]

Learning from Others

Public managers also have, and may actively create, opportunities to communicate with people who have knowledge and insights that might be useful to them. Made popular by management gurus Tom Peters and Robert Waterman, the notion of **"management by walking around"** is intended to convey the value of spontaneous communications that occur in the course of informal interactions with employees and, for that matter, with any important stakeholder group or even with citizens.[99] Although managers who are extraverted and prefer sensory information may be more inclined to learn this way, all public managers may benefit from routine exposure to knowledgeable people in a wide variety of settings.

Informal communications may also be more deliberate. The popular term "networking" conveys the notion that communicating with a group of people who have common interests and relevant expertise may be useful not only as a source of information but also as a way of building confidence in and trust—social capital—among those for whom mutual cooperation and coordination may be beneficial. Hugh Heclo noted the political importance of what he called "issue networks," highly fluid interactions among emotionally committed and knowledgeable activists inside and outside of government who are determined to shape the content of public policy.[100]

A concept related to the issue network is the advocacy coalition, which links policymakers and public managers, important stakeholder groups, think thanks, academic researchers, media organizations, foundations, influential individuals, and advocates with specialized interests. Paul Sabatier and Hank Jenkins-Smith argue that research findings may be influenced by the competition among such coalitions.[101] Public managers who are political appointees are often members of advocacy coalitions, and their learning is heavily influenced by this involvement. Indeed, membership in an advocacy coalition may be an efficient way for researchers to make contact with or have their findings taken seriously by public officials.

This section has described a number of ways in which public managers learn about the content of decisions they must make and the potential consequences of their decisions. The sources discussed include best practices, paradigms or ideologies, scientific research, evidence-based policy and practice, institutions providing analysis and expertise, employees in their organizations, and broader, more inclusive networks.

BEING STRATEGIC

One of the most common prescriptions in the public management literature is that public managers of every type and inclination should think and act strategically.[102] The argument for being strategic as a matter of personal craftsmanship is that public managers, especially those with many different kinds of responsibilities, should create a frame of reference and should act consistently and skillfully in accordance with the logic of that framework. In this way, managers can avoid being put on the defensive by the relentless demands on their time and attention and falling into the habit of making decisions in an ad hoc, unsystematic, and reactive way with little or no appreciation for how issues and decisions are interrelated.

Those who emphasize the extent to which managerial decisions are embedded in political structures and cultures take a different view, however. The combined effects of bounded rationality and political constraints counsel a more modest, but feasible "strategy." In a famous article, "The Science of Muddling Through," political scientist Charles E. Lindblom argued that, in the real world, it is best to be engaged in a process of "successive limited comparisons," by which he meant "building out from the current situation, step by step, and by small degrees." [103] Change in the American political system, governed as it is by a politics of bureaucratic structure that is founded on the U.S. constitutional scheme of governance, is typically incremental. Because of this reality, the public manager is well-advised, the argument goes, to think and act incrementally. More will be accomplished that way than by formulating bold visions that are dismantled in the course of political bargaining. The perfect becomes the enemy of the good.

What Is a Strategy?

As used in this chapter, a **strategy** is a cognitive structure in the mind of the manager, a frame of reference within which thoughts and actions are formulated and reviewed. Barry Bozeman and Jeffrey Straussman define strategic public management as guided by four principles: "concern with the long term, integration of goals and objectives into a coherent hierarchy, recognition that strategic management and planning are not self-implementing, and, most important, an external perspective emphasizing not adapting to the environment but anticipating and shaping of environmental change." [104] In light of the inevitabilities of incrementalism, however, a more circumspect view of being strategic is: Have a broad sense of your purpose and how you would like to accomplish it.

A strategy may be normative; that is, it may originate in managers' ideologies or beliefs about how things *ought* to be done. Alternatively, a strategy may be the product of calculation or a pragmatic weighing of the many substantive, political, and organizational considerations that may affect results or outcomes. Managers of particular types, moreover, may approach "being strategic" in ways that are "true to type"; whether their orientation is ideological or pragmatic, sensing or intuitive, managers may wish to make systematic choices concerning various instruments or tools at their disposal for accomplishing their objectives.

Political contexts, organizational structures and cultures, and individual public managers' proclivities and talents for formulating coherent "big pictures" both enable and constrain the opportunities for strategic public management. Mark Moore writes that "many different strategies are feasible [for public sector organizations] because at any given moment, the politics of a situation can accommodate many different ideas. Moreover, the politics will change . . . in response to particular events, and sometimes even in response to managerial effort. So, if one looks ahead a little bit, the range of possible sustainable political coalitions can be very broad indeed." [105] Some strategic choices, moreover, are substantive, related to the goals of public policy; examples include enforcement versus cooperation, family reunification versus ensuring the safety of the child, and an emphasis on treatment versus an emphasis on prevention. Other strategic choices are related more to the means for accomplishing goals that may be promulgated in statutes, executive orders, or judicial rulings: punishment versus rehabilitation, mandatory versus voluntary compliance, government provision versus contracting with private providers.

Bozeman and Straussman emphasize a useful point: "*Effective* public management and *strategic* public management are not identical."[106] Public managers may be good at particular kinds of tasks or aspects of public management even if they are not particularly strategic about it. The pragmatic adapter to a fluid situation may be just what an ambiguous situation requires, and the strategic thinker may appear to be out of touch with the complexities of particular contexts whose meanings are constantly shifting. Moreover, they say, not all public managers have the qualities of statesmanship that strategic management requires: a broad view, a lively sense of engagement, and intellectual curiosity. Like so many other popular or fashionable notions, strategic public management is not a panacea.

CONCEPTS IN ACTION

Strategy in Iraq (or Not)

Retired Marine Corps general John J. Sheehan described what he learned about the Bush administration's strategies for Iraq and the surrounding region in the course of deciding whether to be a candidate for the position of White House implementation manager for the wars in Iraq and Afghanistan.

What I found in discussions with current and former members of this administration is that there is no agreed-upon strategic view of the Iraq problem or the region. In my view, there are essentially three strategies in play simultaneously.

The first I call "the Woody Hayes basic ground attack," which is basically gaining one yard—or one city block—at a time. Given unconstrained time and resources, one could control the outcome in Iraq and provide the necessary security to move on to the next stage of the process.

The second strategy starts with security but adds benchmarks for both the U.S. and Iraqi participants and applies time constraints that should guide them toward a desired outcome. . . .

The third strategy takes a larger view of the region and the desired end state. Simply put, where does Iraq fit in a larger regional context? . . .

Of the three strategies in play, the third is the most important but, unfortunately, is the least developed and articulated by this administration. . . . There has to be linkage between short-term operations and strategic objectives that represent long-term U.S. and regional interests, such as assured access to energy resources and support for stable, Western-oriented countries.

Source: John J. Sheehan, "Why I Declined to Serve," *Washington Post,* April 16, 2007, Sec. A.

How might public managers go about making strategic sense of the reality in which they are enmeshed?[107] How can they create mental models for understanding ambiguity, emergence, and uncertainty, which is the process by which individuals (or organizations) create the understanding necessary to acting in a principled and informed manner? The discussion that follows describes several different heuristics from among the many found in the public management literature that public managers might employ in "sense-making."

Framing and Reframing

In *Reframing Organizations: Artistry, Choice, and Leadership,* Lee G. Bolman and Terrence E. Deal argue that managers often fail because "they bring too few ideas to the challenges they face. . . . When they don't know what to do, they simply do more of what they do know." [108] Managers, they say, must be able to "reframe" experience in order to identify new and creative possibilities for effective action.[109]

Bolman and Deal identify four distinctive frames of reference, each with its own assumptions and logic, in the literatures on organizations. By applying each frame and its logic, a public manager can gain insights into what is happening, why it is happening, and what might be done.

According to the structural frame, organizations rationally pursue their goals. The purpose of organizational structures is to ensure an efficient division of labor, provide incentives for efficient performance, and facilitate managerial control and coordination. Problems of performance are addressed through realignment of goals, responsibilities, and tasks, typically through reorganizations. Metaphors for this frame are "factory" or "machine." The structural frame is likely to be most useful when goals and information are unambiguous; cause-and-effect relations are clear; technologies and information systems are well developed; conflict, ambiguity, and uncertainty are low; and governance is stable and legitimate.

According to the human resources frame, organizations and people are interdependent in that they need each other: Organizations need ideas, effort, and cooperation, and people need income, opportunities, and satisfaction in their work. Problems of performance are addressed through maintaining a balance between the needs of employees and of the organization and the maintenance of transparent relationships and of opportunities for personal growth. The metaphor for this frame is "family." The human resource frame is likely to be most useful when employees are empowered; morale and motivation are low or deteriorating; adequate resources are available; and diversity, conflict, and uncertainty are low or moderate.

According to the political frame, the distribution of scarce resources and the conflicts associated with differing degrees of power and influence underlie organizational behavior. Organizations are coalitions of individuals and interest groups, and goals and actions emerge from bargaining among stakeholders. Problems of performance are addressed through redistributing power and creating new coalitions. A metaphor for this frame is "jungle." The political frame is likely to be most useful when resources are scarce and shrinking; diversity is high or increasing; and the distribution of power and influence is diffuse or unstable.

According to the symbolic frame, organizations must resolve problems of meaning and value. Events have multiple meanings because people interpret them differently, producing ambiguity and uncertainty. Problems of performance are addressed through creating cultures of shared meanings by means of myths, symbols, ceremonies, and stories. A metaphor for this frame is "theater." The symbolic frame is most likely to be most useful when goals and information are ambiguous; cause-and-effect relations are poorly understood; technologies and information systems are not well developed; and there is considerable cultural diversity within the organization.

Another way of understanding the value of **reframing** is to compare the different interpretations of standard organizational processes using the logic of the four frames. Table 7.1 summarizes the differing interpretations of organizational processes such as decision making, goal setting, and motivation using the four frames. Public managers should be aware that a given process may be viewed in very different ways by those who observe or participate in it.

Richard Heimovics, Robert Herman, and Carole Jurkiewicz Coughlin conducted an empirical test of Bolman and Deal's views on the importance of reframing.[110] Beginning with the proposition that executives of nonprofit organizations are dependent on their external environment for resources to support their missions, the researchers expected to find that executives with reputations for being effective would be more likely to employ the political frame than a comparison group of executives lacking such reputations. Not only did the researchers confirm this expectation, but also they found, as expected, that effective executives were significantly more likely to use multiple frames than executives in the comparison group.

Bolman and Deal use their observation of and experience with managerial performance and their analysis of the prescriptive literature to draw two conclusions. First, in analyzing issues that confront them, managers typically do not use enough frames; often they use only one, and that one is usually the structural frame. Second, being able to reframe problems and issues overcomes rigidities of thought and perception; managers should train themselves to see the layers or dimensions of a problem instead of leaping to a conclusion based on pre- and (too often) misconceptions.

Navigating the Terrain

Several writers have used what amounts to spatial analogies to make sense of the ambiguous, polycentric worlds of public management. Both Richard Haass and Mark Moore urge the public manager to adopt an omnidirectional perspective. In *The Power to Persuade,* Haass advises public managers to "imagine that you are holding a compass." He goes on: "North represents those for whom you work. To the South are those who work for you. East represents colleagues, those in your organization with whom you work. West represents those outside your organization who have the potential to affect matters that affect you." [111] In *Creating Public Value,* Moore defines the directions toward which public managers must face somewhat differently: upward, toward those with some measure of authority over what you

TABLE 7.1 Organizational Processes and the Four Frames

Process	Structural Frame	Human Resource Frame	Political Frame	Symbolic Frame
Strategic planning	Strategies to set objectives and coordinate resources	Gatherings to promote participation	Arenas to air conflicts and realign power	Ritual to signal responsibility, produce symbols, negotiate meanings
Decision making	Rational sequence to produce right decision	Open process to produce commitment	Opportunity to gain or exercise power	Ritual to confirm values and provide opportunities for bonding
Reorganizing	Realign roles and responsibilities to fit tasks and environment	Maintain balance between human needs and formal roles	Redistribute power and form new coalitions	Maintain image of accountability and responsiveness; negotiate new social order
Evaluating	Way to distribute rewards of penalties and control performance	Process for helping individuals grow and improve	Opportunity to exercise power	Occasion to play roles in shared ritual
Approaching conflict	Maintain organizational goals by having authorities resolve conflict	Develop relationships by having individuals confront conflict	Develop power by bargaining, forcing, or manipulating others to win	Develop shared values and use conflict to negotiate meaning
Goal setting	Keep organization headed in right direction	Keep people involved and communication open	Provide opportunity for individuals and groups to make interests known	Develop symbols and shared values
Communication	Transmit facts and information	Exchange information, needs, and feelings	Influence or manipulate others	Tell stories
Meetings	Formal occasions for making decisions	Informal occasions for involvement, sharing feelings	Competitive occasions to win points	Sacred occasions to celebrate and transform the culture
Motivation	Economic incentives	Growth and self-actualization	Coercion, manipulation, and seduction	Symbols and celebrations

Source: Reproduced from Table 15.1 in Lee G. Bolman and Terrence E. Deal, *Reframing Organizations: Artistry, Choice, and Leadership,* 2nd ed. (San Francisco: Jossey-Bass, 1997), 267–268.

do; outward, toward those whose voluntary cooperation and resources you may need; and downward, toward those who work for you and on whose efforts you depend for your own and your organization's success. Both Haass and Moore, therefore, locate public managers at the center of a multipolar space in which challenges and opportunities come from every direction, often simultaneously.

Public management scholars Laurence J. O'Toole Jr., Kenneth J. Meier, and Sean Nicholson-Crotty investigated the relationship to organizational performance of Moore's idea of managing upward, outward, and downward. Based on data from more than one thousand public school districts in Texas, the authors measured the extent to which superintendents interacted with school boards (upward); with local business leaders, other superintendents, state legislators, and the Texas Education Agency (outward); and with school principals (downward). They found that managing outward was consistently associated with higher student performance, but that managing upward or downward had mixed results.[112] Other studies in other types of organizational settings might find different relationships between organizational performance and managerial efforts in each of Moore's directions.

Anticipating How Hard a Problem Will Be

Based on his years of experience as a successful public manager in New York City and the Commonwealth of Massachusetts, Gordon Chase distilled lessons from that experience into a framework that he believed public managers should use to decide how hard it might be to accomplish a goal or objective before they embark on it. Managers should apply this analysis to craft their decisions and their implementation strategies.[113] In Chase's view, obstacles to program implementation come from three sources. The first is operational demands associated with the program concept. These include the people to be served, the services to be delivered, distortions and irregularities that come from screening, incentives to select clients most likely to succeed, inequitable administration, and the controllability of the program. The second source is the nature and availability of resources needed to operate the program, including money and the strings attached to it and the availability and quality of personnel, space, supplies, and technical equipment. The third source of obstacles to program implementation is the need to share authority in accomplishing program goals. Issues of shared authority and retention of support include dealings with overhead agencies, other line agencies, elected officials, higher levels of government, private sector providers, special interest and community groups, and the media.

This way of viewing management challenges has, in Chase's view, several strategic implications. First, the toughest obstacles involve dealing with actors whose cooperation is required but whom you do not and cannot control. Get around them by contracting out the program to avoid "the overhead system" (public personnel, budgeting, and auditing organizations), by using public corporations, or by other tools that bypass political and bureaucratic obstacles, such as the appropriation process.

Second, Chase urges public managers at senior levels to demonstrate competence, loyalty, and reliability to the elected chief executive. "Little, if anything, is more important," he says.

Demonstrated loyalty gives a manager leverage over other actors, allies in struggles over resources and priorities, political clout, and credibility with external groups.

Finally, public managers should follow some rules: anticipate difficulties and act accordingly, do not alienate important actors, remember that relationships are long term and be straight and open, orchestrate meetings carefully, keep moving so that others will have to move, and make cooperation easy.

Working from the Ground Up

According to the conventional view, public policies are formulated and enacted by duly authorized policymakers, then implemented—managed, executed, carried out—by public agencies and their administrators. This kind of top-down or command-and-control management assumes that higher levels of an agency can and should have effective control over lower levels, directing what they do. Management begins with a policy objective or objectives, prescribes for successively lower levels in the organization what must be done if that objective is to be achieved, defines measurable outputs or outcomes that will indicate the degree of success in implementation, and, finally, promulgates the directives and resource allocations that will ensure compliant and effective behavior at each hierarchical level.

Serious problems arise with this strict logic-of-governance view of hierarchy when a large and complex bureaucracy and its numerous agents are expected to produce exactly the intended results and to do so efficiently. Inevitably, "stuff happens," as former secretary of defense Donald Rumsfeld might put it.[114] The writ of policymakers is compromised and weakened as authority is delegated down through various hierarchical levels and intended results and efficiency are compromised. Viewing the world exclusively from the top down obscures the numerous pitfalls that lie in the way of policy achievement, especially when chains of command and delegation linking policy makers and street-level service delivery are long and complex.

Richard F. Elmore has proposed a solution to the tendency to view the world from the top down, which he calls "backward mapping," a concept that although initially applied to public policy design, is equally relevant to public management strategy.[115] **Backward mapping** begins with "a relatively precise target at the lowest level of the system" and defines the capacities and resources needed to meet it. Success at backward mapping, Elmore says, requires a rather deep grasp of "how to use the structure and process of organizations to elaborate, specify, and define policies."[116]

Backward mapping starts with a clear and precise description of the desired outcomes; describes operational or street-level actions and interactions that are most likely to achieve those outcomes; describes, for successively higher levels in the administrative system, what combination of discretion, rules, and resources are needed to sustain the desired operational activities; and, finally, delegates appropriate authority and allocates appropriate resources to each level in the organization to achieve the goals. Backward mapping entails a different kind of learning from the top-down, "forward mapping" described earlier, and that is the important point.

HOW THE WORLD WORKS

The Challenge of Top-Down Management

When Mark W. Everson, former deputy director of management at the Office of Management and Budget and commissioner of the Internal Revenue Service, was appointed president and chief executive officer of the American Red Cross, he received some advice from former director of the National Aeronautics and Space Administration Sean O'Keefe, also an ex-OMB official. In the following excerpt, O'Keefe relays the idea that top-down management may be impossible.

"I told him when he went to the I.R.S., boy, you really know how to put yourself right in the middle of the Cuisinart, don't you. On your best day, people will ignore you; on your worst day, they'll be coming after you with ice picks. I don't think the Red Cross will be that different."

Source: Stephanie Strom, "At Red Cross, A New Head Is Appointed from I.R.S.," *New York Times,* April 19, 2007, Sec. A.

The concept of backward mapping has proven useful not only as a heuristic for management practice but also as a guide to research design. For example, the administration of public assistance programs is the frequent object of public policy reforms intended to encourage able-bodied welfare recipients to make every effort to become self-sufficient. Researchers Marcia Meyers, Bonnie Glaser, and Karin MacDonald use backward mapping to determine the extent to which public managers were successful in refocusing the primary public assistance program on promoting work and self-sufficiency.[117] The researchers analyzed what the new policy emphasis would require of welfare workers in their interactions with welfare clients: "transformation" behavior that ensured that clients received full, work-related information and consistent encouragement toward self-sufficiency. What they actually observed was "instrumental" behavior; most workers limited both information and encouragement to what was necessary for efficient claims processing. If policymakers' intentions were to be fulfilled, much more effort would be needed to acquaint workers with the new policies, train them in the complexities of its administration, and support them in taking a more individualized approach to welfare recipients.

Command-and-control managers are less likely to know what can go wrong until it has already gone wrong because they fail to understand the complex organizational dynamics involved in producing desired results. Backward mapping assumes that public agencies are complex, that there are strong tendencies toward bureau shaping and other self-interested behavior, and that greater reliance on carefully delegated discretion will increase the likelihood of good performance. As Elmore puts it, "The process of framing questions from the top begins with an understanding of what is important at the bottom." [118]

Entrepreneurship

In their accessible and straightforward handbook, *The New Effective Public Manager: Achieving Success in a Changing Government,* Steven Cohen and William Eimicke argue that effective public management is entrepreneurial public management: "active and aggressive effort to overcome constraints and obstacles" inspired by "a positive, can-do attitude. . . . Effective public managers try to make things happen . . . by thinking and acting strategically." [119] Effectiveness has several specific aspects: hiring and retaining good people; developing effective working relationships; structuring systems, tasks, and responsibilities; gathering, organizing, and using information; mastering the budgetary process; shaping organizational goals and strategies; and dealing with the media, legislatures, and interest groups.

The proposition that public managers should think like entrepreneurs, taking risks in order to create value, is controversial.[120] Earlier in this chapter it was suggested that entrepreneurs might be less sensitive to considerations of human relations. Critics of the concept have pointed out that entrepreneurial zeal could conflict with values such as due process, accountability, honesty, fairness, justice, and benevolence. It could also lead to rule bending and breaking and to unwarranted manipulation of the political process. Cohen and Eimicke insist, however, that entrepreneurship does not imply an abandonment of ethical guidelines. Others argue that new values such as innovation, quality, and responsive service are not inimical to traditional values and that entrepreneurs and innovators usually exhibit admirable qualities of commitment to public service and personal integrity.

This section has described what it means for a public manager to be strategic and some different approaches that managers might take. These include framing and reframing, navigating the terrain, anticipating how hard a problem will be, working from the ground up, and entrepreneurship.

LEADERSHIP

Americans take pride in having a government of laws, not of men and women, but they also yearn for what is widely termed **"leadership,"** for people in positions of responsibility who motivate and inspire others, transform situations, solve wicked problems, overcome obstacles, and show the way, intellectually and by personal example, toward better futures that honor the nation's values. But, according to a 2006 study by the Center for Public Leadership at Harvard University's Kennedy School of Government, Americans believe that the country faces a "leadership crisis" and that the quality of leadership is deteriorating.[121]

The yearning for leadership has elicited a large literature on the topic, much of it offering prescriptions for inspirational leadership.[122] Within the domain of public affairs, James MacGregor Burns's *Leadership* popularized the distinction between transformative and transactional leadership, the former concerned with transcendent change of an organization or a people, and the latter with effective interactions between those in leadership roles and those who are subordinate or follow.[123] He also distinguished between intellectual and executive leadership. Other notable leadership treatises include *On Leadership* by John W. Gardner (one-time secretary of the Department of Health, Education and Welfare), *On Becoming a Leader* by Warren G. Bennis, and *Leadership* by former New York City mayor Rudolph Giuliani (with Ken Kurson).[124]

As mentioned briefly in chapter 1, many writers on leadership hold that it is different, and far rarer, than management. According to a popular maxim, "Managers are people who do things right and leaders are people who do the right things." [125] In this view, leadership has a moral dimension, implying vision, exemplary conduct, and principled commitment that are seen and admired by others as transcending expediency, partisanship, and self-interest, or even the efficiency of the status quo. Jonathan R. Tompkins put it this way:

> Government is often thought to be too political, too bureaucratic, and too procedures-oriented to allow for [the pursuit of excellence. But] achieving higher levels of agency functioning is entirely possible for public managers who possess the will and determination to exercise leadership on behalf of the public good. . . . Because government truly matters, public servants bear a moral obligation to help their agencies carry out their missions as effectively as possible.[126]

Other students of leadership argue that although the tasks of leading and managing may differ, the public manager must both lead and manage. Richard Haass, an experienced public manager, insists, "*There is and can be no distinction between leadership and management if you are to be effective.* Direction without means is feckless, and means without direction is aimless. The two—leadership and management—are inseparable." [127] Robert Behn argues that public managers are obligated to lead in order to "help correct some of the imperfections" in the American system of governance. Public managers can contribute to the working of that system by compensating for some of the failures of the legislature, the judiciary, and their elected chief executive." [128] In Brian Cook's view, "Questions about what is effective also raise questions about what is *right.*" [129]

The study of leadership in public administration and management has, according to some scholars, been constrained by the conviction among scholars and practitioners alike that officials in the public sector are, above all, to be responsible to constitutional principles and institutions: to the common good, to duly enacted policy mandates, and to lawful hierarchical authority. Leadership in the public sector is expected to be provided not by administrators but by policymakers: legislative leaders, elected executives, and those appointed to executive positions in the departments, commissions, and agencies that implement public policies. Reflecting this view, scholars and practitioners commonly speak of public servants and public service. Scholars such as Robert Greenleaf and Larry Terry have formulated concepts such as servant-leadership and the leader as conservator of constitutional principles and organizational capabilities.

Such contributions notwithstanding, Montgomery Van Wart observes that despite a substantial mainstream leadership literature, "a distinctive public-sector leadership literature focusing on the significant constraints and unique environments of public sector leaders" has not emerged.[130]

Leadership in Theory

Leadership theories abound. A concise overview of public sector leadership theories has been provided by Janet V. Denhardt and Kelly B. Campbell. They distinguish among approaches that emphasize (1) the traits or attributes of individuals in a position to lead; (2) situations or specific contexts and settings in which leaders and followers interact; (3) organizational transformation based on vision and entrepreneurial initiative by executives; and (4) the realization of ethical and moral values in relationships between leaders and their followers.[131] (See Table 7.2.)

In his comprehensive assessment of what he calls the administrative leadership literature, Van Wart concludes that its strength "has been its hearty normative discussions about the proper roles of administrators in a democratic system. . . . The field has had remarkably few empirical studies that are not largely descriptive and has overly emphasized leadership as an executive function" rather than as a desirable characteristic of management and supervision across a wide variety of functions and roles.[132] Of the large leadership literature, Robert J. House and Ram N. Aditya add the insight that "historically, leadership research has been primarily concerned with generic leadership functions, to the exclusion of specific behavioral manifestations of these functions. Further, the diverse styles (mannerisms) by which leader behaviors are enacted have been largely ignored. The result is that much of our understanding about leadership is not easily operationalized in practical settings." [133]

The essentially normative approach of Philip Selznick illustrates Van Wart's point. Selznick observed in his classic 1957 study, *Leadership in Administration,* "What leaders do is hardly self-evident. And it is likely that much failure of leadership results from an inadequate understanding of its true nature and tasks." Selznick, a sociologist, provides a generic normative account of leadership in large, complex organizations. The tasks of leadership are: (1) defining institutional mission and role; (2) infusing institutional purpose into the organization's social structure; (3) defending institutional values and distinctive identity; and (4) maintaining an appropriate balance of power among the organizations' various interest groups. In summary, "The executive becomes a statesman as he makes the transition from administrative management to institutional leadership." Selznick continues: "[A]uthority and communication must be broadly understood to take account of the social psychology of obedience, perception and co-operation." [134]

More recent examples of normative leadership theory include that of Robert W. Terry, who sees leadership as a skill embodying authenticity, ethics, and spirituality. Authentic lead-

TABLE 7.2 Theories of Leadership in the Public Sector

Leadership Perspective	Goals and Purpose	Learning Objectives	Associated Pedagogies and Sample Approaches
Trait	To identify the traits of effective leaders.	To observe, synthesize, and report the characteristics and behaviors of successful leaders.	Classroom as think tank. Teacher-led, traditional pedagogy based on empirical research and study of the literature. Students may analyze biographies, prepare profiles of leaders, or assess their own traits.
Situational	To understand leadership style differences and the situations for which they are best suited.	To diagnose different organizational situations and choose appropriate behaviors based on model.	Classroom as laboratory. Traditional pedagogy for content and the use of short case studies to practice correct organizational diagnosis, the use of leadership style inventories, role play.
Transformational change	To create and implement planned change and organizational improvements.	To create a compelling vision, to strategically plan and manage multiple management systems and culture.	Classroom as flight simulator. Content based on traditional pedagogy with experiential/ empirical individual applications. Students conduct analyses of organizations based on SWOT [strength, weaknesses, opportunities, threats] or other integrative model, evaluate organizational change processes, and/or use simulations.
Value-based leadership	To create shared, moral leadership based on shared values and democratic norms.	To engage in and facilitate a collaborative leadership process, to inspire and empower leadership at all levels, to enact democratic and public service values.	Classroom as studio. Teacher and student share responsibility for course discussion and direction. The interaction in the classroom is used as part of the educational experience. Instructor both models and provides opportunities for feedback and student self-reflection and awareness, engages students in dialogue, and practices shared leadership through collaboration and facilitation of process. Action research may be used.

Source: Reproduced from Table I in Janet V. Denhardt and Kelly B. Campbell, "Leadership Education in Public Administration: Finding the Fit Between Purpose and Approach," *Journal of Public Affairs Education* 11, no. 3 (2005): 169–179.

ership is genuine and trustworthy because it is based on reflective thought on the part of the leader and a leader-initiated search for common ground among participants.[135] John Bryson and Barbara Crosby also propose a normative theory. They view leadership as promoting positive change under circumstances, such as the American constitutional scheme of checks and balances, where power is widely dispersed (or "shared" as they put it) and political regimes are weak.[136] The role of leadership, therefore, is to create opportunities for mutual gain through reframing problems in ways that enable individuals to perceive, and then act on, their common interests, by forming constituencies of conscience and vision. Effective public leadership is both omnidirectional—concerned with individuals, organizations, and political and legal institutions—and integrative—concerned with synthesizing ideas and interests until the reality of purposefully shared power is attained.

In sharp contrast to these approaches, political scientist Gary Miller offers a theory of leadership that is fundamentally analytical rather than normative.[137] Miller sketches two opposing strategies for managing an organization: optimal contracts, which align the incentives of employees with organizational goals through budget allocations—remuneration, rewards, and similar mechanisms—and leadership, which involves inspiring employees' voluntary and creative cooperation with organizational interests.

Miller's basic argument is clever and straightforward. He asserts, first, that designing optimal incentives is analytically, not to mention practically, impossible. No system of incentives can entirely eliminate noncooperative behavior; no system of formal authority, no system of incentives, can prevent organizational pathologies and inefficiencies—in other words, can preclude—organizations from failing to accomplish their goals or priorities. In the light of that fact, he says that applying repeated game theory (which he regards as appropriate for analyzing managerial strategies because it posits continuing interactions among self-interested organizational participants) yields indeterminate outcomes or multiple equilibriums. Finally, he argues that the role of the manager is to select one of these equilibriums and persuade people to cooperate in its achievement, transcending short term self-interest. Selecting and inspiring cooperation with that particular equilibrium constitutes leadership. Only the manager can foster belief in the certain rewards of cooperation and that "We're all in this together."

How does a manager induce a cooperative equilibrium? Says Miller, "myths and expectations": Activities that convey meaning and inspire loyalty are an important aspect of managerial leadership. Another approach is illuminated by the concept of a "gift exchange" [138] As noted in chapter 6, a manager may offer the "gift" of above-market incomes in the expectation of an employee's reciprocal "gift" of cooperative effort when called upon. The manager initiates job-enhancing opportunities and wins extraordinary cooperation as a result. This "gift exchange" can be construed as both "rational behavior" and "normative or conventional behavior," in other words, as both economic and as socialized behavior. In 1945 Donald Stone, then an official in the old Bureau of the Budget and one of public administration's important leaders, said that the public executive's "success . . . will be, in important measure, determined by his success in developing a body of commonly shared ideas." [139] This is

Miller's concluding point: The task of organizational leadership is to create mutually reinforcing expectations concerning the benefits of cooperative behavior and teamwork on behalf of shared objectives.

In his *Dynamics of Leadership in Public Service,* Van Wart integrates the many aspects of public sector leadership—five major elements and seventy subelements in all—into a "leadership action cycle," which is premised on seventeen specific assumptions. The last of these assumptions illustrates the spirit of his approach: "Leader effectiveness is not a unidimensional concept any more than is leadership itself. It can emphasize technical performance, follower development, organizational alignment, and a public-service and ethical focus, among others. It can balance a number of these perspectives. The proper proportion is a value, not a technical judgment." [140]

Leadership in Practice

At least three different perspectives on leadership as an essential element of public affairs practice can be identified. To leadership believers, which includes authors of inspirational books on leadership, such as Giuliani, the importance of leadership in public life and the need for behavioral skills such as self-awareness, team building, conflict resolution, and effective written and oral communication are self-evident articles of faith.

In contrast, leadership skeptics, which includes many empirical social scientists concerned with government performance, offer a different perspective: (1) "leadership" has never been shown to have any *a priori* theoretical content; leaders are individuals our culture celebrates after the fact, and leadership tends to be in the eye of the beholder; (2) so-called principles of leadership are vacuous proverbs that are either so general as to be useless or are easily invalidated by examples of leaders who clearly violated them. The point is that there is no one right leadership model that has any meaning.

Finally, the leadership pragmatists, such as Jameson Doig and Erwin Hargrove, contend that an emphasis on leadership must not be viewed as a panacea or be restricted to a generic behavioral model. Its meaning must be grounded in research. Pragmatists tend to believe several things. First, leadership emerges from specific contexts. Instances or episodes of leadership that, alas, can be identified only after the fact, are the product of a good fit or match between the skills and attributes of an individual in a leader role and the specific demands of that role in a given time and place. An individual may be regarded as a leader during one phase of his or her life but not during other phases, when the situational fit was less propitious. Second, leadership is elicited by the need for disruptive change in a status quo—it is and ought to be relatively uncommon because disruptive change is very often not an appropriate strategy. Third, individuals with many different skill sets can and have been leaders—there is no lowest common denominator or sufficient condition for leadership. And, finally, leadership is one of several factors that are important to the performance of governance. Others are policy designs, organizations, resources, management, and public service values. Indeed, a leader must recognize that many factors contribute to organizational performance, and that many of them are not under the leader's control.

CONCEPTS IN ACTION

What Is "Bad" Leadership?

Students of leadership have been perplexed by the notion of "bad" leadership. Alan Ehrenhalt, executive editor of *Governing* magazine, recalls that John Randolph once complained that his congressional colleague, Henry Clay, "Clay, was "so brilliant, so capable, and yet so corrupt that like a rotten mackerel in the moonlight, he both shines and stinks." Says Ehrenhalt:

We look for heroes to represent us, although we rarely find them. We take a certain perverse pleasure in unmasking hypocrites and dispatching blowhards who fail to deliver on their promises. The leaders we have trouble dealing with are those of obvious talent and genuine achievement who turn out to have displayed appalling ethical insensitivity—or worse.

Source: Alan Ehrenhalt, "The Paradox of Corrupt Yet Effective Leadership," *New York Times,* September 30, 2002. A fuller discussion of bad leadership, with many examples from public life, is in Barbara Kellerman, *Bad Leadership: What it Is, How it Happens, Why it Matters* (Watertown, Mass.: Harvard Business School Press, 2004).

In the public sector, the context of leadership is almost always organizations in specific political contexts. The possibilities for active leadership, especially when it involves organizational transformation, can either be influenced by or thwarted by the structural and cultural dimensions of public management. Based on the work of Doig and Hargrove, three important aspects of managerial craft crucial to successful leadership in these contingent and uncertain circumstances can be identified: (1) a capacity to engage in systematic analysis of the possibilities for change; (2) an ability to see new possibilities offered by the evolving historical situation and communicate such possibilities to the organizational and political environment; and (3) the manager's desire to "make a difference" and to commit his or her energies and personal reputation toward transformative goals. Leadership is inherently multidimensional, a subject revisited in chapter 10.

DOES MANAGERIAL CRAFTSMANSHIP MATTER?

Both intuition and anecdotal evidence support the proposition that skilled public managers will contribute in a positive way to governmental performance and that incompetent or clueless public managers will cause harm by undermining their agency's effectiveness, eroding its political and public support, and failing to capitalize on opportunities for significant improvements in operations. It is self-evident that good managers are better than bad ones, but it is far from obvious how much good or harm *on average* can be done by individual public managers given the constraints under which they work. Relatively few public managers, however, have the kind of discretion that will enable them to aggressively pursue imaginative, agency-transforming initiatives without restraint. At the very least, political and financial resources are almost always limited relative to visionary ambitions.

Yet there is ample evidence that the ways public managers use their discretion have significant impacts on how, to whom, and with what results public services are produced. Managerial discretion is typically exercised with respect to internal structures and processes of administration; the use of various management tools such as performance incentives, planning, and quality improvement; and goals, missions, priorities, and adaptations to the institutional and political environments.[141] Analyses of the empirical literature on the consequences of these discretionary uses of managerial authority reveals frequent instances of significant managerial impacts on the character, quality, and availability of public services.

The efficacy of managerial craftsmanship is not necessarily robust, however, and scholars disagree over its importance. In her study of the implementation of the federal Temporary Assistance for Needy Families program, Norma M. Riccucci showed that the influence of management on the behaviors and actions of street-level service workers was negligible.[142] Their activities, she argues, are influenced much more by professional norms, work customs, and occupational cultures than by managerial directives. In her ongoing studies of the same kinds of programs, however, Evelyn Brodkin reached virtually the opposite conclusion, that managerial directives affect the fairness and effectiveness of these programs. As noted earlier, public managers confronted with such conflicting findings may need a research broker to sort out the reasons for the disagreements.

It is safe to conclude, all things considered, that managerial craftsmanship, including aspects of both temperament and skill, matters, although exactly how and why it matters varies across organizational and policy contexts. Making good choices concerning strategies and tools can, in a given context, enable public managers to make a difference on a worthwhile, and occasionally even noteworthy, scale. Making questionable choices can matter, too, in the harm it causes.

Consider two more stories: The first concerns Samuel W. Bodman, a public manager and a cabinet officer, who assumed major responsibilities at the federal level and performed them with apparent success; the second is about John D. Ashcroft, another public manager and a cabinet officer, who engendered considerable controversy.

Bodman was confirmed by the Senate as the secretary of energy on February 1, 2005. He previously served in the Bush administration as the deputy secretary of both the Commerce and the Treasury Departments. Before coming to government, Bodman headed Cabot Corporation, a global specialty chemicals and materials company. Earlier in his career, he held positions in the financial services industry as a venture capitalist and as a faculty member at the Massachusetts Institute of Technology, where he had earned a doctor of science degree. He has been described by a knowledgeable observer as "the most qualified secretary [of energy] we've ever had." [143]

Bodman began his tenure at the Department of Energy (DOE) by studying several "fat three-ring briefing binders" on his department's programs. Within months, he was reported to have used a "corporate-style structure" to good effect. His appointees to senior positions, reflecting his belief that the Capitol was where the money is, were praised as "not big ideologues," but as people "very interested and willing to work with both sides of the aisle on the Hill." [144] He was said to hold weekly staff meetings of more than twenty top officials so that they might communicate with each other about their activities and become familiar with the department as a whole.

On April 11, 2006, Bodman sent a memorandum to DOE employees and contractors saying that "all DOE Federal and contractor personnel have the right—and the responsibility—to identify and report concerns associated with safety, quality, environment, health, security, or management of DOE operations without fear of reprisal. . . . In turn, DOE Federal and contractor managers are expected to respond respectfully to these concerns in a prompt and effective manner to ensure efficient operation of programs under their jurisdiction." [145] He was inclined to manage through establishing and enforcing specific, market-oriented goals.

A profile of Bodman in the journal *Science* described him as self-effacing but relishing a challenge and "an engineer, not a scientist." Among the challenges he chose to define for himself were reversing cuts in DOE's budget for basic science and increasing White House support for applied energy initiatives. His success in both and in creating the new position of science adviser to the secretary led to his being characterized as a "hero of science" and praised by independent experts as having "his values in the right location." He has also courted controversy. He dismissed the top science advisory board at DOE, saying he preferred to receive advice from "those on the payroll," including officials at DOE's far-flung laboratories. He speaks little of energy conservation and uses a limousine and SUVs for his entourage, at the same time emphasizing the promise of nuclear energy. Many say his new energy initiatives are too small relative to the problem of achieving energy independence.

Ashcroft, a lawyer and former U.S. senator from Missouri, served as attorney general during George W. Bush's first term. Following the 9/11 terrorist attacks, Ashcroft became the principal advocate for the controversial U.S.A. Patriot Act, which expanded the federal government's powers to combat terrorist threats. There is nothing seriously wrong with the U.S.A. Patriot Act, said an editorial in the Austin, Texas, *American-Statesman.* The cause of all the controversy is instead John Ashcroft himself, "a public official with a penchant for secrecy." The editorial continued: "[T]he Patriot Act would be far less controversial if Ashcroft were not so furtive about when, how, how often and for what it is used." The paper noted that an article about Ashcroft in *U.S. News & World Report* was highly complimentary toward him as a human being; far from the ogre that he is so often portrayed as being, he is a good, smart, and decent man. But, said the editorial, "He barely gives Congress the time of day and is even less forthcoming with the press and the public." [146]

In his interview with *U.S. News & World Report,* Ashcroft noted that his job was nothing less than changing the Justice Department from an agency that prosecutes offenders to one that prevents the most dangerous offenses: terrorism and related acts.[147] "In order to move an institution and its mentality," he said, "sometimes you have to draw very clear lines." Ashcroft defended what many commentators saw as his harsh rhetoric by saying that he needs to let the American people know exactly how he was handling things. For Ashcroft, public management was a matter of changing profoundly the institutionalized values of the Justice Department, the challenge facing virtually every public manager involved in providing for homeland security: changing organizational cultures.

Among his policy priorities, Ashcroft forcefully insisted on uniformity of law enforcement across all the U.S. attorney offices, although, as discussed in chapter 5, typically there are distinct differences in pleadings and sentencing depending on local circumstances. No one told Ashcroft to choose this strategy; he simply believed it was the right thing to do, even though it had been unsuccessfully tried by a predecessor and was intensely controversial within the Justice Department and state law enforcement communities.

Ashcroft believed that his job was not to micromanage but to offer big-picture, results-oriented leadership—what he liked to call "noble inspiration." Critics within the department said that he was isolated from the staff attorneys, that he got information by phone and e-mail rather than through personal contact, and that decision making was opaque.

Bodman and Ashcroft present sharp contrasts in managerial craftsmanship. Bodman's largely rationalist strategy stemmed from a handful of policy convictions and a pragmatic weighing of his challenges and opportunities. His type tends to reflect the problem-oriented style of an engineer—factual and analytical—and the kind of engaging extraversion associated with those who enjoy the social demands of managerial roles. Ashcroft approached his responsibilities in a manner consistent with his devoutly evangelical religious faith, displaying unshakable commitment to principle and the personal aloofness of an inner-directed individual. His strategy, although similar to those of other officials engaged in homeland security, was articulated and pursued with messianic fervor and little patience with the inside-the-Beltway political process. The one characteristic these men clearly had in common was decisiveness: Neither shrank from the challenge of a difficult decision.

Firm conclusions concerning their effectiveness would require deeper investigation, but the evidence supports the view that both made a difference, albeit an incremental one, in their departments. Other energy secretaries have exhibited quite different kinds of craftsmanship, with different consequences for the performance of their departments. In public management, structures and cultures matter. So, too, do public managers and their craft.[148]

Key Concepts

managerial types
deliberation and decision making
rationality
bounded rationality
prospect theory
framing effects
cognitive dissonance
groupthink

psychological biases
best practices
paradigm
ideology
policy analysis
evidence-based policy and practice
think tanks
management by walking around
strategy
reframing
backward mapping
leadership

Analysis and Argument: Test Your Understanding

As the sketch at the end of this chapter suggests, Attorney General John Ashcroft saw himself as a leader at the Department of Justice. Among his initiatives was one to standardize plea bargaining practices in the offices of U.S. attorneys across the country (discussed in chapter 5).

Review the discussion in chapter 5, including Ashcroft's memorandum to U.S. attorneys cited there, and the account below, which provides further details.[149] Next, read the profiles cited below that describe Ashcroft's background and management style.

The following questions ask you to analyze Ashcroft's exercise of craft as a public manager. For each question, use the specific ideas and concepts discussed in this chapter, drawing on evidence from the readings to construct a complete argument, as described in chapter 3, for your response. As an additional exercise, consider collecting similar profiles of Attorney General Michael B. Mukasey and compare and contrast the managerial craft of these two men.

1. How would you characterize Ashcroft's type? What are the potential benefits and drawbacks of this type for a person fulfilling the role of U.S. attorney general?
2. How does Ashcroft tend to deliberate and make decisions?
3. How does Ashcroft tend to learn about the matters that confront him? What sources of information does he tend to rely upon, and which does he tend to ignore?
4. In what ways does Ashcroft exercise strategy in his managerial craft? How would you characterize his strategy?
5. Analyze Ashcroft's capacities and strategies as a leader.

Profiles

Jeffrey Toobin, "Ashcroft's Ascent," *The New Yorker,* April 15, 2002.

"Managing the Departments: Grades for Bush's Cabinet Secretaries," *National Journal,* January 27, 2003.

Vanessa Blum, "Ashcroft's Inner Sanctum," *Legal Times,* October 13, 2003.

Chitra Ragavan, "Ashcroft's Way: America's Top Cop Has Been Demonized and Lionized. He's a Complex Guy All Right, Just Not the Guy Everyone Thinks He Is," *U.S. News & World Report,* January 18, 2004.

Dan Eggen and Paul Kane, "Gonzales Hospital Episode Detailed: Ailing Ashcroft Pressured on Spy Program, Former Deputy Says," *Washington Post,* May 16, 2007.

Review of Ashcroft's Guidance on Plea Bargaining

On September 29, 2003, Attorney General Ashcroft instructed federal prosecutors, who work under the supervision of ninety-three U.S. attorneys in federal court districts, to pursue the most serious readily provable offences. They were prohibited from engaging in fact bargaining or any other "plea agreement that results in the sentencing court having less than a full understanding of all readily provable facts relevant to sentencing." The intent was to reduce the amount of plea bargaining and, incidentally, to reduce district-to-district variation in prosecutorial strategies. Attorney General Richard Thornburgh had pursued a similar strategy in the late 1980s and early 1990s under Presidents Ronald Reagan and George H. W. Bush.

Well over 90 percent of all federal criminal defendants plead out, although, as noted, practices vary across districts. If a significantly higher number of these cases were to go to trial, then court workloads might expand dramatically. Therefore local prosecutors exercise their discretion before charges are filed, using the vagueness of the "readily provable" standard to select the cases most suitable for trial. Ashcroft's instructions, by attempting to centralize, constrain, and standardize local prosecutorial practices, were a direct effort to change the nature of legal practice in U.S. attorneys' offices. The American Civil Liberties Union and similar organizations regarded this policy as a restriction on civil rights. Other legal experts and organizations such as the Heritage Foundation, a conservative think tank, regarded such reductions in prosecutorial discretion as promoting greater equity in sentencing, the goal of the Federal Sentencing Reform Act, and increasing the likelihood that guilty parties will receive proportionate punishment.

The Nevada Department of Corrections newsletter noted that "from Connecticut to California, legislatures and governors are, with a few exceptions, eagerly finding new ways to reduce, rethink or eliminate prison sentences for crimes within their jurisdictions. The result is a somewhat contradictory national crime-fighting agenda: as the Ashcroft Justice Department demands the harshest prison terms and goes out of its way to track federal judges who do not give them, state lawmakers are openly advocating less time for the same crime and giving judges more discretion in choosing punishments." [150] Ashcroft speaks in declarative terms of his responsibilities as a public manager: "I may be the person more responsible for trying to shape the national consciousness in saying that prosecution is not enough for the Justice Department anymore," he told *U.S. News & World Report*. "It has to be actively involved in prevention." "I think clarity is one of the most important features in leadership." Owing to what many regard as a polarizing personality, however, one admirer within the Justice Department observed, "He's become so radioactive that he couldn't announce a free school lunch initiative without people questioning it."

In the last year of the Bush administration, legal scholar Daniel Richman, reflecting on Ashcroft's policy, asked, "How does one figure out what role centralization goals play in the department's sentencing policies?" [151] After all, he continued, "Institutional mind-reading is always a challenge. Sometimes one can work backward and presume intentionality from the natural result of a program. But this line of reasoning only goes so far when dealing with measures that no informed observer would expect to be very successful. Any theoretical model would predict that the informational costs on this hierarchical control project would be prohibitive." He amplified his reasons by quoting law professor Frank Bowman, a former Justice Department attorney:

> The experience of the last decade, during which variants of the same policy [regarding charging and accepting pleas to only the most serious provable offense] have always been in place, strongly suggests that the Justice Dept. cannot meaningfully restrain local United States Attorney's Offices from adopting locally convenient plea bargaining practices.[152]

Ashcroft's departure from the Justice Department at the end of President Bush's first term, the Democratic takeover of Congress in 2006, and controversies over the firing of several U.S. attorneys by Ashcroft's successor put the standardization project on the back burner.

8 Accountability

Accountability is one of the oldest but most elusive issues in the field of public management, and an issue that raises many questions. What does it mean for one actor to hold another accountable? How can public managers be held accountable to constitutional authority? How can political, hierarchical, and citizen principals ensure that bureaucratic agents carry out their wishes? How can managers hold their employees accountable? What should managers do if demands for accountability are in conflict? Because the execution of policies and programs must be delegated, and because public managers and their subordinates must inevitably exercise discretion, accountability is a fundamental concern of public management. Indeed, many of the distinctive challenges of public management, described in chapter 1, are directly concerned with issues of accountability.

The difficulties in pinning down accountability are evident in historical concerns for responsible action by "unelected bureaucrats." Because it often involves competing pressures and expectations from a number of different sources, holding organizations and individuals accountable is no straightforward matter. Structure is the dimension most often used in attempts to ensure accountability, but culture and craft are fundamental as well, even though they are more difficult for external authorities to influence. Therefore, at its core, accountability concerns span the three dimensions of public management.

The following example highlights some of the difficulties of holding organizations accountable in one specific context—public schools. Public School 48 in the South Bronx was operating under an accountability system put in place by a 2002 law commonly referred to as the No Child Left Behind Act, which required states to establish accountability systems and for sanctions to be imposed on schools judged to be "failing."

In the right kind of world, Public School 48 in the South Bronx would be getting all kinds of awards. Though the school serves some of the city's poorest minority children (75 per cent Hispanic, 25 per cent black and all eligible for free lunches), P.S. 48's test scores have soared in the last few years. In 2005, 86 per cent of fourth graders scored proficient in math, and 68.5 per cent in English, placing P.S. 48 near the top of the Bronx's 130 elementary schools.

The principal, John Hughes, has mixed feelings about all the testing that goes on these days, but professionally, he has put that all aside. "The profit margin in this business is test scores," he said. "That's all they measure you by now."

Test prep? "Are you kidding?" he said. "We start in September and we don't stop until the tests are over," in March.

"I can't afford not to do test prep," he said. "Otherwise my kids don't have a chance. It's all by the test numbers. If they score 3's or 4's, they have marketability for getting into one of the city's good middle schools. "With low scores of 2 or 1, out of a maximum of 4, they are stuck in a bad neighborhood school.

In 2004, Chancellor Joel I. Klein attended graduation, praising the test scores and wearing a T-shirt with the P.S. 48 slogan, "Best School in the Universe."

But the universe P.S. 48 gets evaluated in has little to do with the real world. P.S. 48 is measured in the federal No Child Left Behind world, and in that universe, it has been labeled failing.

When Mr. Hughes learned that, last fall, he was outraged, and contacted his supervisors to find out why. "No one could explain," he says. "They'd say, 'It must be this or it must be that.' "

In the No Child world, state and federal officials plug test results from schools that few of them have ever seen into a series of complex formulas. The calculations are so technical that it took city officials many hours over several weeks to finally pinpoint why P.S. 48 was labeled failing.

At one point, the city's top testing officials were not sure whether to use something called the Annual Measurable Objective or the Effective Annual Measurable Objective to calculate P.S. 48's score, and had to confer with state officials.

"If the number-crunchers don't understand," Mr. Hughes said, "how can a principal? And parents? It's crazy." "This federal law," Mr. Hughes added, "is wacky."

P.S. 48's problem? Under the federal law, it is not enough for a school to improve its overall test scores. Every subgroup—blacks, Hispanics, the poor—must also make sufficient progress in English and math. After numerous calls last fall, Mr. Hughes learned that his special-education and English language learner (immigrant) subgroups did not make sufficient progress on the English test.

Subgroup size varies by state; in New York, it is 30 students. Many small schools do not have enough students for subgroups, so they are spared this scrutiny entirely. Cynics have joked that the reason the small-school movement is so popular is that it is the only way to meet federal standards.

P.S. 48 is large, with 970 students. According to the state, it had 31 students in the English language learner subgroup.

Mr. Hughes was sure he had a lot less, but which English language learners the state counts in a subgroup is not straightforward.

Many immigrant students who have been in this country less than six years do not take the regular state English test; they take an alternative state language test that measures their English skills. Still others, who have been in the country or the school too short a time are not supposed to be counted in the subgroup.

Mr. Hughes wanted the names of the 31 students. But though the federal law is four years old, the state has no way to provide subgroup lists to schools. (This is supposed to change soon, when the state implements a new data service.) Instead, city officials spent long hours piecing together the list for Mr. Hughes.

Once the principal saw the names, he realized many did not belong on the list. Typically, they were Hispanics who were given bilingual services when they first arrived. However, once they had been at P.S. 48, teachers realized their problem was not English; it was that they were slow learners and needed special-education services. Most have not been in a language class for two to three years.

A state rule says students cannot be removed from the English learners' subgroup until they pass the English language test. But many cannot pass because of their special-education learning limitations.

In the end, the news was not all bad. Thanks to Mr. Hughes's angry quest, state officials now say they will set up a new process to remove such children from the subgroup list. With that victory, Mr. Hughes's English language learner list shrunk to 25, too small to be counted for the purposes of the No Child Left Behind Law.

Now, his only problem was the special-education subgroup's English score. Special education is the single biggest reason schools are judged failing under the federal law. As a result, the state gives bonus points if that is the only category a school misses. With 34 bonus points, Mr. Hughes assumed P.S. 48 had passed. "They're taking us off the failing list," he said on Friday.

BUT after conferring with the state, city officials e-mailed Mr. Hughes information on Monday that was too technical for him to comprehend but was clearly not good news. "The 34 points can only be applied to the A.M.O., not the E.A.M.O." (For those trying to keep track, that is Annual Measurable Objective rather than Effective Annual Measurable Objective.) Translated into English: if one more special-education child had scored 3, the school of 970 would have gone from failing to successful.

There is hope, however. School officials nationwide have complained that the federal special-education standards are unfair. They have pointed out that children often get special-education services because they are performing two years below their grade, so it is unrealistic to then expect them to pass a regular, grade-level state test.

For four years, the Bush administration dismissed these complaints as the soft bigotry of low expectations. However, recently, under the Secretary of Education, Margaret Spellings, federal officials reversed themselves and acknowledged that this standard is indeed unreasonable.

New rules will soon mean that 30 percent of special-education students are exempted from regular state tests. If that rule had been in place in 2005, P.S. 48 would have easily made its special-education numbers and been judged a success.

Under federal law, a failing school must send letters home offering students the chance to transfer to other schools. Last fall, Mr. Hughes sent home 970 letters. Not one parent removed a child. Unlike state and federal accountability experts, they've seen P.S. 48.[1]

Holding schools—or any individual or organization—accountable is an appealing idea, but such efforts may face many obstacles, some arising from the existing cultures and structures they are embedded in, and some—as the situation at P.S. 48 illustrates—from the seeming disconnect between actual performance and measured performance.

This chapter first discusses the meaning of accountability and frameworks for thinking about it in the context of public organizations. Next, the history of accountability in U.S. government is traced. The remainder of the chapter discusses accountability from structural, cultural, and craft perspectives. Reflecting the dominant role of the structural dimension in accountability relationships, the chapter pays considerable attention to structural mechanisms for ensuring accountability in the executive, legislative, and judicial branches. An additional section discusses performance measurement as a structural tool for ensuring accountability. Following the sections on culture and craft, the chapter concludes with a discussion of the challenges of managing under multiple accountability regimes. In the end-of-chapter exercise, readers consider the multiple accountability pressures facing James Woolsey, director of the Central Intelligence Agency from 1993 to 1995, at the time that CIA employee Aldrich Ames was charged with spying for Russia.

WHAT IS ACCOUNTABILITY?

The difficulty of ensuring accountability is illustrated by and compounded by the vague, incomplete, and multiple understandings of it. Robert D. Behn has observed, "To 'hold people accountable' has become a cliché and, like all clichés, is a substitute for thinking." [2] Accountability shares this characteristic with terms such as "goals," "planning," "learning," or "responsibility," which seem to require no definition and that "start a lot of heads nodding," but often hold different meanings for those who use them.[3] William T. Gormley Jr. has argued that accountability is a "procedural value" that "characterize[s] the process of governance," and, along with other procedural values such as responsiveness, leadership, effectiveness, and fairness, should be invoked only when it is possible to "define them more precisely, to defend them more persuasively, and to place them in the context of other values." [4]

Scholars have attempted to bring precision to definitions and frameworks for accountability in different contexts. Frederick C. Mosher defined accountability in relation to what he termed **objective responsibility,** which "connotes the responsibility of a person or an organization *to* someone else, outside of self, *for* some thing or some kind of performance. It is closely akin to *accountability* or *answerability.*" [5] He distinguished objective responsibility, which reflects the structural dimension of public management, from **subjective responsibility,** which is more closely associated with the cultural dimension, in the sense that it focuses on:

> to whom and for what one *feels* responsible and *behaves* responsibly. This meaning is more nearly synonymous with identification, loyalty, and conscience than it is with

> accountability and answerability. And it hinges more heavily upon background, the processes of socialization, and current associations in and outside the organization than does objective responsibility.[6]

Barbara S. Romzek and Melvin J. Dubnick offer a definition of accountability that reflects Mosher's conceptualization of objective responsibility: "a relationship in which an individual or agency is held to answer for performance that involves some delegation of authority to act."[7] This definition emphasizes the principal-agent nature of the relationship: Principals want to hold agents to whom they delegate authority responsible for their actions.

Herbert A. Simon, Victor A. Thompson, and Donald W. Smithburg offer another definition of accountability that emphasizes its link not only with responsibility but also with responsiveness: "By accountability we mean those methods, procedures, and forces that determine what values will be reflected in administrative decisions. Accountability is the enforcement of responsibility." These authors identify different meanings of "responsibility"—"as a synonym for legal authority," "to denote the compliance with generally accepted moral obligations," or as "responsiveness to other people's values"—and emphasize the last one in their notion of accountability, focusing on "the extent to which administrators are responsive to other persons or groups, in and out of the bureaucracy."[8]

Accountability may also be understood in terms of its purpose or type. Public administration scholar Mark Bovens suggests that public accountability serves five essential functions in a representative democracy: assuring democratic control, enhancing integrity, improving performance, maintaining legitimacy, and providing catharsis after tragedy or failure.[9] Behn points to three typical targets of accountability: for finances, for fairness, and for outcomes, where the first two targets "reflect concerns for *how* government does what it does," and the third target reflects a concern for "*what* government does—what it actually accomplishes."[10]

Romzek and Dubnick have developed a particularly useful framework for analyzing public accountability. They delineate four types of accountability systems based on source of control over an agency's action: whether it originates within or outside the organization, and the extent of that control (see Table 8.1).

TABLE 8.1 Types of Accountability Systems

Degree of Control over Agency Actions	Source of Agency Control	
	Internal	External
High	1. Bureaucratic	2. Legal
Low	3. Professional	4. Political

Source: Barbara S. Romzek and Melvin J. Dubnick, "Accountability in the Public Sector: Lessons from the *Challenger* Tragedy," *Public Administration Review* 47, no. 3 (May/June 1987): 229.

Three of the four systems in this scheme reflect Mosher's concept of objective responsibility and emphasize structural aspects of public management. First, bureaucratic (or hierarchical) accountability is characterized by hierarchical relationships within an organization that are accompanied by and characterized by rules and clearly defined expectations. These types of relationships tend to correlate with the internal, constraining structures described by the framework presented in chapter 5. Second, legal accountability is concerned with "a formal or implied fiduciary (principal/agent) agreement between the public agency and its legal overseer" and by definition is imposed by formal authorities external to the organization. It, too, tends to be manifested in constraining structures. Examples of relationships characterized by legal accountability are those between a legislature and an executive branch agency, between the courts and agencies, and between an agency and its contractors. Third, political accountability emphasizes representativeness and responsiveness of the public manager or organization to a constituency. As Romzek and Dubnick note, "Potential constituencies include the general public, elected officials, agency heads, agency clientele, other special interest groups, and future generations." For this type of accountability, "Regardless of which definition of constituency is adopted, the administrator is expected to be responsive to their policy priorities and programmatic needs." [11] The fourth system in this scheme—professional accountability—reflects Mosher's concept of subjective responsibility and the cultural dimension of public management. This type of accountability relies on the expertise of actors in the organization and is characterized by discretion and deference to professionals and their expertise.

Political scientist Judith E. Gruber has developed a framework for examining different accountability regimes and the specific challenges of ensuring accountability in democracies. She points out that the task of ensuring accountability and controlling bureaucracies is not unique to governments or to democracies, but that it

> takes on special urgency in democracies because unaccountable power flies in the face of the central norms of such political systems. When the legitimacy of a government derives from the consent of the governed, the problem becomes not merely an inability to get the governmental apparatus to act in ways the leaders or citizens wish but also a challenge to the fundamental nature of that government.[12]

Gruber focuses on issues of democratic control of the bureaucracy—that is, control that stems from citizens (related to Romzek and Dubnick's political accountability). Bureaucratic behaviors, she argues, exhibit two dimensions for which they can be held accountable: the procedures they use and the substance of decisions they make. The combination of these dimensions results in four idealized types of bureaucratic actors: autonomous actors, end achievers, procedure followers, and clerks (Table 8.2).

Corresponding systems for ensuring accountability through democratic control, Gruber says, include a "self-control" approach for situations characterized by an autonomous actor (both low substantive and procedural constraints), a participatory approach for situations characterized by a procedure follower (low substantive but high procedural constraints), and a public interest approach for situations characterized by end achievers (high substantive but low procedural constraints). Gruber reserves what she calls an "accountability approach" for

TABLE 8.2 **Idealized Perspectives of Bureaucratic Democracy and Approaches to Democratic Control**

	Substantive Constraint	
Procedural Constraint	**Low**	**High**
Low	Actor: Autonomous actor Approach: Self-control	Actor: End achiever Approach: Public interest
High	Actor: Procedure follower Approach: Participatory	Actor: Clerk

Source: Adapted from Figures 1 and 2 in Judith E. Gruber, *Controlling Bureaucracies: Dilemmas in Democratic Governance* (Berkeley: University of California Press, 1987), 15, 18.

those democratic control mechanisms employed when substantive constraints are low, and that span the range from moderate to high procedural constraints. She characterizes these as focusing on "guaranteeing that decisions are made in an 'appropriate fashion' with only peripheral concern for what the decisions are." At moderate levels of both procedural and substantive constraints, Gruber places "clientele-oriented approaches," which "are more concerned with the substance of decisions made in administrative agencies than with the procedural fact that they are made solely by administrators." [13]

Frameworks such as these can be used as heuristics for identifying the situations, conditions, and characteristics of accountability challenges and possible solutions related to the tasks and environments of public organizations and the possible responses to these challenges from both inside and outside the organization. Near the end of this chapter is an example that shows how one pair of scholars used the Romzek-Dubnick framework to analyze the plane crash that killed Ron Brown, secretary of commerce during the Clinton administration.

ACCOUNTABILITY IN HISTORICAL PERSPECTIVE

Accountability is deeply rooted in constitutional principle. Defined by Alexander Hamilton as "due dependence on the people in a republican sense," the idea of accountability has been central to public administration's claim to constitutional legitimacy from the beginning of the Republic.[14] As James Madison expressed it in Federalist No. 37: "The genius of republican liberty seems to demand . . . not only that all power should be derived from the people, but that those entrusted with it should be kept in dependence on the people."

Often referred to as the accountability clause, Article I, Section 9, clause 7, of the Constitution states: "No Money shall be drawn from the Treasury, but in Consequence of Appropriations made by Law; and a regular Statement and Account of the Receipts and Expenditures of all public Money shall be published from time to time." Clearly, this clause focuses on financial accountability, but many other constitutional provisions also bear on accountability.[15] Congress is required to keep and publish a journal of its proceedings. The president is required to report to Congress on the state of the Union and to publish reasons for vetoing legislation. Criminal defendants must be tried in public. Public officers may be impeached and removed from office. State constitutions contain similar provisions.

CONCEPTS IN ACTION

Representative Democracy as a Form of Accountability

During the administration of President George W. Bush, the recurrent issue of executive branch domination of the federal judiciary through the president's power of appointment was revived. The following excerpt summarizes the argument for the American constitutional scheme of representative democracy as the ultimate protection for an independent judiciary and the ultimate form of democratic accountability.

It is essential to the security of the courts that government have a mechanism that keeps it within its proper bounds and forces it to resist the temptation to swallow up the judiciary in pursuit of its own ends. One way of achieving this security derives from the distinctively American conception of representation. One of the genuinely unique aspects of the Constitution was its dependence on a principle of representation "where all authority flows from and returns at stated periods to, the people." Representation, while having ancient roots, was redefined when it came to America as the pervasive principle on which the entire government rested, even as it comprised only a limited delegation of power. . . . Thus, in America, it became obvious that there was no supreme power except what the people themselves held. . . . They delegated a portion of their power in whatever manner, and for whatever time, they chose.

This unique structure of American government, then, does not divide all power amongst the branches. It divides all *delegated* power amongst the branches, always retaining the role of the people as an overseer of the entire system. Thus, if the executive refused to enforce the orders of the court, or if the legislature tried to impeach the members of the court without warrant, the people would still stand outside of those actions and could pass judgment on them through their retained political powers by holding elected officials accountable for any such breach of trust. Thus, the encroachment into the independence of the judiciary that seemed inevitable under any form of autocratic government is subject to an extrinsic check by the people under their own Constitution. And this role for the people gives meaning to the Constitution's commitment to accountability, without making it necessary to jettison its equally clear commitment to liberty.

Source: Rebecca L. Brown, "Accountability, Liberty, and the Constitution," *Columbia Law Review* 98 (1998): 530–531.

In the largely prebureaucratic America that prevailed between 1789 and the beginnings of the Progressive era, however, accountability was direct, personal, and rather haphazard.[16] Extensive delegation of authority was unnecessary because of the ability at the time to specify in detail "contracts" between legislative principals and administrative agents, as James Hart described in 1925:

> With the theory abroad in the land that the legislature should legislate as little as possible, it was entirely possible for it to debate and prescribe every minute detail and try to anticipate every contingency. And with problems before them of relative simplicity and stability, the laymen who are chosen by popular elections could with less absurdity than today attempt to decide in detail for future events.[17]

Any remaining scope for discretion was left to administrative officers, many of them elected, who functioned independently of executive authority with funds appropriated directly to their offices.[18] According to Dwight Waldo, "The lack of a strong tradition of administrative action . . . contributed to . . . public servants acting more or less in their private capacities." [19] A "spoils system" (to the victor belongs the spoils or privileges of office) of rotation in office dominated nineteenth-century selection and control of administrators, so that officials were beholden to political parties. Intermittent oversight of administration was exercised by legislators, political parties, and the courts.[20]

The issue of accountability became urgent in the latter part of the nineteenth century, when the government grew rapidly and the discretionary authority of public administrators expanded to serve the interests of an industrializing, urbanizing America. Perhaps the most prominent of Progressive-era administrative reforms were rescuing municipal governments from the spoils system's corrupt machines and professionalizing the management of urban services by separating politics from administration. One innovation was the city-manager form of government in which city councils can hire or remove a professional city manager on the basis of merit and the mayor's role is largely ceremonial. The city-manager form contrasts with the mayor-council form where administrative authority rests with the elected mayor. The goal in city-manager governments was accountability that was less political and corruptible and more professional and bureaucratic, that is, administration conducted in compliance with impersonal and lawful rules.

But the so-called politics-administration dichotomy was not the dominant "orthodoxy" that many public administration scholars have claimed that it was. Although Woodrow Wilson is credited with advocating such a dichotomy as doctrine in his famous 1887 essay, "The Study of Administration," his more important observation in that piece is that "there be no danger in power if only it be not irresponsible." [21] In other words, because the founders' political doctrines predated the emergence of American bureaucratic institutions, the doctrines proved inadequate to resolve the issues of accountability raised by widespread resort to administrative discretion. It fell to the emerging professions of public administration and public law to develop new doctrines for new circumstances.

In traditional literature the concept of "responsibility" emphasized by Wilson is often equated with accountability. "[R]esponsibility," Mosher wrote, "may well be the most important word in all the vocabulary of administration, public and private." [22] Noting the importance of the discussion of "responsibility and accountability of the agencies of administration," Wallace Sayre said that these discussions have a common concern: how to reconcile the great, unprecedented growth of administrative power with democratic government.[23] Although no regime of rules can eliminate possibilities for self-interested behavior by subordinate officials, argued John Millett in 1954, "Management guided by [the value of responsibility] abhors the idea of arbitrary authority present in its own wisdom and recognizes the reality of external direction and constraint." [24]

Careful study of the professional literature through most of the twentieth century reveals, then, that traditional public administration thinking emphasized that the function of democratic institutions is to preserve an appropriate balance between administrative capacity to effect the public interest, on the one hand, and the accountability of administrators to democratic authority, and especially to representative and judicial institutions, on the other.[25]

This ideal balance between administrative capacity and accountability comes under constant challenge—some would say redefinition—from the continual emergence of new structures and processes of public administration and management. Such developments often have the effect of lengthening and weakening the chains of delegation linking citizens and their elected representatives to the delivery of publicly supported services. These new structures and techniques include the service and regulatory agencies and administrative technologies created during the legislatively active Progressive, New Deal, and Great Society periods. They also include government corporations, government-sponsored enterprises, and quasi-governmental organizations popular since World War II to ensure a businesslike distance between politics and administration. In addition, the creation of special districts, mixed enterprises, and local-regional corporations at state and local levels of government, and the popularity, especially in times of budgetary stringency and heightened legislative scrutiny, of decentralization, deinstitutionalization, devolution, privatization, and outsourcing have necessitated new structures.

These kinds of developments have increased the distance between those who authorize and appropriate funds for policy and those who deliver the services. Similar to the innovation of city management, these kinds of institutions rely on professional and legal forms of accountability. Said Marshall Dimock, "Using the corporate device . . . involves trusting board members and executives after giving them a firm mandate and discretion." [26] But such developments have drawn sharp criticism from those who fear that accountability and the rule of law are being dangerously weakened. Therefore, among the continually emerging number and variety of structures and techniques are, not surprisingly, those directly concerned with accountability itself.

Among the earliest of these accountability institutions were the Progressives' innovative forms of direct democracy: initiative, referendum, and recall, which allow citizens to propose and vote on laws and constitutional amendments and to remove officials from office, thereby holding elected officials accountable in a direct way for their performance. The initiative and the referendum are popular in many states, especially California, where a 2003 recall vote resulted in Gov. Gray Davis being removed from office.

Another early accountability institution is the General Accounting Office (GAO), now known as the Government Accountability Office. Created by the Budget and Accounting Act of 1921 to audit an executive branch swollen by Progressive reforms and World War I, the GAO, whose chief executive is the comptroller general of the United States with a fifteen-year term, is an agency of the U.S. Congress. The GAO has substantial discretion to investigate fraud, waste, and abuse in the executive branch and to publish reports containing its findings and recommendations. Notes Harvey Mansfield, "The comptroller general retains from his heritage, and has gained by statute, elements of authority that in any other national jurisdiction are lodged with executive officials." [27]

Accountability institutions that emphasize transparency as a way to promote accountable action by federal agencies are laws such as the Freedom of Information Act, which "established a right to information held by government agencies, articulated a presumption that government documents should be publicly accessible, and provided methods for compelling officials to comply with its requirements." [28] Others are the Federal Advisory Committee Act of 1972, which required meetings of federal advisory committees be open to the public, and the Government in the Sunshine Act of 1976, which required meetings of federal commissions be open to the public. Each act contains exemptions for material relating to national security or to certain personnel or law enforcement matters.

In 1978 Congress created the office of inspector general (IG) in many federal agencies, and by 2008 there were sixty-four IG offices. IGs are empowered to conduct and supervise audits of the programs and operations of their agencies with the purpose of identifying and recommending solutions for waste, fraud, and abuse. IGs report to their agency heads, but they are appointed by the president, confirmed by the Senate, and formally protected from political interference. "Neither the head of the establishment nor the officer next in rank below such head shall prevent or prohibit the Inspector General from initiating, carrying out, or completing any audit or investigation, or from issuing any subpoena during the course of any audit or investigation." The President's Council on Integrity and Efficiency and the Executive Council on Integrity and Efficiency were established by Executive Order 12805, May 11, 1992, to "address integrity, economy, and effectiveness issues that transcend individual Government agencies, and increase the professionalism and effectiveness of IG personnel throughout the Government." [29]

Another accountability institution is the protection of whistleblowers, individuals who report misconduct in their agencies or organizations. The first federal legislation with the intent to protect whistleblowers was the Lloyd-La Follette Act of 1912, which guaranteed the right of federal employees to furnish information to Congress. Whistleblower protection became popular in the late twentieth century, especially in the new regulatory agencies such as the Environmental Protection Agency and the Occupational Safety and Health Administration. In the Civil Service Reform Act of 1978, Congress established the Office of

Special Counsel, an independent federal investigative and prosecutorial agency, "to safeguard the merit system by protecting federal employees and applicants from prohibited personnel practices, especially reprisal for whistleblowing." [30] In 1989 Congress enacted the Whistleblower Protection Act "to strengthen and improve protection for the rights of Federal employees, to prevent reprisals, and to help eliminate wrongdoing within the Government."

Because of America's separation of powers and steadily evolving and increasingly complex system of checks and balances, accountability and accountability institutions will also evolve and become more complex as the executive, the legislature, and the courts interpret accountability's requirements and create new forms to ensure them.

ACCOUNTABILITY AND THE STRUCTURAL DIMENSION

Of the three dimensions of public management, the structural dimension encompasses the most familiar and widely used mechanisms for defining and influencing accountability relationships. The primary and secondary checks and balances, discussed in chapter 4, constitute many of these mechanisms. Important structural features and processes associated with four theoretical frameworks—bounded rationality, principal-agent theory, interest group mobilization, and network theory—are featured in William T. Gormley Jr. and Steven J. Balla's analysis of bureaucratic accountability.[31] Indeed, as scholar Robert Gregory put it, "The most pervasive response to perceived 'problems of accountability' is usually drawn from the school of hard rationalism. Formal mechanisms of bureaucratic control are 'tightened up,' in an attempt to cater even more rigorously for whatever contingencies may arise in the exercise of discretionary authority." [32]

Chapter 5 presented a framework that described structures as being constraining or enabling and as emanating from sources of formal authority that were internal or external to the organization. From the various meanings and purposes of accountability described in this chapter, it is clear that most accountability relationships tend to constrain (not enable) the decisions or actions of managers and their subordinates in public organizations. Public managers and their agencies are held accountable primarily to formal authorities external to their organizations, but they must also answer to internal authorities.

This section discusses the structural mechanisms that influence accountability relationships for public managers. The focus is first on the formal authority emanating from the executive, legislative, and judicial branches of government. Authority external to government is also discussed. Some of these mechanisms were mentioned in chapter 4 in the context of the rule of law as checks and balances on administrative activity. The final subsection discusses performance measurement—which, depending on the context, may be constraining or enabling, or may emanate from authority internal or external to the organization—in the context of accountability.

The types of structural accountability mechanisms discussed throughout this section should be of interest to public managers because they shape the environments and conditions in which they work, often constraining their activities and decisions. Although the specific structural mechanisms are oriented toward the federal government, similar mechanisms, such as inspectors general, whistleblower protections, and judicial decrees, are widely present at the state levels of government and sometimes at the local level.

Tools of the Executive Branch

Mechanisms for ensuring accountability—including organizations, institutions, and legal protections—are present within agencies as well as outside of them, but still within the executive branch. These mechanisms include whistleblower protections, IGs, other internal audit and advocate offices, chief financial officers (CFOs), and presidential oversight through the Office of Management and Budget (OMB).

As mentioned above, employees of public agencies who observe and report an incident of illegal or wasteful activity involving their agency are referred to as **whistleblowers.** Their protection by law from reprisals for their revelations is an internal institution aimed to ensure accountability, but external supports also exist. The National Whistleblower Center and the Government Accountability Project are nonprofit organizations that track whistleblower cases and provide assistance and advocacy for their fair treatment under the law.

Another internal structural mechanism for ensuring accountability is the IG office within each agency, department, commission, and entities such as Amtrak.[33] The IG's job, as described by Paul C. Light, is "to audit, investigate, review, assess, analyze, evaluate, oversee, and appraise every problem, abuse, deficiency, and weakness relating to the programs and operations of their establishments." [34] A *Washington Post* columnist recently observed that IGs are "unusual creatures of the federal bureaucracy." Because they are "asked to serve both masters"—the president who appoints them and the Senate that confirms them—they are often in the difficult position of fulfilling their duties "preferably without causing too much embarrassment for their agency heads, usually political appointees." [35]

Additional structural mechanisms for ensuring accountability are present within executive agencies, including audit functions and advocacy or ombudsman services for agency constituents. Examples of the audit function are the Office of the Special Inspector General for Iraq Reconstruction, a temporary agency charged with oversight of Iraq reconstruction projects, and the Defense Contract Audit Agency, located in the Office of the Under Secretary of Defense (Comptroller/Chief Financial Officer) and charged with "providing accounting and financial advisory services regarding contracts and subcontracts to all DoD Components responsible for procurement and contract administration." [36] Examples of within-agency offices that provide advocacy and ombudsman services include the Internal Revenue Service's Taxpayer Advocate Service, an independent organization that ensures that "taxpayer problems which have not been resolved through normal channels, are promptly and fairly handled" and identifies "issues that increase burden or create problems for taxpayers"; and ombudsman offices in agencies such as the Citizens and Immigration Service and the Small Business Administration, that respond to complaints and issues from constituents as well as from employees.[37]

Chief financial officers within each federal agency are tasked with financial accountability. The CFO position was created by the Chief Financial Officers Act of 1990, which has been described as "the most comprehensive and far-reaching financial management improvement legislation since the Budget and Accounting Procedures Act of 1950 . . . lay[ing] a foundation for comprehensive reform of federal financial management." In addition, the act "establishes a leadership structure, provides for long-range planning, requires audited financial statements, and strengthens accountability reporting." [38] Toward these ends, structural changes were also implemented that were external to each agency, described below.

A final example of a structural mechanism for ensuring accountability through the executive branch is the Office of Management and Budget, whose "predominant mission is to assist the President in overseeing the preparation of the federal budget and to supervise its administration in Executive Branch agencies." The scope for doing so is quite broad, as the OMB "evaluates the effectiveness of agency programs, policies, and procedures, assesses competing funding demands among agencies, and sets funding priorities. OMB ensures that agency reports, rules, testimony, and proposed legislation are consistent with the President's Budget and with Administration policies." [39] A Bush administration initiative, the Program Assessment Rating Tool (PART), discussed later in this chapter, is one example of an OMB effort to produce information about federal agency management and performance to inform the budget process.

Within OMB, the CFO Act of 1990 also created a new position, the deputy director for management, and a new subdivision, the Office of Federal Financial Management; together they represent a stronger leadership role for OMB in the financial management of federal agencies.[40] The Office of Information and Regulatory Affairs (OIRA), also within OMB, reviews and coordinates agency rulemaking procedures.[41] OMB is required by the Regulatory Right to Know Act of 2001 to report to Congress each year on the costs and benefits of regulatory action that it reviews.[42] As part of this process, OIRA asks each agency to submit a regulatory impact analysis for "economically significant" regulations.

Tools of the Legislative Branch

In addition to laws such as the Freedom of Information Act and the Whistleblower Protection Act that create institutions specifically concerned with increasing accountability and transparency in federal agencies, structural mechanisms in the legislative branch also aim to ensure accountability of the executive branch. These mechanisms include the hearings, investigative activities, and bill drafting and markup work of the various substantive-area committees of the House and Senate that authorize and reauthorize the work of agencies. Among these committees are the Senate Committee on Agriculture, Nutrition, and Forestry; the House Committee on Energy and Commerce; the appropriations committees of both houses, which annually review and approve budgets for agencies and programs; the House Committee on Oversight and Government Reform; and the Senate Committee on Homeland Security and Governmental Affairs.

The political science literature on the **politics of bureaucratic structure** spurred by Mathew D. McCubbins, Roger G. Noll, and Barry R. Weingast (who are sometimes referred to as "McNollgast") is concerned with the legislature's design (or "appointment") of agencies and programs in the executive branch. At the time agencies or subunits are created, enacting coalitions in legislatures have the opportunity to specify and design accountability mechanisms to reflect their preferences. The aim is to prevent "bureaucratic drift" and induce bureaucrats to comply with the wishes of the enacting coalition.[43] Bureaucratic discretion resulting in drift can occur "when the agency succeeds in choosing a policy in line with agency goals, when those goals *differ* from what the executive and legislature expect *at the appointment stage.*"[44]

If and when bureaucratic noncompliance occurs, the enacting coalition wants it to be detectable and subject to reliable and credible enforcement. Instead of emphasizing **police patrol oversight,** the ongoing monitoring of agencies by oversight committees, "politicians must foresee potential problems and devise solutions as part of the legislation."[45] McNollgast say, "By itself, a system of rewards and punishments is unlikely to be a completely effective solution to the control problem . . . due to the cost of monitoring, limitations in the range of rewards and punishments, and, for the most meaningful forms of rewards and punishments, the cost to the principals of implementing them."[46]

As an alternative, legislators may attempt to shift monitoring responsibilities to constituents through **deck-stacking,** structural opportunities for stakeholders to observe agency deviations from legislative intent, for example, as members of advisory boards.[47] These kinds of structural solutions facilitate **fire alarm oversight,** which brings about responses only when problems are brought to light by citizens, interest groups, journalists, and others. In a typical example of a fire alarm, a 2008 *New York Times* investigation revealed widespread electrical system failures in Iraq military facilities and the electrocution of many troops, and the House Committee on Oversight and Government Reform, which had already been alerted to the problem, scheduled hearings.

An enacting coalition and its supportive constituencies can try to protect and nurture its bureaucratic agents through a variety of structural channels. Terry Moe argues, however, that "legislators tend not to invest in general policy control. Instead, they value 'particularized' control: they want to be able to intervene quickly, inexpensively, and in ad hoc ways to protect or advance the interests of particular clients in particular matters."[48] "Political rationality" may well trump "technical rationality" in designing these structures.

Beyond congressional authorization and oversight through its committees, accountability of executive branch activity is also under scrutiny from the Government Accountability Office. As the legislative branch's investigative equivalent of the IGs, the GAO, known as "the government's watchdog," acts a source of external review.

GAO's work has expanded from its initial activities related to ensuring accountability for expenditures (the traditional audit function) to a broader portfolio of analysis that is concerned with accountability for performance. For example, GAO has been involved in reviewing agency implementation of the Government Performance and Results Act of 1993 and providing guidance for building human capital capacity in federal agencies. The organization's name change in 2004 from General Accounting Office to Government Accountability Office reflected this expansion of its role, as explained by David Walker, who was then the comptroller general:

RULE OF LAW

Making Information Available for Fire Alarm Oversight

For fire alarm oversight to work, stakeholders must be able to find out about the plans and actions of public organizations; that is, their work must be transparent. The excerpt from the Regulatory Flexibility Act illustrates how Congress can ensure that information about agency plans and activities is made available to stakeholders.

Sec. 603. Initial regulatory flexibility analysis.

(a) Whenever an agency is required by section 553 of this title, or any other law, to publish general notice of proposed rulemaking for any proposed rule, or publishes a notice of proposed rulemaking for an interpretative rule involving the internal revenue laws of the United States, the agency shall prepare and make available for public comment an initial regulatory flexibility analysis. . . .

(b) Each initial regulatory flexibility analysis required under this section shall contain—

(1) a description of the reasons why action by the agency is being considered;
(2) a succinct statement of the objectives of, and legal basis for, the proposed rule;
(3) a description of and, where feasible, an estimate of the number of small entities to which the proposed rule will apply;
(4) a description of the projected reporting, recordkeeping and other compliance requirements of the proposed rule, including an estimate of the classes of small entities which will be subject to the requirement and the type of professional skills necessary for preparation of the report or record;
(5) an identification, to the extent practicable, of all relevant Federal rules which may duplicate, overlap or conflict with the proposed rule.

Source: Regulatory Flexibility Act, S. 1974, 95th Cong., 5 U.S.C. 601–612, P.L. 96-354, http://www.fws.gov/policy/library/rgregflexact.pdf.

In fairness, GAO did primarily scrutinize government vouchers and receipts in its early years. The days of accountants in green eyeshades, however, are long gone. Although GAO does serve as the lead auditor of the U.S. government's consolidated financial statements, financial audits are only about 15 percent of GAO's current workload. . . .

Today, most GAO blue-cover reports go beyond the question of whether federal funds are being spent appropriately to ask whether federal programs and policies are meeting their objectives and the needs of society. GAO looks at the results that departments and agencies are getting with the taxpayer dollars they receive. As a strong advocate for truth and transparency in government operations, GAO is committed to ensuring that recent accountability failures, such as Enron and Worldcom, are not repeated in the public sector. To that end, public reporting of our work is vital; virtually every GAO report and congressional testimony is posted on the Internet on the day that it is issued.[49]

Tools of the Judicial Branch

In addition to the general powers of the judiciary discussed in chapter 4, courts may monitor and impose accountability on agencies through a range of structural mechanisms. The degree of judicial deference to managerial judgment affects the extent to which courts are likely to be involved in holding public and private organizations accountable. In *Chevron v. Natural Resources Defense Council* (1984) the U.S. Supreme Court established a judicial standard for deference to administrative agencies. David H. Rosenbloom and Rosemary O'Leary describe the **Chevron doctrine** as follows: "[W]here Congress has spoken clearly to the precise question at issue the rule of law demands agency adherence to its intent. However, if Congress has not addressed the matter precisely, an agency may adopt any reasonable interpretation—regardless of whether a reviewing court may consider some other interpretation more reasonable or sensible." [50] Although subsequent Court opinions have imposed some limitations on the Chevron doctrine, agencies have "considerable flexibility in choosing rule-making procedures and interpreting and enforcing statutes." [51] When other accountability mechanisms are available, especially political or democratic accountability, courts also may be more likely to defer to the legislature's or agency's intent.[52]

Deference to administrative action is not absolute, however, and the remainder of this section considers the judiciary's role in enforcing public agency accountability. Courts get involved in agency accountability as a result of **public law litigation,** where the "object of the litigation is the vindication of constitutional or statutory policies." [53] Such litigation may arise when "citizens or groups contend that some government institution or official has violated a right set forth in the state or federal constitution or statutes." [54] These law suits have dealt with policy areas such as children and family services, pharmaceutical regulation, education, prisons, and environmental hazards.

One option available to a judge in response to such litigation is an **injunction,** "an order that directs a [defendant] to act or refrain from acting in a specified way." [55] In addition to such "negative" relief, plaintiffs may ask for "affirmative" relief—a "decree with provisions which attempt, by directing changes in structure or practice, to undo the damage done to the plaintiffs and others similarly situated." [56] A **decree** is a court order that "seeks to adjust future behavior, not to compensate for past wrong. It is deliberately fashioned rather than logically deduced from the nature of the legal harm suffered. It provides for a complex, on-going regime of performance rather than a simple, one-shot, one-way transfer. Finally, it prolongs and deepens, rather than terminates, the court's involvement with the dispute."[57] Such actions are referred to as **remedies** or **remedial decrees.**[58] For example, a consent decree between the Environmental Protection Agency (EPA) and a number of environmental and labor groups, including the Natural Resources Defense Council and the AFL-CIO, issued by the U.S. district court in San Francisco addressed the EPA's requirements to assess and regulate pesticides under the Food Quality Protection Act of 1996.[59]

Phillip J. Cooper describes the process leading to such remedies as consisting of four basic stages. The first is the "trigger phase" in which plaintiffs bring suit against an agency against a backdrop of political and environmental forces and a history of practices by a public organization. "The cases tend to arise in situations where a number of controversial actions have been taken by one or more government units over time until a trigger level is reached. At that point, one critical action will engender a challenge not only to the most recent event, but to many of the past actions as well."[60]

If a judge determines during the second stage, the "liability phase," that the law was in fact violated and a remedy is called for, the process enters the third stage or "remedy phase," in which the judge determines any negative and affirmative remedies. These choices are "affected by what plaintiffs request, what the case law and statutes allow, and the degree to which proposed remedies actually redress the violation of legally protected rights."[61] Cooper describes three possible types of affirmative remedies: process remedies, performance standards, and specified remedial actions:

> Process remedies include such techniques as ordering formation of advisory committees, dispute resolution procedures, and other devices that will operate to remedy past problems without mandating the particular form of action or the specific goals the government must pursue. Performance standards order specific quantities or types of remedial accomplishments, such as numbers or types of new housing units, racial attendance standards in schools, staffing levels at mental health institutions, or other targets, with the means of attainment left to the discretion of the officials who are the defendants in the suit. Specified remedial actions, such as school busing, modified school attendance zones, or required changes in the size and condition of hospital rooms or prison cells leave defendants with little or no flexibility concerning the remedial goals to be achieved or the means of attaining them.[62]

The fourth stage of the process, as described by Cooper, is the "post decree phase," in which remedies are implemented and refined in response to issues that arise during implementation. Implementation and monitoring of the remedy may be accomplished by either relying on the suit's parties (and the court remains passive), or on the court itself.[63] If the court takes a more active role in overseeing the implementation of the remedy, then two further options exist: Either the court itself can supervise the remedy—conducting hearings, reviewing reports, and so on—or it can appoint an external agent. Because courts are not consistent in labeling these agents, Robert E. Buckholz Jr. and colleagues offer a "function-based" definition for the officers courts might appoint:

- *Masters* "gather information and make recommendations" and "assist the court in formulating the substantive remedy, rather than in implementing it";
- *Monitors* "report on the defendant's compliance with the decree and on the achievement of the decree's goals";
- *Mediators* "handl[e] disputes over the decree's meaning, compliance standards, and the pace of compliance";
- *Administrators* are "normally given powers to supervise, coordinate, approve, or even command actions of the defendants to implement the remedy. . . . Some administrators are granted broad and undefined power to secure implementation"; and
- *Receivers* are a "device of last resort, used only when less intrusive devices have failed to achieve compliance" and are "a more drastic means of implementation than the appointment of an administrator or any lesser administrative agent." [64]

It is important to remember that courts can only deliver decisions or implement remedies in cases that are brought before them. As Donald L. Horowitz put it, "Courts are public decision makers, yet they are wholly dependent on private initiative to invoke their powers: they do not self-start." [65]

Citizen and Stakeholder Involvement

In addition to the structural mechanisms for ensuring public agency accountability through the executive, legislative, and judicial branches, mechanisms and monitors of government accountability are found in the private sector as well. The following list offers a sample of groups that monitor government action and inaction across a range of policy and program areas:

- OMB Watch is a nonprofit formed in 1983 to monitor the actions of the Office of Management and Budget, which OMB Watch argued "remained largely behind the scenes—unaccountable and little understood by the public and public interest groups. By explaining governmental processes and monitoring OMB, OMB Watch helped bring sunshine to this powerful and secretive agency."
- Government Accountability Project is a nonprofit whose "mission is to protect the public interest by promoting government and corporate accountability through advancing occupational free speech and ethical conduct, defending whistleblowers, and empowering citizen activists."
- *Public Citizen,* formed by activist Ralph Nader, is a consumer advocacy organization whose goals include the "fight for openness and democratic accountability in government."
- *Project on Government Oversight,* originally "Project on Military Procurement," is a nonprofit that "investigates and exposes corruption and other misconduct in order to achieve a more accountable federal government."
- *Citizens Against Government Waste* is a nonprofit whose "mission is to eliminate waste, mismanagement, and inefficiency in the federal government."
- *Bank Information Center* is a nonprofit that "advocates for the protection of rights, participation, transparency, and public accountability in the governance and operations of the World Bank, regional development banks, and IMF [International Monetary Fund]." [66]

CONCEPTS IN ACTION

Actions of a Receiver

The state prison system in California was placed into receivership in 2005, following a class action suit that aimed to increase the accountability of the system for adequate care of its inmates. Later, the federal receiver charged with overseeing the system on behalf of the court requested significant resources from the state to improve the system and was met with resistance. The *Wall Street Journal* reported:

A federally appointed receiver assigned to fix the prison health-care system in California says he will force the state to come up with $2.5 billion to begin improvements—just as legislators are confronting a budget shortfall of over $15 billion this fiscal year.

State legislators have failed to approve funds to comply with a federal-court order that California fix its prison hospitals. The federal receiver, J. Clark Kelso, said in an interview that he expects to file a motion in federal court as soon as the first week of August for an order to receive the funds. "Fiscally, the state is near bankrupt. So do I want to take this money and cause chaos and pandemonium? No," says Mr. Kelso. "But I have a court order here, and I must move forward."

The showdown is a side effect of the state's inability to fix problems that have plagued the nation's largest state-prison system for decades. In 2002, a federal judge in the U.S. District Court for the Northern District of California deemed the state's prison health-care system so bad that it violated the constitutional prohibition of cruel and unusual punishment. The judge, Thelton Henderson, ordered the state to improve the system.

The case—part of a 2001 class-action suit against the state that the Prison Law Office, an inmate-advocacy group, filed on behalf of inmates—brought attention to understaffed prison hospitals and inadequately trained caregivers. In one example cited in the suit, a 76-year-old inmate with the onset of cataracts in both eyes was denied surgery and went blind in one eye and partially blind in the other. An inmate under AIDS treatment was denied medical care on eight occasions, in part because authorities didn't believe the inmate was in pain.

The state made little progress in improving prison health care. In 2005, Judge Henderson turned control of the system over to a federal receiver, Robert Sillen, former head of the Santa Clara Valley Health and Hospital System. When matters still didn't improve, the judge in January appointed J. Clark Kelso, a Pacific University law professor, as the new federal receiver. . . .

Mr. Kelso has a reputation as a bureaucracy-busting expert for the state. In 2000, then-Gov. Gray Davis appointed him to take over the state's Department of Insurance. Two years later, Mr. Kelso was appointed to turn around California's technology infrastructure as its chief information officer. "I have been around long enough to know how games are played around here," says Mr. Kelso. "I've done everything possible to avoid a crisis, but time is running out."

Source: Bobby White, "California Balks at Paying Billions to Improve Prison Health Care," *Wall Street Journal*, July 21, 2008, A3.

The involvement of citizens in the processes and decision making of public organizations constitutes another structural accountability mechanism in democratic governments. One such mechanism is **representative bureaucracy,** the degree to which the characteristics of government employees reflect the characteristics of the citizenry at large. The idea is that when bureaucrats exercise discretion, their decisions will at least passively reflect the motivations and concerns of those in the population whom they "represent." [67] Passive representation may proceed to active representation when bureaucrats explicitly seek to reflect in their decisions the wishes of their citizen constituents. Whether passive or active, the idea of representative bureaucracy is related to political accountability from the Romzek and Dubnick framework.

Lael R. Keiser and colleagues conducted a representative bureaucracy study that examined the relationships between teacher gender and female students' test scores in public schools. They found girls' math performance in middle school and high school was positively associated with having female math teachers and that ACT, SAT, and advanced placement scores were higher for girls with female teachers in schools with more female administrators.[68]

Citizen and stakeholder participation in governmental processes and decisions constitutes another mechanism whose aim is to enhance the accountability of government to the people it is intended to serve. A significant part of the Blacksburg Manifesto—a document written in 1990 by faculty members in public administration at Virginia Polytechnic Institute and State University in Blacksburg, Virginia—concerns the importance of citizen participation in government to achieve legitimacy and accountability.[69]

Citizen participation in public processes is enabled through a number of legislative and quasi-judicial tools and processes at the international and U.S. federal, state, and local levels. Lisa Blomgren Bingham, Tina Nabatchi, and Rosemary O'Leary describe these avenues. They discuss quasi-judicial processes, which include mediation (the negotiation of a voluntary resolution of a case with the assistance of a third party), or minitrials, which "involve an abbreviated presentation of evidence and argument to the disputants' senior decision makers, who then attempt to negotiate a settlement." Quasi-legislative processes include e-democracy and study circles and can occur in a number of settings such as town hall meetings or focus groups. Advocates of these processes say they "foster decisional legitimacy, consensus, citizen engagement, public dialogue, reasoned debate, higher decision quality, and fairness among an active and informed citizenry." [70] Whether the processes actually succeed, the authors note, is open to debate and should be pursued with research.

The numerous advisory boards and review panels within agencies and programs, at all levels of government, also constitute citizen and stakeholder participation. The National Academies, made up of the National Academy of Sciences, the Institute of Medicine, the National Academy of Engineering, and the National Research Council, "bring together committees of experts in all areas of scientific and technological endeavor . . . [to] serve *pro bono* to address critical national issues and give advice to the federal government and the public." [71] At the local level, many cities and counties have in place citizen advisory boards or processes for encouraging citizen participation in local decisions.

Performance Measurement

Among the most visible and important aspects of accountability are concerns with agency, program, and individual performance.[72] Indeed, "accountability compels some measure or appraisal of performance, particularly of those individuals and agencies with the authority to act on behalf of the public." [73] As a structural mechanism that may be employed to enhance accountability, **performance measurement** may be imposed by formal authority external to the organization such as the Government Performance and Results Act of 1993 (GPRA) and the Automated Budget and Evaluation System of Texas (ABEST), or by executive initiatives such as the Clinton administration's Reinventing Government (ReGo) plan and the Bush administration's Program Assessment Rating Tool (PART). Or the structural mechanism can be formal authority internal to an organization, as when managers exercise their discretion to implement a measurement system.

Performance measurement is widespread among cities, counties, states, and federal agencies. A number of reform efforts at all levels of government feature performance measurement and are discussed in greater detail in chapter 9. A type of performance measurement has even been applied to the war in Iraq: The U.S. Troop Readiness, Veterans' Care, Katrina Recovery, and Iraq Accountability Appropriations Act of 2007 specified benchmarks for the government of Iraq and required the president to report on progress toward meeting those benchmarks.

The next sections examine the reasons for assessing performance, the types of actors whose performance is measured, the forums and formats for reporting performance measures, the types of performance that are measured, examples of recent performance measurement initiatives, and a discussion of the challenges of measuring performance.

Why Is Performance Measured?

One of the primary uses of performance measurement, argues Harry P. Hatry, is "to establish accountability, so citizens and elected officials can assess what programs have achieved with the funds provided." [74] It is important to note that accountability reasons are not the only ones for measuring performance. Indeed, Hatry lists eleven potential ways that performance information could be used.

1. Respond to elected officials' and the public's demands for accountability.
2. Help formulate and justify budget requests.
3. Help allocate resources throughout the year.
4. Trigger in-depth examinations of why performance problems (or successes) exist.
5. Help motivate personnel to continue improving the program.
6. Formulate and monitor the performance of contractors and grantees (performance contracting).
7. Provide data for special, in-depth program evaluations.
8. Support strategic and other long-term planning efforts (by providing baseline information and later tracking progress).
9. Analyze options and establish priorities.

10. Communicate better with the public and to build trust and support for public services.
11. Above all, help provide services more effectively.[75]

In the literature on performance measurement, **performance analysis** refers to the assessment and interpretation of performance measures to ascertain the specific contribution of the organization or managers, independent of other factors, to organizational performance.[76] Performance analysis can be used to help public managers understand how their own policy and management decisions are linked to outcomes and how systemic and situational factors outside of their control also affect performance.[77] **Performance management,** then, is the use of information from performance measures and performance analysis to improve the management and performance of an organization. **Performance budgeting** refers to the use of performance information to set budget allocations and priorities.

Robert Behn offers another view of the purposes of performance measurement and its relationship to accountability. He argues that performance information may be used for eight different types of purposes, many though not all overlapping with Hatry's list: to evaluate performance; control subordinates; prepare budgets; motivate employees, stakeholders, citizens, and contractors; promote the agency to principals; celebrate accomplishments; learn about what is working and not working; and improve performance.[78] Behn explicitly does not include "promoting accountability" as one of these purposes because of the many different understandings that exist about it: "Depending upon what people mean by accountability, they may promote it by evaluating public agencies, by controlling them, or by motivating them to improve." [79] A first decision that faces an external or internal actor with formal authority, therefore, concerns the purpose(s) measurement is meant to accomplish.

Whether considered from Hatry's or Behn's view, or some other framework, the reasons for performance measurement almost certainly overlap the three dimensions of public management discussed in this book—structure, culture, and craft. The discussion of performance measurement here reflects its fundamental structural features (as measures and processes) and its often central role in promoting and ensuring accountability of agents to principals.

Whose Performance Is Measured?

Typically, public sector measurement efforts at the city, county, state, and federal levels focus on the agency, project, or program. Performance of individuals may be measured as well, perhaps in relation to overarching organizational goals or measures and perhaps in a more limited way to assess the degree to which the agent carries out a principal's wishes. In some cases, the link between individual performance and organizational performance may seem obvious: Arrests made by a police officer are reflected directly in the department's goal of capturing offenders. In other cases, the link is not so obvious: How is the work of a budget officer in the Agency for Healthcare Research and Quality related to organizational performance? This issue arises in part because of the distinction between line and staff positions and in part because of the nature of the work even among line positions.

Other sections of this chapter examine issues related to performance measurement at the organizational or suborganizational level. Here, the focus is on performance measures for individuals.

Performance measurement for individuals, typically linked to the human resource function, raises a unique set of issues, such as what aspects of individual performance should be measured, or how individual performance should be related to organizational goals or outcome measures. A recent GAO report identifies the main practices for linking individual and organizational performance. These include explicitly aligning individual performance goals with those of the broader organization, tracking performance and using the information for management throughout the year, and implementing pay and reward systems that link individual performance with organizational results.[80]

Just as organizations should not be held responsible for factors influencing performance that are out of their control, individuals should not be rewarded (or punished) when their performance improves (or declines) because of factors out of their control. But how to assess these situations presents thorny measurement problems: It may be nearly impossible to identify and measure all such factors and then figure out how to fairly account for them in measurement of an individual's performance.

Another issue that arises is whether and how individual performance should be linked to compensation. Pay-for-performance systems, discussed in chapters 5 and 6, aim to reward employees for performance instead of for tenure or seniority. Yet these systems have proven difficult to implement and sustain.[81] Patricia W. Ingraham argues that this difficulty arises because:

> The effectiveness of [pay-for-performance] systems rests in large part on two conditions: adequate resources and careful performance evaluation. The first condition is largely a political choice; the latter depends squarely on the ability of managers to clarify and communicate performance objectives, as well as to communicate effectively with employees about their success or failure in meeting objectives. Both conditions have been met infrequently in public settings—and in many private settings as well.[82]

An additional complicating issue is that individuals are often involved in team or group work, making measurement of the contribution of each individual quite difficult. Yet for pay for performance to be effective, it must be possible to discriminate performance levels across employees.

How Are Performance Measures Reported?

Performance with regard to any specific measure or dimension may be measured either in its natural metric, such as the average test scores of students in a school or the percentage of welfare recipients working part-time or full-time, or in relation to an external criterion, such as the percentage of students in a school that attained a "proficient" score on a math test or the percentage of welfare clients working more than thirty-five hours a week. Performance may further be expressed in relative terms by comparing a particular measure with that of other programs. Rewards for high performers and/or sanctions for low performers may be based on either relative or criterion-based rankings.

RULE OF LAW

Information to Include in Performance Reports

Legislation authorizing the Workforce Investment Act detailed the types of information that should be included in performance reports for local workforce investment offices.

(d) Information To Be Included in Reports.—
(1) In general.—The reports required in subsection (c) shall include information regarding programs and activities carried out under this title pertaining to—
(A) the relevant demographic characteristics (including race, ethnicity, sex, and age) and other related information regarding participants;
(B) the programs and activities in which participants are enrolled, and the length of time that participants are engaged in such programs and activities;
(C) outcomes of the programs and activities for participants, including the occupations of participants, and placement for participants in nontraditional employment;
(D) specified costs of the programs and activities; and
(E) information necessary to prepare reports to comply with section 188.

Source: Workforce Investment Act of 1998, H.R. 1385, 105th Congress, 112 Stat. 936, P.L. 105-220, http://www.doleta.gov/usworkforce/wia/wialaw.htm#sec185.

Performance information, extracted from administrative data, survey data, subjective or objective assessments, may be compiled by external actors or produced and self-reported within an organization for its own uses. In an effort to enhance accountability of their agents, external authorities may mandate and provide detailed requests for performance information. The GPRA, for example, set forth such requirements.

Entities external to government may also collect information about performance of public organizations. The Fraser Institute, a free market think tank, produces data on waiting times for medical services under the Canadian single payer health insurance system.[83]

A specific type of performance report compiled by external organizations is the **organizational report card.** William Gormley and David L. Weimer define the organizational report card as a "regular effort by an organization to collect data on two or more *other* organizations, transform the data into information relevant to assessing performance, and transmit the information to some audience external to the organizations themselves." Report cards may be used for macro-level purposes, with the ultimate goal of influencing policy, or micro-level purposes, with the goal of helping consumers make choices.[84] Some report cards fulfill both types of purposes. Report cards comparing indicators across states are available in policy areas such as K–12 and higher education, the environment, and economic development, and are published by governments, commercial groups, academics, and nonprofits.[85] One example of an organizational report card is the Hospital Compare system, a joint effort of the Centers for Medicare & Medicare Services (in the Department of Health and Human Services) and the Hospital Quality Alliance (a public-private partnership involving a number of nonprofit as well as government organizations). The system reports on process and outcome of care measures, as well as patient survey results regarding quality of care received while hospitalized, for conditions such as heart attacks, pneumonia, and diabetes and for procedures such as heart bypass, gallbladder removal, and back and neck operations.[86] The data reported through this system are based on medical records submitted voluntarily by hospitals.

For internal accountability purposes, organizations may report performance within the context of a **balanced scorecard,** a reporting method developed in the private sector that draws performance information from four "perspectives": customers, internal organizational, financial, and innovation and learning.[87] Now used in public, for-profit, and nonprofit organizations, the balanced scorecard approach is viewed as a strategic management process that moves beyond measuring financial performance alone.

The Department of Energy uses a balanced scorecard to manage and report performance for its procurement activities. In a reminder that the rule of law is primary whenever information from the balanced scorecard and the law might be in conflict, guidelines note that although the balanced scorecard approach "is intended to be a results oriented, systems focused, organization accomplished assessment, the Department of Energy Acquisition Regulation (DEAR) still requires compliance with specific laws, regulations, and contract terms and conditions." [88]

What Kinds of Performance Are Measured?

Typically, multiple performance measures are collected to provide a broad picture of an organization's efforts and results. These **types of performance measures** include:[89]

- *inputs* (human and material resources used, such as number of staff hours or classroom space used to conduct a welfare-to-work program or textbooks used in K–12 classrooms);
- *outputs* (amount of service, effort, or activity produced or delivered, such as number of clients receiving job training or number of students in advanced placement courses);
- *outcomes* (results or effectiveness of service or effort, such as the number of clients employed at least half time within six months of job training or percentage of students who graduate from high school);
- *efficiency or productivity* (amount of output or outcome achieved in terms of input, costs per participant in welfare-to-work programs, or cost per student);

CONCEPTS IN ACTION

Measures of Performance in Des Moines, Iowa

The city of Des Moines, Iowa, issues a performance report on its goals of having a city that is beautiful, clean, safe, vital, vibrant, fun, accountable, and fair. The excerpt below reports on performance of the police department and includes measures of input, output, efficiency, and impact. The last paragraph also illustrates the use of a relative performance measurement.

The Police Department keeps Des Moines safe by responding to and investigating crimes. Last year the City did not report crime data. Instead, we explained issues affecting the Police Records Management System (RMS). To address the RMS issues, the City created the Police Technology Services Unit. Emergency 911 surcharge fees, Polk County user fees, and salary savings provided $391,000 to hire additional staff. The new unit resolved the problems, and accurate data is [*sic*] again available. . . .

For Fiscal Year 2006, 14,174 Part 1 *Property Crimes* (burglary, larceny, motor vehicle theft, and arson) were reported. The Police Department solved 16.6% of them. This is not only an improvement over the 13% solved in 2003, but exceeds the national average of 16.3% for 2005. For Fiscal Year 2006 1,050 Part 1 *Violent Crimes* (murder, rape, robbery, and aggravated assault) were reported. . . . [The] Des Moines Police solved 58.7% of them. This clearance rate is well above both the national and midwestern averages and indicates an improvement from Fiscal Year 2003.The Police Department also has a high level of citizen satisfaction. 77% of residents are satisfied with the overall quality of police protection. This is an increase over last year's 74%.

Traffic enforcement, however, remains an area of concern for some residents. 52% of residents are satisfied with traffic enforcement on major streets, while 44% are satisfied with enforcement on neighborhood streets. Both of these categories ranked among the top three services that residents want police to emphasize over the next two years.

Survey results are not consistent with police performance in traffic enforcement. . . . [T]he level of traffic enforcement is high compared to other CPM [Center for Performance Measurement] cities of similar size. A similar result was reported last year, which suggests a need to better communicate with residents about the level of performance achieved as well as police efforts to enhance traffic enforcement.

Source: The City of Des Moines, *Building Community: 2006 Performance Report,* January 31, 2007, http://www.ci.des-moines.ia.us/performance/2006report.pdf.

- *demographic/workload characteristics* (descriptions of persons or groups served, such as gender, race/ethnicity, income, family size characteristics);
- *impacts* (the program's value-added, over and above the outcome that would have happened in the absence of the program, such as the number of clients employed in a special job-training program, compared to the employment rate of similar persons who did not participate in the program).

The types of data or performance measures that might be collected for any one program can be endless. As Behn and others have pointed out, the specific measures that are chosen depend on the reason(s) that performance is being measured and on the intended users of that information; no one performance measure will suit all circumstances.[90] For the purpose of measuring effectiveness, Carolyn J. Heinrich suggests choosing a performance measurement system exhibiting the following characteristics:

- performance measures focused on quality, outcomes or results;
- formal report requirements for comparing actual performance with performance goals or standards;
- multiple levels of performance accountability in decentralized programs; and
- market-oriented provisions such as financial/budgetary incentives for performance, as in the [Job Training Partnership Act] program, and plans to use performance information to promote continuous improvement and increased citizen ("customer") satisfaction.[91]

Performance Measurement Initiatives

Governments at the federal, state, and local levels in the United States and internationally engage in performance measurement. This section discusses some high-profile measurement systems that have been implemented as part of reform efforts (discussed further in chapter 9).

The Program Assessment Rating Tool (PART) is a Bush administration initiative that surveys managers in federal agencies in four broad areas: program purpose and design, strategic planning, program management, and program results, that is, the achievement of long-term and annual goals. The survey asks twenty-five questions across these four categories. For example: "Is the program purpose clear?" "Does the program have baselines and ambitious targets and timeframes for its annual measures?" "Does the program have procedures (e.g., competitive sourcing/cost comparisons, IT improvements, appropriate incentives) to measure and achieve efficiencies and cost effectiveness in program execution?" "Has the program demonstrated adequate progress in achieving its long-term outcome performance goals?" Additional questions are asked for specific types of programs, such as block/formula grant or research and development programs.

The PART survey is completed for programs within agencies, with results available online at expectmore.gov. Assessments are compiled by OMB and the agencies. Based on the scores, a program receives an overall assessment in five possible categories. In fiscal year 2007, of the thirty-four programs in the Department of Housing and Urban Development, four were rated "effective," nine rated "moderately effective," nine rated "adequate," five rated "ineffective," and eight were classified as "results not demonstrated."[92]

The information obtained through PART is generally consistent with the requirements of the GPRA, but "goes beyond GPRA in two important ways. First, the PART renders a *judgment* on whether programs are effective by systematically and transparently assessing program management and actual results (what happened). Second, the PART enables decision makers to attach budgetary and management *consequences* to those programs that cannot demonstrate their effectiveness."[93] Indeed, a senior OMB official announced early in the Bush administration's first term that the chief management priority was to link the performance goals of federal programs to agency budgets.[94] Although PART is intended to inform budget decisions, "The relationship between an overall PART rating and the budget is not a rigid calculation. . . . Budgets must still be drawn up to account for changing economic conditions, security needs, and policy priorities."[95]

A number of investigators have undertaken analyses of the Bush administration's budget proposals submitted to Congress to determine if PART evaluations were integrated into the administration's decision making. (Members of Congress and their staffs also have access to PART evaluations, but so far there has been no systematic effort to determine whether the evaluations influence appropriations.) A 2004 GAO analysis found that PART scores had a positive and statistically significant effect on discretionary program funding levels in the president's programs.[96] Analysts John Gilmour and David Lewis found that PART scores for fiscal years 2004 and 2005 and political support influenced "budget choices in expected ways, and the impact of management scores on budget decisions diminished as the political component was taken into account."[97] A third study, by Robert Olsen and Dan Levy, found "the effect of the PART on the allocation of federal resources is positive and nontrivial in size. . . . The effect for small programs—those with relatively low funding levels—is particularly large. . . . However, most federal funds are spent on large programs, for which the estimated PART effects are smaller."[98] Another study by Gilmour and Lewis based on PART scores found that programs administered by appointees, especially Senate-confirmed appointees, get systematically lower management grades than programs managed by careerists even when controlling for differences among programs, substantial variation in management environment, and the policy content of programs themselves. This result confirms the underlying logic for the creation of the merit systems that the Bush administration had been trying to dismantle.[99]

From the available evidence on PART's influence on administration budget making, Donald Moynihan has concluded that "programs deemed . . . ineffective or not demonstrating results are more vulnerable to program cuts or termination" but that the relationship is not strong.[100] PART evaluations may provide candidates for cuts, Moynihan suggests, but OMB officials indicated to him that strong political support for a program mattered more than PART evaluations for how well a program fared during budget season. Further, Moynihan observes that the ambiguous nature of the performance information gathered through the PART process can suit the needs of different actors with different preferences in the political process. These ideas are echoed in the comments of David Walker, who cautioned that "in a political process performance information is likely to be one, but not the only, factor in budgetary decision making. In other words, performance information can change the terms of debate but it will not necessarily determine the ultimate decision." [101]

A second example of a recent performance measurement initiative whose ultimate goal is accountability is the Elementary and Secondary Education Act of 2001, the "No Child Left Behind Act" (NCLB). The NCLB was modeled on education reforms instituted during George W. Bush's tenure as governor of Texas. The act requires that accountability systems be based on academic indicators, be technically rigorous, and apply to progress at all levels and for all subgroups of students. States and school districts must publish annual report cards, with a requisite and detailed program of corrective actions. All states must demonstrate that they have a single statewide accountability system for defining "adequate yearly progress" for all public school students, including those in charter schools, but standards can and do vary widely across states. No single stringent test was forced on the states; in fact, some states, such as New York, chose to adopt more rigorous tests.

Some of the reported difficulties associated with implementing the NCLB may be transition problems, as was the case at P.S. 48. Schools may be penalized because of the structure of the program, which calls for 95 percent of students in each student category to be tested. If a school has ten students in a particular category and one of them is absent and not tested, the school risks failure. In addition, the law allows students in failing schools to transfer to better-performing schools, which can overwhelm these schools and put the quality of their programs in jeopardy. In this system, principals bear the brunt of the burden for accountability, not teachers, superintendents, or others.

Reauthorization hearings for NCLB in fall 2007 focused on how, not whether, to revamp the law. As of April 2008, 144 organizational signatories had indicated their general support for the accountability system that NCLB imposed, even while identifying the following problems with the current system and recommending a number of changes:

> over-emphasizing standardized testing, narrowing curriculum and instruction to focus on test preparation rather than richer academic learning; over-identifying schools in need of improvement; using sanctions that do not help improve schools; inappropriately excluding low-scoring children in order to boost test results; and inadequate funding. Overall, the law's emphasis needs to shift from applying sanctions for failing to raise test scores to holding states and localities accountable for making the systemic changes that improve student achievement.[102]

The experiences of P.S. 48 show how these problems affected one school in particular.

Another measurement system is the Government Performance Project (GPP). The GPP was started in 1996 with a grant from the Pew Charitable Trusts and was initially based at Syracuse University. Since 2006 it has been housed at the Pew Center on the States.[103] Scorecards were published in *Governing* magazine and widely publicized. Because the project is run by nongovernmental organizations, there are no direct consequences attached to the rankings produced by this initiative.

Using criteria-based assessments, the GPP issued letter grades to federal agencies, state governments, and local governments.[104] Assessments were based on "managerial capacity"—government's ability to develop, direct, and control its resources to support the discharge of its policy and program responsibilities in finances, human resources, information technology, and capital. The criteria addressed within-agency capacity by surveying officials in federal, state, or local agencies, analyzing archival documents, and conducting follow-up telephone interviews with government actors and external stakeholders.[105]

A basic question for the GPP has been whether and how capacity is actually related to performance. Amy Kneedler Donahue, Sally Selden, and Patricia Ingraham examined this link, in particular the relationship between human resource capacities and performance of twenty-nine cities.[106] Their study predicted that professionalized personnel systems, such as merit-based systems administered by a city manager, would have higher capacity than would patronage-based personnel systems and that unions were likely to reduce managerial flexibility and degrade managerial capacity. Their empirical findings indicate that unionization slowed down hiring but speeded up terminations and that professionalization of city administration was positively associated with better human resources capacity and management.

A final example of a performance measurement initiative are the so-called Star Ratings for 150 local authorities in England, awarded by the British Social Services Inspectorate in the Department of Health.[107] Both quantitative and qualitative information are used, with the former provided through eleven main performance indicators in the Social Services Performance Assessment Framework. Unlike PART, emphasis is deliberately placed on objective, quantitative indicators in lieu of self reports.

The system uses a "light touch" to motivate public managers by promoting specification of goals and reporting of performance information, and comprehensive audits are conducted only if problems are identified (an example of fire alarm oversight). These rating are intended to evolve toward being more comprehensive, including performance indicators, inspection reports, plans, and evidence from monitoring. Critics of the system argue that it can be misleading to reduce "fiendishly complex" performance to something "simple" implied by the ratings; that quantitative indicators may not fully represent performance, but qualitative information may not be consistent across services, and coverage may be patchy, and that it will be difficult to move from the ratings to "appropriate managerial regimes." [108]

Challenges of Performance Measurement

Some **performance measurement challenges** have already been discussed. This section raises additional concerns, including the actual information contained in measures, incentives that performance measurement creates, suppression of information, attribution problems, performance paradoxes, and political rationality in the process.

One challenge is what to measure and what kind of information is gained. The performance of public and nonprofit sector organizations is widely acknowledged to present performance measurement challenges different from those for-profit organizations, where the bottom line—the ultimate outcome of interest—is profit. For public and nonprofit sector organizations, outputs (interim measures of work done, such as number of welfare

CONCEPTS IN ACTION

Measuring Progress in Iraq

The U.S. military in Iraq attempted to measure the will and ability of Iraqi forces to fight. U.S. military personnel considered quantitative information (such how many Iraqi army and police colonels and lieutenant colonels who are killed each month, a measure of their susceptibility to intimidation by insurgents), but they also recognized its limits and drew on qualitative information for what they call "feel," as reported by U.S. advisory team leaders who live and fight with Iraqis. They ranked leadership capability—"taking the lead in counterinsurgency operations"—and the ability to analyze and disseminate intelligence. Brookings Institution scholar Michael O'Hanlon publishes an Iraq Index, described below, which focuses on quantitative measures.

The Iraq Index is a statistical compilation of economic, public opinion, and security data. This resource will provide updated information on various criteria, including crime, telephone and water service, troop fatalities, unemployment, Iraqi security forces, oil production, and coalition troop strength.

The index is designed to quantify the rebuilding efforts and offer an objective set of criteria for benchmarking performance. It is the first in-depth, non-partisan assessment of American efforts in Iraq, and is based primarily on U.S. government information. Although measurements of progress in any nation-building effort can never be reduced to purely quantitative data, a comprehensive compilation of such information can provide a clearer picture and contribute to a healthier and better informed debate.

Source: Brookings Institution, "Iraq Index," http://www.brookings.edu/iraqindex.

clients served or the number of arrests made) may be easier to observe and measure than outcomes (the desired goals, such as having welfare clients get good jobs and move off welfare or reducing crime). Outputs may be the only type of measure available, as outcomes may not be observed until well after management decisions have to be made. The question, then, is to what extent output measures actually correspond to outcome measures?

A second challenge concerns the time point at which information is collected. Here, the question is whether short-term measures correspond well with longer-term outcomes. These issues are relevant for many public sector organizations such as those concerned with basic scientific research, the environment, health, human services, or national security.

A third challenge is that if organizations are to be held accountable for their performance, then performance measurement must be as accurate as possible, and the link between performance measures and management or organizational actions must be clear. Organizations (just as individuals) should not be penalized or held accountable for factors out of their control. For example, job training programs should not be penalized for serving clients who are more difficult to employ or who are looking for jobs during economic downturns. Performance measurement should somehow account for these external factors; such attribution problems are what performance analysis is meant to address. Yet establishing a clear link between organizational action and any particular measure of performance—taking into account the features of the environment, clients, or other organizational aspects that are out of the control of the manager or frontline workers—can be quite difficult.

A fourth challenge of performance measurement is presented by the pressures and incentives created by these systems, which can be anything but benign. Especially when accompanied by consequences such as sanctions for poor performance or rewards for high performance, performance measurement creates incentives to change the behavior of managers and organization staff.

One incentive that arises is for **creamskimming,** which occurs when agency staff select clients who are likely to be better performers instead of those who are likely to be poor performers in an effort to raise the overall level of performance (of either clients or the organization). Poorly prepared students may be reclassified into special education or learning disabled programs, where they are excluded from a school's reported performance. Although incentives may exist for creamskimming, it is possible that managers and street-level bureaucrats will not act on them. Indeed, one study found that job training workers still chose to serve clients who were most in need, regardless of performance incentives that should have led them to do just the opposite.[109]

Another incentive that performance measurement introduces is for the **suppression of information** that would adversely affect a measure. Especially when performance information is used to make arguments for or against the support of particular programs—that is, when the information is used for political purposes—the "whole story" might not be conveyed, either by public managers themselves or by their political superiors, in the interests of maintaining support for their programs.

A fifth challenge that occurs with performance measurement is the **performance paradox.** Such paradoxes can occur when a weak correlation exists between performance indicators and performance itself, and when performance measures lose their potency over time by failing to discriminate between strong and weak performers.[110] An organization learns to "manage to the test," resulting in "grade inflation." More effort is devoted to the dimensions of performance that are actually monitored and less effort to other dimensions. Such a response is consistent with the multitask principal-agent model described in chapter 5. One criticism of performance measurement systems is that efficiency measures tend to be emphasized at the expense of equity concerns. The reason is that equity is difficult to define and measure and, subsequently, to include in performance assessments. Such problems are related to "data issues, problems of the extent of bounding these questions, and—perhaps most important—the conflict within the society about these issues." [111] A counterargument is that equity is improved, although it may not be explicitly measured, as efficiency or effectiveness of a program improves.

Performance paradoxes may also result from the manipulation of assessments, which can be mitigated by auditing performance measures or adopting more objective measures. An example of such a performance paradox can be found in the measurement of high school dropouts in Houston, Texas, where some schools were reporting no dropouts at all, even though the problem was substantial. The Texas State Auditor's Office and independent research examined the measurement of dropout rates in Houston's system.[112] These analyses found that dropouts had been undercounted and students had been assigned to the special education program, which did not test students for achievement reporting purposes. Actual progress of minority groups was minimal, and retention in grade had increased markedly. In response to these revelations, in 2003 the Texas legislature passed a law that defined how dropout rates must be reported: "dropout rates, including dropout rates and district completion rates for grade levels 9 through 12, computed in accordance with standards and definitions adopted by the National Center for Education Statistics of the United States Department of Education." [113]

A sixth challenge for performance measurement arises from how political rationality affects public organizations. Performance measurement is, for the most part, regarded as a matter of technical rationality. Yet when performance is used for accountability purposes, especially in public sector programs, political rationality enters the picture: Who wants performance information? How will performance information influence the decisions and actions of political actors? Seldom are policymakers interested in performance, effectiveness, or results in a technical or academic sense. Instead, elected officials want to know how performance will affect their agendas, political bases, districts, constituencies, and reelection prospects. Other constituencies for performance information include inspectors general, auditors, budget examiners, personnel officers, advocacy groups, watchdog groups, and other interest groups. Because of political rationality, production of performance information may be done for its symbolic value rather than as an actual tool for management or budgeting.

In a related vein, Beryl Radin criticizes what she characterizes as the "unreal and naïve approach" of those who advocate performance measurement and assume that it is mainly a straightforward matter of defining and measuring performance in an objective way, then providing the performance information to policymakers and public managers, who will draw appropriate conclusions from it and act accordingly. She argues that the generation of information for performance measurement is based on the following false assumptions:

- Information is readily available.
- Information is neutral.
- We know what we are measuring.
- We can define cause-effect relationships in programs.
- Baseline information is available.
- Almost all activities can be measured and quantified.[114]

Radin emphasizes that policies are the product of ideology, interests, and information, and that the use of performance information often depends on whether it is consistent with ideology and interests.

Finally, another challenge is that measured performance may not actually correspond with organizational participants' understandings of performance. Sociologist Renee Anspach argues that "effectiveness" is a socially constructed phenomenon. She investigated the "indigenous or folk methods" actually used by administrators, case managers, families, and clients in community mental health centers to understand the effectiveness of their organizations. She identified the following types of methods the groups used to assess effectiveness:

- Measuring "success" against personal trajectories. Success was valued most in clients least likely to succeed because it enhanced the case manager's sense of efficacy.
- Interpreting acts in the context of relationships. Success was attributable to particular people, not to treatment.
- Using the dramatic incident. Dramatic events came to represent the system as a whole, for good or for ill.
- Relying on the appearance of involvement. Effort was weighted far more than results; effort stood for progress toward results or for results themselves.
- Scaling goals to meet shifting constraints. By lowering expectations, faith can be maintained even in failing programs.[115]

Caseworkers in Anspach's study cited all of these methods for assessing effectiveness, tending to locate sources of failure in the clients or in circumstances, but not in the treatments. These understandings of effectiveness may be coping mechanisms in the face of intense frustrations. The downside of such methods is that "promulgating effectiveness and neutralizing ineffectiveness—while securing resources necessary to a program's survival—may protect a program from critical scrutiny, both by outside evaluators and by program participants."[116] Anspach's work illustrates how understanding performance measurement may contribute to or be affected by the cultural dimension of public management. Such issues are explored further in the next section.

This section as a whole has illustrated important structural features of public management that influence accountability relationships with public organizations. These features include tools, organizations, and institutions available through the executive, legislative, and judicial branches, as well as through external pathways of citizen and stakeholder involvement. One particular structural mechanism, performance measurement, was discussed in detail. Overall, the structural tools discussed in this section shape—and often constrain—a public manager's decisions and actions.

ACCOUNTABILITY AND THE CULTURAL DIMENSION

Although structural tools are the dominant mechanisms under the control of external and internal formal authorities for defining accountability relationships, the cultural dimension also plays important roles in shaping these relationships. These roles range from interactions between culture and structural mechanisms or reforms to the unique contribution of individual values and organizational culture to ensuring responsible action on the part of organizational participants.

For example, ensuring accountability may be one goal of performance measurement in public organizations. Creating a **performance culture** may be crucial to the success of reforms to improve performance, where aspects of such a culture include "a focus on performance and performance data, the prospective high compensation levels, and the competitive spirit" with the idea that "when culture makes performance important, it influences the behavior of people at all levels." [117] In fact, reform efforts at the federal, state, and local levels that aim to improve performance often focus a part of their efforts on bringing about cultural change.

Empirical research supports the link between performance and organizational culture. Indeed, in the private sector management literature, interest in organizational culture has been driven in large part by how it relates to organizational performance.[118] One study identified four important elements of an organizational culture that were positively related to performance: involvement, consistency, adaptability, and mission.[119] Elements of organizational culture are prominent in Hal G. Rainey and Paula Steinbauer's theory of organizational effectiveness in public organizations.[120] Among the cultural elements the authors identify are a "strong" culture linked to accomplishing the organization's mission, professionalism, and motivation of individual actors related to tasks, mission, and public service. Using data from the 1996 Merit Principles Survey, collected by the Merit Systems Protection Board, Gene A. Brewer and Sally Coleman Selden tested the Rainey/Steinbauer model by predicting employees' perceptions of organizational performance in federal agencies.[121] They found empirical support for the model through significant associations with cultural factors of efficacy, teamwork, concern for the public interest, protection of employees, and task and public service motivation.

Yet organizational culture likely contributes to ensuring responsible action even when performance is not formally measured; indeed, culture may be essential for ensuring accountability in such situations. Returning to Mosher's distinction between objective and subjective responsibility (which emphasize the structural and cultural dimensions of public management, respectively), one scholar noted the distinction implies that "[a]ccountability as formal answerability is therefore a necessary but insufficient component of responsibility, in that there is a moral obligation on the individual to answer *for* (explain, justify), both honestly and openly, his or her decisions and actions." [122] In other words, individuals' values, ethics, and motives constitute an "inner check" that can lead to responsible action on the part of public managers, or to lapses in judgment and irresponsible action.

Professional norms and standards serve as guidance for responsible behavior for individuals in public organizations, regardless of the presence of other types of accountability mechanisms. Unique and identifiable norms are developed through professional training and the shared experiences of professionals such as attorneys, doctors, scientists, researchers, teachers, police officers, firefighters, forest rangers, and social service workers, among others. James Q. Wilson describes how professional norms influence individual behavior:

> In bureaucracy, professionals are those employees who receive some significant portion of their incentives from organized groups of fellow practitioners located outside the agency. . . . Because the behavior of a professional is not entirely shaped by organizational incentives, the way such a person defines his or her task may reflect more the standards of the external reference group than the preferences of the internal management.[123]

As identified by Romzek and Dubnick, then, the deference to expertise within an organization is built on the acknowledgment that professional accountability can be assumed or ensured through these externally influenced norms. Professional judgment, and therefore reliance on professional accountability, may be affected by recent performance measurement reforms, Radin writes, because they remove discretion that is at the core of professional accountability, especially when there is "a conflict between quality norms defined by a professional group and the fiscal agenda of the organization." [124] At the same time, professional accountability may be even more important in situations where programs and services previously provided directly by public organizations have been outsourced.[125]

In their book *Working, Shirking, and Sabotage,* political scientists John Brehm and Scott Gates identified the role of professional norms and professionalism in ensuring responsible behavior. They sought to understand whether and why frontline bureaucrats work (comply with the wishes of their hierarchical superiors to perform assigned tasks), shirk (devote their effort to other tasks), or sabotage (actively undermine the work they are supposed to do). Their argument, based on modeling and on empirical analysis of social workers and police officers, is that control over bureaucrats' actions is less likely to be gained by their supervisors' coercive efforts than by their functional and solidary preferences—that is, whether the employee has positive views toward his or her work and colleagues. "To the extent that professionalism provides a signal to supervisors about a bureaucrat's true type, then professionalism and functional preferences help to solve a significant part of the agency problem." This fact, Brehm and Gates argue, points to the importance of the hiring process in selecting employees from the outset who will act responsibly and in ways consistent with the organization's preferences.[126]

How selection and socialization processes ensure accountability is underscored by William Ouchi. He refers to organizations that rely on mechanisms such as clans—contrasting them with market or bureaucratic forms of control—and argues that they are particularly important for ensuring control in loosely coupled organizations:

> [I]f it is not possible to measure either behavior or outputs and it is therefore not possible to "rationally" evaluate the work of the organization, what alternative is there but to carefully select workers so that you can be assured of having an able and committed set of people, and then engaging in rituals and ceremonies which serve the purpose of rewarding those who display the underlying attitudes and values which are likely to lead to organizational success, thus reminding everyone of what they are supposed to be trying to achieve, even if they can't tell whether or not they are achieving it?[127]

CONCEPTS IN ACTION

Clan-like Organizations

In their analysis of accountability frameworks for special education classrooms, Patrick Wolf and Brian Hassel include a discussion of accountability relationships in William Ouchi's clan-like—or what they call "community"—organizations. "Principaled agents" (a term introduced by John DiIulio and discussed in chapter 6 of this book) are mentioned by Wolf and Hassel and are central to the clan-like organizations they observed.

With principled agents delivering services to the organization's clients, community-based agencies often do not overly concern themselves with *ex post* accountability instruments. Their leaders instead tend to rely on their own constant readings of whether the community is thriving and, if not, what might be done to improve its condition. Operators and clients who have performed particularly well in the view of the leader might receive praise during a community gathering or have their roles within the organization enhanced in some way. Operators and clients who have performed poorly in the view of the leader might receive a private admonition, role reduction, or, in extreme cases, banishment from the community.

Source: Patrick J. Wolf and Brian C. Hassel, "Effectiveness and Accountability, Part 1: The Compliance Model," in *Rethinking Special Education for a New Century,* ed. Chester E. Finn Jr., Andrew J. Rotherham, and Charles R. Hokanson Jr. (Washington, D.C.: Thomas B. Fordham Foundation, 2001), 58, http://www.ppionline.org/documents/SpecialEd_ch03.pdf.

Organizational culture contributes to ensuring accountability in tightly coupled organizations, as well. The organizational cultures that characterize high-reliability organizations emphasize discretion and autonomy, implying an emphasis on professional accountability. Perhaps because failure is so visible in high-reliability settings such as nuclear power or air traffic control, the cultures that sustain the continued high functioning of these organizations almost by definition shape their accountability relationships as well.

As illustrated in this section, the cultural dimension of public management in all its forms—the values, ethics, and motives of individuals and the shared culture of organizational participants—can influence responsible behavior and accountability relationships that characterize the organization as a whole. As emphasized by Ouchi and Brehm and

Gates, the selection of employees is critical to shaping culture and ensuring accountability during their tenure in the organization.

ACCOUNTABILITY AND THE CRAFT DIMENSION

The structural and cultural aspects of accountability are often "givens" for public managers, shaping the environments in which they operate, the specific tasks they must fulfill, and the kinds of actions they must induce on the part of subordinates. Yet managers, through their practice of craft, exert influence over accountability relationships and responsible action.[128] In Gary Miller's model of managerial leadership (see chapter 7), the leader selects a focal equilibrium and then induces subordinates to cooperate in order to achieve it. Whenever such equilibria are characterized by accountable and responsible action, managerial craft can guide action toward them.

Either explicit or implicit delegations of authority may require the practice of managerial craft. Therefore, the door is open for managers to influence accountability. Managers may be charged by formal authority with fulfilling specific accountability requirements that constitute a constraining structure under which they must operate. But even responding to specific structural requirements may involve discretion and therefore craft. It is not a foregone conclusion that managers will be fully responsive to such requirements. They can undermine accountability requirements by ignoring or subverting them, or they may even use the requirements as leverage for their own agendas.

The early responses across federal agencies to GPRA (discussed further in chapter 9) illustrate the range of responses to the legal requirement to engage in strategic planning and performance measurement. Beryl Radin has described these responses as follows:

> There are agencies that have engaged in planning as an intellectually rigorous exercise and have taken the requirements both seriously and almost literally. For some agencies, by contrast, the approach might be described as a narrow compliance strategy. In this approach, agencies simply describe what they are already doing but package that description in a way that appears to meet the requirements. Others have used the requirements of GPRA as an opportunity to focus on a specific set of administration or agency initiatives. In this approach, the goals and objectives are crafted as a way to make a case for new, expanded, or refocused policy areas. Still others have focused on measures that will be used for internal management purposes, usually at a program level rather than agency or department level.[129]

This observed variation in response to a specific accountability mechanism—GPRA—illustrates how managers, through exercising discretion, may shape responses to external accountability requirements.

Managers may choose to generate accountability requirements themselves, as a tool for managing and monitoring their subordinates. Implementation of reforms that emphasize particular aspects of accountability enable managers to advance their own agendas. Examples of such manager-led reforms, to be discussed further in chapter 9, include former secretary of defense Robert McNamara's Planning, Programming, and Budgeting System and a number of initiatives at the state and city levels. At the city level, these efforts are sometimes part of CitiStat—a measurement and management system based on CompStat, which William Bratton developed for the New York City Police Department (discussed further in chapter 9).

Because the ways public managers use their discretion have impacts on how, to whom, and with what results public services are delivered, managers inevitably influence accountability and responsible action in public organizations. As these examples illustrate, their responses to and uses of structural mechanisms constitute one way that managerial craft influences accountability relationships.

CONCEPTS IN ACTION

Promoting Accountability through CitiStat

The mayor of Buffalo, New York, demonstrating the exercise of managerial craft, implemented a number of reforms intended to increase the accountability of city agencies as part of the city's CitiStat program.

BUFFALO—Mayor Byron W. Brown today announced the City of Buffalo's Public Integrity and Accountability Plan, which will ensure integrity, transparency, accountability, and ethical behavior in City Hall as well as enhance public confidence in the employees of the City of Buffalo. Since taking office, Mayor Brown has created a written travel policy, and all department heads have had a mandatory ethics training course given by the local Federal Bureau of Investigations office.

"This plan is part of the continuing progress we have made to make City government transparent and accountable through CitiStat Buffalo," said Mayor Brown. "Buffalo is the first city in the nation to televise its CitiStat meetings unedited, so that all citizens can see how their government is functioning and performing. The new Public Integrity and Accountability Plan will enhance policies and procedures that are presently in place."

Details of the Public Integrity and Accountability Plan include the creation of the Office of Inspector General, an independent, centralized office within the Executive Branch that is tasked with addressing government waste, fraud, abuse and complaints. The Office will have the authority to receive and investigate integrity related complaints and incidences of fraud, corruption, and abuse involving city personnel—including elected officials— contractors, vendors and consultants doing business with the City.

Source: City of Buffalo, Office of the Mayor, "Mayor Brown Announces Public Integrity and Accountability Plan," press release, August 2007.

Another is through the responsible (or irresponsible) action by individual public managers and their fidelity to democratic accountability, as emphasized by John Gaus and Carl Friedrich, among others. A precept of **managerial responsibility,** articulated by Anthony M. Bertelli and Laurence E. Lynn Jr. and based on axiomatic principles found in the classical literature of public administration, emphasizes institutionalized values that can ensure the exercise of responsible discretion with respect for democratic values. The elements of the precept are: (1) judgment, which indicates discretion or autonomy; (2) balance, which requires "transparently reasonable" judgment among competing values and which must identify and reconcile "the inevitable conflict among interests, mandates, and desires"; (3) rationality, or the "habitual resort to reason" that "ensure[s] transparent justifications for managerial action"; and (4) accountability, because "[d]irective activity is definitive when the intent of positive law is clear. When it is ambiguous or incomplete, the public manager must exercise judgment as to what the public interest and professionalism require." [130]

Bertelli and Lynn argue that when the possibility for discretion is present, public managers must employ reasonable judgment informed by professionalism and the public interest. Applying the idea to court action in response to institutional reform litigation, they say, "[I]t is improper . . . for a court to place additional structural constraints on a responsibly managed agency, because to do so makes the agency responsible to the court rather than to the polity *through the political branches.*" [131] The Bertelli-Lynn precept of managerial responsibility extends beyond court-mandated reform, applying to public managers in all kinds of settings. As David Weimer has said, the design of governance arrangements for delivering and paying for health care could draw on the precept for understanding of what "responsible public management" might mean in such a system.[132]

Bertelli and Lynn argue that political principals must be able to trust those to whom they delegate authority and to trust them to perform in a reliably responsible way—that is, to exercise an "inner check" as they exercise discretion. Bertelli and Lynn define "irresponsible public management" as managerial action (or inaction) that "disavows judgment or that acts without authority or in an arbitrary, self-serving, ill-informed, and nontransparent fashion." [133] An example of a manager who exhibited such behavior is J. Steven Griles, former deputy secretary of the interior, who continued to meet with former clients of his management consulting firm despite having signed a written agreement not to do so when he entered government service. Griles resigned in 2004 after an eighteen-month investigation by the department's inspector general. Another example is how Federal Aviation Administration middle managers and supervisors responded when they learned of possible safety problems with airplanes flown by Southwest Airlines. They ignored reports from inspectors and even threatened some employees with retaliatory action if they pursued the reported problems.[134]

Exercising responsible judgment is all the more challenging when public managers are faced, as they inevitably are, with multiple accountability relationships, such as the cross-pressures associated with accountability for finances, fairness, and performance. Robert Behn refers to the cross-pressures that result from competing accountability requirements as an **accountability dilemma.** This dilemma, Behn goes on to say, often results in **accountability bias,** in which accountability for finances and accountability for fairness are emphasized because they typically involve more objective, explicit criteria against which to judge than does accountability for performance.[135] Many reform efforts exhibit the pressures such a bias creates: "While management reforms encourage initiative and sometimes even necessitate entrepreneurial behaviors—for example, to continue to provide high levels of service with reduced staff and funding—accountability dynamics continue to reinforce risk-averse rules and process orientations." [136]

Another source of multiple accountability demands is that managers work in organizations whose operating environments are characterized by the rule of law as well as by interest-based politics, separated powers, checks and balances, and organizational cultures. Multiple accountability demands in such environments can create cross-pressures that test the judgment and craftsmanship of even the most conscientious of public managers.

Romzek and Dubnick identify four different ways that managers might respond to multiple accountability demands. One possibility is that a manager may be passive, simply not attempting to manage competing expectations and being subject to "the whims of political fortune." Or a manager may be reactive, dealing with whatever consequences result from a particular action (attention to consequences). A third possibility is that a manager may be adaptive, proactively "assess[ing] emerging situations and tak[ing] anticipatory steps to minimize costly consequences" (attention to consequences and situations). A final possibility is that a manager may be strategic, actively managing the external task environment "to help shape and direct—even control—the emerging accountability dilemma that their organizations might encounter and influence likely consequences" (attention to consequences, situations, and environments).[137]

These types of possible responses can be linked with the Romzek and Dubnick framework for accountability discussed at the beginning of the chapter. It specified four types of accountability: hierarchical (previously referred to as bureaucratic), legal, professional, and political. Each type of accountability implies a particular behavioral response on the part of managers and their organizations (see Table 8.3).

TABLE 8.3 Values and Behavioral Expectations of Different Accountability Types

Type of Accountability	Value Emphasis	Behavioral Expectation
Hierarchical	Efficiency	Obedience to organizational directives
Legal	Rule of law	Compliance with external mandates
Professional	Expertise	Deference to individual judgment and expertise
Political	Responsiveness	Responsive to key external stakeholders

Source: Reproduced from Barbara S. Romzek and Patricia Wallace Ingraham, "Cross Pressures of Accountability: Initiative, Command, and Failure in the Ron Brown Plane Crash," *Public Administration Review* 60, no. 3 (2000): 240–253.

HOW THE WORLD WORKS

Accountability Tensions at the CIA: Structure, Culture, and Craft

In this article from the Web site slate.com, the call for an investigation of an inspector general himself is discussed, illustrating how the IG in this agency is viewed and the roles that the rule of law, organizational culture, craft, and personalities all play in the case. Frederick Hitz, the inspector general at the CIA during the Aldrich Ames spy case, is quoted in this article.

"I didn't get paid to make legal decisions," former CIA officer Michael Scheuer told a congressional panel last spring during testimony on unsavory agency practices like extraordinary rendition. "I got paid to protect Americans." Scheuer has a predilection for this sort of macho straight talk. It's a sentiment one often hears from those who have had to wage the war on terror first-hand: You suits can quibble about the rules, we spies have to think about results. The division of labor may not be a bad thing. Spy agencies should be as zealous as possible in defending the country, even to the point where they chafe at the constraints placed upon them. Independent oversight bodies should set—and uphold—those constraints. Some measure of tension between the two is not just natural, it's productive.

But last week, that tension boiled over when CIA director Michael Hayden launched an investigation into his own agency's inspector general, John Helgerson. Hayden's move to watch the CIA's watchdog is deeply misguided—an effort to neutralize one of the few vestiges of meaningful oversight at the agency, and leave the "legal decisions" to the spies themselves. The intelligence scandals of the past six years, and Mike Hayden's career in particular, demonstrate that this would be a grave mistake.

In Hayden's defense, nobody likes an inspector general. "He is but one man and must correct many, and therefore he cannot be beloved," the Martial Laws of 1629, which first established the office in the military, observed. Like internal affairs investigators in movies about crooked cops, federal IG's are at best ignored and more often loathed by the rank and file. And Helgerson and his staff had been courting particular resentment in recent years. A career agency officer, Helgerson assumed the post in 2002, and his tenure coincided with a period of abuses and controversy—from torture and coercive interrogation of detainees, to extraordinary rendition, to secret "black site" prisons in Europe—like none the agency had experienced since the Watergate era. In 2004, the IG warned that some of the agency's interrogation techniques might violate the Convention Against Torture. More recently, his staff produced a report on CIA failures leading up to 9/11 (a report that Hayden tried to suppress and George Tenet declared "flat wrong"). Hayden's inquisition comes just as the office is finishing a major report on rendition.

Distaste for Helgerson ran highest in the agency's National Clandestine Service (formerly known as the Directorate of Operations)—the front-line human intelligence gatherers who assume identities and run covert operations and assets. For these shadowy professionals, protracted internal investigations are understandably alarming. If a particular practice is authorized by Langley, and approved by the agency's general counsel, an operator wants to believe that he can proceed without the risk that down the line, a second review by the IG may find that he broke the law. Moreover, being the subject of an internal investigation can freeze an officer's career prospects, halting any promotion until the investigation is concluded. Helgerson's investigations sometimes dragged on for years.

Hayden has been credited with restoring some of the morale among the HUMINT ranks, and in this instance, he seems to have taken up their cause. Remember also that Hayden is the new boss at the agency; more than one spook-turned-commentator hints that going after Helgerson might amount to a ham-handed effort to win over the cool kids.

But while morale is unquestionably a crucial issue, let's not lose sight of what is actually happening here: Helgerson is being upbraided for . . . doing his job. One senior intelligence official complained to the *Washington Post* that Helgerson has "a prosecutorial mentality." But shouldn't he, when the CIA stands accused of activities that would make Jack Bauer blush and that in some cases violated the law? The protests bring to mind a sharp-elbowed brute I played basketball with in high school, who, when he wasn't fouling people, always seemed to be grumbling about the ref.

Of course, federal watchdogs are hardly infallible. But the problem lately has not been too much independence, but too little. Consider Howard Krongard, the State Department's inspector general, who stands accused not of assisting, but of actively thwarting, investigations of fraud and abuse by contractors in Iraq. Or NASA's IG, Robert "Moose" Cobb, who reportedly used his position "to interfere in the activities conducted by the investigative and audit divisions within his office." Hayden's move against Helgerson actually coincided with a new bill, passed overwhelmingly by the House of Representatives, that would bolster the authority and autonomy of federal IGs. (The president is threatening a veto.)

There are established procedures for a CIA director to question his IG without threatening the independence of the office. Hayden could go directly to the White House, or to the President's Council on Integrity and Efficiency, which oversees federal watchdogs, and which is run, as Spencer Ackerman points out, by a prep-school crony of the president who would have no trouble icing Helgerson. But by opting to keep the investigation internal, Hayden is undermining not just Helgerson but the structural integrity of the inspector general's office. IGs rely, in their own investigations, on the trust and respect of agency employees. How will this vote of no confidence affect the office's stature?

More pernicious is the possibility that Hayden's investigators will access the IG's files. Employees who alert the inspector general about abuses rely on confidentiality; it allows them to cry foul without jeopardizing their jobs (giving them an important, last-ditch alternative to leaking to the press). If Hayden looks in the files, that promise of confidentiality will no longer be on offer, and the result could have a devastating chilling effect on future internal investigations. But then, it's hard to escape the conclusion that this kind of chilling effect is precisely what Hayden intends. Fred Hitz, the agency's IG from 1990 to 1998, called the investigation "a terrible idea," and told the Los Angeles Times that it looks like Hayden is trying "to call off the dogs."

To get a sense of what can happen when the dogs are called off, we need look no further than Hayden's recent career. Before he left the National Security Agency, where he was director, Hayden originally authorized the infamous warrantless wiretapping program. Hayden's general counsel knew about the program and approved it. And who was his general counsel at the time? Robert Deitz, who followed him to CIA, and whom he just chose to spearhead the investigation of Helgerson. If the NSA's inspector general had a problem with secretly violating federal law, no one ever heard about it, because the office reported only to Hayden and not to Congress. (Helgerson reports to the CIA director and Congress, a two-master system designed to shield him from undue pressure.)

From Watergate to wiretapping, it seems axiomatic that, left to their own devices, spies will overreach. Stifled by secrecy and fearful of being tarred "soft" on national security, Congress has largely abdicated its role in effectively policing American espionage. Now Hayden is seeking to cow his own IG at a time when the agency—and the country—needs that oversight most. I don't trust Mike Hayden, or his subordinates in the field, to be the final arbiter on what our spies can do. That's why Michael Scheuer's division of labor makes sense: We can ask intelligence officers to play by the rules, but it's folly to let them write the rules, as well.

Source: Patrick Radden Keefe, "Don't Hang the Ref: The CIA's Inspector General Must Be Free to Do His Job," Slate, October 16, 2007, http://www.slate.com/id/2175922/.

Barbara Romzek and Patricia Wallace Ingraham used the framework shown in Table 8.3 to analyze the accountability relationships related to the plane crash that killed Secretary of Commerce Ron Brown and his entourage in Bosnia during the Clinton administration. The analysis emphasizes how the crash investigation reflected managerial efforts to reconcile the demands of multiple accountability systems, concluding:

> Entrepreneurial management, which involves cutting red tape (ignoring rules) and pushing the administrative envelope, necessitates standards of accountability that defer to expertise and encourage responsiveness to key stakeholders. When events went awry, entrepreneurial management and leadership rhetoric were downplayed. These officers were judged by whether they had obeyed commands (hierarchical standard) rather than whether their decisions reflected reasonable exercises of their discretion (professional standard). In essence, while the institutional rhetoric and managerial conditions encouraged entrepreneurial behavior, the administrative reality still emphasized a risk-averse, rules-oriented approach to accountability when things went wrong.[138]

Indeed, simultaneously fulfilling the different roles called for by competing accountability demands—hierarchical, legal, professional, and political—may be nothing short of impossible. Tensions between accountability concerns based on responsiveness (the political dimension of the framework) and those based on competence or adherence to hierarchical and legal dimensions may also be evident in relations between public managers in career positions and those who are political appointees.

This chapter has discussed the accountability challenges that arise in public organizations. Because delegation and discretion are inevitable, accountability for performance and responsible action by public organizations and managers is an ongoing concern in our democracy. Although the goal of holding public actors accountable may be unobjectionable and even desirable, figuring out just how to put that goal in operation is enormously complex, as illustrated by the story of P.S. 48 under the NCLB and the discussion throughout the chapter.

Accountability mechanisms tend to be dominated by formal mechanisms and structures, but as this chapter has shown, the cultural and craft components may interact with such structures and ultimately influence responsible behavior of public managers and their subordinates in important ways. In many ways, ensuring accountability is an example of a three-dimensional public management challenge, and other examples are discussed in chapter 10.

Key Concepts

objective responsibility
subjective responsibility
whistleblowers
politics of bureaucratic structure
police patrol oversight
deck-stacking
fire alarm oversight
Chevron doctrine
public law litigation
injunction
decree
remedies/remedial decrees
representative bureaucracy
citizen and stakeholder participation
performance measurement
performance analysis
performance management
performance budgeting
organizational report card
balanced scorecard
types of performance measures
performance measurement challenges
creamskimming
suppression of information
performance paradox
performance culture
managerial responsibility
accountability dilemma
accountability bias

Analysis and Argument: Test Your Understanding

Read the teaching case, " 'James Woolsey and the CIA: The Aldrich Ames Spy Case' (Parts 1 and 2)." [139] This case considers the decisions that James Woolsey, the director of the Central Intelligence Agency from 1993 to 1995, faced once Aldrich Ames was charged with spying for Russia. Ames, a CIA agent for more than thirty years, was incompetent yet had caused incalculable damage to the nation's interests over a long period of time (1985–1994). Inside the agency, his weaknesses had been tolerated, and he had been stereotyped as "not going anywhere." As this case describes, Woolsey faced both internal and external challenges in figuring out how to handle Ames.

In addition, consider the "Accountability Tensions at the CIA: Structure, Culture, and Craft" box on pages 329–331. After reading the case and looking again at the box, consider the questions below regarding the accountability issues raised.

1. Using the Romzek-Dubnick framework of accountability systems, identify the cross-pressures of accountability that Woolsey faced. Make an argument (claims, reasons, evidence, warrants, and acknowledgments and response) to support your answer.
2. This question asks you to analyze this case from the three dimensions of public management. For each question, make an argument to support your answer:
    a. What are the structural and cultural aspects that are "givens" for Woolsey?
    b. What structural and cultural aspects might he be able to change? How?
    c. How would you characterize Woolsey's craft?
    d. What aspects of the environment are "givens" for Woolsey?
    e. How do the factors you identified in the above questions constrain or enable Woolsey's response to the situation? How do they affect his responses to the cross-pressures of accountability that he faces?
3. If Woolsey were guided by a precept of managerial responsibility, what actions would he have taken, and why? Support your answer with an argument.
4. Responsible officials are often described as having had "illustrious" or "distinguished" careers. To what extent should this information be taken into account in exonerating them in the face of one or more instances of "irresponsible" action?
5. According to one observer, the failings of officials responsible for Ames were failures of commission—poor management and poor judgment—but there were no violations of law or agency procedures. "Everyone acted in accordance with 'established mores.' " What do you think of that view?

9 Public Management Reform

The professional field of public administration and management in America originated in the good government reform movements that first took root in the nation's large cities in the early twentieth century. Within a generation they spread to state governments and then to the federal government.[1] Many of the field's most influential ideas—separation of politics and administration, neutral competence of civil servants, efficiency of operations, "scientific management," principles of administration, and the strong executive—far from being products of abstract theorizing or ideology, were the main elements of reform agendas intended to empower public officials to meet the challenges of a growing, industrializing, urbanizing, and diversifying society free from undue political interference and corruption but still with a duty of accountability.

Frederick C. Mosher, one of America's most respected public administration scholars, believed that the emergence of the profession was the consequence of "a fundamental optimism that mankind could direct and control its environment and destiny for the better." [2] That optimism is illustrated by the following account of reform in the organization and management of Missouri's juvenile justice system.

> With prisons around the country filled to bursting, and with states desperate for ways to bring down recidivism rates that rise to 70 and 80 percent, some policymakers are taking a fresh look at treatment-oriented approaches like Missouri's as a way out of America's juvenile justice crisis. Here, large, prison-style "gladiator schools" have been abandoned in favor of 42 community-based centers spread around the state so that now, even parents of inner-city offenders can easily visit their children and participate in family therapy.

The ratio of staff to kids is low: one-to-five. Wards, referred to as "clients," are grouped in teams of 10, not unlike a scout troop. Barring outbursts, they're rarely separated: They go to classes together, play basketball together, eat together, and bunk in communal "cottages." Evenings, they attend therapy and counseling sessions as a group.

Missouri doesn't set timetables for release; children stay until they demonstrate a fundamental shift in character, a policy that detainees say gives kids an added incentive to take the program seriously. Those who are let out don't go unwatched: College students or other volunteers who live in the released youths' community track these youths for three years, helping with job placement, therapy referrals, school issues and drug or alcohol treatment.

The results?

About 8.6 percent of teens who complete Missouri's program are incarcerated in adult prisons within three years of release, according to 2006 figures. (In New York, 75 percent are re-arrested as adults, 42 percent for a violent felony. California's rates are similar.)

Last year, 7.3 percent of teen offenders released from Missouri's youth facilities were recommitted to juvenile centers for new offenses. Texas, which spends about 20 percent more to keep a child in juvenile corrections, has a recidivism rate that tops 50 percent. . . .

Mark Steward, who, as director of the state's Division of Youth Services from 1987 to 2005, oversaw the development of what many experts regard as the best juvenile rehabilitation system in America[, says] "This isn't rocket science. . . . It's about giving young people structure, and love and attention, and not allowing them to hurt themselves or other people. Pretty basic stuff, really. It's just that a lot of these kids haven't gotten the basic stuff." . . .

Many states are trying to bring down high rates of repeat offending by juveniles. Wisconsin now treats some repeat offenders with mental health counselors in hospitals, instead of corrections officers in jails. Illinois offers them drug treatment, job placement or an expedited return to custody. And Washington state targets kids at risk of becoming its most serious offenders with early, intensive anger-management, drug and family therapy.

Research guided these approaches. One 2006 study, for example, found that anger-management, foster-care treatment and family group therapy cut recidivism drastically among teens, resulting in taxpayer savings up to $78,000 per child. Programs that tried to scare kids into living a clean life were money losers, according to the study, conducted by the Washington State Institute for Public Policy.

Missouri employs similar carrot-and-stick techniques. But it takes rehabilitation one step further by normalizing the environments of children in custody, says Barry Krisberg, president of the National Council on Crime and Delinquency, a nonprofit based in Oakland, Calif. . . .

What's been the difference? Good role models help: The girls get to mingle with college students in the campus dining hall and attend campus plays and other cultural events. At the start of the school year they describe their experiences to incoming students during orientation week. But the biggest plus, Schaller says, is that "you have people to talk to here, you have people who truly do care." . . .

> "What is [also] remarkable about Missouri's system is that is has been sustained by conservative and liberal governments," says Krisberg, of the national crime and delinquency council. "They've seen that this is not a left-right issue. In many ways, its a commonsense issue."
>
> A common-cents issue, too since it costs states between $100 and $300 a day to keep a juvenile in so-called "punitive" correctional facilities, according to a 2005 report by the Youth Transition Funders Group, a philanthropy network. Missouri's per capita cost of its juvenile rehabilitation program is $130 a day.
>
> "The fact is that most kids from punitive states get out, get re-arrested, and get thrown back into correctional facilities," Krisberg says. "What amazes me is that taxpayers in these punitive states put up with such rates of failure." [3]

The reform of the juvenile justice system in Missouri appears to be a success. Although the American administrative state reflects a long history of deliberate reforms conceived in optimism and hoping for similarly successful results, the history of governmental change and improvement suggests that reform is very often problematic. A primary reason is that the reform process is influenced by the competition of the three branches for control of administration and by the efforts of each branch to hold the others accountable through the kinds of checks and balances discussed in chapter 4. This state of affairs raises a number of questions. Do policymakers know enough about the complexities of government to be able to design reforms that will largely attain their goals? How can those who design reforms and those who implement them know if a phenomenon as complicated as administrative reform has produced the benefits promised by its advocates? How can policymakers and stakeholders account for and evaluate changes in administrative systems and technologies that occur without the fanfare of being part of a reform initiative?

This chapter takes up these questions and is organized as follows. The next section defines public management reform. Then, an overview is provided of the main reform initiatives that have shaped the American administrative state since the beginning of the Republic. In this account, public management is *the object of reform* by policymakers; that is, it is the product of action external to the executive branch of government. Next is a discussion of public managers as *the initiators or agents of reform,* that is, reform as the product of deliberate action by managers within executive agencies. This discussion considers the principal challenges of designing and achieving public management reforms from the perspective of public managers, including the conceptual and operational design of such reforms. Available evidence concerning the extent to which public management reforms actually improve government performance is then discussed, followed by a detailed case study of manager-initiated organizational reform, CompStat, in the New York City police department. Observations on public management reform as a political process conclude the chapter. In the end-of-chapter exercise, readers analyze the arguments in an academic article that describes and critiques reforms that institute incentives for performance in human service programs.

WHAT IS PUBLIC MANAGEMENT REFORM?

In their book on the subject, European scholars Christopher Pollitt and Geert Bouckaert define **public management reform** as "deliberate changes to the structures and processes of public sector organizations with the objective of getting them (in some sense) to run better." [4] From the three-dimensional perspective of this book, policymakers (external actors) and public managers (internal actors) employ their craft—their temperament, skills, and values—to change a structural and cultural status quo, whether it be of the government as a whole or of a department, bureau, or program, to engineer a better outcome. In the first instance, as Pollitt and Bouckaert suggest, these actors are most apt to use structures as leverage for changing results for the better because, in contrast to people or cultures, structures are most clearly under their control.

Because they are given significant publicity, deliberate reforms, whether externally or internally generated, are the most visible of the many kinds of changes in public management policies and practices that occur with regularity at all levels of government.[5] Among recent initiatives, as was discussed in chapter 8 and will be discussed further below, are the congressionally initiated Government Performance and Results Act of 1993 (GPRA), the Reinventing Government initiative of the Clinton administration, and the President's Management Agenda (PMA) of the George W. Bush administration.

It is important to note, however, that as Michael Barzelay argues, "A focus on initiatives is less helpful in comprehending what governments are actually doing, for two main reasons. First, some changes in public management policy happen without being included in an initiative. . . . Second, focusing on initiatives often permits only a vague understanding of policy content. A clearer understanding requires an effort to specify either the policy instruments or programs of action involved, or both." [6] The adoption of new tools of action, new forms of organization, new ways to perform governmental functions such as budgeting and budget execution and personnel administration, new techniques of communication and coordination, and new managerial strategies for accomplishing organizational change and performance improvement often reflect the efforts of officials operating well below the political radar screen in behalf of specific organizational, programmatic, or personal goals.

The Chief Financial Officers Act of 1990, the creation of the Department of Homeland Security in 2002 and the Directorate of National Intelligence in 2004, state-level reorganizations of child welfare agencies, presidential and gubernatorial reorganizations of executive offices and their functions, and privatization initiatives are reforms that are usually incorporated in well-publicized efforts to improve government performance. Other, more routine measures, such as state-level efforts to facilitate college students' transferring credits from one institution to another, the launching of a Web site that enables citizens to track government performance measures, a city program that recruits and trains high school dropouts to work in home construction, and the adoption of strategic planning and performance measurement processes by an agency's management, although not necessarily publicized as reform initiatives, often contribute in useful ways to making things run better.[7] Such expert-driven reforms often originate in one state or municipality and then quietly diffuse to other jurisdictions through professional networks.

Indeed, many public management scholars regard the seemingly routine, below-the-radar innovations as cumulatively more significant than the more politically visible initiatives. "The bulk of the improvements in government efficiency that have taken place in recent years," wrote George Downs and Patrick Larkey in 1986, "have resulted not so much from overt, grandiose reform schemes as from a host of modest, tactical reforms." [8] As will be further discussed below, that assessment still holds.

IMPLEMENTING AMERICAN DEMOCRACY

Competition among the branches of government for control of the resources of administration often takes the form of public management reform initiatives.[9] These initiatives included President Lyndon Johnson's mandating all federal agencies to adopt the Planning-Programming-Budgeting System (PPBS); Congress's enacting the Budget and Impoundment Control Act of 1974, which created the basic procedures for enacting an annual budget for the federal government; and, in a ruling with clear reform implications for public management, the Supreme Court's articulating a doctrine of judicial deference to administrative discretion in *Chevron U.S.A. v. Natural Resources Defense Council* (1984), which adjusted the boundary between the courts and the executive branch toward greater executive discretion. Reform has been a leitmotif of American politics since the Declaration of Independence.[10]

Prebureaucratic America: The Clerical State

If the Revolution is interpreted as an explosive expression of the desire for radical administrative reform, then the subsequent creation and development of a United States of America represents an administrative reform movement of great moment and complexity. The founders set out to prevent the emergence of a European state of dangerously unaccountable executive power.[11] According to John Gaus, the U.S. contribution to the institutions of democratic governance was the requirement that executive officials submit regularly, either directly or indirectly, to popular vote, a practice then unknown in Europe or elsewhere.[12] Moreover, noted Lloyd Short, "the adoption of a system of single-headed executive departments was a step distinctly in advance of formal English [administrative] development," although "the idea was that agencies were to be run in the same way as the law firms, small businesses, plantations, and military units that agency chieftains came from." [13]

Although not all scholars agree, John Rohr has long maintained that the groundwork for the administrative state that began to emerge in the Progressive Era was actually laid in Philadelphia. He quotes Publius (the *nom de plume* of the authors of *The Federalist:* Alexander Hamilton, John Jay, and James Madison) as insisting that government must be given "an unconfined authority as to all those objects which are intrusted to its management," for "the means ought to be proportional to the *end.*" Thus, says Rohr, Publius takes a managerial view of the Constitution, arguing (in *Federalist* No. 23) that "the persons, from whose agency the attainment of any *end* is expected, ought to possess the *means* by which it is to be attained." [14]

Following his election in 1828, President Andrew Jackson initiated the next significant, whole-of-government public management reform, arguably the first effort at large-scale planned change initiated by the federal executive branch. A **spoils system** of rotation in office replaced the elitist personnel practices of the Federalists, which, more in the English style, preferred government by "gentlemen" of breeding and property. The spoils system dominated nineteenth-century selection and control of administrators (or "clerks," as they were then known), and the oversight of administration exercised by legislators, political parties, and the courts was haphazard.[15]

Although credited with creating the spoils system, Jackson at the same time inaugurated the recognizable beginnings of bureaucratic government in America.[16] The pivotal idea, argues Michael Nelson, was Jackson's notion that federal jobs "admit of being made" so simple that any intelligent person could do them. The need arose to restrain corruption among officeholders unsocialized by specific education, English-style *noblesse oblige*, or what were to become American-style public service values. The result was the creation of agencies with significant internal checks and balances to prevent thievery. To citizens, however, these checks and balances often looked like "red tape," a term that refers to administrative procedures that are redundant or nonfunctional.

But nineteenth-century political parties had little incentive to curb bureaucratic power because they knew their turn would come to use it for their own interests. As a result, nineteenth-century public officials had—as contemporary civil servants continue to have—every incentive to develop political bases of support. Apart from its power of appointment, the executive branch played a relatively minor role in early public administration. As political scientist Daniel Carpenter puts it: "American bureaucracy in the 1800s was a regime of clerkship. In law and in practice, federal agencies existed only to carry out with a minimum of forethought the laws that Congress had passed and that the courts had legitimized and interpreted." [17]

Government by parties, legislatures, and courts was even more pronounced in state and local government.[18] According to John Mabry Mathews, an early participant in public management reform movements, state administration was "decentralized and disintegrated" in part because the functions states perform "have hitherto been of relatively slight magnitude or complexity . . . ; a high degree of state efficiency has not been found necessary to state life." [19] But all was hardly benign. Political scientist Charles Merriam referred pointedly to the pathologies of "corruption, ignorance, indolence, incompetence, favoritism, oppression" that came to characterize spoils system administration and ultimately to undermine it.[20]

Emergence of the Modern Administrative State

Jacksonian traditions were more quintessentially American in their democratic spirit than the European-flavored bureaucratic institutions that began replacing them in the late nineteenth century.[21] Following the Civil War, industrialization, urbanization, and immigration began to transform American society and to strengthen middle-class elites, who viewed spoils-ridden government as corrupt, incompetent, and an impediment to prosperity. In his famous 1887 academic essay, "The Study of Administration," political scientist and future president Woodrow Wilson memorably condemned the "poisonous atmosphere of city government, the crooked secrets of state administration, the confusion, sinecurism, and corruption ever and again discovered in the bureaux at Washington." [22] Promoted by academically oriented activists, the emerging administrative state reflected a number of currents in American thought: a progressive political agenda, the growing authority of science and of the idea of management, the professional development of administrative law, and a spirit of pragmatic empiricism.

The groundwork for change at the federal level was laid by the **civil service reform movement,** the milestone of which was the Pendleton Act of 1883, named after its legislative sponsor, which initiated the trend toward a merit-based civil service protected from political reprisals by tenure in office.[23]As historian Stephen Skowronek argues, "With the legitimacy of the early American state under attack from all sides, government officials finally made the pivotal turn down the bureaucratic road," a road that was already being traveled in Great Britain and was something of a superhighway in continental Europe from the time of the great Prussian autocrats.[24] All levels of government began an inexorable expansion, initially into regulating the private sector and ultimately, as in Europe, into the service and development activities of what would become, during the New Deal, the American welfare state.

The result of these various transformations at local, state, and federal levels of government, which were the product of executive and legislative initiatives, was dramatic, wrote British political scientist Harold Laski in 1923 in the new British journal *Public Administration.* "A state built upon *laissez-faire* has been transformed into a positive [we might say "activist"] state. Vast areas of social life are now definitely within the ambit of legislation; and a corresponding increase in the power of the executive has been the inevitable result." [25] In the same year, John Gaus noted, "The new administration includes a wide share of policy formulation; it requires a large measure of discretion on the part of the civil servant; it claims wide exemption from judicial review of its findings of fact; in brief, we are seeing a development somewhat akin to the rise of the administration in the days when the Tudors and the great monarchs were welding together the modern national state." [26]

Just as America's founders had to confront and overcome the disadvantages of a weak government, evolving ideas about constitutional administration a century later coalesced around a particular idea: the need for strong *elected* executives. Said reformer and scholar Frederick Cleveland, "We have purposely deprived ourselves of responsible executive leadership for fear we shall not be able to control it." [27] The question was whether elected executives had the capacity to administer the rapidly expanding scope and reach of their governments. The seminal development was the Budget and Accounting Act of 1921, a presidential initiative enacted by Congress, which institutionalized the executive budget and put the president for the first time in a position of authority over the entire government, albeit under the watchful eye of Congress and the newly created General Accounting Office.

CONCEPTS IN ACTION

The Bull Moose Party's View of Public Management Reform

In the national election of 1912, the incumbent Republican president, William Howard Taft, and the Democratic nominee, Woodrow Wilson, were challenged by a third party candidate. Former president Theodore Roosevelt ran on the independent Bull Moose Party ticket, whose Progressive public management reform ideas contrasted sharply with the system of political patronage. This is a classic instance of reform as politics and politics as reform. As president, all three men made important contributions to building the modern American administrative state.

We pledge our party to readjustment of the business methods of the National Government and a proper co-ordination of the Federal bureaus, which will increase the economy and efficiency of the Government service, prevent duplications and secure better results to the taxpayers for every dollar expended.

Source: "Panaceas Offered by the New Party; Restriction of Courts, Government Control of Currency and Equal Suffrage," *New York Times,* August 8, 1912, Sec. A.

The Welfare State

Public management reform returned to the top of the political agenda during Franklin D. Roosevelt's presidency and the enormous increase of government power that occurred under his leadership. Following the dramatic expansion of federal executive authority, only grudgingly legitimized by the courts, the 1937 **Brownlow Report** became "a landmark statement of 'managerialism' in public administration." [28] "The President needs help," proclaimed the President's Committee on Administrative Management, in presenting its solution for enabling the nation's chief executive to effectively lead the larger, more powerful executive branch of government crafted during the Great Depression.

The solution to weak executive control over a bureaucracy swelling with New Deal programs "is couched in terms of a more centralized top-down reporting structure based on a private business management analogy, with a large general staff apparatus around the chief executive." [29] The president should be in a position "to coordinate and manage the departments and activities [of the government] in accordance with the laws enacted by the Congress," achievement of which would require an expanded White House staff; stronger management agencies; a strengthened and expanded civil service system; a subordination of independent agencies, administrations, authorities, boards, and commissions to major executive departments; and an independent postaudit of the fiscal transactions of an executive with complete responsibility for accounts and current transactions. "There is nothing [in this program]," Roosevelt insisted, "which is revolutionary, as every element is drawn from our own experience either in government or large-scale business." [30]

The Brownlow Report rapidly faded to political obscurity owing to opposition from a rancorous Congress weary of Roosevelt's self-aggrandizement. Nevertheless the most basic of the reorganization proposals was achieved in 1939, when Congress passed a bill authorizing creation of the **Executive Office of the President,** which recognized the executive role of the president and the concept of administrative management. In the immediate aftermath of World War II, however, Congress struck back at a presidency perceived to have grown so powerful that it threatened to reduce Congress to irrelevance.[31] In a series of legislative enactments, the most significant of which was the Administrative Procedure Act of 1946 (APA), Congress effectively restored legislatively centered public administration *vis-á-vis* a now strengthened federal executive that could be an even more powerful tool for achieving congressional intent.

Following World War II, American public management became the object of a seemingly continuous but disjointed sequence of reform initiatives.[32] As Paul Light sees it, these reforms, some initiated by the executive branch, some by Congress, some by the courts, all reflected the competitive dynamics of the separation of powers, which he traces in detail from 1945 through 1994. Light assigns various themes to these reforms—"scientific management" (relying on expertise), "war on waste" and "watchful eye" (surveillance to prevent corruption and subversion of congressional intent), and "liberation management" (allowing managers greater discretion)—each with its own distinctive theory of the causes and cures of inadequate governmental performance.[33]

Rather than succeeding each other, initiatives reflecting these differing emphases were layered on top of one another, creating additional, poorly articulated structures and processes that acted as checks and balances. Presidential initiatives in the form of John F. Kennedy's New Frontier, Lyndon B. Johnson's Great Society, and Richard M. Nixon's New Federalism brought changes in administrative technologies such as strategic planning, policy analysis, and program evaluation (Johnson's PPBS initiative). Though public management reforms such as PPBS, management by objectives, and zero-based budgeting were often viewed as imitating the private sector, in fact they were political strategies, defended as the techniques of successful corporations to give them a patina of legitimacy, to strengthen the executive branch much as were the reforms of the Progressive Era.

In Francis Rourke's synoptic view of developments in governance during the latter decades of the twentieth century,

> the growth of national bureaucracy in the United States since the 1930s has been a far less important phenomenon than the simultaneous emergence of new ways by which the traditional institutions of American national government—the presidency, Congress, and the courts—have been able to meet and contain the challenge of a bureaucracy that many people prior to World War II anticipated would actually become a fourth branch of government in the postwar period.[34]

These adjustments were seldom part of reform initiatives, and they included a collegial or collective presidency comprising the president and the expanding White House staff to preserve executive hegemony over bureaucracy and the growing use of experts from the private sector to advise policymakers and managers; expansion in the size and proficiency of legislative staffs; an enhancement of the legislature's capacity to do its job; judges becoming "major actors in the policy process, largely as a result of statutes that provide broader opportunities for private parties to challenge the decisions of executive agencies in the courts";[35] and the proliferation of "iron triangles" and "issue networks" linking bureaucrats, interest groups, legislative staff members, and others with a stake in governmental outcomes in networks of communication and cooperation.

A Continuing Wave of Reforms

While these changes were taking place, governments at all levels had begun to use a number of new tools of action: privatization, hybridity, deinstitutionalization, devolution, revenue sharing (or block grants), and personnel system reform. The result, which has been variously called third-party government, indirect government, government by proxy, the hollow state, and virtual government, have had significant implications for federalism, interorganizational and intergovernmental relations, public management, and democratic accountability.

The administration of President Ronald Reagan gave significant impetus to these developments. According to Charles Levine, "By insisting on greater reliance on contracting-out government responsibilities to private sector service providers, the use of user fees for government services, and other alternative service delivery mechanisms, the Reagan administration has accentuated the trend away from the federal government's direct provision of goods and services." [36] As noted in chapter 5, Paul Light has shown that the "true size" of the federal government, which takes into account the extent of third-party government, is much larger than its own payroll; in fact, by the mid-1980s it had risen to approximately four times the size of the federal workforce.[37]

Third-party government has often been celebrated as a way of expanding the role of government in service delivery without increasing the size of government itself. "[W]hat all these varied efforts to involve the public more directly in the administration of government programs reflect," Rourke argued, "is a deep-seated belief on the part of legislative and executive officials that bureaucratic power can best be legitimized by being democratized, by bringing the decisions of public bureaucrats much more closely under the control of private citizens."[38]

A wave of reforms originating in Great Britain and New Zealand in the 1990s became known worldwide as **New Public Management** (NPM). The central idea behind NPM was that public management should mimic private management in its reliance on measured performance and competition. Rather than relying on large bureaucratic agencies (or, as in Europe, nationalized industries), government should be disaggregated into smaller operating agencies linked to policymakers by performance contracts. Such reform concepts did not produce the excitement in America that they did in much of the rest of the world, however. The reason is that most if not all of its features had already become widely used "tools of government" in America in the postwar decades. The focus on policy implementation and the phenomenon of third-party government, which were at the heart of NPM, had already become staples of what was emerging as an American public management movement.

Specifically, beginning in the mid-1950s the U.S. federal government began systematically to privatize public services, using structural instruments such as contracts, user charges, vouchers, and alternative delivery systems, practices pursued with even greater enthusiasm by state and local governments.[39] A concurrent development was the deinstitutionalization of state and county hospital patients and other institutionalized populations, reflecting the growing concern for the civil rights of dependent people and the development of drugs and treatment approaches permitting community-based care for those with chronic conditions. Sometimes such reforms were nonpolitical, but often they were high-visibility political initiatives.

The accelerating popularity of hybrid organizations beginning in the 1960s—examples include the Communication Satellite Corporation (ComSat), the Manpower Demonstration Research Corporation (now known formally as MDRC), and the Corporation for Public Broadcasting (CPB)—reflected several factors: federal budget controls, which force agencies to seek new sources of revenue; evasion of general management laws such as statutory ceilings on personnel and compensation; the popularity of generic, business-focused values; and, in particular, the belief that entity-specific laws and regulations facilitate management flexibility, "even at the cost of accountability to representative institutions."[40]

Further, in the aftermath of the Nixon-era Watergate scandals, the Civil Service Reform Act of 1978, in a historic departure from "protection" as a principle of public personnel administration, abolished the Civil Service Commission and reorganized its functions into the Office of Personnel Management and the Merit Systems Protection Board. The act also created the Senior Executive Service, a cadre of experienced career managers who might be assigned wherever needed by an administration. That the act largely failed to accomplish its goals reflects the competitive politics of controlling the bureaucracy; Congress and the courts largely vindicated the protection principle and thwarted the act's purposes.[41]

Finally, in a continuing effort to maintain control over administration, Congress authorized a number of formal structural reforms, including the Budget and Impoundment

Control Act of 1974, which authorized creation of the Congressional Budget Office (a policy analysis organization responsible to Congress) and the Foreign Intelligence Surveillance Act of 1978, which was intended to compel stricter presidential accountability to Congress and the courts, measures that were later contested by the George W. Bush administration because they unduly weakened the executive authority needed for its "war on terrorism" and its doctrine of the unitary executive.

Managerialism

Beginning in the 1970s, a weakened economy and budgetary shortfalls began pushing American politics in a fiscally conservative direction. One consequence was a heightened emphasis on **managerialism,** born of faith in the efficacy of management and managers as guarantors of efficient and effective public administration. With the exception of the GPRA, discussed in chapter 8 and further below, managerialism has been primarily an executive branch movement.[42]

The Grace Commission

Inspired by a kindred spirit, conservative British prime minister Margaret Thatcher with her aggressive NPM reforms, President Reagan attempted to initiate a new era in American public administration. The goal of his "war on waste" was to shrink the size of government, while increasing its economic efficiency. Although neoliberal (favoring markets over regulation) in spirit, Reagan's reform strategy was quintessentially American and bore little resemblance to NPM.

Reagan's chosen instrument, a throwback to the kinds of initiatives launched by Presidents Theodore Roosevelt and William H. Taft early in the twentieth century, was the President's Private Sector Survey on Cost Control in the Federal Government, known as the Grace Commission after its chair, businessman J. Peter Grace. The commission's objective was to demonstrate how the intrinsically superior methods of the private sector might save billions of dollars by eliminating waste, fraud, and abuse.[43] Its 1984 report called for measures straight out of the business community playbook—objectives-based management, goal clarification, better planning, and the development of performance measures—without, however, acknowledging that prior reforms of a similar character had not accomplished much.[44] This particular report generated no legacy of sustained reform activity and no new ideas beyond the activities of the Partnership for Public Service's Private Sector Council (discussed further below).

Reinventing Government

Less-ephemeral American contributions to the public management reform movement were the publication in 1992 of two influential books, the best-selling *Reinventing Government,* by management consultant David Osborne and local government executive Ted Gaebler, and public management scholar Michael Barzelay's *Breaking through Bureaucracy.*[45] With its universal "steer-don't-row" prescription for "letting managers manage" and canonical principles of administration that echoed those of an earlier era, **reinventing government,** reinforced by Barzelay's proclamation of a postbureaucratic paradigm of governance that relied on coordination and trust, was to provide the text for a new generation of reform-minded activists. These activists included officials associated with the Clinton administration's National Performance Review (NPR)—later renamed the Alliance for Reinventing Government—and the practitioner-dominated National Academy of Public Administration, a congressionally authorized organization of elected fellows and a professional staff.

Beginning in 1993 Vice President Al Gore led an eight-year effort, popularly known as Reinventing Government, to create a federal bureaucracy that was smaller, cheaper, and more effective. "[T]he people who work in government are not the problem," Osborne and Gaebler had proclaimed; "the systems in which they work are the problem." [46] To which Gore added, "The Federal Government is filled with good people trapped in bad systems: budget systems, personnel systems, procurement systems, financial management systems, information systems. When we blame the people and impose more controls, we make the systems worse." [47]

The initial report of the NPR put forward four major themes:

- "cutting red tape," including streamlining the budget process, decentralizing personnel policy, reorienting the inspectors general, and empowering state and local governments;
- "putting customers first," including demanding that service organizations compete and using market mechanisms to solve problems;
- "empowering employees to get results," including decentralizing decision-making power, forming a labor-management partnership, and exerting leadership; and
- "cutting back to basics," including eliminating programs, investing in greater productivity, and reengineering programs to cut costs.[48]

Other specific initiatives of the NPR oriented to performance improvement included:

- benchmarking, which may be described as the process of continuously comparing and measuring against other organizations to gain information that will help an organization to significantly improve its performance. As part of the NPR Federal Benchmarking Consortium, federal agencies work together to benchmark against world-class private companies and high-performing government agencies.
- reinvention labs, which are innovative organizations or activities (there were 325 as of February 1998) that were established to test or prototype radical new ways of doing business and to share their ideas, successes, and lessons across government.[49] No specific rewards or waivers are associated with lab status.
- performance partnerships, in which federal, state, and local governments and service providers jointly design programs and measure program performance. The putative benefits include consolidated funding streams, devolved decision making, and reduced paperwork, with the implied reward of additional funding and other unspecified benefits financed by the increased efficiency.[50]

In addition to these more or less purposeful, high-profile initiatives, the NPR recognized and endorsed governmental improvements of many kinds, such as interagency partnerships, improved human resource management, reducing internal regulations, improving travel management, procurement reform, improvement in support systems, downsizing, fiscal accountability, managing for results, transforming organizational structures, and improving information technology.

The American "reinvention movement" was managerial in its ideological orientation, but it placed far less emphasis on market-mimicking reforms such as competitive contracting with the private sector.[51] Reinvention-inspired reforms instead employed strategies emphasizing the "liberation management" theme of managerial deregulation, quality improvement, employee empowerment, and managerial entrepreneurship. Moreover, as Guy Peters has noted, "Perhaps the one defining feature of reinvention is a disregard of some of the conventions associated with traditional public administration and an associated desire to rethink government operations from the ground up." Peters continues:

RULE OF LAW

Legal Issues in Reinventing Government

In 2003 the state of Maine, in an example of a "reinventing government" reform, enacted the Dirigo Health Reform Act, which went into effect January 1, 2005. The act created a public-private health insurance program that offers lower-cost health plans to self-employed individuals and to employees of small businesses. Under the program, the state enters into contracts with private health insurance carriers and competes with current health plans to offer coverage to employees who work at least twenty hours per week. Employers cover as much as 60 percent of the cost of the premiums, and employees pay the remainder. The state provides premium subsidies on a sliding scale to program participants with annual incomes less than 300 percent of the federal poverty level. The state offers employers subsidies to encourage the participation of employees who meet certain criteria.

Illustrating how the rule of law intervenes in management decision making, representatives of insurers sued the state over its estimate of the assessments, or savings offsets, collected from insurers. The law is meant to reduce charity care and bad debt for insurers, which are required to return the savings to the state in offset payments. Differences in interpretation of the legislature's intention with respect to how the savings offsets are calculated led the act's original proponents to propose a $2.7 million offset. The five-member Dirigo board appointed by Gov. John Baldacci then came up with a figure of $136.8 million, but it was reduced by insurance super-

"The deregulatory movement differs from the widespread use of market models in Europe in part by not having any clear substitute for the rules and hierarchy that are being abolished by reform" and that were intended to ensure democratic control and accountability.[52]

Joel Aberbach and Bert Rockman argue that some NPR recommendations were unarguably good ideas, but their main thrust consisted of slogans and nostrums that could not withstand critical scrutiny. They note that although many of the inefficiencies and restrictive rules NPR decried were legislatively mandated, NPR largely ignored the need for legislative

intendent Alessandro Iuppa to $43.7 million. A later disagreement between the state and the insurance provider over the size of "an experience adjustment payment" led the state to select a new insurance provider.

The Maine Supreme Court on Thursday ruled 5–1 to uphold a "key funding mechanism" in Gov. John Baldacci's (D) Dirigo Health initiative, through which assessments are issued to insurers based on savings generated by the program, the AP/Portland Press Herald reports. Savings-offset payments are among "the most contentious elements of Dirigo," according to the AP/Press Herald.

Former Insurance Superintendent Alessandro Iuppa calculated that the program . . . generated $44 million in savings during its first year. The Maine Association of Health Plans and two other groups sued over the savings figure, arguing that it included additional categories of savings that state lawmakers had not considered when they approved the program. The state argued that the Dirigo board and Iuppa had the expertise to interpret and apply the state Dirigo Health Reform Act. . . .

Justice Donald Alexander, the only dissenter, said Iuppa needed specific criteria to estimate the disputed figure. "Reasonable people do differ, and differ geometrically, in guessing at the meaning of the 'cost savings' provision. And the statute provides no guidance as to how these differences may be resolved," he said.

State Rep. Anglin Treat (D), who helped promote the passage of legislation that created Dirigo Health, said the decision "validates the system we have in place, and it gives us a great deal of encouragement and hope that in moving forward we can continue to expand this program." Baldacci health care adviser Trish Riley said the provision of the law that was in dispute likely will be changed by the Legislature this session. (AP/Portland Press Herald, 6/1).

Source: "Maine Supreme Court Upholds Dirigo Health Funding Mechanism," *Kaiser Daily Health Policy Report,* June 5, 2007, http://www.kaisernetwork.org/daily_reports/rep_index.cfm?hint=3&DR_ID=45363.

reforms, deemphasizing the role of Congress. As for successes, they cite NPR claims concerning "more contracting out, streamlining the hiring process, use of various devices to gauge agency customer opinion and respond to it, greater and more effective use of information technology, streamlining some aspects of procurement, and attention to a variety of internal agency management reforms." [53]

The one feature that was clearly NPM-inspired—Performance-Based Organizations (PBOs), promoted by the Clinton administration as an effort to imitate Great Britain's Next Steps reform—failed to make more than minor inroads on the status quo. The reasons are instructive and have to do with the rule of law. As Andrew Graham and Alasdair Roberts note, the separation of powers meant that "an influential third party—Congress—threatened to complicate negotiations over the content of annual performance agreements." Regarding funding predictability, performance agreements required commitments to budgets for the period covered by the agreements, but future Congresses cannot be bound by the decisions of a sitting Congress. Provisions restricting the termination of chief operating officers for other than performance-related reasons failed because Congress "may not limit the ability of the President to remove appointees, unless those appointees exercise quasi-legislative or quasi-judicial functions that require some independence from the administration." [54] The three PBOs that were created—the Patent and Trademark Office, the Air Traffic Organization (whose services, once considered an "inherently governmental function," were viewed differently by the Clinton and Bush administrations, as described in chapter 5), and the Office of Student Financial Assistance (which was later plagued by scandal)—were denied the kinds of flexibilities that Thatcher could achieve virtually by fiat.

Supporting critical assessments of reinvention, Judith Lombard notes, is that in 1994 Congress, at the administration's behest, amended the Government Employees Training Act of 1958 to change the legal purpose of government training from "training related to official duties" to "training to improve individual and organizational performance." Also, in compliance with administration directives, the Office of Personnel Management reorganized and cut its staff by 50 percent; abolished many midlevel positions; reduced personnel in its training policy, procurement, information technology, financial management, and human resources functions; closed many of its field offices; and privatized its nationwide training and investigation programs. Congress, in typically American fashion, stepped into the vacuum and, beginning in the mid-1990s, began to manage training resource allocations and operations by statute. Unfortunately, as Lombard notes, private sector trainers turned out to lack the special skills needed in federal appropriations, personnel, ethics, and procurement law. A net loss of administrative capacity was the result. [55]

Although the manifestations of the Clinton/Gore Reinventing Government movement have been effaced, the movement lives on as a United Nations-sponsored entity, the Global Forum on Reinventing Government.[56] With the participation of American professional associations, it is one of numerous international forums concerned with the administrative sciences and with public sector reform.

HOW THE WORLD WORKS

Disappearing Initiatives

"They come, they go," say veteran civil servants of the succession of reform initiatives to which they are subject. The day before George W. Bush was to be inaugurated as president of the United States in January 2001, the Web site of the National Partnership for Reinventing Government posted the following announcement.

The National Partnership for Reinventing Government has come to an end, but government reform continues. We thank the Government Printing Office's Federal Depository Library Program and its partner, the Government Documents Department, University of North Texas Libraries, for archiving this website exactly as it appeared on January 19, 2001. NPR's mailing address, phone numbers, and staff e-mail addresses are no longer active.

Source: See http://govinfo.library.unt.edu/npr/index.htm for the archived Web site.

The Government Performance and Results Act

Congress, rather than the executive branch, was responsible for a more durable American public management reform. The **Government Performance and Results Act** (GPRA), enacted in 1993 largely on the initiative of conservative Republicans and signed into law by President Clinton, is now a routine aspect of public management at the federal level and a building block of America's expanding practice of performance management at all levels of government.[57] The act requires each federal agency, in cooperation with Congress and in coordination with the budget process, to formulate forward-looking performance plans and to conduct performance evaluations using agreed-upon performance measures.

The GPRA is intended less to change the administrative status quo than to improve the way it works. John Rohr sees the act as an example of traditional legislative preeminence within the American separation of powers: "By law it requires nothing less than close cooperation between executive branch agencies and congressional subcommittees, first in developing goals and plans and then in evaluating performance measured against these same goals and plans." [58] The Government Accountability Office (GAO), which was tasked with monitoring GPRA's implementation, was not pleased after a decade of executive branch effort, viewing with concern the less-than-whole-hearted use of performance information in government-wide or agency management.[59]

The effects of Congress's decision to enact and implement GPRA has resulted mainly in the proliferation of products on paper: the output of a seemingly far-reaching technocratic effort, with copious documentation, to create plans, performance standards and targets, the measures by which to assess their attainment, and their links to the budget.[60] These paper products are generated in response to GPRA's process requirements. Much of the evaluation of the reforms focuses on the technical adequacy of these paper products and of the processes underlying them. A 1998 review of actual strategic plans by the General Accounting Office focused almost entirely on textual criticism.[61] There was no reported effort to determine if the plans had affected thinking or decision making or if new insights into program administration, achieving efficiency, or the adequacy of priorities had occurred as a result of the planning effort. Little interest has been shown in the changes in priorities or operations brought about by the act.

A 1998 report on GPRA by the National Academy of Public Administration, an early supporter of the act, clearly implied that, on the whole, support for it among senior and midlevel public managers, including those in OMB, and in Congress was uneven and lukewarm. Successful implementation of GPRA, the report's authors warned, will require "sustained political commitment and enthusiastic leadership and visible involvement by senior management. . . . All elements must be actively and constructively involved to achieve the level of consensus required" for accomplishing the Results Act's purposes.[62] The GAO testified before Congress that the federal government

> is a long way from successfully implementing the statutory reforms Congress enacted during the 1990s. Widespread financial system weaknesses, poor record keeping and documentation, weak internal controls, and the lack of cost information have prevented the government from having the information needed to effectively and efficiently manage operations or accurately report a large portion of its assets, liabilities, and costs. There are problems in clearly describing the relationship between performance expectations, requested funding, and consumed resources.[63]

In many ways, the two major U.S. reform initiatives of the 1990s, GPRA and NPR, had opposite implications for public administration. GPRA's success depended on a professionalized bureaucracy able to make detailed objectives, plans, and measurements in consultation with legislative committees. NPR, as an example of what Paul Light calls "liberation management" or "let managers manage," tended to distrust the kind of professionalized administration and complex administrative machinery required by GPRA and its engagement with Congress. The net result of the two reforms has been that changes in the U.S. bureaucracy have been slow and incremental. The status quo will prevail unless an agency enjoys unusually strong and sustained executive leadership or the agency's continued existence is threatened by Congress or the administration and must change to eliminate the threat.

George W. Bush's Management Agenda

In yet another of America's uncoordinated public management reforms, this time initiated by the executive branch, in 2001 the Bush administration promulgated the **President's Management Agenda** (PMA). The agenda emphasized performance-driven, outsourced management in all federal departments and agencies.[64]

PMA was little publicized by the administration and only slowly acknowledged by the professional field as a serious initiative—few outsiders had been involved in its design. The Bush administration's approach required the quarterly scoring of all federal agencies against PMA priorities and other administration initiatives. It also featured the use of the Program Assessment Rating Tool (PART) to evaluate individual program accomplishments in coordination with preparation of the president's annual budget.

The Bush administration's distinctly Thatcherite hostility to the traditional civil service was further demonstrated in its insistence that the permanent personnel of the new Department of Homeland Security be exempt from most civil service rules and managed toward the goal of performance, a model it intended to extend to the entire federal government. These reforms, instituted as part of the legislation creating DHS, have been described as "the most dramatic shift in the direction of management flexibility seen since the founding of the civil service system," a reflection of the New Public Management philosophy underlying the Bush administration's PMA.[65] Congress also authorized the Department of Defense to implement the new National Security Personnel System, which was similar to that of DHS in expanding managerial prerogatives and emphasizing employee performance as a basis for pay increases.

These reforms have been quite controversial among unions representing public sector employees and legislators with significant numbers of public employees in their districts. Because of America's separation of powers, many Bush administration personnel reforms were initially stymied by federal court rulings in response to lawsuits filed by federal employee unions and remained in litigation throughout his presidency. Following the midterm elections of 2006, the Democratic Congress also began to question the administration's undermining of employee bargaining rights.

An important feature of the PMA is the Executive Branch Management Scorecard, which ranks the twenty-six major departments in terms of their performance on five government-wide management initiatives: strategic management of human capital, competitive sourcing, improved financial performance, expanded electronic government, and budget and performance integration. According to the initial scores—green for good, yellow for "needs improvement," red for failure—almost all departments were failing on all five initiatives; these scores apparently reflect the judgments of budget examiners in the OMB. No greens and only a few yellows were awarded; the rest were red. The administration updated the scores quarterly. By mid-2008, a majority of the indicators were green, and very few reds remained. The administration claimed that better management was the reason, but critics argued that the scores were politically manipulated and lacked transparent justifications.

Another, more significant change introduced by the Bush administration was the reformatting of the federal budget. The president's budget was organized by agency, not by the fifty-year-old budget function codes. Accountability was to be centered on departments, not policy areas that cut across agencies. Further, each agency chapter highlighted its major activities and included an assessment of the agency's performance in meeting the objectives of selected programs.

Most experts on public management reform viewed the Bush initiative as a political strategy rather than as a serious effort to change the way the American government is managed or to improve allocative efficiency or performance.[66] As with the NPR, they expected little change in agency capacities or cultures. In the view of Colin Talbot, the Bush administration approach appeared to be in a spirit opposite to Britain's NPM because it was based on old-fashioned, top down, command-and-control systems that used performance information to obtain political leverage over departments and agencies to get them to do what the elected administration wanted.[67]

The many initiatives aimed at reforming government have had surprisingly little political salience, that is, importance to the general public, which has barely been aware of most of them. The one result that anyone did notice was the reduction in the federal workforce by one in seven workers, or 350,000 employees over the course of the Clinton administration (a level that began to rise again during the Bush administration). What is popular with the media and the public is the discovery of incidents of waste, fraud, and abuse—a major scandal, corruption, gross incompetence, tax collectors who abuse citizens, the failure of a major procurement program, or administrative stupidity. But these political disasters may also be political opportunities for public managers to gain attention and convey a sense of urgency for a reform agenda, for seeking solutions to long-range problems, and for overcoming resistance to change.

PUBLIC MANAGERS AS CHANGE AGENTS

The public management reform initiatives discussed in the preceding section have consequences that cumulate to the complex amalgam of structural constraints and enablements and organizational cultures and subcultures that make technically rational management a virtual impossibility. As already noted, however, many public management reforms are internally generated. They are initiated not by legislators, judges, or elected executives but by public managers in departments, bureaus, and offices at all levels of government. Although these reforms may become as politicized as those initiated by external actors, most remain well below the radar screens of partisan politics and achieve visibility primarily among experts and specialists. Some of these managerial reforms are primarily structural; others are intended to alter organizational cultures. Some reforms use restructuring as a means of achieving cultural transformation, as the discussion in chapter 6 suggested.

Strategies for Public Organization Reform

Whether because of external pressures or internal factors, public managers as change agents necessarily engage their organizations as distinctive social and political entities. To do so may seem daunting in that changes to the status quo generally elicit resistance if not outright intransigence. Organization theory is especially relevant to issues concerning this kind of change. Organization theory is "the study of formal structures, internal processes, external constraints, and the ways organizations affect and are affected by their members."[68] Viewed from this perspective, organizational change almost inevitably involves all three dimensions of public management, requiring public managers to employ craftsmanship in identifying strategies, including structural changes, that will alter organizational cultures toward acceptance of the changes and the adoption of new practices.

CONCEPTS IN ACTION

The Value of Early Change

Prof. Steven Kelman of the Kennedy School of Government is credited with introducing substantial change into the federal government's procurement organizations as an Office of Management and Budget official during the Clinton administration. He subsequently organized a study of the change processes he helped initiate. Success breeds success, he concluded, so aim for early, modest successes as a way of opening up greater possibilities for change.

[E]arly wins promote change support . . . not just because of the inherent quality of the experience but also because of feedback [and because they] promote subsequent successful experience through operation of the self-fulfilling prophecy, and this successful experience in turn promotes support. . . . [T]he fate of a change process may get established early on even more than advocates of the early-wins prescription realize. During people's first experiences, the change effort can get propelled on a self-fulfilling path dominated by positive feedback, . . . or it can move on a path to extinction dominated by negative feedback . . . whereby support will eventually get snuffed out. Thus the stakes for early experience with a change are high.

Source: Steven Kelman, *Unleashing Change: A Study of Organizational Renewal in Government* (Washington, D.C.: Brookings Institution Press, 2005), 134.

A large and diverse literature offers approaches to organizational reform and change that draw on organization theory and, explicitly or implicitly, emphasize one or more of the three dimensions of public management: structures, organizational culture, and managerial craftsmanship. But the processes whereby public managers translate opportunities for, as Mark Moore has put it, "creating public value" into actual performance vary widely and inevitably reflect individual managers' distinctive types and perceptions, from systematic and analytical to intuitive and experiential.

Organizational reforms typically require cultural change, and public managers must be willing to invest considerable time and effort in translating structural changes into durable changes in how agencies do their work. They should not be pessimistic about the possibilities, however. Alan Wilkins and William Ouchi have argued that the prospects for changing organizational cultures are not overly daunting.[69] Organizational cultures, they suggest, are seldom so deep that they are immutable or entirely resistant to change, and it is a mistake to think that every organization has a strong culture that will prove resistant to change or adaptation. So long as the basic "paradigm" or the basic foundations of the culture are not threatened, so long as shared commitments are respected, a lot of change can occur.

Following are some approaches to organizational reform that public managers might employ depending on their own inclinations and assessments of the prospects for success.[70]

Using Structures to Promote Change

In chapter 5 it was argued that structures matter to organizational performance. Thomas Hammond showed, for example, how an organization's structure influences its basic agenda and how it pursues its agenda. By changing the basic processes of deliberation and decision making, structural change is a tool for promoting organizational reform.

Economist Susan Rose-Ackerman writes: "[A]n organizational designer must find the mixture of behavioral rules and discretion which assures that officials will be both competent and motivated." The balance between rules and discretion can favor the professionalism of public officials, especially when there is considerable *a priori* uncertainty concerning appropriate behavior. Among the pitfalls of this approach, Rose-Ackerman argues, is that "strong professional norms may themselves conflict with agency goals, and the similar background and training of officials may lead them to band together to suppress criticism of their colleagues or, in extreme cases, to further collusive attempts to undermine agency purposes." [71] The organizational designer may instead choose to emphasize rules that prescribe behavior, forestalling agency problems but at the risk of organizational rigidity and the stifling of professional motivation.

But, Rose-Ackerman points out, "Neither group considers the possibility of relying on direct financial incentives to induce good performance," which requires that the institution of fixed pay scales be abandoned, as in the pay-for-performance schemes discussed in chapter 6. The efficacy of such incentives depends, however, on the ability of officials to make clear connections between financial rewards and the kind of behavior that is to be rewarded. "[E]ven seemingly quite straightforward cases may contain pitfalls which make the design of a workable economic incentive system difficult. . . . [T]he design of a workable scheme of economic incentives depends on the measurability of output, on who can observe this output, and on the risk aversion of officials."[72] If officials are risk averse—if they wish to avoid any possibility that their pay will be affected by factors beyond their control—and if the relationship between behavior and performance is poorly understood—as it often is when those delivering services to clients may be uncertain of how and to what extent clients may actually achieve the desired outcomes—then reliance on professionalism may be superior to economic incentives. In other words, the cultural dimension may come into play.

Public managers often use internal reorganization to accomplish the political objective of reallocating authority and influence within their organizations and at the same time increasing their own authority. As secretary of state in the Bush administration, Condoleezza Rice often reorganized subordinate agencies to increase her control over policymaking and implementation.

Rice reorganized foreign aid administration at the State Department, she said, to improve the coordination of foreign aid programs and increase the accountability of the Agency for International Development (AID). At the time, AID described itself on its Web site as "an independent federal government agency that receives overall foreign policy guidance from the Secretary of State." That description has not changed, even though Rice created an office to coordinate the foreign aid activities of the State Department by, among other things, being responsible for their budgets. To consolidate her control, she appointed the same individual to head the new office and to direct AID, thereby reducing AID's independence. Many AID employees complained that the professionalism of the agency was being compromised to serve an ideological agenda; Rice's appointee was a well-known opponent of U.S. assistance for birth control programs.

Overcoming Resistance to Change

Public managers may be fortunate enough to preside over well-run organizations that need little more than maintenance of operations combined with skill at troubleshooting. More often than not, however, public managers want to make changes in their organizations, promote innovation, introduce best practices, or improve operations in some way. As suggested earlier, they may be under pressure to do so by forces in their external environments. But they may wish to initiate change for reasons of their own or even because they feel an ethical imperative to do so: Why can't we do better?

A well-known approach to change is known as **organizational development.** Organizational development (OD) is concerned primarily with reducing the psychological barriers that can obstruct needed change. The foundational assumption of OD is that organizations do not change unless the people in those organizations do.

A useful application of OD to the public sector is that of David Carnevale, who emphasizes several points. First, individual mind-sets or paradigms, ways of seeing and interpreting the world, "establish the degree of resistance to change." Employees' beliefs help them make sense of things but also may inhibit learning and adaptation. Employees may be reluctant to change their beliefs because they are reluctant to be, or appear to have been, wrong. Within an organization, beliefs are the basis for the "informal organization," the organization's culture. Public managers who would change their agency must, therefore, somehow change people's beliefs. But people may resist such efforts because they fear change. It may be rational for them to do so, especially if they have been victimized in the past by poorly designed and ineptly executed change efforts.[73]

The solution is managerial craftsmanship and, in particular, according to Carnevale, transformational leadership. The OD approach to it relies on **process consultation** that is profoundly democratic in spirit: facilitated group problem-solving. The individuals who are to change are expected and encouraged to participate in formulating the solutions. An objective is to engender trust between change agents and those who must change. It is extremely important not to betray the process, but, if it does not work, it may be necessary to fire people.

The OD approach is quite different from approaches based on principal-agent logic, which rely on structural incentives to align preferences, as in well-designed performance-management systems where rewards and punishments are attached to meeting targets or performance goals. The process consultation approach might well be used to design and garner support for the kind of economic incentives discussed in the preceding section.

Industrial sociologist Patrick Dawson takes a different approach to organizational change. "Conventional change models, based on a situational or contingency framework," argues Dawson, probably including OD in his criticism, exhibit a "tendency to downplay the processual [continuous in a definite manner] and ongoing nature of large-scale operational change." **Processual change** is a dynamic process linking the period when a general awareness of the need to change emerges and the period when new work practices are fully operational, that is, when new cultural roots have matured. "Between these two periods lie the complex non-linear processes of change which may comprise a range of different activities and events." [74] Different actors within the organization are likely to have varying views as to how these processes of change should be characterized.

The change process is affected by the context of change (past, present, and future), by the politics of change (largely those created by external actors) and by the substance or type of change. Their interrelationships are so complex and literally ongoing, however, that neat, rational, prescriptive solutions to the problem of organizational change are certain to be misguided. Dawson writes: "The redefinition of working relationships draws attention to the power-politics of organizational life and the influence of personal and group agendas on the process of organizational decisionmaking. The substance of change and the context in which it takes place also act as determinants on the speed, direction and outcomes of change." [75]

CONCEPTS IN ACTION

Process Consultation for Pay-for-Performance Reforms

Teachers' unions often resist pay-for-performance reforms because they undermine traditional bases for promotion: credentials and seniority. Denver's public school system employed a version of the process consultation concept to gain teacher and administrator support for just such a reform.

ProComp is a groundbreaking compensation system that links teacher pay to the school district's instructional mission. Designed in a partnership between the Denver Classroom Teachers Association and Denver Public Schools, ProComp has received national attention because it rewards teachers for their professional accomplishments while linking pay to student achievement. ProComp was designed by the DPS-DCTA Joint Task Force on Teacher Compensation. The task force included five teachers, five administrators and two citizens appointed by DCTA and DPS. The compensation plan grew out of the Pay for Performance Pilot, a four year project in 16 Denver schools from 1999–2003 that measured teacher objective setting and student growth. Among the findings from the pilot was that teachers who set the highest objectives could have a positive influence on student achievement.

The system accomplishes the following goals:

- Rewards and recognizes teachers for meeting and exceeding expectations
- Links compensation more closely with instructional outcomes for students
- Enables the district to attract and retain the most qualified and effective teachers by offering uncapped annual earnings in a fair system

ProComp has four components that allow teachers to build earnings through nine elements:

Knowledge and Skills—Teachers will earn compensation for acquiring and demonstrating knowledge and skills by completing annual professional development units, through earning additional graduate degrees and national certificates and may be reimbursed up to $1,000 for tuition.

Professional Evaluation—Teachers will be recognized for their classroom skill by receiving salary increases every three years for satisfactory evaluations.

Student Growth—Teachers will be rewarded for the academic growth of their students. They can earn compensation for meeting annual objectives, for exceeding CSAP growth goals and for working in a school judged distinguished based on academic gains and other factors.

Market Incentives—Bonuses can assist the district and schools in meeting specific needs. Teachers in hard to serve schools—those faced with academic challenges—can earn annual bonuses. Bonuses will be available to those filling hard to staff positions—assignments which historically have shortages of qualified applicants.

Source: Denver Public Schools Professional Compensation System for Teachers, http://denverprocomp.org/.

Crafting Innovation

Some approaches to organizational reform emphasize the personal skills and strategies of the public manager as an innovator. "Is it possible to create an innovative organization?" asks Robert Behn. "Is it possible to persuade every individual in the organization that an important part of his or her responsibility is to develop and implement new ways of achieving the organization's purposes?" His answer is yes, if public managers will take the ten hints he offers for creating an **innovative public organization,** hints that are oriented primarily toward motivating street-level workers to become agents of change. For an innovative organization, two conditions must be fulfilled: "[Public managers] must convince frontline workers that the leadership supports the line; and, they must ensure that frontline workers understand the big picture." [76]

Behn's approach—which is conceptually similar to Gary Miller's approach to public sector leadership discussed in chapter 7—is based on what he terms an "implicit contract" with frontline workers that involves a "gift exchange" (see chapter 6): "You produce for us, we'll look after you." Behn's ten hints are summarized in Box 9.1.

In the final analysis, cautions Behn, "Creating an innovative public agency is itself a task of innovation. Each innovative organization will be different. It will be pursuing different purposes. Or it will be pursuing them in a different organizational context, within a different political environment, or within different legal constraints. There is no recipe for replicating an innovation." [77]

Box 9.1

TEN HINTS FOR INVOLVING FRONTLINE WORKERS IN CREATING INNOVATIVE ORGANIZATIONS

CONDITION 1: Frontline Workers Know that Leadership Is on Their Side

Hint 1: Be immediately responsive to requests for improved working conditions (or when they ask for a new photocopier, produce it).

Hint 2: Support mistakes (or sit next to the first honest innovator who is called before a legislative committee).

CONDITION 2: Frontline Workers Understand the Big Picture

Hint 3: Create an explicit mission and related performance measures (or give people a real reason to be innovative).

Hint 4: Broaden job categories (or don't let each individual do only one narrow task).

Hint 5: Move people around (or don't let workers think they need learn only one job for life).

Hint 6: Reward teams, not individuals (or find ways to beat the formal performance-appraisal and promotion systems).

Hint 7: Make the hierarchy as unimportant as possible (or at least walk around without an entourage).

Hint 8: Break down functional units (or don't let the procurement guys tell everyone "no").

Hint 9: Give everyone all the information they need to do the job (or don't let the overhead units hoard the critical data).

Hint 10: Tell everyone what innovations are working (or have frontline workers report their successes to their colleagues).

Source: Robert D. Behn, "Creating an Innovative Organization: Ten Hints for Involving Frontline Workers," *State and Local Government Review* 27, no. 3 (1995), www.govleaders.org/behn_innovation.htm.

RULE OF LAW

Legality of Organizational Change Strategy

In 2005, pursuant to the National Forest Management Act, the secretary of the U.S. Department of Agriculture (USDA) issued rules that employed changes in formal processes to induce cultural change in forest management practices in the field. "The rules . . . cut back on requirements for environmental reviews and safeguards for wildlife, and limited public participation in the development of management plans for individual forests. Instead, they broadened the power of forest managers to decide whether mines, logging operations, cell phone towers or other development would be appropriate uses of forest land." (This rule was mentioned in chapter 5 as an example of an enabling structure.) Environmental groups sued the USDA in an effort to block these changes. On March 30, 2007, Judge Phyllis J. Hamilton of the federal district court in San Francisco struck down the 2005 rules. A private corporation could have pursued this organizational change strategy without hindrance. The U.S. Forest Service could not because of the rule of law. Excerpts from her decision follow.

[O]n January 5, 2005, the USDA published the 2005 Rule, which it asserted was the result of the public comments received through April 7, 2003, to the 2002 Rule. By the USDA's admission, the 2005 Rule "embodies a paradigm shift in land management planning." . . .

Defendants Case characterize the rule as "carr[ying] forward the major themes" contemplated in the 2002 Proposed Rule insofar as the plans under the rule "will be more strategic and less prescriptive in nature." Defendants argue that "the final 2005 Rule did not add anything new, but reduced complexity from the [2002 Rule]." According to defendants, the USDA simply moved details contained in the 2002 Rule to the Forest Service Manual and Handbook. They argue that the "practical effect . . . of this change in location of these standards is minimal at best." According to defendants, the shift was made to give the Forest Service greater flexibility in management. . . .

Plaintiffs, however, claim that the 2005 Rule constitutes a significant departure from prior rules. Plaintiffs take particular issue with the rule's elimination of species viability and diversity requirements, the increased discretion on the part of local agency officials, and the new role that science plays in agency decisions. . . . According to plaintiffs, the 2005 Rule is unprecedented in that, unlike the 2002 Rule, it allows the logging level set in the forest plan to be changed at the local responsible official's discretion at any time and does not require a plan amendment or revision. They also contend that the 2005 Rule allows the prior monitoring program to be altered ministerially; whereas, under the 2002 Rule, the program was to be developed with public participation. . . .

The court concludes that injunctive relief is required. . . . The matter is remanded to the USDA for compliance with the APA, ESA, and NEPA, as discussed above. In particular, the agency must provide notice and comment on the 2005 Rule as required by the APA since the court concludes that the rule was not a "logical outgrowth" of the 2002 Proposed Rule. Additionally, because the 2005 Rule may significantly affect the quality of the human environment under NEPA, and because it may affect listed species and their habitat under ESA, the agency must conduct further analysis and evaluation of the impact of the 2005 Rule in accordance with those statutes.

Source: *Defenders of Wildlife v. American Forest and Paper Association,* C04-4512PJH, and *Citizens for Better Forestry v. U.S. Department of Agriculture,* 05-01144PHJ, http://www.earthjustice.org/library/legal_docs/nfma-decision-3-30-07.pdf.

Recognition and Rewards

A virtue of the Reinventing Government movement was the attention directed to the management of public organizations at all hierarchical levels through the emphasis on reinvention laboratories. Such attention was aimed at increasing the visibility of less-glamorous but nevertheless laudable innovations by conferring special status and bureaucratic leverage on public managers who "cut through red tape," exceeded customer expectations, and unleashed the innovative spirit and skill of their employees.[78] Similar in intent were the Clinton administration's "Hammer Awards," acknowledging agencies and managers who had reinvented successfully (a total of 1,378 were made before Clinton left office) and "Plain Language Awards" to individuals who carried out the public's business in clear, understandable English.

The reinvention laboratories and similar initiatives encouraged public managers to employ the tools of managerial craftsmanship, such as the adoption of best practices, reframing, and working from the ground up, to improve agency operations and performance. Similar encouragement can be created by overhead agencies concerned with budgeting, financial management, and human resources management, or by senior managers' efforts to inject a change/improvement orientation into the deliberation and decision-making processes of subordinate managers. Both the earlier PPBS and the more recent President's Management Agenda, for example, were driven into agency deliberations by OMB and into bureau deliberations by the planning and budgeting offices at the departmental level.

Other useful **recognition activities** include the ongoing Ford Foundation/Kennedy School of Government Innovation in American Government Program, which represents itself as "a significant force in recognizing and promoting excellence and creativity in the public sector." [79] The program is under the auspices of the Ash Institute for Democratic Governance and Innovation at the Kennedy School, which, among other things, supports the Government Innovators Network, a portal to "a marketplace of ideas and examples of government innovation." [80]

HOW THE WORLD WORKS

Buzzwords to Avoid

In its tips to potential applicants for an Innovation in American Government Award, the Kennedy School of Government recommends against overuse of words in the following list. Once a term has acquired the status of an overused buzzword, its further use becomes inadvisable.

Avoid overused words, such as:

- benchmark
- community-based
- customer-based
- empower/ment
- facilitate
- inputs
- integrated services
- need-based
- oriented/orientated
- outcomes
- ownership
- paradigm
- partnership
- preventive/preventative
- self-sustaining
- streamline
- unique

Source: Ash Institute for Democratic Governance and Innovation, "Tips and Samples," http://innovationsaward.harvard.edu/Tips.cfm.

Another recognition activity is the effort by the National Academy of Public Administration to facilitate public management reforms at the agency and program level. A 2007 Excellence in Government conference in Washington, D.C., discussed "New Tools for Implementing Most Efficient Organizations (MEOs)." [81] Other such activities include those of the Council for Excellence in Government, which sponsors awards for inspiring public service; Govleaders.org, "a free on-line resource designed to help government managers cultivate a more effective and motivated public sector workforce"; the numerous professional associations of public officials, including elected officials and administrators, which are useful sources of information and links to resources for managers of agencies, functions, and programs; and the Partnership for Public Service's Private Sector Council (PSC), which "connects experts from America's top corporations with federal leaders to confront government's key management challenges on an operational level" and annually recognizes outstanding public servants and outstanding leaders in both the public and private sectors.[82]

Unfortunately, there is little evidence that the many types of recognition activities change the behavior of public managers in any systematic ways or that the award-seeking that occurs leads to general improvements in government performance. Only a few years after receiving an award, some organizations have abandoned the reform or innovation that was the basis for it, perhaps because the change agent has moved on or conditions giving rise to the change have themselves changed.

DO PUBLIC MANAGEMENT REFORMS IMPROVE GOVERNMENT PERFORMANCE?

Evaluating public management reforms is a dauntingly tricky business. Consider the following characterizations of the Reinventing Government initiatives. From Theo Toonen and Jos Raadschelders's vantage point, the reform represented a rediscovery of classical American public administration.[83] What was new with Reinventing Government was its pro-government spirit as against what went before, especially during the Reagan administration. In sharp contrast, Ezra Suleiman sees the same reforms as a landmark in combining sweeping scope with an anti-government agenda associated with the political right wing. "[A]t the heart of the reinvention-of-government movement lies a skepticism about the existence of a public-service institution."[84]

These conflicting assessments only highlight the difficulty of appraising public management reform in polycentric, ambiguous America and the influence of reform on the actual practice of public management and performance of government.

Public management experts generally agree that insufficient effort is devoted to evaluating public management reforms, especially those that attract the greatest level of political attention. The reasons for this insufficiency are understandable, however. Large-scale reforms often encompass a large number and variety of features that belong to more than one dimension of public management and involve multiple levels of government and multiple entities, all interacting in complex ways. Empirical data of sufficient richness are often difficult or impossible to obtain. Nevertheless, some investigators have attempted ambitious evaluations, albeit usually focused on particular features of the reforms. A great many other researchers have studied a wide variety of the quotidian, processual policy and organizational changes that are constantly occurring at all levels of government. Following are summaries of some of the more successful of these two types of research studies.

James R. Thompson's efforts to evaluate large-scale public management reforms are among the most conceptually ambitious. Thompson undertook to summarize the accomplishments of the NPR. Noting that "NPR incorporates a diverse set of interventions directed toward the achievement of multiple objectives," he summarized and classified its objectives as of first, second, and third order of importance, depending on the extent of internal changes required in agency operations.[85] Of first order importance, and requiring the least extensive internal changes, were downsizing the federal workforce, reducing administrative costs, and reforming administrative systems. Of second order importance were decentralizing authority within agencies, empowering frontline workers, and promoting cultural change in agencies.

Of third order importance, and requiring the most extensive internal change, were improving the quality of public services and improving the efficiency of agency work procedures.

Using this framework, Thompson conducted a broad review of the results of the NPR in terms of satisfying these objectives based on surveys of public employees conducted by the Merit Systems Protection Board. "A broad conclusion," he says, "is that while some success has been achieved with regard to lower, first-order goals, only limited progress has been made toward critical, higher, second- and third-order reinvention objectives. Thus, downsizing and cost reduction objectives have been substantially achieved . . . but there is no evidence of any significant, systemic improvement in quality of services or culture." [86]

Christopher Pollitt and Geert Bouckaert have undertaken perhaps the most broadly ambitious attempts to evaluate the kinds of public management reforms that characterized the era of managerialism.[87] The research has included a broad range of public management reforms across a number of countries and draws on a wide variety of qualitative reports, evaluations, and assessments.

Pollitt studied the consequences of reforms generally associated with the New Public Management. He summarizes the intended results of NPM reforms as follows:

- savings (reduced budget appropriations);
- improved processes (faster, more accessible complaints procedures, quicker turn-around times for repairs or the processing of licenses; "one-stop" service locations; and the like);
- improved efficiency (better input/output ratios, such as more students graduating per full-time equivalent number of staff; the same number of drivers' licenses issued with 20 percent fewer staff);
- greater effectiveness (less crime, poverty, functional illiteracy, homelessness, drug abuse, gender or ethnic inequality; more new jobs created, more contented and trusting citizens); and
- an increase in the overall capacity/flexibility/resilience of the administrative system as a whole (through the recruitment and training of more skilled, more committed public servants).[88]

Although success stories can be found for each of the types of reforms mentioned above, general conclusions are difficult to draw. The evidence often consists of anecdotes, good stories, and "sound bites," rather than systematic, well-documented improvements. Trade-offs are common: Improved client processing, for example, may have occurred at the expense of serving more difficult or needy clients. Says Pollitt: "Cases where there is unmistakable evidence of management reform producing more effective government action are rare." [89]

In later work, Pollitt and Bouckaert identify four levels of results: operational results, process results, improvements in organizational/institutional capacity, and progress toward a goal. Efforts to draw conclusions from available evidence are difficult, Pollitt and Bouckaert say, because "[t]here is often contradictory information and an ambiguous, changing reality." [90] With their work in mind, one might well argue that obtaining unambiguous measures of performance is conceptually almost impossible. There are too many things to measure in a complex reform, and these measures are likely to be highly interrelated. It may be impossible, moreover, to develop any kind of meaningful causal understanding of measured performance.

CONCEPTS IN ACTION

Evaluating Tony Blair's Public Management Reforms

Two British scholars undertook an ambitious evaluation of Prime Minister Tony Blair's public management reforms initiated following the Labour Party's electoral victory in 1997. The applicability of these particular research methods and findings to other countries and other public management reform programs is open to question, but the optimistic tone of the findings is of considerable interest.

In this paper, we have provided the first comprehensive empirical test of the impact of a public management reform program on organizational performance. We have used both external and internal performance measures and a multiple-informant survey, and most of our explanatory variables were derived from several survey items. In these respects, our evidence is stronger than that provided by many other studies of the relationship between public management variables and organizational performance.

Our empirical results across different dimensions of organizational performance indicate that the most effective elements of Labour's reform package are likely to be planning to meet national standards (through information systems and local target ownership), organizational flexibility (via a combination of innovation and leadership commitment), and user voice in service provision. Our results also offer tentative support for service improvement strategies of devolution of service responsibility and non-financial incentives for staff. By contrast, top-down target setting and contestability in local service markets do not appear to be promising routes to public service improvement. The broad pattern of the evidence is consistent with arguments that innovative organizations that use performance management systems and work closely with service users are likely to achieve high standards. More broadly, our analysis provides further evidence that management matters, and that reform can make a difference to public service performance.

Source: Richard M. Walker and George A. Boyne, "Public Management Reform and Organizational Performance: An Empirical Assessment of the U.K. Labour Government's Public Service Improvement Strategy," *Journal of Policy Analysis and Management* 25, no. 2 (2006): 387–388.

President Bush's PMA drew greater attention from evaluators as its consequences began to be felt. The Performance Institute's Center for Government Performance Management, Mercatus Center at George Mason University, Reason Foundation, GAO, Citizens Against Government Waste, and the IBM Center for the Business of Government, among others, have provided continuing surveillance and evaluation of PMA reforms. University-based researchers also began studying these reforms, as described in chapter 8.

COMPSTAT: A CASE STUDY OF ORGANIZATIONAL REFORM

Soon after being appointed commissioner of New York City's police department by Mayor Rudolph Giuliani in 1994, William J. Bratton launched a reform initiative that came to be regarded as so successful in reducing crime that the initiative's core elements were replicated in state and local government jurisdictions across the country. In 1996 this initiative, known as **CompStat,** received an Innovation in American Government Award from the Kennedy School of Government even though it had been operational for only two years. The Kennedy School Case Program published a teaching case, "Assertive Policing, Plummeting Crime," that is widely used in public affairs education.[91] The Harvard Business School also published a teaching case on Bratton's leadership of the NYPD.

What Is CompStat?

Commissioner Bratton and his deputy for operations, an experienced, tough-minded police official named Jack Maple, initially adopted the kind of strategy that had been successful for Bratton when he headed the New York Transit Authority. They rejected the community policing strategy of Bratton's predecessor in favor of a strategy involving four elements: quality-of-life policing, assertive policing, devolving authority to the precincts, and the psychological touch. Bratton publicly announced an ambitious goal of reducing crime in New York City by 10 percent in the first year of the new strategy, thus putting himself on the hook for achieving a specific outcome.

The reform initiative encompassed all three dimensions of public management: structural (precinct commanders were given real authority to devise and implement strategies appropriate to their jurisdictions, whether in pursuit of citywide anticrime strategies or in response to local "hot spots" and special problems); cultural (changing the police mind-set from law enforcement to crime prevention); and craft (Bratton and Maple and their subordinates became personally and intensely involved in managing all aspects of the CompStat process).

That process centered on the creation of an accountability mechanism. Bratton and Maple decided that they wanted to see the numbers on crime by precinct on a regular basis. They quickly discovered, however, that crime statistics were compiled quarterly and primarily for the FBI Uniform Crime Statistics, but not for managerial purposes. The top command staff began to demand weekly crime statistics by precinct. But how could these figures be used as an accountability mechanism? Bratton and Maple devised a series of specific steps:

- make precinct commanders provide briefings to command staff on the weekly numbers, maintain up-to-date pin maps, and prepare acetate overlays;
- bring borough commanders and precinct commanders together on a regular basis to discuss the numbers, and address detailed questions;
- set an ambitious goal on which all personnel would focus: reduce crime by 10 percent;

- institutionalize the weekly meetings: the maps were computerized and became the basis for the discussions, and the name CompStat was coined, referring to computerized comparison crime statistics;
- establish a tradition of tough, unsentimental interactions, resembling interrogations, between command staff and precinct commanders;
- encourage the process to trickle down, so that precinct commanders and tour commanders began using the process; and, as experience was gained,
- refine the model, focusing on:
  accurate and timely intelligence on crime;
  rapid deployment of policing resources;
  effective tactics for addressing problems; and
  relentless follow-up and assessment.

That four-part model became a mantra among CompStat's NYPD leadership.

It is important to note how internal restructuring was essential to this system. As criminal justice scholar Paul O'Connell puts it,

> An emphasis was placed upon the realignment of organizational resources. An ambitious reengineering effort shifted the department from being a centralized, functional organization to a decentralized, geographic organization. A number of centralized, functional units were broken up with their functions (and personnel) redistributed to new geographically decentralized units (precincts). Functional specialists were placed under the command of newly defined geographic managers, thereby moving decision making down the organizational hierarchy.[92]

Bratton and Maple were skilled craftsmen in translating their new structures and processes into changes in the NYPD culture, a fact that is easy to overlook in replicating the model elsewhere. For example, when challenged if he knew how much time it would take to produce pin maps, Maple responded, "Yes, 18 minutes." He had run a test of the process in the busiest precinct. Faced with complaints that precinct commanders and their staffs would be unable to attend meetings, command staff set an earlier time so that no one could claim unavailability. The 10 percent goal for crime reduction was set after weeks of experience with meetings and with detailed analyses of the crime statistics. An extraordinary amount of operational knowledge, credibility, and self-confidence was needed to make the weekly sessions effective. In O'Connell's view, "The department was seeking to institutionalize the organizational learning process." [93]

Why Did CompStat Succeed in New York City?

The answer to the question of why CompStat was so successful with the NYPD is fundamental to replicating the CompStat model not only in other jurisdictions but also in other areas of service delivery. But description alone can only suggest reasons for CompStat's achievements in New York.

HOW THE WORLD WORKS

Bratton's Resignation

His reform of New York City's police department a resounding success, his picture on the cover of a national magazine, William Bratton soon found himself unemployed. Bratton would have been well advised to keep a low profile given Mayor Rudolph Giuliani's temperament, but Bratton's own assertive temperament would never have permitted that. The leadership styles of the two men were apparently incompatible.

Police Commissioner William J. Bratton announced his resignation yesterday after 27 months in office, ending a tenure that saw a precipitous drop in New York City's crime rate and a consequent rivalry for the limelight with Mayor Rudolph W. Giuliani that eventually led to the Commissioner's departure. . . .

[Bratton was] the Giuliani administration's most important Commissioner, a nationally known crime fighter whose popularity in opinion polls exceeded that of any local public official, including Mr. Giuliani. . . . Taking over a department that had just been wracked by a damaging corruption scandal, Mr. Bratton, former chief of the city's Transit Police, engineered a series of management strategies that relied on a block-by-block analysis of computerized crime statistics. Aided by a significant increase in the size of the force begun under the previous Mayor, David N. Dinkins, Mr. Bratton steered the department as crime fell to its lowest levels since the 1960's. . . .

Mr. Bratton was almost universally praised by elected officials around the city yesterday, and several of the Mayor's political rivals seized on the resignation to criticize Mr. Giuliani and accuse him of driving out the Commissioner. . . .

Mr. Giuliani and his staff thought that Mr. Bratton was insufficiently deferential to City Hall, and at one point in 1994 took over the operation of the Police Department's public information office, which was seen as a bastion of pro-Bratton publicity.

The Commissioner, who savored his celebrity in the nation's media capital, had made it clear for the better part of a year that he chafed under the intense scrutiny of his boss. Barely a month went by when there was not another report of a job offer from the private sector, and the Commissioner made no secret of his desire to parlay his popularity into a lucrative corporate position.

Source: David Firestone, "The Bratton Resignation: The Overview; Bratton Quits Police Post; New York Gains over Crime Fed a Rivalry with Giuliani," *New York Times,* March 27, 1996.

A number of factors seem to have contributed to the New York City success story, reflecting structural, cultural, and craft dimensions. First, the timely availability of operational numbers (which had to be created from scratch), the implicit use of performance benchmarking across precincts, and the visibility and actionability that the data-based process gave to the problems of crime were at the core of CompStat's success. Second, the increased discretion allowed precinct commanders, which empowered them in ways that they had not before experienced, and the "deregulation" of policing implicit in the notion of "quality-of-life" policing, were the structural enablers of cultural change within the department. Third, contributing as well were the intense scrutiny of precinct operations; the regularity of the meetings; the wearing down of resistance and building up of a new value system, a process undoubtedly helped by the fact that police departments are paramilitary organizations with strong boundaries (everyone inside faces a common mission and a common danger, and there is a chain of command, a system of discipline). Fourth, the objective was unmistakably clear: reduce crime. Everyone could relate to it. Fifth, Bratton, Maple, and Chief of Patrol Louis Anemone were unusual in their toughness, competence, and determination; it is unlikely that police officials of ordinary managerial talent could have succeeded so quickly and so well. Finally, crime was falling anyway, so many factors associated with it could have been moving in the right direction, although it can be argued that CompStat was significant.

Some researchers argued that long-term cycles in illegal drug use, restrictive gun laws dating to the mid-1980s, expanded police departments and prison systems, demographic trends, and the collective influence of family, community groups, and police, not CompStat, were responsible for crime reduction in New York. Criminal justice scholar Dennis Smith and Bratton rebut these claims: demographics—the crime-prone young male population was actually increasing; drugs—no substantial declines in drug use; gun control—decline in gun crimes probably due to the NYPD strategy, not an exogenous reduction in guns; the economy—improvement in city economy followed, rather than preceded, crime reductions.[94]

CompStat's apparent success does not mean that its implementation posed no problems or challenges. Arguably, there were what was referred to in chapter 8 as performance paradoxes.

Quality-of-life policing—that is, focusing on those crimes and misdemeanors that affect large numbers of citizens directly or indirectly—led to visible and invisible increases in police misconduct, increased tensions with the minority community, and declining confidence in the police department on the part of the general public as high-profile police misconduct and the general adversary relationship between police and civilians became the norm. Complaints, which rose under Bratton, declined under his successor, Howard Safir, as did crime. But the general level of controversy rose. The implication, not clearly substantiated by any performance measures, was that there was a trade-off between a "broken windows" strategy (which punishes routine violations in order to heighten citizen awareness of law enforcement) and police misconduct especially, toward minority young people. Former New York City mayor David Dinkins claimed that the Giuliani administration believed that the ends justify the means, and the public was coming around to the view that police brutality was tolerated.

Certain performance measures, such as gun confiscation, tended to have a corrupting influence on police officers, some of whom, it was said, became unjustifiably more aggressive. Street crime officers were expected to confiscate at least one gun per month. Said one officer: "We frisk 20, maybe 30 people a day. Are they all by the book? Of course not; it's safer and easier to just toss people. And if it's the 25th of the month and you haven't gotten your gun yet? Things can get a little desperate." [95]

Giuliani and Safir responded to such claims with a barrage of statistics, all of which seemed to refute the assertion that the NYPD was out of control. One of the authors of the broken windows strategy said that criticism amounted to an "ideological attack on a successful philosophy of policing." Increases in "misconduct" were held to be a statistical artifact because there was now a Civilian Complaints Review Board, more cops were on the street making more arrests, and few complaints were substantiated.

The statistics seemed to have little effect on public perceptions, however. Even Bratton weighed in against the mayor, also not a surprise given the circumstances of his resignation.

Will CompStat Work Anywhere?

Bratton claimed you can "CompStat" practically anything and raise performance. Some researchers cautioned that the realities of attempting innovation and change in an urban police department or in any other large bureaucracy are more complex than the arguments of CompStat's advocates acknowledge. According to criminal justice specialists James Willis, Stephen Mastrofski, and David Weisburd: "A review of the research literature suggests that the glowing accounts of CompStat's success are fueled mostly by studies that rely on anecdotal evidence or concentrate on the NYPD, the nation's largest and, by any measure, most exceptional police department. To date, there has been little systematic analysis of CompStat in U.S. police departments of different size and organization. Very little is actually known about how CompStat operates." [96]

The Police Foundation conducted a study of three city police departments that had attempted to replicate CompStat: Lowell, Massachusetts; Minneapolis, Minnesota; and Newark, New Jersey. According to the study, "CompStat's creators and advocates present it as a way to transform sluggish, unresponsive police organizations into focused, efficient, and smart organizations." [97] The basic transformational elements are:

- Motivated employees who are guided by a focused mission, disciplined, and stimulated by a rigorous system of direct and personal accountability;
- Organizational nimbleness, or a capacity to deliver resources to places and at times that will nip problems in the bud;
- Organizational decisions informed by knowledge of the problems that require attention beyond that provided by normal organizational routines and facilitated by sophisticated electronic information management and data-analysis systems;
- Problem-solving that reflects collaboration and exchange of ideas among members of an organization, draws on research dealing with successful practices, and acknowledges the experience of other agencies; and

- Decision making in an atmosphere that has an elevated tolerance for risk and encourages new approaches to persistent problems.[98]

The study's fieldwork suggested that the alterations to fundamental organizational structures that would facilitate these changes, and that occurred in New York City, were not fully in place in the three police departments it examined. The study reached a number of other findings.

First, "although Minneapolis provided some relief from the calls-for-service apparatus that dominates the organization of patrol work in most urban police departments, this framework remained virtually untouched by CompStat reform. Indeed, in Newark, rapid response to calls for service was a key element in top leadership's performance agenda for the department. This calls-for-service apparatus is the principal means by which the predominantly non-crime aspects of police work become part of a police department's workload (Mastrofski 1983)." [99]

Second, "organizational flexibility was achieved by one or more of the following: (1) ad hoc changes in who did what usually without altering fundamental job assignment routines, such as officers' shift assignments, (2) district taxi squads not bound by permanent shift assignments, or (3) department-level task forces." Therefore, although "these CompStat programs came to grips with the challenge of organizational flexibility[, they] were unable or unwilling to alter the fundamental constraints that largely determine work schedules and allocation of personnel." [100]

Third, district commanders, in particular, found that CompStat "produced a profound change in the nature of their work as managers. Before CompStat, middle managers did not routinely and proactively pore over reports and scan maps to familiarize themselves with crime problems and identify crime trends. This became a daily imperative, due in no small part to the accountability mechanism to which these activities were so closely tied. . . . This focus on identifying hot spots is, of course, one of the more important objectives of CompStat, which seemed fully realized at these sites." However, "[i]nterest in areas and problems, and the attention accorded them, usually disappeared as soon as crime levels declined and the next hot spot arose. . . . 'Relentless' follow up really meant focusing on a hot spot only until it was no longer hot. This, of course, greatly weakens the capacity of an organization to learn much about the long-term effects of any intervention." [101]

The authors conclude:

> CompStat at these sites did markedly energize middle managers to do something about crime, but in many respects, the pattern that evolved mimicked the reactive forms of policing about which advocates of strategic problem solving have complained. CompStat seemed to engender a pattern of organizational response to crime spikes in hot spots that was analogous to the Whack-a-Mole game found at fairs and carnivals. Moles pop up randomly from holes in the game board, and the object of the game is to whack them with a paddle before they submerge. A premium is placed on responding quickly rather than monitoring problem holes continuously to try to discern patterns in the eruption of moles.

> The pressures on managers to come to the CompStat meeting with problems identified and solutions already implemented were tremendous. Further, managers tended to be reluctant to volunteer "helpful" suggestions for fear that they would create problems for the person whose feet were being held to the fire of accountability lest their colleagues return the favor when their turn arrived. Most of these commanders, moreover, were not in the habit of engaging in free-flowing debate because they had not been socialized to a problem-solving culture that exalts criticism as a means to improve the quality of management decisions. Theirs remained a culture in which the earliest socialization experiences onward emphasized the importance of following orders and deferring to rank. Managers in our three sites seldom sought the input and ideas of law enforcement personnel in other agencies or other professionals outside the department. It was even more rare for them to resort to researchers and their studies. Thus, the solutions selected tended to be parochial, that is, they relied on what those in the agency regarded as tried-and-true methods. CompStat also failed to alter the low tolerance for risk that pervades the culture of police agencies and leads to parochial decision making.
>
> There is . . . an inevitable tension between promoting heightened accountability for outcomes and engaging in the experimental risk taking required to find effective methods, between individual accountability and teamwork, and between organizational flexibility within districts and organizational flexibility between districts. There is a zero-sum element [one party's gain is another's loss] to these paradoxes, making it impossible to maximize both sides. That does not mean that police organizations are doomed to failure, but it does mean that trade-offs of this sort will be inevitable. The art is in finding the best compromises for each organization's circumstances.[102]

The study of how CompStat worked in Lowell yielded similarly interesting insights. CompStat's implementation

> placed greatest emphasis on mission clarification and internal accountability. Members of the department had a strong sense of the department's crime-fighting goal, and district commanders felt highly accountable for identifying and responding to crime problems. Holding officials responsible for attaining valued objectives embraces existing attributes of bureaucracies that are goal oriented and organized hierarchically. Those elements that did not fit easily with existing bureaucratic structures were much less developed. The department was unable or unwilling to shift substantially toward geographic operational command, flexibility, data-driven analysis, innovations in problem solving, or external accountability. The collective benefits of existing bureaucratic structures—formalization, routine, and functional specialization—make them difficult to surrender for the promise of uncertain gains.[103]

Further, CompStat's "reinforcement of the bureaucratic hierarchy of policing stifles creative problem solving approaches. CompStat . . . was in good part a response to what was seen as bureaucratic dysfunction in the New York City Police Department. However, . . . CompStat itself may also be prone to bureaucratic dysfunction, though of a very different type than that which spawned the program."[104]

Will CompStat work in any kind of agency? The above discussion suggests that implementation of a public management reform that, at first glance, seems relatively straightforward is bound to be problematic even when the settings are in fundamental respects the same. When the settings are different, as they are in child protection services, public school systems, or counterterrorism operations, the problems are sure to multiply. Some considerations that bear on the success of replication are whether the following conditions are met:

- repetitive operations;
- ease of assembling the chain of command in one location;
- hierarchical managerial control;
- adequate resources;
- adequate, timely data;
- political support sufficient to withstand criticism and opposition; and
- local talent sufficient for the intense demands of the process.

Those who advocate the use of CompStat-like procedures to, for example, manage illegal immigration and border protection might want to proceed with great care in the light of these conditions.

In summary, CompStat will not "work" anywhere, in any jurisdiction, or with any public service unless considerable care is taken to replicate those features of CompStat that were operative in the NYPD. But policy and service improvements may well follow from the aggressive use of operational data by managers, by "relentless follow-up," and by other actions that were part of the CompStat model. If the goal is cultural change, however, then public managers are well advised to attend to the details of the model, fitting it to its context with great care.

REFORM AS A POLITICAL PROCESS

In recent years, dissatisfaction with the status quo and impulses to fix the government have often taken the form of bureaucracy-bashing. As William Gormley has noted, "Legislators, chief executives, and judges have beaten up on one another. Even more frequently, they have beaten up on bureaucrats. Not to be outdone, federal bureaucrats have beaten up on state bureaucrats, who in turn have beaten up on local bureaucrats." [105] This kind of punitive reformism, as Gormley notes, is in the Madisonian spirit of checks and balances, which make tension and conflict inevitable in American politics and in public management.

Chronic dissatisfaction with the status quo has its costs, however. An ill-tempered electorate can become surly and cynical and endorse actions that are thoughtlessly misdirected or mindlessly punitive. Public anger toward government can provoke action by elected officials that is hasty, ill-considered, or opportunistic. Meritorious bond issues, ballot initiatives, and tax increases may be impossible to pass; tax caps, term limits, appropriations with restrictive provisions, hiring freezes, denial of appointments, and other antigovernment measures may be approved with little consideration for their consequences. Public discontent need not have a specific justification, however. Regimes of ordinary competence are also condemned and frequently replaced simply because they become emblematic of "bureaucracy" or of a tiresome status quo: a convenient scapegoat for candidates for office and frustrated voters.

HOW THE WORLD WORKS

The Downside of Reorganization

In an interview podcast in June 2008, Michael Chertoff, secretary of the Homeland Security Department, complained about the frequent reorganizations of his department by Congress.

"Every time Congress mandates a reshuffling of the boxes, that tends to set us back," Chertoff says. "Whether people believe this is the perfect organizational set-up or not, the one thing I can tell you is you can't grow a plant by tearing up the roots every six months. And I hope the next secretary gets the benefit of some stability to really let things flourish before they start to monkey around with the organizational chart."

Source: Homeland Security Inside & Out, http://homestation.typepad.com/hlsinsideandout/2008/06/interview-with.html.

With the ground constantly moving under their feet, public managers may be tempted merely to hunker down: to mollify critics, avoid provocative actions, and manage defensively so as not to jeopardize their careers. The toll on the morale, creativity, and sustained attention to effective service of civil servants can be high. The administrators of public policies face pressures that test and often defeat even the most skilled among them while seeming to reward reactive and self-seeking opportunists. But the result, ineffectual public management, is seldom acknowledged as a consequence of reform, rather than as a justification for it. Vigorous and far-seeing administration is only infrequently the product of reform, and not for long, because the shadow of future reprisals for bungling hangs ominously over the present.

The news is not all bad, however. Whether motivated by pressures from external sources such as legislatures and powerful stakeholders or by their own desire to improve organizational performance or to strengthen policy control over subordinate officials and offices, public managers may use their own internal authority to become agents of organizational change. Public managers may redesign processes of deliberation and decision making, introduce new administrative technologies or abolish old ones, introduce new "best practices," reallocate responsibilities, create new positions not requiring legislative authorization, issue guidelines concerning performance of tasks and functions, or introduce new information technologies and communications methods. Their chances of succeeding may be higher if their reforms remain below the political radar, because a controversial change may invite legislative scrutiny and intervention.

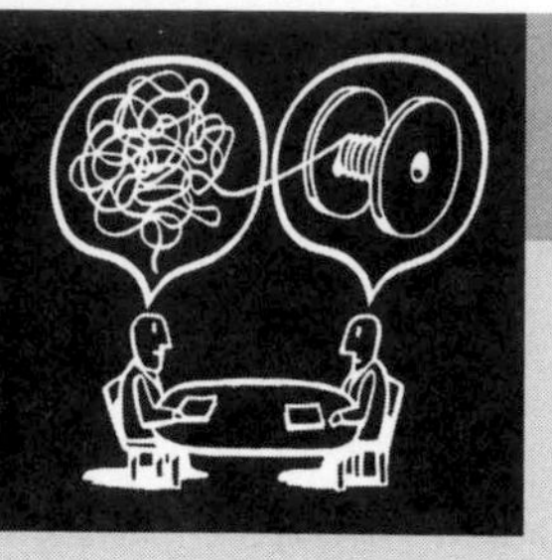

CONCEPTS IN ACTION

NASA Reforms Contributed to Tragedies?

A series of reforms intended to make the National Aeronautics and Space Administration (NASA) more efficient and responsive to changed circumstances may have increased the likelihood of the two tragic and consequential space shuttle accidents.

In interviews, a cross-section of scientists, engineers and historians of technology universally expressed admiration for the efforts of NASA engineers and officials to determine what caused the Columbia disaster and take steps to fix problems. But they also unanimously voiced another thought: with a few important exceptions, NASA has lost its status as a technical powerhouse.

"There's been a steady decay in the competence and the feeling that you're really dealing with scientific peers," said Dr. Van Allen, who with his group at the University of Iowa has sent instruments on mission after mission with NASA over the decades.

Reliance on outside contractors has left personnel at NASA centers like the Goddard Space Flight Center in Greenbelt, Md., and the Marshall Space Flight Center in Huntsville, Ala., with little hands-on expertise. "They don't really know what's going on," Dr. Van Allen said. "They do what they are supposed to, in a very narrow sense, on a day-to-day basis."

Devastating assessments come not just from scientists who were present at the program's creation, and who still carry a special pride for the inspired daring of those early days. Daniel Baker, who led a space sciences laboratory at Goddard from 1987 to 1994, said that in the 1990's, when NASA cut some of the last in-house programs that let young engineers and scientists build satellites themselves, the technical decline slid from steady to precipitous.

"I think that's disastrous," Dr. Baker, now director of the University of Colorado"s laboratory for atmospheric and space physics, said. "NASA has lost some of its nerve, maybe some of its sense of purpose."

Scientists said that the agency's original sense of mission and can-do spirit had largely given way to a civil-service culture, with a maze of bureaucratic rules, overlaid by a risk-averse approach that permeated NASA after the Challenger explosion in 1986. As a result, these experts said, it was difficult to attract ambitious young talent.

Source: James Glanz, "Loss of the Shuttle: Bureaucrats Stifled Spirit of Adventure, NASA's Critics Say," *New York Times,* February 18, 2003.

At times reform seems to represent change for its own sake, its methods poorly related to its goals, but the inclination to improve the status quo, whether by external or internal actors, is to be expected. If citizens insist, as Americans do, that they are sovereign, and if they differ among themselves as to what the public good requires, then candidates for elective office will compete vigorously to win control over the powers of the state to tax, spend, and regulate economic activity. Moreover, public managers are, if circumstances permit, likely to be proactive toward their responsibilities and opportunities. In Herbert Kaufman's famous study of federal bureau chiefs, all of them were proactive, goal oriented, willing to buck the tide.[106] In fact, they were chosen for those qualities. In addition, Kaufman notes, others in their political environments will not allow public managers to be wholly passive; they will make demands and expect responses. The resulting uncertainty of administration is an inevitable concomitant of our political practices and, it can be argued, the price we pay for the long-term stability of our governing arrangements.

The positive legacies of public management reform must also be emphasized, however. America has been transformed from a sparsely settled agrarian wilderness into a positive state capable of promoting the welfare and security of its citizens and arguably the most powerful nation on earth. Despite extraordinary complexity—America has more government than any nation in the world—the private, nonprofit, and public sectors; federal, state, and local governments; and executive, judicial, and legislative branches somehow contrive to achieve growth, stability, and worldwide influence in a remarkably diverse society.

Key Concepts

public management reform
spoils system
civil service reform movement
Brownlow Report
Executive Office of the President
New Public Management
managerialism
reinventing government
Government Performance and Results Act
President's Management Agenda
organizational development
process consultation
processual change
innovative public organization
recognition activities
CompStat
quality-of-life policing

Analysis and Argument: Test Your Understanding

Read the article by Carolyn J. Heinrich, "False or Fitting Recognition? The Use of High Performance Bonuses in Motivating Organizational Achievements," *Journal of Policy Analysis and Management* 26, no. 2 (2005): 281–304, which makes an argument concerning the effectiveness of a popular public management reform: using bonuses to motivate public organizations and their employees to improve their performance. If access to the full article is not possible, read the excerpted sections below from the working paper. Then consider the following:

1. Identify the elements of argument in Heinrich's article: claims, reasons, evidence, warrants, and qualifications (and responses).
2. What dimensions of public management, and what particular concepts or ideas within those dimensions, are reflected in this argument?
3. Reflecting on the material covered in this book and in your course, can you think of other arguments (or counterarguments) to complement or respond to the Heinrich article? Construct an argument to support your position.

Lamenting the lack of public confidence in government and calling for the "revitalization" of the public service, the 2003 Report of the National Commission on the Public Service identified ineffective or perverse incentive systems as a deep cause of government underperformance. . . . Quoting a federal government employee, the National (Volcker) Commission report conveyed the strong criticism that "there is no incentive structure, no recognition of hard work . . ." to effectively motivate employees and organizational achievements in the public sector.[107]

Currently, states have the opportunity to compete for high performance bonuses each year in the Food Stamps, Temporary Assistance for Needy Families (TANF), and Workforce Investment Act (WIA) programs; the total amount of bonuses awarded in these programs in fiscal/program year 2003 was $48 million, $200 million and $16.6 million, respectively. . . . As the use of high performance bonuses has expanded, however, concerns are growing about the design and implementation of these systems, the incentives they create for bureaucratic behavior, and their effectiveness in improving program administration and outcomes. . . .

The underlying (agency theory) logic is that the principal determines what is an efficient or competitive level of effort on the part of agents (employees) and then shares some portion of the organizational surplus (in the form of compensation or bonuses) with those employees who supply this level of effort or more. . . . With effort rationally tied to rewards, employees have an incentive to work harder to achieve organizational goals; and with employees working harder, organizational performance should also improve. Another broad finding in this literature is that *higher-powered* incentives attract higher quality employees who are more productive. Incentive power is commonly defined as the ratio of performance-contingent pay to fixed pay, where a stronger link between performance and total compensation is expected to produce a greater incentive to work hard. . . .

[D]istinct from agency theory's emphasis on self-serving, individualistic motives, stewardship theory emphasizes collective goals and public managers who highly value cooperative behavior even when their interests and those of the principal diverge. . . . Public-service motivation diverges from agency theory in asserting that individuals act to contribute to the public good in order to satisfy their personal needs and goals, rather than in response to incentives offered by organizations for performance. . . . [C]hoices in incentive system design have to be made with careful attention to the distinctive characteristics, goals and context of public organizations, including employee culture and relations, the nature of services produced or delivered, the ease and effectiveness with which performance is measured and monitored, and the extent to which environmental factors influence organizational achievements. . . .

In the WIA performance bonus system, the U.S. Department of Labor (USDOL) has set a minimum and maximum amount for performance bonuses awarded to qualifying states—$750,000 to $3,000,000—contingent on the availability of performance bonus funding. If every state/territory was awarded the maximum bonus in a given year, the total bonus allocation would be $156 million, which is less than 5 percent of the total WIA program funding in program year (PY) 2003. In fact, only $16.6 million in performance bonuses were awarded in PY 2003, or less than 0.5 percent of the total training grants ($3,369 million) to states. . . . In the process of making the WIA performance bonus awards, states are asked to indicate how they plan to spend the performance bonus monies that they receive. A review of these proposals for performance bonus uses in the first few years of the WIA program shows that most states propose to invest the funds in making program improvements, either through new initiatives or enhancements to current program infrastructure and services. . . . [I]t seems apparent that states do not create any expectations that the bonuses will be used to increase individual employee compensation. . . . This suggests that WIA employees would probably have to possess a strong public-service ethic or a steward-like interest in achieving the organization's performance goals—or possibly a desire for public recognition related to their own career concerns or ambitions—if the prospect of high performance bonus awards were to have any direct influence on their behavior. . . .

Although these processes and criteria for evaluating state WIA program performance appear to be explicit and uncomplicated in the guidelines published by the DOL, the lack of standardization in processes for establishing performance expectations and lingering doubts about the quality/accuracy of data and methods used in making performance calculations have contributed to risks (or perceptions thereof) that the system will not fairly appraise states' performance. . . .

Both theory and the empirical findings of this study suggest that the design and implementation of the WIA performance bonus system is far from ideal, and that it has likely done little to improve the incentive system and performance of this program (at either individual or organizational levels). The incentive power of the system—in terms of the ratio of performance-contingent funding made available to total funding—is low and declining, and states' proposed uses of the funds do not include bonuses for individual employees, such as increases in compensation or other rewards for exceptional employee efforts or achievements. In addition, empirical analyses showed that participant characteristics affected states' measured performance, such that states serving more disadvantaged individuals (e.g., high school dropouts) were less likely to qualify for a performance bonus. And furthermore, the sizes of the bonuses received by states that did satisfy the basic performance bonus criteria bore no relationship to their performance levels relative to other states, to the extent to which they exceeded their performance goals, or to improvements in their performance over time. . . .

At the same time, theory also suggests that low-powered incentives may still be functional or even desirable in systems where performance is measured with less precision or greater noise, as they may reduce pressures to perform that encourage strategic or "gaming" behavior intended to increase measured performance (rather than the value or impact of the program). In addition, state organizations and their employees might still be motivated to achieve the public recognition associated with being identified as a "high performer," whether due to individual employee career concerns or reputational interests of the organization, which could in turn influence its ability to attract high-performing workers and achieve high performance in the future. It is also possible that although states propose to use bonus funds for program investments rather than individual bonuses, some employees might be motivated by their personal identification with a particular organizational goal or program or their advocacy of a special interest that is supported with the funds (i.e., by public-service motives).

In this regard, probably the most discouraging finding of this study is that public employees can influence states' measured performance by engaging in strategic behaviors such as limiting individuals' access to WIA program services. Findings of other studies . . . indicate that WIA program administrators are aware of (and have acted on) the risks to their organization's performance created by the failure of performance standard negotiation processes to adequately adjust for factors such as client population characteristics and economic conditions. . . . The persistence of these risks, gaming responses, and management expectations for opportunistic behavior unfortunately also make it unlikely (at least in theory) that steward-like relationships will develop (or a public-service ethic will prevail) among employees and motivate them to identify with and work hard toward organizational performance goals. Other research on high performance bonus systems confirms that these experiences are not unique to the WIA performance bonus system. . . . Evidence of these problems in public performance incentive systems is also not limited to U.S. government programs. . . .

The implications of these problems are that recognition and rewards are probably too often (or more often) false than fitting; that is, they are not linked to exceptional performance or performance improvements and are probably not commensurate with sincere efforts to achieve organizational goals. As currently designed and implemented, the incentives generated by high performance bonus systems appear more likely to be "ineffective or perverse," and thus, I conclude that they are not (in their present form) the solution to the public sector motivation and performance problems identified by the 2003 Report of the National Commission on the Public Service.

10 Managing in Three Dimensions

Public managers continuously make judgments: Do I have a problem that requires my time and attention? Is it a routine problem, well within my capabilities and possibly better left to subordinates to resolve under my watchful eye? Or does, or might, the situation present a distinctive challenge, extraordinary in scope and complexity, beyond my ability to resolve on my own? What do I need to know, and do, now? And, by the way, are issues and problems already on the agenda proceeding toward a satisfactory resolution or outcome?

In the public sector, it cannot be overemphasized that even routine problems may be difficult to solve because doing so then requires choices that have controversial political ramifications. Opening or closing a facility such as a drug rehabilitation center or a prison often involves engaging community groups with strong feelings in the matter. The perennial problem of closing obsolete military bases, for which technically rational solutions are relatively easy to formulate, is nevertheless one of the most difficult problems to resolve politically. "Routine" does not necessarily mean "easy." But in the case of the distinctive challenges of public management enumerated in chapter 1, controversy is virtually guaranteed. The consequences of success or failure can make or break, or at least seriously undermine, a public manager or even a political administration, as was the case with Hurricane Katrina.

Consequential situations—routine or extraordinary—will almost always call for decisions and actions that involve more than one of the three dimensions of public management: structure, culture, and craft. Public managers who are unprepared to manage in all three dimensions are likely to be ill-equipped to deal with the kinds of problems that have significant political and programmatic ramifications for their effectiveness and reputations. The reform of policing in New York City was shown to involve all three dimensions of public management: the use of extraordinary craftsmanship by departmental managers to design and implement structural reform and induce change in the values of the police department's rank and file. Such situations are by no means rare.

What does it mean to "manage in three dimensions" as an intentional, ongoing strategy? What kinds of deliberation, decision making, and reflection are associated with three-dimensional resolutions of complex problems? What if resources available for three-dimensional management are lacking or there is opposition to the actions and decisions such management requires? What if three-dimensional management is impossible? These kinds of questions are addressed here.

Consider the following account of a complex public agency transformation and note how all dimensions are in play.

Prior to the mid-1990s, the Veterans Health Administration (VHA) suffered from "a tarnished reputation of bureaucracy, inefficiency, and mediocre care." [1] In 1994 Kenneth W. Kizer was appointed chief executive officer of the VHA and undersecretary for health affairs of the Veterans Administration (VA). Following his departure in 1999, according to a subsequent evaluation, "the VHA has quite possibly outperformed all other aspects of U.S. health care" despite relatively tight resource constraints.[2] "Increasingly, VA performance compares favorably with the best performers in areas where performance is, in fact, measured and performance data are available." [3]

Kizer is credited with being a dynamic policy entrepreneur who was the principal change agent in the VHA's transformation from an organization serving indigent veterans and those with service-related conditions to one providing broader access to high-quality care to veterans in general. An outsider to the VA, Kizer was a physician specializing in emergency medicine who had held several senior positions in California's public health system.[4] In 1995 he promulgated his blueprint for the VHA's future, *Vision for Change.* According to Kizer, "Rapid change is possible in a large, politically sensitive, financially stressed publicly administered healthcare system" if you create and maintain a constant focus on "a clear vision of the future and a coherent transformation plan having concrete and concise goals and performance measures." [5]

A major feature of the plan was to strengthen the VHA's control over health services delivery by replacing four largely ineffective regions, thirty-three networks, and 159 independent medical centers. In their place were created twenty-two Veterans Integrated Service Networks (VISNs), each with its own budgeting and planning authority. They were coordinated from the center so as to ensure resource allocation among networks proportionate to need through the implementation of the Veterans Equitable Resource Allocation (VERA), a capitation-based resource allocation system. With the support of a popular secretary of Veterans Affairs, the VHA overcame congressional and stakeholder skepticism and obtained legislative support for a less hospital-focused, more accessible system of care, including eligibility reform, contractual authority, and enrollment changes. As Kizer put it, "The VISNs had to be created out of whole cloth. . . . [They] are the VHA's chief tools of transformation. In both image and substance, they are sweeping away the old view—prevalent inside and outside the VHA—that it was a kind of public works program in building construction and lifetime jobs. Such a culture of stasis is typical of large bureaucracies, which tend to focus on self-propagation at the expense of purpose." [6] Among the other tools he employed were electronic medical records and a universal access and identification card for patients, to integrate the separate parts of the system.

Kizer also established performance criteria for the VISNs that were, in his view, simple and related to organizational objectives, including patients' satisfaction and compliance with external review criteria. To reduce tensions between VHA headquarters and the VISN directors, the measures were jointly determined. VISN directors are eligible for performance bonuses, and data on VISN performance are disseminated throughout the VHA, increasing competitive pressures for performance improvement (at the cost of some initial demoralization).

At the end of his four-year term, Kizer's transformation came under criticism from legislators and interest groups concerned that the rebalancing of medical care away from hospital-based and chronic treatment toward acute and outpatient care threatened facilities and specialties that provided jobs and important services not elsewhere available, and he was not confirmed for a second term. Two able successors continued the reinvention process until officials of the Bush administration began curtailing VHA authority to conform with its privatization agenda just when the VHA was coming under pressure from the wars in Afghanistan and Iraq.[7]

A 2004 evaluation nevertheless concluded, "Veterans are increasingly satisfied by changes in the VA health system. On the American Customer Satisfaction Index, the VA bested the private sector's mean healthcare score of 68 on a 100-point scale with scores of 80 for ambulatory care, 81 for inpatient care, and 83 for pharmacy services for the past 3 years. Similar improvements have been achieved in each value domain." [8]

As chief executive of the VHA, Kizer made a judgment concerning the need for the agency's organizational transformation and made its achievement his overriding priority. It was a judgment that reflected his personal style, values, and motives; another individual in his position might well have sized up the situation and acted differently. Kizer also grasped the importance of his own leadership to such a transformation, the need to alter the values that constituted the VHA's culture, and how the reorganization could promote cultural change.

Using strategies similar to those of William Bratton in New York City, Kizer reorganized the VHA, devolving responsibility to lower levels and infusing it with purpose, using performance incentives, another structural change. As with Bratton, Kizer's qualities of leadership—a basic feature of his craft—enabled him to build momentum for change among VHA professionals who, although concerned for their personal situations, respected Kizer's professionalism and commitment to quality care for veterans. The professional culture of serving veterans began to respond in a positive way to his leadership skills. Also, as with Bratton, Kizer could not entirely overcome political opposition from those who perceived their interests as threatened by his changes and to whom the big picture of success mattered little, and he was forced to leave his position prematurely. Kizer, like Bratton, left a legacy of achievement through three-dimensional management that not only enhanced his reputation but also provided valuable insights into how others might successfully meet public management's distinctive challenges.

CONCEPTS IN ACTION

Cognitive Dissonance Surrounding the VHA's Success

In his *New York Times* column, economist Paul Krugman discussed the transformation of the Veterans Health Administration in the context of contemporary health care reform debates. Krugman saw an example of a familiar psychological phenomenon discussed in chapter 7: cognitive dissonance.

I don't want to idealize the veterans' system. In fact, there's reason to be concerned about its future: will it be given the resources it needs to cope with the flood of wounded and traumatized veterans from Iraq? But the transformation of the V.H.A. is clearly the most encouraging health policy story of the past decade. So why haven't you heard about it?

The answer, I believe, is that pundits and policy makers don't talk about the veterans' system because they can't handle the cognitive dissonance. (One prominent commentator started yelling at me when I tried to describe the system's successes in a private conversation.) For the lesson of the V.H.A.'s success story—that a government agency can deliver better care at lower cost than the private sector—runs completely counter to the pro-privatization, anti-government conventional wisdom that dominates today's Washington.

The dissonance between the dominant ideology and the realities of health care is one reason the Medicare drug legislation looks as if someone went down a checklist of things that the veterans' system does right, and in each case did the opposite. For example, the V.H.A. avoids dealing with insurance companies; the drug bill shoehorns insurance companies into the program even though they serve no real function. The V.H.A. bargains effectively on drug prices; the drug bill forbids Medicare from doing the same.

Source: Paul Krugman, "Health Care Confidential," *New York Times,* January 27, 2006.

In this concluding chapter, three-dimensional public management is placed in both conceptual and practical perspective. It emerges as a form of deliberation and decision making that views managerial problems from multiple perspectives and formulates strategies that use as many dimensions as the circumstances and the public manager's judgment deem appropriate. Although successful three-dimensional public management may often seem to be a product largely of intuition, such management will be more effective if supported and sustained by processes of deliberation and decision making that engage and utilize an organization's fiscal, material, and human resources in a positive and focused way. Managing in three dimensions does not inevitably mean using all three dimensions to address every issue. It does mean the ability to devise managerial strategies that are more than one-dimensional and, if appropriate, that utilize all three.

This chapter is organized as follows. The next section reviews and elaborates on the overlaps among the three dimensions of public management. Then, the idea of managing in the black—managing in circumstances that call for three-dimensional strategies of action, change, or reform—is described, including a section that delineates a model deliberative process that incorporates three-dimensional analysis and the use of the method of argument. The following section discusses the kinds of conundrums and dilemmas that inevitably confront a multidimensional public manager and then considers circumstances that may be so fraught with difficulties—so many conundrums, dilemmas, conflicts, and constraints—that entrepreneurial strategies must yield to survival or coping strategies. Next, the chapter returns to the role of argument as an aspect of multidimensional public management. After consideration of whether some public managers' jobs are "impossible," two detailed accounts are presented—one in which a public manager failed to manage in the black and one in which a public manager successfully and consistently did so. The end-of-chapter exercise asks readers to use the model deliberative process described in the chapter to analyze the multiple dimensions of the U.S. Postal Service's response to the anthrax crisis in 2001.

OVERLAPPING DIMENSIONS

Most managerial strategies are, as emphasized throughout the book, likely to involve two or more dimensions. Figure 10.1, which is based on Figure 2.1 (page 47), depicts the three dimensions of public management as three intersecting circles. In this depiction, a public management problem might be confined to a single dimension and, as such, may even be a routine problem. Often, however, more than one dimension will be involved. Four possible combinations of the three dimensions are depicted in Figure 10.1. Three involve two dimensions: structure and craft (I), structure and culture (II), and culture and craft (III). The area of maximum overlap—among structure, culture, and craft—is shown in black at the center of the diagram. These overlaps are further explained in the discussion that follows.

Structure and Craft

The dimensions of structure and craft interact with each other in two different ways. Because structures both enable and constrain managerial discretion, the requirements of effective management may vary by legislated or court-ordered agency structures and processes. And deliberation may lead public managers to conclude that internal reorganizations of some kind might further their purposes by clarifying responsibilities, improving the exchange of information, and bringing the right people to the table.

FIGURE 10.1 Public Management's Three Dimensions

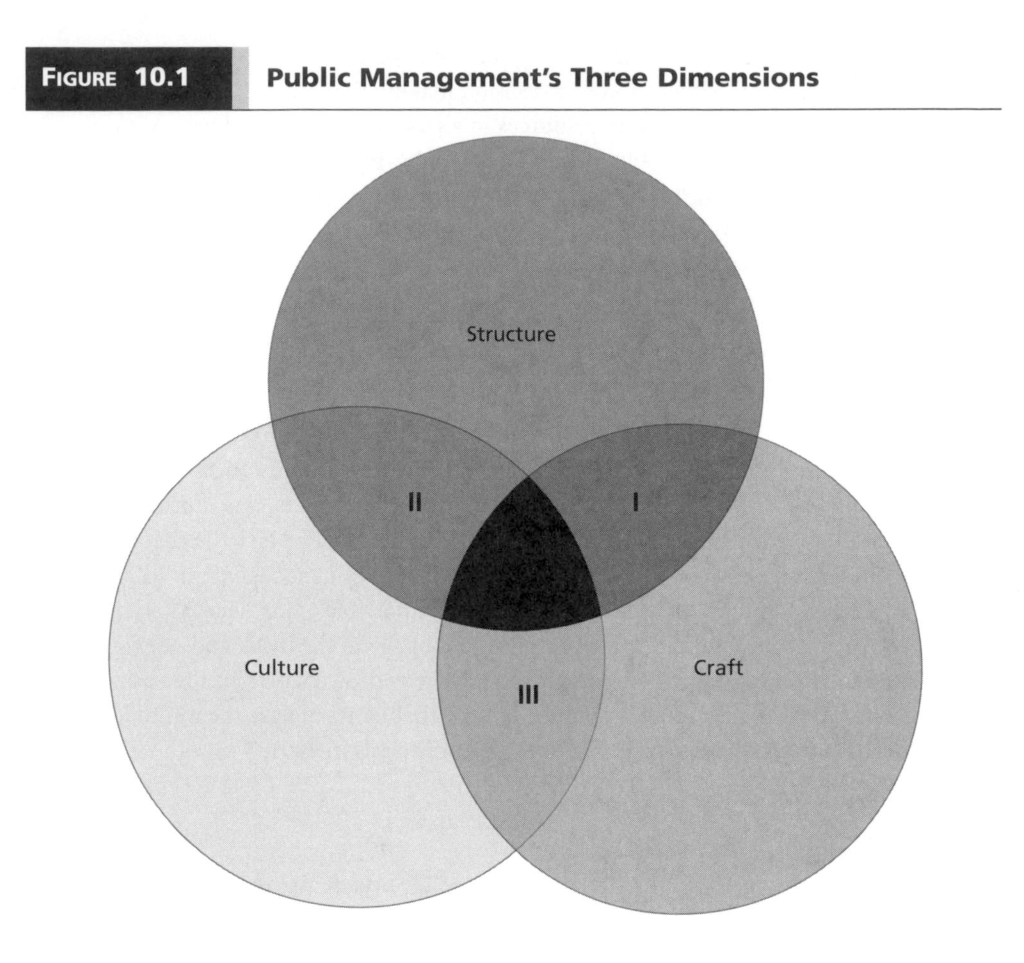

First, consider the way organizational structure influences how managerial craft is practiced. In chapter 1 James Q. Wilson's four types of public organizations—production, procedural, craft, and coping—and Patrick Dunleavy's distinctions among the budgetary structures of public organizations—core, agency, and program—were said to elicit different management strategies. A managerial focus on efficiency is more likely in a production organization, but in coping organizations, public managers are more likely to be engaged in leadership activities: resolving conflicts inside and outside the agency, defining goals, raising morale, and the like. Using similar reasoning, managers in agencies with large core budgets are more likely to be concerned with seeking larger budgets and with the constraints that accompany them than managers in agencies with large program budgets, where resources are passed through to other levels of government.

Managerial craft will be different in still other ways in organizations that take the form of networks or voluntary associations rather than hierarchies. In the absence of leverage afforded by hierarchical accountability mechanisms, managers will of necessity seek to build cooperation among participants by promoting information exchange and the identification of common interests, to provide resources of information and coordination to participants to enhance the benefits of interdependence, and to troubleshoot and solve problems that arise in network relationships. Network and association managers may need to resolve or ameliorate tensions between the priorities of the individual organizations and those of the network. To facilitate decision making and conflict resolution, network participants may create hierarchical mechanisms with which they agree to cooperate. Indeed, some degree of centralization has been shown to enhance network effectiveness by reducing the costs of coordination.

A distinctive set of issues for managerial craft arises in organizations structured as private, nonprofit entities. As noted in chapter 5, the nonprofit form is a tool for organizing collective action. Managers of charitable nonprofits are typically accountable to numerous community interests and values both for legitimacy and for resources. What was termed "third-party government" in chapter 9 involves the extensive and growing use of nonprofits by government to deliver public services. Problems can arise on both sides of the relationship: Public managers face a loss of control and weak accountability, and nonprofit managers face conflicts between the priorities of public agencies providing grants and contracts and the missions and priorities of their own organizations. An extensive literature on nonprofit management explores public-nonprofit relationships in considerable detail.[9]

Second, public managers often exercise their craft by deliberately restructuring their organizations or their relations with other organizations. Or they may advocate legislative authorization for larger-scale and more permanent reorganizations. These reorganizations may be undertaken for any number of reasons: to enable or constrain their subordinates on behalf of organizational or public policy goals; to ensure compliance with policy directives from the political branches or the courts; to promote operational economies or efficiencies; to change processes of deliberation and decision so that they better support a manager's leadership style or learning and information needs (transcending the limitations of organization stovepipes, for example); to create or alter patterns of work and shape organizational work environments; or to change allocations of political influence within the organization. The operative reasons may not be stated as such, however. A political shake-up may be depicted as having greater efficiency as a goal.

Seemingly straightforward applications of managerial craft to employ structural tools to achieve greater efficiency can encounter strong political opposition. Michael P. Jackson, the deputy secretary of the Department of Homeland Security (DHS), drew sharp criticism when he told a congressional hearing of plans to downsize and limit the responsibilities of the Federal Protective Service, the agency that hires contract guards to provide security for nearly nine thousand government buildings nationwide.[10] Jackson said the goal was to bring discipline to the agency's activities, which had been criticized for lack of oversight, and to increase reliance on local police. Legislators objected that such moves would expose federal employees to greater risks of crime and terrorist attacks because there would be fewer guards on-site and employees would have to depend on local police responses to 911 calls. Jackson promised to secure agreements with local police departments to ensure adequate response and employee security.

Structure and Culture

Organizational structures are often the basis for the emergence of identifiable cultures and subcultures. Structural arrangements therefore can contribute to cultural conflict within and between organizations. Public managers can make constructive use of this important interaction between structures and cultures, as when a reorganization changes internal cultures in specific ways that minimize or eliminate conflict. Kizer's consolidation of control over the administration of health services for veterans enabled the transformation of the VHA's culture away from hospital-based care for service-related injuries toward an emphasis on accessible outpatient services of high quality to a wider community of veterans, with measurable results.

The processes by which deliberation and decision making are organized—that is, whether the strategic or policy planning process is transparent, whether policy decisions are reached systematically or in an ad hoc manner, whether deliberation is confined to a few or allows broad participation—also interact with organizational cultures. Such processes can be used to define roles for organizational participants, empowering them, for example, by providing access to forums and opportunities to influence important organizational actions. Legislators like to create specific offices to further constituent interests to ensure that those interests have a place at the decision-making table. Role-defined behaviors become a basis for the formation of cultures: Including policy analysis and program evaluation officials in organizational budget making, for example, enhances the status and influence of these specialized skills in the wider organizational culture.

Insight into the interaction between the structures of deliberation and organization subcultures was provided by Michael Cohen, James March, and Johan Olsen in their famous **"garbage can model"** of organizational choice.[11] In many organizations, participation in the processes of deliberation and decision making may be fluid, and participants opportunistic. Those whose concerns are with putting problems on the agenda vie with those who are determined to "sell" preferred solutions. All participants bring their personal ambitions, motivations, and reputations to the table. The outcome of the deliberation might or might not be related to its original purpose, much less to technical or even political rationality. It will all depend on the mix of "stuff" (garbage) that participants dump into the process (can). Anticipating such possibilities, managers can structure deliberation to minimize them.

A clear example of the interaction between structure and culture is the debate over the 2004 reorganization of three entities in the Interior Department: the Office of the Assistant Secretary for Indian Affairs, the Bureau of Indian Affairs (BIA), and the Office of the Special Trustee for American Indians. The goal of the reorganization was reform of Indian trust management (by law, the Interior Department serves as trustee for American Indian tribal assets) and improving the delivery of services to the American Indian and Alaska Native communities. According to an official summary of the complex statute, the congressionally approved reorganization

> provides a uniform method to pass individual Indian land ownership from one generation to the next—creating a Federal Indian probate code that replaces the multiple individual State laws now governing Indian probate activity. This new law requires small interests in land to pass exclusively to single heirs when there is no will involved. The act provides greater flexibility for individuals and Tribes to consolidate and acquire interests during the probate process. The measure makes the Department of the Interior's Land Acquisition Pilot Program permanent and allows a Tribe, or an Indian co-owner, to request a sale of a highly fractionated parcel of land for the purposes of making that parcel whole under a single owner.[12]

Many Indian leaders saw the issue as a clash between "business culture" and "the culture of Native America." *Indian Country Today* reported that at a congressional hearing,

> tribal leaders, up against management axioms that hold sway from business meetings to board rooms and high government office, stood their ground against the promise of improved services to client tribes. They argued not for a changeless BIA, but for a tribally driven improvement process that won't sacrifice the treaty-based federal trust obligation to business efficiency. . . . Harold Frazier, chairman of the Cheyenne River Sioux Tribe in South Dakota, insisted that local restructuring of the reservation-based bureau agencies is the only path to efficiency with BIA resources. "We lead that way of life that they would never know unless they led it. It's time to take a stand against this reorganization." [13]

One tribal member noted, however, that the reorganization would not standardize tribes; instead, it would standardize the systems tribes work with.

The interdependence of the structural and cultural dimensions is commonly observed in state and local public management. After less than three weeks on the job, Bryan, Texas, police chief Tyrone Morrow announced a reorganization of his department. Three former divisions concerned with patrol, investigations, and administration were combined into two: operations and operations support. The stated purpose was to change a culture in which investigators considered themselves "a step above" patrol officers into one in which the priority would be "boots on the ground" patrolling Bryan's neighborhoods. "We're not going to have egos and people who don't want to play in the sandbox with the others," Morrow said. "We're going to support our field operations to facilitate our primary mission, which is crime control." [14] Accompanying the reorganization were a promotions and reassignments plan that would place Morrow's personnel choices in strategic administrative positions, presumably to reinforce the intent of the reorganization. Concurrently, the former chief of investigations announced his retirement, removing an impediment to cultural change.

Culture and Craft

Public managers may seek to change organizational cultures by using their personalities and skills to inspire behaviors that support the organization's goals. An important function of organizational leadership is to motivate cooperation with organizational purposes through a combination of inducements such as various forms of personal recognition and effective communication of the value to the organization of cooperative behavior. Kizer used reorganization to accomplish cultural change, but his change strategy also included mobilizing support for cultural transformation from policymakers and the effective communication of his vision in various formats and forums.

The Illinois Department on Aging (IDOA) provides an example of how managerial craft can be used to transform an organization's culture. The IDOA is responsible for carrying out the mandates of the federal Older Americans Act of 1965 through the department's Community Care Program (CCR) and Case Coordination Units (CCUs).[15] When Victor L. Wirth assumed the position of IDOA director in 1990, the state of Illinois and its agencies were under severe fiscal stress, the agency's culture emphasized risk aversion and compliance, and relationships among the department, the CCUs, service providers, and aging advocacy groups were hostile. In only a year on the job—he resigned for personal reasons in 1991—Wirth, by the testimony of all relevant stakeholders, successfully refocused his department's operations on client service, induced cooperative relationships with providers, and complied with the governor's budget directives.

Wirth had the advantage of prior experience in IDOA in a number of positions. Observers credit his success as director to maintaining open communications with agency employees and including them in decision making. The theme of these efforts was the need to support street-level workers in providing services to older persons. At the same time, he reduced paperwork by 60 percent to 70 percent by accepting the recommendations of a task force dominated by the CCUs, which had the effect of reducing the emphasis on complying with rules and protocols. According to Wirth, the task force "helped tremendously in drawing the group together because it is the first time the department had ever really come to the CCUs and said, 'Would you be our partners?' "[16] Through these and other measures—he made small structural changes such as combining advisory committees and appointing outside rather than inside chairpersons for these committees—Wirth, unlike his longtime predecessor, used a personal style of deliberation and decision making and his knowledge of the agency to build trust, minimize internal conflicts, and, in the manner suggested by Gary Miller (discussed in chapter 7), induced cooperation around politically necessary goals.

Barbara Koremenos and Laurence Lynn employed game theory reasoning similar to Miller's to analyze the dynamics of the transformation Wirth brought about at IDOA:

> Wirth's problem was noncooperation originating at the top of the agency and institutionalized primarily at the division manager level, from where it was transmitted downward to the field. At lower levels, Wirth had ideological allies whom he could easily mobilize to squeeze the division managers into line. This is not a universal principle of public management, however. In a social service agency where noncooperation originates at lower levels, . . . a better strategy . . . might be the opposite of Wirth's: to recruit middle management to monitor the field and deliver rewards and sanctions sufficient to overcome resistance to change. What works, therefore, will depend on the internal dynamics of the agency.[17]

Wirth's intuition—that leadership could transform the culture of his formerly hunkered-down agency—proved to be highly effective in the particular context in which he found himself. As Koremenos and Lynn point out, in different contexts, and with managers of other types, a different strategy might well succeed and Wirth and his strategy might have failed.

Structure, Culture, and Craft

The need for managerial effectiveness is especially urgent when public managers operate in situations that are extraordinary in scope and consequence. In chapter 1, such situations were called **distinctive challenges of public management.** They can be summarized as follows:

- dealing with issues that lie in part outside one's sphere of authority and influence;
- meeting the often conflicting expectations of powerful stakeholders;
- confronting situations that may arise and begin to spin out of control without warning and before adequate information can be obtained;
- responding to warnings of potential problems for which the costs and risks of various solutions, as well as of doing nothing, are high;
- overcoming the inertia or resistance associated with recalcitrant organizational cultures;
- ensuring the accountability of agents; and
- coping with unanticipated changes in priorities, tasks, or workloads.

Combinations of effective enabling structures, functional organizational cultures, and managerial leadership and skill can result in effective responses to these kinds of challenges. Doing the combining constitutes **managing in the black.**

Overlaps among structure, culture, and craft are necessarily complex and may range from mutually reinforcing to conflictual. In most instances, reorganizing an agency to re-root its culture requires managerial leadership and skill. Moreover, structural and cultural considerations influence the exercise of managerial craft. The scope for individual contributions to government performance depends on the type of organization, the hierarchical position of the public manager within the organization, the nature of the manager's employment contract, the extent of managerial autonomy or independence afforded by the manager's political environment, and the strength and functionality of various cultures and subcultures within and outside the organization.

Effective combinations of public management's three dimensions, therefore, will vary by the specifics of the situation: Structural change may not be necessary, cultures may be functional, and subordinates may be experienced and effective, all of which eases the burden of leadership. Public management positions therefore impose sharply differentiated and widely varying pressures and demands on their incumbents, and managerial craftsmanship must be sensitive to the contexts and resulting challenges of a particular position. Public managerial practice can in no sense be regarded as merely a generic, by-the-book, "one best way" activity.

Diagnosing a situation and making good decisions concerning what kinds of strategies might be appropriate will depend not only on the facts of a situation but also on the public manager's particular temperament and skill set. One manager might decide not to reorganize but to address organizational interdependence through more effective communications, and another might decide that only structural change will provide the capacity to address similar problems that might arise in the future. A manager might be particularly adept at crisis management but less effective in managing day-to-day operations, where a manager with different temperament and skills might excel.

MANAGING IN THE BLACK

How do public managers identify the combination of dimensions that is appropriate to the problem or issue at hand? For many, it is a matter of intuition, not calculation, of instinctively recognizing the importance of managerial direction and leadership, of appropriate organizational arrangements, and of the taken-for-granted beliefs and values of those who are employed at various levels of governance. But, as the discussion of reframing in chapter 7 suggested, intuition may not be a reliable foundation for effective action if it is based on a restricted range of experience or a dogmatic certainty that only leadership or only reorganization or only changing hearts and minds will suffice to solve a problem.

To guard against faulty intuition, in one's self or one's advisers, public managers would do well to incorporate into their deliberations—both their personal thought processes and the formal strategic planning or staff consultation processes they rely on—what might be termed a "model deliberative process" that ensures adequate scanning of a full range of possibilities, drawing on the three dimensions of public management and the method of argument.

A Model Deliberative Process

The basic steps of a **model deliberative process** that supports three-dimensional thinking and action are based on the analytic technique of reframing discussed in chapter 7. The model process examines a situation through multiple perspectives such as the three dimensions that constitute the approach used in this book.[18] Its steps are straightforward.

First, each of the three dimensions is used as a lens through which to observe and analyze the facts of particular managerial situations. A public manager-as-analyst examines the formal structural and procedural aspects of a situation, the facts that reveal an organization's institutionalized values and beliefs, and the potential contribution of managerial style, skill, and judgment.

Second, the manager-as-analyst integrates and synthesizes the insights gained from these three dimensions, addressing questions such as: How might the formal organization enable and constrain individual public managers to further organizational objectives more effectively? Are some classes of structures and techniques likely to be more effective than others in overcoming the specific problems at issue and, if so, why? How does the organization's culture affect the prospects for success of restructuring? What type of leadership and direction will be needed to promote organizational change efforts, both cultural and structural? The manager should draw not only on the broad dimensions of structure, culture, and craft, but also on specific frameworks, concepts, theories, and ideas within each dimension. As described in chapter 3, these ideas can be used as warrants for analyses and arguments.

Third, the manager-as-analyst formulates a strategy, or alternative strategies, to address the particular challenges at hand. Potentially effective strategies may emphasize one, two, or all three dimensions of public management. If employees are likely to see needed change as consistent with their values, cultural resistance may not be a factor. If it is primarily a matter of changing employee commitments, restructuring may not be necessary. If it is a matter of replacing a particular subordinate, then craft alone, a managerial decision, may be all that is needed. Good strategic choices, however, will be grounded on a consideration of how all three dimensions are or might be effectively employed.

Finally, after arriving at this stage through internal analysis and argument, the manager-as-analyst formulates persuasive arguments intended for external consumption to support these potentially effective strategies. Arguments with different emphases might be used in different forums—executive branch budget reviews, legislative testimony, public statements, internal advocacy—to build momentum for the strategy's adoption.

A particular problem in the analytic process—how to distinguish structurally induced behavior, culturally conditioned behavior, and craft-induced behavior—can be approached in the following way. An individual's actions and behavior can be said to be structurally induced if a change in the constraints faced by that individual (frontline employee, professional, or manager) would lead to a change in his or her behavior. Would a reduction in caseloads lead to more effective processing of each case? An individual's behavior can be said to be culturally conditioned if any individual in the agency would probably have behaved in the same way under similar circumstances, and if changing the formal constraints faced by that individual would not inevitably lead to a change in his or her behavior. Suppose that following a reduction in caseloads, caseworkers still process cases in the same way because that is "the way we do things around here." Other aspects of culture include the ethics, values, and motives of individuals in an organization, which may not reflect common approaches of all organizational participants. A manager's behavior can be said to be a manifestation of managerial craft if it is likely that other managers in exactly the same circumstances would have acted or decided differently depending on their personalities, skills, styles, or motives.

Any situation, action, or behavior can reflect one, two, or all three dimensions. A reorganization of agency tasks might lead to changes in frontline employee behavior that are directly task-oriented but not to those elements of task performance that are values-oriented. Moreover, different individuals might balance possible conflicts between task-oriented and values-oriented behavior in different ways, some resisting change in routines or, alternatively, embracing it creatively. These considerations add complexity to three-dimensional analysis, but they also reinforce the need for it. Assumptions that organizational participants can simply be reorganized into having different values, or that values will defeat all efforts at reorganization, or that individual styles, skills, and personalities do not matter are all likely to be mistaken and, if accepted, to lead to poorly conceived managerial strategies.

Some unique three-dimensional managerial challenges can be identified. Consider the following examples.

Connecting the Dots

Public managers may confront situations in which bits of information potentially relevant to defining and possibly addressing a problem are widely dispersed among both known and unknown locations within or beyond the manager's jurisdiction. If assembled and analyzed, these bits—dots—might reveal a clearer picture of the problem and provide a basis for addressing it. Any particular official with such information may, however, be unaware of what others might know or do know. In the absence of prior habits of cooperation, connecting these dots may be costly and time-consuming, and the results of efforts to do so may still be ambiguous.

A well-known example of such a **connecting-the-dots problem** was assessing the terrorist threat prior to the attacks of September 11, 2001. Bits of potentially relevant information were scattered throughout the intelligence community, but, because of factors relating to public policy structures, organizational cultures, and managerial craft, they were never assembled for analysis. Connecting-the-dots problems also arise when criminal suspects or individuals posing threats to homeland security are moving across various surveillance and law enforcement jurisdictions or when individuals suffering chronic mental illness or other debilitating conditions experience acute episodes or become criminal suspects while away from their home jurisdictions and service providers. Service workers, supervisors, and managers must try to assemble information relevant to accurate diagnosis and appropriate intervention.

In the immediate situation, the premium is likely to be on managerial craft: skill in identifying relevant sources of information, eliciting cooperation, and using partial information to create perceptive conjectures or hypotheses as to the precise nature of the situation. Where situations involving connecting-the-dots problems for organizational managers are common, however, all three dimensions come into play in creating institutional arrangements that ensure timely and effective responses. Effective diagnosis and intervention will require structures, such as networks, incident command protocols, resource-sharing agreements, and communications systems; attitudes that regard cooperation and information sharing built on trust as normal and taken-for-granted; and managerial leadership in mobilizing preexisting structures and cultures on behalf of the immediate challenge quickly and nondefensively.

A good example of a three-dimensional solution to a connecting-the-dots problem is the hot line created by the Veterans Affairs Department to prevent suicides by veterans in distress. Urged to call the hot line by a VA official, a veteran named Robert told the social worker who answered that he wanted to "just lay down in the river and never get up." According to a *New York Times* account, the social worker "gave an assistant Robert's phone number to find his address and alert local police to stand by. The chain of care resembled a relay race, with one runner trying not [to] let go of the baton until the next runner had it in hand." [19] The hot lines enable counselors for the first time "to instantly check a veteran's medical records and then combine emergency response with local follow-up services." VA leadership saw to it that structures were in place and staffed by those with a cultural commitment to veterans' suicide prevention.

Structural solutions to many connecting-the-dots problems that depend on timely information sharing may encounter privacy issues, as statutes and regulations that preclude organizations from releasing certain information at all or without consent or court approval.[20] Such concerns arise in counterterrorism and homeland security activities, law enforcement, medical diagnosis and treatment, the determination of benefits eligibility, and the administration of financial transactions. Some organizational cultures encourage such sharing, while others emphasize information protection and nondisclosure. In emergency situations, connecting the dots may, therefore, require a high order of leadership skill and timing and, alas, even that might not be enough.

Confronting a Crisis

Public managers may confront the need to manage under emergency conditions where lives and property are at stake. Hurricane Katrina confronted officials at all levels of government with unprecedented demands on their time, resources, and managerial acumen, and many of them lost credibility in the aftermath. Similar demands followed the September 11 attacks, and a formerly controversial mayor, Rudolph Giuliani, became a popular hero. But situations amounting to a crisis may arrive from oblique angles. In November 2007 officials in the District of Columbia, from the mayor on down, were suddenly confronted with the indictment and arrest of two midlevel officials in the Office of Tax and Revenue, who were accused of stealing tens of millions of dollars even though auditors had long warned that something—they did not know what—was amiss in revenue administration.

If an agency faces a likelihood of crises, contingency planning is a reasonable structural response. Crisis scenarios are created and simulated, and officials evaluate their responses to the simulated circumstances to determine what additional preparations are needed to ensure an adequate response should an actual crisis occur. Their plans might include the preparation of protocols to allocate responsibilities and guide action in an emergency. Preparation may require negotiations, which can be contentious; police and fire departments may disagree over which agency should be the first responder to particular kinds of emergency or what frequencies should be used on radios; public and nonprofit agencies may disagree over the sharing of responsibilities and resources. The possibility of such conflicts makes discussion and negotiation prior to an emergency all the more necessary. This kind of anticipatory planning is more likely, though far from guaranteed, with organizations that regularly face emergencies.

At the federal level, DHS created the National Incident Management System (NIMS), described as follows:

> While most emergency situations are handled locally, when there's a major incident help may be needed from other jurisdictions, the state and the federal government. NIMS was developed so responders from different jurisdictions and disciplines can work together better to respond to natural disasters and emergencies, including acts of terrorism. NIMS benefits include a unified approach to incident management; standard command and management structures; and emphasis on preparedness, mutual aid and resource management.[21]

CONCEPTS IN ACTION

Preparing for the Crisis of Hurricane Katrina

An example of best practices in preparing for likely crises, published on the Federal Emergency Management Agency Web site, is that of Harris County, Texas, where Houston is located, prior to Hurricane Katrina.

KEYS TO SUCCESS

Long before Hurricane Katrina ever made landfall, the Harris County Citizen Corps laid the groundwork for success with its pre-incident organization and its partnerships with local volunteer groups and area businesses. These two factors allowed the Harris County Citizen Corps to mobilize and organize its resources quickly and efficiently to serve the thousands of evacuees sheltered in Houston-area sites.

Pre-Incident Organization. The Harris County Citizen Corps organized itself for large-scale emergencies through the formation of a Citizen Corps Council and the tracking of Council member capabilities. Upon joining the council, each Citizen Corps Council member completes a survey, which describes the resources and capabilities s/he can provide. This capabilities awareness allowed Hurricane Katrina responders to gain easy access to information on where resources were located and how they could be employed.

Establishing Partnerships. The Harris County Citizen Corps also established partnerships with volunteer organizations and area businesses. Included among these partners were the United Way, Catholic Charities, and Volunteer Houston, the major clearinghouse for volunteer opportunities in the Houston area. When the number of spontaneous volunteers arriving at Reliant Park leveled off during the Hurricane Katrina response, Volunteer Houston was tasked with managing corporate volunteer commitments. These commitments included local businesses (e.g. Shell, Halliburton, etc.) that provided groups of employees willing to volunteer for shelter activities for a specific period of time. These partnerships became "force multipliers," as pre-incident contacts with a few area organizations led to the mobilization of large groups of volunteers.

Source: "Harris County Texas Citizens Corps' Response to Hurricane Katrina," http://www.fema.gov/pdf/emergency/nims/lessons_learned_tx_katrina.pdf.

Crises may evoke the kinds of pathologies of deliberation and decision making discussed in chapter 7, prominently including groupthink. Also, cultural conflicts between and within agencies may be exacerbated. The leak of sensitive or embarrassing information may cause officials to "circle the wagons" and become unthinkingly defensive when they should be using deliberation and decision-making processes to address problems. Unwelcome realities are a test of managerial leadership and craft. Giuliani was widely praised for his leadership—appearing on the scene with inspirational courage—in mobilizing the New York City's post-9/11 response. In sharp contrast, the ineffectual responses of Bush administration officials to Hurricane Katrina were widely criticized and had long-lasting political repercussions.

Transforming an Organization

Chapter 9 suggested that public managers often find themselves acting as change agents within their organizations. As director of the Federal Emergency Management Agency in the 1990s, James Lee Witt earned a reputation for successful agency transformation.[22] The story in this chapter's introduction of how the VHA reinvented itself is a another example of a management-led agency transformation: A manager's judgment that better performance was both feasible and necessary proved to be correct. In this particular case, the motivation to do so was primarily internal. A public manager other than Kenneth Kizer might have chosen a less-ambitious strategy of "muddling through," as the VHA had done prior to his directorship. In contrast, when Thomas Garthwaite was under strong external pressures to transform the Los Angeles County Board of Health Services, he strove for three-dimensional transformation. His particular situation, however, did not afford him the political support and benefit of the doubt enjoyed by Kizer, and Garthwaite's transformation failed.

By definition, transforming an organization involves premeditation on the part of the public manager and is the kind of challenge for which the model deliberative process is especially recommended. Some public managers may approximate such a process through largely informal, make-it-up-as-you-go-along activities. Others may prefer to conduct the kinds of analyses associated with a formal or deliberate strategic planning process. A well-known example of a strategic planning process, designed for use in public and nonprofit organizations, is described by John M. Bryson. His *Strategic Planning for Public and Nonprofit Organizations: A Guide to Strengthening and Sustaining Organizational Achievement* features a "strategy change cycle," which includes actions such as "setting the organization's direction," "making internal and external assessments," "making fundamental decisions," and "continually monitoring and assessing the results." [23] Real-world strategic planning in political environments is bound to deviate from any specific model procedure, but such a model can serve as a template or checklist against which actual planning may be reviewed in order to prevent deliberation from degenerating into garbage cans.

Although agency transformations often involve all dimensions of public management, not all do. The institution of a well-conceived performance measurement and management function may lead to improved results even in the absence of reorganization or direct challenges to internal norms and values. Similarly, a reorganization of structures and processes of deliberation can better align agency responsibilities and planning activities with its policy mandates. It is, however, hard to imagine a case of significant transformation in which managerial craft exercised on behalf of systematic deliberation does not play a catalytic, creative, or sustaining role.

Responding to Early Warning

Public managers may receive early warnings of possible crises or dangers. These warnings may be speculative and controversial predictions of possibilities in the distant future for which no specific organization is responsible, such as the earliest concerns about global warming in the 1970s. The warnings may be of more specific but still uncertain events that could materialize at any time and affect specific organizations. Emergency preparedness experts were confident that New Orleans eventually would be struck by a devastating hurricane, but no one could say when. Even when a warning concerns an existing problem such the discovery of leaks in the storm drains under downtown Chicago, the response may not be adequate. The city planned repairs that did not proceed rapidly enough, leading to severe downtown flooding following a heavy rainfall on April 13, 1992. Emergency management agencies, therefore, are obligated to be prepared to respond to warnings of immediate concern that are nevertheless far from certain.

Analytical journalist Malcolm Gladwell writes that it may be wrong to look backward to see if there were warning signs of a devastating event and then conclude that if there were, they *should* have been heeded.[24] Many public managers face continuous, repeated warnings of varying degrees of specificity and credibility about a great many potential dangers. The vast majority of them, Gladwell says, turn out to be wrong. Therefore, not all threats can or should be taken seriously. There will always be more warnings than resources, and there will always be lots of "noise," or interpretable material, in the flow of information, some of it deliberately created by enemies or opponents. It is necessary, Gladwell says, to set priorities

In these kinds of situations, as in so many decision-making situations, psychological factors come into play. People are apt to be more sensitive to warnings similar to past failures or warnings of events that have already been anticipated. They are apt to have mindsets and be biased in their assessments of threats. Gladwell's analysis of why Israeli leaders failed to react to the threat of the Yom Kippur war in 1973 is convincing on this point. Warned on the morning of October 6 that the attack would occur later that day, the Israelis did nothing, and the attack did in fact occur later that day. But many such warnings had been received from the same sources in the past, the Israelis had prepared for an attack, and nothing had happened. Similarly, foam shedding from the space shuttle launch vehicle's external fuel tanks had become such common occurrences that they were not considered to be warnings of impending trouble until trouble happened.

In general, early warnings and the responses to them are likely to reflect all three dimensions of public management: structural and procedural arrangements that either encourage or discourage and impede the communication and interpretation of such warnings; cultural factors that predispose employees to react to warnings in certain ways, ranging from shrugging them off to overreacting; and inclinations and deliberative skills of public managers, similarly ranging from eye-rolling skepticism to "the sky is falling" zeal. Prudence suggests, however, that ignoring early warning and its implications altogether is unwise.

HOW THE WORLD WORKS

Early Warnings of Global Warming

Beginning in the late 1970s, as the following story indicates, expert, media, and public opinion on climate change underwent what may be described as a climate change. The new view, that the world was facing not a new ice age, as some had thought, but the prospect of global warming constituted an early warning that governments, and especially the Environmental Protection Agency (EPA), would in all likelihood be required to take action to reduce greenhouse gas emissions.

In April 2007, a generation later, the U.S. Supreme Court ordered the EPA to explain why its refusal to regulate carbon dioxide emissions from motor vehicles was in compliance with the Clean Air Act. In December the EPA responded with a report concluding that greenhouse gases must be controlled. According to a *New York Times* account quoting agency officials, the White House told the agency that "an e-mail message containing the document would not be opened." This meant the report had no official status. In mid-2008 the EPA issued a version of the report that showed how warming might be dealt with and then proclaimed that no action would be taken.

[In the 1970s] new studies convinced an increasing number of scientists that, given a choice between warming and cooling, it was the greenhouse effect that would dominate sooner or later. Theoretical work on aerosols suggested that human smog and dust might not cool the atmosphere very much after all. At most, the increased pollution might bring a mild cooling that would only temporarily mask greenhouse warming. Other studies suggested that the greenhouse effect might already be changing the weather. Computer models, although still provisional, tended to agree that the rising level of CO2 would bring a degree or so of warming within decades. Any statement that invoked supercomputers commanded strong respect from the public, and from most scientists too.

Climate experts were quick to explain the new findings. A well-respected geochemist, Wallace Broecker, took the lead in 1975, warning in an influential *Science* magazine article that the world might be poised on the brink of a serious rise of temperature. "Complacency may not be warranted," he said. "We may be in for a climatic surprise." In 1977, the National Academy of Sciences weighed in with a major study by a panel of experts who warned that temperatures might rise to nearly catastrophic levels during the next century or two. The report, announced at a press conference during the hottest July the nation had experienced since the 1930s, was widely noted in the press.

Science journalists, by now closely attuned to the views of climate scientists, promptly reflected the shift of opinion. Media talk of a ruinous new ice age continued through the winter of 1976–1977, which was savagely cold in the Eastern half of the United States. But that was the end of it. From 1978 on, nearly all articles on climate in the *New York Times* were oriented toward greenhouse warming. In the *Readers' Guide* listing of U.S. popular articles, warnings about climate were more or less evenly divided between heating and cooling up to 1977, but then articles about global warming took over almost completely.

As an example of the change, in 1976 the *U.S. News & World Report* described (with strong qualifications) the theories that the world would be getting cooler. The very next year the same magazine reported that "The world may be inching into a prolonged warming trend that is the direct result of burning more and more fossil fuels. . . ." The ice-age theories, said the article, "are being convincingly opposed by growing evidence of human impact." Similarly, in 1976 *Business Week* had explained both sides of the debate but reported that "the dominant school maintains that the world is becoming cooler." Just one year later, the magazine declared that CO2 "may be the world's biggest environmental problem, threatening to raise the world's temperature" with horrendous long-term consequences.

Source: Spencer Weart, "The Public and Climate Change," in *The Discovery of Global Warming,* http://www.aip.org/history/exhibits/climate/Public.htm#L000.

Creative Problem Solving

Managers in all sectors are frequently urged, or expected, to think and act creatively in addressing difficult problems. Creative solutions are often dubbed "innovations" because they represent heretofore unheard of approaches to vexing situations. Over the past half century, creative problem solving (CPS) has become the subject of a considerable research literature, consultancies, and management development and training activities. The CPS tool box may be a source of useful approaches to public managers attempting to manage in the black.

A recent example of a creative solution to a familiar problem—an **innovation—** is the use of fake speed bumps in roadways to get drivers to slow down. Authorities install two-dimensional panels, or painted areas, that create the optical illusion of being three dimensional and cost a fraction of the real thing. Even when motorists get used to them, the ersatz speed bumps may function in a manner equivalent to flashing yellow lights, warning drivers to slow down. When bus and high-occupancy vehicle lanes were first introduced, they were innovative solutions to traffic congestion, as was the use of Polaroid and digital photography in criminal investigations. Another example of creativity is a device given to domestic violence victims under court-ordered protection that enables them to send a signal to police if threatened by an abuser.

The issue is how public managers might elicit ideas, insights, and solutions that are far from obvious, that require imagination, or that might appear to be at variance with "the way we do things." Exhorting colleagues and subordinates to "think outside the box," and rewarding promising results of doing so, might help. So, too, might bringing in people known to be creative, to be (constructive) contrarians, or to have considerable imagination and the ability to think in a nonlinear, what-if-we-look-at-it-this-way manner that makes heretofore hidden solutions emerge. Although, as chapter 7 suggested, organized brainstorming has its downsides, it might stimulate open-mindedness about how to define and address problems and bring new insights and creative thinking to the table.

Managers might also want to consider using specific techniques that have proven to have value in stimulating creativity. One is mind mapping, in which participants are urged to identify and visually suggest possible associations among facts, ideas, claims, and other elements of a problem situation until new patterns and relationships emerge that might be the basis of creative solutions.[25] A well-known CPS process originating with the work of Alex Osborn and Sidney J. Parnes involves several stages of fact-finding, idea generation, and solution identification.[26] The model deliberative process described earlier in this chapter itself might be used as the basis for creativity exercises involving multidimensional reframing of problem situations. The point of all such processes is to dissolve interpersonal, organizational, and cultural barriers to the generation and consideration of fresh ideas.

Managing People

Public managers must decide whether and how to hire, supervise, reward, train, promote, and discipline employees in their organizations. In recent years management of these tasks became known as "human resource management" or "human capital management," reflecting the shift in emphasis from a primarily structural approach to managing employees to an approach that engages all three dimensions. Reforms to personnel systems have introduced flexibility, managerial discretion, pay for performance, and decentralization.[27] And with these changes comes the need for three-dimensional management.

The leadership and best practices literatures are both concerned with managing people. Among works mentioned in chapter 7, Richard N. Haass's *The Bureaucratic Entrepreneur: How to be Effective in Any Unruly Organization* offers down-to-earth, practical advice to managers on, for example, organizing staff, being a successful boss, delegation, and showing loyalty down. Not surprisingly, says Haass, treating your people as you yourself want to be treated is a good way to be effective. In *Caught Between the Dog and the Fireplug, or How to Survive in Public Service,* Kenneth H. Ashworth, an experienced practitioner, insists that good bosses figure out a way to work for those under them; they delegate but are accessible for advice and counsel; and they keep people focused on the mission of the organization.[28] Earning respect and loyalty, then, is a matter of showing respect and loyalty to one's own people.

People management is necessarily three dimensional. All three dimensions are evident, for example, in a "self-assessment" developed by the Government Accountability Office for agency managers to use in weighing their human capital policies and needs:

1. Strategic Planning: Establish the agency's mission, vision for the future, core values, goals and objectives, and strategies.
2. Organizational Alignment: Integrate human capital strategies with the agency's core business practices.
3. Leadership: Foster a committed leadership team and provide reasonable continuity through succession planning.
4. Talent: Recruit, hire, develop, and retain employees with the skills for mission accomplishment.
5. Performance Culture: Empower and motivate employees while ensuring accountability and fairness in the workplace.[29]

An increased focus on the cultural and craft dimensions of management that affect human capital policies is consistent with the ideas of John Brehm and Scott Gates, and William Ouchi, discussed in chapter 8. These ideas emphasize the importance of the hiring function as perhaps the best way to ensure that employees would act in ways consistent with the organization's mission.[30]

Connecting the dots, confronting a crisis, transforming an organization, responding to an early warning, creative problem solving, managing people: Each of these challenges is likely to be most successfully met—to the extent possible—by three-dimensional public management. Yet managing in the black is not restricted to these six situations; it might be beneficial or even essential for a number of other situations or tasks that public managers face. Eugene Bardach's concepts of managerial craftsmanship and interagency collaborative capacity reflect the importance of all three dimensions for facing the design challenges of successfully managing interagency networks or collaborations.[31] Across a range of situations and challenges, the model deliberative process can be used as a tool for managing in the black.

CONUNDRUMS OF THREE-DIMENSIONAL MANAGEMENT

In their comprehensive monograph *Public Management Reform: A Comparative Analysis*, Christopher Pollitt and Geert Bouckaert point out that no matter what strategy a public manager may choose, the process of moving forward is far from straightforward.[32] Their chapter, "Trade-offs, Balances, Limits, Dilemmas, and Paradoxes," discusses a number of the intellectual and practical difficulties that challenge the craftsmanship of any public manager attempting to manage in the black.

Such difficulties may be termed **conundrums:** intractable or difficult problems that may constitute no-win situations. The types of conundrums identified by Pollitt and Bouckaert include:

- *Trade-offs:* Because resources are scarce, achieving more of one good thing means settling for less of another good thing. Decentralizing agency decision making, empowering field offices, and outsourcing functions and responsibilities usually occur at the expense of policy control and accountability. The adoption of "quality of life" policing may lead to reductions in crime but a rising level of citizen complaints because of increased police-citizen interactions.
- *Limits:* Public managers may encounter absolute constraints on what they may do even if it means accepting considerable inefficiency. The Internal Revenue Service was prohibited by arcane budget scoring rules from hiring additional auditors and was forced to hire private contractors to collect delinquent taxes at greater cost. U.S. aid agencies are able to purchase less food to feed victims of drought or civil conflict because of rules requiring the use of U.S.-grown commodities and U.S.-flag transportation, both of which are more expensive than goods and services from abroad.
- *Dilemmas:* Public managers may confront choices between undesirable, often incommensurable alternatives. NASA managers must occasionally choose between canceling a shuttle flight and throwing flight schedules into disarray, which jeopardizes program goals, and allowing a flight to proceed, thereby incurring an unknown risk of a catastrophic accident.
- *Paradoxes:* Public managers may encounter situations with seemingly contradictory aspects that nevertheless may be true. The paradoxes of performance discussed in chapter 8 are examples. Public managers may face the reality that being opportunistic and disingenuous is politically safer than exhibiting integrity and a commitment to quality. And then there is the adage: "We never have time to do it right, but we always have time to do it over."
- *Contradictions:* A contradiction is an extreme trade-off: If you have one desirable thing, you cannot have another desirable thing. For example, allowing interest groups or representative groups of citizens to have a veto over program implementation alternatives may reduce the prospects for technically and economically efficient solutions to near zero. Democracy cancels out efficiency, which are both in the public interest.[33]

To Pollitt and Bouckaert's list might be added:

- *Unintended consequences:* Unintended consequences are outcomes of a managerial strategy, usually unanticipated and unwelcome, that complicate, undermine, or nullify the *intended* consequences. For example:

> In 1692 John Locke, the English philosopher and a forerunner of modern economists, urged the defeat of a parliamentary bill designed to cut the maximum permissible rate of interest from 6 percent to 4 percent. Locke argued that instead of benefiting borrowers, as intended, it would hurt them. People would find ways to circumvent the law, with the costs of circumvention borne by borrowers. To the extent the law was obeyed, Locke concluded, the chief results would be less available credit and a redistribution of income away from "widows, orphans and all those who have their estates in money."[34]

- *Externalities:* Externalities occur when the actions of a government agency or a business firm affect the well-being of others in either positive or negative ways. Construction of a hospital or a shopping center, while a benefit to patients and customers, may create aggravating traffic congestion for those who must use nearby roads.
- *A Hobson's Choice:* A Hobson's choice is one that involves a take-it-or-leave-it proposition. Managers in weak bargaining positions may be offered this-or-nothing settlements of disputes.

Why make a point of conundrums? Public managers who launch reforms are often surprisingly unsophisticated or soft-minded about conundrums that they are likely to encounter. They may be motivated by wishful thinking or ideological conviction more than by careful planning or rational anticipation of potential problems. To attract sufficient political support, policymakers often create expectations and demand results that are entirely unrealistic, placing their agents, who must deal with the conundrums, in difficult or untenable situations.

Pollitt and Bouckaert cite some interesting and popular conundrums in public management.[35] Public managers may, for example, be directed to increase political control of the bureaucracy and at the same time empower subordinates to manage and/or empower consumers; promote entrepreneurship, risk taking, and innovation and at the same time raise citizen trust in the certainty of effectiveness; increase efficiency by saving money and at the same time increase effectiveness (the notion that government can cost less and work better); improve staff morale and dedication and at the same time downsize and outsource; reduce agency complexity and at the same time improve agency coordination; and improve quality and at the same time cut costs. Failure to accomplish incompatible objectives may doom the offending public manager to political reprisals and loss of reputation by whichever side is most aggrieved, or maybe by all sides. As with all management in the black, such possibilities may be minimized by deliberation that is carefully three-dimensional.

MANAGING IN THE BLACK AS ARGUMENT

As has been emphasized throughout this book, effective public management, and certainly managing in the black, places a special premium on the ability to make persuasive arguments. A persuasive argument has a better chance of prevailing with skeptics and heightening support than an argument that is defective because it lacks one of the constituent elements of a sound argument. A defective argument is, in effect, no argument at all but an assertion, an opinion, or a declaration without logic or evidence. Warning an important stakeholder group to "get on the train or it will leave the station without you" is not an argument and, as the case of public manager Rod Hickman will illustrate, not likely to further a manager's purposes.

As was noted in chapter 3, arguments put forward in political forums and in real time are often not pristine examples of an ideal argument. They may contain enough elements of sound argument to be effective, however. The following illustrates managerial argument in real time with both its strengths and its flaws.

On September 25, 1998, Thomas Garthwaite, the deputy under secretary for health of the Department of Veterans Affairs, appeared before the House Subcommittee on Human Resources to testify on behalf of the VHA's efforts to improve the quality of medical services to veterans.[36] As successor to Kenneth Kizer, an acknowledged successful manager of the VHA, Garthwaite was attempting to justify the types of reforms, many of them controversial, that Kizer had implemented and that he was continuing to support.

Garthwaite's testimony contains an explicit argument with the following elements. He claims that "the quality of VA healthcare has measurably improved in the last three years [and that], using standard quality of care measures employed in the private sector, VA performance is superior [to the private sector] across the board." His reason for claiming this unprecedented improvement is that "no other healthcare system in the U.S. can match the extent of change that has occurred in the veterans' healthcare system since [deliberate] efforts to restructure the system were launched in late 1995." His evidence, which is highly detailed and often technical, is of two types: (1) evidence concerning the specific changes taking place at the VHA—a shift from inpatient to outpatient care and from specialty to primary care, routine customer satisfaction surveys, electronic records management (altogether, about twenty-five points like this); and (2) evidence concerning how VA quality of care indicators are superior to those of the private sector; for example, "an editorial by the Chairman of Surgery at Duke University endorsed VA's approach as one that will improve the quality of surgical care throughout the nation."

Furthermore, Garthwaite says that VERA (the Veterans Equitable Resource Allocation), which allocates budgetary resources across VHA activities, "rectifies problems perpetuated by previous funding systems by providing networks [of medical care providers] with two national workload prices for two types of patients—those with routine (Basic Care) needs and those with complex/chronic healthcare needs (Complex Care)." He says that "Comparing FY 1998 funding with FY 1996 (the baseline year for VERA), fifteen networks have received overall increases while seven networks have received decreases." That is, real reallocation is taking place.

The warrant that links his claim to his reasons and the evidence on which both are based is that when a change strategy is implemented and performance improvements are observed, the change strategy can reasonably be considered a contributing cause of the improvements. In this particular case, the numerous change processes initiated by the VHA in 1995 were expressly designed to improve the quality of care provided by the VHA. Change has involved "reengineering VHA's operational structure, diversifying its funding base, streamlining processes, implementing 'best practices,' improving information management, reforming eligibility rules, expanding contracting authority, and changing the culture of VA healthcare, among other things." In other words, Garthwaite is asserting a causal relationship between this type of change strategy, which is largely structural, and the documented improvements in quality of care.

Garthwaite acknowledges some qualifications to his argument. He says that comparable data to permit quality comparisons between the public and private sectors are not available for all aspects of quality. In VHA's favor, he acknowledges that "the patients who fill VA clinics and hospitals are more medically complicated and socially needy than the U.S. population overall." He adds, "It is not only the largest fully integrated healthcare system in the U.S., but it is also among the most complex healthcare systems in the world because of its multiple missions—missions which are at the same time complementary, competing and conflictive." More specifically, he notes:

> While VERA is an effective methodology for allocating resources at the network level, it is recognized that VERA may not be as useful to the networks at the facility level. This is due to significant differences at the facility level that, in the aggregate, are not a factor when allocating at the network level.

He cites one response to this acknowledgment:

> In March 1998 Price Waterhouse LLP issued a report on its evaluation of VERA. The report concluded that VERA was a well designed system, is ahead of other global budgeting systems, and met VHA's goals of simplicity, equity and fairness.

Garthwaite's argument and its various elements are not as clear in the actual testimony as they might be, which is typical of real-world arguments. That it is convincing as it stands is largely because his claims are clear and attention-getting and the weight of the evidence supporting them is almost overwhelming. Garthwaite might have been even more convincing, however, had he organized his testimony to more explicitly *argue* his case.

His claim attracts attention because it says that not only have VHA services improved, but also that they are now of the same or better quality than those of the private sector, a truly arresting statement. Although the claim is stated clearly enough, it is not to be found either at the beginning or at the end of his testimony, where it might have had even greater impact on his audience. A bold, up-front placement would have his audience's complete attention. His reason is also stated clearly enough but, again, is not as well placed as it might have been. He could have said, following his claim: "The reason for these dramatic improvements is that we have made a concerted, comprehensive effort that was deliberately designed to bring it about." In its specificity and amount, the evidence is, as noted, impressive. Here is an expert putting his expertise on exhibit to an important audience. The two long lists of points of evidence might, however, have been given more thematic coherence. As it stands, the lists seem unedited, almost laundry lists, and the relative importance of the many specific points is difficult to discern.

His principle is—and this, too, is common in real-world arguments—only weakly stated. Garthwaite comes across as primarily concerned with the operations, not the fundamental theory, of the change processes. Kizer, Garthwaite's boss, had made numerous statements concerning the importance of articulating clear goals and sustaining a focus on the change process. A concise restatement of Kizer's ideas would have strengthened Garthwaite's testimony.[37] In addition, the few acknowledgments impart a sense of professional integrity to the statement, although most are self-serving, albeit in a good sense. Garthwaite was not blowing smoke. Again, and this is a judgment call, he might have been somewhat more forthright concerning uncertainties that professional health care providers would surely recognize in the VHA's efforts to date. This frankness would have been appreciated by professionals reading the testimony later.

As emphasized in chapter 3, constructing a complete, well-reasoned argument and using the three-dimensional framework are no guarantee of managerial persuasiveness. Instead, these are tools that can be employed to synthesize insights from diverse sources and to construct reasoned cases for managerial strategies. To do less is to be less than responsible.

HOW THE WORLD WORKS

Do the Media Undermine Argumentation?

In his *Washington Post* column, David Broder criticized the media for undermining the quality of argument during televised debates among presidential candidates in the campaign leading up to the 2008 election.

During Thursday night's Democratic presidential debate . . . , New Mexico Gov. Bill Richardson was given a chance to answer the question about offering driver's licenses to illegal immigrants. . . .

. . . Richardson . . . said that when the legislature sent him a bill allowing illegal immigrants to obtain driver's licenses, "I signed it. My law enforcement people said it's a matter of public safety. . . . We wanted more people to be insured. When we started with this program, 33 percent of New Mexicans were uninsured. Today, it's 11 percent. Traffic fatalities have gone down. It's a matter of public safety." . . .

. . . [O]f course, none of the other candidates was ever asked, "What about the public safety argument cited by Richardson?" . . . The TV impresarios are so eager for headlines, they rarely pause to ask the candidates for evidence to support their opinions or assertions. It is bang-bang, but rarely because-and-here's-proof. . . . [T]he implications of [the candidates'] positions go unexplored, because there's always another candidate, another topic, another headline clamoring for attention.

Source: David Broder, "Debates in Need of Rescue," *Washington Post,* November 11, 2007, Sec. B.

ARE SOME PUBLIC MANAGEMENT JOBS IMPOSSIBLE?

Cautionary notes in the discussion up to this point raise this question: In the face of conundrums, together with the other distinctive challenges of managing in the public sector, are some public sector jobs simply too hard to do with any degree of real success? Many jobs may be thankless, but are some of them impossible? Garthwaite, a success in Washington, D.C., failed in Los Angeles County. But was managing the L.A. County health department at that particular time an impossible job?

Dimensions of Impossibility

Erwin Hargrove, a political scientist, and John C. Glidewell, a psychologist, and a group of their collaborators might think so. *Impossible Jobs in Public Management,* a volume edited and partially written by Hargrove and Glidewell, grew out of the intuition that some public management jobs, especially in state and local government, are so difficult as to be virtually undoable.[38] Contributors were recruited to write research papers about some of these jobs with the goal of identifying the underlying explanations for the phenomenon of impossibility. The writers met to consider the dimensions of impossibility or possibility inherent in jobs they studied. Hargrove and Glidewell summarized and elaborated on the results of their collaboration. The resulting model of impossibility identified four dimensions of possibility/impossibility:

- the legitimacy (or deservingness) of the public manager's clientele. Children, those in need of medical treatment, veterans, and farmers are usually regarded as deserving of public support, but welfare recipients, suspected and convicted criminals, suspected terrorists, and the chronically mentally ill are viewed, if not as undeserving, at least as intractable.
- the intensity of conflict among the agency's constituencies. Should welfare mothers be given income support or forced to go to work? Should prisoners be punished or rehabilitated? Should the mentally ill be hospitalized or sustained in their own communities? Such issues are likely to produce intense, protracted political conflict.
- public confidence in the authority of the public manager's profession. Physicians, agricultural extension agents, maternal and child health nurses are held in esteem, but inner city school superintendents (Paul Vallas, discussed later in this chapter, was a clear and arguably rare exception), social workers, and corrections officers have relatively low professional status.
- the strength of the agency "myth," the extent of sustained public commitment to an ideal worth pursuing and public understanding and acceptance of the difficulties and altruistic sacrifice inherent in providing the service. Fire departments, public health agencies, and many environmental protection agencies usually enjoy good reputations for serving the public interest, but welfare agencies, many local law enforcement agencies, and urban school boards are often not accorded the benefit of the doubt by a skeptical public.

Impossible jobs are those in which the commissioners "must serve irresponsible and intractable clients in intense conflicts with more legitimate clients for public resources; must satisfy multiple and intensely polarized, active constituencies; possess professional, scientific authority that commands little public respect; and are guided by weak, controversial myths that cannot sustain policy continuity." [39] In contrast, officials with "possible" jobs serve a legitimate clientele with little political conflict and enjoy public respect for their expertise and for the effectiveness of their agencies.

The Case of Rod Hickman

Roderick Q. Hickman was sworn in as secretary of the California Department of Corrections (CDC), on November 17, 2003, the first day of Gov. Arnold Schwarzenegger's administration. A little more than two years later, near the end of February 2006, Hickman abruptly resigned.

On their basis of their research, Hargrove and Glidewell might well have warned Hickman about his future. The position of corrections commissioner was, according to their analytical framework, the quintessential "impossible job." Still, the circumstances were ripe with possibility.

Hickman seemed ideal for the challenges of his new position. When named to the post, he was serving as the CDC's chief deputy director for field operations. Prior to that assignment, he was assistant deputy director of operations and programs of CDC's Institutions Division. Before that, he was the northern regional administrator for the Institutions Division and was warden of Mule Creek State Prison in Amador County. Hickman began his CDC career in June 1979 as a correctional officer at the California Institution for Men, in Chino. At the same time, he earned degrees in public administration and attended courses in leadership development and often spoke to professional and community groups.

Schwarzenegger had campaigned on the promise to solve the problems of overcrowding, violence, rising costs, poor medical care, and high rates of recidivism that were overwhelming California's prison system. Although a system insider, Hickman was committed to shifting the emphasis away from punishment toward rehabilitation. He said his mission was "to bring social sector organizations into prison and parole reform." [40] Corrections employees and advocates for prison reform were optimistic that Hickman would be able to bring about real and constructive change in the agency. His leadership team devoted long hours to crafting the specific measures that they believed would accomplish the governor's and Hickman's reform goals.

Within a year, however, Hickman was under fire from an unexpected quarter: "the labor union that represented him for 20 years. . . . When Gov. Arnold Schwarzenegger appointed [him], correctional officers rejoiced that, finally, one of their own would be running the show. At the same time, skeptics questioned whether he would stand up to the union, a formidable force inside the prisons and beyond." Unexpectedly, union leaders were soon routinely bashing Hickman and labeling him "an embarrassment." [41] A *Los Angeles Times* article reported that, in an interview,

> Hickman said he does not worry about the attacks on his performance, but that he receives many calls and e-mails from officers and supervisors concerned about the criticism and supportive of his work. Pulling out his hand-held computer, Hickman shared two new e-mail messages—one from an associate warden, another from a sergeant—praising a recent videotape he distributed on the code of silence. "We're heading in a new direction," Hickman said. The prison guards union "can get on the train or get left at the station." [42]

On the news of Hickman's departure, a union spokesman said, "Our members are tired, they're demoralized, we have an unclear chain of command, and the management team is in complete disarray. It all happened under Mr. Hickman's watch." [43]

Criticism also began to be heard from the other side: the reform groups that had put their faith in Schwarzenegger and Hickman. The leader of one such group wrote Hickman an open letter:

> Over the past seven years, we have united in a statewide communication system and daily newsletter to report to California media and legislators the tragic fiscal and human loss happening in voter-financed penal institutions. As you know, our action system is called United for No Injustice, Oppression, or Neglect (U.N.I.O.N.). We consist of a coalition of organizations and individuals dedicated to reforming the criminal justice system from arrest through parole. . . . During the past seven years, we have brought to everyone's attention in CDC and the legislature thousands of instances of unbearable incompetence which result in needless suffering and dying and lawsuits costing taxpayers millions, if not billions of dollars which could better be used to actually rehabilitate and/or to prevent crime from ever happening.[44]

In an editorial, the *Los Angeles Times* cited an example of the mounting frustrations:

> In 2004, the state expanded a program begun under Gov. Gray Davis to send nonviolent parole violators to halfway houses, home detention, or jail-based drug treatment programs. It was a badly needed effort to reduce the prison population and cut recidivism by helping addicts get the kind of treatment they weren't getting in prison. A year later, as a victims' rights group, heavily supported by the guards union, was running misleading commercials claiming that the program was endangering the public, Hickman abruptly dropped it. Then he had to revive it two months later under orders from a federal judge.[45]

As a reason for his resignation, Hickman cited dwindling support from the governor and his staff for the reforms he had initiated. California's "political environment and the power of special interests work against efforts to bring about lasting reform." [46] Opposition from the correction officers union, whose contract gave its leaders influence over any change in the workplace, became a particular liability and appeared to cause the governor's office to back away from Hickman's aggressive program. Reform groups in turn expressed disappointment at the slow pace of change. Finally, legislators began weighing in, questioning

Hickman's progress. The situation had repercussions nationwide. Said the chief of corrections in Ohio, "Nobody believes you can do your craft there. Nobody is going to come to a place where the environment just makes it impossible to do the business of corrections." [47] (Hickman was replaced by his deputy.)

Following his resignation, even the media distanced themselves from the once popular Hickman. The *Los Angeles Times* editorialized as follows:

> Running this state's prisons is a thankless job. On one side are legislators demanding quick fixes to intractable problems and federal courts that are dividing up responsibility over the prisons piecemeal; on the other is a guards union wielding its enormous political clout to squelch most changes. Hickman, standing in the middle, had only one ally he could count on: Gov. Arnold Schwarzenegger, who now seems to have moved on to other things. . . . [Hickman] may be remembered as a man who said all the right things but did few of them, buffeted as he was by competing interests and problems beyond his control.[48]

Impossible Job? Manage in the Black

Often, say Hargrove and Glidewell, the tenure of those with impossible jobs "is short and their accomplishments are limited, but they persist in doing the best they can until they burn out or are fired." [49] Coping, in other words, may be the only way to secure any gains at all when the odds are against you. Coping is one way of "managing in the black."

But that view is too pessimistic. Jobs with reputations as being impossible need not be entirely beyond the influence of effective managerial leadership, of the value of deliberation within a three-dimensional analytic framework. The Federal Emergency Management Agency, Veterans Health Administration, and Alabama's child welfare agencies, all regarded at one time as exceedingly difficult if not impossible to manage, experienced turnarounds and achieved real excellence after sustained periods of capable management.[50] Such management will almost invariably be not only three-dimensional but also cognizant of the complex patterns of overlap and interdependence among the three dimensions.

Hickman may well have erred by overemphasizing the power of his craft and the efficacy of structural/procedural techniques and underemphasizing the primary importance of the organization's culture and its potential influence on both craft and structure. He persisted in a strategy of aggressive entrepreneurship in circumstances that called for a different strategy—employing the power of professionalism and expertise, which Hickman possessed in abundance. His persistent use of rewards and punishments alienated his most powerful rival, the union, and that alienation was a significant contributor to his undoing. Hickman might also have taken greater care to heed the advice of experts such as Mark Moore and Gordon Chase, discussed in chapter 7, to spend more time "managing upward" and preserving the all-important support of his boss, the governor.[51]

But such persistence appeared to be less a matter of miscalculation than of Hickman's temperament. To waste an opportunity to lead by merely coping must have seemed unthinkable to him. More calculation might have helped. Had the deliberation that he undertook with his staff been more systematically three-dimensional, he might have successfully managed in the black, perhaps not achieving all that he hoped for but more than he did.

PAUL VALLAS: A MANAGER IN THE BLACK

This book has included numerous examples of public managers attempting to deal with the distinctive challenges of public management. That stories of flawed performance have outnumbered clear-cut success stories is not accidental. Flawed or unexceptional performance is, unfortunately, more common that unequivocal success. Moreover, there is usually less to be learned from success than from the more ordinary or problematic experiences of public managers. Complex interrelationships among actions and consequences within and between the three dimensions are more likely to be revealed when all does not go well than when it does.

The book concludes with a success story, however. It is not unequivocal success, but it is arguably the more interesting because success is almost never uncontroversial in government. According to a saying of Confucius:

> Tzu King asked: "What would you say of the man who is liked by all his fellow townsmen?" "That is not sufficient," was the reply. "What is better is that the good among his fellow townsmen like him, and the bad hate him."

Paul G. Vallas assumed responsibility for the New Orleans Recovery School District at the beginning of the 2007–2008 school year. The situation he confronted was fraught with exceptional challenges: the aftermath of Hurricane Katrina and the long-standing problems in the New Orleans public schools stemming from poverty and a dysfunctional administration. At the end of the previous school year, fewer than half of the district's students were showing up for school. Said one expert on the Louisiana public schools, "I'm just not sure there's very much room to accomplish anything." [52] But Vallas was no stranger to the challenges of urban public education. Although he was not a professional educator, he had been superintendent of the public school systems of Chicago and Philadelphia and had earned a reputation as someone who could make public schools work better for students. The belief was widespread that if anyone could accomplish something in New Orleans, it was Paul Vallas.

How does a public manager acquire a reputation described as "gold plated" while undertaking such difficult assignments?[53] First, Vallas is regarded as a nontraditional superintendent. Though he has run for public office, he is more of a political technocrat—described by one observer as "charismatic in a wonky sort of way"—whose roots are in the Daley family political machine in Chicago. "The argument in favor of non-traditional leadership has been that managerial experience is more important to running a school system than educational background." [54] And so is political savvy.[55]

Nationally, public school administration in the 1980s and part of the 1990s was, according to one account, "dominated by the idea of decentralization, of devolving power to the individual school site, its principal, teachers and parents." Vallas and many of his peers began strengthening the power of the central office to gain greater control over standards, curricula, facilities, teacher assignments, and resource allocation. One goal was to prevent bad schools from becoming worse by making them "dumping grounds for those with the least seniority" and restricting their access to resources.[56]

Second, Vallas might be regarded as a nontraditional manager. According to someone who observed him and is an admirer:

> Tall and ungainly, Vallas is nonetheless a charming, intellectually imposing man, a charismatic bully. In many situations, he simply steamrolls most of those around him. . . . He does what he wants—sometimes rashly—and bristles at any whiff of opposition. Known to berate underlings, educators, and members of the press alike, Vallas has a leadership style that seems more a product of his Greek roots and intellect than of any management book or bureaucratic experience. . . . Self-assured and capable of torrential speech, Vallas only rarely admits to doubt or fault.[57]

Effective public management does not depend upon having the ideal managerial temperament. His outsized skills, however, have been at the root of many of the controversies he has generated.

Vallas is an instructive example of a three-dimensional public manager *because* he does not conform to stereotypes that emphasize vision, stewardship, compromise, unfailing courtesy, and other platonic virtues. By all accounts charismatic, physical, energetic, and passionate, he self-consciously but for the most part intuitively uses his craft—in other words, his unique personality and leadership style—to confront the specific structural and cultural realities of the administrative systems in which he works and to devise strategies that result in measurable improvements. He is an inveterate user of structures and processes to transform dysfunctional public school system cultures. He manages "in the black."

Chicago

When Chicago mayor Richard M. Daley was given control over his city's public schools by the state legislature in 1995, he appointed Vallas as superintendent, and school improvement became one of the mayor's top priorities. Chicago's public schools had once been described by President Ronald Reagan's secretary of education as the worst in the nation. The 1995 school reform legislation gave the mayor, school board, superintendent, and local parents, teachers, and community members greatly expanded powers over the system and established the structural framework within which Vallas would work.

Vallas had important qualifications for running an urban school district. He had served five years as Chicago's budget director. "Budgets were a snap for him, large bureaucracies were not intimidating, and he had no previous allegiances within the school system to hold him back from asking hard questions or demanding new solutions." [58] By the end of his tenure in Chicago, more eighth graders than third graders were meeting national norms—meaning students were performing better the longer they were in the system.[59]

> During his tenure, from 1995 to 2001, Vallas racked up a long string of accomplishments that would be the envy of nearly any superintendent. The budget was quickly put in order. Vallas rehabbed old schools and built attractive new ones. Test scores reported to the public rose nearly every year, two union contracts were negotiated without any strikes, and a host of new programs—summer school, afterschool programs, alternative schools, new magnet programs—were all created. Most important, for perhaps the first time in Chicago's history, low-performing schools were pressured to do better, and students and their parents encountered a system that did not just pass everyone through regardless of what they learned.[60]

Despite his accomplishments, "Vallas fatigue" led to criticism. According to one account, he

> was nearly always battling someone or something. During his time as schools chief, he took on the reform groups, the local school councils, the education schools, the state board of education, and the education research community. His verbal attacks on teachers and the teacher union were not matched by any significant attempts to address problems with teacher quality. At one point he threatened to cancel all field trips. At another, he threatened not to participate in the state's testing program. The public ate it up, but that kind of endless battle could last only so long.[61]

He says of himself: "I don't burn out. I burn other people out." [62]

Critics argued that Vallas lacked a sophisticated or flexible education vision, or ready access to one. Over and again during his last year, the mayor called on Vallas for new ideas, to "think outside the box." But Vallas, "deeply suspicious of the reform groups whom he says 'exploited' failing schools, critical of ed-school policy experts, and antagonistic toward the independent research shop set up at the University of Chicago, seemed to have been focused on political and managerial" rather than the priorities of professional educators. "Even after six years running the Chicago schools, Vallas still talked about time on task rather than methods or quality: more kindergarten, double periods of reading for struggling students, summer school, mandatory extended day.[63]

As in the cases of William Bratton and Kenneth Kizer, who also managed "in the black," Vallas found himself under fire. Student test scores were rising, but not fast enough for the mayor, who eventually decided to replace Vallas.[64] Said someone familiar with the situation, "The most obvious political explanation for his departure was that, from the mayor's perspective, Vallas grew too big for his britches. Like many other deputies before him . . . too much adulation can become a problem. Daley is famous in Chicago for firing staffers who steal his headlines." [65] Vallas's tenure as superintendent in Chicago lasted six years. His replacement was thirty-six-year-old Arne Duncan, little-known but liked by professional educators.

Philadelphia

Vallas became superintendent of the Philadelphia public schools, which had been taken over by the state, in 2002. He immediately became involved in overseeing the biggest privatization effort in any district in the country.[66] Many observers believed that the success of the public-private partnerships would make or break his reputation. His impact turned out to be much broader, however.

Vallas's political background was an evident asset in his new situation. His experience in politics, including campaigning for governor of Illinois after relinquishing his school post there,

> showed in the way he interacts with teachers and parents as he made his stops around the city. He put them at ease like an old pol, cracking quick jokes and swapping updates on common acquaintances before handing them a little spiral notebook and asking them to jot down complaints or problems in it. Vallas almost seemed more at ease with school kids and strangers than with members of his staff, who sometimes flinched perceptibly when he compliments them, taking his kind words as preludes to bigger work assignments.[67]

Unlike previous school administrators, Vallas got on well with the teachers' union and other critical stakeholder groups.

Vallas was said to hate not only the danger that suffused public schools in Philadelphia but also the way so many of the schools looked: "like dark and ugly penal colonies, small fortresses of concrete and brick with windows that no one can see through." He was said to wonder whether there is a connection between the brutality of the schools' appearance and the brutality that often takes place within them. An observer accompanied him on a visit to one of his schools to celebrate a new mural that had been painted on a school wall depicting several current students surrounded by basketballs, comets, and books. The school was one of seventeen where Vallas had commissioned murals. "The schools should be the most impressive buildings in the community," he said, "not the most run-down." [68]

Vallas's moves won praise virtually across the board in Philadelphia, "from Republican state legislators pushing hard for school privatization to city activists who can't stand that part of his program." "I don't remember a superintendent ever being on a honeymoon for three years," said Ted Kirsch, the local union president. He continued:

> He's imposed stricter discipline enforcement and assigned the most unruly kids to alternative facilities, a strategy that has reduced by half the number of Philadelphia schools considered "persistently dangerous" by federal standards. More positively, Vallas expanded the number of children who receive early childhood instruction by about 50 percent, lowering the shelf life of textbooks down to three years, pioneering the idea of a standardized curriculum for high schools, bringing advanced placement and college preparatory classes to every high school—"even where the students don't think they're going to college," he insists—and pursuing the structural reorganization of virtually every middle and high school in the city. All that on top of big changes in finance, human resources, capital planning and technology.[69]

On Vallas's departure from the Philadelphia schools, one observer said:

> I know, he is not a miracle worker. I know, any successes of the school district in the last five years may have had more to do with the fact that the district had $300 million in additional funding to play with after the state takeover than with the guy at the top. I know, there are people in town who think that he played fast and loose with the schools budget. But he brought an enormous amount of energy to a job that is known for sapping it right out of your bone marrow. [This is a] job that really may be impossible for one person to do.[70]

New Orleans

Reflecting his intuitive grasp of context and culture, in New Orleans Vallas appeared to be convinced that the approaches he had used in Chicago and Philadelphia were ill-suited to his new responsibilities. "There's much deeper poverty here," Vallas said. "So you take deep poverty and then you compound that by the aftermath of the hurricane, by the physical, psychological, emotional damage inflicted by the hurricane. It's like the straw that breaks the camel's back." [71]

In Vallas's view, the culture of New Orleans schools had to change; school personnel needed to accept that they were, in effect, substitute families. "You begin to make the schools community centers," he said. "The whole objective here is to keep the schools open through the dinner hour, and keep schools open 11 months out of the year." [72] Said one New Orleans teacher: "What he brings is high expectations, of course, but also a sense of urgency. You can hear it in his voice." [73] Said Vallas of his strategy in New Orleans: "I've actually prepared a checklist that we're giving to all the teachers and the parents the first week of school." His impact was immediate: Early in his first school year, the truancy rate had already dropped to 15 percent.

Said one observer, "As an educator for the past 14 years, I've heard it all. I've heard promises being made and nothing being the result. Superintendent Vallas is promoting technology in the classrooms. It's here. He's saying every classroom will be painted before students actually come into the school. That is being done. He really has come in with everything that he's promised." [74] Other teachers regarded Vallas's high expectations as naïve and unrealistic, however, and they remained skeptical as to whether he could keep all his promises or if he even understood what he was up against. After almost a year on the job, according to one account, "On one level the transformation has already been total. . . . [T]he schools are being administered with a vigor that would have been unrecognizable here before the storm." [75] Once again, Paul Vallas appeared to be very much in his element.

Vallas's long-term influence in Chicago and Philadelphia is hard to gauge. Individuals who show that "it can be done" often leave elevated expectations concerning what is attainable after they have moved on. Indeed, organizations may outgrow the need for this type of leadership, and a change of managers may be beneficial for all concerned. Leadership that is intense, demanding, and charismatic can also create, as noted above, a kind of fatigue that leads successor administrations to "consolidate the gains" and manage in a lower key, which may allow some unraveling of earlier accomplishments and the reappearance of old power relationships.

Confucius also said this, however: "Do not wish for quick results, nor look for small advantages. If you seek quick results, you will not reach the ultimate goal. If you are led astray by small advantages, you will never accomplish great things." Managing in the black is ultimately about being effective in adapting means to ends rather than the other way around. Knowing what those means are—structure, culture, and craft—and combining and integrating them in creative ways, and with due regard for the rule of law, is unlikely to win universal acclaim. As several examples in this book have suggested, doing so may even cost you your job. To be effective, to manage in the black, requires intellectual, behavioral, and emotional strengths of a high, and in many cases of an extraordinary, order. But that is the kind of challenge the founders of the Republic created for those who would "run a constitution." [76] And there are few deeper satisfactions than meeting such challenges successfully.

Key Concepts

garbage can model
distinctive challenges of public management
managing in the black
model deliberative process
connecting-the-dots problem
innovation
conundrums
impossible jobs

Analysis and Argument: Test Your Understanding

Read the teaching case, "Charting a Course in a Storm: US Postal Service and the Anthrax Crisis," published by the Case Program of the John F. Kennedy School of Government at Harvard University.[77] It tells the story of how Postal Service officials confronted the crisis created by the discovery that deadly anthrax was being sent through the U.S. mail, causing illness and death to recipients, postal workers, and others. Faced with the possibility that the entire postal system would have to be shut down due to a contingency for which there had been no prior planning, officials had to devise solutions and devise them quickly.

After studying the case, use the model deliberative process described earlier in this chapter to analyze it. Use the questions below to guide your analysis. Be as precise as possible, drawing on specific facts and quotes from the case, and making complete arguments (claims, reasons, evidence, warrants, and acknowledgments and responses).

1. How did the three dimensions of public management—structures and processes, institutionalized values and organizational cultures, and managerial skill and craftsmanship—come into play in the way USPS employees responded to the unfolding anthrax crisis? (You should be able to identify at least five examples of each dimension.)

2. Use concepts introduced throughout this book to illustrate how these various factors manifested themselves in resolving the anthrax crisis. Such concepts might include: street-level bureaucracy, backward-mapping, principal-agent relationships, roots of culture, cross pressures of accountability, deliberation and decision making, leadership.
3. Do you consider this case a public management success story? If so (or if not), what were the main reasons for the success (or failure)? Cite specific evidence—facts, indicators—you used in drawing your conclusion.

Notes

CHAPTER 1

1. U.S. Senate, *Hurricane Katrina: A Nation Still Unprepared: Special Report of the Committee on Homeland Security and Governmental Affairs* (Washington, D.C.: Government Printing Office, 2006), http://www.gpoaccess.gov/serialset/creports/katrinanation.html; and U.S. House of Representatives, *A Failure of Initiative: Final Report of the Select Bipartisan Committee to Investigate the Preparation for and Response to Hurricane Katrina* (Washington, D.C.: Government Printing Office, 2006), http://www.gpoaccess.gov/katrinareport/fullreport.pdf.
2. Martha Derthick, "Where Federalism Didn't Fail," *Public Administration Review,* (Special Issue, 2007): 43.
3. John R. Harrald, "Planning for Disaster," *TomPaine. CommonSense,* August 29, 2006, http://www.tompaine.com/articles/2006/08/29/planning_for_disaster.php.
4. James Q. Wilson, "The Rise of the Bureaucratic State," *The Public Interest* 41 (1975): 77–103; William E. Nelson, *The Roots of American Bureaucracy, 1830–1900* (Cambridge: Harvard University Press, 1982).
5. H. B. Learned, *The President's Cabinet* (New Haven: Yale University Press, 1912), 55, quoted by Michael Nelson, "A Short, Ironic History of American National Bureaucracy," *The Journal of Politics* 44 (1982): 751.
6. John A. Rohr, *Civil Servants and Their Constitutions* (Lawrence: University Press of Kansas, 2002), 78, 80.
7. In addition to the references cited in this section, see also E. Barker, *The Development of Public Services in Western Europe: 1660–1930* (London: Oxford University Press, 1944); H. G. Creel, "The Beginnings of Bureaucracy in China: The Origins of the Hsien," *Journal of Asian Studies* 23 (1964): 155–184; Henri Fayol, "Industrial and General Administration," *Bulletin de la societe de l'industrie minerale,* no. 3 (1916); Frank J. Goodnow, *Politics and Administration: A Study in Government* (New York: Russell and Russell, 1900); Luther Gulick and Lyndall Urwick, eds., *Papers on the Science of Administration* (New York: Institute of Public Administration, 1937); Harold Joseph Laski, *Authority in the Modern State* (New Haven: Yale University Press, 1919); Harold Joseph Laski, "The Growth of Administrative Discretion," *Journal of Public Administration* 1 (1923): 92–100; A. Lepawsky, *Administration: The Art and Science of Organization and Management* (New York: Alfred A. Knopf, 1949); H. Rosenberg,

Bureaucracy, Aristocracy and Autocracy: The Prussian Experience, 1660–1815 (Boston: Beacon Press, 1958); Leonard D. White, *Introduction to the Study of Public Administration,* rev. ed. (New York: Macmillan, 1935); Woodrow Wilson, "The Study of Administration," *Political Science Quarterly* 2 (1885): 197–222; Laurence E. Lynn Jr., "Public Management: A Concise History of the Field," in *The Oxford Handbook of Public Management,* ed. E. Ferlie, L. Lynn, and C. Pollitt (London and New York: Oxford University Press, 2005), 27–50; and Nicholas Henry, "Public Administration's Century in a Quandary," in *Public Administration and Public Affairs,* 10th ed. (Upper Saddle River, N.J.: Pearson Prentice Hall, 2007), 26–47.

8. Nelson, "A Short, Ironic History," 748.
9. Joel D. Aberbach and Bert A. Rockman, "Problems of Cross-National Comparison," in *Public Administration in Developed Democracies: A Comparative Study,* ed. Donald C. Rowat (New York: Marcel Dekker, 1988), 419–440, 421.
10. H. George Frederickson and Kevin B. Smith, *The Public Administration Theory Primer* (Boulder: Westview Press, 2003), 98.
11. James Q. Wilson, *Bureaucracy: What Government Agencies Do and Why They Do It* (New York: Basic Books, 1989), 375.
12. Richard F. Elmore, "Graduate Education in Public Management: Working the Seams of Government," *Journal of Policy Analysis and Management* 6, no. 1 (1986): 69.
13. Barry Bozeman, "Preface," in *Public Management: The State of the Art,* ed. Barry Bozeman (San Francisco: Jossey-Bass, 1993), xiii.
14. Luther Gulick, "Notes on the Theory of Organization," in *Papers on the Science of Administration,* ed. L. Gulick and L. Urwick (New York: Institute of Public Administration, 1937), 3–13.
15. Henry Mintzberg, *The Nature of Managerial Work* (Harper and Row, 1973).
16. Peter Hupe, *Government Performance in Micro-Networks: Towards a Theory of Functional Discretion* (paper presented at the conference on Performance in the Public Sector, Katholieke Universiteit Leuven, June 1–3, 2006).
17. Elmore, "Graduate Education in Public Management," 81; see also Mark Moore, *Creating Public Value: Strategic Management in Government* (Cambridge: Harvard University Press, 1995).
18. Herbert A. Simon, *Administrative Behavior,* 4th ed. (New York: Free Press, 1997), 91.
19. Wilson, *Bureaucracy,* 158–173.
20. Patrick Dunleavy, *Democracy, Bureaucracy and Public Choice* (New York: Harvester, 1991).
21. Gordon Chase and Elizabeth C. Reveal, *How to Manage in the Public Sector* (Reading, Mass.: Addison-Wesley, 1983).
22. Information in this section and for Figure 1.1 was drawn from correspondence with Amanda Bryans and Amanda Quesenberry in the Office of Head Start, as well as organization charts at: Health and Human Services Department, http://www.hhs.gov/about/orgchart.html; Administration for Children and Families, http://www.acf.hhs.gov/orgs/opschart0903.html; and Administration for Children's Services, http://www.nyc.gov/html/acs/downloads/pdf/org_chart.pdf.
23. In addition to the references cited in this section, see also Robert D. Behn, "What Right Do Public Managers Have to Lead?" *Public Administration Review* 58, no. 3 (1998): 209–224; Brian J. Cook, "Politics, Political Leadership, and Public Management," *Public Administration Review* 58, no. 3 (1998): 225–230; and Herbert Kaufman, "Administrative Decentralization and Political Power," *Public Administration Review* 29, no. 1 (1969): 3–15.
24. Harold D. Lasswell, *Politics: Who Gets What, When, How* (New York: Whittlesey House, 1936).
25. E. E. Schattschneider, *Politics, Pressures and the Tariff* (Hamden, Conn.: Archon Books, 1963 [1935]), 288.
26. James MacGregor Burns, *Leadership* (New York: Harper and Row, 1978), 18.
27. Wilson, "The Study of Administration," 197–222; Frank J. Goodnow, *Politics and Administration: A Study in Government* (New York: Russell and Russell, 1900).

28. Terry Moe, "The Politics of Structural Choice: Toward a Theory of Public Bureaucracy," in *Organization Theory: From Chester Barnard to the Present and Beyond,* ed. Oliver E. Williamson (New York: Oxford University Press, 1990), 116–153.
29. Ibid., 143.
30. Laurence E. Lynn Jr., "Public Management," in *Handbook of Public Administration,* ed. B. Guy Peters and Jon Pierre (London: Sage, 2003), 21.
31. Moe, "The Politics of Structural Choice, 143.
32. Nina Bernstein, "Security Rules Tie Foreigners with Red Tape," *New York Times,* April 6, 2004.
33. Marty Davis, "Managing the Unexpected," *ASK* magazine, November 2004, http://appel.nasa.gov/ask/issues/20/20s_managing_davis.php.
34. David Anderson, "The Great Chicago Flood," *Horizon* magazine, August 1999, 2; see also Transit Cooperative Research Program and National Cooperative Highway Research Program, *Making Transportation Tunnels Safe and Secure,* TCRP Report 86/NCHRP Report 525, Transportation Security, vol. 12 (Washington, D.C.: National Academies/National Research Council, Transportation Research Board, 2006), 37–39.
35. Office of Personnel Management, *Results from the 2006 Federal Human Capital Survey,* http://www.fhcs2006.opm.gov/Published/FHCS_2006_Report.pdf.
36. James L. Perry and Lois Recascino Wise, "The Motivational Bases of Public Service," *Public Administration Review* 50, no. 3 (1990).
37. Joel D. Aberbach, Robert D. Putnam, and Bert A. Rockman, *Bureaucrats and Politicians in Western Democracies* (Cambridge: Harvard University Press, 1981), 125, 230–231.
38. Norma M. Riccucci, *Unsung Heroes: Federal Executives Making a Difference* (Washington, D.C.: Georgetown University Press, 1995).
39. Carolyn Ban, *How Do Public Managers Manage? Bureaucratic Constraints, Organizational Culture, and the Potential for Reform* (San Francisco: Jossey-Bass, 1995).
40. Jane Hannaway, *Managers Managing: The Workings of an Administrative System* (New York: Oxford University Press, 1989), 141, 147–148.
41. Douglas Yates, *Bureaucratic Democracy: The Search for Democracy and Efficiency in American Government* (Cambridge: Harvard University Press, 1982).
42. Frank J. Goodnow, *1902 Comparative Administrative Law: An Analysis of the Administrative Systems, National and Local, of the United States, England, France, and Germany* (New York: G. P. Putnam's Sons), 10, quoted in Lynn, "Public Management," 19.
43. Graham T. Allison, *Public and Private Management: Are They Fundamentally Alike in All Unimportant Respects?* (proceedings for the Office of Personnel Management Public Management Research Conference, Washington, D.C., November 19–20, 1979), 27–38.
44. Hal G. Rainey and Young Han Chun, "Public and Private Management Compared," in *The Oxford Handbook of Public Management,* 72–102. See also Jack Knott, "Comparing Public and Private Management: Cooperative Effort and Principal-Agent Relationships," *Journal of Public Administration Research and Theory* (1993); Christopher Pollitt, "Public Sector, Private Sector—Where Would We Be without a Few Good Stereotypes?" in *The Essential Public Manager* (Maidenhead, Berks., U.K.: Open University Press, 2003), 1–25; Hal G. Rainey, *Understanding and Managing Public Organizations* (San Francisco: Jossey-Bass, 2003); and Wilson, *Bureaucracy.*
45. Donald Kettl and James Fesler, *The Politics of the Administrative Process* (Chatham, N.J.: Chatham House Publishers, 1996), 10.
46. For further information on these issues, see, for example, Harvey S. Rosen and Ted Gayer, *Public Finance,* 8th ed. (Boston: McGraw-Hill Irwin, 2008).
47. Charles Wolf Jr., *Markets or Governments: Choosing Between Imperfect Alternatives,* 2nd ed. (Cambridge: MIT Press, 1993). In a related work, Barry Bozeman calls such phenomena

"bureaupathologies." Barry Bozeman, *Bureaucracy and Red Tape* (Upper Saddle River, N.J.: Prentice Hall, 2000).

48. Wolf, *Markets or Governments,* 69–70.
49. Allison Jr., *Public and Private Management: Are They Fundamentally Alike in All Unimportant Respects?*
50. Michael Barzelay and Babak J. Armajani, *Breaking through Bureaucracy* (Berkeley: University of California Press, 1992); David Osborne and Ted Gaebler, *Reinventing Government* (Reading, Mass.: Addison-Wesley, 1992).
51. Christopher Pollitt and Geert Bouckaert, *Public Management Reform: A Comparative Perspective,* 2nd ed. (Oxford: Oxford University Press, 2004).
52. Barry Bozeman, *All Organizations are Public: Bridging Public and Private Organizational Theories* (San Francisco: Jossey-Bass, 1987).
53. Rainey and Chun, "Public and Private Management Compared," 72–102.
54. Ibid.
55. Santa Falcone, "Self-Assessments and Job Satisfaction in Public and Private Organizations," *Public Productivity & Management Review* 14, no. 4 (1991): 385–396.
56. Ibid.
57. Katharine Karl and Cynthia Sutton, "Job Values in Today's Workforce: A Comparison of Public and Private Sector Employees," *Public Personnel Management* 27, no. 4 (1998): 515–528.
58. Robert Golembiewski, Robert Boudreau, Ben-Chu Sun, and Huaping Lou, "Estimates of Burnout in Public Agencies," *Public Administration Review* 58, no. 1 (1998): 59–65.
59. Office of Personnel Management, *Federal Human Capital Survey,* 2006.
60. Rainey and Chun, "Public and Private Management Compared," 93.
61. Lynn, "Public Management," 17.
62. In addition to the references cited in this section, see also Linda Kaboolian, "The New Public Management: Challenging the Boundaries of the Management vs. Administration Debate," *Public Administration Review* 58, no. 3 (1998): 189–193; Donald F. Kettl, "Public Administration at the Millennium: The State of the Field," *Journal of Public Administration Research and Theory* 10, no. 1 (2000): 7–34; Larry D. Terry, "Administrative Leadership, Neo-Managerialism, and the Public Management Movement," *Public Administration Review* 58, no. 3 (1998): 194–200.
63. Lynn, "Public Management"; Laurence E. Lynn Jr., *Public Management: Old and New* (New York: Routledge, 2006).
64. Lynn, "Public Management," 15; see also Lynn, *Public Management: Old and New.*
65. Ibid., 10.
66. The three-dimensional framework was initially developed in Lynn, "Public Management."
67. Petula Dvorak and David Nakamura, "Fenty Fires 6 in Girls' Deaths: Four Children Had Not Been Seen for Months," *Washington Post,* January 15, 2008, A01.

CHAPTER 2

1. Presidential Commission on the Space Shuttle Challenger Accident, *Report to the President* (Washington, D.C.: National Aeronautics and Space Administration, 1986).
2. Presidential Commission on the Space Shuttle Challenger Accident, *Implementation of the Recommendations* (Washington, D.C.: National Aeronautics and Space Administration, 1987).
3. John Schwartz and Matthew L. Wald, "Echoes of Challenger: Shuttle Panel Considers Longstanding Flaws in NASA's System," *New York Times,* April 13, 2003.
4. Richard Blomberg, Statement to the House Subcommittee on Space and Aeronautics, April 18, 2002.

5. Shuttle Competitive Source Task Force, *Final Report* (Washington, D.C.: RAND Corporation, 2002).
6. "Honesty and Denial at NASA," *Nature*, September 4, 2003, 1.
7. Graham T. Allison, *The Essence of Decision: Explaining the Cuban Missile Crisis* (Boston: Little, Brown, 1972).
8. Gareth Morgan, *Images of Organization* (Thousand Oaks, Calif.: Sage, 1996).
9. Henry Mintzberg, "Managing Government, Governing Management," *Harvard Business Review* (May/June 1996): 75.
10. Lee G. Bolman and Terrence E. Deal, *Reframing Organizations: Artistry, Choice, and Leadership* (San Francisco: Jossey-Bass, 2003).
11. Geeta Anand, "Who Gets Health Care? Rationing in an Age of Rising Costs, *Wall Street Journal*, September 12, 2003, Sec. A.
12. Texas Politics, "Bureaucracy," http://texaspolitics.laits.utexas.edu.
13. Steve Vogel, "The Young Lions of Able Troop: To the Cadre on the Front Lines of Improving Care at Walter Reed, The Challenge Can Rival Combat," *Washington Post*, April 10, 2008, B1.
14. Jean-Claude Thoenig, "Institutional Theories and Public Institutions: Traditions and Appropriateness," in *Handbook of Public Administration*, ed. B. Guy Peters and Jon Pierre (London: Sage, 2003), 129.
15. Philip Selznick, *TVA and the Grass Roots*, quoted in Jane E. Fountain, *Building the Virtual State: Information Technology and Institutional Change* (Washington, D.C.: Brookings Institution Press, 2001), 92.
16. *Report of Columbia Accident Investigation Board*, vol. 1 (Washington, D.C.: National Aeronautics and Space Administration, 2003), 138, http://www.nasa.gov/columbia/home/CAIB_Vol1.html.
17. Ibid., 169.
18. Anne M. Khademian, *Working with Culture: The Way the Job Gets Done in Public Programs* (Washington, D.C.: CQ Press, 2002).
19. Alyssa Rosenberg, "Army Facility Wins National Quality Award," Govexec.com, December 5, 2007.
20. Sewell Chan, "City Official Pleads Guilty in Ferry Crash," *New York Times*, April 23, 2005, Sec. B.
21. Justin Blum, "Officials Earn High Marks on the Hill," *Washington Post*, August 9, 2005, Sec. A.
22. "Departure of a Pragmatist," *New York Times*, September 8, 2006, Sec. A.
23. *Report of Columbia Accident Investigation Board*, 197.
24. Max Weber, *Economy and Society*, ed. G. Roth and R. Wittich (Berkeley: University of California Press, 1978).
25. Diane Vaughan, *The Challenger Launch Decision: Risky Technology, Culture, and Deviance at NASA* (Chicago: University of Chicago Press, 1996), in *Report of Columbia Accident Investigation Board*, 130.
26. *Report of Columbia Accident Investigation Board*, 180; Todd R. La Porte and Paula M. Consolini, "Working in Practice but Not in Theory," *Journal of Public Administration Research and Theory* 1 (1991): 19–47.
27. *Report of Columbia Accident Investigation Board*, 180.
28. Ibid.
29. Government Accountability Office, "United Nations: Oil for Food Program Provides Lessons Learned from Future Sanctions and Ongoing Reform" *(GAO-06-711T)*, May 2, 2006.
30. "The U.N. Oil for Food Scandal," March 22, 2004, http://www.washingtontimes.com/op-ed/20040321-101405-2593r.htm.
31. Claudia Rosett, "The Oil-for-Food Scam: What Did Kofi Annan Know, and When Did He Know It?" *Commentary*, May 2004, http://www.defenddemocracy.org/publications/publications_show.htm?doc_id=228669.

32. Ibid.
33. Paul A. Volcker, Richard J. Goldstone, Mark Pieth, and the Independent Inquiry Committee in to the United Nations Oil-for-Food Programme, *The Management of the United Nations Oil-for-Food Programme,* vol. 1, September 7, 2005, http://www.iic-offp.org/Mgmt_Report.htm, 47.

CHAPTER 3

1. In addition to the citations throughout this chapter, see also Christopher Hood and Michael Jackson, *Administrative Argument* (Aldershot, U.K.: Dartmouth, 1991); Michael Barzelay, "How to Argue about the New Public Management," *International Public Management Journal* 2, no. 2 (1999): 183–216.
2. Arthur W. Macmahon, "Specialization and the Public Interest," in *Democracy in Federal Administration,* ed. Orrin Bryte Conway Jr. (Washington, D.C.: U.S. Department of Agriculture Graduate School, 1955), 40.
3. David M. Walker, "Facing Facts about America's True Financial Conditions and Fiscal Outlook: The Outlook Is Grim and Will Get Worse Unless We Act Soon," *Business Economics,* July 2004. For further information, see, for example, the March 4, 2007, *60 Minutes* interview with David Walker, http://www.pgpf.org/multimedia/, as well as the numerous presentations and reports on the GAO Web site: http://www.gao.gov/cghome/cghomeformer.htm.
4. Press release, "Peter G. Peterson Commits $1 Billion Toward Solving America's Most Significant Economic Challenges," February 15, 2008, http://www.petergpetersonfoundation.org/news.asp.
5. Press release, "David M. Walker, U.S. Comptroller General, Announces Early Departure to Head New Public Interest Foundation," February 15, 2008, http://www.gao.gov/press/cgdeparture 2152008.pdf.
6. Alberto R. Gonzales, "Prepared Remarks for Attorney General Alberto R. Gonzales at the Georgetown University Law Center," January 24, 2006, http://www.usdoj.gov/ag/speeches/2006/ag_speech_0601241.html.
7. *Rebuilding Lives. Restoring Hope. Strengthening Communities. Breaking the Cycle of Incarceration and Building Brighter Futures in Chicago.* Final Report of the Mayoral Policy Caucus on Prisoner Reentry, January 2006, http://egov.cityofchicago.org/webportal/COCWebPortal/COC_EDITORIAL/MPCFinalReport.pdf.
8. "Message from the Mayor," regarding City of Chicago prisoner reentry initiatives, http://egov.cityofchicago.org/city/webportal/portalContentItemAction.do?contentOID=536951276&contenTypeName=COC_EDITORIAL&topChannelName=Dept&blockName=Mayors+Office%2FTest%2FI+Want+To&context=dept&channelId=0&programId=0&entityName=Mayors+Office&deptMainCategoryOID=-536882061.
9. Ibid.
10. We employ the terminology used by Wayne C. Booth, Gregory G. Colomb, and Joseph M. Williams, *The Craft of Research,* 2nd ed. (Chicago: University of Chicago Press, 2003); Joseph M. Williams and Gregory G. Colomb, *The Craft of Argument,* 3rd ed. (New York: Pearson Longman, 2007); and Joseph M. Williams et al., *The Craft of Argument, with Readings* (New York: Longman, 2003). Stephen E. Toulmin, *The Uses of Argument,* updated ed. (Cambridge: Cambridge University Press, 2003), 89–96, refers to main elements of an argument as "claims," "data," "warrants," "qualifiers," and "backing," where "backing" provides the fundamental justification for a warrant. Stephen Toulmin, Richard Rieke, and Allan Janik, *An Introduction to Reasoning,* 2nd ed. (New York: Macmillan, 1984), 25–27, 85–87, refer to the main elements of argument as "claims," "grounds," "warrants," and "backing." They consider "qualifiers" to be at the "second level of analysis" for an argument. Toulmin's work contains an explicit role for qualifications, but this is

not found in Williams and Colomb or in Williams et al., who argue that qualifications may play a part in each element of the argument and therefore are not a separate element.

11. Booth, Colomb, and Williams, *The Craft of Research,* 140.
12. Stuart Hampshire, *Justice Is Conflict* (Princeton: Princeton University Press, 1999), 45.
13. Williams and Colomb, *The Craft of Argument,* 133.
14. Gonzales, "Prepared Remarks," 2006.
15. Giandomenico Majone, *Evidence, Argument, and Persuasion in the Policy Process* (New Haven: Yale University Press, 1989), 21–22.
16. W. James Bradley and Kurt C. Schaefer, *The Uses and Misuses of Data and Models: The Mathematization of the Human Sciences* (Thousand Oaks, Calif.: Sage Publications, 1998), 161–163.
17. Ibid., 162.
18. Ibid., 164.
19. See, for example, Peter deLeon, "Introduction: The Evidentiary Base for Policy Analysis: Empiricist versus Postpositivist Positions," *Policy Studies Journal* 26 (1998): 109–113; Laurence E. Lynn Jr., "A Place at the Table: Policy Analysis: Its Postpositive Critics, and the Future of Practice," *Journal of Policy Analysis and Management* 18 (1999): 411–425.
20. Donald P. Moynihan, "What Do We Talk About When We Talk About Performance? Dialogue Theory and Performance Budgeting, *Journal of Public Administration Research and Theory* 16, no. 2 (2006): 167.
21. Bradley and Schaefer, *The Uses and Misuses of Data and Models,* 164–171.
22. Williams et al., *The Craft of Argument, with Readings,* 156.
23. Particularly useful resources showing examples of warrants and their use are "The Logic of Your Argument: Warranting Claims and Reasons," in Williams and Colomb, *The Craft of Argument,* 203–231; and "Warranting Claims and Reasons," in ibid., 154–177.
24. Toulmin, *The Uses of Argument,* 93.
25. Toulmin, Rieke, and Janik, *An Introduction to Reasoning,* 386.
26. Booth, Colomb, and Williams, *The Craft of Research,* 179–181.
27. Terry Moe, "The Politics of Structural Choice: Toward a Theory of Public Bureaucracy," in *Organization Theory: From Chester Barnard to the Present and Beyond,* ed. Oliver E. Williamson (New York: Oxford University Press, 1990), 116–153.
28. Web sites for the Kennedy School Case Program and Electronic Hallway are, respectively, http://www.ksgcase.harvard.edu/ and http://www.hallway.org.
29. Adapted from Laurence E. Lynn Jr., "Welcome to the Case Method!" 1999, Electronic Hallway, http://www.hallway.org.
30. See also Barbara Minto, *The Pyramid Principle: Logic in Writing and Thinking,* 3rd ed. (London: Financial Times Prentice Hall, 2002); Booth, Colomb, and Williams, *The Craft of Research;* Jonathan Brock, "MORETOOLS: A Framework for Analyzing Management Dilemmas," Electronic Hallway, http://www.hallway.org; Judith R. Gordon, *Organizational Behavior: A Diagnostic Approach,* 7th ed. (Upper Saddle River, N.J.: Prentice Hall, 2001); and Laurence E. Lynn Jr., *Teaching and Learning with Cases: A Guidebook* (New York: Chatham House Publishers, 1999).
31. Melvin J. Dubnick, "Spirited Dialogue: The Case for Administrative Evil: A Critique," *Public Administration Review* 60, no. 5 (2000): 464–474.
32. Guy B. Adams and Danny L. Balfour, "Spirited Dialogue: The Authors' Response," *Public Administration Review* 60, no. 5 (2000): 481–482.
33. Herbert A. Simon, *Models of Man* (New York: Wiley, 1957); Herbert A. Simon, "Rationality as Process and as Process of Thought," *American Economic Review* 68 (1978): 1–16; see also Jonathan Bendor, "Herbert A. Simon: Political Scientist," *Annual Review of Political Science* 6 (June 2003): 433–471.

34. Testimony of Secretary Michael Chertoff, U.S. Department of Homeland Security, before the Senate Committee on Homeland Security and Governmental Affairs, September 12, 2006, http://www.dhs.gov/dhspublic/display?content=5825.
35. Nanotechnology Workgroup, Science Policy Council, U.S. Environmental Protection Agency, "Nanotechnology White Paper," February 2007, EPA 100/B-07/001, http://www.epa.gov/OSA/pdfs/nanotech/epa-nanotechnology-whitepaper-0207.pdf.
36. The President's Commission to Strengthen Social Security, *Strengthening Social Security and Creating Personal Wealth for All Americans,* December 21, 2001, http://www.csss.gov/reports/Final_report.pdf.
37. Los Angeles City Controller and Sjoberg Evashenk Consulting Inc., "Review of the Los Angeles Fire Department Management Practices," January 26, 2006, http://www.lacity.org/ctr/audits/ctraudits18035136_01262006.pdf.
38. Interview with David Walker, *60 Minutes,* March 4, 2007, http://www.pgpf.org/multimedia/.
39. Jeffrey Leib, "FAA Official Defends Air-Traffic Staffing," *Denver Post,* October 13, 2005, Sec. B.
40. Office of the Chancellor, District of Columbia Public Schools, *Year 1 Plan,* http://www.k12.dc.us/chancellor/documents/First%20year%20plan.pdf.

CHAPTER 4

1. Thomas Paine, *Common Sense* (Philadelphia: W. and T. Bradford, 1791), http://www.earlyamerica.com/earlyamerica/milestones/commonsense/text.html.
2. Michael Mullane, "The Rule of Law," *NPR Morning Edition,* June 5, 2006.
3. Andrew Graham and Alasdair Roberts, "The Agency Concept in North America: Failure, Adaptation, and Incremental Change," in *Unbundled Government: A Critical Analysis of the Global Trend to Agencies, Quangos and Contractualisation,* ed. Christopher Pollitt and Colin Talbot (London and New York: Routledge, 2004), 146.
4. Ibid., 147.
5. Daniel Primbs, "There's No Such Thing as a Federal Mandate?" *Public Interest Institute Brief* 64 (July 1998).
6. *Printz v. United States,* 521 U.S. 898 (1997), http://www.law.cornell.edu/supct/html/95-1478.ZO.html.
7. Souter's dissent in *Printz v. United States* is at http://www.law.cornell.edu/supct/html/95-1478.ZD1.html.
8. *Printz v. United States,* majority opinion.
9. Gary Wamsley et al., "Public Administration and the Governance Process: Shifting the Political Dialogue," in Gary L. Wamsley et al., *Refounding Public Administration* (Beverley Hills, Calif.: Sage, 1990), www.cpap.vt.edu/current/wamsley_etal.pdf.
10. *Massachusetts Constitution,* Part The First, art. XXX (1780).
11. A useful online source of definitions related to the rule of law is at http://www.quickmba.com/law/sys/. Articles from the electronic journal of the former United States Information Agency offer a comprehensive overview of how the U.S. court system works. See http://usinfo.state.gov/journals/itdhr/0999/ijde/ijde0999.htm. Access to a comprehensive body of informative links for the federal government, the states, and other sources of law is at http://www.lawsource.com/also/#[United%20States].
12. For an annotated text of the U.S. Constitution from Cornell University Law School, see http://www.law.cornell.edu/constitution/index.html.
13. On administrative law, see David H. Rosenbloom, *Administrative Law for Public Managers* (Boulder, Colo.: Westview Press, 2003); and Phillip J. Cooper, *Public Law and Public Administration,* 4th ed. (Itasca, Ill.: F. E. Peacock, 2006).

14. Rosenbloom, *Administrative Law for Public Managers.*
15. Ibid., 17.
16. *Clinton v. Cedar Rapids and the Missouri River Railroad,* 24 Iowa 455 (1868). The author of the opinion, John Forrest Dillon, was a justice of the Iowa Supreme Court, who was later appointed to the federal bench by President Ulysses S. Grant.
17. David R. Berman, *Local Government and the States: Autonomy, Politics, and Policy* (Armonk, N.Y.: M. E. Sharpe, 2003), 19.
18. For texts of state constitutions and related materials, consult http://www.constitution.org/cons/usstcons.htm. For individual state information, go to http://www.findlaw.com/11stategov/. For detailed information on the characteristics of state constitutions, see Christopher W. Hammons, "Was James Madison Wrong? Rethinking the American Preference for Short, Framework-Oriented Constitutions," *American Political Science Review* 93, no. 4 (1999): 837–149. See also G. Alan Tarr, *Understanding State Constitutions* (Princeton: Princeton University Press, 1998).
19. G. Alan Tarr, "Interpreting the Separation of Powers in State Constitutions," *NYU Annual Survey of American Law* 59 (2003): 330.
20. Ibid., 338.
21. For overviews of federalism and intergovernmental relations, see Beryl A. Radin, "The Instruments of Intergovernmental Management," in *Handbook of Public Administration,* ed. B. Guy Peters and Jon Pierre (London and Thousand Oaks, Calif.: Sage Publications, 2003), 607–618; Lester M. Salamon, ed., *The Tools of Government Action: A Guide to the New Governance* (Oxford and New York: Oxford University Press, 2002); and Nicholas Henry, *Public Administration and Public Affairs,* 10th ed. (Upper Saddle River, N.J.: Pearson Prentice-Hall, 2007), 349–392.
22. Henry, *Public Administration and Public Affairs,* 350.
23. A complete list of constitutional checks and balances is available online at http://www.usconstitution.net/consttop_cnb.html. See also Rafael La Porta et al., "Judicial Checks and Balances," *Journal of Political Economy* 112, no. 2 (2004): 445–470; and James Madison, "Federalist No. 47," in *The Federalist Papers,* ed. C. Rossiter (New York: New American Library, 1961), or any other edition of these seminal papers.
24. An authoritative discussion of separation of powers and checks and balances is maintained at http://caselaw.lp.findlaw.com/data/constitution/article01/01.html.
25. *Shoemaker v. United States,* 147 U.S. 282, 301 (1893).
26. John A. Rohr, *Civil Servants and Their Constitutions* (Lawrence: University Press of Kansas, 2002), 101.
27. Kroll Web site, http://www.kroll.com.
28. For Kroll's reports on the Los Angeles Police Department, see http://www.krollworldwide.com/about/library/lapd/.
29. "Summarizing the Monitor's Evaluation of Compliance with the Consent Decree as of the Quarter Ending March 31, 2006," http://www.krollworldwide.com/ library/lapd/ LAPD_Q19_Appendix_A_05-15-2006.pdf.
30. General Accounting Office, "Head Start: Research Provides Little Information on Impact of Current Program" (Washington, D.C.: GAO, 1997).
31. Reports available at http://www.acf.hhs.gov/programs/opre/hs/impact_study/#reports.
32. See http://www.fseee.org/ for detailed information.
33. See Case 3:04-cv-04512-PJH Document 101 Filed 03/30/2007, U.S. District Court for the Northern District of California.
34. Paula Dobbyn, "Biologist Files Suit Targeting Logging Roads," *Anchorage Daily News,* May 20, 2006.
35. *Garcetti v. Ceballos,* 547 U.S. 410 (2006), http://www.supremecourtus.gov/opinions/05pdf/04-473.pdf.

36. Ibid., 3–4.
37. "ABA Administrative Procedure Data Base," Florida State University College of Law, http://www.law.fsu.edu/library/admin/.
38. Rosenbloom, *Administrative Law for Public Managers.*
39. Ibid., 13.
40. Stephen D. Sugarman, "Cases in Vaccine Court—Legal Battles over Vaccines and Autism," *New England Journal of Medicine* 357, no. 13 (September 27, 2007): 1275–1277, http://content.nejm.org/cgi/content/full/357/13/1275.
41. National Vaccine Injury Compensation Program, Strategic Plan, April 2006, http://www.hrsa.gov/vaccinecompensation/strategic_plan.htm.
42. AutismVox, http://www.autismvox.com/what-the-government-said/.
43. Rosemary O'Leary, *The Ethics of Dissent: Managing Guerrilla Government* (Washington, D.C.: CQ Press, 2005).
44. Jonathan D. Moreno and Richard O. Hynes, "Guidelines for Human Embryonic Stem Cell Research," *Nature Biotechnology* 23 (2005): 793–794.
45. David L. Weimer, "The Puzzle of Private Rulemaking: Expertise, Flexibility, and Blame Avoidance in U.S. Regulation," *Public Administration Review* 66 (July/August 2006): 569–582.
46. Ibid., 578.
47. J. C. Nelson et al., "When Doctors Go to War," *New England Journal of Medicine* 352 (April 2005): 1497–1499; Steven H. Miles, *Oath Betrayed: Torture, Medical Complicity, and the War on Terror* (New York: Random House, 2006).
48. Laurence E. Lynn Jr., "Has Governance Eclipsed Government?" in Robert F. Durant, ed., *Oxford Handbook of American Bureaucracy* (London and New York: Oxford University Press, 2009).
49. Laurence E. Lynn Jr., Carolyn J. Heinrich, and Carolyn J. Hill, *Improving Governance: A New Logic for Empirical Research* (Washington, D.C.: Georgetown University Press, 2001). See also Laurence E. Lynn Jr., Carolyn J. Heinrich, and Carolyn J. Hill, "Studying Governance and Public Management: Challenges and Prospects," *Journal of Public Administration Research and Theory* 10, no. 2 (2000): 233–261.
50. For other definitions, see Laurence E. Lynn Jr., *Public Management: Old and New* (London: Routledge, 2006); and Michael Hill and Peter Hupe, *Implementing Public Policy* (London: Sage, 2008).
51. Geoffrey Vickers, *The Art of Judgment: A Study of Policymaking* (New York: Harper and Row, 1983); Lynn, Heinrich, and Hill, *Improving Governance*; Gary L. Wamsley, "The Agency Perspective: Public Administrators as Agential Leader," in Wamsley et al., *Refounding Public Administration.*
52. Human Rights Watch, "The Road to Abu Ghraib," September 21, 2006, http://hrw.org/reports/2004/usa0604/. Other sources of information on Abu Ghraib are Phillip Carter, "The Road to Abu Ghraib," *Washington Monthly,* November 2004; Mark Danner, *Torture and Truth: America, Abu Ghraib, and the War on Terror* (New York: New York Review of Books, 2004); Karen J. Greenberg and Joshua L. Dratel, eds., *The Torture Papers: The Road to Abu Ghraib* (New York: Cambridge University Press, 2005); and Guy B. Adams, Danny L. Balfour, and George E. Reed, "Abu Ghraib, Administrative Evil, and Moral Inversion: The Value of 'Putting Cruelty First,' " *Public Administration Review* 66, no. 5 (September/October 2006): 680–693.
53. For additional discussion of managing according to the rule of law, see Yong S. Lee with David H. Rosenbloom, *A Reasonable Public Servant: Constitutional Foundations of Administrative Conduct in the United States* (Armonk, N.Y.: M. E. Sharpe, 2005); and Anthony M. Bertelli, "Strategy and Accountability: Structural Reform Litigation and Public Management," *Public Administration Review* 64 (2004): 28–42.
54. *Rapanos v. United States,* 547 U.S. 715 (2006), http://laws.findlaw.com/us/000/04-1034.html.

55. John A. Rohr, "The Administrative State and Constitutional Principle," in *A Centennial History of the American Administrative State,* ed. Ralph Clark Chandler (New York: Free Press, 1987), 145, 148.
56. For further reading concerning alternative concepts of managerial responsibility, see Guy B. Adams and Danny L. Balfour, *Unmasking Administrative Evil,* rev. ed. (Armonk, N.Y.: M. E. Sharpe, 2004); Martha S. Feldman and Anne M. Khademian, "Managing for Inclusion: Balancing Control and Participation," *International Journal of Public Management* 3, no. 2 (2000): 149–168; Linda deLeon and Peter deLeon, "The Democratic Ethos and Public Management," *Administration & Society* 34, no. 2 (2002): 229–250.
57. Wamsley et al., "Public Administration and the Governance Process."
58. Michael W. Spicer and Larry D. Terry, "Legitimacy, History, and Logic: Public Administration and the Constitution," *Public Administration Review* 53, no. 3 (May/June 1993): 239–246.
59. H. George Frederickson, *The Spirit of Public Administration* (San Francisco: Jossey-Bass, 1997), 229.
60. Anthony Michael Bertelli and Laurence E. Lynn Jr., *Madison's Managers: Public Administration and the Constitution* (Baltimore: Johns Hopkins University Press, 2006), 65.
61. Rosenbloom, *Administrative Law for Public Managers.*
62. *City of Boerne v. Flores,* 521 U.S. 507 (1997).
63. *Harlow v. Fitzgerald,* 457 U.S. 800 (1982); *Anderson v. Creighton,* 483 U.S. 635 (1987).
64. Yong S. Lee, "The Judicial Theory of a Reasonable Public Servant," *Public Administration Review* 64 (July 2004): 425. See also Charles R. Wise, "Suits against Federal Employees for Constitutional Violations: A Search for Reasonableness," *Public Administration Review* 45, no. 6 (November/December 1985): 845–856.
65. R. Jeffrey Smith, "Worried CIA Officers Buy Legal Insurance," *Washington Post,* September 11, 2006, Sec. A.
66. Herbert Kaufman, "The Confines of Leadership," in *The Administrative Behavior of Federal Bureau Chiefs* (Washington, D.C.: Brookings Institution, 1981), 91–138.
67. Ibid., 91.
68. Phillip J. Cooper, *Public Law and Public Administration,* 3rd ed. (Itasca, Ill.: F. E. Peacock, 2000).
69. See Donald L. Horowitz, "The Courts as Guardians of the Public Interest," *Public Administration Review* 37, no. 2 (March/April 1977): 148–154, for supplemental reading that complements this case and that raises additional questions for discussion.
70. Plaintiff-employees have now withdrawn their request that they be reinstated as employees of the Alabama Mental Health Board. This completely eliminates their reinstatement claims from the case.
71. [From original *Wyatt* decision.] The Alabama Mental Health Board is also responsible for other State mental health facilities, such as that located at Searcy Hospital, Mount Vernon, Alabama. However, in this case this Court is not concerned with the operation of the facility at Searcy, since plaintiffs have not properly raised the "adequacy of treatment" afforded by the State of Alabama to patients at Searcy Hospital. Plaintiffs, in their post-trial briefs, argue that they have properly raised the "adequacy of treatment" afforded the patients at Searcy Hospital; however, this Court finds that the defendants were not fairly apprised that plaintiffs intended to include Searcy and the pleadings in this case do not so reflect.
72. [From original *Wyatt* decision.] Searcy, located at Mount Vernon, Alabama.
73. [From original *Wyatt* decision.] No evidence was presented on the point, but the plaintiffs in their post-trial brief advised this Court that Bryce Hospital has not conformed with the standards of the Social Security Administration to the point of becoming eligible for federal funds under the Medicare and Medicaid programs. Plaintiffs' counsel further advised in their brief that Bryce Hospital had not applied for certification for eligibility for these funds.

CHAPTER 5

1. Katherine McIntire Peters, "Partners in Crimefighting," Government Executive.com, February 2, 2005.
2. For example, centralization, formalization, red tape, and complexity are the dimensions of organizational structure listed by Hal G. Rainey, *Understanding and Managing Public Organizations, 3rd ed.* (San Francisco: Jossey-Bass, 2003).
3. James D. Thompson. *Organizations in Action: Social Science Bases of Administrative Theory* (New York: McGraw-Hill, 1967), 51.
4. Derek S. Pugh et al., "Dimensions of Organization Structure," *Administrative Science Quarterly* 13, no. 1 (1968): 65–105.
5. W. Richard Scott, *Organizations: Rational, Natural, and Open Systems* (Upper Saddle River, N.J.: Prentice Hall, 1998), 227.
6. Lee G. Bolman and Terrence E. Deal, *Reframing Organizations: Artistry, Choice, and Leadership,* 2nd ed. (San Francisco: Jossey-Bass, 1997), 38–39.
7. Morten Egeberg, "How Bureaucratic Structure Matters: An Organizational Perspective," in *Handbook of Public Administration,* ed. B. Guy Peters and Jon Pierre (London: Sage Publications, 2003), 116–126, 117.
8. Elinor Ostrom, "An Agenda for the Study of Institutions," *Public Choice* 48, no. 1 (1986): 5.
9. Ibid.
10. Lester M. Salamon, *The Tools of Government: A Guide to the New Governance* (Oxford: Oxford University Press, 2002).
11. Barry Bozeman, *Bureaucracy and Red Tape* (Upper Saddle River, N.J.: Prentice Hall, 2000), 12.
12. Department of Health and Human Services, Centers for Medicare & Medicaid Services, "Medicare Program: Revisions to Payment Policies, etc., Final Rule," *Federal Register,* Part II 42 CFR Parts 405, 410 et al., December 1, 2006.
13. U.S. Department of Agriculture, Forest Service, "Final Rule on National Forest System Land Management Planning," *Federal Register,* vol. 70, no. 3, 36 CFR Part 219, RIN 0596-AB86, January 5, 2005.
14. Quoted by Leonard D. White, *Introduction to the Study of Public Administration* (New York: Macmillan, 1926).
15. In addition to the references cited in this section, see Laurence E. Lynn Jr., "The Myth of the Bureaucratic Paradigm: What Traditional Public Administration Really Stood For," *Public Administration Review* 61 (2001): 144–160; and Kenneth J. Meier and Gregory C. Hill, "Bureaucracy in the Twenty-First Century," in *The Oxford Handbook of Public Management,* ed. Ewan Ferlie, Laurence E. Lynn Jr., and Christopher Pollitt (Oxford and New York: Oxford University Press, 2005), 51–71.
16. Laurence E. Lynn Jr., *Managing the Public's Business: The Job of the Government Executive* (New York: Basic Books, 1980), 106.
17. Jack H. Knott and Gary J. Miller, *Reforming Bureaucracy: The Politics of Institutional Choice* (Englewood Cliffs, N.J.: Prentice-Hall, 1987).
18. Bolman and Deal, *Reframing Organizations.*
19. Frederick W. Taylor, *Principles of Scientific Management* (New York: Harper, 1911).
20. Luther H. Gulick, "Notes on the Theory of Organization," in *Papers on the Science of Administration,* ed. Luther Gulick and Lyndall Urwick (New York: Institute of Public Administration, 1937).
21. Laurence E. Lynn Jr., *Public Management: Old and New* (London: Routledge, 2006).
22. Donald F. Kettl, "The Global Revolution in Public Management: Driving Themes, Missing Links," *Journal of Policy Analysis and Management* 16 (1997): 449.

23. Paul C. Light, *Thickening Government: Federal Hierarchy and the Diffusion of Accountability* (Washington, D.C.: Brookings Institution, 1995); and Paul C. Light, "Fact Sheet on the Continued Thickening of Government," Brookings Institution, July 23, 2004.
24. Light, "Fact Sheet."
25. Ibid.
26. Scott, *Organizations,* 311.
27. John W. Meyer and Brian Rowan, "Institutionalized Organizations: Formal Structure as Myth and Ceremony," *American Journal of Sociology* 83 (1977): 340–363.
28. Thomas H. Hammond, "Agenda Control, Organizational Structure, and Bureaucratic Politics," *American Journal of Political Science* 30, no. 2 (1986): 379–420, 382.
29. Ibid., 393, 400.
30. Ibid., 400, 402.
31. Ibid., 416.
32. Charles Perrow, "A Framework for the Comparative Analysis of Organizations," *American Sociological Review* 32, no. 2 (1967): 194–208. Also see Rainey, *Understanding and Managing Public Organizations,* 192–193.
33. John Ashcroft, "Memo Regarding Policy on Charging Criminal Defendants," U.S. Department of Justice, September 22, 2003.
34. Adam Liptak and Eric Lichtblau, "New Plea Bargain Limits Could Swamp Courts, Experts Say," *New York Times,* September 24, 2003, Sec. A.
35. Michael Lipsky, *Street-Level Bureaucracy* (New York: Russell Sage Foundation, 1980).
36. In addition to the sources cited in this section, see Evelyn Z. Brodkin, "Inside the Welfare Contract: Discretion and Accountability in State Welfare Administration," *Social Service Review* 71, no. 1 (1997): 1–33; Marcia K. Meyers and Susan Vorsanger, "Street-Level Bureaucrats and the Implementation of Public Policy," in *Handbook of Public Administration,* 245–255; Norma M. Riccucci, *How Management Matters: Street-Level Bureaucrats and Welfare Reform* (Washington, D.C.: Georgetown University Press, 2005); and Steven Rathgeb Smith, "Street-Level Bureaucracy and Public Policy," in *Handbook of Public Administration,* 354–365.
37. Lipsky, *Street-Level Bureaucracy.*
38. Liptak and Lichtblau, "New Plea Bargain Limits Could Swamp Courts," 2003.
39. This example is based on information in Max Leimgruber, "Agricultural Inspections on the California-Mexico Border: The Impacts of Public Policy," *Public Administration & Management: An Interactive Journal* 8, no. 3 (2003), 215–224.
40. Ibid., 219.
41. Ibid.
42. See, for example, Janice Johnson Dias and Steven Maynard-Moody, "For-Profit Welfare: Contracts, Conflicts, and the Performance Paradox," *Journal of Public Administration Research and Theory* 17, no. 2 (2007): 189–211.
43. Patricia W. Ingraham and Amy Kneedler Donahue, "Dissecting the Black Box Revisited: Characterizing Government Management Capacity," in *Governance and Performance: New Perspectives,* ed. Carolyn J. Heinrich and Laurence E. Lynn Jr. (Washington, D.C.: Georgetown University Press, 2000), 292–318.
44. Patricia W. Ingraham, Philip G. Joyce, and Amy Kneedler Donahue, *Government Performance: Why Management Matters* (Baltimore: Johns Hopkins University Press, 2003).
45. Ingraham and Donahue, "Dissecting the Black Box Revisited"; Ingraham, Joyce, and Donahue, *Government Performance.*
46. Government Performance Project, http://www.gpponline.org/.
47. Aaron Wildavsky, *The Politics of the Budgetary Process,* 2nd ed. (Boston: Little, Brown, 1974), 4.

48. In addition to ibid., see Robert T. Golembiewski and Jack Rabin, eds., *Public Budgeting and Finance,* 4th ed. (New York: Marcel Dekker, 1997); Irene S. Rubin, *The Politics of Public Budget: Getting and Spending, Borrowing and Balancing* (Chatham, N.J.: Chatham House, 1990); Robert L. Bland and Irene S. Rubin, *Budgeting: A Guide for Local Governments* (Washington, D.C.: International City/County Management Association, 1997); Allen Schick, *The Federal Budget: Politics, Policy, Process,* rev. ed. (Washington, D.C.: Brookings Institution, 2000); and the journal *Public Budgeting and Finance.*
49. William A. Niskanen Jr., *Bureaucracy and Representative Government* (New York: Aldine-Atherton, 1971).
50. For a critical appraisal of this theory, see André Blais and Stéphane Dion, eds., *The Budget-Maximizing Bureaucrat: Appraisals and Evidence* (Pittsburgh: University of Pittsburgh Press, 1991).
51. Patrick Dunleavy, "The Bureau-Shaping Model," in *Democracy, Bureaucracy and Public Choice* (Englewood Cliffs, N.J.: Prentice-Hall, 1992), 174–209.
52. Ibid., 202.
53. Laurence E. Lynn Jr., "The Budget-Maximizing Bureaucrat: Is There a Case?" in *The Budget-Maximizing Bureaucrat,* 59–83, 64.
54. Ibid., 64.
55. Ibid., 65.
56. A comprehensive discussion of personnel issues is in Donald F. Kettl and James W. Fesler, *The Politics of the Administrative Process,* 3rd ed. (Washington, D.C.: CQ Press, 2005), especially "Part III: People in Government Organizations," 163–223. See also Donald E. Klingner and John Nalbandian, *Public Personnel Management: Contexts and Strategies,* 5th ed. (Upper Saddle River, N.J.: Prentice Hall, 2003).
57. Patricia W. Ingraham, "Striving for Balance: Reforms in Human Resource Management," in *The Oxford Handbook of Public Management,* 521–536.
58. Ibid.
59. George T. Milkovich and Alexandra K. Wigdor, eds., *Pay for Performance: Evaluating Performance Appraisal and Merit Pay* (Washington D.C.: National Research Council, 1991), 3.
60. See, for example, Howard Risher, *Pay for Performance: A Guide for Federal Managers* (Washington, D.C.: IBM Center for the Business of Government, 2004); Milkovich and Wigdor, *Pay for Performance.*
61. See, for example, Iris Bohnet and Susan C. Eaton, "Does Performance Pay Perform? Conditions for Success in the Public Sector," in *For the People: Can We Fix Public Service?* ed. John D. Donahue and Joseph S. Nye Jr. (Washington, D.C.: Brookings Institution, 2003), 238–254; and Milkovich and Wigdor, *Pay for Performance.*
62. Paul Milgrom and John Roberts, "Bounded Rationality and Private Information," in *Economics Organization & Management* (Englewood Cliffs, N.J.: Prentice Hall, 1992), 127.
63. In addition to the references cited in this section, see Kenneth Arrow, "The Economics of Agency," in *Principals and Agents,* ed. John Pratt and Richard Zeckhauser (Boston: Harvard Business School Press, 1985).
64. Avinash Dixit, "Incentives and Organizations in the Public Sector: An Interpretive Review," *Journal of Human Resources* 37, no. 4 (2002): 696–727; Aidan R. Vining and David L. Weimer, "Economic Perspectives on Public Organizations," in *The Oxford Handbook of Public Management,* 209–233; and Terry Moe, "The New Economics of Organization," *American Journal of Political Science* 28, no. 4 (1984): 739–777.
65. Moe, "The New Economics of Organization," 757.
66. Ibid., 755.

67. Carolyn J. Hill, "Casework Job Design and Client Outcomes in Welfare-to-Work Programs," *Journal of Public Administration Research and Theory* 16, no. 2 (2006): 263–288.
68. Bengt Holmstrom and Paul Milgrom, "Multitask Principal-Agent Analyses: Incentive Contracts, Asset Ownership, and Job Design," *Journal of Law, Economics, and Organization* 7, Special Issue (1991): 24–52, 27.
69. Ibid., 26.
70. B. Douglas Bernheim and Michael D. Whinston, "Common Agency," *Econometrica* 54, no. 4 (July 1986): 923–942.
71. For a fuller discussion, see Anthony M. Bertelli and Laurence E. Lynn Jr., "Policy Making in the Parallelogram of Forces: Common Agency and Human Services," *Policy Studies Journal* 32 (August 2004): 297–315.
72. Oliver Williamson, "The Economics of Organization," *American Journal of Sociology* 87 (1981): 548–577; Oliver Williamson, *The Mechanisms of Governance* (New York: Oxford University Press, 1996).
73. For economic policy, see Avinash Dixit, *The Making of Economic Policy: A Transaction Cost Politics Perspective* (Cambridge: MIT Press, 1996); antitrust rules, Paul L. Joskow, "Transaction Cost Economics, Antitrust Rules, and Remedies," *Journal of Law, Economics, and Organization* 18, no. 1 (2002): 95–116; contracting out, Trevor L. Brown and Matthew Potoski, "Transaction Costs and Institutional Explanations for Government Service Production Decisions," *Journal of Public Administration Research and Theory* 13, no. 4 (2003): 441–468; and contracting out mental health services, Anne M. Libby and Neal T. Wallace, "Effects of Contracting and Local Markets on Costs of Public Mental Health Services in California," *Psychiatric Services* 49 (1998): 1067–71.
74. In addition to the references cited in this section, see Steven J. Kelman, "Contracting," in *The Tools of Government*, 282–318; Stephen Rathgeb Smith, "NGOs and Contracting," in *The Oxford Handbook of Public Management*, 591–614; Jacques S. Gansler, *Moving Toward Market-Based Government: The Changing Role of Government as the Provider* (Arlington, Va.: IBM Endowment for the Business of Government, 2003); Symposium on "Public Values in an Era of Privatization," *Harvard Law Review* 116, no. 5 (2003); John D. Donahue, *The Privatization Decision: Public Ends, Private Means* (New York: Basic Books, 1989); E. S. Savas, *Privatization and Public-Private Partnerships* (New York: Chatham House, 2000).
75. Laurence E. Lynn Jr., "Social Services and the State: The Public Appropriation of Private Charity," *Social Service Review* 76 (March 2002): 58–82.
76. Brown and Potoski, "Transaction Costs and Institutional Explanations."
77. Ibid., 444.
78. Michael Moss, "U.S. Struggling to Get Soldiers Updated Armor," *New York Times*, August 14, 2005, Sec. A.
79. See http://www.whitehouse.gov/omb/circulars/a076/a76_rev2003.pdf. This document is revised periodically.
80. Executive Order 13180—Air Traffic Performance-Based Organization, *Federal Register*, Part VII, vol. 65, no. 238, December 7, 2000.
81. Executive Order 13264—Amendment to Executive Order 13180, Air Traffic Performance-Based Organization, *Federal Register*, vol. 67, no. 110, June 4, 2002.
82. Robert Poole, "Controllers, FAA Mistaken on Privatization," *Air Traffic Control Reform Newsletter*, Reason Foundation, Issue 9, December 2002.
83. David H. Rosenbloom and Suzanne J. Piotrowski, "Outsourcing the Constitution and Administrative Law Norms," *American Review of Public Administration* 35, no. 2 (June 2005): 103–121, 110.
84. Oliver Hart, Andrei Shleifer, and Robert W. Vishny, "The Proper Scope of Government: Theory and an Application to Prisons," *Quarterly Journal of Economics* (November 1997): 1127–61.

85. Ibid., 1129. In a related paper, Timothy Besley and Maitreesh Ghatak also use an incomplete contracting framework, but allow private sector producers to be value-driven. Their model is sufficiently general to include a special case of profit-maximizing producers, but the model focuses on asset specificity and hold-up problems, and the primary applications of interest are the relationships between governments and nongovernmental organizations in developing countries in deciding on inputs and financing for public projects. See "Government versus Private Ownership of Public Goods," *Quarterly Journal of Economics* 116, no. 4 (November 2001): 1443–72.
86. Hart, Shleifer, and Vishny, "The Proper Scope of Government, 1159.
87. Gilbert M. Gaul, "Bad Practices Net Hospitals More Money: High Quality Often Loses Out in the 40-Year-Old Program," *Washington Post,* July 24, 2005, Sec. A.
88. In addition to the references cited in this section, see Robert D. Behn and Peter A. Kant, "Strategies for Avoiding the Pitfalls of Performance Contracting," *Public Productivity and Management Review* 22, no. 4 (1999): 470–489; Trevor L. Brown and Matthew Potoski, "Managing Contract Performance: A Transaction Costs Approach," *Journal of Policy Analysis and Management* 22, no. 2 (2003): 275–297; Trevor L. Brown, Matthew Potoski, and David M. Van Slyke, "Managing Public Service Contracts: Aligning Values, Institutions, and Markets," *Public Administration Review* (May/June 2006): 323–331; National State Auditors Association, "Contracting for Services: A National State Auditors Association Best Practices Document," June 2003, http://www.nasact.org/onlineresources/downloads/BP/06_03-Contracting_Best_Practices.pdf.
89. Donald F. Kettl, *Sharing Power: Public Governance and Private Markets* (Washington, D.C.: Brookings Institution, 1993).
90. Phillip J. Cooper, *Governing by Contract: Challenges and Opportunities for Public Managers* (Washington, D.C.: CQ Press, 2003), 13.
91. Ibid.; Steven Kelman, "Strategic Contracting Management," in *Market-Based Governance: Supply Size, Demand Side, Upside, Downside,* ed. John D. Donahue and Joseph S. Nye Jr. (Washington, D.C.: Brookings Institution, 2002), 88–102.
92. Kelman, "Strategic Contracting Management," 89.
93. H. Brinton Milward and Keith G. Provan, "The Hollow State: Private Provision of Public Services," in *Public Policy for Democracy,* ed. Helen Ingram and Steven Rathgeb Smith (Washington, D.C.: Brookings Institution, 1993); Donald F. Kettl, *Government by Proxy: (Mis?)Managing Federal Programs* (Washington, D.C.: CQ Press, 1988); Lester M. Salamon, "Rethinking Public Management: Third-Party Government and the Changing Forms of Government Action," *Public Policy* 29 (Summer 1981): 255–275.
94. H. Brinton Milward and Keith G. Provan, "Governing the Hollow State," *Journal of Public Administration Research and Theory* 10, no. 2 (2000): 359–379.
95. Paul C. Light, *The True Size of Government* (Washington, D.C.: Brookings Institution, 1999); Paul C. Light, "Fact Sheet on the New True Size of Government," working paper, Brookings Institution, 2003.
96. Light, "Fact Sheet," Table 1.
97. Milward and Provan, "The Hollow State."
98. Richard F. Elmore, "Graduate Education in Public Management: Working the Seams of Government," *Journal of Policy Analysis and Management* 6, no. 1 (Autumn 1986): 74.
99. See, for example, the dedicated issues of *Public Administration Review* (December 2006) and *International Journal of Public Management* 10, no. 1 (2007).
100. Walter W. Powell, "Neither Market nor Hierarchy: Network Forms of Organization," *Research in Organizational Behavior,* 12 (Greenwich, Conn.: JAI Press, 1990), 295–336.
101. In addition to the references cited in this section, see Robert Agranoff and M. McGuire, *Collaborative Public Management: New Strategies for Local Governments* (Washington, D.C.:

Georgetown University Press, 2003); Eugene Bardach, *Getting Agencies to Work Together: The Practice and Theory of Managerial Craftsmanship* (Washington, D.C.: Brookings Institution, 1998); Stephen Goldsmith and William D. Eggers, *Governing by Network: The New Shape of the Public Sector* (Washington, D.C.: Brookings Institution Press, 2004); Erik-Hans Klijn, "Networks and Inter-organizational Management: Challenging, Steering, Evaluation, and the Role of Public Actors in Public Management," in *The Oxford Handbook of Public Management,* 257–281; Laurence E. Lynn Jr., "Policy Achievement as a Collective Good: A Strategic Perspective on Managing Social Programs," in *Public Management: The State of the Art,* ed. Barry Bozeman (San Francisco: Jossey-Bass, 1993), 108–133; Jodi R. Sandfort, "The Structural Impediments to Front-line Human Service Collaboration: Examining Welfare Reform at the Front-lines," *Social Service Review* 73, no. 3 (1999): 314–339.

102. Laurence J. O'Toole Jr., "Treating Networks Seriously: Practical and Research-Based Agendas in Public Administration," *Public Administration Review* 57 (1997): 45–52, 45.
103. Keith G. Provan and H. Brinton Milward, "Do Networks Really Work? A Framework for Evaluating Public Sector Organization Networks," *Public Administration Review* 61 (2001): 414–423.
104. Ann Marie Thompson and James L. Perry, "Collaboration Processes: Inside the Black Box," *Public Administration Review* 66, no. 1 (2006): 20–32.
105. Carolyn J. Hill and Laurence E. Lynn Jr., "Producing Human Services: Why Do Agencies Collaborate?" *Public Management Review* 5, no. 1 (2003): 63–81; Marcia K. Meyers, "Organizational Factors in the Integration of Services for Children," *Social Service Review* 67, no. 4 (1993): 547–575.
106. Robert I. Agranoff and Michael McGuire, "Big Questions in Public Network Management Research," *Journal of Public Administration Research and Theory* 11 (2001): 295–326, 297–298, 305.
107. Sandra Van Thiel, *Quangos: Trends, Causes and Consequences* (Burlington, Vt.: Ashgate, 2001).
108. Thomas H. Stanton and Ronald C. Moe, "Government Corporations and Government-Sponsored Enterprises," in *The Tools of Government,* 80–116.
109. "Statement by Secretary Henry M. Paulson, Jr. on Treasury and Federal Housing Finance Agency Action to Protect Financial Markets and Taxpayers," U.S. Department of the Treasury press release, September 7, 2008.
110. Ibid.
111. In addition to the references cited in this section, see Elizabeth T. Boris and C. Eugene Steuerle, eds., *Nonprofits and Government: Collaboration and Conflict* (Washington, D.C.: Urban Institute, 2006); Walter W. Powell and Richard Steinberg, eds., *The Nonprofit Sector: A Research Handbook,* 2nd ed. (New Haven: Yale University Press, 2006).
112. Burton Weisbrod, ed., *The Voluntary Nonprofit Sector* (Lexington, Mass.: D. C. Heath, 1977).
113. Ibid., 59.
114. Henry B. Hansmann, "The Role of Nonprofit Enterprise," *Yale Law Journal* 89, no. 5 (1980): 835–901, 844.
115. Ibid., 849, 851.
116. Edward L. Glaeser and Andrei Shleifer, "Not-for-Profit Entrepreneurs," *Journal of Public Economics* 81 (2001): 99–115, 100.
117. Lester M. Salamon, "Of Market Failure, Voluntary Failure, and Third-Party Government: Toward a Theory of Government-Nonprofit Relations in the Modern Welfare State," *Journal of Voluntary Action Research* 16, no. 1–2 (1987): 29–49.
118. Avner Ben-Ner and Theresa Van Hoomissen, "Nonprofit Organizations in the Mixed Economy: A Demand and Supply Analysis," *Annals of Public and Cooperative Economics* 62 (1991): 519–550, 544.

119. See also Dana Brakman Reiser, "Dismembering Civil Society: The Social Cost of Internally Undemocratic Nonprofits," *Oregon Law Review* 82 (Fall 2003): 829–900.
120. In addition to the references cited in this section, see Christoph Badelt, "Entrepreneurship in Nonprofit Organizations: Its Role in Theory and in the Real World Nonprofit Sector," in *The Study of the Nonprofit Enterprise: Theories and Approaches,* ed. Helmut Anheier and Avner Ben-Ner (New York: Kluwer, 2003); and Dennis R. Young, "Entrepreneurs, Managers, and the Nonprofit Enterprise," in *The Study of the Nonprofit Enterprise.*
121. Susan Rose-Ackerman, "Altruism, Nonprofits, and Economic Theory," *Journal of Economic Literature* 34 (June 1996): 719.
122. Dennis R. Young, *If Not For Profit, For What? A Behavioral Theory of the Nonprofit Sector Based on Entrepreneurship* (Lexington, Mass.: D. C. Heath, 1983), 99.
123. Stephen Rathgeb Smith and Michael Lipsky, *Nonprofits for Hire: The Welfare State in the Age of Contracting* (Cambridge: Harvard University Press, 1993).
124. Richard Steinberg and Bradford H. Gray, " 'The Role of Nonprofit Enterprise' in 1992: Hansmann Revisited," *Nonprofit and Voluntary Sector Quarterly* 22 (Winter 1993): 297–316.
125. Henry B. Hansmann, "Economic Theories of Nonprofit Organization," in *The Nonprofit Sector: A Research Handbook,* ed. Walter W. Powell (New Haven: Yale University Press, 1987), 27–42; Estelle James and Susan Rose-Ackerman, *The Nonprofit Enterprise in Market Economics* (New York: Harwood Academic Publishers, 1986).
126. Henry B. Hansmann, "The Changing Roles of Public, Private, and Nonprofit Enterprise in Education, Health Care, and Other Human Services," in *Individual and Social Responsibility: Child Care, Education, Medical Care, and Long-Term Care In America,* ed. Victor R. Fuchs (Chicago: University of Chicago Press, 1996), 249.
127. Paul C. Light, "Fact Sheet on the Continued Crisis in Charitable Confidence," Brookings Institution, 2004.
128. Laurence E. Lynn Jr. and Steven Rathgeb Smith, "The Performance Challenge in Nonprofit Organizations," working paper, February 17, 2007.
129. Karen Eggleston and Richard Zeckhauser, "Government Contracting for Health Care," in *Market-Based Governance: Supply Side, Demand Side, Upside, Downside,* ed. John D. Donahue and Joseph S. Nye Jr. (Washington, D.C.: Brookings Institution, 2002).
130. Ibid., 42.
131. Ibid., 44.
132. Moe, "The Politics of Structural Choice."
133. In addition to the references cited in this section, see Terry Moe, "The Politics of Structural Choice: Toward a Theory of Public Bureaucracy," in *Organization Theory: From Chester Barnard to the Present and Beyond,* ed. Oliver E. Williamson (New York: Oxford University Press, 1990), 116–153; Mathew D. McCubbins, Roger G. Noll, and Barry R. Weingast, "Administrative Procedures as Instruments of Political Control," *Journal of Law, Economics, and Organization* 3, no. 2 (1987): 243–277; Knott and Miller, "The Politics of Reform," in *Reforming Bureaucracy,* 189–276; B. Guy Peters, "The Politics of Tool Choice," in *The Tools of Government,* 552–564.
134. "Prioritization of Health Services: A Report to the Governor and the 73rd Oregon Legislative Assembly," Oregon Health Services Commission, Office for Oregon Health Policy and Research, Department of Administrative Services, March 2005, http://www.oregon.gov/das/ohppr/hsc/docs/bireport05-07.pdf.
135. Geeta Anand, "Who Deserves Health Care? Rationing Becomes a Reality as Costs Skyrocket," *Wall Street Journal,* December 3, 2003.
136. Susan Bartlett Foote, "Focus on Locus: Evolution of Medicare's Local Coverage Policy," *Health Affairs* 22, no. 4 (2003): 137–146.

137. Peter Q. Eichacker, Charles Natanson, and Robert L. Danner, "Surviving Sepsis—Practice Guidelines, Marketing Campaigns, and Eli Lilly," *New England Journal of Medicine* 355, no. 16 (2006), 1640–42; and Jeff Donn and Marilynn Marchione, "Federal Doctors Fault Eli Lilly for Blood Infection Drug Push," *Associated Press Newswires,* October 18, 2006.
138. John E. Chubb and Terry M. Moe, *Politics, Markets, and America's Schools* (Washington, D.C.: Brookings Institution, 1990).
139. Ibid., 34.

CHAPTER 6

1. *Report of the Columbia Accident Investigation Board,* vol. 1 (Washington, D.C.: National Aeronautics and Space Administration, 2003), 101–102, http://www.nasa.gov/columbia/home/CAIB_Vol1. html.
2. For comprehensive treatments of organizational culture, see Linda Smircich, "Concepts of Culture and Organizational Analysis," *Administrative Science Quarterly* 28 (1983): 339–358; Harrison M. Trice and Janice M. Beyer, *The Cultures of Work Organizations* (Englewood Cliffs, N.J.: Prentice Hall, 1993); Edgar H. Schein, *Organizational Culture and Leadership,* 2nd ed. (San Francisco: Jossey-Bass, 1992); J. Steven Ott, *The Organizational Culture Perspective* (Chicago: Dorsey Press, 1989). See Ott's chapter 3 appendix for many different definitions of organizational culture found in the literature.
3. Lee G. Bolman and Terrence E. Deal, *Reframing Organizations* (San Francisco: Jossey-Bass, 1991), 270; Terrence E. Deal and Allan A. Kennedy, *Corporate Cultures: The Rites and Rituals of Corporate Life* (London: Penguin, 1982); James Q. Wilson, *Bureaucracy: What Government Agencies Do and Why They Do It* (New York: Basic Books, 1991), 91.
4. Schein, *Organizational Culture and Leadership,* 12.
5. Trice and Beyer, *The Cultures of Work Organizations,* 32.
6. Jean-Claude Thoenig, "Institutional Theories and Public Institutions: Traditions and Appropriateness," in *Handbook of Public Administration,* ed. B. Guy Peters and Jon Pierre (London: Sage, 2003), 129; Philip Selznick, *TVA and the Grass Roots,* quoted in Jane E. Fountain, *Building the Virtual State: Information Technology and Institutional Change* (Washington, D.C.: Brookings Institution Press, 2001), 92.
7. James March and Johan Olsen, *Rediscovering Institutions* (New York: Free Press, 1989), 22.
8. In addition to the references cited in this section, see Herbert Kaufman, *The Forest Ranger: A Study in Administrative Behavior* (Washington, D.C.: Resources for the Future, 1960); Philip Selznick, *Leadership in Administration* (Evanston, Ill.: Row, Peterson, 1957); Dwight Waldo, *The Administrative State* (Somerset, N.J.: Ronald Press, 1949).
9. Woodrow Wilson, "The Study of Administration," *Political Science Quarterly* 2 (1887): 216.
10. John Dickinson, *Administrative Justice and the Supremacy of Law in the United States* (New York: Russell and Russell, 1927), 277.
11. John M. Gaus, "The Responsibility of Public Administration," in *The Frontiers of Public Administration,* ed. John M. Gaus, Leonard D. White, and Marshall E. Dimock (Chicago: University of Chicago Press, 1936), 26–44, 40; Anthony M. Bertelli and Laurence E. Lynn Jr., *Madison's Managers: Public Administration and the Constitution* (Baltimore, Md.: Johns Hopkins University Press, 2006).
12. Bertelli and Lynn, *Madison's Managers.*
13. Herman Finer, "Administrative Responsibility in Democratic Government," *Public Administration Review* 1 (1940): 336.

14. Carl J. Friedrich, "Public Policy and the Nature of Administrative Responsibility," in *Public Policy: A Yearbook of the Graduate School of Public Administration, Harvard University, 1940,* ed. Carl Friedrich and Edward Mason (Cambridge: Harvard University Press, 1940), 3–24.
15. John A. Rohr, *To Run a Constitution: The Legitimacy of the Administrative State* (Lawrence: University Press of Kansas, 1986), 181.
16. Robert B. Denhardt, *The Pursuit of Significance: Strategies for Managerial Success in Public Organizations* (Belmont, Calif.: Wadsworth, 1993), 20.
17. H. George Frederickson, *The Spirit of Public Administration* (San Francisco: Jossey-Bass, 1997), 229.
18. Chester Irving Barnard, *The Functions of the Executive* (Cambridge: Harvard University Press, 1938).
19. Fritz J. Roethlisberger and William J. Dickson, *Management and the Worker* (Cambridge: Harvard University Press, 1939), cited by William G. Ouchi and Alan L. Wilkins, in "Organizational Culture," *Annual Review of Sociology* 11 (1985): 457–483.
20. Herbert A. Simon, *Administrative Behavior: A Study of Decision-Making Processes in Administrative Organization,* 3rd ed. (New York: Free Press, 1976), 148, 149.
21. Robert B. Denhardt, "Bureaucratic Socialization and Organizational Accommodation," *Administrative Science Quarterly* 13, no. 3 (1968): 441–450, 449.
22. Edgar Schein, "Organizational Culture," Working Paper #2088-88 (Cambridge: MIT Sloan School of Management, December 1988), 1.
23. Ouchi and Wilkins, "Organizational Culture."
24. Thomas J. Peters and Robert H. Waterman, *In Search of Excellence: Lessons from America's Best-Run Companies* (New York: Harper and Row, 1982); Deal and Kennedy, *Corporate Cultures;* Schein, "Organizational Culture and Leadership."
25. Schein, "Organizational Culture," 3.
26. Barry Bozeman, *Public Values and Public Interest: Counterbalancing Economic Individualism* (Washington, D.C.: Georgetown University Press, 2007), 117.
27. Dwight Waldo, "Development of Theory of Democratic Administration," *American Political Science Review* 46, no. 1 (1952): 81–103, 97.
28. Torben Beck Jørgensen and Barry Bozeman, "Public Values: An Inventory," *Administration & Society* 39, no. 3 (2007): 354–381.
29. Ibid., 377.
30. Barry Bozeman, *All Organizations are Public: Bridging Public and Private Organizational Theories* (San Francisco: Jossey-Bass, 1987).
31. Jon Elster, *Local Justice* (New York: Russell Sage Foundation, 1992), 143.
32. Laurence E. Lynn Jr., *Teaching and Learning with Cases* (Chappaqua, N.Y.: Seven Bridges Press, 1999), 7, 9, 11.
33. W. Richard Scott. *Organizations: Rational, Natural and Open Systems,* 4th ed. (Upper Saddle River, N.J.: Prentice Hall, 1998), 211.
34. Wilson, *Bureaucracy,* 64–65.
35. Marc Allen Eisner and Kenneth J. Meier, "Presidential Control versus Bureaucratic Power: Explaining the Reagan Revolution in Antitrust," *American Journal of Political Science* 34, no. 1 (1990): 269–287.
36. Ibid., 283.
37. Alice Rivlin, *Systematic Thinking for Social Action* (Washington, D.C.: Brookings Institution, 1971), 4.
38. Laurence E. Lynn Jr., "A Place at the Table: Policy Analysis, Its Postpositive Critics, and the Future of Practice," *Journal of Policy Analysis and Management* 18, no. 3 (1999): 411–424.

39. Rivlin, *Systematic Thinking for Social Action,* 5.
40. Martha S. Feldman, *Order without Design: Information Production and Policy Making* (Stanford: Stanford University Press, 1989).
41. Christopher Pollitt, *The Essential Public Manager* (Maidenhead, U.K.: Open University Press, 2003), 133.
42. Herbert A. Simon, Victor A. Thompson, and Donald W. Smithburg, *Public Administration* (New Brunswick, N.J.: Transaction Publishers, 1991), 539.
43. In addition to the references cited in this section, see Terry L. Cooper, *The Responsible Administrator: An Approach to Ethics for the Administrative Role,* 5th ed. (San Francisco: Jossey-Bass, 2006); Linda deLeon, "On Acting Responsibly in a Disorderly World: Individual Ethics and Administrative Responsibility," in *Handbook of Public Administration,* 569–580; Kathryn G. Denhardt, *The Ethics of Public Service* (New York: Greenwood Press, 1988); J. Patrick Dobel, "Public Management as Ethics," in *The Oxford Handbook of Public Management,* ed. Ewan Ferlie, Laurence E. Lynn Jr., and Christopher Pollitt (Oxford: Oxford University Press, 2005), 156–181.
44. Frederickson, *The Spirit of Public Administration,* 171.
45. Office of Government Ethics, "Background and Mission," http://www.usoge.gov/about/background_mission.aspx.
46. Office of Government Ethics, *Public Financial Disclosure: A Reviewer's Reference,* 2nd ed., November 2004.
47. See also the OECD report cited in Pollitt, *The Essential Public Manager;* OECD, *Principles for Managing Ethics in the Public Service,* PUMA Policy Brief no. 4, May 1998.
48. Pollitt, *The Essential Public Manager,* 147.
49. Ibid., 133.
50. For further information on assumptions of rational choice theory and its variants, see chapter 2, "The Nature of Rational Choice Theory," in Donald P. Green and Ian Shapiro, *Pathologies of Rational Choice Theory: A Critique of Applications in Political Science* (New Haven: Yale University Press, 1994), 13–32.
51. James H. David, F. David Schoorman, and Lex Donaldson, "Toward a Stewardship Theory of Management," *Academy of Management Review* 22, no. 1 (1997): 37.
52. Principal-agent theory and stewardship theory were used to examine the government-nonprofit contracting relationship in David M. Van Slyke, "Agents or Stewards: Using Theory to Understand the Government-Nonprofit Social Service Contracting Relationship," *Journal of Public Administration Research and Theory* 17, no. 2 (2007): 157–187.
53. John D. DiIulio Jr., "Principled Agents: The Cultural Bases of Behavior in a Federal Government Bureaucracy," *Journal of Public Administration Research and Theory* 4, no. 3 (1994): 277–318, 282.
54. Ibid., 316.
55. James L. Perry and Lois Recascino Wise, "The Motivational Bases of Public Service," *Public Administration Review* 50, no. 3 (1990): 368.
56. H. George Frederickson and David K. Hart, "The Public Service and the Patriotism of Benevolence," *Public Administration Review* 45 (September/October 1985): 547–553, 549.
57. Philip E. Crewson, "Public-Service Motivation: Building Empirical Evidence of Incidence and Effect," *Journal of Public Administration Research and Theory* 7, no. 4 (1997): 499–518; Gene A. Brewer and Sally Coleman Selden, "Whistle Blowers in the Federal Civil Service: New Evidence of the Public Service Ethic," *Journal of Public Administration Research and Theory* 8, no. 3 (1998): 413–439; Katherine C. Naff and John Crum, "Working for America: Does Public Service Motivation Make a Difference?" *Review of Public Personnel Administration* 19, no. 4 (1999): 5–16; Bradley E. Wright, "Public Service Motivation: Does Mission Matter?" *Public Administration Review* 67, no. 1 (2007): 54–64; and Sanjay K. Pandey, Bradley E. Wright, and Donald P.

Moynihan, "Public Service Motivation and Interpersonal Citizenship Behavior in Public Organizations: Testing a Preliminary Model," *International Public Management Journal* 11, no. 1 (2008): 89–108.

58. Bradley E. Wright and Sanjay K. Pandey, "Public Service Motivation and the Assumption of Person-Organization Fit: Testing the Mediating Effect of Value Congruence," *Administration & Society* 40, no. 5 (2008): 502–521.
59. In addition to the references cited in this section, see Marissa Golden, *What Motivates Bureaucrats? Politics and Administration during the Reagan Years* (New York: Columbia University Press, 2000); Frederickson, *The Spirit of Public Administration*; James L. Perry and Annie Hondeghem, eds., *Motivation in Public Management: The Call of Public Service* (Oxford: Oxford University Press, 2008).
60. Roger C. Mayer, James H. Davis, and F. David Schoorman, "An Integrative Model of Organizational Trust," *Academy of Management Review* 20, no. 3 (1995): 709–734, 712.
61. Russell Hardin, *Collective Action* (Baltimore: Johns Hopkins University Press, 1982); Robert Axelrod, *The Evolution of Cooperation* (New York: Basic Books, 1984).
62. Jurian Edelenbos and Erik-Hans Klijn, "Trust in Complex Decision-Making Networks: A Theoretical and Empirical Exploration," *Administration & Society* 39, no. 1 (2007): 25–50.
63. Ibid.; Erik-Hans Klijn, "Networks and Inter-organizational Management: Challenging, Steering, Evaluation, and the Role of Public Actors in Public Management," in *The Oxford Handbook of Public Management*, 257–281.
64. Joop Koppenjan and Erik-Hans Klijn, *Managing Uncertainties in Networks: A Network Approach to Problem Solving and Decision Making* (New York: Routledge, 2004).
65. David M. Kreps uses concepts from economic theory, such as transaction costs, focal points, information asymmetries, and contracts, to explain corporate culture. See David M. Kreps, "Corporate Culture and Economic Theory," in *Perspectives on Positive Political Economy*, ed. James E. Alt and Kenneth A. Shepsle (Cambridge: Cambridge University Press, 1990), 90–143.
66. Terry M. Moe, "The Politics of Structural Choice: Toward a Theory of Public Bureaucracy," in *Organization Theory: From Chester Barnard to the Present and Beyond* (New York: Oxford University Press, 1990), 134.
67. David L. Weimer, "Institutionalizing Neutrally Competent Policy Analysis: Resources for Promoting Objectivity and Balance in Consolidating Democracies," *Policy Studies Journal* 33, no. 2 (2005): 132, 138.
68. Carolyn Ban, *How Do Public Managers Manage? Bureaucratic Constraints, Organizational Culture, and the Potential for Reform* (San Francisco: Jossey-Bass, 1995).
69. Sanjay K. Pandey, David H. Coursey, and Donald P. Moynihan, "Organizational Effectiveness and Bureaucratic Red Tape," *Public Performance and Management Review* 30, no. 3 (2007): 398–425.
70. Ibid., 416.
71. For detailed accounts, see, for example, W. Richard Scott, "Unpacking Institutional Arguments," in *The New Institutionalism in Organizational Analysis*, ed. Walter W. Powell and Paul J. DiMaggio (Chicago: University of Chicago Press, 1991); and W. Richard Scott, *Organizations: Rational, Natural, and Open Systems*, 4th ed. (Upper Saddle River, N.J.: Prentice Hall, 1998).
72. For further information on the creation of the Department of Energy and clashes of cultures, see Federation of American Scientists, http://www.fas.org/sgp/library/pfiab/root.html.
73. Government Accountability Office, "Department of Homeland Security: Addressing Management Challenges that Face Immigration Enforcement Agencies" (GAO-05-664T), Testimony of Richard M. Stana, Director, Homeland Security and Justice Issues, May 5, 2005, 5, 8.
74. Fountain, *Building the Virtual State*.

75. Rosemary O'Leary and Susan Summers Raines, "Lessons Learned from Two Decades of Alternative Dispute Resolution Programs and Processes at the U.S. Environmental Protection Agency," *Public Administration Review* 61, no. 6 (2001): 682–692, 687.
76. Martha Derthick, *Agency under Stress: The Social Security Administration in American Government* (Washington, D.C.: Brookings Institution 1990), 47.
77. Steven Rathgeb Smith and Michael Lipsky, *Nonprofits for Hire: The Welfare State in the Age of Contracting* (Cambridge: Harvard University Press, 1993), 95. See also Lester M. Salamon, "The Marketization of Welfare: Changing Nonprofit and For-Profit Roles in the American Welfare State," *Social Service Review* 67, no. 1 (1993): 16–39.
78. Barbara S. Romzek and Jocelyn M. Johnston, "Reforming Medicaid through Contracting: The Nexus of Implementation and Organizational Culture," *Journal of Public Administration Research and Theory* 9, no. 1 (1999): 107–139, 136, 135.
79. Karl E. Weick, "Educational Organizations as Loosely Coupled Systems," *Administrative Science Quarterly* 21, no. 1 (1976): 1–19.
80. John W. Meyer and Brian Rowan, "Institutional Organizations: Formal Structure as Myth and Ceremony," *American Journal of Sociology* 83 (1977): 357.
81. In addition to the references cited in this section, see Charles Perrow, *Normal Accidents: Living with High Risk Technologies* (New York: Basic Books, 1984); Karl E. Weick, "Organizational Culture as a Source of High Reliability," *California Management Review* 29, no. 2 (1987): 112–127; Todd R. LaPorte and Paula M. Consolini, "Working in Practice but Not in Theory: Theoretical Challenges of High-Reliability Organizations," *Journal of Public Administration Research and Theory* 1, no. 1 (1991): 19–47.
82. Todd R. LaPorte, "High-Reliability Organizations: Unlikely, Demanding and At Risk," *Journal of Contingencies and Crisis Management* 4, no. 2 (1996): 64.
83. Ibid., 65.
84. Todd R. LaPorte and H. George Frederickson, "Airport Security, High Reliability, and the Problem of Rationality," *Public Administration Review* 62, no. 1 (2002): 33–43.
85. In addition to the references cited in this section, see *Organization Science, Special Issue: Organizational Learning: Papers in Honor of (and by) James G. March* 2, no. 1 (1991).
86. Eric W. K. Tsang, "Organizational Learning and the Learning Organization: A Dichotomy between Descriptive and Prescriptive Research," *Human Relations* 50, no. 1 (1997): 73–89; see also C. Marlene Fiol and Marjorie A. Lyles, "Organizational Learning," *Academy of Management Review* 10, no. 4 (1985): 803–813.
87. B. Hedberg, "How Organizations Learn and Unlearn," in *Handbook of Organizational Design*, ed. Paul C. Nystrom and William H. Starbuck (London: Oxford University Press, 1981), 6.
88. Chris Argyris and Donald A. Schön, *Organizational Learning: A Theory of Action Perspective* (Reading, Mass.: Addison-Wesley), 2, 29.
89. Barbara Levitt and James G. March, "Organizational Learning," *Annual Review of Sociology* 14 (1988): 320.
90. Tsang, "Organizational Learning and the Learning Organization.
91. Swee C. Goh, "Toward a Learning Organization: The Strategic Building Blocks," *SAM Advanced Management Journal* 63, no. 2 (1998): 15–22.
92. Baiyin Yang, Karen E. Watkins, and Victoria J. Marsick, "The Construct of the Learning Organization: Dimensions, Measurement, and Validation," *Human Resource Development Quarterly* 15 (2004): 31–55.
93. Julianne Mahler, "Influences of Organizational Culture on Learning in Public Agencies," *Journal of Public Administration Research and Theory* 7, no. 4 (1997): 519–540, 521.

94. Jostein Askim, Åge Johnsen, and Knut-Andreas Christophersen, "Factors Behind Organizational Learning from Benchmarking: Experiences from Norwegian Municipal Benchmarking Networks," *Journal of Public Administration Research and Theory* 18, no. 2 (2008): 297–320; Donald P. Moynihan, "Goal-Based Learning and the Future of Performance Management," *Public Administration Review* 65, no. 2 (2005): 203–216;. Thomas A. Birkland, *Lessons of Disaster: Policy Change after Catastrophic Events* (Washington, D.C.: Georgetown University Press, 2006); and Donald P. Moynihan, "Learning under Uncertainty: Networks in Crisis Management," *Public Administration Review* 68, no. 2 (2008): 350–361.
95. Levitt and March, "Organizational Learning," 335.
96. In James L. Perry, *Handbook of Public Administration* (San Francisco: Jossey-Bass, 1996), see Sandra J. Hale, "Achieving High Performance in Public Organizations," a highly prescriptive piece with a section on "Learning" (136–150), described as the most important value of a high performance organization. Its elements include innovation, risk taking, training and the right tools, communication, and work measurement. In the same source, Douglas C. Eade, a consultant with twenty-five years of experience with more than three hundred public and nonprofit organizations, writes in another prescriptive piece, "Leading and Managing Strategic Change" (499–510), that personal mastery is an important discipline in a learning organization, its spiritual foundation.
97. Anne M. Khademian, *Working with Culture: The Way the Job Gets Done in Public Programs* (Washington, D.C.: CQ Press, 2002), 24.
98. Barnard, *The Functions of the Executive.*
99. Schein, "Organizational Culture," 5.
100. DiIulio, "Principled Agents," 314.
101. Janet A. Weiss, "Public Management and Psychology," in *The State of Public Management,* ed. Donald Kettl and Brint Milward (Baltimore: Johns Hopkins University Press, 1996).
102. Wilson, *Bureaucracy,* 95.
103. Janet A. Weiss and Sandy Kristin Piderit, "The Value of Mission Statements in Public Agencies," *Journal of Public Administration Research and Theory* 9, no. 2 (1999): 193–223, 221.
104. Khademian, *Working with Culture,* 3.
105. In ibid., see Box 5.1, page 119, for a full set of guidelines.
106. Barry Bozeman, *Government Management of Information Mega-Technology: Lessons from the Internal Revenue Service's Tax Systems Modernization* (Washington, D.C.: IBM Center for the Business of Government, 2002).
107. Laurie E. Paarlberg, James L. Perry, and Annie Hondeghem, "From Theory to Practice: Strategies for Applying Public Service Motivation," in *Motivation in Public Management: The Call of Public Service,* ed. James L. Perry and Annie Hondeghem (London: Oxford University Press, 2008).
108. Paarlberg, Perry, and Hondeghem, "From Theory to Practice" (working paper version), 3.
109. Ibid., 6, 11, 15, 19, 23.
110. DiIulio, "Principled Agents," 315.
111. Trice and Beyer, *The Cultures of Work Organizations,* 356.
112. Wilson, *Bureaucracy,* 92.
113. George T. Milkovich and Alexandra K. Wigdor, eds., *Pay for Performance: Evaluating Performance Appraisal and Merit Pay* (Washington, D.C.: National Academy Press, 1991),126.
114. George A. Akerlof, "Contracts as Partial Gift Exchange," *Quarterly Journal of Economics* 97, no. 4 (November 1982): 543–569.
115. Christopher Hood, "Control, Bargains, and Cheating: The Politics of Public-Service Reform," *Journal of Public Administration Research and Theory* 12, no. 3 (2002): 309–332, 310.

116. Ibid., 310.
117. Donald P. Moynihan, "The Normative Model in Decline? Public Service Motivation in the Age of Governance," in *Motivation in Public Management,* 248.

CHAPTER 7

1. Sources include Jennifer Oldham, "Thomas Garthwaite: Tempers Flare Over King/Drew Advisors," *Los Angeles Times,* October 12, 2005; Laurence Darmiento, "Critical Conditions," *Los Angeles Business Journal,* July 22, 2002; and Charles Ornstein and Tracy Weber, "3 King/Drew Deaths Blamed on Lapses," *Los Angeles Times,* April 6, 2005.
2. Charles Ornstein, Tracy Weber, and Jack Leonard, "King-Harbor Fails Final Check, Will Close Soon," *Los Angeles Times,* August 11, 2007.
3. David Nakamura, "Fenty Fills Another Key Cabinet Position," *Washington Post,* October 3, 2006; Lena H. Sun, "Metro Chief Ready for Next Move," *Washington Post,* October 4, 2006.
4. David Nakamura and Nikita Stewart, "Tangles over City Budget Reflect a Deeper Divide; Despite Mayor's Promise of 'Open Government,' Some Council Members Say They Feel Shut Out," *Washington Post,* May 4, 2008, C7.
5. Jonetta Rose Barras, "Dan Tangherlini: The Wizard's Assistant," *Examiner.com,* October 5, 2006.
6. Laurence E. Lynn Jr., "Public Management," in *Handbook of Public Administration,* ed. B. Guy Peters and Jon Pierre (London: Sage Publications, 2003), 14–24.
7. Herbert Kaufman, *The Administrative Behavior of Federal Bureau Chiefs* (Washington, D.C.: Brookings Institution, 1981), 136.
8. Luther Gulick, "Notes on the Theory of Organization," in *Papers on the Science of Administration,* ed. Luther Gulick and Lyndall F. Urwick (New York: Institute of Public Administration, Columbia University, 1937), 1–46.
9. Roscoe C. Martin, "Paul H. Appleby and His Administrative World," in *Public Administration and Democracy: Essays in Honor of Paul H. Appleby,* ed. Roscoe C. Martin (Syracuse, N.Y.: Syracuse University Press, 1965), 8.
10. Frederick C. Mosher, *Democracy and the Public Service* (New York: Oxford University Press, 1968), 210. Discussion in this section draws on Lynn, "Public Management."
11. John D. Millett, *Management in the Public Service: The Quest for Effective Performance* (New York: McGraw-Hill, 1954), 401.
12. Ibid.
13. Robert D. Behn, "Case Analysis Research and Managerial Effectiveness: Learning How to Lead Organizations up Sand Dunes," in *Public Management: The State of the Art,* ed. Barry Bozeman (San Francisco: Jossey-Bass, 1993), 40–54.
14. A more extensive review of this literature is in Laurence E. Lynn Jr., *Public Management as Art, Science and Profession* (Chatham, N.J.: Chatham House, 1996), 65–86.
15. Graham T. Allison Jr., "Public and Private Management: Are They Fundamentally Alike in All Unimportant Respects?" *Proceedings for the Public Management Research Conference,* OPM Document 127-53-1 (Washington, D.C.: Office of Personal Management, November 19–20, 1979), 38.
16. J. Patrick Dobel, Review of Erwin C. Hargrove and John C. Glidewell, *Impossible Jobs* (Lawrence: University Press of Kansas, 1990), in *Journal of Policy Analysis and Management* 11, no. 1 (1992): 144–147.
17. Kenneth H. Ashworth, *Caught Between the Dog and the Fireplug, or How to Survive in Public Service* (Washington, D.C.: Georgetown University Press, 2001); Steven Cohen and William Eimicke, *The Effective Public Manager: Achieving Success in a Changing Government* (San

Francisco: Jossey-Bass, 2002); Philip Heymann, *The Politics of Public Management* (New Haven: Yale University Press, 1987); Robert Reich, *Public Management in a Democratic Society* (Englewood Cliffs, N.J.: Prentice Hall, 1990); Robert D. Behn, *Leadership Counts: Lessons for Public Managers from the Massachusetts Welfare, Training, and Employment Program* (Cambridge: Harvard University Press, 1991); and Mark H. Moore, *Creating Public Value: Strategic Management in Government* (Cambridge: Harvard University Press, 1995).

18. Norma Riccucci, *Unsung Heroes: Federal Execucrats Making a Difference* (Washington, D.C.: Georgetown University Press, 1995); Paul Light, *Sustaining Innovation: Creating Nonprofit and Government Organizations that Innovate Naturally* (San Francisco: Jossey-Bass, 1998); Eugene Bardach, *Getting Agencies to Work Together* (Washington, D.C.: Brookings Institution, 1998).
19. Cohen and Eimicke, *The Effective Public Manager*; Richard N. Haass, *The Bureaucratic Entrepreneur: How to Be Effective in Any Unruly Organization* (Washington, D.C.: Brookings Institution, 1999).
20. Moore, *Creating Public Value.*
21. Robert D. Behn, "Management by Groping Along," *Journal of Policy Analysis and Management* 8 (1988): 651.
22. Richard N. Haass, *The Power to Persuade: How to be Effective in Government, the Public Sector, or Any Unruly Organization* (New York: Houghton, Mifflin, 1994), 230.
23. This section is adapted from Laurence E. Lynn Jr., *Managing Public Policy* (Boston: Little, Brown, 1987), 116–119. For a discussion of the predictive value of the Myers-Briggs test, see Bryan Caplan, "Stigler-Becker versus Myers-Briggs: Why Preference-Based Explanations Are Scientifically Meaningful and Empirically Important," *Journal of Economic Behavior & Organization* 50 (2003): 391–405.
24. Material on the Myers-Briggs Type Indicator is from Isabel Briggs Myers and Peter B. Myers, *Gifts Differing* (Palo Alto, Calif.: Consulting Psychologists Press, 1980).
25. "In general, the MBTI and its scales yielded scores with strong internal consistency and test-retest reliability estimates, although variation was observed." Robert M. Capraro and Mary Margaret Capraro, "Myers-Briggs Type Indicator Score Reliability across Studies: A Meta-Analytic Reliability Generalization Study," *Educational and Psychological Measurement* 62 (2002): 590.
26. Myers and Myers, *Gifts Differing,* 4.
27. William L. Gardner and Mark J. Martinko, "Using the Myers-Briggs Type Indicator to Study Managers: A Literature Review and Research Agenda," *Journal of Management* 22 (1996): 59.
28. Ibid., 64.
29. Yves-C. Gagnon, "The Behavior of Public Managers in Adopting New Technologies," *Public Performance and Management Review* 24 (2001): 337–350.
30. For an interesting analysis, see J. A. Chatman, D. F. Caldwell, and C. A. O'Reilly, "Managerial Personality and Performance: A Semi-Idiographic Approach," *Journal of Research in Personality* 33 (1999): 514–545.
31. Jameson W. Doig and Erwin C. Hargrove, *Leadership and Innovation: A Biographical Perspective on Entrepreneurs in Government* (Baltimore: Johns Hopkins University Press, 1987), 7–8, 14.
32. Laurence E. Lynn Jr., "The Reagan Administration and the Renitent Bureaucracy," in *The Reagan Presidency and the Governing of America,* ed. Lester M. Salomon and Michael S. Lund (Washington, D.C.: Urban Institute Press, 1985), 339–370.
33. Herbert A. Simon, "On the Concept of Organizational Goal," *Administrative Science Quarterly* 9 (1964): 21; Herbert A. Simon, *Models of Man* (New York: Wiley, 1957); Herbert A. Simon, "Rationality as Process and as Process of Thought," *American Economic Review* 68 (1978): 1–16; see also Jonathan Bendor, "Herbert A. Simon: Political Scientist," *Annual Review of Political Science* 6 (June 2003): 433–471.

34. S. Kenneth Howard, "Analysis, Rationality, and Administrative Decision Making," in *Toward a New Public Administration: The Minnowbrook Perspective,* ed. Frank Marini (Scranton, Pa.: Chandler, 1971), 287.
35. John M. Pfiffner, "Administrative Rationality," *Public Administration Review* 20, no. 3 (1960): 125–132, 128.
36. Anthony M. Bertelli and Laurence E. Lynn Jr., *Madison's Managers: Public Administration and the Constitution* (Baltimore: Johns Hopkins University Press, 2006).
37. See Herbert A. Simon, "Rationality as Process and as Process of Thought," *American Economic Review* 68 (1978): 1–16; and John Conlisk, "Why Bounded Rationality?" *Journal of Economic Literature* 34 (1998): 669–700.
38. For additional discussion of choice overload, see Barry Schwartz, *The Paradox of Choice: Why More Is Less* (New York: Ecco, HarperCollins, 2005).
39. Amos Tversky and Daniel Kahneman, "Rational Choice and the Framing of Decisions," in *Rational Choice: The Contrast between Economics and Psychology,* ed. Robin M. Hogarth and Melvin W. Reder (Chicago: University of Chicago Press, 1986), 67–94.
40. John Billings, "Promoting the Dissemination of Decision Aids: An Odyssey in a Dysfunctional Health Care Financing System," *Health Affairs Web Exclusive,* October 7, 2004, http://content.healthaffairs.org/cgi/reprint/hlthaff.var.128v1.pdf, 128–132.
41. B. J. McNeil et al., "On the Elicitation of Preferences for Alternative Therapies," *New England Journal of Medicine* 306, no. 21 (1982): 1259–62.
42. A. Edwards et al., "Presenting Risk Information—A Review of the Effects of 'Framing' and Other Manipulations on Patient Choice," *Journal of Health Communication* 6, no. 1 (2001): 61–82, cited by Billings, "Promoting the Dissemination of Decision Aids."
43. L. Festinger, *A Theory of Cognitive Dissonance* (Stanford, Calif.: Stanford University Press, 1957).
44. Irving L. Janis, *Victims of Groupthink* (Boston: Houghton Mifflin, 1972), 9. For further discussion, see Gregory Moorhead and Richard Ference, "Group Decision Fiascoes Continue: Space Shuttle Challenger and a Revised Groupthink Framework," *Human Relations* 44 (1991): 539–550; and J. K. Esser, "Alive and Well after 25 Years: A Review of Groupthink Research," *Organizational Behavior and Human Decision Processes* 73 (1998): 116–141.
45. Adapted from Lynn, *Managing Public Policy,* 95–97.
46. Daniel Kahneman and Jonathan Renshon, "Why Hawks Win," *Foreign Policy* (January/February 2007), http://www.foreignpolicy.com/story/cms.php?story_id=3660.
47. Shankar Vedantam, "Iraq War Naysayers May Have Hindsight Bias," *Washington Post,* October 2, 2006, Sec. A.
48. Shankar Vedantam, "Repeated Warnings Have Diminishing Returns," *Washington Post,* November 20, 2006, Sec. A.
49. Ibid.
50. Eldar Shafir, "Choosing versus Rejecting: Why Some Options are Both Better and Worse Than Others," *Memory & Cognition* 21 (1993): 546–556, quoted in Barry Schwartz, "Mr. Bland Goes to Washington," *New York Times,* November 7, 2006.
51. Daniel L. Schacter, "The Fog of War," *New York Times,* April 5, 2004.
52. Daniel Gilbert, "I'm O.K., You're Biased," *New York Times,* April 16, 2006.
53. Daniel Gilbert, "He Who Cast the First Stone Probably Didn't," *New York Times,* July 24, 2006.
54. Quoted by Jared Sandberg, "Brainstorming Works Best if People Scramble for Ideas on Their Own," *Wall Street Journal,* June 13, 2006.
55. Michael D. Cohen, James G. March, and Johan P. Olsen, "A Garbage Can Model of Organizational Choice," *Administrative Science Quarterly* 17, no. 1 (March 1972): 1–25.
56. Jane Addams, *Democracy and Social Ethics* (Champaign, Ill.: University of Illinois Press, 2001 [1902]).

57. Chris Argyris and Donald A. Schön, *Organizational Learning: A Theory of Action Perspective* (Reading, Mass.: Addison-Wesley, 1978). See also Chris Argyris, *Overcoming Organizational Defenses: Facilitating Organizational Learning* (Boston: Allyn and Bacon, 1990).
58. For an interesting discussion, see Stephen Fineman, "Emotion and Managerial Learning," *Management Learning* 28 (1997): 13–25. Note the existence of a journal devoted to managerial learning.
59. Eugene Bardach, "From Practitioner Wisdom to Scholarly Knowledge and Back Again," *Journal of Policy Analysis and Management* 7 (1987): 188–199; Giandomenico Majone, *Evidence, Argument, and Persuasion in the Policy Process* (New Haven: Yale University Press, 1989).
60. Frederick Taylor, *The Principles of Scientific Management* (New York: W. W. Norton, 1967), 25; Robert Kanigel, *The One Best Way: Frederick Winslow Taylor and the Enigma of Efficiency* (New York: Penguin Books, 1997).
61. Herbert A. Simon, "The Proverbs of Administration," *Public Administration Review* 6 (November/December 1946): 53, 66.
62. Harry P. Hatry et al., *Excellence in Managing* (Washington, D.C.: The Urban Institute, 1991).
63. Laurence E. Lynn Jr., "The Budget-Maximizing Bureaucrat: Is There a Case?" in *The Budget-Maximizing Bureaucrat: Appraisals and Evidence,* ed. André Blais and Stéphane Dion (Pittsburgh: University of Pittsburgh Press, 1991), 59.
64. Richard T. Pascale and Anthony G. Athos, *The Art of Japanese Management* (London: Alan Lane, 1982); Thomas J. Peters and Robert H. Waterman, *In Search of Excellence: Lessons from America's Best-Run Companies* (New York: Harper and Row, 1982).
65. Selected GAO Best Practices Work, http://www.gao.gov/bestpractices/.
66. Government Accountability Office, "Results-Oriented Cultures: Using Balanced Expectations to Manage Senior Executive Performance" (GAO-02-966), 2002.
67. National Governors Association, http://www.nga.org/Files/pdf/CBPBROCHURE.pdf.
68. National Alliance to End Homelessness, http://www.naeh.org/section/tools/essentials; United Nations, http://pbpu.unlb.org/pbpu/default.aspx?id=1; Finance Center, http://www.finance project.org/index.cfm?page=23.
69. Thomas Kuhn, *The Structure of Scientific Revolutions* (Chicago: University of Chicago Press, 1962).
70. Ian Heath, "Paradigm and Ideology," 2003, http://www.modern-thinker.co.uk/1a%20-%20 Paradigm.htm.
71. Henry Mintzberg, "Managing Government, Governing Management," *Harvard Business Review* 74, no. 3 (1996): 75–84.
72. Beryl A. Radin, *Challenging the Performance Movement: Accountability, Complexity, and Democratic Values* (Washington, D.C.: Georgetown University Press, 2006), 19.
73. Linda DeLeon and Peter DeLeon, "The Democratic Ethos and Public Management," *Administration & Society* 34 (2002): 229–250.
74. Lisa Anderson, *Pursuing Truth, Exercising Power: Social Science and Public Policy in the Twenty-First Century* (New York: Columbia University Press, 2003), 13.
75. Aaron Wildavsky, *Speaking Truth to Power: The Art and Craft of Policy Analysis* (Boston: Little, Brown, 1979), 16.
76. James L. Sundquist, "Research Brokerage: The Weak Link," in *Knowledge and Policy: The Uncertain Connection,* ed. Laurence E. Lynn Jr. (Washington, D.C.: National Academy of Sciences, 1978).
77. Hugh Heclo, *A Government of Strangers: Executive Politics in Washington* (Washington, D.C.: Brookings Institution, 1977), 151.
78. For a critical assessment of the role of scientific research in policy making, see Carol H. Weiss, "The Haphazard Connection: Social Science and Public Policy," *International Journal of Educational Research* 23 (1995): 137–150.

79. Lawrence W. Sherman, "Misleading Evidence and Evidence-Led Policy: Making Social Science More Experimental," *Annals of the American Academy of Political and Social Science* 589 (2003): 6.
80. Steven I. Miller and Marcel Fredericks, "Social Science Research Findings and Educational Policy Dilemmas: Some Additional Distinctions," *Education Policy Analysis Archive* 8 (2000), http://epaa. asu.edu/epaa/v8n3/.
81. Sharon Begley, "Alzheimer's Field Blocking Research into Other Causes?" *Wall Street Journal,* April 9, 2004, Sec. B; Sharon Begley, "Scientists World-Wide Battle a Narrow View of Alzheimer's Cause," *Wall Street Journal,* April 16, 2004, Sec. A.
82. Gio Batta Gori, "The Bogus 'Science' of Secondhand Smoke," *Washington Post,* January 30, 2007.
83. Sherman, "Misleading Evidence and Evidence-Led Policy," 226. The entire volume 589 of *The Annals of the American Academy of Political and Social Science,* consists of papers on evidence-based policymaking and public management. Jon Glasby, Kieran Walshe, and Gill Harvey, eds., *Evidence & Policy* 3, no. 3 (2007), is a special issue on evidence-based practice. It is an edited selection of papers from the British ESRC (Economic and Social Research Council) seminar series, addressing the question, what counts as "evidence" in "evidence-based practice"?
84. Evidence-Based Policy Help Desk, http://www.evidencebasedpolicy.org/. See also http://coexgov. securesites.net/index.php?keyword=a432fbc34d71c7.
85. Carolyn J. Heinrich, "Evidence-Based Policy and Performance Management: Challenges and Prospects in Two Parallel Movements," *American Review of Public Administration* 37, no. 3 (2007): 255–277.
86. Ibid. 274.
87. Sherman, "Misleading Evidence and Evidence-Led Policy," 229–230.
88. Institute of Education Sciences, What Works Clearinghouse, http://ies.ed.gov/ncee/wwc/.
89. Sherman, "Misleading Evidence and Evidence-Led Policy."
90. David C. Hoaglin et al., *Data for Decisions: Information Strategies for Policymakers* (Cambridge: Abt Books, 1982).
91. Bent Flyvbjerg, "Five Misunderstandings about Case-Study Research," *Qualitative Inquiry* 12 (2006): 242.
92. Andrew Rich, *Think Tanks, Public Policy, and the Politics of Expertise* (New York: Cambridge University Press, 2004), provides considerable insight into the evolution and role of think tanks in American policymaking. See also James McGann, ed., *Think Tanks and Policy Advice in the United States: Academics, Advisors and Advocates* (New York: Routledge, 2007).
93. Daniel Guttman and Barry Willner, *The Shadow Government: The Government's Multi-Billion-Dollar Giveaway of its Decision-Making Powers to Private Management Consultants, "Experts," and Think Tanks* (New York: Pantheon Books, 1976).
94. James McGann, "US Think-Tanks Casualties in the War of Ideas," openDemocracy, December 20, 2005, http://www.opendemocracy.net/democracy-think_tank/us_thinktanks_3137.jsp.
95. "Conclusions Are Reported on the Teaching of Abstinence," Associated Press, April 15, 2007.
96. Gardiner Harris, "F.D.A. Limits Role of Advisers Tied to Industry," *New York Times,* March 22, 2007.
97. Frances B. Phillips and Joshua Sharfstein, "A Medicaid Provision to Repeal: New ID Requirement Imperils Public Health," *Washington Post,* March 4, 2007, Sec. B.
98. Kevin Freking for the Associated Press, "Welfare, Abstinence Chief Resigns," *Washington Post,* April 2, 2007.
99. Peters and Waterman, *In Search of Excellence.* See also David Boud and Heather Middleton, "Learning from Others at Work: Communities of Practice and Informal Learning," *Journal of Workplace Learning* 15 (2003): 194–202.
100. Hugh Heclo, "Issue Networks and the Executive Establishment," in *The New American Political System,* ed. Anthony King (Washington, D.C.: American Enterprise Institute, 1978), 106.

101. Paul Sabatier and Hank Jenkins-Smith, *Policy Change and Learning: An Advocacy Coalition Approach* (Boulder, Colo.: Westview Press, 1993).
102. John M. Bryson, *Strategic Planning for Public and Nonprofit Organizations,* rev. ed. (San Francisco: Jossey-Bass, 1995); David L. Weimer and Aidan R. Vining, "Thinking Strategically about Adoption and Implementation," in *Policy Analysis: Concepts and Practice* (Upper Saddle River, N.J.: Prentice Hall, 2005); Mark H. Moore, "Managing for Value: Organizational Strategy in For-Profit, Nonprofit, and Governmental Organizations," *Nonprofit and Voluntary Sector Quarterly* 29 (2000): 183–204; and Peter Smith Ring and James L. Perry, "Strategic Management in Public and Private Organizations: Implications of Distinctive Contexts and Constraints," *Academy of Management Review* 10 (1985): 276–286.
103. Charles E. Lindblom, "The Science of Muddling Through," *Public Administration Review* 19, no. 2 (Spring 1959): 81.
104. Barry Bozeman and Jeffrey D. Straussman, *Public Management Strategies: Guidelines for Managerial Effectiveness* (San Francisco: Jossey-Bass, 1990), 29–30.
105. Moore, *Creating Public Value,* 94.
106. Bozeman and Straussman, *Public Management Strategies,* 203.
107. The activity of "sense making" is a subject for research in social and cognitive psychology, sociology, decision making, and organizations, among other fields. For further discussion, see Karl E. Weick, *Sensemaking in Organizations* (Thousand Oaks, Calif.: Sage, 1995).
108. Lee G. Bolman and Terrence E. Deal, *Reframing Organizations: Artistry, Choice, and Leadership* (San Francisco: Jossey-Bass, 1991), 4.
109. Lee G. Bolman and Terrence E. Deal, *Reframing Organizations,* 3rd ed. (San Francisco: Jossey-Bass, 2003), is the best source of additional readings on framing and reframing. The chapter, "Bringing It All Together," is a case study on how a newly appointed public high school principal uses reframing to assess the problems he faces and potential solutions to them.
110. Richard D. Heimovics, Robert D. Herman, and Carole L. Jurkiewicz Coughlin, "Executive Leadership and Resource Dependence in Nonprofit Organizations: A Frame Analysis," *Public Administration Review* 53, no. 5 (1993): 419–427.
111. Haass, *The Power to Persuade,* 2. See also Dan H. Fenn Jr., "Finding Where the Power Lies in Government," *Harvard Business Review* 57 (1979): 144–153.
112. Laurence J. O'Toole Jr., Kenneth J. Meier, and Sean Nicholson-Crotty, "Managing Upward, Downward, and Outward: Networks, Hierarchical Relationships, and Performance," *Public Management Review* 7, no. 1 (2005): 45–68.
113. Gordon Chase, "Implementing a Human Service Program: How Hard Will It Be?" *Public Policy* 27 (1979): 385–435. For an example, see L. C. Steenbergen et al., "Kentucky's Graduated Driver Licensing Program for Young Drivers: Barriers to Effective Local Implementation," *Injury Prevention* 7 (2001): 286–291.
114. U.S. Department of Defense, Office of the Assistant Secretary of Defense (Public Affairs), News Transcript, Presenter: Secretary of Defense Donald H. Rumsfeld, April 11, 2003, http://www.defenselink.mil/transcripts/transcript.aspx?transcriptid=2367.
115. Richard Elmore, "Backward Mapping: Implementation Research and Policy Decisions," *Political Science Quarterly* 94 (1979–1980): 601–616. For an example, see Caroline Dyer, "Researching the Implementation of Educational Policy: A Backward Mapping Approach," *Comparative Education* 35 (1999): 45–61.
116. Elmore, "Backward Mapping," 606.
117. Marcia K. Meyers, Bonnie Glaser, and Karin MacDonald, "On the Front Lines of Welfare Delivery: Are Workers Implementing Policy Reforms?" *Journal of Policy Analysis and Management* 17, no. 1 (1998): 1–22.

118. Elmore, "Backward Mapping."
119. Steven Cohen and William Eimicke, *The New Effective Public Manager: Achieving Success in a Changing Government*, 2nd ed. (San Francisco: Jossey-Bass, 1995). For additional discussion of political entrepreneurship, see Mark Schneider and Paul Teske, "Toward a Theory of the Political Entrepreneur: Evidence from Local Government," *American Political Science Review* 86 (1992): 737–747; and Carl J. Bellone and George Frederick Goerl, "Reconciling Political Entrepreneurship and Democracy," *Public Administration Review* 52 (1992): 130–134.
120. S. Borins, "What Border? Public Management Innovation in the United States and Canada," *Journal of Policy Analysis and Management* 19 (2000): 46–74.
121. T. L. Pittinsky et al., *National Leadership Index 2006: A National Study of Confidence in Leadership* (Cambridge: John F. Kennedy School of Government Center for Public Leadership, 2006).
122. Amazon.com lists nearly twenty thousand books with the word "leadership" in the title. Two classic academic studies are Bernard M. Bass, *Bass & Stogdill's Handbook of Leadership* (New York: Free Press, 1990); and Edgar H. Schein, *Organizational Culture and Leadership*, 3rd ed. (San Francisco: Jossey-Bass, 2004).
123. James MacGregor Burns, *Leadership* (New York: Harper Perennial, 1982).
124. John W. Gardner, *On Leadership* (New York: Free Press, 1993); Warren G. Bennis, *On Becoming a Leader*, rev. ed. (Cambridge: Perseus Publishing, 2003); Rudolph W. Giuliani, *Leadership* (New York: Miramax Books, 2002).
125. Warren Bennis and Burt Nanus, *Leaders: The Strategies for Taking Charge* (New York: Harper and Row, 1985), 21.
126. Jonathan R. Tompkins, *Organization Theory and Public Management* (Belmont, Calif.: Thomson Wadsworth, 2005), 400.
127. Haass, *The Power to Persuade*, 103.
128. Robert D. Behn, "What Right Do Public Managers Have to Lead?" *Public Administration Review* 58 (1998): 209.
129. Brian J. Cook, "Politics, Political Leadership and Public Management," *Public Administration Review* 58 (1998): 227.
130. Montgomery Van Wart, "Public-Sector Leadership Theory: An Assessment," *Public Administration Review* 63 (2003): 224.
131. Janet V. Denhardt and Kelly B. Campbell, "Leadership Education in Public Administration: Finding the Fit Between Purpose and Approach," *Journal of Public Affairs Education* 11 (2005): 169–179. For additional discussion, see Peter Northouse, *Leadership Theory and Practice*, 4th ed. (Thousand Oaks, Calif.: Sage, 2006).
132. Van Wart, "Public-Sector Leadership Theory," 224, 225.
133. Robert J. House and Ram N. Aditya, "The Social Scientific Study of Leadership: Quo Vadis?" *Journal of Management* 23 (1997): 465.
134. Philip Selznick, *Leadership in Administration: A Sociological Interpretation* (Berkeley: University of California Press, 1984), quotes on pp. 22, 4, and 31.
135. See, for example, Robert W. Terry, *Authentic Leadership: Courage in Action* (San Francisco: Jossey-Bass, 1993).
136. John M. Bryson and Barbara C. Crosby, *Leadership for the Common Good: Tackling Public Problems in a Shared-Power World* (San Francisco: Jossey-Bass, 1992).
137. Gary J. Miller, "Managerial Dilemmas: Political Leadership in Hierarchies," in *The Limits of Rationality*, ed. Karen Schweers Cook and Margaret Levi (Chicago: University of Chicago, 1990), 324–357.
138. George A. Akerlof, "Labor Contracts as Partial Gift Exchange," *Quarterly Journal of Economics* 97 (1982): 543–569.

139. Donald C. Stone, "Notes on the Governmental Executive: His Role and His Methods," *Public Administration Review* 5 (1945): 210–225.
140. Montgomery Van Wart, *Dynamics of Leadership in Public Service: Theory and Practice* (Armonk, N.Y.: M. E. Sharpe, 2005), xix.
141. Carolyn J. Hill and Laurence E. Lynn Jr., "Is Hierarchical Governance in Decline?" *Journal of Public Administration Research and Theory* 15 (2005): 173–195.
142. Norma M. Riccucci, *How Management Matters: Street-Level Bureaucrats and Welfare Reform* (Washington, D.C.: Georgetown University Press, 2005).
143. Eli Kintisch, "With Energy to Spare, an Engineer Makes the Case for Basic Research," *Science,* March 10, 2006, 1369–70.
144. Justin Blum, "Officials Earn High Marks on the Hill," *Washington Post,* August 9, 2005, Sec. A.
145. Samuel W. Bodman, "Memorandum for all Federal and Contractor Employees; subject: Employee Concerns Statement," April 11, 2006, http://hss.energy.gov/deprep/news/Documents/SecyPolicy.pdf.
146. "Ashcroft's Style of Secretness Harmful to American Justice," *Austin American-Statesman,* January 24, 2004, A14.
147. Chitra Ragavan, "Ashcroft's Way," *U.S. News and World Report,* January 26, 2004.
148. For examples of how career public managers matter, see Riccucci, *Unsung Heroes.*
149. U.S. Department of Justice, "Memo Regarding Policy on Charging Criminal Defendants," September 9, 2003.
150. "NDOC Newsletter," October-November 2003.
151. Daniel C., Richman, "Federal Sentencing in 2007: The Supreme Court Holds—The Center Doesn't," *Yale Law Journal* 117 (2008): 11. Available at SSRN: http://ssrn.com/abstract=1096694.
152. Ibid.; Frank O. Bowman III, "Beyond Band-Aids: A Proposal for Reconfiguring Federal Sentencing after *Booker,*" *University of Chicago Legal Forum* 149 (2005): 193.

CHAPTER 8

1. Michael Winerip, "Bitter Lesson: A Good School Gets an 'F,' " *New York Times,* January 11, 2006.
2. Robert D. Behn, "What Do We Mean by Accountability, Anyway?" in *Rethinking Democratic Accountability* (Washington, D.C.: Brookings Institution Press, 2001), 6. See also Mark Bovens, "Public Accountability," in *The Oxford Handbook of Public Management,* ed. Ewan Ferlie, Laurence E. Lynn Jr., and Christopher Pollitt (Oxford: Oxford University Press, 2005), 182–208.
3. Behn, "What Do We Mean by Accountability, Anyway?" 6.
4. William T. Gormley Jr., "Institutional Policy Analysis: A Critical Review," *Journal of Policy Analysis and Management* 6, no. 2 (1987): 153–169, 155, 161.
5. Frederick C. Mosher, *Democracy and the Public Service* (New York: Oxford University Press, 1968), 7.
6. Ibid., 8.
7. Barbara S. Romzek and Melvin J. Dubnick, "Accountability," in *The International Encyclopedia of Public Policy and Administration,* ed. Jay M. Shafritz (Boulder, Colo.: Westview Press, 1998), 6–11.
8. Herbert A. Simon, Victor A. Thompson, and Donald W. Smithburg, *Public Administration* (New Brunswick, N.J.: Transaction Publishers, 1991), 513.
9. Mark Bovens, "Public Accountability," in *The Oxford Handbook of Public Management,* 191–192.
10. Robert D. Behn, *Rethinking Democratic Accountability* (Washington, D.C.: Brookings Institution, 2001), 9–10.
11. Barbara S. Romzek and Melvin J. Dubnick, "Accountability in the Public Sector: Lessons from the *Challenger* Crisis," *Public Administration Review* 47 (May/June 1987): 227–238, 229.

12. Judith E. Gruber, *Controlling Bureaucracies: Dilemmas in Democratic Governance* (Berkeley: University of California Press, 1987), 5.
13. Ibid., 22–23, 20.
14. Anthony Bertelli and Laurence E. Lynn Jr., *Madison's Managers* (Baltimore: Johns Hopkins University Press, 2006), 206.
15. Robert S. Barker, "Government Accountability and Its Limits," *Issues of Democracy* 5, no. 2 (August 2000).
16. Laurence E. Lynn Jr., *Public Management: Old and New* (London: Routledge, 2007).
17. James Hart, *The Ordinance Making Powers of the President of the United States,* reprinted in *Johns Hopkins University Studies in Historical and Political Science,* vol. XLIII, no. 3 (Baltimore: Johns Hopkins University Press, 1925), 1–359, 268.
18. Laurence E. Lynn Jr., "The Myth of the Bureaucratic Paradigm: What Traditional Public Administration Really Stood For," *Public Administration Review* 61 (2001): 144–160.
19. Dwight Waldo, *The Administrative State: A Study of the Political Theory of American Public Administration,* 2nd ed. (New York: Holmes and Meier Publishers, 1984), 11.
20. Lynn, "The Myth of the Bureaucratic Paradigm."
21. Woodrow Wilson, "The Study of Administration," *Political Science Quarterly* 2 (1887): 197–222, 213.
22. Mosher, *Democracy and the Public Service,* 7.
23. Wallace S. Sayre, "Trends of a Decade in Administrative Values," *Public Administration Review* 11 (1951): 1–9, 5; Bertelli and Lynn, *Madison's Managers.*
24. John D. Millett, *Management in the Public Service: The Quest for Effective Performance* (New York: McGraw-Hill, 1954), 403.
25. Lynn, "The Myth of the Bureaucratic Paradigm"; Bertelli and Lynn, *Madison's Managers.*
26. Marshall C. Dimock, "Review: Government Corporations," *Public Administration Review* 49 (1989): 85.
27. Harvey C. Mansfield Sr., "Review: The Quest for Accountability," *Public Administration Review* 41 (2001): 397–401, 397.
28. Alasdair Roberts, *Blacked Out: Government Secrecy in the Information Age* (Cambridge: Cambridge University Press, 2006), 14.
29. IGNet, http://www.ignet.gov/pande/mission1.html.
30. U.S. Office of Special Counsel, http://www.osc.gov/intro.htm.
31. William T. Gormley Jr. and Steven J. Balla, *Bureaucracy and Democracy: Accountability and Performance,* 2nd ed. (Washington, D.C.: CQ Press, 2008).
32. Robert Gregory, "Accountability in Modern Government," in *Handbook of Public Administration,* ed. B. Guy Peters and Jon Pierre (London: Sage Publications, 2003), 562.
33. A full list of inspectors general and further resources is available at http://www.ignet.gov.
34. Paul C. Light, *Monitoring Government: Inspectors General and the Search for Accountability* (Washington, D.C.: Brookings Institution, 1993), 17.
35. Stephen Barr, "Administration Opposes Bill on Inspectors General," *Washington Post,* October 2, 2007, Sec. D.
36. Defense Contract Audit Agency, http://www.dcaa.mil.
37. Taxpayer Advocate Service, http://www.irs.gov/advocate/article/0,,id=97392,00.html. For a list of ombudsman offices that are members of the Federal Coalition of Ombudsmen, see http://www.federalombuds.ed.gov/membership.html.
38. General Accounting Office, "The Chief Financial Officers Act: A Mandate for Federal Financial Management Reform," GAO/AFMD-12.19.4 (Washington, D.C.: General Accounting Office, 1991), 1.

39. Office of Management and Budget, "OMB's Mission," http://www.whitehouse.gov/omb/organization/role.html.
40. General Accounting Office, "The Chief Financial Officers Act."
41. See Executive Order 12866, September 30, 1993.
42. For example, see Office of Management and Budget, Office of Information and Regulatory Affairs, *2007 Report to Congress on the Benefits and Costs of Federal Regulations and Unfunded Mandates on State, Local, and Tribal Entities,* http://www.whitehouse.gov/omb/inforeg/2007_cb/2007_cb_final_report.pdf.
43. Mathew D. McCubbins, Roger G. Noll, and Barry R. Weingast, "Administrative Procedures as Instruments of Political Control," *Journal of Law, Economics, and Organization* 3, no. 2 (1987): 243–277; Mathew D. McCubbins, Roger G. Noll, and Barry R. Weingast, "Structure and Process, Politics and Policy: Administrative Arrangements and the Political Control of Agencies," *Virginia Law Review* 75, no. 2 (1989): 431–482.
44. Randall L. Calvert, Mathew D. McCubbins, and Barry R. Weingast, "A Theory of Political Control and Agency Discretion," *American Journal of Political Science* 33 (1989): 588–611, 605.
45. Murray J. Horn and Kenneth A. Shepsle, "Administrative Arrangements and the Political Control of Agencies," *Virginia Law Review* 75 (1989): 499–508, 503
46. McCubbins, Noll, and Weingast, "Administrative Procedures as Instruments of Political Control of Law," 249.
47. Mathew McCubbins and Thomas Schwartz, "Congressional Oversight Overlooked: Police Patrols versus Fire Alarms," *American Journal of Political Science* 28 (1984): 16–79.
48. Terry M. Moe, "The Politics of Bureaucratic Structure," in *Can the Government Govern?* ed. John E. Chubb and Paul E. Peterson (Washington, D.C.: Brookings Institution, 1989), 278.
49. David M. Walker, "GAO Answers the Question: What's in a Name?" *Roll Call,* July 19, 2004.
50. David H. Rosenbloom and Rosemary O'Leary, *Public Administration and Law,* 2nd ed. (New York: Marcel Dekker, 1997), 64.
51. David H. Rosenbloom and Robert S. Kravchuk, *Public Administration: Understanding Management, Politics, and Law in the Public Sector,* 6th ed. (Boston: McGraw Hill, 2005), 426.
52. See, for example, Lisa Schwartz Bressman, "Deference and Democracy," *George Washington University Law Review* 75, no. 4 (2007): 761–803.
53. Abram Chayes, "The Role of the Judge in Public Law Litigation," *Harvard Law Review* 89, no. 7 (May 1976): 1281–1316, 1284.
54. Phillip J. Cooper, *Hard Judicial Choices: Federal District Court Judges and State and Local Officials* (New York: Oxford University Press, 1988), 13.
55. David I. Levine et al., *Remedies: Public and Private,* 4th ed. (St. Paul, Minn.: Thomson/West, 2006), 33.
56. Cooper, *Hard Judicial Choices,* 14.
57. Chayes, "The Role of the Judge in Public Law Litigation," 1298.
58. Cooper, *Hard Judicial Choices.* See also Levine et al., *Remedies: Public and Private*; Robert E. Buckholz Jr. et al., "The Remedial Process in Institutional Reform Litigation," *Columbia Law Review* 78, no. 4 (May 1978): 784–929; Robert C. Wood, ed., *Remedial Law: When Courts Become Administrators* (Amherst: University of Massachusetts Press, 1990).
59. Environmental Protection Agency, "The Food Quality Protection Act (FQPA) Background," http://www.epa.gov/opp00001/regulating/laws/fqpa/backgrnd.htm.
60. Cooper, *Hard Judicial Choices,* 17.
61. Ibid., 20.
62. Ibid., 20–21.
63. Buckholz et al., "The Remedial Process in Institutional Reform Litigation."
64. Ibid., 827, 827, 828, 830, 834, 836.

65. Donald L. Horowitz, "The Courts as Guardians of the Public Interest," *Public Administration Review* 37, no. 2 (March/April 1977): 148–154.
66. OMBWatch, http://www.ombwatch.org; Government Accountability Project, http://www.whistleblower.org; Public Citizen, http://www.citizen.org; Project on Government Oversight, http://www.pogo.org; Citizens Against Government Waste, http://www.cagw.org; Bank Information Center, http://www.bicusa.org.
67. Norton Long, "Bureaucracy and Constitutionalism," *American Political Science Review* 46, no. 3 (1952): 808–818; Frederick Mosher, *Democracy and the Public Service,* 2nd ed. (New York: Oxford University Press, 1982).
68. Lael R. Keiser et al., "Lipstick and Logarithms: Gender, Institutional Context, and Representative Bureaucracy," *American Political Science Review* 96, no. 3 (2002): 553–564.
69. Gary Wamsley et al., *Refounding Public Administration* (London: Sage, 1990).
70. Lisa Blomgren Bingham, Tina Nabatchi, and Rosemary O'Leary, "The New Governance: Practices and Processes for Stakeholder and Citizen Participation in the Work of Government," *Public Administration Review* 65, no. 5 (2005): 547–558, 553, 554.
71. National Academies, http://www.nationalacademies.org/about/.
72. In addition to the references cited in this section, see also Gormley and Balla, *Bureaucracy and Democracy: Accountability and Performance*; Donald P. Moynihan, *The Dynamics of Performance Management: Constructing Information and Reform* (Washington, D.C.: Georgetown University Press, 2008); Rita M. Hilton and Philip G. Joyce, "Performance Information and Budgeting in Historical and Comparative Perspective," in *Handbook of Public Administration,* 402–412; Office of Management and Budget, *Primer on Performance Measurement* (Washington, D.C.: Office of Management and Budget, 1995), http://govinfo.library.unt.edu/npr/library/resource/gpraprmr.html; Colin Talbot, "Performance Measurement," in *The Oxford Handbook of Public Management,* 494–496.
73. Carolyn J. Heinrich, "Measuring Public Sector Performance and Effectiveness," in *Handbook of Public Administration,* 25.
74. Harry P. Hatry, *Performance Measurement: Getting Results,* 2nd ed. (Washington, D.C.: Urban Institute Press, 2006), 3–4.
75. Ibid., 196.
76. Lawrence M. Mead, "Performance Analysis," in *Policy Into Action: Implementation Research and Welfare Reform,* ed. Mary Clare Lennon and Thomas Corbett (Washington, D.C.: Urban Institute Press, 2003); Heinrich, "Measuring Public Sector Performance and Effectiveness."
77. Heinrich, "Measuring Public Sector Performance and Effectiveness."
78. Robert D. Behn, "Why Measure Performance? Different Purposes Require Different Measures," *Public Administration Review* 63, no. 5 (2003): 586–606. See also Colin Talbot, "Performance Management," in *The Oxford Handbook of Public Management,* 491–517.
79. Behn, "Why Measure Performance?" 588.
80. General Accounting Office, "Results-Oriented Cultures: Creating a Clear Linkage between Individual Performance and Organizational Success," GAO 03-488 (Washington, D.C.: General Accounting Office, 2003).
81. Christopher Pollitt and Geert Bouckaert, *Public Management Reform: A Comparative Analysis,* 2nd ed. (Oxford: Oxford University Press, 2004), 126–127.
82. Patricia W. Ingraham, "Striving for Balance: Reforms in Human Resource Management," in *The Oxford Handbook of Public Management,* 521–536.
83. The Fraser Institute, http://www.fraserinstitute.ca/admin/books/chapterfiles/WYT2005pt2.pdf#.
84. William T. Gormley Jr. and David L. Weimer, *Organizational Report Cards* (Cambridge: Harvard University Press, 1999), 3.

85. Charles K. Coe and James R. Brunet, "Organizational Report Cards: Significant Impact or Much Ado about Nothing?" *Public Administration Review* 66, no. 1 (2006): 90–100.
86. Hospital Compare, http://www.hospitalcompare.hhs.gov.
87. Robert S. Kaplan and David P. Norton, "The Balanced Scorecard—Measures that Drive Performance," *Harvard Business Review* (January–February 1992): 71–79; see also http://www.balancedscorecard.org.
88. U.S. Department of Energy, Office of Procurement and Assistance Management, "Balanced Scorecard: Performance Measurement and Performance Management Program for Federal Procurement and Major Site and Facility Management Contractor Purchasing Systems," January 2005, http://management.energy.gov/documents/BSCProgramDescriptionDocument Jan2005.pdf.
89. Hatry, *Performance Measurement,* 14–24.
90. Behn, "Why Measure Performance?"
91. Heinrich, "Measuring Public Sector Performance and Effectiveness," 29.
92. Expectmore.gov, Department of Housing and Urban Development Programs, http://www.whitehouse.gov/omb/expectmore/agency/025.html.
93. Jonathan D. Breul, "PARTing Is Such Sweet Sorrow," in *The Business of Government* (Washington, D.C.: IBM Center for the Business of Government, 2004), http://www.businessofgovernment.org/pdfs/Forum.pdf, 62–66.
94. Kellie Lunney, "OMB Deputy Says Performance-Based Budgeting Is Top Priority," June 20, 2001, GovernmentExecutive.com.
95. Office of Management and Budget, "Rating the Performance of Federal Programs," in *Budget of the United States Government, Fiscal Year 2004* (Washington, D.C.: U.S. Government Printing Office), 47–53.
96. Government Accountability Office, "Performance Budgeting: Observations on the Use of OMB's Program Assessment Rating Tool for the Fiscal Year 2004 Budget" (GAO-04-174), 42.
97. John B. Gilmour and David E. Lewis, "Does Performance Budgeting Work? An Examination of the Office of Management and Budget's PART Scores," *Public Administration Review* 66 (2006): 742.
98. Robert Olsen and Dan Levy, "Program Performance and the President's Budget: Do OMB's PART Scores Really Matter?" Working paper PP04-80, Mathematica Policy Research, October 2004, abstract.
99. John B. Gilmour and David E. Lewis, "Political Appointees and the Competence of Federal Program Management," *American Politics Research* 34, no. 1 (2006): 22–50. Other findings from this study suggest that insulation from political presidential control may enhance program performance, that political conflict might undermine the technical rationality of program design, and that policy preferences might contaminate evaluations of program performance.
100. Moynihan, *The Dynamics of Performance Management,* 130.
101. David Walker, Comptroller General of the United States, testimony before the U.S. Senate Subcommittee on Federal Financial Management, Government Information, and International Security, Committee on Homeland Security and Governmental Affairs, Washington, D.C., June 14, 2005, quoted in Government Accountability Office, "21st Century Challenges: Performance Budgeting Could Help Promote Necessary Reexamination (GAO-05-709T)," 1.
102. "Fair Test, "Joint Organizational Statement on No Child Left Behind (NCLB) Act," October 21, 2004, http://www.fairtest.org/.
103. Pew Center on the States, http://www.gpponline.org/.
104. Patricia W. Ingraham, Philip G. Joyce, and Amy Kneedler Donahue, *Government Performance: Why Management Matters* (Baltimore: Johns Hopkins University Press, 2003); http://www.

govexec.com/gpp/reportcard.htm. Since the program moved to the Pew Center on the States, it assesses only state governments.

105. Patricia W. Ingraham, Philip G. Joyce, and Amy Kneedler Donahue, "Assessing Management," in *Government Performance,* 28–49.
106. Amy Kneedler Donahue, Sally Coleman Selden, and Patricia W. Ingraham, "Measuring Government Management Capacity: A Comparative Analysis of City Human Resource Management Systems," *Journal of Public Administration Research and Theory* 10, no. 2 (2000): 381–411.
107. Healthcare Commission, http://ratings2005.healthcarecommission.org.uk/more_information.asp.
108. Tony Cutler and Barbara Waine, "Advancing Public Accountability? The Social Services Star Ratings," *Public Money and Management* 23 (2003): 125–128.
109. James J. Heckman, Jeffrey A. Smith, and Christopher Taber, "What Do Bureaucrats Do? The Effects of Performance Standards and Bureaucratic Preferences on Acceptance into the JTPA Program," in *Advances in the Study of Entrepreneurship, Innovation, and Growth,* ed. G. Libecap (Greenwich, Conn.: JAI Press, 1996), 191–217.
110. Sandra Van Thiel and Frans L. Leeuw, "The Performance Paradox in the Public Sector," *Public Performance and Management Review* 25, no. 3 (2002): 267–281.
111. Beryl A. Radin, *Challenging the Performance Movement: Accountability, Complexity, and Democratic Values* (Washington, D.C.: Georgetown University Press, 2006), 97.
112. Walt Haney, "The Myth of the Texas Miracle in Education," *Education Policy Analysis Archives* 8, no. 41 (August 19, 2000).
113. SB 186, 78th Texas Legislature, Texas Education Code § 39.051(b)(2).
114. Radin, *Challenging the Performance Movement.*
115. Renee R. Anspach, "Everyday Methods for Assessing Organizational Effectiveness," *Social Problems* 38, no. 1 (February 1991): 1–19.
116. Ibid., 16.
117. Howard Risher, *Pay for Performance: A Guide for Federal Managers* (Washington, D.C.: IBM Center for the Business of Government, 2004), 27.
118. See, for example: Guy S. Saffold III, "Culture Traits, Strength, and Organizational Performance: Moving Beyond 'Strong' Culture," *Academy of Management Review* 13, no. 4 (1988): 546–558; Daniel R. Denison and Aneil K. Mishra, "Toward a Theory of Organizational Culture and Effectiveness," *Organization Science* 6, no. 2 (1995): 204–223; George A. Marcoulides and Ronald H. Heck, "Organizational Culture and Performance: Proposing and Testing a Model," *Organization Science* 4, no. 2 (1993): 209–225.
119. Denison and Mishra, "Toward a Theory of Organizational Culture and Effectiveness."
120. Hal G. Rainey and Paula Steinbauer, "Galloping Elephants: Developing Elements of a Theory of Effective Government Organizations," *Journal of Public Administration Research and Theory* 9, no. 1 (1999): 1–32.
121. Gene A. Brewer and Sally Coleman Selden, "Why Elephants Gallop: Assessing and Predicting Organizational Performance in Federal Agencies," *Journal of Public Administration Research and Theory* 10, no. 4 (2000): 685–711.
122. Paul G. Thomas, "Accountability: Introduction" in *Handbook of Public Administration,* 560.
123. James Q. Wilson, *Bureaucracy: What Government Agencies Do and Why They Do It* (New York: Basic Books, 1989), 60.
124. Radin, *Challenging the Performance Movement,* 238.
125. Donald F. Kettl, *The Transformation of Governance: Public Administration for Twenty-First Century America* (Baltimore: Johns Hopkins University Press, 2002); Barbara S. Romzek, "Where the Buck Stops: Accountability in Reformed Public Organizations," in *Transforming*

Government: Lessons from the Reinvention Laboratories, ed. Patricia W. Ingraham, James R. Thompson, and Ronald P. Sanders (San Francisco: Jossey-Bass, 1998), 193–219; Lynn, *Public Management: Old and New.* See also Stephen Page, "The Web of Managerial Accountability: The Impact of Reinventing Government," *Administration & Society* 38, no. 2 (May 2006): 166–197.

126. John Brehm and Scott Gates, *Working, Shirking, and Sabotage: Bureaucratic Response to a Democratic Public* (Ann Arbor: University of Michigan Press, 1999), 202.
127. William G. Ouchi, "A Conceptual Framework for the Design of Organizational Control Mechanisms," *Management Science* 25, no. 9 (1979): 833–848, 844.
128. In addition to the references cited in this section, see also Kevin P. Kearns, *Managing for Accountability: Preserving the Public Trust in Public and Nonprofit Organizations* (San Francisco: Jossey-Bass, 1996).
129. Beryl A. Radin, "The Government Performance and Results Act (GPRA): Hydra-headed Monster or Flexible Management Tool?" *Public Administration Review* 58, no. 4 (1998): 313.
130. Anthony M. Bertelli and Laurence E. Lynn Jr., "Managerial Responsibility," *Public Administration Review* 63, no. 3 (2003), 261–262.
131. Ibid., 260.
132. David L. Weimer, "Medical Governance: Are We Ready to Prescribe?" *Journal of Policy Analysis and Management* 26, no. 2 (2007): 217–229.
133. Bertelli and Lynn, "Managerial Responsibility," 262.
134. See, for example, Matthew L. Wald, "Inspectors for F.A.A. Say Violations Were Ignored," *New York Times,* April 3, 2008.
135. Behn, *Rethinking Democratic Accountability,* 10–12, 11–13.
136. Barbara S. Romzek and Patricia Wallace Ingraham, "Cross Pressures of Accountability: Initiative, Command, and Failure in the Ron Brown Plane Crash," *Public Administration Review* 60, no. 3 (2000), 241; see also Beryl A. Radin, *The Accountable Juggler: The Art of Leadership in a Federal Agency* (Washington, D.C.: CQ Press, 2002).
137. Romzek and Dubnick, "Accountability," 11.
138. Romzek and Ingraham, "Cross Pressures of Accountability," 240–253, 250.
139. The first and second parts of this case are available through the Kennedy School of Government's Case Program, http://www.ksgcase.harvard.edu/.

CHAPTER 9

1. Anthony M. Bertelli and Laurence E. Lynn Jr., *Madison's Managers: Public Administration and the Constitution* (Baltimore: Johns Hopkins University Press, 2006).
2. Frederick C. Mosher, "The American Setting," in *American Public Administration: Past, Present and Future,* ed. Frederick C. Mosher (University: University of Alabama Press, 1975), 3.
3. Todd Lewan, "Mo. Tries New Approach on Teen Offenders," December 29, 2007, http://www.ncsl.org/programs/cyf/Y41107v2_n20.htm#mo. The author was a FoxNews reporter.
4. Christopher Pollitt and Geert Bouckaert, *Public Management Reform: A Comparative Analysis* (Oxford: Oxford University Press, 2004), 8.
5. A useful overview of American federal government reform initiatives is James P. Pfiffner, "The American Tradition of Administrative Reform," in *The White House and the Blue House: Government Reform in the United States and Korea,* ed. Yong Hyo Cho and H. George Frederickson (Lanham, Md.: University Press of American, 1998).
6. Michael Barzelay, "Politics of Public Management Reform in OECD Countries" (paper presented at the II International Congress of CLAD on State and Public Administration Reform, Margarita Island, Venezuela, October 14–18, 1997).

7. These examples are from the Web site of the "Government Innovators Network," maintained by the Ash Institute for Democratic Governance and Innovation at Harvard University's Kennedy School of Government, http://www.innovations.harvard.edu/.
8. George W. Downs and Patrick D. Larkey, *The Search for Government Efficiency: From Hubris to Helplessness* (New York: Random House, 1986), 259.
9. This section draws on and adapts materials from Bertelli and Lynn, *Madison's Managers*; and Laurence E. Lynn Jr., *Public Management: Old and New* (London and New York: Routledge, 2006).
10. For additional information on the emergence of the American administrative state, see Jack H. Knott and Gary J. Miller, *Reforming Bureaucracy: The Politics of Institutional Choice* (Englewood Cliffs, N.J.: Prentice Hall, 1987); James A. Morone, *The Democratic Wish: Popular Participation and the Limits of American Government* (New Haven: Yale University Press, 1998); and Laurence J. O'Toole Jr., "Doctrines and Developments: Separation of Powers, the Politics-Administration Dichotomy, and the Rise of the Administrative State," *Public Administration Review* 47, no. 1 (1987): 17–25.
11. Richard J. Stillman II, "American versus European Public Administration: Does Public Administration Make the Modern State, or Does the State Make Public Administration?" in *The Modern State and its Study: New Administrative Sciences in a Changing Europe and the United States,* ed. Walter J. M. Kickert and Richard J. Stillman II (Cheltenham, U.K.: Edward Elgar Publishing, 1999), 247–260; Dwight Waldo, *The Administrative State: Second Edition with New Observations and Reflections* (New York: Holmes and Meier Publishers, 1984).
12. John Gaus, "The Responsibility of Public Administration," in *The Frontiers of Public Administration,* ed. John M. Gaus, Leonard D. White, and Marshall E. Dimock (Chicago: University of Chicago Press, 1936), 26–44. At the time of the American Revolution, Edmund Burke, in *Thoughts on the Cause of the Present Discontents,* was, according to Gaus, "describing for the first time a consistent theory of party government in which the responsibility for the direction of administration is vested in the leaders of the majority party of the legislature" (page 30).
13. Lloyd M. Short, *The Development of National Administrative Organization in the United States* (Baltimore: Johns Hopkins University Press, 1923), 75, quoted by Michael Nelson, in "A Short, Ironic History of American National Bureaucracy," *The Journal of Politics* 44 (1982): 751, 756.
14. John A. Rohr, *To Run a Constitution* (Lawrence: University Press of Kansas, 1986), 148.
15. Laurence E. Lynn Jr., "The Myth of the Bureaucratic Paradigm: What Traditional Public Administration Really Stood For," *Public Administration Review* 61 (2000): 144–160.
16. Matthew Crenson, *The Federal Machine: Beginnings of Bureaucracy in Jacksonian America* (Baltimore: Johns Hopkins University Press, 1975); James W. Fesler, "The Presence of the Administrative Past," in *American Public Administration: Patterns of the Past,* ed. James W. Fesler (Washington, D.C.: American Society for Public Administration, 1982), 1–27; Nelson, "A Short, Ironic History."
17. Daniel P. Carpenter, *The Forging of Bureaucratic Autonomy: Reputations, Networks, and Policy Innovation in Executive Agencies, 1862–1928* (Princeton: Princeton University Press, 2001), 38.
18. Bertelli and Lynn, *Madison's Managers.*
19. John Mabry Mathews, *Principles of American State Administration* (New York: D. Appleton, 1917), 20.
20. Charles E. Merriam, "Public Administration and Political Theory," *Journal of Social Philosophy* 5 (1940): 305.
21. Material in the following section has been adapted from Laurence E. Lynn Jr., "The Study of Public Management in the United States: Management in the New World and a Reflection on

Europe," in *The Study of Public Management in Europe and the US: A Competitive Analysis of National Distinctiveness,* ed. Walter J. M. Kickert (London: Routledge, 2008), 233–262.
22. Woodrow Wilson, "The Study of Administration," in *Classics of Public Administration,* 4th ed., ed. Jay M. Shafritz and Albert C. Hyde (Stamford, Conn.: Wadsworth/Thomson Learning, 1997), 16.
23. See Paul P. Van Riper, *History of the United States Civil Service* (Evanston, Ill.: Row, Peterson, 1958).
24. Stephen Skowronek, *Building a New American State: The Expansion of Administrative Capacities, 1877–1920* (New York: Cambridge University Press, 1982), 165.
25. Harold Joseph Laski, "The Growth of Administrative Discretion," *Journal of Public Administration* 1 (1923): 92.
26. John M. Gaus, "The New Problem of Administration," *Minnesota Law Review* 8 (1923–1924): 220.
27. Frederick A. Cleveland, "Popular Control of Government," *Political Science Quarterly* 34 (1919): 252.
28. Christopher Hood and Michael W. Jackson, *Administrative Argument* (Aldershot, U.K.: Dartmouth Publishing, 1991), 135; Andrew Dunsire, *Administration: The Word and the Science* (New York: John Wiley and Sons, 1973); Judith A. Merkle, *Management and Ideology: The Legacy of the International Scientific Management Movement* (Berkeley: University of California Press, 1980).
29. Hood and Jackson, *Administrative Argument.*
30. President's Committee on Administrative Management, *Report of the Committee with Studies of Administrative Management in the Federal Government* (Washington, D.C.: Government Printing Office, 1937), iv.
31. David H. Rosenbloom, *Building a Legislative-Centered Public Administration: Congress and the Administrative State, 1946–1999* (Tuscaloosa: University of Alabama Press, 2000).
32. Ibid.; Bertelli and Lynn, *Madison's Managers.*
33. Paul C. Light, *The Tides of Reform: Making Government Work, 1945–1995* (New Haven: Yale University Press, 1997).
34. Francis E. Rourke, "Bureaucracy in the American Constitutional Order," *Political Science Quarterly* 102 (1987): 218.
35. Ibid., 226.
36. Charles H. Levine, "The Federal Government in the Year 2000: Administrative Legacies of the Reagan Years," *Public Administration Review* 46, no. 3 (1986): 198.
37. Paul C. Light, *The True Size of Government* (Washington, D.C.: Brookings Institution, 1999).
38. Rourke, "Bureaucracy in the American Constitutional Order," 231.
39. J. Steven Ott, Albert C. Hyde, and Jay M. Shafritz, eds., *Public Management: The Essential Readings* (Chicago: Lyceum/Nelson-Hall, 1991), 110.
40. Ronald C. Moe, "The Emerging Federal Quasi Government: Issues of Management and Accountability," *Public Administration Review* 61 (2001): 291.
41. Donald P. Moynihan, "Protection versus Flexibility: The Civil Service Reform Act, Competing Administrative Doctrines, and the Roots of the Contemporary Public Management Debate," *Journal of Policy History* 16, no. 1 (2004): 1–33.
42. An early and illuminating discussion of managerialism is Christopher Pollitt, *Managerialism and the Public Services: The Anglo-American Experience* (London: Blackwell, 1991).
43. Downs and Larkey, *The Search for Government Efficiency*; J. Peter Grace, *Report of the President's Private Sector Survey on Cost Control* (Washington, D.C.: Government Printing Office, 1984).
44. Downs and Larkey, *The Search for Government Efficiency.*
45. David Osborne and Ted Gaebler, *Reinventing Government: How the Entrepreneurial Spirit Is Transforming the Public Sector* (Reading, Mass.: Addison-Wesley, 1992); Michael Barzelay, with

Babak J. Armajani, *Breaking through Bureaucracy: A New Vision for Managing in Government* (Berkeley: University of California Press, 1992).

46. Osborne and Gaebler, *Reinventing Government,* xviii.
47. Al Gore, *From Red Tape to Results: Creating a Government that Works Better & Costs Less: Report of the National Performance Review* (Washington, D.C.: Government Printing Office, 1993), 2.
48. Ibid., 6–7.
49. Additional information on reinvention labs is at http://govinfo.library.unt.edu/npr/library/papers/bkgrd/whatis.html.
50. Additional information on performance partnerships is at http://govinfo.library.unt.edu/npr/library/fedstat/2572.html.
51. Joel D. Aberbach and Bert A. Rockman, "Reinventing Government or Reinventing Politics? The American Experience," in *Politicians, Bureaucrats and Administrative Reform,* ed. B. Guy Peters and Jon Pierre (London: Routledge, 2001), 24–34.
52. B. Guy Peters, "A North American Perspective on Administrative Modernisation in Europe," in Walter J. M. Kickert, ed., *Public Management and Administrative Reform in Western Europe* (Cheltenham, U.K.: Edward Elgar Publishing, 1997), 251–266, 255.
53. Aberbach and Rockman, "Reinventing Government or Reinventing Politics?" 31.
54. Andrew Graham and Alasdair Roberts, "The Agency Concept in North America: Failure, Adaptation, and Incremental Change," in *Unbundled Government: A Critical Analysis of the Global Trend to Agencies, Quangos and Contractualisation,* ed. Christopher Pollitt and Colin Talbot (New York: Routledge, 2004), 140–163, 146, 147.
55. Judith M. Lombard, "Reinventing Human Resource Development: Unintended Consequences of Clinton Administration Reforms," *International Journal of Public Administration* 26, no. 10–11 (2003): 1114.
56. UN Public Administration Network, http://www.unpan.org/globalforums.asp.
57. Beryl A. Radin, "Intergovernmental Relationships and the Federal Performance Movement," in *Quicker, Better, Cheaper? Managing Performance in American Government,* ed. Dall W. Forsythe (Albany, N.Y.: Rockefeller Institute Press, 2001), 285–306.
58. Rohr, *To Run a Constitution,* 84.
59. Government Accountability Office, "Results-Oriented Government: GPRA Has Established a Solid Foundation for Achieving Greater Results," GAO-04-594T, 2004.
60. Office of Management and Budget, *Government-Wide Performance Plan, Budget of the United States Government, Fiscal Year 1999* (Washington, D.C.: U.S. Government Printing Office, 1998).
61. General Accounting Office, *Managing for Results: Agencies' Annual Performance Plans Can Help Address Strategic Planning Challenges,* GAO/GGD-98-44, 1998.
62. National Academy of Public Administration, *Effective Implementation of the Government Performance and Results Act* (Washington, D.C.: National Academy of Public Administration, 1998), vii, 29.
63. Government Accounting Office, "Performance Budgeting: Current Developments and Future Prospects," GAO-03-595T, 2003, 17.
64. The Bush administration's public management reforms are discussed in Jonathan Breul, "Three Bush Administration Management Reform Initiatives: The President's Management Agenda, Freedom to Manage Legislative Proposals, and the Program Assessment Rating Tool," *Public Administration Review* 67, no. 1 (January/February 2007): 21–26; and James P. Pfiffner, "The First MBA President: George W. Bush as Public Administrator," *Public Administration Review* 67, no. 1 (January/February 2007): 6–20.
65. Donald P. Moynihan, "Homeland Security and the U.S. Public Management Policy Agenda," *Governance: An International Journal of Policy, Administration and Institutions* 18, no. 2 (2005):

171–196. See also Douglas A. Brook and Cynthia L. King, "Civil Service Reform as National Security," *Public Administration Review* 67, no. 3 (2007): 397–405.

66. This point is discussed further in Moynihan, "Homeland Security"; and James R. Thompson, "The Federal Civil Service: The Demise of an Institution," *Public Administration Review* 66, no. 4 (July/August 2006): 496–503.
67. Colin Talbot, "Executive Agencies: Have They Improved Management in Government?" *Public Money and Management* 24 (2004): 104–112.
68. Jonathan R. Tompkins, *Organization Theory and Public Management* (Belmont, Calif.: Thomson Wadsworth, 2005), 1.
69. Alan L. Wilkins and William G. Ouchi, "Efficient Cultures: Exploring the Relationship between Culture and Organizational Performance," *Administrative Science Quarterly* 28 (1983): 468–481.
70. Other sources of strategies include Ellen Schall, "Notes from a Reflective Practitioner of Innovation," in *Innovation in American Government: Challenges, Opportunities, and Dilemmas*, ed. Alan A. Altschuler and Robert D. Behn (Washington, D.C.: Brookings Institution Press, 1997), http://www.govleaders.org/schall.htm; Steven Cohen and William B. Eimicke, *Tools for Innovators: Creative Strategies for Managing Public Sector Organizations* (San Francisco: Jossey-Bass, 1997); David Osborne and Peter Plastrik, *The Reinventor's Fieldbook: Tools for Transforming Your Government* (San Francisco: Jossey-Bass, 2000); David Osborne and Peter Plastrik, *Banishing Bureaucracy: The Five Strategies of Reinventing Government* (Reading, Mass.: Addison-Wesley, 1997); Geraldine O'Brien, "Participation as the Key to Successful Change—A Public Sector Case Study," *Leadership and Organization Development Journal* 23, no. 8 (2002): 442–455; Robert B. Denhardt, *The Pursuit of Significance: Strategies for Managerial Success in Public Organizations* (Belmont, Calif.: Wadsworth, 1993); Peter Senge, *The Fifth Discipline* (New York: Doubleday, 1990).
71. Susan Rose-Ackerman, "Reforming Public Bureaucracy through Economic Incentives?" *Journal of Law, Economics and Organization* 2, no. 1 (1986): 131, 132.
72. Ibid., 131, 133.
73. David G. Carnevale, "The Issue of Change," in *Organizational Development in the Public Sector* (New York: Westview Press, 2003), 39–60.
74. Patrick Dawson, "Beyond Conventional Change Models: A Processual Perspective," *Asia Pacific Journal of Human Resources* 34 (December 1996): 57–70, 57, 64.
75. Ibid., 68.
76. Robert D. Behn, "Creating an Innovative Organization: Ten Hints for Involving Frontline Workers," *State and Local Government Review* 27, no. 3 (1995).
77. Ibid.
78. Patricia W. Ingraham, James R. Thompson, and Ronald P. Sanders, eds., *Transforming Government: Lessons from the Reinvention Laboratories* (San Francisco: Jossey-Bass, 1997).
79. Innovations in American Government Award, http://www.innovations.harvard.edu/award_landing.html.
80. Government Innovators Network, http://www.innovations.harvard.edu/.
81. "New Tools for Implementing 'Most Efficient Organizations' (MEO)," *Proceedings from the National Academy of Public Administration Symposium*, Washington, D.C., February 8, 2006, http://www.napawash.org/_images/FINAL_MEO_Symposium3_27_06.pdf.
82. Council for Excellence in Government, http://www.excelgov.org/; Partnership for Public Service, http://ourpublicservice.org/OPS/programs/psc/.
83. Theo A. J. Toonen and Jos C. N. Raadschelders, "Public Sector Reform in Western Europe" (paper presented at the Conference on Comparative Civil Service Systems, School of Public and Environmental Affairs, Indiana University, Bloomington, April 5–8, 1997).
84. Ezra Suleiman, *Dismantling Democratic States* (Princeton: Princeton University Press, 2003), 47.

85. James Thompson, "Reinvention as Reform: Assessing the National Performance Review," *Public Administration Review* 60, no. 6 (2000): 508–521, 509.
86. Ibid., 510.
87. Christopher Pollitt and Geert Bouckaert, "Results: Through a Glass Darkly," in *Public Management Reform: A Comparative Analysis,* 2nd ed. (New York: Oxford University Press, 2004), 103–142.
88. Christopher Pollitt, "Is the Emperor in His Underwear? An Analysis of the Impacts of Public Management Reform," *Public Management* 2 (2000): 181–199, 185–186.
89. Ibid., 194.
90. Pollitt and Bouckaert, "Results: Through a Glass Darkly," 104.
91. J. Buntin, "Assertive Policing, Plummeting Crime: The NYPD Takes on Crime in New York City," Harvard University, John F. Kennedy School of Government Case Study Program series, #C16-99-1530.0, 1999.
92. Paul E. O'Connell, "Using Performance Data for Accountability: The New York City Police Department's CompStat Model of Police Management," in *Managing for Results 2002,* ed. Mark A. Abramson and John M. Kamensky (Lanham, Md.: Rowman and Littlefield, 2001), 179–224.
93. Ibid.
94. Dennis C. Smith, with William J. Bratton, "Performance Management in New York City: Compstat and the Revolution in Police Management," in *Quicker, Better, Cheaper?* 453–482.
95. David Kocieniewski, "Success of Elite Police Unit Exacts a Toll on the Streets," *New York Times,* February 15, 1999.
96. James J. Willis, Stephen D. Mastrofski, and David Weisburd, *CompStat in Practice: An In-Depth Analysis of Three Cities* (Washington, D.C.: Police Foundation, 2003), 3.
97. Ibid., 73.
98. Ibid.
99. Ibid., 73–74; Stephen D. Mastrofski, "The Police and Noncrime Services: Measuring Performance in Criminal Justice Agencies," *Sage Criminal Justice System Annuals,* vol. 18, ed. Gordon P. Whitaker and Charles David Phillips (Beverly Hills, Calif.: Sage Publications, 1983), 33–62.
100. Willis, Mastrofski, and Weisburd, *CompStat in Practice,* 74.
101. Ibid., 74–75.
102. Ibid., 77.
103. James J. Willis, Stephen D. Mastrofski, and David Weisburd, "CompStat and Bureaucracy: A Case Study of Challenges and Opportunities for Change," *Justice Quarterly* 21 (September 2004): 491.
104. Ibid., 493.
105. William T. Gormley Jr., *Taming the Bureaucracy: Muscles, Prayers, and Other Strategies* (Princeton: Princeton University Press, 1989), 224.
106. Herbert Kaufman, "The Confines of Leadership," in *The Administrative Behavior of Federal Bureau Chiefs* (Washington, D.C.: Brookings Institution, 1981), 91–138.
107. Report of the National Commission on the Public Service, *Urgent Business for America: Revitalizing the Federal Government for the 21st Century* (Washington, D.C.: Brookings Institution, 2003), 9.

CHAPTER 10

1. Jonathan B. Perlin, Robert M. Kolodner, and Robert H. Roswell, "The Veterans Health Administration: Quality, Value, Accountability, and Information as Transforming Strategies for Patient-Centered Care," *American Journal of Managed Care* 20 (2004): 828–836, 829.

2. Adam Oliver, "The Veterans Health Administration: An American Success Story?" *Milbank Quarterly* 85 (2007), http://www.milbank.org/quarterly/8501feat.html.
3. Perlin, Kolodner, and Roswell, "The Veterans Health Administration," 835.
4. Oliver, "The Veterans Health Administration: An American Success Story?"
5. Veterans Health Administration, http://www.cancercare.on.ca/documents/CQCOKenKizer Summary.pdf.
6. Gary J. Young, *Transforming Government: The Revitalization of the Veterans Health Administration* (Arlington, Va.: The PricewaterhouseCoopers Endowment for the Business of Government, 2000), 25.
7. Oliver, "The Veterans Health Administration: An American Success Story?"
8. Ibid.
9. See, for example, Helmut K. Anheier, *Nonprofit Organizations: Theory, Management, Policy* (London and New York: Routledge, 2005); Peter F. Drucker, *Managing the Nonprofit Organization* (New York: Collins Business, 2005); and Gary M. Grobman, *The Nonprofit Handbook: Everything You Need to Know to Start and Run Your Nonprofit Organization,* 5th ed. (Harrisburg, Pa.: White Hat Communications, 2008).
10. Mary Beth Sheridan, "Plan to Cut Federal Security Unit Decried," *Washington Post,* June 21, 2007, Sec. A.
11. Michael D. Cohen, James G. March, and Johan P. Olsen, "A Garbage Can Model of Organizational Choice," *Administrative Science Quarterly* 17, no. 1 (March 1972): 1–25.
12. U.S. Department of the Interior, Bureau of Indian Affairs, "Performance and Accountability Report, Fiscal Year 2005," 13.
13. Jerry Reynolds, "BIA Reorganizations Shows Culture Gap," *Indian Country Today,* March 22, 2004, http://www.indiancountry.com/content.cfm?id=1079970122.
14. April Avison, "Changes Starting at Bryan PD," *The Eagle,* Bryan-College Station, Texas, September 29, 2007, Sec. A.
15. This account is adapted from Barbara Koremenos and Laurence E. Lynn Jr., "Leadership of a State Agency: An Analysis Using Game Theory," in *The State of Public Management,* ed. Donald F. Kettl and Brinton Milward (Baltimore: Johns Hopkins University Press, 1996), 213–240.
16. Ibid., 232.
17. Ibid., 235.
18. For additional material on reframing, see Lee G. Bolman and Terrence E. Deal, *Reframing Organizations: Artistry, Choice, and Leadership,* 3rd ed. (San Francisco: Jossey-Bass, 2003), esp. chapters "Integrating Frames for Effective Practice" and "Bringing It All Together: Change and Leadership in Action"; Jonathan R. Tompkins, "Excellence in Government," in *Organization Theory and Public Management* (Belmont, Calif.: Thomson Wadsworth, 2005); Ian Palmer and Richard Dunford, "Reframing and Organizational Action: The Unexplored Link," *Journal of Organizational Change Management* 9 (1996): 12–25; Christine M. Pearson and Judith A. Clair, "Reframing Crisis Management," *The Academy of Management Review* 23 (1998): 509–576.
19. Patricia Cohen, "Talking Veterans Down from Despair," *New York Times,* April 22, 2008.
20. For information on information sharing concerning terrorism, law enforcement, and other aspects of national security, see Information Sharing Environment, http://www.ise.gov/index.html.
21. National Incident Management System, http://www.fema.gov/emergency/nims/index.shtm.
22. See Patrick S. Roberts, "FEMA and the Prospects for Reputation-Based Autonomy," *Studies in American Political Development* 20, no. 1 (April 2006): 57–87; and James Lee Witt and James Morgan, *Stronger in the Broken Places: Nine Lessons for Turning Crisis into Triumph* (New York: Times Books, 2003).

23. John M. Bryson, *Strategic Planning for Public and Nonprofit Organizations: A Guide to Strengthening and Sustaining Organizational Achievement,* 3rd ed. (San Francisco: Jossey-Bass, 2004). See also Richard D. Young, "Perspectives on Strategic Planning in the Public Sector," http://www.ipspr.sc.edu/publication/Perspectives%20on%20Strategic%20Planning.pdf. For a scholarly and more critical account of the concept of strategic planning, see Henry Mintzberg, *The Rise and Fall of Strategic Planning* (New York: Free Press, 1994).
24. Malcolm Gladwell, "Connecting the Dots: The Paradox of Intelligence Reform," *The New Yorker,* March 10, 2003, 83–89.
25. Study Guides and Strategies, http://www.studygs.net/mapping/.
26. Creativity Manual, http://www.ideastream.com/create/.
27. Ibid.
28. Richard N. Haass, *The Bureaucratic Entrepreneur: How to be Effective in Any Unruly Organization* (Washington, D.C.: Brookings Institution, 1999); Kenneth H. Ashworth, *Caught Between the Dog and the Fireplug, or How to Survive in Public Service* (Washington, D.C.: Georgetown University Press, 2001).
29. Government Accountability Office, "Human Capital: A Self-Assessment Checklist for Agency Leaders," GAO/OCG-00-14G, 2000, 10.
30. John Brehm and Scott Gates, *Working, Shirking, and Sabotage: Bureaucratic Response to a Democratic Public* (Ann Arbor: University of Michigan Press, 1999); William G. Ouchi, "A Conceptual Framework for the Design of Organizational Control Mechanisms," *Management Science* 25, no. 9 (1979): 833–848. The importance of employee screening and hiring is also emphasized by Anthony M. Bertelli and Laurence E. Lynn Jr., in *Madison's Managers: Public Administration and the Constitution* (Baltimore: Johns Hopkins University Press, 2006).
31. Eugene Bardach, *Getting Agencies to Work Together: The Practice and Theory of Managerial Craftsmanship* (Washington, D.C.: Brookings Institution Press, 1998).
32. Christopher Pollitt and Geert Bouckaert, *Public Management Reform: A Comparative Analysis,* 2nd ed. (London and New York: Oxford University Press, 2004).
33. Ibid.
34. Rob Norton, "Unintended Consequences," *The Concise Encyclopedia of Economics,* http://www.econlib.org/library/Enc/UnintendedConsequences.html.
35. Pollitt and Bouckaert, *Public Management Reform,* 164.
36. Thomas L. Garthwaite, Deputy Under Secretary for Health of the Department of Veterans Affairs, testimony before the U.S. House of Representatives Subcommittee on Human Resources, Committee on Government Reform and Oversight, Washington, D.C., September 25, 1998, http://www.va.gov/OCA/testimony/hgrc/25SE981A.asp.
37. See Kenneth W. Kizer, "The 'New VA': A National Laboratory for Health Care Quality Management," *American Journal of Medical Quality* 14 (1999): 3–20.
38. Erwin C. Hargrove and John C. Glidewell, eds., *Impossible Jobs in Public Management* (Lawrence: University Press of Kansas, 1990).
39. Ibid., 8.
40. Frances Hesselbein, "Seeing Things Whole," *Leader to Leader* 37 (Summer 2005): 4–6, 5.
41. Jennifer Warren, "Roderick Q. Hickman's Reform Agenda Has Riled the State's Correctional Officers Association," *Los Angeles Times,* November 15, 2004.
42. Ibid.
43. Jennifer Warren, "State Chief of Prisons Resigns after 2 Years on Job," *Los Angeles Times,* February 26, 2006.
44. B. Cayenne Bird, "Open Letter to Rod Hickman: Prison Guards and Wardens Are Out of Control!," October 18, 2005, http://www.americanchronicle.com/articles/viewArticle.asp?articleID=3024.

45. Editorial, "Prisons and the Brick Wall," *Los Angeles Times*, February 28, 2006.
46. Jennifer Warren, "State Prison Reform in Jeopardy—The Recent Resignation of the Corrections Chief Raises Doubts about the Governor's Commitment to Overhaul the System," *Los Angeles Times*, March 7, 2006.
47. Ibid.
48. Editorial, "Prisons and the Brick Wall."
49. Hargrove and Glidewell, *Impossible Jobs in Public Management*, 25.
50. A history and status of the lawsuit that instigated the reforms is at http://www.youthlaw.org/publications/fc_docket/alpha/rcvwally/. An assessment of the reforms themselves is *Making Child Welfare Work: How the R.C. Lawsuit Forged New Partnerships to Protect Children and Sustain Families*, Bazelon Center for Mental Health Law, Washington, D.C., May 1998.
51. See John J. DiIulio, "Managing a Barbed-Wire Bureaucracy: The Impossible Job of Corrections Commissioner," in Hargrove and Glidewell, *Impossible Jobs in Public Management*, 49–71.
52. Adam Nossiter, "A Tamer of Schools Has Plan in New Orleans," *New York Times*, September 24, 2007.
53. Ibid.
54. Alan Greenblatt, "The Impatience of Paul Vallas," *Governing magazine*, September 2002.
55. For additional discussion of public school reform, see William Ouchi, "Making Public Schools Work: Management Reform as Key," *Academy of Management Journal* 48, no. 6 (2005): 929–934.
56. Ibid.
57. Alexander Russo, "Political Educator," *Education Next* (Winter 2003), http://www.hoover.org/publications/ednext/3354931.html.
58. Ibid.
59. Greenblatt, "The Impatience of Paul Vallas."
60. Russo, "Political Educator."
61. Ibid.
62. Adam Nossiter, "Against Odds, New Orleans Schools Fight Back," *New York Times*, April 30, 2008.
63. Ibid.
64. Greenblatt, "The Impatience of Paul Vallas."
65. Russo, "Political Educator."
66. Greenblatt, "The Impatience of Paul Vallas."
67. Ibid.
68. Ibid.
69. Ibid.
70. "Paul Vallas Leaving," *The Next Mayor*, http://blogs.phillynews.com/dailynews/nextmayor/2007/04/paul_vallas_leaving.html.
71. Nossiter, "A Tamer of Schools Has Plan in New Orleans."
72. Ibid.
73. John Merrow, "New Orleans Chief Tackles Rebuilding Shattered System," *The News Hour*, October 2, 2007, http://www.pbs.org/newshour/bb/education/july-dec07/nola_10-02.html.
74. Ibid.
75. Nossiter, "Against Odds."
76. John A. Rohr, *To Run a Constitution: The Legitimacy of the American Administrative State* (Lawrence: University Press of Kansas, 1986).
77. This case is for sale by the Kennedy School of Government Case Program, at http://www.ksgcase.harvard.edu/, Case No. C16-03-1692.0.

Credits

Credits are a continuation from page iv.

CHAPTER 2 Public Management's Three Dimensions

Excerpts from the *Final Report of the Return to Flight Task Group* courtesy of the National Aeronautics and Space Administration.

CHAPTER 3 Analysis and Argument in Public Management

Text quote from Alberto R. Gonzales, "Prepared Remarks for Attorney General Alberto R. Gonzales at the Georgetown University Law Center," courtesy of the U.S. Department of Justice.

Text quote from "Message from the Mayor," regarding report of the Mayoral Policy Caucus on Prisoner Reentry, courtesy of the Mayor's Office, City of Chicago, Richard M. Daly, mayor.

Figure 3-1, Elements of an Argument, from *The Craft of Argument, with Readings,* by Joseph M. Williams, Gregory G. Colomb, Jonathan D'Errico, and Karen Tracey. Copyright © 2003 by Addision Wesley Longman, Inc. Reprinted by permission of Pearson Education, Inc.

Jeffrey Leib, "FAA Official Defends Air-Traffic Staffing," *Denver Post,* October 13, 2005, Sec. B. Reprinted with permission of the *Denver Post.*

Matthew Franck, "State Is Chastised over Foster Adoption Rates," *St. Louis Post-Dispatch,* October 28, 2005, Sec. D. Reprinted with permission of the *St. Louis Post-Dispatch,* copyright © 2005.

CHAPTER 4 Public Management's Backbone: The Rule of Law

Box 4.3, Letter from Rep. Pete Hoekstra to President George W. Bush, courtesy of the U.S. House of Representatives, House Permanent Select Committee on Intelligence.

CHAPTER 5 Public Management: The Structural Dimension

Katherine McIntire Peters, "Partners in Crimefighting," from Management Matters, govexec.com, February 2, 2005. Reprinted with permission from GovernmentExecutive.com. Copyright © 2005 by National Journal Group, Inc. All rights reserved.

Figure 5-1, Organization Chart for Head Start Program Run by Southern Illinois University Edwardsville, from the SIUE Head Start/Early Head Start Policies and Procedures Manual. Courtesy of the East St. Louis Center, Southern Illinois University Edwardsville.

Sam Dillon, "Long Reviled, Merit Pay Gains Among Teachers," *New York Times,* June 18, 2007. Copyright © 2007 by the *New York Times.* All rights reserved. Used by permission and protected by the Copyright Laws of the United States.

Table 5.2, from "When Can Public Policy Makers Rely on Private Markets? The Effective Provision of Social Services." *The Economic Journal* 110 (March, 2000): table 1, C40. Reprinted with permission from Wiley-Blackwell. All rights reserved.

Otto Kreisher, "Appropriators Skewer Army over Contracting Abuse, Care," *CongressDailyPM,* February 27, 2008. Reprinted with permission from National Journal's *CongressDailyPM,* February 27, 2008. Copyright © 2008 by National Journal Group, Inc. All rights reserved.

Patricia Kime and Christopher P. Cavas, "U.S. Coast Guard Takes Control of Patrol Boat Program: Ends Contract with Lockheed Martin, Northrop Grumman," *DefenseNews,* March 15, 2007. Reprinted with permission.

Collaboration among Public and Private Organizations, from "A Brief Overview of Caring Communities," Family and Community Trust, Jefferson City, Missouri. All rights reserved.

CHAPTER 6 Public Management: The Cultural Dimension

Excerpts from the *Report of the Columbia Accident Investigation Board* courtesy of the National Aeronautics and Space Administration.

Table 6.1, Values Found in Recent Public Administration Literature, adapted from Torben Beck Jørgensen and Barry Bozeman, "Public Values: An Inventory," *Administration & Society* 39, no. 3 (2007): 360–361. Reproduced with permission of Sage Publications Inc. Journals in the format Textbook via Copyright Clearance Center.

David W. Chen, "New Jersey Police Win Praise for Efforts to End Profiling," *New York Times,* September 6, 2007. Copyright © 2007 by the *New York Times.* All rights reserved. Used by permission and protected by the Copyright Laws of the United States.

Box 6.1, ASPA Code of Ethics, reprinted with permission of the American Society for Public Administration (ASPA), www.aspanet.org.

Jonathan Karp, "At the Pentagon, an 'Encyclopedia of Ethical Failure.' " *Wall Street Journal,* May 14, 2007. Reprinted by permission of the *Wall Street Journal.* Copyright © 2007 Dow Jones & Company, Inc. All Rights Reserved Worldwide. License number 2022080984967.

"The Right Stuff," *New York Times,* December 27, 2005, Sec. A. Copyright © 2005 by the *New York Times.* All rights reserved. Used by permission and protected by the Copyright Laws of the United States.

Joby Warrick and Walter Pincus, "Lessons of Iraq Aided Intelligence on Iran: Officials Cite New Caution and a Surge in Spying," *Washington Post,* December 5, 2007, Sec. A. Copyright © 2007 the *Washington Post.* All rights reserved. Used by permission and protected by the Copyright Laws of the United States.

CHAPTER 7 Public Management: The Craft Dimension

Table 7.1, Organizational Processes and the Four Frames, reproduced from Lee G. Bolman and Terrence E. Deal, *Reframing Organizations: Artistry, Choice, and Leadership,* 2nd ed. (San Francisco: Jossey-Bass), table 15.1. Reprinted with permission from Wiley-Blackwell. All rights reserved.

Table 7.2, Theories of Leadership in the Public Sector, reproduced from Janet V. Denhardt and Kelly B. Campbell, "Leadership Education in Public Administration: Finding the Fit between Purpose and Approach," *Journal of Public Affairs Education* 11, no. 3 (2005), table 1. Reproduced with permission.

CHAPTER 8 Accountability

Michael Winerip, "Bitter Lesson: A Good School Gets an 'F.' " *New York Times,* January 11, 2006. Copyright © 2006 by the *New York Times.* All rights reserved. Used by permission and protected by the Copyright Laws of the United States.

Table 8.1, Types of Accountability Systems, from Barbara S. Romzek and Melvin J. Dubnick, "Accountability in the Public Sector: Lessons from the *Challenger* Tragedy," *Public Administration Review* 47, no. 3 (May/June 1987): 229. Reprinted with permission from Wiley-Blackwell. All rights reserved.

Table 8.2, Idealized Perspectives of Bureaucratic Democracy and Approaches to Democratic Control, adapted from Judith E. Gruber, *Controlling Bureaucracies: Dilemmas in Democratic Governance* (Berkeley: University of California Press, 1987), 15, 18. Reprinted with permission from the University of California Press. All rights reserved.

Rebecca L. Brown, "Accountability, Liberty, and the Constitution," *Columbia Law Review* 98 (1998): 530–531. Copyright 1998 by Columbia Law Review Association, Inc. Journals in the format Textbook via Copyright Clearance Center.

Bobby White, "California Balks at Paying Billions to Improve Prison Health Care," *Wall Street Journal,* July 21, 2008, A3. Reprinted by permission of the *Wall Street Journal.* Copyright © 2008 Dow Jones & Company, Inc. All Rights Reserved Worldwide. License number 2022081466089.

City of Des Moines, *Building Community: 2006 Performance Report,* January 31, 2007, 19. Copyright © City of Des Moines 2006. Used with permission.

Table 8.3, Values and Behavioral Expectations of Different Accountability Types, from Barbara S. Romzek and Patricia Wallace Ingraham, "Cross Pressures of Accountability: Initiative, Command, and Failure in the Ron Brown Plane Crash," *Public Administration Review* 60, no. 3: 240–253. Reprinted with permission from Wiley-Blackwell. All rights reserved.

Patrick Radden Keefe, "Don't Hang the Ref: The CIA's Inspector General Must Be Free to Do His Job," *Slate,* October 16, 2007. Reprinted with permission from Slate.com and the *Washington Post.* Newsweek Interactive. All rights reserved.

CHAPTER 9 Public Management Reform

Todd Lewan, "Mo. Tries New Approach on Teen Offenders," December 29, 2007. Copyright 2007 by the National Conference of State Legislatures.

"Maine Supreme Court Upholds Dirigo Health Funding Mechanism," *Kaiser Daily Health Policy Report*, June 5, 2007. Reprinted with permission from the Henry J. Kaiser Family Foundation.

Denver Public Schools Professional Compensation System for Teachers, http://denverpro-comp.org/. Used by permission of Denver Public Schools.

Box 9.1, Ten Hints for Involving Frontline Workers in Creating Innovative Organizations, adapted from Robert D. Behn, "Creating an Innovative Organization: Ten Hints for Involving Frontline Workers," *State and Local Government Review* 27, no. 3 (1995). Reprinted with permission of the Carl Vinson Institute of Government at the University of Georgia.

Excerpts from *Defenders of Wildlife v. American Forest and Paper Association* and *Citizens for Better Forestry v. U.S. Department of Agriculture* courtesy of Earthjustice.

David Firestone, "The Bratton Resignation: The Overview; Bratton Quits Police Post; New York Gains over Crime Fed a Rivalry with Giuliani," *New York Times*, March 27, 1996. Copyright © 1996 by the *New York Times*. All rights reserved. Used by permission and protected by the Copyright Laws of the United States.

James Glanz, "Loss of the Shuttle: Bureaucrats Stifled Spirit of Adventure, NASA's Critics Say," *New York Times*, February 18, 2003. Copyright © 2003 by the *New York Times*. All rights reserved. Used by permission and protected by the Copyright Laws of the United States.

Carolyn J. Heinrich, "False or Fitting Recognition? The Use of High Performance Bonuses in Motivating Organizational Achievements," *Journal of Policy Analysis and Management* 26, no. 2 (2005): 281–304. Reprinted with permission.

CHAPTER 10 Managing in Three Dimensions

Spencer Weart, "The Public and Climate Change," in *The Discovery of Global Warming*. Copyright © 2008 Spencer Weart and American Institute of Physics.

Alan Greenblatt, "The Impatience of Paul Vallas," *Governing Magazine*, September 2002. Copyright © 2002. Reprinted with permission from *Governing Magazine*.

Alexander Russo, "Political Educator," *Education Next* (Winter 2003). Copyright © 2003 by *Education Next*, the Hoover Institution.

Name Index

Page numbers followed by *t* refer to tables.

Subject Index

Page numbers followed by *f* refer to figures and those followed by *t* refer to tables.